THE WORLD ALMANAC®
ATLAS
of the WORLD

Maps created by

MapQuest.com, Inc.

MAPQUEST.COM™   WORLD ALMANAC BOOKS

World Almanac Education Group Staff

Editorial Director
William A. McGeveran, Jr.

Director–Purchasing and Production
Edward A. Thomas

Managing Editor
Lori Wiesenfeld

Associate Editors
Mette Bahde, David M. Faris, Kevin Seabrooke

Desktop Production Manager
Lisa Lazzara

Publisher
Ken Park

Cover Design
Eileen Svajger

MapQuest.com/Digital Mapping Services Staff

Project Managers
Keith Winters, Robert Woolley

Project Coordinators
Matt DiBerardino, Andrew Green, Matt Tharp

Research & Compilation
Marley Amstutz, Laura Hartwig, Bill Truninger

Research Librarian
Craig Haggit

GIS
Dave Folk, Mark Leitzell

Cartographers
Brian Goudreau, Kendall Marten, Jeff Martz, Hylon Plumb

Editors
Robert Harding, Dana Wolf

Production Support
Shawna Roberts

TABLE OF CONTENTS

PORTRAIT OF THE U.S., CENSUS 2000

THE WORLD IN THE 21ST CENTURY

4 **WORLD**

6 **ASIA and OCEANIA**
8 Japan
9 North Korea, South Korea, Taiwan
10 China
11 Vietnam, Laos, Cambodia, Mongolia
12 Thailand, Myanmar (Burma), Philippines
13 Indonesia, Brunei, Singapore, Malaysia
14 Australia
15 Papua New Guinea, New Zealand, Federated States of Micronesia
16 Marshall Is., Nauru, Solomon Is., Tuvalu
17 Kiribati, Fiji, Palau, Tonga
18 Vanuatu, New Caledonia & Dependencies, Samoa, American Samoa
19 Nepal, Maldives, Bhutan, Sri Lanka
20 India
21 Bangladesh, Pakistan
22 Afghanistan, Iran, Turkmenistan
23 Kazakhstan, Uzbekistan, Kyrgyzstan, Tajikistan
24 Iraq, Kuwait, Saudi Arabia
25 Bahrain, Qatar, United Arab Emirates, Yemen, Oman
26 Lebanon, Israel, Jordan
27 Turkey, Cyprus, Syria

28 **EUROPE**
30 Great Britain & Northern Ireland
31 Republic of Ireland
32 Denmark, Netherlands
33 Belgium, Liechtenstein, Luxembourg
34 France
35 Monaco, Switzerland
36 Portugal, Malta, Gibraltar, Andorra
37 Spain
38 Italy
39 Austria, Vatican City, San Marino
40 Germany
41 Poland
42 Czech Republic, Slovakia
43 Hungary, Romania
44 Russia
45 Armenia, Georgia, Azerbaijan
46 Estonia, Latvia, Lithuania
47 Belarus, Ukraine
48 Slovenia, Croatia, Bosnia & Herzegovina, F.Y.R. Macedonia
49 Albania, Yugoslavia
50 Moldova, Bulgaria
51 Greece
52 Iceland, Norway
53 Sweden, Finland

54 **AFRICA**
56 Egypt, Libya
57 Algeria, Tunisia, Morocco
58 Western Sahara, Cape Verde, Mali, Mauritania
59 Chad, Niger, Sudan
60 Eritrea, Djibouti, Ethiopia, Somalia
61 Kenya, Uganda, Rwanda, Burundi
62 Senegal, The Gambia, Guinea, Guinea-Bissau
63 Sierra Leone, Côte d'Ivoire, São Tomé & Príncipe, Liberia
64 Ghana, Burkina Faso, Benin, Togo
65 Nigeria, Cameroon
66 Equatorial Guinea, Republic of the Congo, Gabon, Central African Republic
67 Comoros, Democratic Republic of the Congo, Zambia
68 Tanzania, Malawi, Mozambique
69 Mauritius, Zimbabwe, Botswana, Madagascar
70 Angola, Namibia, Seychelles
71 South Africa, Swaziland, Lesotho

72 **SOUTH AMERICA**
74 Argentina
75 Paraguay, Uruguay
76 Chile
77 Peru, Bolivia
78 Colombia
79 Ecuador, Venezuela
80 Guyana, Suriname, French Guiana
81 Brazil

82 **NORTH AMERICA**
84 Mexico
85 Belize, Guatemala
86 Honduras, El Salvador, Costa Rica
87 Nicaragua, Panama
88 Cuba, Jamaica
89 Dominican Republic, Haiti, Bahamas, Turks & Caicos Is.
90 Puerto Rico, Antigua & Barbuda, St. Kitts & Nevis, Dominica
91 St. Lucia, Barbados, St. Vincent & the Grenadines, Grenada, Trinidad & Tobago
92 Canada
93 Canadian Provincial & Territorial Flags
94 Alberta
95 British Columbia
96 Manitoba
97 New Brunswick
98 Newfoundland
99 Northwest Territories, Nunavut
100 Nova Scotia, Prince Edward Island
101 Ontario, Québec
102 Southern Ontario
103 Southern Québec
104 Saskatchewan
105 Yukon Territory

POLAR REGIONS

106 Arctic Regions, Greenland
107 Antarctica

108 WORLD INDEX

UNITED STATES

126 U.S. Political
127 U.S. Physical
128 Alabama
129 Alaska
130 Arizona
131 Arkansas
132 California
133 Colorado
134 Connecticut
135 Delaware
136 Florida
137 Georgia
138 Hawaii
139 Idaho
140 Illinois
141 Indiana
142 Iowa
143 Kansas
144 Kentucky
145 Louisiana
146 Maine
147 Maryland
148 Massachusetts
149 Michigan
150 Minnesota
151 Mississippi
152 Missouri
153 Montana
154 Nebraska
155 Nevada
156 New Hampshire
157 New Jersey
158 New Mexico
159 New York
160 North Carolina
161 North Dakota
162 Ohio
163 Oklahoma
164 Oregon
165 Pennsylvania
166 Rhode Island
167 South Carolina
168 South Dakota
169 Tennessee
170 Texas
171 Utah
172 Vermont
173 Virginia
174 Washington
175 West Virginia
176 Wisconsin
177 Wyoming

178 STATE INDEXES

General

⊛ National Capital
★ Territorial Capital
• Other City

International Boundary
(subject area)

International Boundary
(non-subject)

Internal Boundary
(state, province, etc.)

----- Disputed Boundary

Perennial River

Intermittent River

⊥⊥⊥⊥ Canal

／ Dam

U.S. States, Canadian Provinces & Territories
(additions and changes to general legend)

★ State Capital
◦ County Seat

Built Up Area

State Boundary

County Boundary

National Park

Other Park, Forest, Grassland

Indian, Other Reservation

▪ Point of Interest
▲ Mountain Peak
·········· Continental Divide
········· Time Zone Boundary

——— Limited Access Highway
——— Other Major Road

(90) Highway Shield

PROJECTION

The only true representation of the Earth, free of distortion, is a globe. Maps are flat, and the process by which the geographic locations (latitude and longitude) are transformed from a three-dimensional sphere to a two-dimensional flat map is called a Projection.

For a detailed explanation of Projections, see *MapScope* in Volume 2 of *Funk & Wagnalls New Encyclopedia.*

TYPES OF SCALE

VISUAL SCALE

Every map has a bar scale, or a Visual Scale, that can be used for measuring. It shows graphically the relationship between map distance and ground distance.

Miles

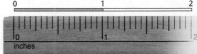

One inch represents 1 mile

Kilometers

One centimeter represents 10 kilometers

REPRESENTATIVE FRACTION

The scale of a map, expressed as a numerical ratio of map distance to ground distance, is called a Representative Fraction (or RF). It is usually written as 1/50,000 or 1:50,000, meaning that one unit of measurement on the map represents 50,000 of the same units on the ground.

This example is used on pages 20, 21 for India, Bangladesh, and Pakistan.

— The Globe is centered on the continent of Asia, as shown on pages 6, 7.

— The subject countries are shown in a stronger red/brown color.

LOCATOR

U.S. CENSUS 2000

The following four pages look at results from Census 2000. Some highlights:

- The U.S. population increased a remarkable 13.2% over 1990.
- Most growth was in the South and West. California had the largest increase (4,111,627) and Nevada had the largest percentage increase (66.3%).
- The Hispanic population grew 57.9% since 1990, reaching 35.3 million, or 12.5% of the total population.

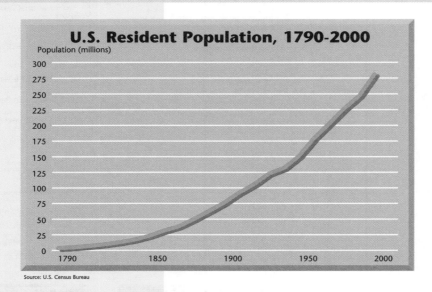

U.S. Resident Population, 1790-2000

Population (millions)

Source: U.S. Census Bureau

United States Resident Population per Census

Year	Population
2000	281,421,906
1990	248,709,873
1980	226,542,199
1970	203,302,031
1960	179,323,175
1950	151,325,798
1940	132,164,569
1930	123,202,624
1920	106,021,537
1910	92,228,496
1900	76,212,168
1890	62,979,766
1880	50,189,209
1870	38,558,371
1860	31,443,321
1850	23,191,876
1840	17,063,353
1830	12,860,702
1820	9,638,453
1810	7,239,881
1800	5,308,483
1790	3,929,214

Source: U.S. Census Bureau

Population Density, 2000
(persons per sq. mi., land area only)

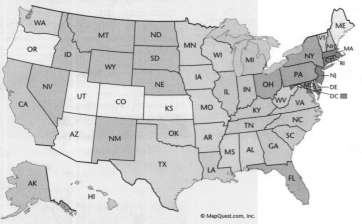

© MapQuest.com, Inc.

Most People per Sq. Mi.

Washington, D.C.	9,378.0
New Jersey	1,134.5
Rhode Island	1,003.2
Massachusetts	809.8
Connecticut	702.9

Fewest People per Sq. Mi.

Alaska	1.1
Wyoming	5.1
Montana	6.2
North Dakota	9.3
South Dakota	9.9

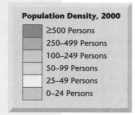

Population Density, 2000

- ≥500 Persons
- 250–499 Persons
- 100–249 Persons
- 50–99 Persons
- 25–49 Persons
- 0–24 Persons

New Apportionment in U.S. House of Representatives

© MapQuest.com, Inc.

Apportionment is the process of dividing the 435 seats in the U.S. House of Representatives among the states. The apportionment calculation is based upon the total resident population of each state as determined by the latest U.S. Census.

Change after Census 2000

- Gain two seats
- Gain one seat
- No change
- Lose one seat
- Lose two seats

red fig. — Number of seats in 108th Congress (January 2003)

Percent Change in State Population, 1990-2000

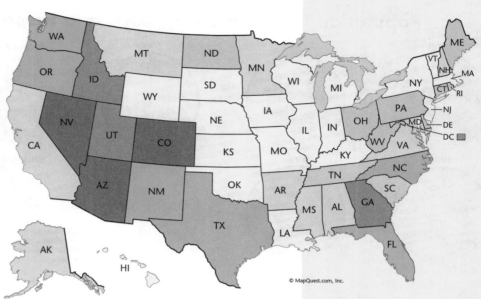

Percent Change, 1990–2000	
	≥30.0% increase
	25.0–29.9% increase
	20.0–24.9% increase
	15.0–19.9% increase
	10.0–14.9% increase
	5.0–9.9% increase
	0–4.9% increase
	decrease

© MapQuest.com, Inc.

Population by State, 1990-2000

Source: U.S. Census Bureau

State	2000 Pop.	1990 Pop.	Percent Change
Alabama	4,447,100	4,040,587	10.1
Alaska	626,932	550,043	14.0
Arizona	5,130,632	3,665,228	40.0
Arkansas	2,673,400	2,350,725	13.7
California	33,871,648	29,760,021	13.8
Colorado	4,301,261	3,294,394	30.6
Connecticut	3,405,565	3,287,116	3.6
Delaware	783,600	666,168	17.6
District of Columbia	572,059	606,900	-5.7
Florida	15,982,378	12,937,926	23.5
Georgia	8,186,453	6,478,216	26.4
Hawaii	1,211,537	1,108,229	9.3
Idaho	1,293,953	1,006,749	28.5
Illinois	12,419,293	11,430,602	8.6
Indiana	6,080,485	5,544,159	9.7
Iowa	2,926,324	2,776,755	5.4
Kansas	2,688,418	2,477,574	8.5
Kentucky	4,041,769	3,685,296	9.7
Louisiana	4,468,976	4,219,973	5.9
Maine	1,274,923	1,227,928	3.8
Maryland	5,296,486	4,781,468	10.8
Massachusetts	6,349,097	6,016,425	5.5
Michigan	9,938,444	9,295,297	6.9
Minnesota	4,919,479	4,375,099	12.4
Mississippi	2,844,658	2,573,216	10.5
Missouri	5,595,211	5,117,073	9.3
Montana	902,195	799,065	12.9
Nebraska	1,711,263	1,578,385	8.4
Nevada	1,998,257	1,201,833	66.3
New Hampshire	1,235,786	1,109,252	11.4
New Jersey	8,414,350	7,730,188	8.9
New Mexico	1,819,046	1,515,069	20.1
New York	18,976,457	17,990,455	5.5
North Carolina	8,049,313	6,628,637	21.4
North Dakota	642,200	638,800	0.5
Ohio	11,353,140	10,847,115	4.7
Oklahoma	3,450,654	3,145,585	9.7
Oregon	3,421,399	2,842,321	20.4
Pennsylvania	12,281,054	11,881,643	3.4
Rhode Island	1,048,319	1,003,464	4.5
South Carolina	4,012,012	3,486,703	15.1
South Dakota	754,844	696,004	8.5
Tennessee	5,689,283	4,877,185	16.7
Texas	20,851,820	16,986,510	22.8
Utah	2,233,169	1,722,850	29.6
Vermont	608,827	562,758	8.2
Virginia	7,078,515	6,187,358	14.4
Washington	5,894,121	4,866,692	21.1
West Virginia	1,808,344	1,793,477	0.8
Wisconsin	5,363,675	4,891,769	9.7
Wyoming	493,782	453,588	8.9

Distribution of Population by Region, 1900, 1950, 2000

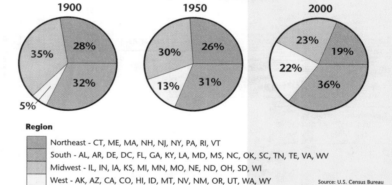

1900	1950	2000
35%, 28%, 32%, 5%	30%, 26%, 13%, 31%	23%, 19%, 22%, 36%

Region

- Northeast - CT, ME, MA, NH, NJ, NY, PA, RI, VT
- South - AL, AR, DE, DC, FL, GA, KY, LA, MD, MS, NC, OK, SC, TN, TE, VA, WV
- Midwest - IL, IN, IA, KS, MI, MN, MO, NE, ND, OH, SD, WI
- West - AK, AZ, CA, CO, HI, ID, MT, NV, NM, OR, UT, WA, WY

Source: U.S. Census Bureau

U.S. Center of Population

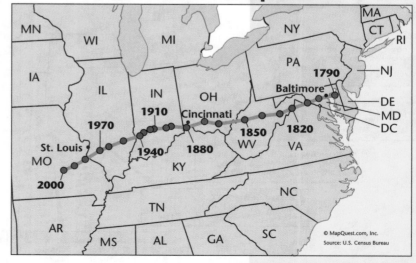

© MapQuest.com, Inc.
Source: U.S. Census Bureau

U.S. Center of Population = center of population gravity, or the point on which the U.S. would balance if it were a rigid plane, assuming all individuals weigh the same and exert influence proportional to their distance from a central point

Population Breakdown by Race and Hispanic or Latino Origin

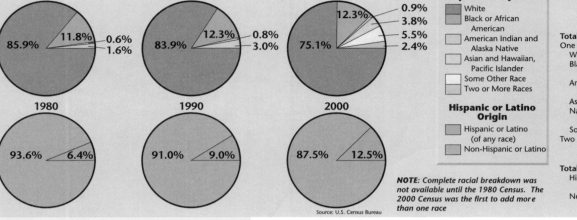

Population by Race
- White
- Black or African American
- American Indian and Alaska Native
- Asian and Hawaiian, Pacific Islander
- Some Other Race
- Two or More Races

Hispanic or Latino Origin
- Hispanic or Latino (of any race)
- Non-Hispanic or Latino

NOTE: *Complete racial breakdown was not available until the 1980 Census. The 2000 Census was the first to add more than one race*

Source: U.S. Census Bureau

Population by Race and Hispanic or Latino Origin, 2000 Census

	Population	Percen
RACE		
Total population	281,421,906	100.0
One race	274,595,678	97.6
White	211,460,626	75.1
Black or African American	34,658,190	12.3
American Indian and Alaska Native	2,475,956	0.9
Asian	10,242,998	3.6
Native Hawaiian and Other Pacific Islander	398,835	0.1
Some other race	15,359,073	5.5
Two or more races	6,826,228	2.4
HISPANIC OR LATINO ORIGIN		
Total population	281,421,906	100.0
Hispanic or Latino (of any race)	35,305,818	12.5
Not Hispanic or Latino	246,116,088	87.5

20 Largest Metropolitan Areas, 2000 Census

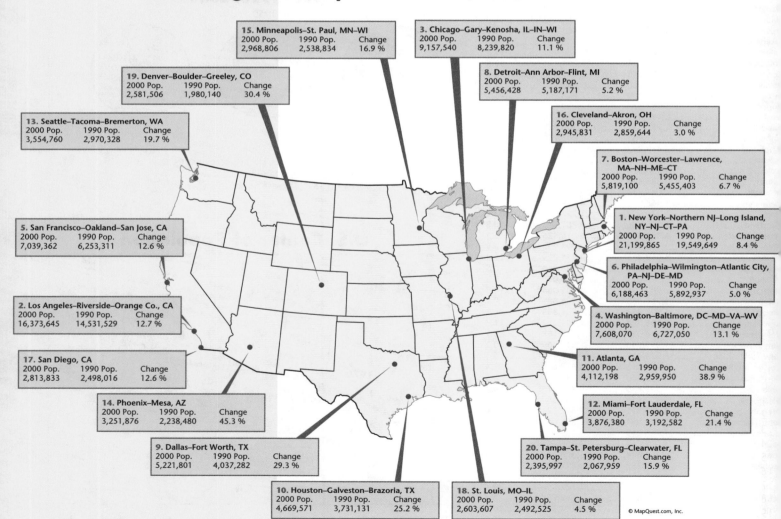

15. Minneapolis–St. Paul, MN–WI
2000 Pop.	1990 Pop.	Change
2,968,806	2,538,834	16.9 %

3. Chicago–Gary–Kenosha, IL–IN–WI
2000 Pop.	1990 Pop.	Change
9,157,540	8,239,820	11.1 %

19. Denver–Boulder–Greeley, CO
2000 Pop.	1990 Pop.	Change
2,581,506	1,980,140	30.4 %

8. Detroit–Ann Arbor–Flint, MI
2000 Pop.	1990 Pop.	Change
5,456,428	5,187,171	5.2 %

13. Seattle–Tacoma–Bremerton, WA
2000 Pop.	1990 Pop.	Change
3,554,760	2,970,328	19.7 %

16. Cleveland–Akron, OH
2000 Pop.	1990 Pop.	Change
2,945,831	2,859,644	3.0 %

7. Boston–Worcester–Lawrence, MA–NH–ME–CT
2000 Pop.	1990 Pop.	Change
5,819,100	5,455,403	6.7 %

5. San Francisco–Oakland–San Jose, CA
2000 Pop.	1990 Pop.	Change
7,039,362	6,253,311	12.6 %

1. New York–Northern NJ–Long Island, NY–NJ–CT–PA
2000 Pop.	1990 Pop.	Change
21,199,865	19,549,649	8.4 %

6. Philadelphia–Wilmington–Atlantic City, PA–NJ–DE–MD
2000 Pop.	1990 Pop.	Change
6,188,463	5,892,937	5.0 %

2. Los Angeles–Riverside–Orange Co., CA
2000 Pop.	1990 Pop.	Change
16,373,645	14,531,529	12.7 %

4. Washington–Baltimore, DC–MD–VA–WV
2000 Pop.	1990 Pop.	Change
7,608,070	6,727,050	13.1 %

17. San Diego, CA
2000 Pop.	1990 Pop.	Change
2,813,833	2,498,016	12.6 %

11. Atlanta, GA
2000 Pop.	1990 Pop.	Change
4,112,198	2,959,950	38.9 %

14. Phoenix–Mesa, AZ
2000 Pop.	1990 Pop.	Change
3,251,876	2,238,480	45.3 %

12. Miami–Fort Lauderdale, FL
2000 Pop.	1990 Pop.	Change
3,876,380	3,192,582	21.4 %

9. Dallas–Fort Worth, TX
2000 Pop.	1990 Pop.	Change
5,221,801	4,037,282	29.3 %

20. Tampa–St. Petersburg–Clearwater, FL
2000 Pop.	1990 Pop.	Change
2,395,997	2,067,959	15.9 %

10. Houston–Galveston–Brazoria, TX
2000 Pop.	1990 Pop.	Change
4,669,571	3,731,131	25.2 %

18. St. Louis, MO–IL
2000 Pop.	1990 Pop.	Change
2,603,607	2,492,525	4.5 %

© MapQuest.com, Inc.

20 Largest Cities, 2000 Census

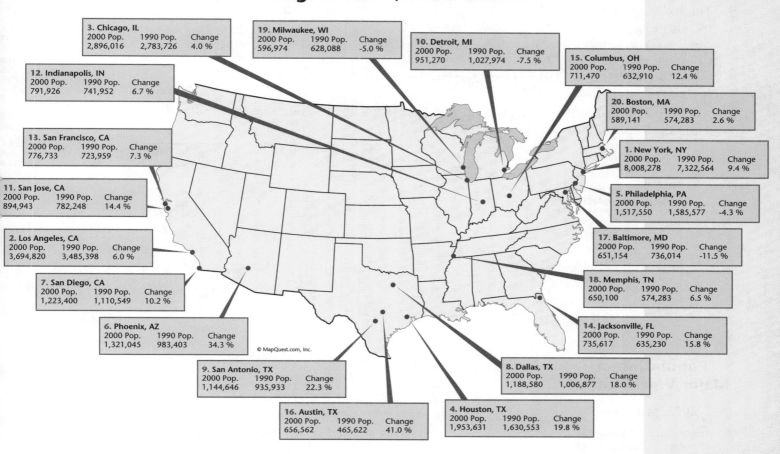

3. Chicago, IL
2000 Pop. 2,896,016 | 1990 Pop. 2,783,726 | Change 4.0 %

19. Milwaukee, WI
2000 Pop. 596,974 | 1990 Pop. 628,088 | Change -5.0 %

10. Detroit, MI
2000 Pop. 951,270 | 1990 Pop. 1,027,974 | Change -7.5 %

15. Columbus, OH
2000 Pop. 711,470 | 1990 Pop. 632,910 | Change 12.4 %

12. Indianapolis, IN
2000 Pop. 791,926 | 1990 Pop. 741,952 | Change 6.7 %

20. Boston, MA
2000 Pop. 589,141 | 1990 Pop. 574,283 | Change 2.6 %

13. San Francisco, CA
2000 Pop. 776,733 | 1990 Pop. 723,959 | Change 7.3 %

1. New York, NY
2000 Pop. 8,008,278 | 1990 Pop. 7,322,564 | Change 9.4 %

11. San Jose, CA
2000 Pop. 894,943 | 1990 Pop. 782,248 | Change 14.4 %

5. Philadelphia, PA
2000 Pop. 1,517,550 | 1990 Pop. 1,585,577 | Change -4.3 %

2. Los Angeles, CA
2000 Pop. 3,694,820 | 1990 Pop. 3,485,398 | Change 6.0 %

17. Baltimore, MD
2000 Pop. 651,154 | 1990 Pop. 736,014 | Change -11.5 %

7. San Diego, CA
2000 Pop. 1,223,400 | 1990 Pop. 1,110,549 | Change 10.2 %

18. Memphis, TN
2000 Pop. 650,100 | 1990 Pop. 574,283 | Change 6.5 %

6. Phoenix, AZ
2000 Pop. 1,321,045 | 1990 Pop. 983,403 | Change 34.3 %

14. Jacksonville, FL
2000 Pop. 735,617 | 1990 Pop. 635,230 | Change 15.8 %

© MapQuest.com, Inc.

9. San Antonio, TX
2000 Pop. 1,144,646 | 1990 Pop. 935,933 | Change 22.3 %

8. Dallas, TX
2000 Pop. 1,188,580 | 1990 Pop. 1,006,877 | Change 18.0 %

16. Austin, TX
2000 Pop. 656,562 | 1990 Pop. 465,622 | Change 41.0 %

4. Houston, TX
2000 Pop. 1,953,631 | 1990 Pop. 1,630,553 | Change 19.8 %

Percent of Population by Race and Hispanic or Latino Origin for the 20 Largest Cities

City		2000 Population	White	Black or African American	American Indian, Alaska Native	Asian	Hawaiian & Other Pacific Islander	Some Other Race	Two or More Races	Hispanic or Latino (of any race)
1	New York ....NY	8,008,278	44.7	26.6	0.5	9.8	0.1	13.4	4.9	27.0
2	Los Angeles ....CA	3,694,820	46.9	11.2	0.8	10.0	0.2	25.7	5.2	46.5
3	Chicago IL	2,896,016	42.0	36.8	0.4	4.3	0.1	13.6	2.9	26.0
4	Houston ....TX	1,953,631	49.3	25.3	0.4	5.3	0.1	16.5	3.1	37.4
5	Philadelphia..........PA	1,517,550	45.0	43.2	0.3	4.5	0.0	4.8	2.2	8.5
6	Phoenix ....AZ	1,321,045	71.1	5.1	2.0	2.0	0.1	16.4	3.3	34.1
7	San Diego ....CA	1,223,400	60.2	7.9	0.6	13.6	0.5	12.4	4.8	25.4
8	Dallas ....TX	1,188,580	50.8	25.9	0.5	2.7	0.0	17.2	2.7	35.6
9	San Antonio ....TX	1,144,646	67.7	6.8	0.8	1.6	0.1	19.3	3.7	58.7
10	Detroit ....MI	951,270	12.3	81.6	0.3	1.0	0.0	2.5	2.3	5.0
11	San Jose ....CA	894,943	47.5	3.5	0.8	26.9	0.4	15.9	5.0	30.2
12	Indianapolis..........IN	791,926	69.3	25.3	0.3	1.4	0.0	2.0	1.6	3.9
13	San Francisco ....CA	776,733	49.7	7.8	0.4	30.8	0.5	6.5	4.3	14.1
14	Jacksonville ....FL	735,617	64.5	29.0	0.3	2.8	0.1	1.3	2.0	4.2
15	Columbus ....OH	711,470	67.9	24.5	0.3	3.4	0.1	1.2	2.6	2.5
16	Austin ....TX	656,562	65.4	10.0	0.6	4.7	0.1	16.2	3.0	30.5
17	Baltimore..........MD	651,154	31.6	64.3	0.3	1.5	0.0	0.7	1.5	1.7
18	Memphis ....TN	650,100	34.4	61.4	0.2	1.5	0.0	1.5	1.0	3.0
19	Milwaukee ....WI	596,974	50.0	37.3	0.9	2.9	0.1	6.1	2.7	12.0
20	Boston ....MA	589,141	54.5	25.3	0.4	7.5	0.1	7.8	4.4	14.4

Source: U.S. Census Bureau

THE WORLD IN THE 21ST CENTURY

The following four pages look at the growing world population and the latest trends in health and mortality. Some highlights:

• The world population has passed 6.1 billion, with 1.3 billion people in China alone.

• By 2050 the world population may pass 11 billion, with most of the growth in urban areas and developing countries.

• The highest life expectancies and lowest infant mortality rates are in North America, Western Europe, and Australia.

Percent Increase in Urban Population, 2000–2015

- 55 and over
- 35–54
- 20–34
- 10–19
- 0–9
- No data

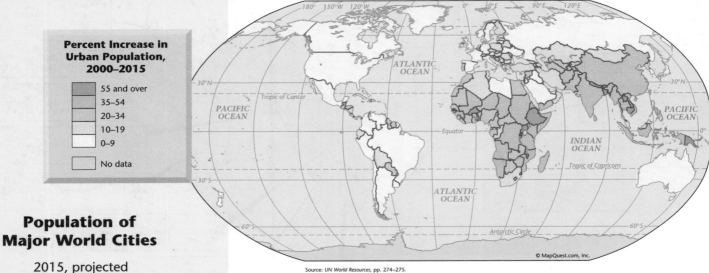

Source: *UN World Resources*, pp. 274–275.

Urban Population Growth, 2000–2015

The world population will become increasingly urbanized in the early 21st century. It is predicted that the largest increases in urban population will occur in Africa and southern and eastern Asia.

Population of Major World Cities

2015, projected

1	Tokyo	28,887,000
2	Mumbai	26,218,000
3	Lagos	24,640,000
4	São Paulo	20,320,000
5	Mexico City	19,180,000
6	Shanghai	17,969,000
7	New York	17,602,000
8	Kolkata	17,305,000
9	Delhi	16,860,000
10	Beijing	15,572,000
11	Los Angeles	14,217,000
12	Buenos Aires	13,856,000
13	Seoul	12,980,000
14	Rio de Janeiro	11,860,000
15	Osaka	10,609,000

These figures are for "urban agglomerations," which are densely populated urban areas, larger than the cities by themselves.

Source: UN, Dept. for Economic and Social Information and Policy Analysis

© MapQuest.com, Inc.

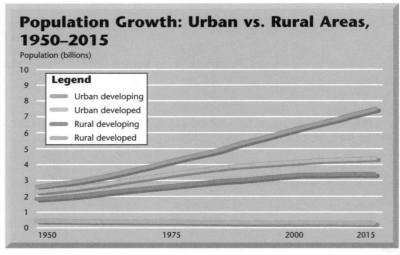

Population Growth: Urban vs. Rural Areas, 1950–2015

Population (billions)

Legend
- Urban developing
- Urban developed
- Rural developing
- Rural developed

Source: *UN World Resources*, p. 146.

Population growth in rural areas will taper off where it has not already. But urban growth will increase, especially in the developing nations.

Developed regions include United States, Canada, Japan, Europe, and Australia and New Zealand.

Developing regions include Africa, Asia (excluding Japan), South America and Central America, Mexico, and Oceania (excluding Australia and New Zealand). The European successor states of the former Soviet Union are classified as developed regions, while the Asian successor states are classified as developing regions.

Population Density, 2000

Population

Persons per sq. mi.		Persons per sq. km.
520 and over		200 and over
260–519		100–199
130–259		50–99
25–129		10–49
1–24		1–9
under 1		under 1

© MapQuest.com, Inc.

World population total (May 1, 2001): 6,144,488,802

Source: International Programs Center, U.S. Census Bureau

Population Density, Largest Countries

2000
People per square mile

China	330
India	800
United States	70
Indonesia	290
Brazil	50
Russia	20

2050
People per square mile

China	360
India	1,400
United States	100
Indonesia	450
Brazil	70
Russia	20

The world is becoming more crowded in the 21st century. In mid-2000, China already had the highest population in the world, with an estimated 1.3 billion inhabitants, more than one-fifth of the total population. India had passed 1 billion, while the United States had the world's third-largest population, with about 281 million, followed by Indonesia, Brazil, and Pakistan.

Source: U.S. Census Bureau

Anticipated World Population Growth

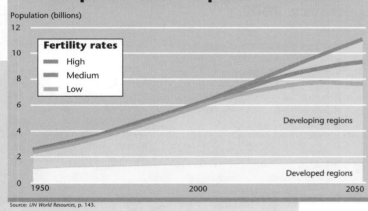

Population (billions)

Fertility rates
- High
- Medium
- Low

Developing regions

Developed regions

Source: *UN World Resources*, p. 143.

The world population has grown from about 2 billion in 1950 to more than 6 billion today, and could almost double by 2050. Most of the growth will continue to occur in developing regions, where fertility rates (number of children born per woman of childbearing age) are relatively high.

Where the fertility rate is around 2 children per woman of childbearing age, the population will tend to stabilize. This figure indicates roughly that couples, over a lifetime, are replacing themselves without adding to the population.

Population experts at the United Nations actually give three different projections for future population growth. Under a **high** fertility-rate projection, which assumes rates would stabilize at an average of 2.6 in high-fertility regions and 2.1 in low-fertility regions, the global population would reach 11.2 billion by 2050. Under a **medium** projection, which assumes rates would ultimately stabilize at around replacement levels, the population would rise to 9.4 billion by 2050. Under a **low** fertility-rate projection, which assumes rates would eventually stabilize at lower-than-replacement levels, the world population would still reach about 7.7 billion by 2050.

Population Projections by Continent

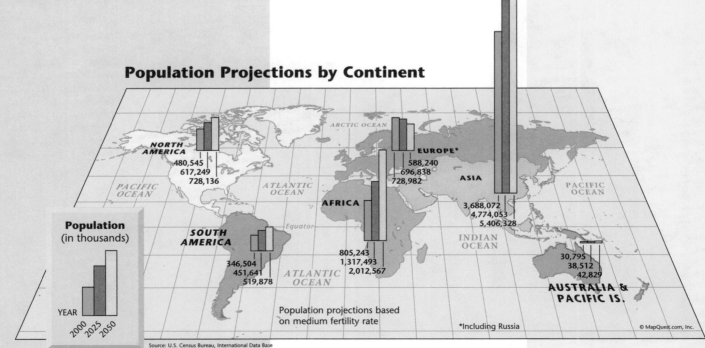

NORTH AMERICA
480,545
617,249
728,136

EUROPE*
588,240
696,838
728,982

ASIA
3,688,072
4,774,053
5,406,328

AFRICA
805,243
1,317,493
2,012,567

SOUTH AMERICA
346,504
451,641
519,878

AUSTRALIA & PACIFIC IS.
30,795
38,512
42,829

Population (in thousands)

YEAR
2000 2025 2050

Population projections based on medium fertility rate

*Including Russia

© MapQuest.com, Inc.

Source: U.S. Census Bureau, International Data Base

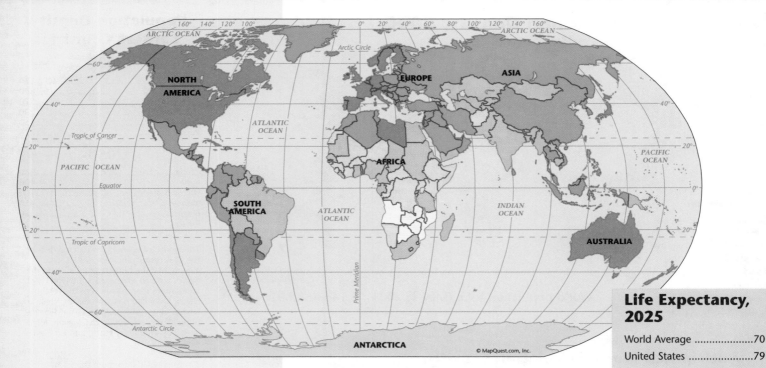

World Life Expectancy, 2000

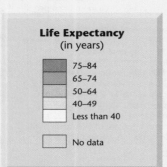

Life Expectancy
(in years)

- 75–84
- 65–74
- 50–64
- 40–49
- Less than 40

- No data

Life expectancy at birth is a common measure of the number of years a person may expect to live. There are many factors, such as nutrition, sanitation, health and medical services, that contribute to helping people live longer.

As some of the above factors improve in the developing countries, life expectancy there should increase. But most of Sub-Saharan Africa will have less than average life expectancies.

Although it is not indicated here, females almost always have a longer life expectancy than males.

World Life Expectancy, 2025

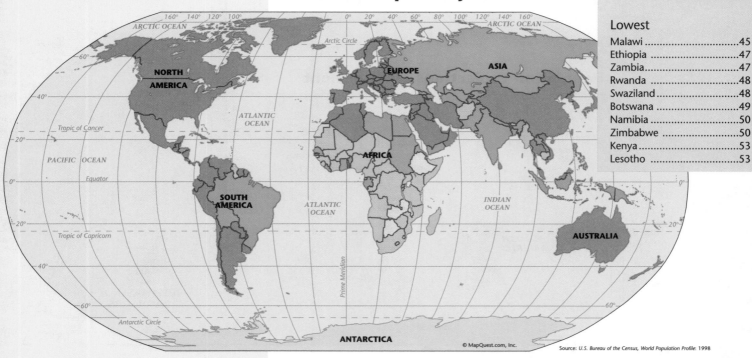

Life Expectancy, 2025

World Average	70
United States	79

Highest

Andorra	84
Austria	84
Australia	83
Canada	82
Cyprus	82
Dominica	82
Israel	82
Japan	82
Kuwait	82
Monaco	82
San Marino	82
Singapore	82
Taiwan	82

Lowest

Malawi	45
Ethiopia	47
Zambia	47
Rwanda	48
Swaziland	48
Botswana	49
Namibia	50
Zimbabwe	50
Kenya	53
Lesotho	53

Source: U.S. Bureau of the Census, World Population Profile: 1998

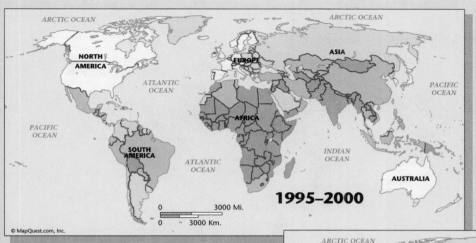

1995–2000

© MapQuest.com, Inc.

Infant Mortality Averages, 2015–2020

by continent with highest and lowest country

World Average 35

Africa 55	Europe 8
Sierra Leone 114	Albania 20
Mauritius 8	Austria
	& 14 others..........5
Asia 32	
Afghanistan 118	North America 22
Japan 4	Haiti 82
	Canada...................5
	U.S. 5
Australia & Oceania ..15	
Papua	South America 23
New Guinea 37	Guyana.................37
Australia 5	Chile......................9

Infant Mortality

Infant mortality means the number of deaths before the age of one per 1,000 live births. It is a fairly common way of judging how healthy a country is. Presently there are about 14 countries with infant mortality rates lower than that of the United States.

With improvements in sanitation and health care, it is expected that infant mortality will decline substantially in the 21st century. However, it will continue to be a serious problem especially in Sub-Saharan Africa and other developing regions

Infant Mortality Rate
(per 1,000 live births)

- 85–169
- 50–85
- 25–49
- 10–24
- Less than 10
- No data

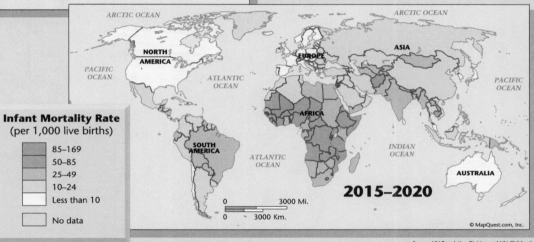

2015–2020

© MapQuest.com, Inc.

Source: UN Population Division and UN Children's Fund

Food & Nutrition

There has been a general trend towards better nutrition, but Sub-Saharan Africa remains a problem area: increasing numbers of people will be suffering from undernutrition.

On a worldwide basis, the food supply seems adequate. Unfortunately the availability of food and the distribution of people don't always match up.

Undernutrition in Developing Countries, 1969-2010

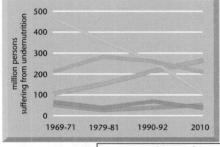

million persons suffering from undernutrition

500 / 400 / 300 / 200 / 100 / 0

1969-71   1979-81   1990-92   2010

Fertility

This rate is the number of births related to the number of women of childbearing age. Currently the rate for developed nations is about 1.6, but it is about 2.9 in developing nations.

Africa shows the slowest reduction in the fertility rate. With improvements in infant mortality and the implementation of family planning programs, the rate should stabilize.

Average Daily per Capita Calorie Supply, 1999

by continent
with highest and lowest country

PORTUGAL 3,768
CROATIA 2,617
ISRAEL 3,542
AFGHANISTAN 1,755
UNITED STATES 3,754
HAITI 1,977
VENEZUELA 2,229
PAPUA NEW GUINEA 2,186
TUNISIA 3,388
SOMALIA 1,555
ARGENTINA 3,176
NEW ZEALAND 3,152

Source: UN Food and Agriculture Organization,
UN Population Division,
U.S. Department of Agriculture

© MapQuest.com, Inc.

Legend
- Latin America and the Caribbean
- Near East and North Africa
- Sub-Saharan Africa
- East and Southeast Asia
- South Asia

Trends in Fertility Rates

Legend
- Africa
- Asia
- South and Central America
- Developed
- Developing

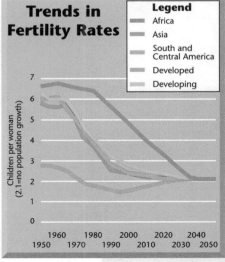

Children per woman (2.1=no population growth)

7 / 6 / 5 / 4 / 3 / 2 / 1 / 0

1950 1960 1970 1980 1990 2000 2010 2020 2030 2040 2050

Source: UN Population Division

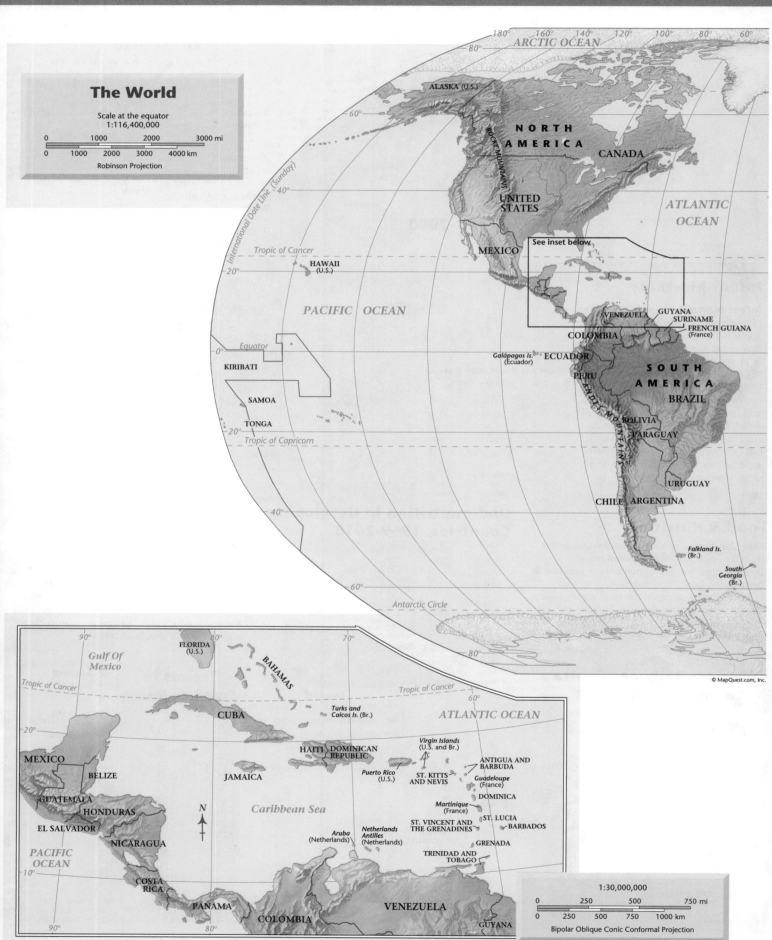

The World

Scale at the equator
1:116,400,000

0   1000   2000   3000 mi

0   1000   2000   3000   4000 km

Robinson Projection

ARCTIC OCEAN

ALASKA (U.S.)

NORTH AMERICA

CANADA

ROCKY MOUNTAINS

UNITED STATES

ATLANTIC OCEAN

MEXICO

International Date Line (Sunday)

Tropic of Cancer

HAWAII (U.S.)

See inset below

PACIFIC OCEAN

VENEZUELA   GUYANA   SURINAME   FRENCH GUIANA (France)

COLOMBIA

Galápagos Is. (Ecuador)   ECUADOR

Equator

KIRIBATI

PERU   SOUTH AMERICA   BRAZIL

ANDES MOUNTAINS

SAMOA   BOLIVIA

TONGA   PARAGUAY

Tropic of Capricorn

URUGUAY

CHILE   ARGENTINA

Falkland Is. (Br.)

South Georgia (Br.)

Antarctic Circle

© MapQuest.com, Inc.

Gulf Of Mexico   FLORIDA (U.S.)   BAHAMAS

Tropic of Cancer   Tropic of Cancer

Turks and Caicos Is. (Br.)   ATLANTIC OCEAN

CUBA

Virgin Islands (U.S. and Br.)

MEXICO   HAITI   DOMINICAN REPUBLIC   ANTIGUA AND BARBUDA

BELIZE   Puerto Rico (U.S.)   ST. KITTS AND NEVIS   Guadeloupe (France)

JAMAICA   DOMINICA

GUATEMALA   Martinique (France)   ST. LUCIA

HONDURAS   Caribbean Sea   ST. VINCENT AND THE GRENADINES   BARBADOS

EL SALVADOR   N

NICARAGUA   Aruba (Netherlands)   Netherlands Antilles (Netherlands)   GRENADA

PACIFIC OCEAN   TRINIDAD AND TOBAGO

COSTA RICA

1:30,000,000

0   250   500   750 mi

0   250   500   750   1000 km

PANAMA   VENEZUELA

COLOMBIA   GUYANA

Bipolar Oblique Conic Conformal Projection

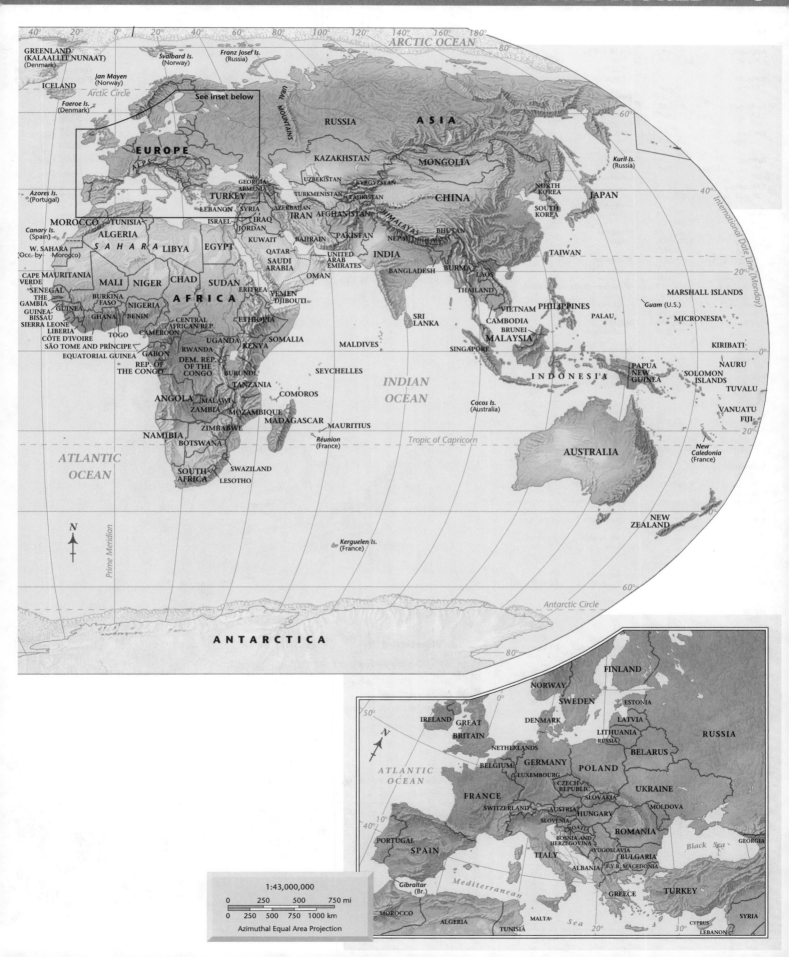

ARCTIC OCEAN

GREENLAND
(KALAALLIT NUNAAT)
(Denmark)

ICELAND

Jan Mayen
(Norway)

Svalbard Is.
(Norway)

Franz Josef Is.
(Russia)

Arctic Circle

Faeroe Is.
(Denmark)

See inset below

URAL MOUNTAINS

RUSSIA

ASIA

EUROPE

ALPS

Kuril Is.
(Russia)

Azores Is.
(Portugal)

KAZAKHSTAN

MONGOLIA

NORTH
KOREA

JAPAN

GEORGIA
ARMENIA

UZBEKISTAN

KYRGYZSTAN

CHINA

TURKEY

TURKMENISTAN

TAJIKISTAN

SOUTH
KOREA

MOROCCO TUNISIA

LEBANON SYRIA

AZERBAIJAN

IRAN AFGHANISTAN

HIMALAYAS

ISRAEL

IRAQ

JORDAN

PAKISTAN

BHUTAN

TAIWAN

International Date Line (Monday)

Canary Is.
(Spain)

ALGERIA

LIBYA

EGYPT

KUWAIT

BAHRAIN

NEPAL

W. SAHARA
(Occ. by
Morocco)

SAHARA

QATAR
SAUDI
ARABIA

UNITED
ARAB
EMIRATES

INDIA

BANGLADESH

BURMA

CAPE
VERDE

MAURITANIA

MALI

NIGER

CHAD

SUDAN

OMAN

LAOS

MARSHALL ISLANDS

SENEGAL
THE
GAMBIA

ERITREA

YEMEN

THAILAND

Guam (U.S.)

GUINEA-
BISSAU

GUINEA

BURKINA
FASO

NIGERIA

AFRICA

DJIBOUTI

VIETNAM

PHILIPPINES

MICRONESIA

PALAU

SIERRA LEONE

GHANA

BENIN

ETHIOPIA

CAMBODIA

LIBERIA

TOGO

CENTRAL
AFRICAN REP.

CAMEROON

BRUNEI

KIRIBATI

CÔTE D'IVOIRE

SÃO TOME AND PRÍNCIPE

UGANDA

SOMALIA

MALDIVES

MALAYSIA

EQUATORIAL GUINEA

GABON

KENYA

SRI
LANKA

NAURU

REP. OF
THE CONGO

DEM. REP.
OF THE
CONGO

RWANDA

SINGAPORE

INDONESIA

PAPUA
NEW
GUINEA

SOLOMON
ISLANDS

BURUNDI

SEYCHELLES

INDIAN
OCEAN

TUVALU

ANGOLA

TANZANIA

COMOROS

MALAWI

ZAMBIA

MOZAMBIQUE

MADAGASCAR

MAURITIUS

Cocos Is.
(Australia)

VANUATU

FIJI

ZIMBABWE

NAMIBIA

BOTSWANA

Réunion
(France)

Tropic of Capricorn

New
Caledonia
(France)

AUSTRALIA

ATLANTIC
OCEAN

SOUTH
AFRICA

SWAZILAND

LESOTHO

N

Prime Meridian

Kerguelen Is.
(France)

NEW
ZEALAND

Antarctic Circle

ANTARCTICA

1:43,000,000

0   250   500   750 mi

0   250 500 750 1000 km

Azimuthal Equal Area Projection

FINLAND

NORWAY

SWEDEN

ESTONIA

IRELAND

GREAT
BRITAIN

DENMARK

LATVIA

RUSSIA

LITHUANIA

RUSSIA

ATLANTIC
OCEAN

NETHERLANDS

BELGIUM

GERMANY

POLAND

BELARUS

LUXEMBOURG

CZECH
REPUBLIC

UKRAINE

FRANCE

SWITZERLAND

SLOVAKIA

MOLDOVA

AUSTRIA

HUNGARY

SLOVENIA

ROMANIA

CROATIA

PORTUGAL

SPAIN

ITALY

BOSNIA AND
HERZEGOVINA

YUGOSLAVIA

GEORGIA

Black Sea

BULGARIA

Gibraltar
(Br.)

ALBANIA

F.Y.R. MACEDONIA

Mediterranean

GREECE

TURKEY

MOROCCO

ALGERIA

TUNISIA

MALTA

Sea

CYPRUS
LEBANON

SYRIA

MAJOR CITIES

Country/City	Population
Afghanistan	(metro)
Kabul	2,029,000
Bahrain	
Manama	151,000
Bangladesh	(metro)
Dhaka	8,545,000
Bhutan	
Thimphu	8,900
Brunei	
Band. Seri Begawan	51,000
Cambodia	
Phnom Penh	800,000
China	
Shanghai	7,500,000
Hong Kong	6,502,000
Beijing	5,700,000
Tianjin	4,500,000
Shenyang	3,600,000
Wuhan	3,200,000
Guangzhou	2,900,000
Chongqing	2,700,000
Harbin	2,500,000
Chengdu	2,500,000
Zibo	2,200,000
Xi'an	2,200,000
Nanjing	2,091,000
Cyprus	
Nicosia	193,000
India	(metro)
Mumbai	
(Bombay)	12,572,000
Kolkata	
(Calcutta)	10,916,000
Delhi	8,375,000
Madras	5,361,000
Hyderabad	4,280,000
Bangalore	4,087,000
Indonesia	
Jakarta	9,113,000
Surabaya	2,664,000
Bandung	2,356,000
Medan	1,844,000
Iran	
Tehran	6,750,000
Mashhad	1,964,000
Iraq	(metro)
Baghdad	4,336,000
Israel	
Jerusalem	585,000
Japan	
Tokyo	7,968,000
Yokohama	3,320,000
Osaka	2,600,000
Nagoya	2,151,000
Sapporo	1,774,000
Kyoto	1,464,000
Kobe	1,420,000
Fukuoka	1,296,000
Kawasaki	1,209,000
Hiroshima	1,115,000
Jordan	(metro)
Amman	1,183,000
Kazakhstan	
Almaty	
(Alma-Ata)	1,064,000
North Korea	
P'yŏngyang	2,741,000

Country/City	Population
South Korea	
Seoul	10,231,000
Pusan	3,814,000
Taegu	2,449,000
Kuwait	
Kuwait	29,000
Kyrgyzstan	
Bishkek	589,000
Laos	
Vientiane	377,000
Lebanon	(metro)
Beirut	1,826,000
Malaysia	(metro)
Kuala Lumpur	1,236,000
Maldives	
Male	55,000
Mongolia	
Ulaanbaatar	536,000
Myanmar (Burma)	(metro)
Yangon	
(Rangoon)	3,873,000
Nepal	
Kathmandu	419,000
Oman	
Muscat	85,000
Pakistan	(metro)
Karachi	5,181,000
Lahore	2,953,000
Faisalabad	1,104,000
Islamabad	204,000
Philippines	
Manila	1,655,000
Qatar	
Doha	236,000
Russia (Asian)	
Novosibirsk	1,368,000
Yekaterinburg	1,277,000
Omsk	1,161,000
Chelyabinsk	1,084,000
Saudi Arabia	(metro)
Riyadh	2,619,000
Jeddah	1,492,000
Singapore	
Singapore	3,737,000
Sri Lanka	
Colombo	615,000
Syria	
Damascus	1,549,000
Halab (Aleppo)	1,542,000
Taiwan	
Taipei	1,770,000
Tajikistan	
Dushanbe	529,000
Thailand	(metro)
Bangkok	6,547,000
Turkey (Asian)	
Ankara	2,938,000
İzmir	2,130,000
Turkmenistan	
Ashgabat	407,000
United Arab Emirates	
Abu Dhabi (metro)	799,000
Uzbekistan	(metro)
Tashkent	2,282,000
Vietnam	(metro)
Ho Chi Minh City	3,521,000
Hanoi	1,236,000
Yemen	(metro)
Sanaa	927,000

International comparability of city population data is limited by various data inconsistencies.

© MapQuest.com, Inc.

Gross National Product (GNP) per capita

- $36,410
- $21,500
- $8625
- $2785
- $695
- $0
- No data

Vegetation

- Unclassified Highlands and Ice Cap
- Tundra and Alpine Tundra
- Coniferous Forest
- Midlatitude Deciduous Forest
- Subtropical Broadleaf Evergreen Forest
- Mixed Forest
- Midlatitude Scrub
- Midlatitude Grassland
- Desert
- Tropical Seasonal and Scrub
- Tropical Rain Forest
- Tropical Savanna

Asia: Population, by nation (in millions)*

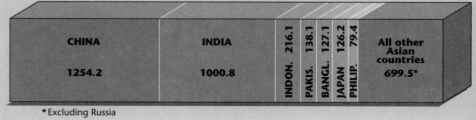

CHINA	INDIA	INDON.	PAKIS.	BANGL.	JAPAN	PHILIP.	All other Asian countries
1254.2	1000.8	216.1	138.1	127.1	126.2	79.4	699.5*

*Excluding Russia

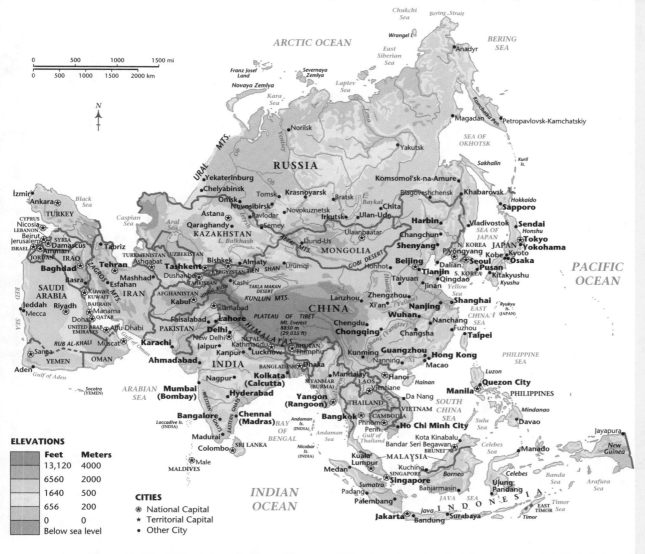

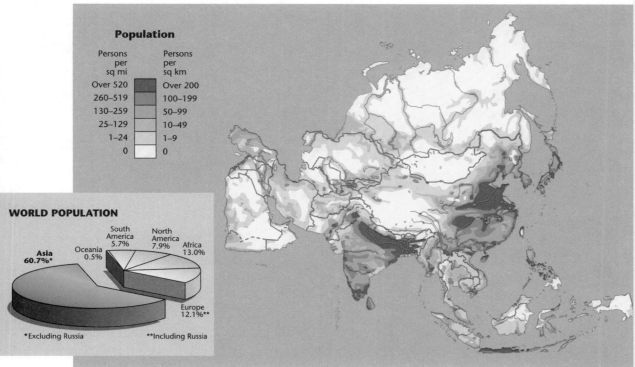

ELEVATIONS

Feet	Meters
13,120	4000
6,560	2000
1,640	500
656	200
0	0
Below sea level	

CITIES
- ⊛ National Capital
- ★ Territorial Capital
- • Other City

Population

Persons per sq mi	Persons per sq km
Over 520	Over 200
260–519	100–199
130–259	50–99
25–129	10–49
1–24	1–9
0	0

WORLD POPULATION

- Asia 60.7%*
- Oceania 0.5%
- South America 5.7%
- North America 7.9%
- Africa 13.0%
- Europe 12.1%**

*Excluding Russia   **Including Russia

CLIMATE

Average daily temperature °F range — High, Low
Average monthly precipitation Inches

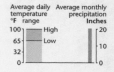
ALMATY, Kazakhstan

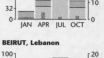
BEIRUT, Lebanon

COLOMBO, Sri Lanka

DHAKA, Bangladesh

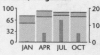
HONG KONG, China

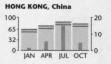
JAKARTA, Indonesia

NEW DELHI, India

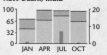
RIYADH, Saudi Arabia

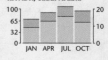
TEHRAN, Iran

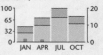
TIANJIN, China

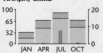
TOKYO, Japan

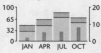
YAKUTSK, Russia

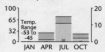

Inset I (Hokkaido)

La Pérouse Strait
Point Soya
Cape Soya
Rebun
Rishiri
Wakkanai
Sea of Okhotsk
Teshio
Kitami Mts.
Mombetsu
Haboro
Cape Shiretoko
Kunashir (Russia)
Asahikawa
Ishikari
Kitami
Asahi Dake 2290 m (7513 ft)
Nemuro Strait
Cape Kamui
HOKKAIDO
Nemuro
Cape Erimo
Otaru
Yubari
Sapporo
Obihiro
Chitose
Tokachi
Kushiro
Tomakomai
HIDAKA MTS.
Okushiri
Muroran
Oshima Pen.
Uchiura Bay
Hakodate
Matsumae
Tsugaru Strait

Main map

SOUTH KOREA
P'ohang
Pusan
Korea Strait
Sea of Japan
Noto Peninsula
Toyama Bay
Oki Is.
Dogo
Dozen
Wakasa Bay
Cape Hino
Matsue
Tottori
HYOGO
Maizuru
SHIMANE
Yonago
TOTTORI
Ibaraki
KYOTO
Gotsu
Chugoku Mts.
OKAYAMA
Amagasaki
Nishinomiya
SHIGA
Masuda
HIROSHIMA
Okayama
Kurashiki
Himeji
Kobe
Akashi
Suita
Hiroshima
YAMAGUCHI
Fukuyama
Takamatsu
KAGAWA
Awaji
Sakai
OSAKA
MIE
Yamaguchi
Kure
Iwakuni
Inland Sea
Yao
Neyagawa
Higashiosaka
Shimonoseki
Ube
Osaka
NARA
Tokuyama
Niihama
TOKUSHIMA
Wakayama
Kitakyushu
FUKUOKA
Matsuyama
Kochi
Tokushima
WAKAYAMA
Tanabe
Fukuoka
SAGA
Kurume
OITA
EHIME
KOCHI
Tosa Bay
Sasebo
Saga
Oita
Uwajima
Cape Muroto
Nakadori
NAGASAKI
Omuta
Nagasaki
KYUSHU
Burgo Channel
Cape Ashizuri
SHIKOKU
Fukue
Fukue
Kumamoto
Aso 1592 m (5223 ft)
Nobeoka
Yatsushiro
KUMAMOTO
MIYAZAKI
Amakusa Is.
Koshiki Is.
Miyazaki
KAGOSHIMA
Miyakonojo
East China Sea
Satsuma Peninsula
Kagoshima
Osumi Pen.
Cape Sata
Osumi Strait
Osumi Is.
Yaku
Kuchino
Nakano
Suwanose
Akuseki
Takara
Tanega
Tokara Islands

Main map (Honshu/east)

HOKKAIDO (see inset)
Okushiri
Muroran
Oshima Pen.
Hakodate
Matsumae
Mutsu
Cape Henashi
Aomori
Hirosake
AOMORI
Towada L.
Hachinohe
Miyako
Morioka
IWATE
Akita
Ou Mts.
Kitakami
AKITA
MIYAGI
Mogami
Tsuruoka
Ishinomaki
YAMAGATA
Sendai
Ishinomaki Bay
Yamagata
Zao 1841 m (6040 ft)
Ryotsu
Sado
Niigata
Fukushima
NIIGATA
Aizuwakamatsu
Koriyama
Iwaki
Nagaoka
FUKUSHIMA
HONSHU
Joetsu
ISHIKAWA
Nagano
Nikko
TOCHIGI
IBARAKI
Hitachi
Toyama
GUMMA
Utsunomiya
Mito
Kanazawa
TOYAMA
Maebashi
Ashikaga
Kawaguchi
Komatsu
Japanese Alps
Asama 2542 m (8340 ft)
Koshigaya
Matsumoto
SAITAMA
Omiya
Kashiwa
Fukui
NAGANO
Tokorozawa
Ichikawa
FUKUI
Yariga 3180 m (10,433 ft)
Urawa
Matsudo
Tsuruga
GIFU
Kofu
Hachioji
TOKYO
Funabashi
Gifu
Shirane 3192 m (10,472 ft)
Sagamihara
Chiba
Ichinomiya
YAMANASHI Machida
Ichihara
Otsu
AICHI
Fuji KANAGAWA
Tokyo
SHIGA
Kasugai
Fuji 3776 m (12,388 ft)
Yokohama
Takatsuki
Nagoya
Okazaki
Yokosuka
Kawasaki
Hirakata
Toyota
SHIZUOKA
Fujisawa
CHIBA
Yokkaichi
Shimizu
Numazu
Boso Pen.
Ise
Toyohashi
Hamamatsu
Izu Pen.
Cape Nojima
Ise Bay
Sagami Bay
Nii
Kozu
Izu Islands
Miyake
Mikura
PACIFIC OCEAN
Hachijo
Bonin Is. (see inset)

Japan legend (center box)

Japan
⊛ National Capital
• Other City
1:7,500,000
0 50 100 150 mi
0 50 100 150 km
Lambert Conformal Conic Projection

Inset II (Ryukyu Islands)

Amami
Naze
Amami Islands
Kakeroma
Tokuno
Okino Erabu
Yoron
Kume
Okinawa Islands
Okinawa
Gushikawa
Naha
RYUKYU ISLANDS
Senkaku Islands
OKINAWA
Yonaguni
Hirara
Miyako
Ishigaki
Iriomote
Sakishima Islands
0 50 100 mi
0 50 100 km

Inset III (Bonin/Volcano Islands)

Nishino
Muko
Chichi
Haha
Bonin Islands
Kita
Iwo Jima
Volcano Islands
Minami
0 50 100 mi
0 50 100 km

Japan (bottom-left box)

Japan
Capital: Tokyo
Area: 145,850 sq. mi.
377,850 sq. km.
Population: 126,182,000
Largest City: Tokyo
Language: Japanese
Monetary Unit: Yen

Japan: Map Index

Prefectures
Aichi	C3
Akita	D2
Aomori	D1
Chiba	D3
Ehime	B3
Fukui	C3
Fukuoka	A3
Fukushima	D2
Gifu	C3
Gumma	C2
Hiroshima	B3
Hokkaido	D1, Inset I
Hyogo	B3
Ibaraki	D2
Ishikawa	C2
Iwate	D2
Kagawa	B3
Kagoshima	A4
Kanagawa	C3
Kochi	B3
Kumamoto	A3
Kyoto	B3
Mie	C3
Miyagi	D2
Miyazaki	A3
Nagano	C2
Nagasaki	A3
Nara	B3
Niigata	C2
Oita	A3
Okayama	B3
Okinawa	Inset II
Osaka	B3
Saga	A3
Saitama	C2
Shiga	C3
Shimane	B3
Shizuoka	C3
Tochigi	C2
Tokushima	B3
Tokyo	C3
Tottori	B3
Toyama	C2
Wakayama	B3
Yamagata	C2
Yamaguchi	A3
Yamanashi	C3
Yao	B3
Yatsushiro	A3

Cities and Towns
Aizuwakamatsu	C2
Akashi	B3
Akita	D2
Amagasaki	B3
Aomori	D1
Asahikawa	Inset I
Ashikaga	C2
Awaji	B3
Chiba	D3
Chitose	Inset I
Fujisawa	C3
Fukue	A3
Fukui	C2
Fukuoka	A3
Fukushima	D2
Fukuyama	B3
Funabashi	D3
Gifu	C3
Gotsu	B3
Gushikawa	Inset II
Haboro	Inset I
Hachinohe	D1
Hachioji	C3
Hakodate	D1, Inset I
Hamamatsu	C3
Higashiosaka	B3
Himeji	B3
Hirakata	B3
Hirara	Inset II
Hirosake	D1
Hiroshima	B3
Hitachi	D2
Ibaraki	B3
Ichihara	D3
Ichikawa	D3
Ichinomiya	C3
Ise	C3
Ishinomaki	D2
Iwaki	D2
Iwakuni	B3
Izuhara	A3
Joetsu	C2
Kagoshima	A4
Kanazawa	C2
Kashiwa	D3
Kasugai	C3
Kawagoe	C3
Kawaguchi	C3
Kawasaki	C3
Kitakyushu	A3
Kitami	Inset I
Kobe	B3
Kochi	B3
Kofu	C3
Komatsu	C2
Koriyama	D2
Koshigaya	C3
Kumamoto	A3
Kurashiki	B3
Kure	B3
Kurume	A3
Kushiro	Inset I
Kyoto	B3
Machida	C3
Maebashi	C2
Maizuru	B3
Masuda	A3
Matsudo	C3
Matsue	B3
Matsumae	D1, Inset I
Matsumoto	C2
Matsuyama	B3
Mito	D2
Miyako	D2
Miyakonojo	A4
Miyazaki	A4
Mombetsu	Inset I
Morioka	D2
Muroran	D1, Inset I
Mutsu	D1
Nagano	C2
Nagaoka	C2
Nagasaki	A3
Nagoya	C3
Naha	Inset II
Nara	B3
Naze	Inset II
Nemuro	Inset I
Neyagawa	B3
Niigata	C2
Niihama	B3
Nikko	C2
Nishinomiya	B3
Nobeoka	A3
Numazu	C3
Obihiro	Inset I
Oita	A3
Okayama	B3
Okazaki	C3
Omiya	C3
Omuta	A3
Osaka	B3
Otaru	Inset I
Otsu	B3
Ryotsu	C2
Saga	A3
Sagamihara	C3
Sakai	B3
Sapporo	Inset I
Sasebo	A3
Sendai	D2
Shimizu	C3
Shimonoseki	A3
Shizuoka	C3
Suita	B3
Takamatsu	B3
Takatsuki	B3
Tanabe	B3
Tokorozawa	C3
Tokushima	B3
Tokuyama	A3
Tokyo, capital	C3
Tomakomai	Inset I
Tottori	B3
Toyama	C2
Toyohashi	C3
Toyonaka	B3
Toyota	C3
Tsuruga	C3
Tsuruoka	C2
Ube	A3
Urawa	C3
Utsunomiya	C2
Uwajima	A3
Wakayama	B3
Wakkanai	Inset I
Yamagata	D2
Yamaguchi	A3
Yao	B3
Yatsushiro	A3

© MapQuest.com, Inc.

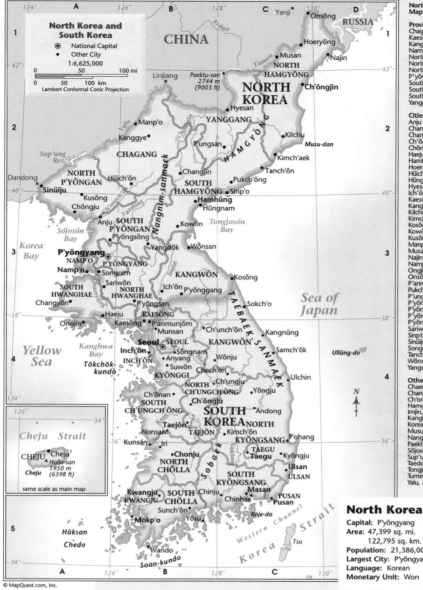

North Korea and South Korea

⊛ National Capital
● Other City

1:6,625,000

0   50   100 mi
0   50   100 km

Lambert Conformal Conic Projection

Taiwan

⊛ National Capital
● Other City

1:10,292,000

0   30   60 mi
0   30   60 km

Lambert Conformal Conic Projection

© MapQuest.com, Inc.

© MapQuest.com, Inc.

North Korea

Capital: P'yŏngyang
Area: 47,399 sq. mi.
122,795 sq. km.
Population: 21,386,000
Largest City: P'yŏngyang
Language: Korean
Monetary Unit: Won

South Korea

Capital: Seoul
Area: 38,330 sq. mi.
99,301 sq. km.
Population: 46,885,000
Largest City: Seoul
Language: Korean
Monetary Unit: Won

Taiwan

Capital: Taipei
Area: 13,969 sq. mi.
36,189 sq. km.
Population: 22,113,000
Largest City: Taipei
Language: Mandarin Chinese
Monetary Unit: New Taiwan dollar

Japan: Map Index

Yokkaichi C3
Yokohama C3
Yokosuka C3
Yonago B3
Yubari ....Inset I

Other Features

Akuseki, island..............A4
Amakusa, island A3
Amami, island ....Inset II
Amami, islands ....Inset II
Asahi Dake, mt. ....Inset I
Asama, mt. C2
Ashizuri, cape B3
Aso, mt. A3
Awaji, island B3
Biwa, lake B3
Bonin, islands ....Inset III
Boso, peninsula D3
Bungo, channel B3
Chichi, island ....Inset III
Chugoku, mts. B3
Dogo, island B2
Dozen, island B2
East China, sea A4
Erimo, cape ....Inset I
Fuji, mt. C3
Fukue, island A3
Hachijo, island C3
Haha, island ....Inset III
Henashi, cape C1
Hidaka, mts. ....Inset I
Hino, cape B3
Hokkaido, island ...D1, Inset I
Honshu, island C2
Iki, island A3
Inland, sea B3
Iriomote, island ......Inset II
Ise, bay C3
Ishigaki, island ....Inset II
Ishikari, river ....Inset I
Ishinomaki, bay D2
Ishizuchi, mt. B3
Iwo Jima, island .....Inset III
Izu, islands C3
Izu, peninsula C3
Japan, sea B2
Japanese Alps, mts. C3
Kakeroma, island ....Inset II
Kamui, cape ....Inset I
Kii, channel B3
Kii, peninsula B3
Kita, island ....Inset III
Kitakami, river D2
Kitami, mts. ....Inset I
Korea, strait A3
Koshiki, islands A4
Kozu, island C3
Kuchino, island A4
Kume, island ....Inset II
Kyushu, island A4
La Pérouse, strait ....Inset I
Mikura, island C3
Minami, island ......Inset III
Miyake, island C3
Miyako, island ....Inset II
Mogami, river D2
Muko, island ....Inset III
Muroto, cape B3
Nakadori, island A3
Nakano, island A4
Nemuro, strait ....Inset I
Nii, island C3
Nishino, island ......Inset III
Nojima, cape D3
Noto, peninsula C2
Okhotsk, sea ....Inset I
Oki, islands B2
Okinawa, island ......Inset II
Okinawa, islands ......Inset II
Okino Erabu, island......Inset II
Okushiri, island .....C1, Inset I
Oshima, peninsula ..D1, Inset I
Osumi, islands A4
Osumi, peninsula.........A4
Osumi, strait A4
Ou, mts. D2
Rebun, island ....Inset I
Rishiri, island ....Inset I
Ryukyu, islands ......A4, Inset II
Sado, island C3
Sagami, bay C3
Sakishima, islands ....Inset II
Sata, cape A4
Satsuma, peninsula A4
Senkaku, islands ....Inset II
Shikoku, island B3
Shimonoseki, strait A3
Shinano, river C2
Shiono, cape B3
Shirane, mt. C3
Shiretoko, cape ....Inset I
Soya, point ....Inset I
Suwanose, island A4
Takara, island A4
Tanega, island A4
Tenryu, river C3
Teshio, river ....Inset I
Tokachi, river ....Inset I
Tokara, islands A4
Tokuno, island ....Inset II
Tone, river C2
Tosa, bay B3
Towada, lake D1
Toyama, bay C2
Tsu, island A3
Tsugaru, strait ....D1, Inset I
Uchiura, bay ....Inset I
Volcano, islands .....Inset III
Wakasa, bay B3
Yaku, island A4
Yariga, mt. C3
Yonaguni, island .....Inset II
Yoron, island ....Inset II
Yoshino, river B3
Zao, mt. D2

North Korea: Map Index

Provinces

Chagang B2
Kaesŏng B3
Kangwŏn B3
Namp'o A3
North Hamgyŏng C1
North Hwanghae B3
North P'yŏngan A2
P'yŏngyang A3
South Hamgyŏng B2
South Hwanghae A3
South P'yŏngan A3
Yanggang B2

Cities and Towns

Anju A3
Changjin B2
Changyŏn A3
Ch'ŏngjin C2
Chŏngju A3
Haeju A3
Hamhŭng B3
Hoeryŏng C1
Hŭich'ŏn B2
Hŭngnam B3
Hyesan B2
Ich'ŏn B3
Kaesŏng B4
Kanggye B2
Kilchu C2
Kimch'aek C2
Kosŏng C3
Kowŏn B3
Kusŏng A3
Manp'o B2
Musan C1
Najin D1
Namp'o A3
Ongjin A3
Onsŏng C1
P'anmunjŏm B4
Pukch'ŏng C2
P'ungsan B2
P'yŏnggang B3
P'yŏngsan B3
P'yŏngsŏng A3
P'yŏngyang, capital A3
Sariwŏn A3
Sinp'o B3
Sinŭiju A2
Songnim A3
Tanch'ŏn C2
Wŏnsan B3
Yangdŏk B3

Other Features

Chaeryŏng, river A3
Changjin, river B2
Ch'ŏngch'ŏn, river A3
Hamgyŏng, mts. C2
Imjin, river B3
Kanghwa, bay A4
Korea, bay A3
Musu-dan, point C2
Nangnim-sanmaek, mts. ..B3
Paektu-san, mt. B2
Sŏjosŏn, bay A3
Sup'ung, reservoir A2
Taedong, river A3
Tongjosŏn, bay B3
Tumen, river C1
Yalu, river B2

South Korea: Map Index

Provinces

Cheju ....Inset
Inch'ŏn B4
Kangwŏn B4
Kwangju B5
Kyŏnggi B4
North Chŏlla B5
North Ch'ungch'ŏng B4
North Kyŏngsang C4
Pusan C5
Seoul B4
South Chŏlla B5
South Ch'ungch'ŏng B4
South Kyŏngsang C5
Taegu C5
Taejŏn B4
Ulsan C5

Cities and Towns

Andong C4
Anyang B4
Chech'ŏn C4
Cheju ....Inset
Chinhae C5
Chinju C5
Chonju B5
Ch'ŏnan B4
Ch'ŏngju B4
Ch'unch'ŏn B4
Ch'ungju B4
Inch'ŏn B4
Iri B5
Kangnŭng C4
Kimch'ŏn C4
Kunsan B5
Kwangju B5
Kyŏngju C5
Masan C5
Mokp'o B5
Munsan B4
Nonsan B4
P'ohang C4
Pusan C5
Samch'ŏk C4
Seoul, capital B4
Sokch'o C3
Sŏngnam B4
Sunch'ŏn B5
Suwŏn B4
Taegu C5
Taejŏn B4
Ulchin C4
Ulsan C5
Wŏnju B4
Wando B5
Yŏngju C4
Yŏsu B5

Other Features

Cheju, island ....Inset
Cheju, strait ....Inset
Halla-san, mt. ....Inset
Han, river B4
Hŭksan Chedo, islands ...A5
Kanghwa, bay A4
Koje-do, island C5
Korea, strait C5
Kum, river B4
Naktong, river C5
Soan-kundo, islands B5
Sobaek, mts. C5
Taebaek-Sanmaek, mts. ..C3
Tŏkchŏk-kundo, islands ..A4
Ullŭng-do, island D4
Western, channel C5

Taiwan: Map Index

Cities and Towns

Changhua B1
Chiai B2
Chilung B1
Chunan B1
Chungho B1
Chungli B1
Fangliao B2
Fengshan B2
Fengyüan B1
Hengch'un B2
Hsinchu B1
Hsinchuang B1
Hsintien B1
Hsinying B2
Hualien B2
Ilan B1
Kangshan B2
Kaohsiung B2
Makung A2
Miaoli B1
Nant'ou B1
Panch'iao B1
P'ingtung B2

Shanchung B1
T'aichung B1
T'ainan B2
Taipei, capital B1
T'aitung B2
Tanshui B1
T'aoyüan B1
Touliu B2
Yungho B1

Other Features

Choshui, river B2
Chungyang, range B2
East China, sea B1
Kaop'ing, river B2
Lan, island B2
Lü, island B2
Luzon, strait B2
P'enghu (Pescadores),
islands A2
Pescadores, channel A2
Philippine, sea B2
South China, sea A2
Taiwan, strait A1
Tanshui, river B1
Tsengwen, river B2
Yü Shan, mt. B2

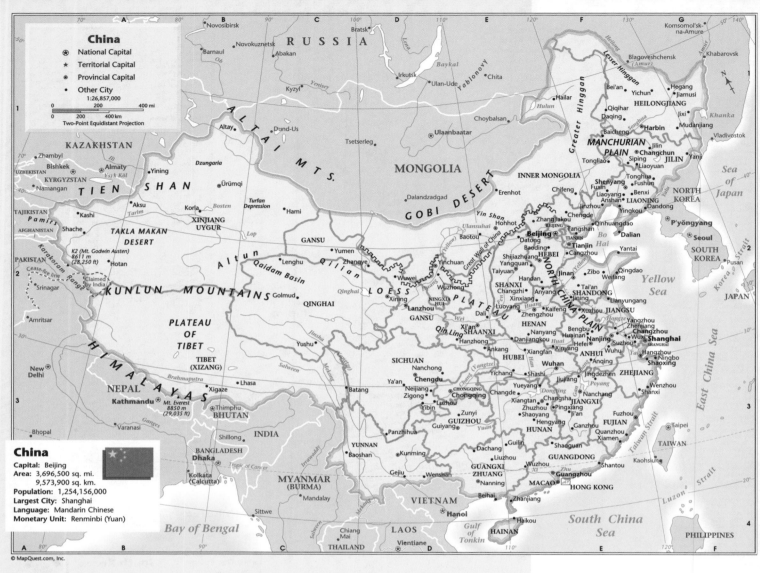

China
- ⊛ National Capital
- ★ Territorial Capital
- ◉ Provincial Capital
- ● Other City

1:26,857,000

0 — 200 — 400 mi
0 — 200 — 400 km
Two-Point Equidistant Projection

China
Capital: Beijing
Area: 3,696,500 sq. mi.
9,573,900 sq. km.
Population: 1,254,156,000
Largest City: Shanghai
Language: Mandarin Chinese
Monetary Unit: Renminbi (Yuan)

© MapQuest.com, Inc.

Hong Kong S.A.R.
- ● City

1:1,800,000

0 — 10 — 20 mi
0 — 10 — 20 km
Transverse Mercator Projection

© MapQuest.com, Inc.

China:
Map Index

Internal Divisions
Provinces
Anhui E2
Fujian E3
Gansu C1, D2
Guangdong E3
Guizhou D3
Hainan D4
Hebei E2
Heilongjiang F1
Henan E2
Hubei E3
Hunan E3
Jiangsu E2
Jiangxi E3
Jilin F1
Liaoning F1
Qinghai C2
Shaanxi D2
Shandong E2
Shanxi E2
Sichuan D2
Yunnan C3
Zhejiang E3

Autonomous Regions
Guangxi Zhuang D3
Inner Mongolia D1
Ningxia Hui D2
Tibet (Xizang) B2
Xinjiang Uygur B1

Independent Municipalities
Beijing E1
Chongqing D3
Shanghai F2
Tianjin E2

Special Administrative Regions (S.A.R.)
Hong Kong .... E3, Inset
Macao E3

Cities and Towns
Aberdeen .... Inset
Aksu B1
Altay B1
Ankang D2
Anqing E2
Anshan F1

Anyang E2
Baicheng F1
Baoding E2
Baoshan C3
Baotou E1
Batang C3
Bei'an F1
Beihai D3
Beijing, capital E2
Bengbu E2
Benxi F1
Cangzhou E2
Changchun F1
Changde E3
Changsha E3
Changzhi E2
Changzhou E2
Chek Keng .... Inset
Chengde E1
Chengdu D2
Chifeng E1
Chongqing D3
Chung Hau .... Inset
Dachang D2
Dali D2
Dalian F2
Dandong F1
Danjiangkou E2
Daqing F1
Datong E1
Erenhot E1
Fushun F1
Fuxin F1
Fuzhou E3
Ganzhou E3
Gejiu D3
Golmud C2
Guangzhou E3
Guilin D3
Guiyang D3
Haikou E4
Hailar E1
Hami C1
Handan E2
Hangzhou F2
Hanzhong D2
Harbin F1
Hefei E2
Hegang G1
Hengyang E3
Hohhot E1
Hotan A2

Huainan E2
Jiamusi G1
Ji'an E3
Jilin F1
Jinan E2
Jingdezhen E3
Jining E2
Jinzhou F1
Jiujiang E3
Jixi G1
Kaifeng E2
Kashi A2
Korla B1
Kowloon .... Inset
Kunming D3
Lanzhou D2
Lenghu C2
Lhasa C3
Lianyungang E2
Liaoyang F1
Liaoyuan F1
Liuzhou D3
Lo Wu .... Inset
Luoyang E2
Luzhou D3
Mudanjiang F1
Nanchang E3
Nanchong D2
Nanjing E2
Nanning D3
Nanyang E2
Neijiang D2
New Kowloon .... Inset
Ningbo F3
Panzhihua D3
Pingxiang E3
Qingdao F2
Qinhuangdao E2
Qiqihar F1
Quanzhou E3
Sai Kung .... Inset
Shache A2
Shanghai F2
Shantou E3
Shanxi E2
Shaoguan E3
Shaoxing F3
Shaoyang E3
Shashi E2
Sha Tin .... Inset
Shek Pik .... Inset
Shenyang F1

Shijiazhuang E2
Siping F1
Suzhou F2
Tai'an E2
Taiyuan E2
Tangshan E2
Tianjin E2
Tonghua F1
Tongliao E1
Tsuen Wan .... Inset
Tuen Mun .... Inset
Ürümqi B1
Weifang E2
Wenshan D3
Wenzhou F3
Wuhan E2
Wuhu E3
Wuwei D2
Wuxi F2
Wuzhong D2
Wuzhou D3
Xiamen E3
Xi'an D2
Xiangfan E2
Xiangtan E3
Xigaze B3
Xining D2
Xinxiang E2
Xinyang E2
Xuzhou E2
Ya'an D2
Yangquan E2
Yangzhou E2
Yanji F1
Yantai F2
Yibin D3
Yichang E2
Yichun F1
Yinchuan D2
Yingkou F1
Yining B1
Yuen Long .... Inset
Yueyang E3
Yumen C2
Yushu C2
Zhangjiakou E1
Zhangye D2
Zhanjiang E3
Zhengzhou E2
Zhenjiang E2
Zhuzhou E3
Zibo E2

Zigong D3
Zunyi D3

Other Features
Altai, mts. B1
Altun, range B2
Bayan Har, range C2
Bo Hai, gulf E2
Bosten, lake B1
Brahmaputra, river B3
Chang (Yangtze), river ... D2, E2
Deep, bay .... Inset
Dongting, lake E3
Dzungaria, desert basin ... B1
East China, sea F3
Fen, river E2
Gan, river E3
Gobi, desert D1
Greater Hinggan, range ... F1
Great Wall of China D2
Han, river E2
Heilong (Amur), river F1
Himalayas, mts. B3
Hong Kong, island ... Inset
Hongze, lake E2
Huai, river E2
Huang (Yellow), river ... D2, E2
Hulun, lake E1
Indus, river A2
Jinsha (Yangtze), river ... C2
Khanka, lake G1
Kunlun, mts. B2
K2 (Godwin Austen), mt. ... A2
Lantau, island .... Inset
Lesser Hinggan, range ... F1
Liao, river F1
Loess, plateau D2
Lop, lake C1
Manchurian, plain F2
Mekong, river C2
Nan Ling, mts. E3
New Territories, island ....Inset
North China, plain E2
Pamirs, region A2
Poyang, lake E3
Qaidam, basin C2
Qilian, range D2
Qinghai, lake D2
Qin Ling, mts. D2
Salween, river C2
Songhua, river F1
South China, sea ......E4, Inset

Stonecutters (S.I.), island..Inset
Tai, lake F2
Taiwan, strait E3
Takla Makan, desert B2
Tanggula, range C2
Tarim, river B1
Tibet, plateau B2
Tien Shan, range A1
Tonkin, gulf D4
Turfan, depression C1
Ulansuhai, lake D2
Wei, river D2
Xi, river E3
Yalu, river F1
Yangtze, river ... C2, D2
Yellow, sea F2
Yin Shan, mts. D1
Yuan, river E3
Zhu, river E3

Vietnam: Map Index

Cities and Towns
Bac Lieu A5
Bien Hoa B4
Buon Me Thuot B4
Ca Mau A5
Cam Ranh B4
Can Tho A4
Cao Bang B1
Chau Doc A4
Da Lat B4
Da Nang B3
Dien Bien Phu A2
Dong Hoi B3
Ha Giang A1
Haiphong B2
Hanoi, capital A2
Hoa Binh A2
Ho Chi Minh City B4
Hon Gai B2
Hue B3
Khe Sanh B3
Kontum B3
Lang Son B1
Lao Cai A1
Long Xuyen A4
My Tho B4
Nam Dinh B2
Nha Trang B4
Phan Rang B4
Phan Thiet B4
Pleiku B4
Quang Ngai B3
Quang Tri B3
Qui Nhon B4
Rach Gia A4
Soc Trang A5
Son La A2
Tay Ninh B4
Thai Nguyen A2
Thanh Hoa A2
Tuy Hoa B4
Viet Tri A2
Vinh A2
Vung Tau- Con Dao B4
Yen Bai A2

Other Features
Annam, mts. A2
Ba, river B3
Black (Da), river A2
Ca, river A2
Central, highlands B4
Con Son, islands B5
Cu Lao Thu, island B4
Dao Phu Quoc, island .. A4
Dong Nai, river B4
Fan Si Pan, mt. A1
Gam, river A1
Lo, river A1
Ma, river A2
Mekong, delta B5
Mekong, river A4
Mui Bai Bung, point A5
Ngoc Linh, mt. B3
Red (Hong), river A2
Tonkin, gulf B2

Vietnam
Capital: Hanoi
Area: 127,246 sq. mi.
  329,653 sq. km.
Population: 77,311,000
Largest City: Ho Chi Minh City
Language: Vietnamese
Monetary Unit: Dong

Vietnam
⊛ National Capital
● Other City
1:14,333,000
0 50 100 150 200 mi
0 50 100 150 200 km
Lambert Conformal Conic Projection

Laos: Map Index

Cities and Towns
Attapu D4
Ban Houayxay A1
Champasak C4
Louang Namtha A1
Luang Prabang B2
Muang Khammouan C3
Muang Khong C4
Muang Khôngxédôn C4
Muang Paklay A2
Muang Pakxan B2
Muang Vangviang B2
Muang Xaignabouri A2
Muang Xay B1
Muang Xépôn D3
Muang Xon B1
Pakse C4
Phôngsali B1
Saravan D4
Savannakhet C3
Vientiane, capital B3
Xam Nua C1
Xiangkhoang B2

Other Features
Annam, range C3
Banghiang, River D4
Bolovens, plateau D4
Kong, river D4
Luang Prabang, range .. A3
Mekong, river A1, C3
Nam Ngum, reservoir .. B2
Ou, river B1
Phou Bia, mt. B2
Xiangkhoang, plateau .. B2

Laos
Capital: Vientiane
Area: 91,429 sq. mi.
  236,085 sq. km.
Population: 5,407,000
Largest City: Vientiane
Language: Lao
Monetary Unit: New kip

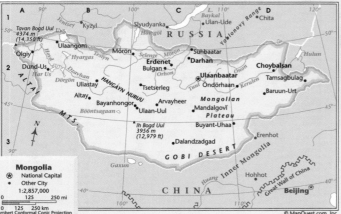

Laos
⊛ National Capital
● Other City
1:14,533,000
0 50 100 mi
0 50 100 km
Lambert Conformal Conic Projection

© MapQuest.com, Inc.

Cambodia
⊛ National Capital 1:8,573,000
● Other City
◆ Ruins
0 50 100 mi
0 50 100 km
Conic Projection

© MapQuest.com, Inc.

Cambodia
Capital: Phnom Penh
Area: 70,238 sq. mi.
  181,964 sq. km.
Population: 11,627,000
Largest City: Phnom Penh
Language: Khmer
Monetary Unit: New riel

Cambodia: Map Index

Cities and Towns
Batdambang B2
Kampong Cham D4
Kampong Chhnang C3
Kampong Saom B5
Kampong Thum C3
Kampot C4
Kracheh E3
Krong Kaoh Kong A4
Lumphat F2
Phnom Penh, capital C4
Phnum Tbeng Meanchey .. C2
Phumi Samraong B1
Pouthisat B3
Prey Veng D4
Senmonorom F3
Siempang E1
Siemreab B2
Sisophon B2
Sre Ambel B4
Stoeng Treng D2
Svay Rieng D4
Takev C5

Other Features
Angkor Thom, ruins B2
Angkor Wat, ruins B2
Aoral, mt. C3
Cardamom, mts. B3
Dangrek, mts. B1
Mekong, river D2
San, river D2
Sen, river C2
Sreng, river B2
Thailand, gulf B4
Tonle Sap, lake B2, C3
Tonle Sap, river B2

Mongolia: Map Index

Cities and Towns
Altay B2
Arvayheer C2
Baruun-Urt D2
Bayanhongor C2
Bulgan C2
Buyant-Uhaa D3
Choybalsan D2
Dalandzadgad C3
Darhan C2
Dund-Us B2
Erdenet C2
Mandalgovĭ C2
Mörön C2
Ölgiy A2
Öndörhaan D2
Sühbaatar C2
Tamsagbulag D2
Tsetserleg C2
Ulaangom B2
Ulaan-Uul D3
Ulaanbaatar, capital ... C2
Uliastay B2

Other Features
Altai, mts. B2
Bööntsagaan, lake B2
Dörgön, lake B2
Dzavhan, river B2
Gobi, desert C3
Hangayn, mts. B2
Har Us, lake B2
Hovd, river B2
Hövsgöl, lake C1
Hyargas, lake B2
Ih Bogd Uul, mt. C3
Kerulen, river D2
Mongolian, plateau D2
Onon, river D2
Orhon, river C2
Selenge Mörön, river .. C2
Tavan Bogd Uul, mt. ... A2
Tesiyn, river B2
Tuul, river C2
Uvs, lake B1

Mongolia
Capital: Ulaanbaatar
Area: 604,800 sq. mi.
  1,566,839 sq. km.
Population: 2,617,000
Largest City: Ulaanbaatar
Language: Mongolian
Monetary Unit: Tughrik

Mongolia
⊛ National Capital
● Other City
1:2,857,000
0 125 250 mi
0 125 250 km
Lambert Conformal Conic Projection

© MapQuest.com, Inc.

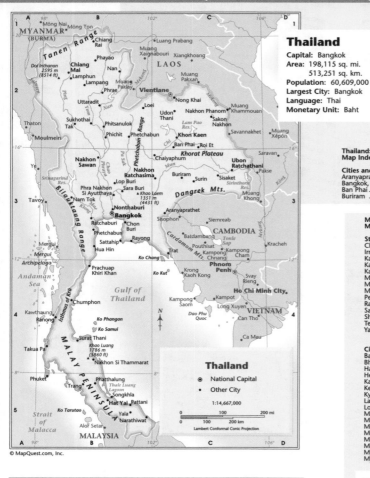

Thailand

Capital: Bangkok
Area: 198,115 sq. mi.
513,251 sq. km.
Population: 60,609,000
Largest City: Bangkok
Language: Thai
Monetary Unit: Baht

Thailand:
Map Index

Cities and Towns
Aranyaprathet	C3
Bangkok, *capital*	B3
Ban Phai	C2
Buriram	C3
Chaiyaphum	C3
Chiang Mai	B2
Chiang Rai	B2
Chon Buri	B3
Chumphon	B4
Hat Yai	B5
Hua Hin	B3
Khon Kaen	C2
Lampang	B2
Lamphun	B2
Loei	B2
Lop Buri	B3
Nakhon Phanom	C2
Nakhon Ratchasima	C3
Nakhon Sawan	B2
Nakhon Si Thammarat	B4
Nam Tok	B3
Nan	B2
Narathiwat	B5
Nong Khai	C2
Nonthaburi	B3
Pattani	B5
Phatthalung	B5
Phetchabun	B2
Phetchaburi	B3
Phichit	B2
Phitsanulok	B2
Phrae	B2
Phra Nakhon Si Ayutthaya	B3
Phuket	B5
Prachuap Khiri Khan	B4
Ranong	B4
Ratchaburi	B3
Rayong	B3
Roi Et	C2
Sakon Nakhon	C2
Sara Buri	B3
Sattahip	B3
Sisaket	C3
Songkhla	B5
Sukhothai	B2
Surat Thani	B4
Surin	C3
Tak	B2
Takua Pa	B4
Trang	B5
Trat	C3
Ubon Ratchathani	C3
Udon Thani	C2
Uttaradit	B2
Yala	B5

Other Features
Bilauktaung, *range*	B3
Chao Phraya, *river*	B2
Chi, *river*	C2
Dangrek, *mts.*	C3
Dawna, *range*	B2
Inthanon, *mt.*	B2
Khorat, *plateau*	C3
Ko Chang, *island*	C3
Ko Kut, *island*	C4
Ko Phangan, *island*	B4
Ko Samui, *island*	B4
Ko Tarutao, *island*	B5
Kra, *isthmus*	B4
Laem, *mt.*	B3
Lam Pao, *reservoir*	C2
Luang, *mt.*	B4
Mae Klong, *river*	B3
Malacca, *strait*	B5
Malay, *peninsula*	B5
Mekong, *river*	C2
Mun, *river*	C3
Nan, *river*	B2
Pa Sak, *river*	B2
Phetchabun, *range*	B3
Ping, *river*	B2
Salween, *river*	A2
Sirinthorn, *reservoir*	C3
Srinagarind, *reservoir*	B3
Tanen, *range*	B2
Thailand, *gulf*	B4
Thale Luang, *lagoon*	B5
Yom, *river*	B2

Myanmar (Burma):
Map Index

States and Divisions
Chin, *state*	B2
Irrawaddy, *division*	B3
Kachin, *state*	C1
Karen, *state*	C3
Kayah, *state*	C2
Magwe, *division*	B2
Mandalay, *division*	B2
Mon, *state*	C3
Pegu, *division*	B3
Rakhine, *state*	B2
Sagaing, *division*	B2
Shan, *state*	C2
Tenasserim, *division*	C3
Yangon (Rangoon), *division*	C3

Cities and Towns
Bassein	B3
Bhamo	C1
Haka	B2
Henzada	B3
Kawthaung	C4
Keng Tung	C2
Kyaukpyu	B2
Lashio	C2
Loi-kaw	C2
Mandalay	C2
Maymyo	C2
Meiktila	C2
Mergui	C3
Monywa	B2
Moulmein	C3
Myingyan	B2
Myitkyina	C1
Pa-an	C3
Pegu	C3
Prome	B2
Putao	C1
Sagaing	B2
Shwebo	B2
Sittwe	B2
Tamu	B1
Taunggyi	C2
Tavoy	C3
Toungoo	C2
Yangon (Rangoon), *capital*	C3
Ye	C3

Other Features
Andaman, *sea*	B3
Arakan Yoma, *mts.*	B2
Bengal, *bay*	B3
Bilauktaung, *range*	C3
Cheduba, *island*	B2
Chin, *hills*	B2
Chindwin, *river*	B1
Coco, *islands*	B3
Hkakabo Razi, *mt.*	C1
Irrawaddy, *river*	B2
Martaban, *gulf*	C3
Mekong, *river*	C2
Mergui, *archipelago*	C4
Mouths of the Irrawaddy, *delta*	B3
Preparis, *island*	B3
Ramree, *island*	B2
Salween, *river*	C2
Shan, *plateau*	C2
Sittang, *river*	C2
Tavoy, *point*	C3
Thailand, *gulf*	C4

Myanmar (Burma)

Capital: Yangon (Rangoon)
Area: 261,228 sq. mi.
676,756 sq. km.
Population: 48,081,000
Largest City: Yangon (Rangoon)
Language: Burmese
Monetary Unit: Kyat

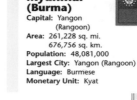

Philippines

Capital: Manila
Area: 115,860 sq. mi.
300,155 sq. km.
Population: 79,346,000
Largest City: Manila
Languages: Pilipino, English
Monetary Unit: Philippine peso

Philippines:
Map Index

Regions
Bicol	B3
Cagayan Valley	B2
Central Luzon	A3
Central Mindanao	C5
Central Visayas	B4
*Cordillera Autonomous Region	B2
Eastern Visayas	C4
Ilocos	B2
*Moslem Mindanao Autonomous Region	B5
National Capital Region	B3
Northern Mindanao	C4
Southern Mindanao	C5
Southern Tagalog	B3
Western Mindanao	B5
Western Visayas	B4

Cities and Towns
Angeles	B3
Bacolod	B4
Baguio	B2
Basilan	B5
Batangas	B3
Bislig	C4
Butuan	C4
Cabanatuan	B3
Cadiz	B4
Cagayan de Oro	C4
Calapan	B3
Calbayog	C3
Cebu	B4
Cotabato	C5
Dagupan	B2
Davao	C5
Dipolog	B4
Dumaguete	B4
General Santos	C5
Iligan	C4
Iloilo	B4
Jolo	B5
Laoag	B2
Laoang	C3
Legazpi	B3
Lipa	B3
Lucena	B3
Mamburao	B3
Mandaue	B4
Manila, *capital*	B3
Masbate	B3
Naga	B3
Olongapo	B3
Ormoc	C4
Pagadian	B5
Puerto Princesa	A4
Quezon City	B3
Roxas	B4
San Carlos	B4
San Fernando	B2
San Pablo	B3
Silay	B4
Surigao	C4
Tacloban	C4
Tuguegarao	B2
Vigan	B2
Zamboanga	B5

Other Features
Agusan, *river*	C4
Apo, *volcano*	C5
Babuyan, *channel*	B2
Babuyan, *islands*	B1
Balabac, *island*	A5
Balabac, *strait*	A5
Bashi, *channel*	B1
Basilan, *island*	B5
Bataan, *peninsula*	B3
Batan, *islands*	B1
Bohol, *island*	C4
Bohol, *sea*	C4
Cagayan, *islands*	B4
Cagayan, *river*	B2
Cagayan Sulu, *island*	A5
Calamian, *islands*	A4
Caramoan, *peninsula*	B3
Catanduanes, *island*	C3
Cebu, *island*	B4
Celebes, *sea*	B5
Cordillera Central, *mts.*	B2
Corregidor, *island*	B3
Cuyo, *islands*	B4
Davao, *gulf*	C5
Dinagat, *island*	C4
Diuata, *mts.*	C4
Jolo, *island*	B5
Laguna de Bay, *lake*	B3
Lamon, *bay*	B3
Leyte, *island*	C4
Lingayen, *gulf*	B2
Luzon, *island*	B3
Luzon, *strait*	B2
Manila, *bay*	B3
Marinduque, *island*	B3
Masbate, *island*	B3
Mayon, *volcano*	B3
Mindanao, *island*	C5
Mindoro, *island*	B3
Mindoro, *strait*	B3
Moro, *gulf*	B5
Negros, *island*	B4
Palawan, *island*	A4
Panay, *gulf*	B4
Panay, *island*	B4
Philippine, *sea*	C3
Pulangi, *river*	C5
Samar, *island*	C3
Samar, *sea*	B3
Siargao, *island*	C4
Sibuyan, *island*	B3
Sibuyan, *sea*	B3
Sierra Madre, *mts.*	B2
South China, *sea*	A3
Sulu, *archipelago*	A5
Sulu, *sea*	A4
Tablas, *island*	B3
Tawi Tawi, *island*	A5
Visayan, *islands*	B4
Visayan, *sea*	B4
Zambales, *mts.*	B3
Zamboanga, *peninsula*	B5

*Not on map

© MapQuest.com, Inc.

Indonesia: Map Index

Cities and Towns

Amahai	D2
Ambon	D2
Balikpapan	C2
Banda Aceh	A1
Bandar Lampung	B2
Bandung	B2
Banjarmasin	C2
Baubau	D2
Bengkulu	B2
Bogor	B2
Cilacap	B2
Cirebon	B2
Denpasar	C2
Ende	D2
Fakfak	E2
Gorontalo	D1
Jakarta, capital	B2
Jambi	B2
Jayapura	F2
Kediri	C2
Kendari	D2
Kupang	D3
Madiun	C2
Magelang	C2
Malang	C2
Manado	D1
Manokwari	E2
Mataram	C2
Medan	A1
Merauke	F2
Padang	B2
Palangkaraya	B2
Palembang	B2
Palu	C2
Pangkalpinang	B2
Parepare	C2
Pekalongan	B2
Pekanbaru	B1
Pematangsiantar	A1

Pontianak	B2
Raba	C2
Samarinda	C2
Semarang	C2
Sorong	E2
Sukabumi	C2
Surabaya	C2
Surakarta	C2
Tanjungpinang	B1
Tarakan	C1
Tasikmalaya	B2
Tegal	B2
Ternate	D1
Ujung Pandang	D2
Waingapu	D2
Yogyakarta	C2

Other Features

Agung, mt.	C2
Alor, island	D2
Arafura, sea	E2
Aru, islands	E2
Babar, island	D2
Bali, island	C2
Banda, sea	D2
Bangka, island	B2
Belitung, island	B2
Biak, island	E2
Borneo, island	C1
Buru, island	D2
Celebes (Sulawesi), island	D2
Celebes, sea	D1
Ceram, island	D2
Ceram, sea	D2
Digul, river	E2
Enggano, island	B2
Flores, island	C2
Flores, sea	C2
Greater Sunda, islands	B2
Halmahera, island	D1

Irian Jaya, region	E2
Java, island	C2
Java, sea	C2
Jaya, mt.	E2
Kahayan, river	C2
Kai, islands	E2
Kalimantan, region	C2
Kerinci, mt.	B2
Krakatau, island	B2
Lesser Sunda, islands	C2
Lingga, island	B2
Lombok, island	C2
Madura, island	C2
Makassar, strait	C2
Malacca, strait	A1
Mentawai, islands	A2
Misool, island	E2
Moa, island	D2
Molucca, sea	D2
Moluccas, islands	D2

Morotai, island	D1
Muna, island	D2
Natuna Besar, island	B1
New Guinea, island	F2
Nias, island	A1
Obi, island	D2
Peleng, island	D2
Savu, sea	D2
Semeru, mt.	C2
Siberut, island	A2
Simeulue, island	A1
South China, sea	C1
Sudirman, range	E2
Sula, islands	D2
Sulu, sea	C1
Sumatra, island	B2
Sumba, island	C2
Sumbawa, island	C2
Talaud, islands	D1
Tanimbar, islands	E2

Indonesia

Capital: Jakarta
Area: 741,052 sq. mi.
  1,919,824 sq. km.
Population: 216,108,000
Largest City: Jakarta
Language: Bahasa Indonesian
Monetary Unit: New rupiah

Timor, island	D2
Timor, sea	D3
Waigeo, island	E2
Wetar, island	D2
Yapen, island	E2

Brunei

Capital: Bandar Seri
  Begawan
Area: 2,226 sq. mi.
  5,767 sq. km.
Population: 323,000
Largest City: Bandar Seri Begawan
Language: Malay
Monetary Unit: Brunei dollar

Brunei: Map Index

Cities and Towns

Badas	A2
Bandar Seri Begawan, capital	B2
Bangar	C2
Batang Duri	B2
Jerudong	B2
Kerangan Nyatan	B3
Kuala Abang	B2
Kuala Belait	A2
Labi	A3
Labu	C2
Lumut	A2
Medit	B2
Muara	C1
Seria	A2
Sukang	B3
Tutong	B2

Other Features

Belait, river	B3
Brunei, bay	C1
Brunei, river	B2
Bukit Pagon, mt.	C3
Pandaruan, river	C2
South China, sea	A2
Temburong, river	C2
Tutong, river	B2

Singapore: Map Index

Cities and Towns

Bedok	B1
Bukit Panjang	B1
Bukit Timah	B1
Changi	B1
Choa Chu Kang	A1
Jurong	A1
Kranji	A1
Nee Soon	B1
Punggol	B1
Queenstown	B1
Sembawang	B1
Serangoon	B1
Singapore, capital	B1
Tampines	B1
Thong Hoe	A1
Toa Payoh	A1
Tuas	A1
Woodlands	B1

Other Features

Ayer Chawan, island	A2
Bukum, island	B2
Johor, strait	B1

Singapore

Capital: Singapore
Area: 247 sq. mi.
  640 sq. km.
Population: 3,532,000
Largest City: Singapore
Languages: Mandarin Chinese, English, Malay, Tamil
Monetary Unit: Singapore dollar

Keppel, harbor	B2
Pandan, strait	A2
Semakau, island	B2
Senang, island	B2
Sentosa, island	B2
Singapore, island	B1
Singapore, strait	B2
Tekong, island	C1
Timah, hill	B1
Ubin, island	B1

Singapore

Malaysia: Map Index

Cities and Towns

Alor Setar	A1
Batu Pahat	B2
George Town	A2
Ipoh	B2
Johor Baharu	B2
Kelang	A2
Keluang	B2
Kota Baharu	B1
Kota Kinabalu	C1
Kuala Lumpur, capital	A2
Kuala Terengganu	B2

Kuantan	B2
Kuching	C2
Melaka	B2
Miri	D2
Muar	B2
Sandakan	D2
Seremban	B2
Sibu	C2
Tawau	D2
Telok Anson	A2

Other Features

Banggi, island	D1
Baram, river	D2
Crocker, range	D1
Kinabalu, mt.	D1
Kinabatangan, river	D2
Labuan, island	D2
Langkawi, island	A1
Malacca, strait	A1
Malay, peninsula	A1
Pahang, river	B2
Peninsular Malaysia, region	B2
Perak, river	A2
Pinang, island	A2
Rajang, river	C2
Sabah, state	D2
Sarawak, state	C2
Tahan, mt.	B2

Malaysia

Capital: Kuala Lumpur
Area: 127,584 sq. mi.
  330,529 sq. km.
Population: 21,376,000
Largest City: Kuala Lumpur
Language: Malay
Monetary Unit: Ringgit

© MapQuest.com, Inc.

**Australia:
Map Index**

States and Territories
Australian Capital Territory......D3
New South Wales D3
Northern Territory C2
Queensland D2
South Australia C2
Tasmania D4
Victoria D3
Western Australia B2

Aboriginal Lands
Alawa-Ngandji C1
Balwina B2
Central Australia B2
Central Desert B2
Daly River B1
Haasts Bluff C2
Nganyatjara B2
Petermann B2
Pitjantjatjara C2
Waani/Garawa C1
Yandeyarra A2
Unnamed B2
Unnamed C1
Unnamed D1

Cities and Towns
Adelaide, S.A., capital ..C3, Inset II
Albany, W.A. A3
Albury, N.S.W. D3
Alice Springs, N.T. C2
Altona, Vic. ....Inset I
Armadale, W.A. ....Inset I
Armidale, N.S.W. E3
Asquith, N.S.W. ....Inset IV
Auburn, N.S.W. ....Inset IV
Balcatta, W.A. ....Inset I
Bald Hills, Qld. ....Inset III
Ballarat, Vic. D3
Bankstown, N.S.W. ....Inset IV
Bayswater, W.A. ....Inset I
Beenleigh, Qld. ....Inset III
Belmont, W.A. ....Inset I
Bendigo, Vic. D3
Berwick, Vic. ....Inset V
Blacktown, N.S.W. ....Inset IV
Botany, N.S.W. ....Inset IV

Bourke, N.S.W. D3
Bowen, Qld. D2
Box Hill, Vic. ....Inset V
Brighton, S.A. ....Inset II
Brighton, Qld. ....Inset III
Brighton, Vic. ....Inset V
Brisbane, Qld.,
  capital ....E2, Inset III
Broadmeadows, Vic. ....Inset V
Broken Hill, N.S.W. D3
Broome, W.A. ....Inset III
Bunbury, W.A. A3
Bundaberg, Qld. E2
Burnside, S.A. ....Inset II
Byford, W.A. ....Inset I
Cairns, Qld. D1
Campbelltown, S.A. ....Inset II
Campbelltown, N.S.W. ....Inset IV
Canberra, A.C.T.,
  national capital D3
Cannington, W.A. ....Inset I
Canterbury, N.S.W. ....Inset IV
Carnarvon, W.A. A2
Castle Hill, N.S.W. ....Inset IV
Caulfield, Vic. ....Inset V
Ceduna, S.A. C3
Charleville, Qld. D2
Charters Towers, Qld. D2
Chelsea, Vic. ....Inset V
Chermside, Qld. ....Inset III
City Beach, W.A. ....Inset I
Cleveland, Qld. ....Inset III
Cloncurry, Qld. D2
Coburg, Vic. ....Inset V
Coober Pedy, S.A. C2
Coopers Plains, Qld. ....Inset III
Cranbourne, Vic. ....Inset V
Cronulla, N.S.W. ....Inset IV
Dampier, W.A. A2
Dandenong, Vic. ....Inset V
Darwin, N.T., capital C1
Dee Why, N.S.W. ....Inset IV
Devonport, Tas. D4
Doncaster, Vic. ....Inset V
Dubbo, N.S.W. D3
Elizabeth, S.A. ....Inset II
Eltham, Vic. ....Inset V
Emerald, Qld. D2
Enfield, S.A. ....Inset II
Epping, N.S.W. ....Inset IV
Esperance, W.A. B3
Essendon, Vic. ....Inset V
Fairfield, N.S.W. ....Inset IV
Ferntree Gully, Vic. ....Inset V
Ferny Grove, Qld. ....Inset III

Frankston, Vic. ....Inset V
Fremantle, W.A. ....A3, Inset I
Geelong, Vic. D3
Geraldton, W.A. A2
Gladstone, Qld. E2
Glenelg, S.A. ....Inset II
Glen Forrest, W.A. ....Inset I
Gold Coast, Qld. E2
Goodna, Qld. ....Inset III
Gosford, N.S.W. E3
Gosnells, W.A. ....Inset I
Grafton, N.S.W. E3
Grange, S.A. ....Inset II
Greenslopes, Qld. ....Inset III
Griffith, N.S.W. D3
Gympie, Qld. E2
Heidelberg, Vic. ....Inset V
Hobart, Tas., capital D4
Holland Park, Qld. ....Inset III
Holroyd, N.S.W. ....Inset IV
Hornsby, N.S.W. ....Inset IV
Hurstville, N.S.W. ....Inset IV
Inala, Qld. ....Inset III
Ipswich, Qld. ....Inset III
Kalamunda, W.A. ....Inset I
Kalgoorlie-Boulder, W.A. B3
Katherine, N.T. C1
Keilor, Vic. ....Inset V
Kelmscott, W.A. ....Inset I
Kersbrook, S.A. ....Inset II
Kwinana, W.A. ....Inset I
Kwinana Beach, W.A. ....Inset I
La Perouse, N.S.W. ....Inset IV
Launceston, Tas. D4
Leichhardt, N.S.W. ....Inset IV
Lilydale, Vic. ....Inset V
Lismore, N.S.W. E2
Liverpool, N.S.W. ....Inset IV
Lobethal, S.A. ....Inset II
Logan, Qld. ....Inset III
Longreach, Qld. D2
Mackay, Qld. D2
Mandurah, W.A. A3
Manly, Qld. ....Inset III
Manly, N.S.W. ....Inset IV
Marion, S.A. ....Inset II
Maryborough, Qld. E2
Melbourne, Vic.,
  capital ....D3, Inset V
Melville, W.A. ....Inset I
Merredin, W.A. A3
Midland, W.A. ....Inset I
Mildura, Vic. D3
Mitcham, S.A. ....Inset II
Mona Vale, N.S.W. ....Inset IV
Moorabbin, Vic. ....Inset V

Mordialloc, Vic. ....Inset V
Moree, N.S.W. D2
Morningside, Qld. ....Inset III
Mosman Park, W.A. ....Inset I
Mount Barker, S.A. ....Inset II
Mount Gambier, S.A. D3
Mount Gravatt, Qld. ....Inset III
Mount Isa, Qld. C2
Mount Nebo, Qld. ....Inset III
Mullaloo, W.A. ....Inset I
Narrogin, W.A. A3
Nedlands, W.A. ....Inset I
Newcastle, N.S.W. E3
Newman, W.A. A3
Newmarket, Qld. ....Inset III
Noarlunga, S.A. ....Inset II
North Adelaide, S.A. ....Inset II
Northcote, Vic. ....Inset V
North Sydney, N.S.W. ....Inset IV
Nunawading, Vic. ....Inset V
Oakleigh, Vic. ....Inset V
Orange, N.S.W. D3
Parramatta, N.S.W. ....Inset IV
Perth, W.A., capital ...A3, Inset I
Petrie, Qld. ....Inset III
Pickering Brook, W.A. ....Inset I
Port Adelaide, S.A. ....Inset II
Port Augusta, S.A. C3
Port Hedland, W.A. A2
Port Lincoln, S.A. C3
Port Macquarie, N.S.W. E3
Port Pirie, S.A. C3
Prahran, Vic. ....Inset V
Preston, Vic. ....Inset V
Queenstown, Tas. D4
Randwick, N.S.W. ....Inset IV
Redcliffe, Qld. ....Inset III
Redland Bay, Qld. ....Inset III
Reynella, S.A. ....Inset II
Ringwood, Vic. ....Inset V
Rockdale, N.S.W. ....Inset IV
Rockhampton, Qld. E2
Roma, Qld. D2
Ryde, N.S.W. ....Inset IV
St. Ives, N.S.W. ....Inset IV
St. Kilda, S.A. ....Inset II
St. Kilda, Vic. ....Inset V
Salisbury, S.A. ....Inset II
Samford, Qld. ....Inset III
Sandgate, Qld. ....Inset III
Scarborough, W.A. ....Inset I
Spearwood, W.A. ....Inset I
Springvale, Vic. ....Inset V
Stirling, W.A. ....Inset I
Stirling, S.A. ....Inset II
Sunshine, Vic. ....Inset V

Sutherland, N.S.W. ....Inset IV
Sydney, N.S.W.,
  capital ....E3, Inset IV
Tamworth, N.S.W. E3
Taree, N.S.W. E3
Tea Tree Gully, S.A. ....Inset II
Tennant Creek, N.T. C1
Tom Price, W.A. A2
Toowoomba, Qld. E2
Townsville, Qld. D1
Unley, S.A. ....Inset II
Victoria Park, W.A. ....Inset I
Victoria Point, Qld. ....Inset III
Wagga Wagga, N.S.W. D3
Wanneroo, W.A. ....Inset I
Warrnambool, Vic. D3
Waverley, Vic. ....Inset V
Weipa, Qld. D1
Whyalla, S.A. C3
Willoughby, N.S.W. ....Inset IV
Wollongong, N.S.W. E3
Woodside, S.A. ....Inset II
Woodville, S.A. ....Inset II
Woomera, S.A. C3
Wyndham, W.A. B1
Wynnum, Qld. ....Inset III

Other Features
Arafura, sea C1
Arnhem, cape C1
Arnhem Land, region C1
Ashburton, river A2
Ashmore and Cartier, islands B1
Australian Alps, mts. D3
Barkly, tableland C1
Bass, strait D3
Bate, bay ....Inset IV
Blue, mts. E3
Botany, bay ....Inset IV
Brisbane, river ....Inset III
Burdekin, river D1
Canning, river ....Inset I
Cape York, peninsula D1
Carpentaria, gulf C1
Coral, sea E1
Daly, river C1
Darling, range A3
Darling, river D3
Drysdale River Natl. Park B1
Eyre, lake C2
Eyre, peninsula C3
Fitzroy, river B1
Flinders, range C3
Flinders, river D1
Frome, lake C3
Gairdner, lake C3

Garden, island ....Inset I
Gascoyne, river A2
Gibson, desert B2
Gilbert, river D1
Great Artesian, basin D2
Great Australian, bight B3
Great Barrier, reef D1
Great Dividing, range D1, D3
Great Sandy, desert B2
Great Victoria, desert B2
Gregory Natl. Park C1
Grey, range D2
Groote Eylandt, island C1
Hamersley, range A2
Hobsons, bay ....Inset V
Jackson, port ....Inset IV
Kakadu Natl. Park C1
Kangaroo, island C3
Kimberley, plateau B1
King Leopold, range B1
Kosciusko, mt. D3
Lakefield Natl. Park D1
Leeuwin, cape A3
Leichhardt, river D1
Leveque, cape B1
Logan, river ....Inset III
Macdonnell, ranges C2
Melville, island C1
Mitchell, river D1
Moreton, bay ....Inset III
Murchison, river A2
Murray, river C3
Murrumbidgee, river D3
Musgrave, ranges C2
New England, range E3
North West, cape A2
Nullarbor, plain B3
Port Phillip, bay ....Inset V
Roper, river C1
Rudall River Natl. Park B2
St. Vincent, gulf ....Inset II
Samsonvale, lake ....Inset III
Simpson, desert C2
Simpson Desert Natl. Park C2
Spencer, gulf C3
Swan, river ....Inset I
Tasman, sea E3
Timor, sea B1
Torrens, lake C2
Torrens, river ....Inset II
Torrens, strait D1
Uluru (Ayers Rock) C2
Victoria, river C1
Witjira Natl. Park C2
Yampi, sound B1
York, cape D1

Australia

Capital: Canberra
Area: 2,966,200 sq. mi.
  7,684,456 sq. km.
Population: 18,784,000
Largest City: Sydney
Language: English
Monetary Unit: Australian dollar

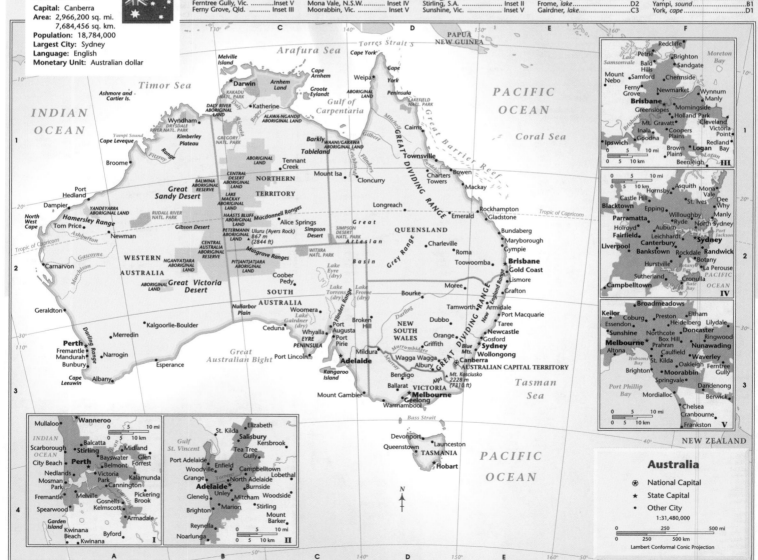

Australia
⊛ National Capital
★ State Capital
• Other City
1:31,480,000

Papua New Guinea:
Map Index

Cities and Towns
Alotau B3
Arawa B2
Daru A2
Goroka A2
Kavieng B2
Kerema A2
Kimbe B2
Lae A2
Lorengau A2
Madang A2
Morehead A2
Mount Hagen A2
Popondetta A2
Port Moresby, capital A2
Rabaul B2
Vanimo A2
Wabag A2
Wau A2
Wewak A1

Other Features
Admiralty, islands A2
Bismarck, archipelago A2
Bismarck, range A2
Bismarck, sea A2
Bougainville, island B2
Buka, island B2
Central, range A2
Coral, sea A3
D'Entrecasteaux, islands B2
Feni, islands B2
Fly, river A2
Gazelle, peninsula B2
Green, islands B2
Huon, peninsula A2
Karkar, island A2
Lihir, group B2
Louisiade, archipelago B3
Manus, island A2
Markham, river A2

Milne, bay B3
Murray, lake A2
Mussau, island A2
New Britain, island B2
New Guinea, island A2
New Hanover, island B2
New Ireland, island B2
Ninigo, group A2
Nuguria, islands A2
Owen Stanley, range A2
Papua, gulf A2
Purari, river A2
Ramu, river A2
Rossel, island B3
St. George's, channel B2
Sepik, river A2
Solomon, sea B2
Tabar, islands B2
Tagula, island B3
Tanga, islands B2
Tauu, islands A2
Torres, strait A2
Trobriand, islands B2
Umboi, island A2
Whiteman, range A2
Wilhelm, mt. A2
Witu, island A2
Woodlark (Muyua), island..B2

Papua New Guinea

Capital: Port Moresby
Area: 178,704 sq. mi.
    462,964 sq. km.
Population: 4,705,000
Largest City: Port Moresby
Language: English
Monetary Unit: Kina

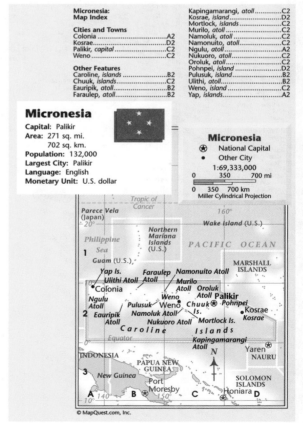

Papua New Guinea
⊛ National Capital
• Other City
1:23,692,000
0   150   300 mi
0   150   300 km
Mercator Projection

© MapQuest.com, Inc.

New Zealand

Capital: Wellington
Area: 104,454 sq. mi.
    270,606 sq. km.
Population: 3,662,000
Largest City: Auckland
Language: English
Monetary Unit: New Zealand dollar

New Zealand:
Map Index

Cities and Towns
Alexandra A4
Ashburton B3
Auckland B2
Blenheim B3
Christchurch B3
Collingwood B3
Dunedin B4
East Coast Bays B2
Gisborne C2
Greymouth B3
Hamilton C2
Hastings C2
Hicks Bay C2
Invercargill A4
Kaeo B2
Kaikoura B3
Kaitaia B2
Kawhia B2
Lower Hutt B3
Manukau B2
Milford Sound A3
Napier C2
Nelson B3
New Plymouth B2
Oamaru B4
Palmerston North C3
Queenstown A3
Rotorua C2
Taumaruni C2
Taupo C2
Tauranga C2
Timaru B3
Waimamaku B2
Wanganui C2
Wellington, capital B3
Westport B3
Whakatane C2
Whangarei B2

Other Features
Aspiring, mt. A3
Banks, peninsula B3
Canterbury, bight B3
Canterbury, plains A4
Clutha, river A4
Cook, mt. B3
Cook, strait B3
Coromandel, peninsula C2
East, cape C2
Egmont, cape B2
Egmont, mt. B2
Farewell, cape B3
Foveaux, strait A4
Great Barrier, island C2
Hawea, lake A3
Hawke, bay C2
Ngauruhoe, mt. C2
North, cape B1
North, island B2
North Taranaki, bight B2
Palliser, cape C3
Pegasus, bay B3
Plenty, bay C2
Puysegur, point A4
Rangitikei, river C2
Raukumara, range C2
Ruahine, range C2
Ruapehu, mt. C2
South, island A3
Southern Alps, mts. A3
Southland, plains A4
South Taranaki, bight B2
South West, cape A4
Stewart, island A4
Tararua, range C3
Tasman, bay B3
Tasman, sea A2
Taupo, lake C2
Te Anau, lake A4
Tekapo, lake B3
Three Kings, islands B1
Tongariro, mt. C2
Waikato, river C2
Wairau, river B3
Waitaki, river B3
Wanaka, lake A3

MAJOR CITIES

Australia
Sydney   3,935,000
Melbourne   3,322,000
Brisbane   1,548,000
Perth   1,319,000
Adelaide   1,083,000

New Zealand
Auckland   998,000
Wellington   335,000
Christchurch   331,000
Hamilton   159,000
Dunedin   112,000

**Papua New
Guinea**   (metro)
Morobe   439,725
Western   398,376
 Highlands
Southern   390,240
 Highlands
Eastern   316,802
 Highlands
Madang   288,317
Port Moresby   271,813

New Zealand
⊛ National Capital
• Other City
1:16,077,000
0   150   300 mi
0   150   300 km
Lambert Conformal Conic Projection

© MapQuest.com, Inc.

Micronesia:
Map Index

Cities and Towns
Colonia A2
Kosrae D2
Palikir, capital C2
Weno C2

Other Features
Caroline, islands B2
Chuuk, islands C2
Eauripik, atoll B2
Faraulep, atoll B2

Kapingamarangi, atoll C2
Kosrae, island D2
Mortlock, islands C2
Murilo, atoll C2
Namoluk, atoll C2
Namonuito, atoll C2
Ngulu, atoll A2
Nukuoro, atoll C2
Oroluk, atoll C2
Pohnpei, island D2
Pulusuk, island B2
Ulithi, atoll B2
Weno, island C2
Yap, islands A2

Micronesia

Capital: Palikir
Area: 271 sq. mi.
    702 sq. km.
Population: 132,000
Largest City: Palikir
Language: English
Monetary Unit: U.S. dollar

Micronesia
⊛ National Capital
• Other City
1:69,333,000
0   350   700 mi
0   350   700 km
Miller Cylindrical Projection

© MapQuest.com, Inc.

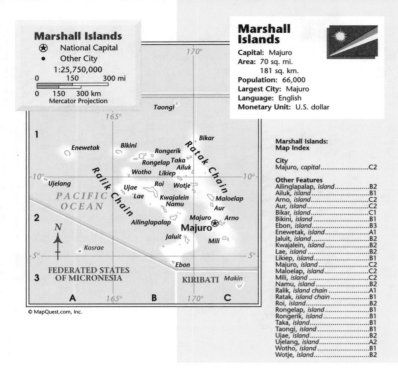

Marshall Islands
* ⊛ National Capital
* ● Other City
1:25,750,000

0   150   300 mi
0   150   300 km
Mercator Projection

© MapQuest.com, Inc.

Marshall Islands
Capital: Majuro
Area: 70 sq. mi.
     181 sq. km.
Population: 66,000
Largest City: Majuro
Language: English
Monetary Unit: U.S. dollar

Marshall Islands:
Map Index

City
Majuro, capital C2

Other Features
Ailinglapalap, island B2
Ailuk, island B1
Arno, island C2
Aur, island C2
Bikar, island C1
Bikini, island B1
Ebon, island B3
Enewetak, island A1
Jaluit, island B2
Kwajalein, island B2
Lae, island B2
Likiep, island B1
Majuro, island C2
Maloelap, island C2
Mili, island C2
Namu, island B2
Ralik, island chain A1
Ratak, island chain B1
Roi, island B2
Rongelap, island B1
Rongerik, island B1
Taka, island B1
Taongi, island B1
Ujae, island B2
Ujelang, island A2
Wotho, island B1
Wotje, island B2

Nauru
* ⊛ National Capital
* ● Other City
1:135,000

0   1   2 mi
0   1   2 km
Lambert Conformal Conic Projection

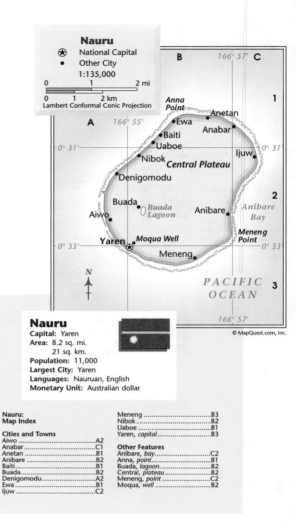

© MapQuest.com, Inc.

Nauru
Capital: Yaren
Area: 8.2 sq. mi.
     21 sq. km.
Population: 11,000
Largest City: Yaren
Languages: Nauruan, English
Monetary Unit: Australian dollar

Nauru:
Map Index

Cities and Towns
Aiwo A2
Anabar C1
Anetan B1
Anibare B2
Baiti B1
Buada B2
Denigomodu A2
Ewa B1
Ijuw C2

Meneng B3
Nibok B2
Uaboe B1
Yaren, capital B3

Other Features
Anibare, bay C2
Anna, point B1
Buada, lagoon B2
Central, plateau B2
Meneng, point C2
Moqua, well B2

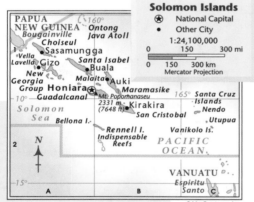

Solomon Islands:
Map Index

Cities and Towns
Auki B1
Buala A1
Gizo A1
Honiara, capital A1
Kirakira B2
Sasamungga A1

Other Features
Bellona, island A2
Choiseul, island A1
Guadalcanal, island A1
Indispensable, reefs B2
Malaita, island B1
Maramasike, island B1
Nendo, island C2
New Georgia Group,
    islands A1
Ontong Java, island A1
Popomanaseu, mt. A1
Rennell, island B2
San Cristobal, island B2
Santa Cruz, islands C2
Santa Isabel, island A1
Solomon, sea A2
Utupua, island C2
Vanikolo, islands C2
Vella Lavella, island A1

Solomon Islands
* ⊛ National Capital
* ● Other City
1:24,100,000

0   150   300 mi
0   150   300 km
Mercator Projection

Solomon Islands
Capital: Honiara
Area: 10,954 sq. mi.
     28,378 sq. km.
Population: 455,000
Largest City: Honiara
Language: English
Monetary Unit: Dollar

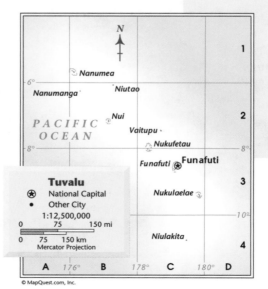

Tuvalu
Capital: Funafuti
Area: 9.4 sq. mi.
     24.4 sq. km.
Population: 11,000
Largest City: Funafuti
Languages: Tuvaluan, English
Monetary Unit: Tuvalu dollar,
     Australian dollar

Tuvalu:
Map Index

City
Funafuti, capital C3

Other Features
Funafuti, island C3
Nanumanga, island B2
Nanumea, island B1
Niulakita, island C4
Niutao, island B2
Nui, island B2
Nukufetau, island C2
Nukulaelae, island C3
Vaitupu, island C2

Tuvalu
* ⊛ National Capital
* ● Other City
1:12,500,000

0   75   150 mi
0   75   150 km
Mercator Projection

© MapQuest.com, Inc.

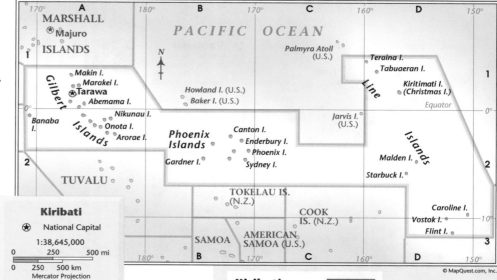

Fiji:
Map Index

Cities and Towns
Galoa B3
Labasa B2
Lami B3
Lautoka A2
Lomawai A3
Nabouwalu B2
Nadi B2
Naduri B2
Nakodu B2
Navua B3
Suva, *capital* B3
Vunisea B3

Other Features
Beqa, *island* B3
Bligh Water, *sound*......B2
Cicia, *island*................C2
Cikobia, *island*............C1
Gau, *island* B3
Great Sea, *reef* B1
Kadavu, *island*............B3
Kadavu, *passage*..........A3
Kioa, *island* C2

Koro, *island* B2
Koro, *sea* C3
Lakeba, *island*............C3
Lakeba, *passage*..........C3
Lau, *island group* C2
Laucala, *island*............C2
Moala, *island group*....B3
Nadi, *bay* A2
Navua, *river* A3
Ono, *island* B3
Ovalau, *island*............B2
Qamea, *island*............C2
Qelelevu, *island*..........C2
Rabi, *island*................C2
Soso, *bay*......................B3
Taveuni, *island* C2
Tomanivi, *mt.*..............B2
Udu, *point* C2
Vanua Balavu, *island*..C2
Vanua Levu, *island*......B2
Vatu Lele, *island*........A3
Vetauua, *island*..........C1
Viti Levu, *island*..........A2
Vunaniu, *bay*..............A3
Washington, *cape*........A3
Yasawa, *island group* A2

Kiribati

⊛ National Capital

1:38,645,000

0 250 500 mi
0 250 500 km
Mercator Projection

Kiribati

Capital: Tarawa
Area: 313 sq. mi.
811 sq. km.
Population: 86,000
Largest City: Tarawa
Languages: I-Kiribati (Gilbertese), English
Monetary Unit: Australian dollar

Kiribati:
Map Index

City
Tarawa, *capital* A1

Other Features
Abemama, *island* A1
Arorae, *island*..................A2

Banaba, *island*..................A2
Canton, *island* B2
Caroline, *island*................D2
Enderbury, *island* B2
Flint, *island* D3
Gardner, *island* B2
Gilbert, *islands*................A1
Kiritimati (Christmas), *island*..D1
Line, *islands* D1
Makin, *island* A1
Malden, *island* D2
Marakei, *island*................A1
Nikunau, *island*................A2
Onota, *island* A2
Phoenix, *island*................B2
Starbuck, *island*..............B2
Sydney, *island*..................B2
Tabuaeran, *island*............D1
Teraina, *island*................D1
Vostok, *island*..................D3

Fiji

⊛ National Capital
● Other City

1:8,900,000

0 50 100 mi
0 50 100 km
Azimuthal Equal Area Projection

Fiji

Capital: Suva
Area: 7,056 sq. mi.
18,280 sq. km.
Population: 813,000
Largest City: Suva
Languages: Fijian, Hindi, English
Monetary Unit: Fiji dollar

© MapQuest.com, Inc.

Tonga

⊛ National Capital
● Other City

1:11,000,000

0 75 150 mi
0 75 150 km
Mercator Projection

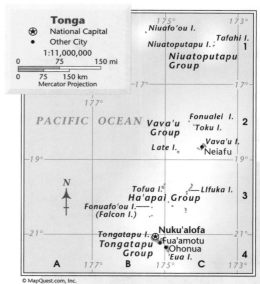

© MapQuest.com, Inc.

Tonga

Capital: Nuku'alofa
Area: 301 sq. mi.
780 sq. km.
Population: 109,000
Largest City: Nuku'alofa
Languages: Tongan, English
Monetary Unit: Pa'anga

Palau:
Map Index

Cities and Towns
Kloulklubed......................B3
Koror, *capital*..................B3
Melekeok C3
Meyungs............................B3
Ngaramasch......................B4
Ngerkeel............................B3
Ngermechau......................C2
Ngetbong..........................C2
Ollei C2

Other Features
Angaur, *island* B4
Arakabesan, *island*........B3
Arekalong, *peninsula*......C2

Babelthuap, *island*..........C3
Cormoran, *reef*..............B2
Eli Malk, *island* B3
Helen, *reef*..................Inset
Kayangel, *islands* C1
Koror, *island* C3
Kossol, *passage*..............C2
Kossol, *reef* C2
Merir, *island* ....Inset
Ngemelis, *islands*............B4
Peleliu, *island* B4
Philippine, *sea*................B2
Pulo Anna, *island*........Inset
Sar, *passage* B3
Sonsoral, *island*............Inset
Tobi, *island* ....Inset
Urukthapel, *island*..........B3

Palau

⊛ National Capital
● Other City

1:1,900,000

0 5 10 mi
0 5 10 km
Lambert Conformal Conic Projection

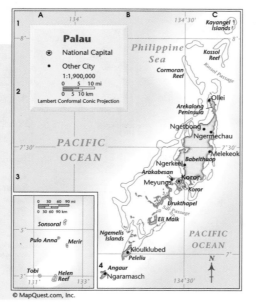

© MapQuest.com, Inc.

Palau

Capital: Koror
Area: 177 sq. mi.
458 sq. km.
Population: 18,000
Largest City: Koror
Languages: English, Sonsorolese,
Angaur, Japanese, Tobi, Palauan
Monetary Unit: U.S. dollar

Tonga:
Map Index

Cities and Towns
Fua'amotu B4
Neiafu C2
Nuku'alofa, *capital*........B4
Ohonua C4

Other Features
'Eua, *island* C4
Fonuafo'ou (Falcon), *island* B3
Fonualei, *island*............C2

Ha'apai, *island group*......B3
Late, *island* C2
Lifuka, *island*................C3
Niuafo'ou, *island* B1
Niuatoputapu, *island* C1
Niuatoputapu, *island group*..C1
Tafahi, *island*................C1
Tofua, *island* B3
Toku, *island* C2
Tongatapu, *island*..........B4
Tongatapu, *island group*....B4
Vava'u, *island* C2
Vava'u, *island group*......C2

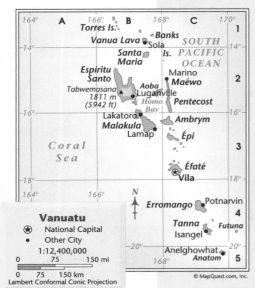

Vanuatu

Capital: Vila
Area: 4,707 sq. mi.
12,194 sq. km.
Population: 189,000
Largest City: Vila
Languages: French, English, Bislama
Monetary Unit: Vatu

Vanuatu:
Map Index

Cities and Towns
Anelghowhat	C5
Isangel	C4
Lakatoro	B3
Lamap	B3
Luganville	B2
Marino	C2
Potnarvin	C4
Sola	B1
Vila, *capital*	C3

Other Features
Ambrym, *island*	C3
Anatom, *island*	C5
Aoba, *island*	B2
Banks, *islands*	B1
Coral, *sea*	C3
Éfaté, *island*	C3
Épi, *island*	C3
Erromango, *island*	C4
Espiritu Santo, *island*	B2
Futuna, *island*	C4
Homo, *bay*	B2
Maéwo, *island*	C2
Malakula, *island*	B3
Pentecost, *island*	C3
Santa Maria, *island*	B2
Tabwemasana, *mt.*	B2
Tanna, *island*	C4
Torres, *islands*	B1
Vanua Lava, *island*	B1

Vanuatu
⊛ National Capital
• Other City
1:12,400,000
0   75   150 mi
0   75   150 km
Lambert Conformal Conic Projection

© MapQuest.com, Inc.

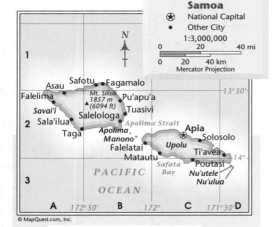

Samoa

⊛ National Capital
• Other City
1:3,000,000
0   20   40 mi
0   20   40 km
Mercator Projection

© MapQuest.com, Inc.

Samoa

Capital: Apia
Area: 1,093 sq. mi.
2,832 sq. km.
Population: 230,000
Largest City: Apia
Languages: Samoan, English
Monetary Unit: Tala

Samoa:
Map Index

Cities and Towns
Apia, *capital*	C2
Asau	A2
Fagamalo	B1
Falelatai	B2
Falelima	A2
Matautu	C2
Poutasi	C3
Pu'apu'a	B2
Safotu	B1
Sala'ilua	A2
Salelologa	B2

Solosolo	C2
Taga	A2
Ti'avea	D2
Tuasivi	B2

Other Features
Apolima, *island*	B2
Apolima, *strait*	B2
Manono, *island*	B2
Nu'utele, *island*	D3
Nu'ulua, *island*	D3
Safata, *bay*	C3
Savai'i, *island*	A2
Silisili, *mt.*	B2
Upolu, *island*	C2

New Caledonia

★ Territorial Capital
• Other City
1:19,650,000
0   125   250 mi
0   125   250 km
Lambert Conformal Conic Projection

© MapQuest.com, Inc.

New Caledonia:
Map Index

Cities and Towns
Bourail	C2
Koné	C2
Koumac	C2
Nouméa, *capital*	C2
Thio	C2

Other Features
Astrolabe, *reefs*	C2

Avon, *islands*	A2
Bélep, *islands*	C2
Chesterfield, *islands*	A2
Coral, *sea*	B2
D'Entrecasteaux, *reefs*	C1
Huon, *islands*	B1
Lifou, *island*	D2
Loyalty, *islands*	C2
Maré, *island*	D2
New Caledonia, *island*	C2
Ouvéa, *island*	C2
Pines, *island*	D2
Sandy, *island*	B2

New Caledonia

Capital: Nouméa
Area: 8,548 sq. mi.
21,912 sq. km.
Population: 197,000
Largest City: Nouméa
Language: French
Monetary Unit: CFA Franc

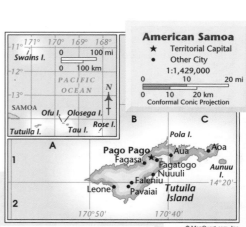

American Samoa

★ Territorial Capital
• Other City
1:1,429,000
0   10   20 mi
0   10   20 km
Conformal Conic Projection

© MapQuest.com, Inc.

American Samoa:
Map Index

Cities and Towns
Aoa	C1
Aua	C1
Fagasa	B1
Fagatogo	B1
Faleniu	B1
Leone	B2
Nuuuli	B1
Pago Pago, *capital*	B1
Pavaiai	B2

Other Features
Aunuu, *island*	C1
Ofu, *island*	A1
Olosega, *island*	A1
Pola, *island*	C1
Rose, *island*	A1
Swains, *island*	A1
Tau, *island*	A1
Tutuila, *island*	A1, C2

American Samoa

Capital: Pago Pago
Area: 77 sq. mi.
199 sq. km.
Population: 64,000
Largest City: Pago Pago
Language: Samoan, English
Monetary Unit: U.S. dollar

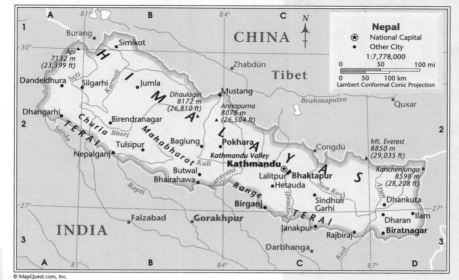

Nepal map labels: Burang, Simikot, CHINA, Zhabdün, Tibet, Api 7132 m (23,399 ft), Dandeldhura, Silgarhi, Jumla, Mustang, Brahmaputra, Quxar, Dhangarhi, Birendranagar, Dhaulagiri 8172 m (26,810 ft), Annapurna 8078 m (26,504 ft), Congdü, Mt. Everest 8850 m (29,035 ft), Kanchenjunga 8598 m (28,208 ft), Pokhara, Kathmandu Valley, Kathmandu, Lalitpur, Bhaktapur, Hetauda, Dhankuta, Baglung, Tulsipur, Nepalganj, Butwal, Bhairahawa, Sindhuli Garhi, Birganj, Dharan, Ilam, Faizabad, Gorakhpur, Janakpur, Rajbiraj, Biratnagar, Darbhanga, INDIA, HIMALAYAS, TERAI, CHURIA, MAHABHARAT, Range, Seti, Karnali, Bheri, Sarda, Kali, Narayani, Rapti, Bagmati, Sun Kosi, Arun, Kosi

© MapQuest.com, Inc.

Nepal:
Map Index

Cities and Towns
Baglung B2
Bhairahawa B2
Bhaktapur C2
Biratnagar D3
Birendranagar B2
Birganj C2
Butwal B2
Dandeldhura A2
Dhangarhi A2
Dhankuta D2
Dharan D3
Hetauda C2
Ilam D3
Janakpur C3
Jumla B2
Kathmandu, *capital* C2
Lalitpur C2
Mustang B2
Nepalganj B2
Pokhara B2
Rajbiraj C3
Silgarhi B2
Simikot B1
Sindhuli Garhi B2
Tulsipur B2

Other Features
Annapurna, *mt.* B2
Api, *mt.* A2
Arun, *river* D2
Bagmati, *river* C2
Bheri, *river* B2
Churia, *mts.* B2
Dhaulagiri, *mt.* B2
Everest, *mt.* C2
Himalayas, *mts.* B2
Kali, *river* B2
Kanchenjunga, *mt.* D2
Karnali, *river* B2
Kathmandu, *valley* B2
Mahabharat, *range* B2
Narayani, *river* B2
Rapti, *river* B2
Sarda, *river* A2
Seti, *river* A2
Sun Kosi, *river* C2
Terai, *region* A2, C3

Maldives

Capital: Male
Area: 115 sq. mi.
    298 sq. km.
Population: 300,000
Largest City: Male
Language: Divehi
Monetary Unit: Rufiyaa

Nepal

Capital: Kathmandu
Area: 56,827 sq. mi.
    147,220 sq. km.
Population: 24,303,000
Largest City: Kathmandu
Language: Nepali
Monetary Unit: Rupee

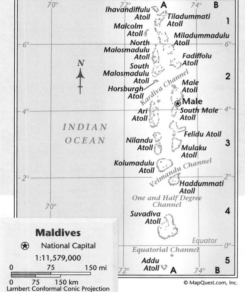

Maldives map labels: Ihavandiffulu Atoll, Tiladummati Atoll, Malcolm Atoll, Miladummadulu Atoll, North Malosmadulu Atoll, Fadiffolu Atoll, South Malosmadulu Atoll, Horsburgh Atoll, Male Atoll, Male, South Male Atoll, Ari Atoll, Felidu Atoll, INDIAN OCEAN, Nilandu Atoll, Mulaku Atoll, Kolumadulu Atoll, Kardiva Channel, Veimandu Channel, Haddummati Atoll, One and Half Degree Channel, Suvadiva Atoll, Equatorial Channel, Addu Atoll, Equator

© MapQuest.com, Inc.

Maldives:
Map Index

City
Male, *capital* A2

Other Features
Addu, *atoll* A5
Ari, *atoll* A5
Equatorial, *channel* A5
Fadiffolu, *atoll* A2
Felidu, *atoll* A3
Haddummati, *atoll* A4
Horsburgh, *atoll* A2
Ihavandiffulu, *atoll* A1
Kardiva, *channel* A2
Kolumadulu, *atoll* A3
Malcolm, *atoll* A1
Male, *atoll* A2
Miladummadulu, *atoll* A1
Mulaku, *atoll* A3
Nilandu, *atoll* A3
North Malosmadulu, *atoll* A2
One and Half Degree, *channel* ...A4
South Male, *atoll* A3
South Malosmadulu, *atoll* A2
Suvadiva, *atoll* A4
Tiladummati, *atoll* A1
Veimandu, *channel* A3

Sri Lanka:
Map Index

Provinces
Central B4
Eastern C4
North Central B3
Northern B2
North Western B4
Sabaragamuwa B5
Southern B5
Uva C5
Western A4

Cities and Towns
Amparai C4
Anuradhapura B3
Batticaloa C4
Colombo, *capital* A5
Dehiwala-Mt. Lavinia A5
Galle B5
Hambantota C5
Jaffna B2
Kalutara A5
Kandy B4
Kilinochchi B2
Kurunegala B4
Mankulam B2
Mannar A3
Matale B4
Matara B6
Moratuwa A5
Mullaittivu B2
Negombo A4
Nuwara Eliya B5
Point Pedro B2
Polonnaruwa C4
Pottuvil C5
Puttalam A3
Sri Jayawardenepura, *capital* A5
Trincomalee C3
Vavuniya B3

Other Features
Adam's, *peak* B4
Adam's Bridge, *shoal* A3
Aruvi, *river* B3
Bengal, *bay* C3
Delft, *island* A2
Dondra Head, *cape* B6
Jaffna, *lagoon* B2
Kalu, *river* B5
Kelani, *river* B4
Mahaweli Ganga, *river* B4
Mannar, *gulf* A3
Mannar, *island* A3
Palk, *strait* B2
Pidurutalagala, *mt.* B4
Trincomalee, *harbor* C3
Yan, *river* B3

Sri Lanka

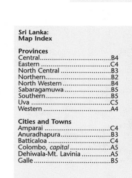

Capital: Colombo,
    Sri Jayawardenepura
Area: 25,332 sq. mi.
    65,627 sq. km.
Population: 19,145,000
Largest City: Colombo
Language: Sinhalese
Monetary Unit: Rupee

Sri Lanka map labels: INDIA, Palk Strait, Point Pedro, Jaffna, Delft Island, Jaffna Lagoon, Kilinochchi, Mannar Island, Mullaittivu, Mankulam, NORTHERN, Adam's Bridge, Mannar, Gulf of Mannar, Vavuniya, Trincomalee, Trincomalee Harbor, Anuradhapura, NORTH CENTRAL, Bay of Bengal, Puttalam, Polonnaruwa, NORTH WESTERN, CENTRAL, Batticaloa, Kurunegala, EASTERN, Negombo, Kandy, Matale, Amparai, Adam's Peak 2243 m (7360 ft), Pidurutalagala 2524 m (8281 ft), Dehiwala-Mt. Lavinia, Colombo, Nuwara Eliya, SABARAGAMUWA, UVA, Ratnapura, Pottuvil, Moratuwa, WESTERN, Sri Jayawardenepura, Kalutara, Galle, SOUTHERN, Hambantota, INDIAN OCEAN, Matara, Dondra Head, Aruvi, Yan, Kelani, Kalu

Bhutan map labels: CHINA, Chomo Lhari 7314 m (23,997 ft), Kula Kangri 7554 m (24,783 ft), Cona, HIMALAYAS, Lingshi, Punakha, Lhuntshi, Tibet, Tashigang, Paro, Thimphu, Tongsa, Shamgong, Louri, Chhukha, Geylegphug, Sarbhang, Phuntsholing, Duars, INDIA, Brahmaputra, Wong, Sankosh, Tongsa, Dangme, Lhobrak

© MapQuest.com, Inc.

Bhutan

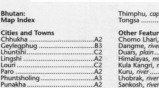

Capital: Thimphu
Area: 18,147 sq. mi.
    47,013 sq. km.
Population: 1,952,000
Largest City: Thimphu
Language: Dzongkha
Monetary Unit: Ngultrum

Bhutan:
Map Index

Cities and Towns
Chhukha A2
Geylegphug B3
Lhuntshi C2
Lingshi A2
Louri C2
Paro A2
Phuntsholing A3
Punakha A2
Sarbhang B3
Shamgong B2
Tashigang C2
Thimphu, *capital* A2
Tongsa B2

Other Features
Chomo Lhari, *mt.* A1
Dangme, *river* C2
Duars, *plain* A3
Himalayas, *mts.* A1
Kula Kangri, *mt.* B1
Kuru, *river* C2
Lhobrak, *river* C2
Sankosh, *river* A2
Tongsa, *river* B2
Wong, *river* A2

Maldives
⊛ National Capital
1:11,579,000
0   75   150 mi
0   75   150 km
Lambert Conformal Conic Projection

Bhutan
⊛ National Capital
• Other City
1:6,053,000
0   25   50   75 mi
0   25   50   75 km
Lambert Conformal Conic Projection

Nepal
⊛ National Capital
• Other City
1:7,778,000
0   50   100 mi
0   50   100 km
Lambert Conformal Conic Projection

Sri Lanka
⊛ National Capital
• Other City
1:6,400,000
0   40   80 mi
0   40   80 km
Mercator Projection

© MapQuest.com, Inc.

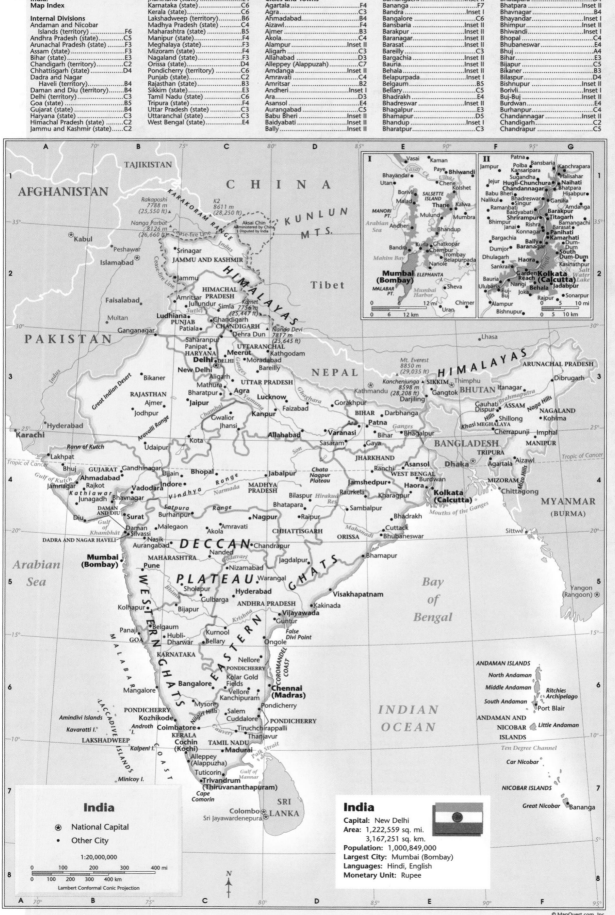

India:
Map Index

Internal Divisions
Andaman and Nicobar
  Islands (territory) F6
Andhra Pradesh (state) C5
Arunachal Pradesh (state) ...F3
Assam (state) F3
Bihar (state) E3
Chandigarh (territory) C2
Chhattisgarh (state) D4
Dadra and Nagar
  Haveli (territory) B4
Daman and Diu (territory) ...B4
Delhi (territory) C3
Goa (state) B5
Gujarat (state) B4
Haryana (state) C3
Himachal Pradesh (state) ...C2
Jammu and Kashmir (state) ..C2

Jharkhand (state) E4
Karnataka (state) C6
Kerala (state) C6
Lakshadweep (territory) B6
Madhya Pradesh (state) C4
Maharashtra (state) B5
Manipur (state) F4
Meghalaya (state) F3
Mizoram (state) F4
Nagaland (state) F3
Orissa (state) D5
Pondicherry (territory) C6
Punjab (state) C2
Rajasthan (state) B3
Sikkim (state) E3
Tamil Nadu (state) C6
Tripura (state) F4
Uttar Pradesh (state) C3
Uttaranchal (state) C3
West Bengal (state) E4

Cities and Towns
Agartala F4
Agra C3
Ahmadabad B4
Aizawl F4
Ajmer B3
Akola C4
Alampur ....Inset II
Allahabad C3
Allahabad D3
Alleppey (Alappuzha) C7
Amdanga ....Inset II
Amravati C4
Amritsar C2
Andheri ....Inset I
Ara D3
Asansol E4
Aurangabad C5
Babu Bheri ....Inset II
Baidyabati ....Inset II
Bally ....Inset II

Bamangachi ....Inset II
Bananga F7
Bandra ....Inset I
Bangalore C6
Bansbaria ....Inset II
Barakpur ....Inset II
Baranagar ....Inset II
Barasat ....Inset II
Bareilly C3
Bargachia ....Inset II
Bauria ....Inset II
Behala ....Inset II
Belapurpada ....Inset I
Belgaum B5
Bellary C5
Bhadrakh E4
Bhadreswar ....Inset II
Bhagalpur E3
Bhamapur D5
Bhandup ....Inset I
Bharatpur C3

Bhatapara D4
Bhatpara ....Inset II
Bhavnagar B4
Bhayandar ....Inset I
Bhimpur ....Inset II
Bhiwandi ....Inset I
Bhopal C4
Bhubaneswar E4
Bhuj A4
Bihar E3
Bijapur B5
Bikaner B3
Bilaspur D4
Bishnupur ....Inset II
Borivli ....Inset I
Buj-Buj ....Inset II
Burdwan E4
Burhanpur C4
Chandannagar ....Inset II
Chandigarh C2
Chandrapur C5

Chembur ....Inset I
Chene ....Inset I
Chennai (Madras) D6
Cherrapunji F3
Chirner ....Inset I
Cochin (Kochi) C7
Coimbatore C6
Cuddalore C6
Cuttack E4
Daman B4
Darbhanga E3
Darjiling E3
Dehra Dun C2
Delhi C3
Dhulagarh ....Inset II
Dibrugarh F3
Dispur F3
Diu B4
Dum-Dum ....Inset II
Dumjor ....Inset II
Faizabad D3
Gandhinagar B4
Ganganagar B3
Gangtok E3
Garden Reach ....Inset II
Garulia F3
Gauhati F3
Gaya E4
Ghatkopar ....Inset I
Gorakhpur D3
Gulbarga C5
Guntur D5
Gwalior C3
Halisahar ....Inset II
Haora ....E4, Inset II
Hisapbur ....Inset II
Hubli-Dharwar C5
Hugli-Chunchura ....Inset II
Hyderabad C5
Imphal F4
Indore C4
Itanagar F3
Jabalpur C4
Jadabpur ....Inset II
Jaipur C3
Jammu B2
Jamnagar B4
Jampur ....Inset II
Jamshedpur E4
Janai ....Inset II
Jejur ....Inset II
Jhansi C3
Jodhpur B3
Joka ....Inset II
Jullundur C2
Junagadh B4
Kakinada D5
Kalwa ....Inset I
Kaman ....Inset I
Kamarhati ....Inset II
Kanchipuram C6
Kanchrapara ....Inset II
Kanpur D3
Kansaripara ....Inset II
Kasinathpur ....Inset II
Kathgodam C3
Kharagpur E4
Kohima F3
Kolhapur B5
Kolkata (Calcutta) ......E4, Inset II
Kolshet ....Inset I
Konnagar ....Inset II
Kota C4
Kozhikode C6
Kurla ....Inset I
Kurnool C5
Lakhpat A4
Lucknow D3
Ludhiana C2
Madurai C7
Malad ....Inset I
Malegaon B4
Mangalore B6
Mathura C3
Meerut C3
Moradabad C3
Mulund ....Inset I
Mumbai (Bombay) ....B5, Inset I
Mumbra ....Inset I
Mysore C6
Naihati ....Inset II
Nalikul ....Inset II
Nanded C5
Nangi ....Inset II
Nanole ....Inset I
Nasik B4
Nellore C6
New Delhi, capital C3
Nizamabad C5
Ongole C5
Panaji B5
Panihati ....Inset II
Patiala C2
Patna E3
Paye ....Inset I
Polba ....Inset II
Pondicherry C6
Port Blair F6
Pune B5
Raipur D4
Rajkot B4
Ramanbati ....Inset II
Ranchi E4
Raurkela D4
Rishra ....Inset II
Saharanpur Panipat C3
Salem C6
Sambalpur D4
Sankrail ....Inset II
Sasaram D4
Sheva ....Inset I
Shillong F3
Sholapur C5
Shrirampur ....Inset II
Silvassi B4
Simla C2
Singur ....Inset II
Sonarpur ....Inset II
South Dum-Dum ....Inset II
Srinagar B2
Sugandha ....Inset II
Surat B4
Thane ....Inset I
Thanjavur C6
Tiruchchirappalli C6
Titagarh ....Inset II
Trivandrum
  (Thiruvananthapuram) C7

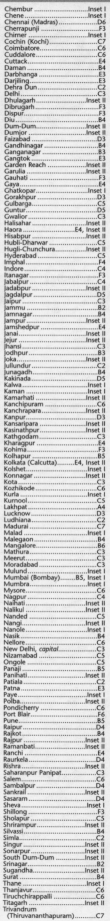

India

⊛ National Capital

• Other City

1:20,000,000

0 100 200 300 400 mi

0 100 200 300 400 km

Lambert Conformal Conic Projection

India
Capital: New Delhi
Area: 1,222,559 sq. mi.
  3,167,251 sq. km.
Population: 1,000,849,000
Largest City: Mumbai (Bombay)
Languages: Hindi, English
Monetary Unit: Rupee

© MapQuest.com, Inc.

Bangladesh

National Capital
• **Other City**

1:7,491,000

0   50   100 mi
0   50 100 km

Azimuthal Equal Area Projection

© MapQuest.com, Inc.

Bangladesh

Capital: Dhaka
Area: 57,295 sq. mi.
148,433 sq. km.
Population: 127,118,000
Largest City: Dhaka
Language: Bengali
Monetary Unit: Taka

Bangladesh:
Map Index

Cities and Towns
Barisal D6
Bogra C4
Brahmanbaria E5
Chalna C6
Chandpur D5
Chittagong E6
Comilla E5
Cox's Bazar E7
Dhaka, capital D5
Dinajpur B3
Faridpur C5
Jaipurhat B3
Jamalpur C4
Jessore C5
Khulna C6
Kushtia C5
Mymensingh D4
Narayanganj D5
Noakhali E6
Pabna C4
Patuakhali D6
Rajshahi B4
Rangamati F6

Rangpur C3
Saidpur B3
Sirajganj C4
Sylhet E4
Tangail C4

Other Features
Atrai, river B4
Barind, region B4
Bengal, bay D7
Brahmaputra, river D3
Chittagong Hills, region ...F5
Ganges, river B4
Jamuna, river C4
Karnaphuli, reservoir F6
Karnaphuli, river E6
Keokradong, mt. F7
Madhumati, river C5
Madhupur Tract, region ...D4
Meghna, river D5
Mouths of the Ganges,
delta C7
Old Brahmaputra, river ...C4
Padma, river D5
Sundarbans, region C7
Surma, river E3
Tista, river C2

India: Map Index
Trombay ....Inset I
Tuticorin C7
Udaipur B4
Ujjain C4
Uluberia ....Inset II
Uran ....Inset I
Utan ....Inset I
Vadodara B4
Varanasi D3
Vasai ....Inset I
Vellore C6
Vijayawada D5
Visakhapatnam D5
Warangal C5

Other Features
Amindivi, islands B6
Andaman, islands F6
Androth, island B6
Arabian, sea ....A5, Inset I
Aravalli, range B3
Bengal, bay E5
Bhima, river C5
Brahmaputra, river F3
Car Nicobar, island F7
Cauvery, river C6
Chambal, river C3
Chata Nagpur, plateau D4
Comorin, cape C7
Coromandel, coast D6
Deccan, plateau C5
Eastern Ghats, mts. C6
Elephanta, island ....Inset I
False Divi, point D5
Ganges, river E3
Ghaghara, river D3
Godavari, river C5
Great Indian, desert B3
Great Nicobar, island F7
Himalayas, mts. C2, E3
Hirakud, reservoir D4
Hugli, river ....Inset II
Indus, river C2
Kalpeni, island B7
Kamet, mt. C2
Kanchenjunga, mt. E3
Karakoram, range C1
Kathiawar, peninsula B4
Kavaratti, island B6
Khambhat, gulf B4
Khasi, hills F3
Kolar, gold fields C6
Krishna, river C5
Kutch, gulf A4
Laccadive, islands B6
Little Andaman, island F6
Mahanadi, river D4
Mahim, bay ....Inset I
Malabar, coast B6
Malabar, point ....Inset I
Mannar, gulf C7
Manori, point ....Inset I
Middle Andaman, island ...F6
Minicoy, island B7
Mizo, hills F4
Mouths of the Ganges, delta ...E4
Mumbai, harbor ....Inset I
Naga, hills F3
Nanda Devi, mt. C2
Narmada, river C4
Nicobar, islands F7
Nilgiri, hills C6
North Andaman, island F6
Palk, strait C7
Rann of Kutch, mud flat ...B4
Ritchies, archipelago F6
Salsette, island ....Inset I
Salt Water, lake ....Inset II
Satpura, range C4
Son, river D4
South Andaman, island F6
Sutlej, river C2
Ten Degree, channel F7
Ulhas, river ....Inset I
Vasai, creek ....Inset I
Vindhya, range C4
Western Ghats, mts. B5
Yamuna, river C3

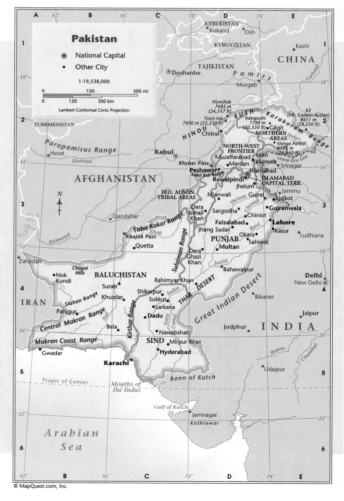

Pakistan

National Capital
• **Other City**

1:19,538,000

0   150   300 mi
0 150 300 km

Lambert Conformal Conic Projection

© MapQuest.com, Inc.

Pakistan

Capital: Islamabad
Area: 339,697 sq. mi.
880,044 sq. km.
Population: 138,123,000
Largest City: Karachi
Languages: Urdu, English
Monetary Unit: Pakistani rupee

Pakistan:
Map Index

Internal Divisions
Azad Kashmir Province D2
Baluchistan Province B4
Federally Administrated
Tribal Areas C3
Islamabad Capital Territory ...D2
Northern Areas D2
North-West Frontier Province ...D2
Punjab Province D3
Sind Province C5

Cities and Towns
Bahawalpur D4
Bela C4
Chiniot D3
Chitral D2
Dadu C4
Dera Ghazi Khan D3
Dera Ismail Khan D3
Faisalabad D3
Gilgit E2
Gujranwala E3
Gujrat E3
Gwadar B5
Hyderabad C5
Islamabad, capital D3
Jhang Sadar D3
Jhelum D3
Karachi C5
Kasur E3
Khuzdar C4
Lahore E3
Larkana C4
Mardan D2
Mianwali D3
Mirpur Khas C5
Multan D3
Muzaffarabad D2
Nawabshah C4
Nok Kundi B4

Okara D3
Panjgur B4
Peshawar D2
Quetta C3
Rahimyar Khan D4
Rawalpindi D3
Sahiwal D3
Sargodha D3
Shikarpur C4
Sialkot E3
Sukkur C4
Surab C4

Other Features
Arabian, sea B6
Central Makran, range B4
Chagai, hills B4
Chenab, river D3
Hindu Kush, mts. D2
Indus, river C4, E2
Jhelum, river D3
Karakoram, range E2
Khojak, pass C3
Khyber, pass D2
Kirthar, range C4
Konar, river D2
K2 (Godwin Austen), mt. ...E2
Makran Coast, range B5
Mouths of the Indus, delta ...C5
Nal, river B4
Nanga Parbat, mt. E2
Nara, canal C4
Nowshak, mt. D2
Rakaposhi, mt. E2
Ravi, river D3
Safed Koh, range D3
Siahan, range B4
Sulaiman, range C4
Sutlej, river D4
Thar, desert C4
Tirich Mir, mt. D2
Toba Kakar, range C3
Zhob, river C3

Afghanistan: Map Index

Cities and Towns

Asadabad	C2
Baghlan	B1
Balkh	B1
Bamian	B2
Baraki Barak	B2
Chaghcharan	B2
Charikar	B1
Farah	A2
Feyzabad	C1
Gardez	B2
Ghazni	B2
Herat	A2
Jalalabad	C2
Kabul, capital	B2
Khowst	B2
Konduz	B1

Kowt-e Ashrow	B2
Lashkar Gah	A2
Mazar-e Sharif	B1
Meymaneh	A1
Qalat	B2
Qaleh-ye Now	A2
Qaleh-ye Panjeh	C1
Qandahar	B2
Samangan	B1
Sar-e Pol	B1
Sheberghan	B1
Shindand	A2
Taloqan	B1
Tarin Kowt	B2
Zaranj	A2
Zareh Sharan	B2

Farah, river	A2
Fuladi, mt.	B2
Gowd-e Zereh, lake	A3
Hamun-e Saberi, lake	A2
Harirud, river	A2
Helmand, river	A2
Hindu Kush, range	B1
Kabul, river	B2
Khojak, pass	B2
Khyber, pass	C2
Konar, river	C1
Konduz, river	B1
Morghab, river	A1
Nowshak, mt.	C1
Panj, river	C1
Paropamisus, range	A2
Registan, region	A2
Shibar, pass	B2
Vakhan, region	C1

Other Features

Amu Darya, river	B1
Arghandab, river	B2

Afghanistan

Capital: Kabul
Area: 251,825 sq. mi.
  652,396 sq. km.
Population: 25,825,000
Largest City: Kabul
Languages: Pashto, Dari Persian
Monetary Unit: Afghani

Iran

Capital: Tehran
Area: 632,457 sq. mi.
  1,638,490 sq. km.
Population: 65,180,000
Largest City: Tehran
Languages: Persian, Turkic, Luri, Kurdish
Monetary Unit: Rial

Iran: Map Index

Cities and Towns

Abadan	B3
Ahvaz	B3
Arak	B3
Ardabil	B2
Bakhtaran	B3
Bam	D4
Bandar Beheshti	E4
Bandar-e Abbas	D4
Bandar-e Anzali	B2
Bandar-e Bushehr	C4
Bandar-e Khomeyni	C2
Bandar-e Torkeman	C2
Birjand	D3
Dezful	B3

Esfahan	C3
Hamadan	B3
Ilam	B3
Iranshahr	E4
Jask	D4
Karaj	C2
Kashan	C3
Kerman	D3
Khorramabad	B3
Khorramshahr	B3
Khvoy	A2
Mashhad	D2
Neyshabur	D2
Orumiyeh (Urmia)	A2
Qazvin	B2
Qom	C3
Rasht	B2
Sabzevar	D2
Sanandaj	B2
Sari	C2
Shahr-e Kord	C3
Shiraz	C4
Sirjan	D4
Tabriz	A2
Tehran, capital	C2
Yasuj	C3
Yazd	C3
Zabol	E3
Zahedan	E4
Zanjan	B2

Other Features

Aras, river	B2

Atrak, river	D2
Azerbaijan, region	B2
Bakhtiari, region	B3
Baluchistan, region	E4
Caspian, sea	C2
Damavand, mt.	C2
Dasht-e Kavir, desert	D3
Dasht-e Lut, desert	D3
Elburz, mts.	C2
Halil, river	D4
Hamun-e Jaz Murian, lake	D4
Hashtadan, region	E3
Hormuz, strait	D4
Karun, river	B3
Kavir-e Namak, desert	D3
Kerman, region	D4
Kharg, island	C4
Khorasan, region	D2
Khuzestan, region	B3
Kopet, mts.	D2
Kul, river	D4
Larestan, region	C4
Mand, river	C4
Mazandaran, region	C2
Oman, gulf	D5
Persian, gulf	C4
Qareh, river	B3
Qeshm, island	D4
Shatt al-Arab, river	B3
Urmia, lake	B2
Yazd, region	C3
Zagros, mts.	B3

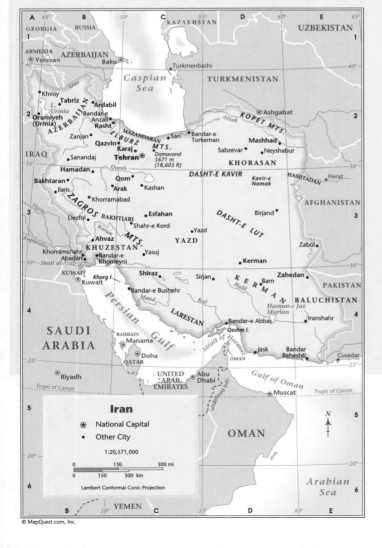

Turkmenistan: Map Index

Cities and Towns

Ashgabat, capital	C3
Bakhardok	C2
Bayramaly	D3
Büzmeyin	C2
Chardzhou	D2
Cheleken	A2
Dashhowuz	C2
Ensenguly	A3
Gazanjyk	B2
Gumdag	B2
Gushgy	D3
Gyzylarbat	B2
Kerki	D3
Mary	C3
Nebitdag	B2

Tedzhen	C3
Turkmenbashi	A2

Other Features

Amu Darya, river	D2
Caspian, sea	A2
Etrek, river	B3
Garabil, plateau	D3
Garabogazköl, lake	A2
Gushgy, river	D3
Kara-Kum, canal	D3
Kara-Kum, desert	C2
Kopet, mts.	B2
Murgab, river	D3
Sarygamysh Koli, lake	B2
Sumbar, river	B2
Tedzhen, river	C3
Turan, lowland	C2

Turkmenistan

Capital: Ashgabat
Area: 188,417 sq. mi.
  488,127 sq. km.
Population: 4,366,000
Largest City: Ashgabat
Languages: Turkmen, Russian, Uzbek
Monetary Unit: Manat

© MapQuest.com, Inc.

Beyneu	B2
Ekibastuz	D1
Embi	B2
Esil	C1
Kokshetau	C1
Leninsk	D2
Lepsi	D2
Oral	B1
Öskemen (Ust-Kamenogorsk)	E1
Pavlodar	D1
Petropavl	C1
Qaraghandy (Karaganda)	D2
Qostanay	C1
Qyzylorda	C2
Rudnyy	C1
Saryshaghan	D2
Semey (Semipalatinsk)	E1
Shalqar	B2
Shymkent (Chimkent)	C2
Taldyqorghan	D2
Temirtau	D1
Zaysan	E2
Zhambyl (Dzhambul)	D2
Zhezqazgham	C2

Other Features

Alakol, lake	E2
Aral, sea	B2
Balkhash, lake	D2
Betpak Dala, plain	C2
Caspian, depression	B2
Caspian, sea	A2
Ili, river	D2
Irtysh, river	D1
Ishim, river	C1
Kazakh Upland, region	C2
Khan-Tengri, mt.	E2
Muyun Kum, desert	D2
Syrdarya, river	C2
Tengiz, lake	C1
Tobol, river	C1
Torghay, plateau	C1
Ural, river	B2
Ustyurt, plateau	B2
Zaysan, lake	E2

Kazakhstan

Capital: Astana (Aqmola)
Area: 1,049,200 sq. mi.
 2,718,135 sq. km.
Population: 16,825,000
Largest City: Almaty (Alma-Ata)
Language: Kazakh
Monetary Unit: Tenge

Kazakhstan: Map Index

Cities and Towns

Astana (Aqmola), capital	D1
Almaty (Alma-Ata)	D2
Aqtau	B2
Aqtobe	B1
Aral	C2
Arqalyq	C1
Atbasar	C1
Atyrau	B2
Ayagöz	E2
Balkhash	D2

Kazakhstan

⊛ National Capital
• Other City

1:26,667,000

0 — 125 — 250 mi
0 — 125 — 250 km

Lambert Conformal Conic Projection

© MapQuest.com, Inc.

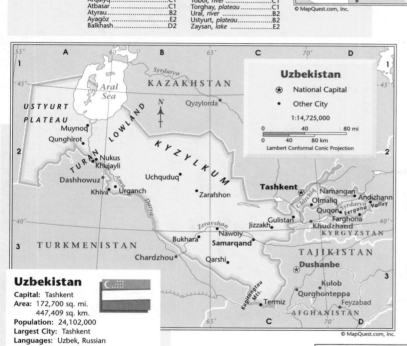

Uzbekistan

✪ National Capital
• Other City

1:14,725,000

0 — 40 — 80 mi
0 — 40 — 80 km

Lambert Conformal Conic Projection

Uzbekistan

Capital: Tashkent
Area: 172,700 sq. mi.
 447,409 sq. km.
Population: 24,102,000
Largest City: Tashkent
Languages: Uzbek, Russian
Monetary Unit: Ruble

Uzbekistan: Map Index

Cities and Towns

Andizhan	D2
Bukhara	B3
Farghona	D2
Gulistan	C2
Jizzakh	C2
Khujayli	A2
Muynoq	A2
Namangan	D2
Nawoiy	C2
Nukus	A2
Olmaliq	C2
Qarshi	C3
Qunghirot	A2
Quqon	D2
Samarqand	C3
Tashkent, capital	C2
Termiz	C3
Uchquduq	B2
Urganch	B2
Zarafshon	B2

Other Features

Amu Darya, river	B2
Aral, sea	A2
Chirchiq, river	C2
Fergana, valley	D2
Kyzylkum, desert	B2
Syrdarya, river	D2
Turan, lowland	A2
Ustyurt, plateau	A2
Zeravshan, river	B2

Kyrgyzstan: Map Index

Cities and Towns

At-Bashy	D2
Balykchy	E1
Bishkek, capital	D1
Cholpon-Ata	E1
Jalal-Abad	C2
Jangy-Bazar	B2
Karakol	F1
Kara-Say	F2
Kyzyl-Kyya	E2
Naryn	E2
Osh	C2
Özgön	C2
Sary Tash	C3
Songköl	D2
Sülüktü	A3
Talas	C1
Tash Kömür	C2
Tokmok	D1
Toktogul	C2

Other Features

Alay, mts.	C3
Chatkal, river	B2
Chu, river	D1
Jengish Chokusu, mt.	G1
Kyzyl-Suu, river	C3
Naryn, river	E2
Tien Shan, mts.	E2
Toxkan, river	E2
Ysyk-Köl, lake	E1

Kyrgyzstan

Capital: Bishkek
Area: 76,642 sq. mi.
 198,554 sq. km.
Population: 4,546,000
Largest City: Bishkek
Language: Kirghiz
Monetary Unit: Som

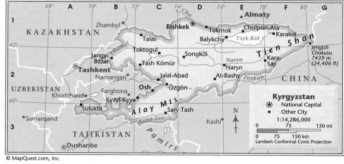

Kyrgyzstan

⊛ National Capital
• Other City

1:14,286,000

0 — 75 — 150 mi
0 — 75 — 150 km

Lambert Conformal Conic Projection

© MapQuest.com, Inc.

Tajikistan

Capital: Dushanbe
Area: 55,300 sq. mi.
 143,264 sq. km.
Population: 6,103,000
Largest City: Dushanbe
Language: Tajik
Monetary Unit: Ruble

Tajikistan: Map Index

Cities and Towns

Dangara	A1
Dushanbe, capital	A1
Jirgatol	B1
Kalai Khum	B1
Kansay	A1
Khorugh	B2
Khudzhand	A1
Konibodom	B1
Kulob	A2
Morghob	B1
Navabad	A1
Norak	A1
Panj	A2
Panjakent	A1
Qurghonteppa	A2
Tursunzoda	A1
Uroteppa	A1
Zarafobod	A1

Other Features

| Alay, mts. | B1 |
| Bartang, river | B1 |

Darya, river	A2
Imeni Ismail Samani, mt.	B1
Kofarnihon, river	A2
Morghob, river	B1
Oqsu, river	C2

Pamirs, mts.	B2
Panj, river	A1
Pyandzh, river	B1
Qarokul, lake	B1
Surkhob, river	B1

Syrdarya, river	A1, B1
Turkestan, mts.	A1
Vahsh, river	A1
Zeravshan, river	A1
Zeravshan, mts.	A1

Tajikistan

✪ National Capital
• Other City

1:7,622,000

0 — 40 — 80 mi
0 — 40 — 80 km

Lambert Conformal Conic Projection

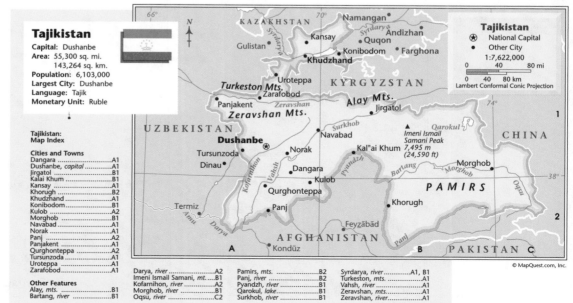

© MapQuest.com, Inc.

Iraq: Map Index

Cities and Towns

Amarah, al- C2
Baghdad, *capital* B2
Baqubah B2
Basra C2
Dahuk B1
Diwaniyah, ad- C2
Fallujah, al- B2
Hadithah, al- B2
Hillah, al- B1
Irbil B1
Karbala C2
Khanaqin C2
Kirkuk B1
Kut, al- C2
Mosul B1
Najaf, an- C2
Nasiriyah, an- C2
Qayyarah, al- B1
Ramadi, ar- B2
Rutbah, ar- B2

Samarra B2
Samawah, as- C2
Sulaymaniyah, as- C1
Tall Afar B1
Tikrit B2
Umm Qasr C2

Other Features

Babylon, *ruins* B2
Diyala, *river* C2

Euphrates, *river* C2
Great Zab, *river* B1
Haji Ibrahim, *mt.* B1
Little Zab, *river* B1
Mesopotamia, *region* B2
Milh, *lake* B2
Persian, *gulf* C3
Shatt al-Arab, *river* C2
Syrian, *desert* B2
Tigris, *river* B1

Iraq

Capital: Baghdad
Area: 167,975 sq. mi.
435,169 sq. km.
Population: 22,427,000
Largest City: Baghdad
Language: Arabic
Monetary Unit: Dinar

Iraq

⊛ National Capital
• Other City

1:12,765,000

0   100   200 mi
0   100   200 km

Lambert Conformal Conic Projection

© MapQuest.com, Inc.

Kuwait

⊛ National Capital
• Other City

1:4,667,000

0   25   50 mi
0   25   50 km

Lambert Conformal Conic Projection

© MapQuest.com, Inc.

Kuwait

Capital: Kuwait
Area: 6,880 sq. mi.
17,924 sq. km.
Population: 1,991,000
Largest City: Kuwait
Language: Arabic
Monetary Unit: Dinar

Kuwait: Map Index

Cities and Towns

Abdali B1
Ahmadi, al- C2
Fuhayhil, al- C2
Hawalli C2
Jahrah, al- B2
Khiran, al- C3
Kuwait, *capital* B2
Qasr as-Sabiyah B2
Rawdatayn, ar- B2
Sulaybikhat, as- B2
Wafrah, al- B3

Other Features

Bubiyan, *island* C2
Faylakah, *island* C2
Kuwait, *bay* B2
Persian, *gulf* C2
Wadi al-Batin, *river* A2
Warbah, *island* C1

Saudi Arabia

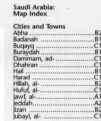

Capital: Riyadh
Area: 865,000 sq. mi.
2,240,933 sq. km.
Population: 21,505,000
Largest City: Riyadh
Language: Arabic
Monetary Unit: Riyal

Saudi Arabia: Map Index

Cities and Towns

Abha B2
Badanah B1
Buqayq C1
Buraydah B1
Dammam, ad- C1
Dhahran C1
Hail B1
Harad B2
Hillah, al- B2
Hufuf, al- C2
Jawf, al- A1
Jeddah A2
Jizan B2
Jubayl, al- C1

Khamis Mushayt B2
Kharj, al- B1
Mecca A2
Medina A1
Najran B2
Qalat Bishah B2
Qunfudhah, al- A2
Rafha B1
Ras al-Khafji C1
Ras Tanura C1
Riyadh, *capital* B1
Sulayyil, as- B2
Tabuk A1
Taif, at- B2
Turayf A1
Unayzah B1
Wajh, al- A1
Yanbu al-Bahr A1

Other Features

Asir, *region* B2
Dahna, ad-, *desert* B1
Farasan, *islands* B2
Hasa, al-, *region* C1
Hijaz, al-, *region* A1
Jabal Tuwayq, *mts.* B2
Nafud, an-, *desert* B1
Najd, *region* B1
Persian, *gulf* C1
Red, *sea* A1
Rub al-Khali
(Empty Quarter), *desert* ...C2
Sabkhat Matti, *salt flat* C2
Sawda, *mt.* B2
Syrian, *desert* A1
Umm as-Samim, *salt flat* ...C2
Wadi al-Hamd, *river* A1

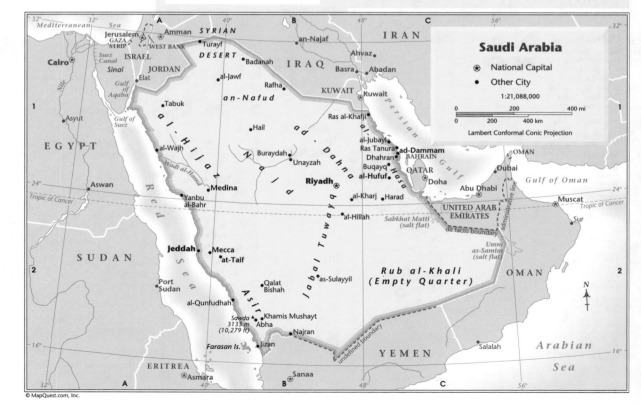

Saudi Arabia

⊛ National Capital
• Other City

1:21,088,000

0   200   400 mi
0   200   400 km

Lambert Conformal Conic Projection

© MapQuest.com, Inc.

Bahrain and Qatar

⊛ National Capital
• Other City

1:2,842,000

0   10   20 mi
0   10 20 km
Transverse Mercator Projection

Map labels: Manama, Jiddah, al-Muharraq, Mina Salman, Sitrah, Umm an-Nasan, Askar, ar-Ruways, Ras Rakan, Persian Gulf, BAHRAIN, al-Mamtalah, Ras Laffan, Gulf of Bahrain, Ras al-Barr, Hawar Is. (disputed between Qatar & Bahrain), al-Khawr, al-Jumayliyah, Dukhan, QATAR, Doha, Umm Bab, al-Wakrah, Umm Said (Musayid), SAUDI ARABIA, Dawhat as-Salwa, Tuwayyir al-Hamir 103 m (338 ft), Ras Abu Qumayyis, SAUDI ARABIA

© MapQuest.com, Inc.

Bahrain and Qatar: Map Index

Bahrain

Cities and Towns
Askar	B1
Mamtalah, al-	B2
Manama, capital	B1
Mina Salman	B1

Other Features
Bahrain, gulf	A2
Hawar, islands	B2
Jiddah, island	A1
Muharraq, al-, island	B1
Ras al-Barr, cape	B2
Sitrah, island	B1
Umm an-Nasan, island	A1

Qatar

Cities and Towns
Doha, capital	D3
Dukhan	B3
Jumayliyah, al-	C2
Khawr, al-	D2
Ruways, ar-	C1
Umm Bab	B3
Umm Said (Musayid)	D4
Wakrah, al-	D3

Other Features
Dawhat as-Salwa, bay	B3
Ras Laffan, cape	D2
Ras Rakan, cape	C1
Tuwayyir al-Hamir, hill	C4

Bahrain
Capital: Manama
Area: 268 sq. mi.
   694 sq. km.
Population: 629,000
Largest City: Manama
Language: Arabic
Monetary Unit: Dinar

Qatar
Capital: Doha
Area: 4,412 sq. mi.
   11,430 sq. km.
Population: 724,000
Largest City: Doha
Language: Arabic
Monetary Unit: Riyal

United Arab Emirates

⊛ National Capital
• Other City

1:11,579,000

0   50   100   150 mi
0   50 100 150 km
Lambert Conformal Conic Projection

Map labels: IRAN, Strait of Hormuz, Persian Gulf, QATAR, Doha, Umm Said, ash-Sham, Ras al-Khaymah, Umm al-Qaywayn, OMAN, Sharjah, Ajman, Dubai, Masfut, al-Fujayrah, Abu Dhabi, al-Ayn, Suhar, ar-Ruways, Tarif, Salamiyah (salt flat), al-Qabil, OMAN, Matti (salt flat), Aradah, an-Nashshash, SAUDI ARABIA

© MapQuest.com, Inc.

United Arab Emirates (U.A.E.)

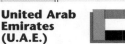

Capital: Abu Dhabi
Area: 30,000 sq. mi.
   77,720 sq. km.
Population: 2,344,000
Largest City: Abu Dhabi
Language: Arabic
Monetary Unit: Dirham

United Arab Emirates: Map Index

Cities and Towns
Abu Dhabi, capital	C2
Ajman	C2
Aradah	B3
Ayn, al-	C2
Dubai	C2
Fujayrah, al-	D2
Masfut	D2
Nashshash, an-	C3
Ras al-Khaymah	C2

Ruways, ar-	B2
Sham, ash-	D1
Sharjah	C2
Tarif	B2
Umm al-Qaywayn	C2

Other Features
Hormuz, strait	D1
Matti, salt flat	B3
Oman, gulf	D2
Persian, gulf	B1
Salamiyah, salt flat	C3

Yemen: Map Index

Cities and Towns
Aden	B2
Ahwar	B2
Amran	A1
Ataq	B2
Balhaf	B2
Bayda, al-	B2
Dhamar	A2
Ghaydah, al-	C1
Habarut	C1
Hadiboh	C2
Hajjah	A1
Hawf	C1
Hazm, al-	A1
Hudaydah, al-	A2
Ibb	A2
Lahij	A2
Madinat ash-Shab	A2
Marib	B1
Maydi	A1

Mocha (Mukha, al-)	A2
Mukalla, al-	B2
Qalansiyah	C2
Qishn	C1
Rida	A2
Sadah	A1
Sanaa, capital	A1
Sanaw	C1
Sayhut	C1
Saywun	B1
Shabwah	B1
Taizz	A2
Zabid	A2

Other Features
Abd al-Kuri, island	C2
Aden, gulf	B2
Arabian, sea	C2
Bab al-Mandab, strait	A2
Hadhramaut, district	B1
Jabal an-Nabi Shuayb, mt.	A1
Jabal Zuqar, island	A2
Kamaran, island	A1

Perim, island	A2
Ras al-Kalb, cape	B2
Ras Fartak, cape	C1
Red, sea	A2
Socotra, island	C2
The Brothers, islands	C2
Wadi al-Masilah, river	B1

Yemen

Capital: Sanaa
Area: 205,356 sq. mi.
   532,010 sq. km.
Population: 16,942,000
Largest City: Sanaa
Language: Arabic
Monetary Unit: Riyal

Map labels: SAUDI ARABIA, Rub al-Khali, OMAN, Abha, Najran, Farasan Is., Jizan, Sadah, Sanaw, Habarut, Salalah, Maydi, al-Hazm, Hawf, al-Ghaydah, Ras Fartak, Kamaran, Hajjah, Amran, Saywun, Wadi al-Masilah, Qishn, Jabal an-Nabi Shuayb 3760 m (12,336 ft), Sanaa, Marib, Shabwah, Sayhut, HADHRAMAUT, Red Sea, Jabal Zuqar, al-Hudaydah, Dhamar, Rida, Ataq, al-Mukalla, Ras al-Kalb, Arabian Sea, Zabid, Ibb, al-Bayda, Mocha (al-Mukha), Taizz, Balhaf, Lahij, Ahwar, ERITREA, Bab al-Mandab, Madinat ash-Shab, Aden, Gulf of Aden, Assab, Perim, Qalansiyah, Hadiboh, The Brothers, Socotra, Abd al-Kuri, DJIBOUTI

© MapQuest.com, Inc.

Yemen

⊛ National Capital
• Other City

1:13,000,000

0   75   150 mi
0   75 150 km
Lambert Conformal Conic Projection

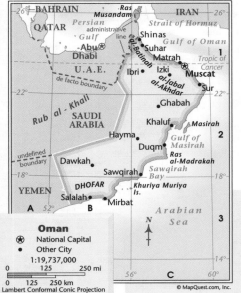

Map labels: BAHRAIN, QATAR, Ras Musandam, IRAN, Persian Gulf, administrative line, Strait of Hormuz, Abu Dhabi, Shinas, Gulf of Oman, al-Batinah, Suhar, U.A.E., Matrah, Tropic of Cancer, Ibri, Izki, al-Jabal al-Akhdar, Muscat, de facto boundary, Sur, Rub al-Khali, Ghabah, SAUDI ARABIA, Khaluf, Masirah, Hayma, Gulf of Masirah, Duqm, Ras al-Madrakah, undefined boundary, Dawkah, Sawqirah, Sawqirah Bay, YEMEN, DHOFAR, Khuriya Muriya Is., Salalah, Mirbat, Arabian Sea

© MapQuest.com, Inc.

Oman

⊛ National Capital
• Other City

1:19,737,000

0   125   250 mi
0   125   250 km
Lambert Conformal Conic Projection

Oman: Map Index

Cities and Towns
Dawkah	B2
Duqm	C2
Ghabah	C2
Hayma	C2
Ibri	C1
Izki	C1
Khaluf	C2
Matrah	C1

Mirbat	B3
Muscat, capital	C1
Salalah	B3
Sawqirah	C2
Shinas	C1
Suhar	C1
Sur	C1

Other Features
Arabian, sea	C3
Batinah, al-, region	C1
Dhofar, region	B3

Hormuz, strait	C1
Jabal al-Akhdar, al-, mts.	C1
Khuriya Muriya, islands	C3
Masirah, gulf	C2
Masirah, island	C2
Oman, gulf	C1
Persian, gulf	B1
Ras al-Madrakah, cape	C2
Ras Musandam, cape	C1
Sawqirah, bay	C2

Oman

Capital: Muscat
Area: 118,150 sq. mi.
   305,829 sq. km.
Population: 2,447,000
Largest City: Muscat
Language: Arabic
Monetary Unit: Rial Omani

Lebanon

Capital: Beirut
Area: 3,950 sq. mi.
10,233 sq. km.
Population: 3,563,000
Largest City: Beirut
Languages: Arabic, French
Monetary Unit: Pound

Lebanon: Map Index

Cities and Towns

Amyun A1
Baalbek B1
Babda A2
Batrun, al- A1
Beirut, capital A2
Bint Jubayl B1
Bsharri B1
Damur, ad- A1
Duma A1
Halba B1
Hirmil, al- B1
Jazzin A2
Jubayl A1
Juniyah A2
Marj Uyun A2
Nabatiyah at-Tahta, an- ...A2
Qubayyat, al- B1
Rashayya A2
Riyaq B2
Sidon (Sayda) A2
Sur (Tyre) A2
Tripoli (Tarabulus) A1
Zahlah A2

Other Features

Anti-Lebanon, mts. B1
Awwali, river B1
Bekaa, valley B1
Byblos, ruins A1
Hermon, mt. B1
Ibrahim, river A1
Kebir, river B1
Lebanon, mts. B1
Litani, river B1
Orontes, river B1
Qurnat as-Sawda, mt. B1

© MapQuest.com, Inc.

Israel

⊛ National Capital
• Other City
⊥⊥⊥ Canal

1:2,838,000

0   20   40 mi
0 20 40 km

Cassini-Soldner Transverse
Cylindrical Projection

© MapQuest.com, Inc.

Jordan: Map Index

Cities and Towns

Amman, capital A2
Aqabah, al- A3
Azraq ash-Shishan B2
Bair B2
Irbid A1
Jafr, al- B2
Jarash A1
Karak, al- A2
Maan A2
Madaba A2
Mafraq, al- B1
Mudawwarah, al- B3
Qatranah, al- A2
Ramtha, ar- B1
Ras an-Naqb A2
Salt, as- A1
Tafilah, at- A2
Zarqa, az- B1

Other Features

Aqaba, gulf A3
Arabah, al-, river A2
Dead Sea, lake A2
Jabal Ramm, mt. A3
Jordan, river A2
Petra, ruins A2
Syrian, desert B1
Tiberias, lake A1
Wadi as-Sirhan, depression .B2

Jordan

Capital: Amman
Area: 34,342 sq. mi.
88,969 sq. km.
Population: 4,561,000
Largest City: Amman
Language: Arabic
Monetary Unit: Dinar

Jordan

⊛ National Capital
• Other City

1:3,250,000

0   50   100 mi
0   50   100 km

Lambert Conformal Conic Projection

© MapQuest.com, Inc.

Israel

Capital: Jerusalem
Area: 7,992 sq. mi.
20,705 sq. km.
Population: 5,750,000
Largest City: Jerusalem
Languages: Hebrew, Arabic
Monetary Unit: New Shekel

Israel: Map Index

Districts

Central B1
Haifa B1
Jerusalem B2
Northern B1
Southern B2
Tel Aviv B1

Cities and Towns

Acre (Akko) B1
Ashdod B2
Ashqelon B2
Beersheba B2
Dimona B2
Elat B3
Hadera B1
Haifa B1
Herzliyya B1
Holon B1
Jerusalem, capital B2
Lod (Lydda) B2
Mizpe Ramon B2
Nahariyya B1
Nazareth B1
Netanya B1
Petah Tiqwa B1
Qiryat Gat B2
Qiryat Shemona B1
Ramat Gan B1
Ramla B2
Rehovot B2
Tel Aviv-Jaffa B1
Tiberias B1
Yotvata B3
Zefat B1

Other Features

Aqaba, gulf B3
Arabah, al-, river B2
Besor, river B2
Dead, sea B2
Galilee, region B1
Haifa, bay B1
Jezreel (Esdraelon), plain .B1
Jordan, river B1
Judea, plain B2
Masada, ruins B2
Meron, mt. B1
Negev, region B2
Ramon, mt. B2
Samarian, hills B1
Sharon, plain B1
Tiberias (Galilee), lake ..B1
Zevulun, plain B1

Turkey

Capital: Ankara
Area: 300,948 sq. mi.
779,658 sq. km.
Population: 65,599,000
Largest City: İstanbul
Language: Turkish
Monetary Unit: Lira

Turkey
⊛ National Capital
● Other City
1:11,125,000
0   75   150 mi
0 75 150 km
Lambert Conformal Conic Projection

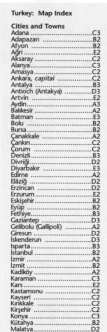

Turkey: Map Index

Cities and Towns

Adana	C3
Adapazarı	B2
Afyon	B2
Ağrı	E2
Aksaray	C3
Alanya	C3
Amasya	C2
Ankara, *capital*	C2
Antalya	B3
Antioch (Antakya)	D3
Artvin	E2
Aydın	A3
Balıkesir	A2
Batman	E3
Bolu	B2
Bursa	B2
Çanakkale	A2
Çankırı	C2
Çorum	C2
Denizli	B3
Divriği	D2
Diyarbakır	E3
Edirne	A2
Elâzığ	D2
Erzincan	D2
Erzurum	E2
Eskişehir	B2
Eyüp	B2
Fethiye	B3
Gaziantep	D3
Gelibolu (Gallipoli)	A2
Giresun	D2
İskenderun	B3
Isparta	B3
İstanbul	B2
İzmir	A2
İzmit	A2
Kadıköy	A2
Karaman	C3
Kars	E2
Kastamonu	C2
Kayseri	C2
Kırıkkale	C2
Kırşehir	C2
Konya	C3
Kütahya	B2
Malatya	D2

Manisa	A2
Maraş	D3
Mardin	E3
Mersin	C3
Muğla	B3
Muş	E2
Niğde	C2
Ordu	D2
Samsun	D2
Siirt	E3

Silifke	C3
Sinope	C2
Sivas	D2
Tarsus	C3
Tekirdağ	A2
Thrace	D2
Trabzon	D2
Urfa	D3
Usak	B2

Üsküdar	B2
Van	E2
Zonguldak	B2

Other Features

Aegean, *sea*	A3
Anatolia, *region*	C2
Antalya, *gulf*	B3
Ararat (Ağrı Dağı), *mt.*	F2
Aras, *river*	E2

Atatürk, *reservoir*	D3
Beyşehir, *lake*	B3
Black, *sea*	C1
Bosporus, *strait*	B2
Burdur, *lake*	B3
Büyük Menderes, *rivers*	A3
Ceyhan, *river*	D3
Cilician Gates, *pass*	C3
Çoruh, *river*	E2
Çukorova, *region*	C3

Eğridir, *lake*	B2
Erciyas Dağı, *mt.*	C2
Euphrates, *river*	E3
Great Zab, *river*	E3
Iskenderum, *gulf*	C3
Keban, *reservoir*	D2
Kızıl Irmak, *river*	C2
Kura, *river*	E2
Marmara, *sea*	A2
Mediterranean, *sea*	B4

Murat, *river*	E2
Pontic, *mts.*	C2
Sakarya, *river*	B2
Seyhan, *river*	C3
Taurus, *mts.*	B3
Tigris, *river*	E2
Tuz, *lake*	C2
Ulu Dağ (Mt. Olympus), *mt.*	B2
Van, *lake*	E2
Yesilirmak, *river*	D2

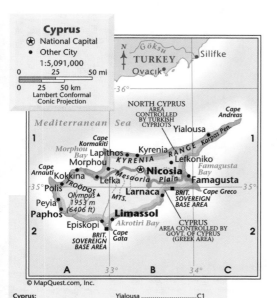

Cyprus
⊛ National Capital
● Other City
1:5,091,000
0   25   50 mi
0 25 50 km
Lambert Conformal Conic Projection

Cyprus

Capital: Nicosia
Area: 3,572 sq. mi.
9,254 sq. km.
Population: 754,000
Largest City: Nicosia
Languages: Greek, Turkish
Monetary Unit: Pound

Cyprus: Map Index

Cities and Towns

Episkopi	A2
Famagusta	B1
Kokkina	A1
Kyrenia	B1
Lapithos	B1
Larnaca	B2
Lefka	A1
Lefkoniko	B1
Limassol	B2
Morphou	A1
Nicosia, *capital*	B1
Paphos	A2
Peyia	A2
Polis	A1

Yialousa	C1

Other Features

Akrotiri, *bay*	B2
Andreas, *cape*	C1
Arnauti, *cape*	A2
British Sovereign Base Area	A2, B2
Famagusta, *bay*	C1
Gata, *cape*	B2
Greco, *cape*	C2
Karpas, *peninsula*	C1
Kormakiti, *cape*	A1
Kyrenia, *range*	B1
Mesaoria, *plain*	B1
Morphou, *bay*	A1
Olympus, *mt.*	A2
Troödos, *mts.*	A2

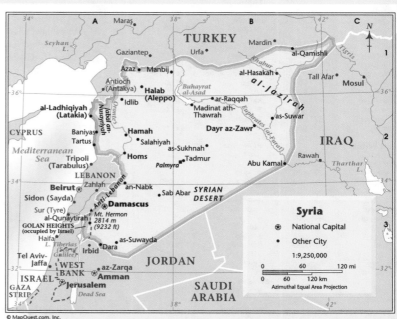

Syria

Capital: Damascus
Area: 71,498 sq. mi.
185,228 sq. km.
Population: 17,214,000
Largest City: Damascus
Language: Arabic
Monetary Unit: Pound

Syria
⊛ National Capital
● Other City
1:9,250,000
0   60   120 mi
0 60 120 km
Azimuthal Equal Area Projection

Syria: Map Index

Cities and Towns

Abu Kamal	B2
Azaz	A1
Baniyas	A2
Damascus, *capital*	A3
Dara	A3
Dayr az-Zawr	B2
Halab (Aleppo)	A1
Hamah	A2
Hasakah, al-	B1
Homs	A2
Idlib	A2
Ladhiqiyah, al- (Latakia)	A2
Madinat ath-Thawrah	B2
Manbij	A1
Nabk, an-	A2
Qamishli, al-	B1

Qunaytirah, al-	A3
Raqqah, ar-	B2
Sab Abar	A3
Salahiyah	A2
Sukhnah, as-	B2
Suwar, as-	B2
Suwayda, as-	A3
Tadmur	B2
Tartus	A2

Other Features

Anti-Lebanon, *mts.*	A3
Buhayrat al-Asad, *lake*	A2
Euphrates (al-Furat), *river*	B2
Golan Heights, *occupied territory*	A3
Hermon, *mt.*	A3
Jabal an-Nusayriyah, *mts.*	A2
Jazirah, al-, *region*	B1
Khabur, *river*	B1

Mediterranean, *sea*	A2
Orontes, *river*	A2
Palmyra, *ruins*	B2
Syrian, *desert*	B3
Tigris, *river*	C1

MAJOR CITIES

Albania
Tirana 244,000

Andorra
Andorra la Vella 16,000

Armenia (metro)
Yerevan 1,278,000

Austria
Vienna 1,540,000

Azerbaijan (metro)
Baku 1,848,000

Belarus (metro)
Minsk 1,708,000

Belgium (metro)
Brussels 948,000
Antwerp 456,000

Bosnia and Hercegovina
Sarajevo 416,000

Bulgaria
Sofia 1,117,000

Croatia (metro)
Zagreb 981,000

Czech Republic
Prague 1,200,000

Denmark
Copenhagen 632,000

Estonia
Tallinn 424,000

Finland
Helsinki 532,000

France
Paris 2,152,000
Lyon 1,260,000
Marseille 1,200,000

Georgia (metro)
Tbilisi 1,342,000

Germany
Berlin 3,458,000
Hamburg 1,708,000
Munich 1,226,000
Cologne 964,000
Frankfurt 647,000
Essen 612,000
Dortmund 597,000
Stuttgart 586,000
Düsseldorf 571,000
Leipzig 549,000

Great Britain
London 7,074,000
Birmingham 1,021,000
Leeds 727,000
Glasgow 616,000
Sheffield 530,000
Bradford 483,000
Liverpool 468,000
Edinburgh 449,000

Greece (metro)
Athens 3,073,000

Hungary
Budapest 1,897,000

Iceland
Reykjavík 105,000

Ireland
Dublin 482,000

Italy
Rome 2,645,000
Milan 1,304,000
Naples 1,046,000
Turin 920,000
Palermo 688,000
Genoa 654,000

Latvia
Riga 821,000

Liechtenstein
Vaduz 5,000

Lithuania
Vilnius 580,000

Luxembourg
Luxembourg 77,000

F.Y.R. Macedonia
Skopje 430,000

Malta
Valletta 7,000

Moldova
Chişinău 656,000

Monaco
Monaco 27,000

Netherlands
Amsterdam 717,000
Rotterdam 591,000

Norway
Oslo 492,000

Poland
Warsaw 1,633,000
Łódź 820,000
Kraków 745,000
Wrocław 642,000

Portugal
Lisbon 582,000

Romania
Bucharest 2,037,000

Russia (European)
Moscow 8,368,000
St. Petersburg 4,232,000
Nizh. Novgorod 1,376,000
Samara 1,184,000
Ufa 1,093,000
Kazan 1,076,000
Perm 1,031,000
Rostov-na-Donu 1,014,000
Volgograd 999,000

San Marino
San Marino 3,000

Slovakia
Bratislava 452,000

Slovenia
Ljubljana 273,000

Spain
Madrid 2,867,000
Barcelona 1,509,000
Valencia 747,000
Seville 697,000

Sweden
Stockholm 718,000

Switzerland
Zürich 342,000
Bern 129,000

Turkey (European)
İstanbul 6,620,000

Ukraine
Kiev 2,630,000
Kharkiv 1,555,000
Dnipropetrovsk 1,147,000
Donetsk 1,088,000
Odesa 1,046,000

Yugoslavia (metro)
Belgrade 1,204,000

International comparability of city population
data is limited by various data inconsistencies.

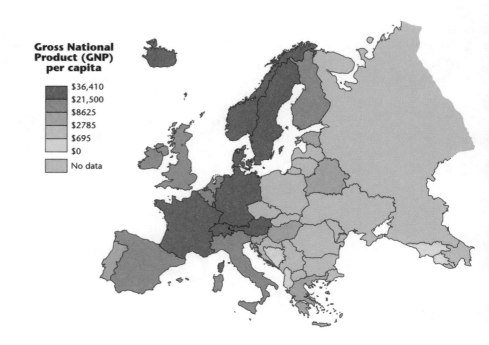

Gross National Product (GNP) per capita

- $36,410
- $21,500
- $8625
- $2785
- $695
- $0
- No data

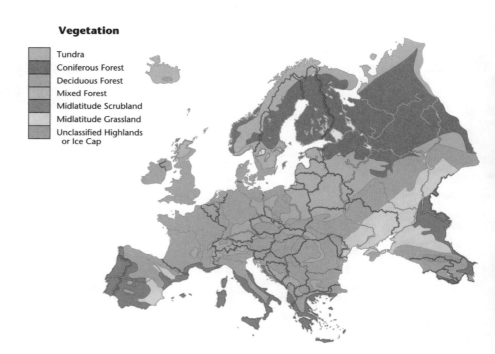

Vegetation

- Tundra
- Coniferous Forest
- Deciduous Forest
- Mixed Forest
- Midlatitude Scrubland
- Midlatitude Grassland
- Unclassified Highlands or Ice Cap

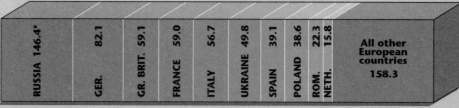

Europe: Population, by nation (in millions)*

RUSSIA 146.4* | GER. 82.1 | GR. BRIT. 59.1 | FRANCE 59.0 | ITALY 56.7 | UKRAINE 49.8 | SPAIN 39.1 | POLAND 38.6 | ROM. 22.3 | NETH. 15.8 | All other European countries 158.3

*Including Asian Russia as well as the more populous European portion of the country.

© MapQuest.com, Inc.

CITIES
- ⊛ National Capital
- ★ Territorial Capital
- • Other City

ELEVATIONS

Feet	Meters
13,120	4000
6560	2000
1640	500
656	200
0	0
Below sea level	

CLIMATE

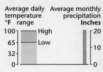

Average daily temperature °F range — High / Low
Average monthly precipitation Inches

ARKHANGELSK, Russia

ATHENS, Greece

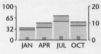

COPENHAGEN, Denmark

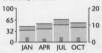

DUBLIN, Ireland

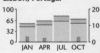

LISBON, Portugal

MOSCOW, Russia

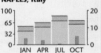

NAPLES, Italy

ODESA, Ukraine

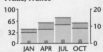

PARIS, France

REYKJAVÍK, Iceland

TROMSØ, Norway

VIENNA, Austria

Population

Persons per sq mi	Persons per sq km
Over 520	Over 200
260–519	100–199
130–259	50–99
25–129	10–49
1–24	1–9
0	0

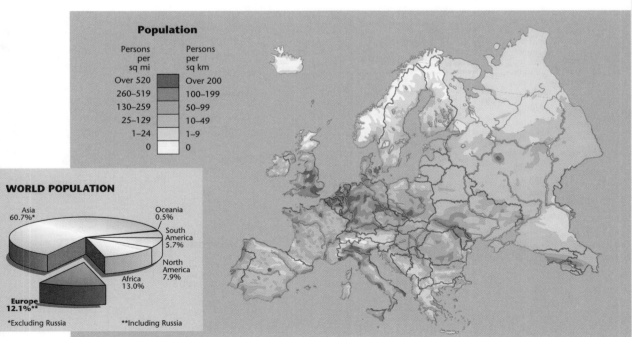

WORLD POPULATION

- Asia 60.7%*
- Oceania 0.5%
- South America 5.7%
- North America 7.9%
- Africa 13.0%
- Europe 12.1%**

*Excluding Russia
**Including Russia

Great Britain

⊛ National Capital
● Other City

1:4,375,000

| 0 | 25 | 50 | 75 | 100 mi |

| 0 | 25 | 50 | 75 | 100 | 125 | 150 km |

Lambert Conformal Conic Projection

Great Britain

Capital: London
Area: 94,251 sq. mi.
244,174 sq. km.
Population: 59,133,000
Largest City: London
Language: English
Monetary Unit: Pound

Great Britain: Map Index

CHANNEL ISLANDS
Features
Alderney, island..........Inset II
Guernsey, island..........Inset II
Jersey, island..........Inset II
St. Malo, gulf..........Inset II
Sark, island..........Inset II

ENGLAND
Cities and Towns
Aylesbury..........Inset III
Banbury..........C3
Barnsley..........C3
Barnstaple..........B3
Barrow-in-Furness..........B2
Basildon..........Inset III
Bath..........C3
Bedford..........C3
Berwick-upon-Tweed..........C2
Birkenhead..........B3
Birmingham..........C3
Blackburn..........C3
Blackpool..........C3
Bolton..........C3
Boston..........C3
Bournemouth..........C4
Bradford..........C3
Braintree..........Inset III
Brentwood..........Inset III
Brighton..........C4
Bristol..........C3
Burnley..........C3
Bury..........C3
Bury St. Edmunds..........D3
Buxton..........C3
Camberley..........Inset III
Cambridge..........D3
Canterbury..........D3
Carlisle..........C2
Chatham..........Inset III
Chelmsford..........D3, Inset III
Cheltenham..........C3
Chester..........C3
Chesterfield..........C3
Chichester..........C4
Colchester..........D3
Coventry..........C3
Cowes..........C4
Crawley..........Inset III
Crewe..........C3
Darlington..........C2
Derby..........C3
Doncaster..........C3
Dorchester..........C4
Dorking..........Inset III
Dover..........D3
Dudley..........C3
Dunstable..........Inset III
Durham..........C2
Eastbourne..........D4
Ely..........D3
Epsom..........Inset III
Ewell..........Inset III
Exeter..........B4
Farnham..........Inset III
Felixstowe..........D3
Fleetwood..........C3
Folkestone..........D3
Gateshead..........C2
Gillingham..........D3
Glastonbury..........C3
Gloucester..........C3
Gosport..........C4
Grantham..........C3
Gravesend..........Inset III
Great Yarmouth..........D3
Grimsby..........C3
Guildford..........C3
Halifax..........C3
Harlow..........Inset III
Harrogate..........C2
Haslemere..........Inset III
Hastings..........D4
Hereford..........C3
Hertford..........Inset III
High Wycombe..........Inset III
Hove..........C4
Huddersfield..........C3
Ipswich..........D3
Kendal..........C2
Kenilworth..........C3
Kidderminster..........C3
King's Lynn..........D3
Kingston upon Hull..........C3
Kingston upon Thames..........Inset III
Lancaster..........C2
Launceston..........B4
Leeds..........C3
Leicester..........C3
Lewes..........D4
Lichfield..........C3
Lincoln..........C3
Liverpool..........C3
London, capital....C3, Inset III
Lowestoft..........D3
Luton..........C3
Maidstone..........D3
Manchester..........C3
Margate..........D3
Matlock..........C3
Middlesbrough..........C2
Newcastle-under-Lyme..........C3
Newcastle upon Tyne..........C2
Newmarket..........D3
Newquay..........B4
Northallerton..........C2
Northampton..........C3
North Shields..........C2
Norwich..........D3
Nottingham..........C3
Oldham..........C3
Oxford..........C3
Penrith..........C2
Penzance..........B4
Peterborough..........C3
Plymouth..........B4
Poole..........C4
Portsmouth..........C4
Preston..........C3
Reading..........C3
Reigate..........Inset III
Rochdale..........C3
Rotherham..........C3
St. Albans..........C3, Inset III

Republic of Ireland

Capital: Dublin
Area: 27,137 sq. mi.
70,303 sq. km.
Population: 3,632,000
Largest City: Dublin
Languages: English, Irish
Monetary Unit: Punt, Euro

Republic of Ireland:
Map Index

Counties
Carlow C2
Cavan C2
Clare B2
Cork B3
Donegal B1
Dún Laoghaire-Rathdown ...C2
Fingal C2
Galway B2
Kerry B2
Kildare C2
Kilkenny C2
Laois C2
Leitrim B1
Limerick B2
Longford C2
Louth C2
Mayo B2
Meath C2
Monaghan C1
Offaly C2
Roscommon B2
Sligo B1
South Dublin C2
Tipperary North Riding B2
Tipperary South Riding B2
Waterford C2
Westmeath C2
Wexford C2
Wicklow C2

Monaghan C1
Mullingar C2
Naas C2
Nenagh B2
Port Laoise C2
Roscommon B2
Roscrea C2
Rosslare C2
Shannon B2
Sligo B1
Swords C2
Tipperary B2
Tralee B2
Trim C2
Tuam B2
Tullamore C2
Waterford C2
Westport B2
Wexford C2
Wicklow C2
Youghal C3

County Boroughs
Cork B3
Dublin D2
Galway B2
Limerick B2
Waterford C2

Cities and Towns
Ardara B1
Arklow C2
Athlone C2
Ballina B1
Bantry B3
Blarney B3
Carlingford C1
Carlow C2
Carrick-on-Shannon B2
Cashel C2
Castlebar B2
Cavan C2
Clara C2
Clifden A2
Clonmel C2
Cóbh B3
Cork B3
Dingle A2
Donegal B1
Drogheda C2
Dublin, *capital* C2
Dundalk C2
Dungarvan C2
Dún Laoghaire C2
Ennis B2
Ennistymon B2
Galway B2
Kildare C2
Kilkee B2
Kilkenny C2
Killarney B2
Letterkenny C1
Lifford C1
Limerick B2
Longford C2
Mallow B2
Maynooth C2

Other Features
Achill, *island* A2
Allen, *lake* B1
Aran, *islands* B2
Bantry, *bay* B3
Barrow, *river* C2
Benwee Head, *cape* B1
Blackwater, *river* B2
Blackwater, *river* C1
Boggeragh, *mts.* B2
Boyne, *river* C2
Caha, *mts.* B3
Carlingford, *lake* C1
Carnsore, *point* C2
Carrantuohill, *mt.* B3
Celtic, *sea* B3
Clear, *cape* B3
Conn, *lake* B1
Connaught, *province* B2
Connemara, *region* B2
Corrib, *lake* B2
Derg, *lake* B2
Dingle, *bay* A2
Donegal, *bay* B1
Erne, *river* B1
Errigal, *mt.* B1
Finn, *river* C1
Foyle, *inlet* C1
Galway, *bay* B2
Grand, *canal* C2
Irish, *sea* D2
Killala, *bay* B1
Knockboy, *mt.* B3
Lee, *river* B3
Leinster, *province* C2
Loop Head, *cape* B2
Malin Head, *cape* C1
Mask, *lake* B2
Maumturk, *mts.* B2
Mizen Head, *cape* B3
Moher, *cliffs* B2
Munster, *province* B2
Ree, *lake* B2
Royal, *canal* C2
Saint George's, *channel* ...C3
Shannon, *river* B2
Suir, *river* C2
Twelve Pins, *mt.* B2
Ulster, *province* C1
Wicklow, *mts.* C2
Wicklow Head, *cape* D2

Great Britain: Map Index
St. Austell B4
St. Helens C3
Salford C3
Salisbury C3
Scarborough C2
Scunthorpe C3
Sheffield C3
Shrewsbury C3
Slough ....Inset III
Solihull C4
Southampton C4
Southend-on-Sea D3
Southport C2
South Shields C3
Stafford C3
Stevenage ....Inset III
Stoke-on-Trent C3
Stratford-upon-Avon C3
Sunderland C2
Swindon C3
Taunton C3
Telford C3
Tewkesbury C3
Thetford D3
Tiverton C4
Tonbridge ....Inset III
Torbay B4
Trowbridge C3
Truro B4
Tunbridge Wells D3
Wakefield C3
Walsall C3
Warrington C3
Warwick C3
Watford ....Inset III
Westminster ....Inset III
Whitehaven B2
Wigan C3
Winchester C3
Windsor ....Inset III
Wolverhampton C3
Worcester C3
Yeovil C4
York C2

Other Features
Avon, *river* C3
Black Country, *region* C3
Bristol, *channel* B3
Cheviot, *hills* C2
Cotswold, *hills* C3
Cumbrian, *mts.* B2
Dartmoor, *plateau* B4
Dee, *river* B3
Dover, *strait* D4
English, *channel* C4
Exmoor, *plateau* B3
Fens, *region* C3
Flodden Field, *plain* C2
Humber, *river* D3
Irish, *sea* B3
Lake, *district* B2
Land's End, *promontory* B4
Liverpool, *bay* B3
Lyme, *bay* C4
Mersey, *river* C3
Midlands, *region* C3
North, *sea* D2
North Downs, *hills* C3
North Foreland,
  promontory D3
Ouse, *river* C2, D3
Pennines, *mts.* C3
Scafell Pike, *mt.* B2
Scilly, *islands* A4
Severn, *river* C3
South Downs, *hills* C3
Spithead, *channel* C4
Start, *point* B4
Tees, *river* C2
Thames, *river* ....C3, Inset III
Trent, *river* C3
Tweed, *river* C2
Tyne, *river* C2
Wash, *bay* D3
Wight, *island* C4
Wye, *river* C3
Yare, *river* D3

ISLE OF MAN
City
Douglas B2

NORTHERN IRELAND
Cities and Towns
Armagh A2
Ballymena A2
Bangor B2
Belfast B2
Coleraine A2
Holywood B2
Larne B2
Londonderry A2
Newry A2
Omagh A2
Strabane A2
Strangford B2

Other Features
Antrim, *mts.* A2

Ireland

⊛ National Capital
• Other City

1:3,960,000

| 0 | 30 | 60 mi |
| 0 | 30 | 60 km |

Lambert Conformal Conic Projection

© MapQuest.com, Inc.

Bann, *river* A2
Erne, *river* A2
Foyle, *lake* A2
Foyle, *river* A2
Giant's Causeway,
  headland A2
Irish, *sea* B3
Lough Erne, *lake* A2
Mourne, *mts.* A2
Neagh, *lake* A2
North, *channel* A2
Rathlin, *island* A2
Slieve Donard, *mt.* B2
Sperrin, *mts.* A2
Upper Lough Erne, *lake* ...A2

SCOTLAND
Cities and Towns
Aberdeen C1
Aviemore B1
Ayr B2
Campbeltown B2
Clydebank B2
Cupar B2
Dornoch B1
Dumfries B2
Dundee B2
Dunfermline B2
Elgin B1
Fort William B2
Fraserburgh C1
Glasgow B2
Greenock B2
Hamilton B2
Hawick B2
Inverness B1
Kilmarnock B2
Kirkcaldy B2
Kirkwall ....Inset I
Kyle of Lochalsh B1
Lairg B1

Lerwick ....Inset I
Mallaig B1
Montrose C2
Motherwell B2
Newtown St. Boswells C2
Oban B2
Paisley B2
Perth B2
Peterhead C1
Pitlochry B2
Portree A1
St. Andrews B2
Scone B2
Sconser A1
Stirling B2
Stornoway A1
Stranraer B2
Thurso B1
Ullapool B1
Wick B1

Other Features
Arran, *island* B2
Barra, *island* A2
Bass Rock, *islet* C2
Bell Rock (Inchcape),
  reef C2
Ben Nevis, *mt.* B2
Bute, *island* B2
Cheviot, *hills* C2
Clyde, *estuary* B2
Clyde, *river* B2
Coll, *island* A2
Colonsay, *island* A2
Dee, *river* C1
Dornoch, *estuary* B1
Duncansby, *cape* B1
Dunsinane, *mt.* B2
Eigg, *island* A2
Fair, *island* ....Inset I
Forth, *estuary* C2
Forth, *river* B2

Grampian, *mts.* B2
Hebrides, *sea* A2
Hoy, *island* ....Inset I
Inner Hebrides, *islands* ...A2
Islay, *island* B2
Jura, *island* B2
Katrine, *lake* B2
Kinnairds, *cape* C1
Lammermuir, *hills* C2
Lewis, *island* A1
Linnhe, *lake* A2
Lomond, *lake* B2
Lorne, *estuary* A2
Mainland, *island* .....Inset I
Merrick, *mt.* B2
Minch, *strait* A1
Moray, *estuary* B1
Mull, *island* A2
Ness, *lake* B1
North Uist, *island* A1
Ochil, *hills* B2
Orkney, *islands* ......Inset I
Outer Hebrides, *islands* ...A1
Rhum, *island* A2
Sanday, *island* ....Inset I
Shetland, *islands* ....Inset I
Sidlaw, *hills* B2
Skye, *island* A1
Solway, *estuary* B2
Southern Uplands, *mts.* ...B2
South Ronaldsay,
  island ....Inset I
South Uist, *island* A1
Spey, *river* B1
Stronsay, *island* .....Inset I
Tay, *estuary* B2
Tay, *lake* B2
Tay, *river* B2
Tiree, *island* A2
Tweed, *river* C2
Unst, *island* ....Inset I
Westray, *island* ......Inset I

Wrath, *cape* B1
Yell, *island* ....Inset I

WALES
Cities and Towns
Aberystwyth B3
Bangor B3
Caerleon C3
Caernarfon B3
Cardiff B3
Carmarthen B3
Conwy B3
Fishguard B3
Holyhead B3
Lampeter B3
Llandrindod Wells B3
Merthyr Tydfil B3
Milford Haven B3
Mold B3
Newport C3
Pembroke B3
Port Talbot B3
Rhondda B3
St. David's B3
Swansea B3
Welshpool B3

Other Features
Anglesey, *island* B3
Bala, *lake* B3
Brecon Beacons, *mts.* B3
Bristol, *channel* B3
Cambrian, *mts.* B3
Cardigan, *bay* B3
Dee, *river* B3
Lleyn, *peninsula* B3
Menai, *strait* B3
Snowdon, *mt.* B3
Teifi, *river* B3
Tywi, *river* B3
Usk, *river* C3
Wye, *river* C3

Denmark

Capital: Copenhagen
Area: 16,639 sq. mi.
43,080 sq. km.
Population: 5,357,000
Largest City: Copenhagen
Language: Danish
Monetary Unit: Krone

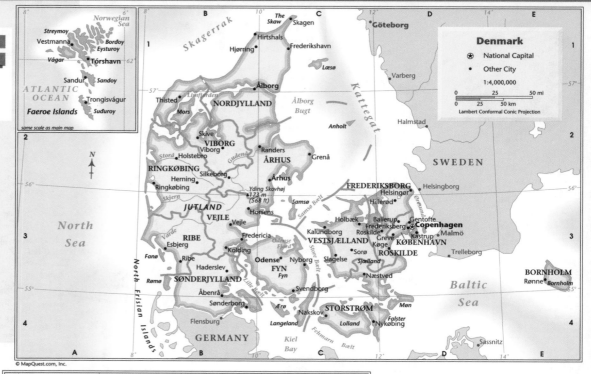

Denmark:
Map Index

Counties
Århus C2
Bornholm E3
Frederiksborg D2
Fyn C3
København D3
Nordjylland B2
Ribe B3
Ringkøbing B3
Roskilde D3
Sønderjylland B3
Storstrøm C4
Vejle B3
Vestsjælland C3
Viborg B2

Cities and Towns
Åbenrå B3
Ålborg B1
Århus C2
Ballerup D3
Copenhagen, capital ..D3
Esbjerg B3
Fredericia B3
Frederiksberg D3
Frederikshavn C1
Gentofte D3
Grenå C2
Greve D3
Haderslev B3
Helsingør D3
Herning B2
Hillerød D3
Hirtshals B1
Hjørring B1
Holbæk C3
Holstebro B2
Horsens B3
Kalundborg C3
Kastrup D3
Køge D3
Kolding B3
Næstved C3
Nakskov C4
Nyborg C3
Nykøbing C4
Odense C3
Randers C2
Ribe B3
Ringkøbing B2
Rønne E3
Roskilde D3
Sandur ....Inset
Silkeborg B2
Skagen C1
Skive B2
Slagelse C3
Sønderborg B4
Sorø C3
Svendborg C3
Thisted B2
Tórshavn ....Inset
Trongisvágur ....Inset
Vejle B3
Vestmanna ....Inset
Viborg B2

Other Features
Ærø, island C4
Ålborg, bay C2
Anholt, island D3
Baltic, sea E3
Borðoy, island ....Inset
Bornholm, island E3
Eysturoy, island ......Inset
Faeroe, islands ....Inset
Falster, island D4
Fanø, island B3
Fehmarn, strait C4
Fyn, island C3
Gudenå, river B2
Jutland, peninsula ...B3
Kattegat, strait C2
Læsø, island C1
Langeland, island C4
Lille, strait B3
Limfjorden, channel ..B2
Lolland, island C4
Møn, island D4
Mors, island B2
North, sea A3
North Frisian, islands ..B4
Norwegian, sea ....Inset
Odense, fjord D3
Øresund, sound D3
Rømø, island B3
Samsø, island C3
Samsø, strait C3
Sandoy, island ....Inset
Sjælland, island C3
Skagerrak, strait B1
Skaw, cape C1
Skjern, river B3
Storå, river B2
Store, strait C3
Streymoy, island .....Inset
Suðuroy, island ....Inset
Vágar, island ....Inset
Varde, river B3
Yding Skovhøj, hill ...B2

Netherlands

Capital: Amsterdam
Area: 16,033 sq. mi.
41,536 sq. km.
Population: 15,808,000
Largest City: Amsterdam
Language: Dutch
Monetary Unit: Guilder, Euro

Netherlands:
Map Index

Provinces
Drenthe D2
Flevoland C2
Friesland C1
Gelderland D2
Groningen D1
Limburg C3
North Brabant C3
North Holland B2
Overijssel D2
South Holland B2
Utrecht C2
Zeeland A3

Cities and Towns
Alkmaar B2
Almelo D2
Amersfoort C2
Amsterdam, capital ..B2
Apeldoorn C2
Arnhem C3
Assen D2
Bergen op Zoom B3
Breda B3
Delft B2
Delfzijl D1
Den Helder B2
Deventer D2
Doetinchem D3
Dordrecht B3
Edam C2
Ede C2
Eindhoven C3
Emmeloord C2
Emmen D2
Enschede D2
Gouda B2
Groningen D1
Haarlem B2
Heerenveen C2
Heerlen C4
Hengelo D2
Hilversum C2
Hoogeveen D2
Hoorn C2
Leeuwarden C1
Leiden B2
Lelystad C2
Maastricht C4

Meppel D2
Middelburg A3
Nijmegen C3
Oss C3
Otterlo C2
Roermond D3
Rotterdam B3
Scheveningen B2
Schiedam B3
's Hertogenbosch C3
Sittard C4
Sneek C1
The Hague B2
Tilburg C3
Utrecht C2
Venlo D3
Vlaardingen B3
Vlissingen A3
Weert C3
Zaanstad B2
Zwolle D2

Other Features
Ameland, island C1
Eems, river D1
Flevoland, polder C2
IJssel, river D2
IJsselmeer, sea C2
Maas, river C3, D3
Neder Rijn, river C3
New Waterway, channel ..B3
Northeast, polder C2
North Holland, canal ..B2
North Sea, canal B2
Oosterschelde, channel ..A3
Overflakkee, island ..B3
Princess Margriet, canal ..C1
Schiermonnikoog, island ..D1
Schouwen, island A3
Terschelling, island ..C1
Texel, island B1
Tholen, island B3
Vaalserberg, mt. D4
Vlieland, island B1
Waal, river C3
Waddenzee, sound ...C1
Walcheren, island A3
Westerschelde, channel ..A3
West Frisian, islands ..B1
Wilhelmina, canal C3
Zuid-Willemsvaart, canal ..C3

Belgium

Belgium Map Index

Internal Divisions
Antwerp (province)............C1
Brussels Cap. Region.........C2
East Flanders (province) B2
Flanders (region)..............C1
Flemish Brabant (province) C2
Hainaut (province).............B2
Liège (province)................D2
Limburg (province)............D1
Luxembourg (province) D3
Namur (province)..............C2
Walloon Brabant
  (province) C2
Wallonia (region)..............C2
West Flanders (province)....B1

Cities and Towns
Aalst C2
Anderlecht C2
Antwerp C1
Arlon D3
Ath B2
Bastogne D2
Binche C2
Brugge B1

Brussels, *capital*................C2
Charleroi............................C2
Chimay...............................C2
Dinant C2
Gembloux C2
Genk D2
Ghent B1
Halle C2
Hasselt D2
Ixelles C2
Knokke B1
Kortrijk B2
La Louvière C2
Leuven C2
Liège D2
Limbourg D2
Malmédy E2
Mechelen C1
Mons B2
Mouscron B2
Namur C2
Neufchâteau.......................D3
Oostende A1
Poperinge A2
Roeselare B2
Schaerbeek C2
Sint-Niklaas C1
Sint-Truiden D2

Spa.....................................D2
Tournai...............................B2
Turnhout.............................C1
Uccle C2
Verviers..............................D2
Wavre C2
Ypres A2
Zeebrugge B1

Other Features
Albert, *canal* C1
Ardennes, *plateau*.............D2
Botrange, *mt.*.....................E2
Brugge-Ghent, *canal*.........B1
Dender, *river*......................B2
Kempenland, *region* D1
Leie, *river*..........................B2
Maas, *river* D1
Meuse, *river*.......................D2
Oostende-Brugge,
  canal................................B1
Ourthe, *river*......................D2
Rupel, *river*........................C1
Sambre, *river*.....................C2
Schelde, *river* B2
Semois, *river*......................D3
Senne, *river*........................C2

Belgium

Capital: Brussels
Area: 11,787 sq. mi.
  30,536 sq. km.
Population: 10,182,000
Largest City: Brussels
Languages: Flemish, French, German
Monetary Unit: Belgian franc, Euro

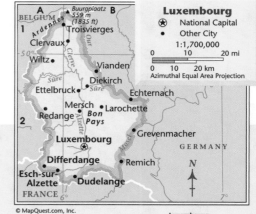

Luxembourg

Luxembourg Map Index

Cities and Towns
Clervaux B1
Diekirch B2
Differdange A2
Dudelange B2
Echternach B2
Esch-sur-Alzette A2
Ettelbruck B2
Grevenmacher B2
Larochette B2
Luxembourg, *capital*............B2
Mersch B2
Redange A2
Remich B2
Troisvierges B1
Vianden B2
Wiltz A2

Other Features
Alzette, *river* B2
Ardennes, *plateau* A1
Bon Pays, *region* B2
Buurgplaatz, *mt.* B1
Clerve, *river* B1
Mosel, *river* B2
Our, *river* B1
Sûre, *river* A2, B2

Luxembourg

Capital: Luxembourg
Area: 999 sq. mi.
  2,588 sq. km.
Population: 429,000
Largest City: Luxembourg
Languages: French, German
Monetary Unit: Luxembourg franc, Euro

Liechtenstein

Capital: Vaduz
Area: 62 sq. mi.
  161 sq. km.
Population: 32,000
Largest City: Vaduz
Language: German
Monetary Unit: Swiss franc

Liechtenstein Map Index

Cities and Towns
Balzers B2
Eschen B1
Gamprin B1
Malbun B2
Mauren B1
Planken B1
Ruggell B1
Schaan B2
Schellenberg B1
Triesen B2
Triesenberg B2
Vaduz, *capital*...................B2

Other Features
Alps, *range* A2
Grauspitz, *mt.* B2
Rhine, *canal*......................B1, B2
Rhine, *river* A1, A2
Samina, *river* B2

© MapQuest.com, Inc.

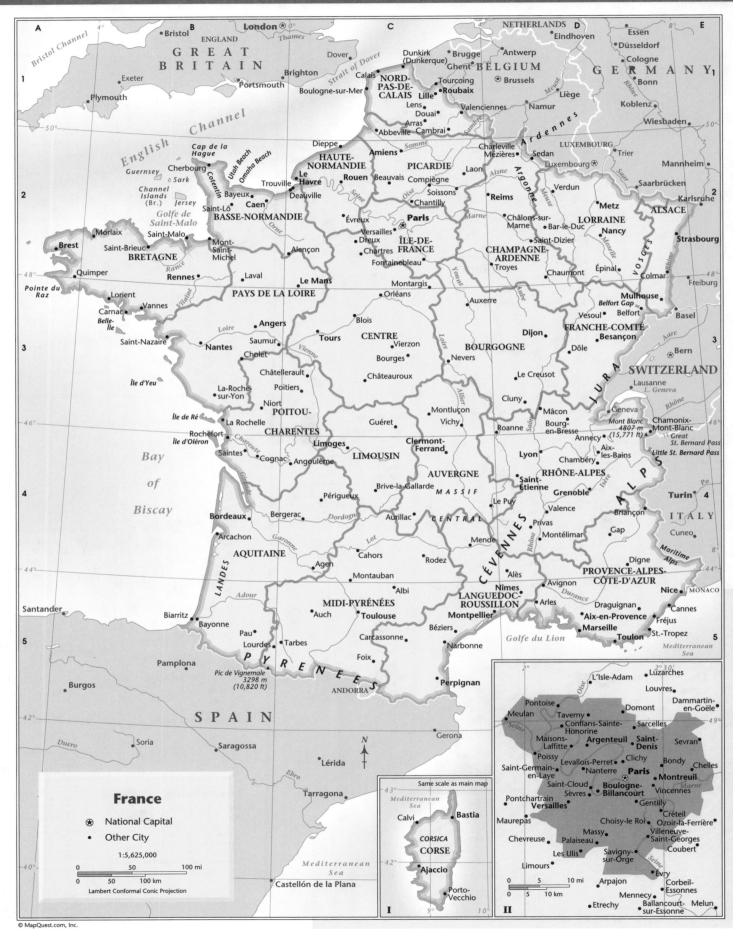

France

⊛ National Capital

• Other City

1:5,625,000

0   50   100 mi

0   50   100 km

Lambert Conformal Conic Projection

Same scale as main map

© MapQuest.com, Inc.

Switzerland

Capital: Bern
Area: 15,943 sq. mi.
41,303 sq. km.
Population: 7,275,000
Largest City: Zürich
Languages: German, French, Italian
Monetary Unit: Swiss franc

Switzerland
National Capital
Other City
1:3,090,000
0 20 40 mi
0 20 40 km
Lambert Conformal Conic Projection
FRANCE
GERMANY
AUSTRIA
ITALY
LIECHTENSTEIN
Vaduz
Black Forest
Freiburg
Tuttlingen
Mulhouse
Belfort
SCHAFFHAUSEN
Schaffhausen
BASEL-STADT
Basel
BASEL-LAND
Olten
Aarau
AARGAU
Baden
Frauenfeld
THURGAU
Winterthur
ZÜRICH
Zürich
Uster
Sankt Gallen
AUSSER-RHODEN (APPENZELL)
INNER-RHODEN
SANKT GALLEN
L. Constance (Bodensee)
Delémont
JURA
SOLOTHURN
Solothurn
Biel
La Chaux-de-Fonds
NEUCHÂTEL
Neuchâtel
Burgdorf
Bern
BERN
Sempach
LUZERN
Luzern
Zug
ZUG
Einsiedeln
SCHWYZ
Schwyz
GLARUS
Glarus
Walensee
Sarnen
Stans
NIDWALDEN
OBWALDEN
URI
Altdorf
Glarner Alpen
Rhätikon
Chur
Arosa
Davos
Scuol
Landeck
GRAUBÜNDEN
Rhaetian Alps
Engadine Valley
St. Moritz
Piz Bernina 4049 m (13,284 ft)
Poschiavo
Ortiles
Sondrio
Dole
Pontarlier
JURA MOUNTAINS
Yverdon
VAUD
Fribourg
FRIBOURG
Thun
Brienz
Interlaken
Thunersee
Brienzersee
Staubbach Falls
Tödi 3239 m (10,627 ft)
St. Gotthard Tunnel
St. Gotthard Pass
Lausanne
Montreux
Gstaad
Jungfrau 4166 m (13,667 ft)
Lötschberg Tunnel
Bernese Alps
Nyon
L. Geneva
GENEVA
Geneva
Monthey
Sierre
Sion
Rhône
Brig
Simplon Tunnel
VALAIS
ALPS
Martigny
Pennine Alps
Zermatt
Matterhorn 4505 m (14,780 ft)
Monte Rosa 4634 m (15,203 ft)
Domodossola
Lepontine Alps
TICINO
Locarno
Bellinzona
Lugano
L. Maggiore
L. of Lugano
L. Como
Varese
Como
Annecy
Mont Blanc 4807 m (15,771 ft)
Aosta
Albertville

© MapQuest.com, Inc.

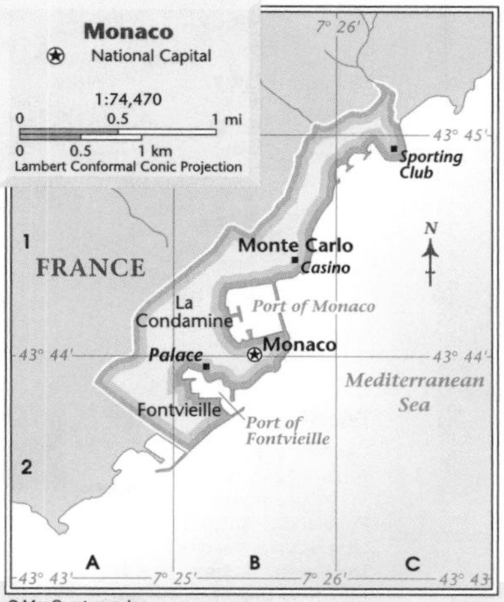

Monaco
National Capital
1:74,470
0 0.5 1 mi
0 0.5 1 km
Lambert Conformal Conic Projection
FRANCE
Sporting Club
Monte Carlo
Casino
La Condamine
Port of Monaco
Palace
Monaco
Mediterranean Sea
Fontvieille
Port of Fontvieille

© MapQuest.com, Inc.

Monaco: Map Index

Districts
- Fontvieille A2
- La Condamine B1
- Monaco, *capital* B1
- Monte Carlo B1

Other Features
- Casino B1
- Fontvieille, *port* B2
- Monaco, *port* B1
- Palace B2
- Sporting Club C1

Monaco

Capital: Monaco
Area: 0.75 sq. mi.
1.94 sq. km.
Population: 32,000
Language: French
Monetary Unit: French franc or Monégasque franc

Switzerland: Map Index

Cantons
- Aargau C1
- Appenzell Ausser-Rhoden D1
- Appenzell Inner-Rhoden D1
- Basel-Land B1
- Basel-Stadt B1
- Bern B2
- Fribourg B2
- Geneva A2
- Glarus D2
- Graubünden D2
- Jura B1
- Lucerne C1
- Neuchâtel A2
- Nidwalden C2
- Obwalden C2
- Sankt Gallen D1
- Schaffhausen C1
- Schwyz C1
- Solothurn B1
- Thurgau C1
- Ticino C2
- Uri C2
- Valais B2
- Vaud A2
- Zug C1
- Zürich C1

Cities and Towns
- Aarau C1
- Altdorf C2
- Baden C1
- Basel B1
- Bellinzona D2
- Bern, *capital* B2
- Biel B1
- Bolligen B2
- Bulle B2
- Chur D2
- Davos D2
- Einsiedeln C1
- Fribourg B2
- Frutigen B2
- Geneva A2
- Horgèn C1
- Interlaken B2
- La Chaux-de-Fonds A1
- Lausanne A2
- Locarno C2
- Lucerne C1
- Lugano C3
- Montreux A2
- Morges A2
- Neuchâtel A2
- St. Moritz D2
- Sankt Gallen D1
- Schaffhausen C1
- Schwyz C1
- Sempach C1
- Sion B2
- Thun B2
- Uster C1
- Winterthur C1
- Yverdon A2
- Zermatt B2
- Zug C1
- Zürich C1

Other Features
- Aare, *river* B1, B2
- Alps, *mts.* B2
- Bernese Alps, *mts.* B2
- Biel, *lake* B1
- Brienzersee, *lake* B2
- Constance (Bodensee), *lake* D1
- Doubs, *river* A1
- Dufourspitze, *mt.* B3
- Engadine, *valley* D2
- Geneva, *lake* A2
- Inn, *river* D2
- Jungfrau, *mt.* B2
- Jura, *mts.* A2
- Lepontine Alps, *mts.* C2
- Lucerne, *lake* C2
- Lugano, *lake* C3
- Maggiore, *lake* C3
- Matterhorn, *mt.* B3
- Neuchâtel, *lake* A2
- Pennine Alps, *mts.* B2
- Reuss, *river* C2
- Rhaetian Alps, *mts.* D2
- Rhine, *river* C1, D2
- Rhône, *river* B2
- St. Gotthard, *pass* C2
- St. Gotthard, *tunnel* C2
- Splügen, *pass* D2
- Staubbach, *falls* B2
- Thunersee, *lake* B2
- Ticino, *river* C2
- Walensee, *lake* D1
- Zürichsee, *lake* C1

France

Capital: Paris
Area: 210,026 sq. mi.
544,109 sq. km.
Population: 58,978,000
Largest City: Paris
Language: French
Monetary Unit: Franc, Euro

France: Map Index

Regions
- Alsace D2
- Aquitaine B4
- Auvergne C4
- Basse-Normandie B2
- Bourgogne C3
- Bretagne B2
- Centre C3
- Champagne-Ardenne D2
- Corse Inset I
- Franche-Comté D3
- Haute-Normandie C2
- Île-de-France C2
- Languedoc-Roussillon C5
- Limousin C4
- Lorraine D2
- Midi-Pyrénées C5
- Nord-Pas-de-Calais C1
- Pays De La Loire B3
- Picardie C2
- Poitou-Charentes C3
- Provence-Alpes-Côte-d'Azur D4
- Rhône-Alpes D4

Cities and Towns
- Abbeville C1
- Agen C4
- Aix-en-Provence D5
- Aix-les-Bains D4
- Ajaccio Inset I
- Albi C5
- Alençon C2
- Alès D4
- Amiens C2
- Angers B3
- Angoulême C4
- Annecy D4
- Arachon B4
- Argenteuil Inset II
- Arles D5
- Arpajon Inset II
- Arras C1
- Auch C5
- Aurillac C4
- Auxerre C3
- Avignon D5
- Ballancourt-sur-Essonne Inset II
- Bar-le-Duc D2
- Bastia Inset I
- Bayeux B2
- Bayonne B5
- Beauvais C2
- Belfort D3
- Bergerac C4
- Besançon D3
- Béziers C5
- Biarritz B5
- Blois C3
- Bondy Inset II
- Bordeaux B4
- Boulogne-Billancourt Inset II
- Boulogne-sur-Mer C1
- Bourg-en-Bresse D3
- Bourges C3
- Brest A2
- Briançon D4
- Brive-la-Gallarde C4
- Caen B2
- Cahors C4
- Calais C1
- Calvi Inset I
- Cambrai C1
- Cannes D5
- Carcassonne C5
- Carnac B3
- Châlons-sur-Marne D2
- Chambéry D4
- Chamonix-Mont-Blanc D4
- Chantilly C2
- Charleville Mézières D2
- Chartres C2
- Châteauroux C3
- Châtellerault C3
- Chaumont D2
- Chelles Inset II
- Cherbourg B2
- Chevreuse Inset II
- Choisy-le Roi Inset II
- Cholet B3
- Clermont-Ferrand C4
- Clichy Inset II
- Cluny D3
- Cognac B4
- Colmar D2
- Compiègne C2
- Conflans-Sainte-Honorine Inset II
- Corbeil-Essonnes Inset II
- Coubert Inset II
- Créteil Inset II
- Dammartin-en-Goële Inset II
- Deauville C2
- Dieppe C2
- Digne D4
- Dijon D3
- Dôle D3
- Domont Inset II
- Douai C1
- Draguignan D5
- Dreux C2
- Dunkirk (Dunkerque) C1
- Épinal D2
- Etrechy Inset II
- Évreux C2
- Évry Inset II
- Foix C5
- Fontainebleau C2
- Fréjus D5
- Gap D4
- Gentilly Inset II
- Grenoble D4
- Guéret C3
- Laon C2
- La Rochelle B3
- La-Roche-sur-Yon B3
- Laval B2
- Le Creusot D3
- Le Havre C2
- Le Mans C2
- Lens C1
- Le Puy C4
- Les Ulis Inset II
- Levallois-Perret Inset II
- Lille C1
- Limoges C4
- Limours Inset II
- L'Isle-Adam Inset II
- Lorient B3
- Lourdes B5
- Louvres Inset II
- Luzarches Inset II
- Lyon D4
- Mâcon D3
- Maisons-Laffitte Inset II
- Marseille D5
- Massy Inset II
- Maurepas Inset II
- Melun Inset II
- Mende C4
- Mennecy Inset II
- Metz D2
- Meulan Inset II
- Montargis C2
- Montauban C4
- Montélimar D4
- Montluçon C3
- Montpellier C5
- Montreuil Inset II
- Mont-Saint-Michel B2
- Morlaix B2
- Mulhouse D3
- Nancy D2
- Nanterre Inset II
- Nantes B3
- Narbonne C5
- Nevers C3
- Nice D5
- Nîmes D5
- Niort B3
- Orléans C3
- Ozoir-la-Ferrière Inset II
- Palaiseau Inset II
- Paris, *capital* C2, Inset II
- Pau B5
- Périgueux C4
- Perpignan C5
- Poissy Inset II
- Poitiers C3
- Pontchartrain Inset II
- Pontoise Inset II
- Porto-Vecchio Inset I
- Privas D4
- Quimper A2
- Reims D2
- Rennes B2
- Roanne D3
- Rochefort B4
- Rodez C4
- Roubaix C1
- Rouen C2
- Saint-Brieuc B2
- Saint-Cloud Inset II
- Saint-Denis Inset II
- Saint-Dizier D2
- Saintes B4
- Saint-Étienne D4
- Saint-Germain-en-Laye Inset II
- Saint-Lô B2
- Saint-Malo B2
- Saint-Nazaire B3
- Saint-Tropez D5
- Sarcelles Inset II
- Saumur B3
- Savigny-sur-Orge Inset II
- Sedan D2
- Sevran Inset II
- Sèvres Inset II
- Soissons C2
- Strasbourg D2
- Tarbes C5
- Taverny Inset II
- Toulon D5
- Toulouse C5
- Tourcoing C1
- Tours C3
- Trouville C2
- Troyes D2
- Valence D4
- Valenciennes C1
- Vannes B3
- Verdun D2
- Versailles C2, Inset II
- Vesoul D3
- Vichy C3
- Vierzon C3
- Villeneuve-Saint-Georges Inset II
- Vincennes Inset II

Other Features
- Adour, *river* B5
- Aisne, *river* D2
- Allier, *river* C3
- Alps, *range* D4
- Ardennes, *region* D1
- Argonne, *forest* D2
- Aube, *river* D3
- Belfort, *gap* D3
- Belle, *island* B3
- Biscay, *bay* B4
- Blanc, *mt.* D4
- Cévennes, *mts.* C4
- Charente, *river* B4
- Corsica, *island* Inset I
- Cotentin, *peninsula* B2
- Dordogne, *river* C4
- Dover, *strait* C1
- Durance, *river* D5
- English, *channel* B2
- Garonne, *river* C4
- Geneva, *lake* D3
- Gironde, *river* B4
- Hague, *cape* B2
- Isère, *river* D4
- Jura, *mts.* D3
- Landes, *region* B5
- Lion, *gulf* D5
- Little St. Bernard, *pass* D4
- Loire, *river* C3
- Lot, *river* C4
- Maritime Alps, *range* D4
- Marne, *river* C2, Inset II
- Massif Central, *plateau* C4
- Meuse, *river* D2
- Moselle, *river* D2
- Oise, *river* C2, Inset II
- Oléron, *island* B4
- Omaha, *beach* B2
- Orne, *river* B2
- Pyrenees, *range* C5
- Rance, *river* B2
- Raz, *point* A3
- Ré, *island* B3
- Rhine, *river* D2
- Rhône, *river* D4
- Saint-Malo, *gulf* B2
- Sambre, *river* C1
- Saône, *river* D3
- Seine, *river* C2, Inset II
- Somme, *river* C2
- Utah, *beach* B2
- Vienne, *river* C3
- Vignemale, *mt.* B5
- Vilaine, *river* B3
- Vosges, *mts.* D2
- Yeu, *island* B3
- Yonne, *river* C2

© MapQuest.com, Inc.

Portugal: Map Index

Districts

Aveiro	A2
Beja	A4
Braga	A2
Bragança	B2
Castelo Branco	B2
Coimbra	A2
Évora	B3
Faro	A4
Guarda	B2
Leiria	A3
Lisbon	A3
Oporto (Porto)	A2
Portalegre	B3
Santarém	A3
Setúbal	A3
Viana do Castelo	A2
Vila Real	B2
Viseu	B2

Cities and Towns

Abrantes	A3
Almada	A3
Amadora	A3
Aveiro	A2
Barreiro	A3
Beja	B3
Braga	A2
Bragança	B2
Caidasm da Rainha	A3
Castelo Branco	B3
Chaves	B2
Coimbra	A2
Covilhã	B2
Elvas	B3
Estoril	A3
Évora	B3
Faro	B4
Figueira da Foz	A2
Grândola	A3
Guarda	B2
Guimarães	A2
Lagos	A4
Leiria	A3
Leixões	A2
Lisbon, capital	A3
Mafra	A3
Moura	B3
Odemira	A4
Oeiras	A3
Oporto (Porto)	A2
Peniche	A3
Portalegre	B3
Portimão	A4
Queluz	A3
Santarém	A3
Setúbal	A3
Sines	A4
Valença	A1
Viana do Castelo	A2
Vila do Conde	A2
Vila Nova de Gaia	A2
Vila Real	B2
Vila Real de Santo Antonio	B4
Viseu	B2

Other Features

Algarve, region	A4
Cádiz, gulf	B4
Carvoeiro, cape	A3
Chança, river	B4
Douro, river	B2
Espichel, cape	A3
Estrela, mt.	B2
Estrela, mts.	B2
Guadiana, river	B3
Lima, river	A2
Minho, river	A1
Mondego, cape	A2
Mondego, river	B2
Roca, cape	A3
Sado, river	A3
São Vicente, cape	A4
Seda, river	B3
Setúbal, bay	A3
Sor, river	B3
Sorraia, river	A3
Tagus, river	A3
Tâmega, river	B2
Zêzere, river	A3

Portugal

Capital: Lisbon
Area: 35,672 sq. mi.
 92,415 sq. km.
Population: 9,918,000
Largest City: Lisbon
Language: Portuguese
Monetary Unit: Escudo, Euro

© MapQuest.com, Inc.

Malta

Capital: Valletta
Area: 122 sq. mi.
 316 sq. km.
Population: 382,000
Largest City: Valletta
Languages: Maltese, English
Monetary Unit: Maltese lira

Malta: Map Index

Cities and Towns

Birkirkara	B2
Birzebbuga	C3
Dingli	B2
Mellieha	B2
Nadur	B1
Qormi	B2
Rabat	B2
San Pawl il-Bahar	B2
Siggiewi	B2
Sliema	C2
Valletta, capital	C2
Victoria	A1
Zabbar	C2
Zebbug	A1
Zurrieq	B2

Other Features

Comino, island	B1
Cominotto, island	B1
Filfla, island	B3
Gozo, island	A1
Grand, harbor	C2
Malta, island	B2
Marsaxlokk, bay	C3
Mellieha, bay	B2
North Comino, channel	B1
Saint Paul's, bay	B2
South Comino, channel	B2

Gibraltar

Area: 2.25 sq. mi.
 5.83 sq. km.
Population: 29,000
Language: English
Monetary Unit: British Pound

Gibraltar: Map Index

Features

Catalan, bay	A2
Detached, mole	A2
Eastern, beach	A2
Fortress Headquarters	A3
Gibraltar, bay	A2
Gibraltar, harbor	A2
Gibraltar, strait	A4
Governor's Residence	A2
Great Europa, point	A4
Highest point	A3
Little, bay	A4
Mediterranean, sea	A3
North, mole	A2
North Front, airfield	A1
Rosia, bay	A3
Saint Michael's, cave	A3
Sandy, bay	A3
Signal, hill	A2
South, mole	A2
The Rock, prom.	A3

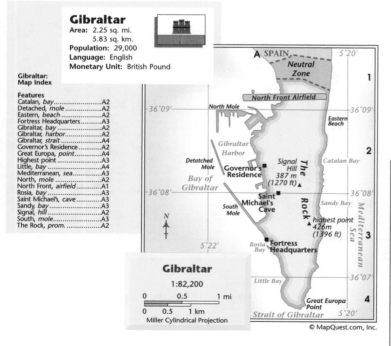

© MapQuest.com, Inc.

Gibraltar

1:82,200

0	0.5	1 mi
0	0.5	1 km

Miller Cylindrical Projection

Andorra

Capital: Andorra la Vella
Area: 181 sq. mi.
 469 sq. km.
Population: 66,000
Largest City: Andorra la Vella
Language: Catalan
Monetary Unit: French franc

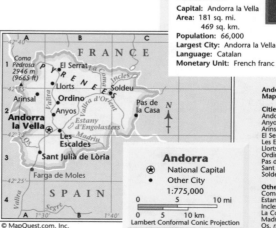

© MapQuest.com, Inc.

Andorra

1:775,000

0	5	10 mi
0	5	10 km

Lambert Conformal Conic Projection

Andorra: Map Index

Cities and Towns

Andorra la Vella, capital	B2
Anyos	B2
Arinsal	A2
El Serrat	B1
Les Escaldes	B2
Llorts	B1
Ordino	B2
Pas de la Casa	C2
Sant Julià de Lòria	A3
Soldeu	B2

Other Features

Coma Pedrosa, mt.	A1
Estany d'Engolasters, lake	B2
Incles, river	C1
La Coma, river	B1
Madriu, river	B3
Os, river	A3
Pyrenees, range	A1
Valira, river	A2
Valira d'Orient, river	B2

Spain:
Map Index

Regions

Andalusia	D4
Aragón	F2
Asturias	C1
Balearic Islands	G3
Basque Country	E1
Canary Islands	Inset I
Cantabria	D1
Castile-La Mancha	E3
Castile-León	D1, E1
Catalonia	G2
Estremadura	C3
Galicia	C1
La Rioja	E1
Madrid	E2
Murcia	F4
Navarra	F1
Valencia	F2, F3

Cities and Towns

Águilas	F4
Albacete	F3
Alcalá de Henares	Inset II
Alcañiz	F2
Alcázar de San Juan	E3
Alcira	F3
Alcobendas	Inset II
Alcorcón	E2, Inset II
Alcoy	F3
Algeciras	D4
Alicante	F3
Almadén	D3
Almansa	F3
Almendralejo	C3
Almería	E4
Antequera	D4
Aranda de Duero	E2
Aranjuez	E2
Astorga	C1
Ávila	D2
Avilés	D1
Badajoz	C3
Badalona	H2
Baracaldo	E1
Barcelona	H2
Baza	E4
Béjar	D2
Benavente	D1
Benidorm	F3
Bilbao	E1
Burgos	E1
Cáceres	C3
Cádiz	C4
Calatayud	F2
Cartagena	F4
Castellón de la Plana	F3
Ceuta	D5
Cieza	F3
Ciudadela	H2
Ciudad Real	E3
Ciudad Rodrigo	C2
Córdoba	D4
Cornellá de Llogregat	G2
Coslada	Inset II
Cuenca	E2
Don Benito	D3
Dos Hermanas	D4
Écija	D4
Elche	F3
El Ferrol	B1
Figueras	H1
Fuenlabrada	Inset II
Gerona	H1
Getafe	E2, Inset II
Gijón	D1
Granada	E4
Guadalajara	E2
Guecho	E1
Guernica y Luno	E1
Hellín	F3
Hospitalet	H2
Huelva	C4
Huesca	F1
Ibiza	G3
Jaén	E4
Jerez de la Frontera	C4
La Coruña	B1
La Laguna	Inset I
La Roda	E3
Las Palmas	Inset I
Leganés	Inset II
León	D1
Lérida	G2
Linares	E3
Logroño	E1
Loja	D4
Lorca	F4
Lucena	D4
Lugo	C1
Madrid, capital	E2, Inset II
Mahón	J3
Málaga	D4
Marbella	D4
Mataró	H2
Medina del Campo	D2
Mérida	C3
Mieres	D1
Miranda de Ebro	E1
Monforte	C1
Morón de la Frontera	D4
Móstoles	Inset II
Murcia	F4
Orense	C1
Oviedo	D1
Palencia	D1
Palma	H3
Pamplona	F1
Plasencia	C2
Ponferrada	C1
Pontevedra	B1
Puertollano	D3
Reinosa	D1
Reus	G2
Sabadell	H2
Sagunto	F3
Salamanca	D2
San Baudilio de Llobregat	G2
San Fernando	C4
San Sebastián	F1
Santa Coloma de Gramanet	H2
Santa Cruz de Tenerife	Inset I
Santander	E1
Santiago de Compostela	B1
Segovia	D2
Seville	D4
Soria	E2
Talavera de la Reina	D3
Tarragona	G2
Tarrasa	H2
Telde	Inset I
Teruel	F2
Toledo	D3
Tomelloso	E3
Torrejón de Ardoz	Inset II
Torrelavega	D1
Torrente	F3
Tortosa	G2
Úbeda	E3
Valdepeñas	E3
Valencia	F3
Valladolid	D2
Vich	H2
Vigo	B1
Villarreal de los Infantes	F3
Vitoria	E1
Yecla	F3
Zafra	C3
Zamora	D2
Zaragoza	F2

Other Features

Alarcón, reservoir	E3
Alboran, sea	E4
Alcántara, reservoir	C3
Almendra, reservoir	C2
Aneto, mt.	G1
Balearic, islands	G3
Balearic, sea	G3
Béticos, mts.	D4
Biscay, bay	D1
Brava, coast	H2
Buendía, reservoir	E2
Cabrera, island	H3
Cádiz, gulf	C4
Canaray, islands	Inset I
Cantábrica, mts.	D1
Cijara, reservoir	D3
Duero, river	D2
Ebro, river	F1
Esla, river	D2
Finisterre, cape	B1
Formentera, island	G3
Fuerteventura, island	Inset I
Gata, cape	E4
Gibraltar, strait	D5
Gomera, island	Inset I
Gran Canaria, island	Inset I
Gredos, mts.	D2
Guadalquivir, river	D4
Guadarrama, mts.	D2
Guadiana, river	C3
Hierro, island	Inset I
Ibérico, mts.	E1
Ibiza, island	G3
Jarama, river	Inset II
Júcar, river	F3
Lanzarote, island	Inset I
La Palma, island	Inset I
Majorca, island	H3
Mediterranean, sea	E4
Mequinenza, reservoir	F2
Meseta, plateau	D3
Miño, river	B1
Minorca, island	H2
Morena, mts.	D4
Mulhacén, mt.	E4
Nao, cape	G3
Nevada, mts.	E4
Orellana, reservoir	D3
Ortegal, cape	C1
Palos, cape	F4
Pyrenees, mts.	F1
Ricobayo, reservoir	D2
Segura, river	E3
Sol, coast	D4
Tagus, river	D3
Tenerife, island	Inset I
Toledo, mts.	D3
Tormes, river	D2
Tortosa, cape	G2
Valdecañas, reservoir	D3
Valencia, gulf	G3
Zújar, reservoir	D3

Spain

Capital: Madrid
Area: 194,898 sq. mi.
504,917 sq. km.
Population: 39,168,000
Largest City: Madrid
Language: Spanish
Monetary Unit: Peseta, Euro

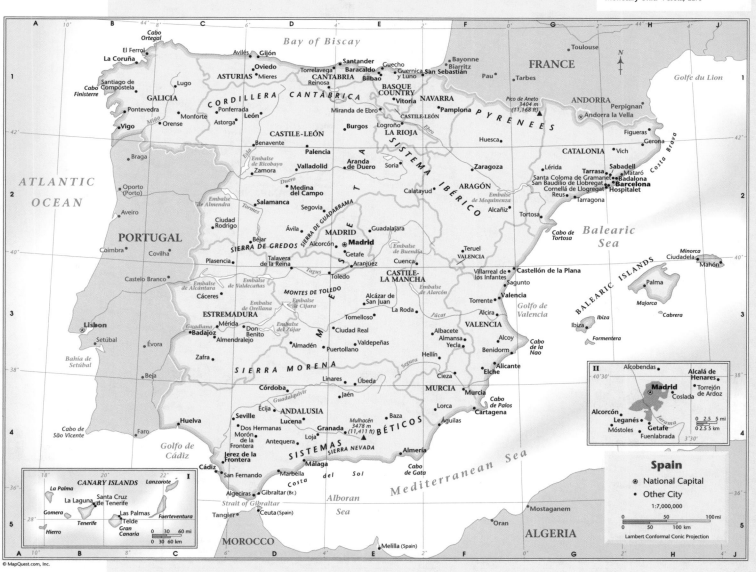

Italy

⊛ National Capital

• Other City

1:5,614,000

0   50   100   150 mi

0   50   100   150 km

Lambert Conformal Conic Projection

Italy
Capital: Rome
Area: 116,333 sq. mi.
         301,381 sq. km.
Population: 56,735,000
Largest City: Rome
Language: Italian
Monetary Unit: Lira, Euro

Austria
- ⊛ National Capital
- • Other City
- 1:4,714,000

0   25   50 mi
0 25 50 km
Lambert Conformal Conic Projection

© MapQuest.com, Inc.

Austria:
Map Index

Provinces
Burgenland E3
Carinthia C4
Lower Austria D2
Salzburg C3
Styria D3
Tirol B3, C4
Upper Austria C2
Vienna E2
Vorarlberg A3

Cities and Towns
Amstetten D2
Baden E2
Bad Ischl C2
Braunau C2
Feldkirch A3
Fürstenfeld E3
Gmünd D2
Graz D3
Hieflau D3
Innsbruck B3
Kapfenberg D3
Klagenfurt D4
Köflach D3
Kufstein C3
Lech B3
Leoben D3
Lienz C4
Linz D2
Mistelbach E2
Salzburg C3

Sankt Pölten D2
Steyr D2
Stockerau E2
Vienna, capital E2
Villach C4
Vöcklabruck C2
Wels C2
Wiener Neustadt E3
Wolfsberg D4

Other Features
Alps, range B3
Bavarian Alps, range B3
Brenner, pass B3
Carnic Alps, range C4
Constance, lake A3
Danube, river D2
Drava, river C4
Enns, river D3
Grossglockner, mt. C3
Hohe Tauern, mts. C3
Inn, river B3, C2
Karawanken, range D4
Mur, river D3
Mürz, river D3
Neusiedler, lake E3
Niedere Tauern, range C3
Ötztal Alps, range B4
Salzach, river C3
Salzburg Alps, range C3
Semmering, pass D3
Traun, river D2
Ybbs, river D2
Zillertal Alps, range B3

Austria
Capital: Vienna
Area: 32,378 sq. mi.
83,881 sq. km.
Population: 8,139,000
Largest City: Vienna
Language: German
Monetary Unit: Schilling, Euro

Italy:
Map Index

Regions
Abruzzi C2
Apulia C2
Basilicata C2
Calabria D3
Campania C2
Emilia-Romagna B1
Friuli-Venezia Giulia C1
Latium C2
Liguria B1
Lombardy B1
Marche C2
Molise C2
Piedmont A1
Puglia C2
Sardinia B3
Sicily C3
Trentino-Alto Adige B1
Tuscany B2
Umbria C2
Valle d'Aosta A1
Veneto B1

Cities and Towns
Agrigento C3
Alessandria B1
Alghero B2
Ancona C2
Aosta A1
Aquileia C1
Arezzo B2
Ascoli Piceno C2
Asti B1
Avellino C2
Bari C2
Barletta D2
Belluno C1
Benevento C2
Bergamo B1
Bologna B1
Bolzano B1
Brescia B1
Brindisi D2
Cagliari B3
Caltanissetta C3
Campobasso C2
Canossa B1
Capua C2
Carbonia B3
Caserta C2
Castel Gandolfo C2
Catania C3
Catanzaro D3
Cefalù C2
Chieti C2
Chioggia C2
Civitavecchia B2
Como B1
Cortina d'Ampezzo C1
Cortona B2
Cosenza D3
Cremona B1
Crotone D3
Cuneo A1
Enna C3
Faenza B1
Ferrara B1
Florence B2
Foggia C2
Forlì C2
Frosinone C2
Gaeta C2
Gela C3

Genoa B1
Gorizia C1
Grosseto B2
Isernia C2
L'Aquila C2
La Spezia B1
Latina C2
Lecce D2
Livorno B2
Lucca B2
Macerata C2
Manfredonia C2
Mantova (Mantua) B1
Marsala C3
Matera D2
Merano B1
Messina C3
Milan B1
Modena B1
Monopoli D2
Montepulciano B2
Monza B1
Naples C2
Novara B1
Nuoro B2
Olbia B2
Oristano B2
Otranto D2
Padova (Padua) B1
Palermo C3
Parma B1
Pavia B1
Perugia C2
Pesaro C2
Pescara C2
Pisa B2
Pistoia B2
Placenza B1
Potenza C2
Prato B2
Ragusa C3
Ravenna C1
Reggio di Calabria C3
Reggio nell'Emilia B1
Rieti C2
Rimini C1
Rome, capital C2
Rovigo B1
Salerno C2
San Gimignano B2
San Remo A2
San Severo C2
Sassari B2
Savona B2
Siena B2
Siracusa C3
Sondrio B1
Sorrento C2
Spoleto C2
Syracuse (Siracusa) C3
Taranto D2
Teramo C2
Termoli C2
Terni C2
Torre del Greco C2
Trapani C3
Trento B1
Treviso C1
Trieste C1
Turin A1
Udine C1
Venice C1
Ventimiglia A2
Vercelli B1

Verona B1
Vicenza B1
Viterbo C2

Other Features
Adige, river B1
Adriatic, sea C2
Alps, mts. A1, B1
Apennines, range B1
Arno, river B2
Asinara, island B2
Blanc, mt. A1
Bolsena, lake B2
Botte Donato, mt. D3
Bracciano, lake C2
Brenner, pass B1
Cagliari, gulf B3
Campagna di Roma, region C2
Caprara, point C2
Capri, island C2
Carbonara, cape B3
Cervati, mt. C2
Cimone, mt. B1
Como, lake B1
Corno, mt. C2
Dolomites, range B1
Egadi, islands C3
Elba, island B2
Etna, mt. C3
Garda, lake B1
Gennargentu, mts. B2
Genoa, gulf B1
Giglio, island B2
Ionian, sea D3
Ischia, island C2
Ligurian, sea A2
Lipari, islands C3
Lombardy, plain B1
Lugano, lake B1
Maggiore, lake B1
Maremma, region B2
Mediterranean, sea C3
Messina, strait C3
Montalto, mt. C3
Montecristo, island B2
Naples, bay C2
Oglio, river B1
Pantelleria, island C3
Passero, cape C3
Pianosa, island B2
Piave, river C1
Po, river A1, B1
Pontine, islands C2
Pontine, marshes C2
Rosa, mt. A1
Salerno, gulf C2
Sangro, river C2
San Pietro, island B3
Santa Maria di Leuca, cape D3
Sant'Antioco, island B3
Sardinia, island C3
Sicily, island C3
Sicily, strait B3
Spartivento, cape D3
Stromboli, island C3
Taranto, gulf D2
Testa del Gargano, point D2
Teulada, cape B3
Tiber, river C2
Tirso, river B2
Trasimeno, lake C2
Tyrrhenian, sea B2
Ustica, island C3
Venice, gulf C1
Vesuvius, volcano C2

Vatican City
Area: 108.7 acres
Population: 811
Languages: Italian, Latin
Monetary Unit: Lira

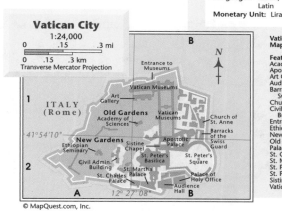

Vatican City
1:24,000

0   .15   .3 mi
0 .15 .3 km
Transverse Mercator Projection

© MapQuest.com, Inc.

Vatican City:
Map Index

Features
Academy of Sciences B1
Apostolic Palace B2
Art Gallery B1
Audience Hall B2
Barracks of the
Swiss Guard B1
Church of St. Anne B1
Civil Administration
Building A2
Entrance to Museums B1
Ethiopian Seminary A2
New Gardens A2
Old Gardens A1
Palace of Holy Office B2
St. Charles Palace B2
St. Martha Palace B2
St. Peter's Basilica B2
St. Peter's Square B2
Sistine Chapel B2
Vatican Museums B1

San Marino
Capital: San Marino
Area: 24 sq. mi.
62 sq. km.
Population: 25,000
Largest City: San Marino
Language: Italian
Monetary Unit: Italian lira

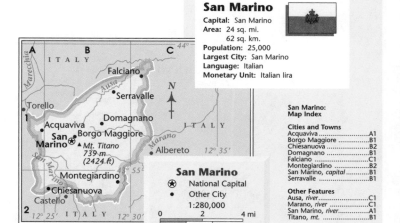

San Marino
- ⊛ National Capital
- • Other City
- 1:280,000

0   2   4 mi
0 2 4 km
Gauss-Krüger Projection

© MapQuest.com, Inc.

San Marino:
Map Index

Cities and Towns
Acquaviva A1
Borgo Maggiore B1
Chiesanuova B2
Domagnano B1
Faetano C1
Montegiardino B2
San Marino, capital B1
Serravalle B1

Other Features
Ausa, river C1
Marano, river C1
San Marino, river A1
Titano, mt. B1

North Sea

DENMARK

Sønderborg · Flensburg · Rødby Havn · *Rügen* · Sassnitz · **Baltic Sea** · *Bornholm (Den.)*

Schleswig · *Kiel Bay* · *Fehmarn* · Puttgarden

North Frisian Is. · *Helgoland* · **Kiel** · Neumünster · *Mecklenburg Bay* · Stralsund · Greifswald · *Pomeranian Bay*

East Frisian Is. · Cuxhaven · **SCHLESWIG-HOLSTEIN** · Lübeck · Wismar · Güstrow · Rostock · Świnoujście

Wilhelmshaven · Nordenham · Bremerhaven · **HAMBURG** · Schwerin · **MECKLENBURG-WESTERN POMERANIA** · Neubrandenburg · Szczecin

Emden · Oldenburg · **BREMEN** · *Lüneburger* · *Schweriner See* · *Müritz* · Neustrelitz · Schwedt

NETHERLANDS · Groningen · **Bremen** · *Lüneburg Heide* · Uelzen · Wittenberge · *Haven* · POLAND

Nordhorn · **NORTHERN** · **LOWER SAXONY** · Nienburg · Stendal · Brandenburg · **BERLIN** · Frankfurt an der Oder

Arnhem · **Osnabrück** · **Hannover** · Wolfsburg · Potsdam · Spandau · **Berlin** · Gorzów Wielkopolski

Bocholt · **Münster** · **Bielefeld** · Hameln · Hildesheim · **Magdeburg** · Luckenwalde · Eisenhüttenstadt

Kleve · Recklinghausen · Detmold · Salzgitter · Goslar · Halberstadt · Bernburg · Dessau · Wittenberg · Guben · Zielona Góra

Gelsenkirchen · Marl · Hamm · **NORTH RHINE-WESTPHALIA** · Paderborn · *Harz* · **SAXONY-ANHALT** · Cottbus

Bottrop · Herne · Lünen · Lippstadt · Northeim · Eisleben · Halle · Riesa · Bautzen · Görlitz

Oberhausen · **Duisburg** · **Dortmund** · **Bochum** · Büren · Göttingen · Nordhausen · **Leipzig** · Meissen · **Dresden** · Zittau

Moers · Witten · Hagen · Arnsberg · **Kassel** · Mühlhausen · **Chemnitz** · Freiberg · **SAXONY** · Liberec

Mülheim an der Ruhr · **Essen** · Ratingen · **Wuppertal** · Remscheid · *Ruhr* · *Fulda* · *Werra* · Eisenach · Gotha · Weimar · Naumburg · Gera · Jena

Krefeld · Neuss · Solingen · Remscheid · Siegen · Eisenach · Erfurt · Zwickau · **ERZGEBIRGE**

Düsseldorf · Leverkusen · Bergisch Gladbach · **HESSE** · **THURINGIA** · *Fichtelberg 1214 m (3983 ft)*

Mönchengladbach · **Cologne** · Siegen · Marburg · *Thuringian Forest* · Suhl · Plauen · Karlovy Vary

Maastricht · **Aachen** · **Bonn** · Giessen · Wetzlar · Coburg · Hof · *Frankenwald* · **CZECH REPUBLIC**

Liège · Remagen · *Rhine* · *Lahn* · Fulda · Coburg · Schweinfurt · Kulmbach · Prague

BELGIUM · Koblenz · Bad Ems · *Taunus* · **Frankfurt am Main** · Bayreuth · *Fichtelgebirge* · Plzeň

Eifel · *Mosel* · Bingen · Hanau · Offenbach · Schweinfurt · Bamberg · Weiden · Karlovy Vary

LUXEMBOURG · Trier · **Wiesbaden** · Mainz · Bad Kreuznach · **Darmstadt** · *Odenwald* · Würzburg · Erlangen · Amberg · *Oberpfälzer Wald*

Luxembourg · **HÜNSRUCK** · **RHINELAND-PALATINATE** · Worms · *Spessart* · *Main* · Fürth · **Nuremberg** · *Bohemian Forest*

SAARLAND · Ludwigshafen am Rhein · **Mannheim** · Ansbach · *Franconian Jura* · Regensburg · Straubing

Metz · **Saarbrücken** · Kaiserslautern · Neunkirchen · Heidelberg · Speyer · *Danube* · Ingolstadt · *Isar* · *Bayerischer Wald*

Nancy · Pirmasens · **Karlsruhe** · Heilbronn · Schwäbisch Gmünd · Heidenheim · **BAVARIA** · Landshut · Passau

Strasbourg · Pforzheim · Ludwigsburg · Esslingen · *Neckar* · Göppingen · Augsburg · Dachau

FRANCE · Baden-Baden · **Stuttgart** · Tübingen · Reutlingen · Ulm · *Lech* · **Munich**

Black Forest · *Swabian Jura* · *Danube* · Rosenheim · *Inn* · Salzburg · **AUSTRIA**

Mulhouse · Freiburg · Singen · Memmingen · Kaufbeuren · *Starnberger See* · Garmisch · *Chiem See* · Bad Reichenhall

Basel · Constance · Ravensburg · Kempten · *Ammersee* · Oberammergau · **Bavarian Alps**

Zürich · *L. Constance* · Friedrichshafen · Lindau · Hindelang · *Zugspitze 2962 m (9718 ft)* · Garmisch-Partenkirchen

Lucerne · Vaduz · **LIECHTENSTEIN** · **BADEN-WÜRTTEMBERG** · Innsbruck

SWITZERLAND · Chur · **ITALY** · Bolzano · ALPS

Germany

Capital:	Berlin
Area:	137,735 sq. mi.
	356,826 sq. km.
Population:	82,087,000
Largest City:	Berlin
Language:	German
Monetary Unit:	Mark, Euro

Germany

⊛ National Capital

● Other City

1:4,066,000

0 25 50 75 mi

0 25 50 75 km

Lambert Conformal Conic Projection

© MapQuest.com, Inc.

Poland

Capital: Warsaw
Area: 120,727 sq. mi.
312,764 sq. km.
Population: 38,609,000
Largest City: Warsaw
Language: Polish
Monetary Unit: Zloty

Poland:
Map Index

Cities and Towns

Biała Podlaska	F2
Białystok	F2
Bielsko-Biała	D4
Bydgoszcz	C2
Bytom	D3
Chełm	F3
Chojnice	C2
Chorzów	D3
Ciechánow	E2
Częstochowa	D3
Darłowo	C1
Elbląg	D1
Ełk	F2
Gdańsk	D1
Gdynia	D1
Gliwice	D3
Głogów	C3
Gorzów Wielkopolski	B2
Grudziądz	D2
Hel	D1
Jelenia Góra	B3
Katowice	D3
Kielce	E3
Kołobrzeg	B1
Konin	D2
Koszalin	C1
Kraków	D3
Krosnow	E4
Kutno	D2
Legnica	C3
Leszno	C3
Łódź	D3
Łomża	F2
Lublin	F3
Nowy Sącz	E4
Nysa	C3
Olsztyn	E2
Opole	C3
Ostrołęka	E2
Piła	C2
Piotrków Trybunalski	D3
Płock	D2
Poznań	C2
Przemyśl	F4
Puck	D1
Puławy	E3
Radom	E3
Ruda Śląska	D3
Rybnik	D3
Rzeszów	F3
Szczecinek	C2
Siedlce	F2
Sieradz	D3
Skierniewice	E3
Słupsk	C1
Sosnowiec	D3
Suwałki	F1
Świnoujście	B2
Szczecin	B2
Tarnobrzeg	E3
Tarnów	E3
Toruń	D2
Tychy	D3
Ustka	C1
Wałbrzych	C3
Warsaw, capital	E2
Władysławowo	D1
Włocławek	D2
Wodzisław Śląski	D3
Wrocław	C3
Zabrze	D3
Zakopane	D4
Zamość	F3
Zielona Góra	B3

Other Features

Baltic, sea	B1
Beskid, mts.	D4
Bug, river	E2, F3
Carpathian, mts.	E4
Frisches Haff, bay	D1
Gdańsk, gulf	D1
High Tatra, mts.	D4
Mamry, lake	E1
Narew, river	E2
Neisse, river	B3
Noteć, river	C2, D2
Oder, river	B2, C3
Pilica, river	E3
Pomeranian, bay	B1
Rysy, mt.	D4
San, river	F3
Silesia, region	C3
Śniardwy, lake	E2
Sudeten, mts.	B3
Vistula, river	D2, E3
Warta, river	B2, C2
Wieprz, river	F3

Poland

⊛ National Capital
• Other City
⊥⊥⊥ Canal

1:6,687,500

| 0 | 50 | 100 mi |
| 0 | 50 | 100 km |

Lambert Conformal Conic Projection

© MapQuest.com, Inc.

Germany:
Map Index

States

Baden-Württemberg	B4
Bavaria	B4
Berlin	C2
Brandenburg	C2
Bremen	B2
Hamburg	B2
Hesse	B3
Lower Saxony	B2
Mecklenburg-Western Pomerania	C2
North Rhine-Westphalia	A3
Rhineland-Palatinate	A4
Saarland	A4
Saxony	C3
Saxony-Anhalt	B3
Schleswig-Holstein	B2
Thuringia	B3

Cities and Towns

Aachen	A3
Amberg	B4
Ansbach	B4
Arnsberg	B3
Augsburg	B4
Bad Ems	A3
Baden-Baden	A4
Bad Kreuznach	A4
Bad Reichenhall	C5
Bamberg	B4
Bautzen	C3
Bayreuth	B4
Bergisch Gladbach	A3
Berlin, capital	C2
Bernburg	B3
Bielefeld	B2
Bingen	A4
Bocholt	A3
Bochum	A3
Bonn	A3
Bottrop	A3
Brandenburg	C2
Bremen	B2
Bremerhaven	B2

Brunswick	B2
Büren	B3
Chemnitz	C3
Coburg	B3
Cologne	A3
Constance	B5
Cottbus	C3
Cuxhaven	B2
Dachau	B4
Darmstadt	B4
Dessau	C3
Detmold	B3
Dortmund	A3
Dresden	C3
Duisburg	A3
Düsseldorf	A3
Eberswalde	C2
Eisenach	B3
Eisenhüttenstadt	C2
Eisleben	B3
Emden	A2
Erfurt	B3
Erlangen	B4
Essen	A3
Esslingen	B4
Flensburg	B1
Frankfurt am Main	B3
Frankfurt an der Oder	C2
Freiberg	C3
Freiburg	A5
Friedrichshafen	B5
Fulda	B3
Fürth	B4
Garmisch-Partenkirchen	B5
Gelsenkirchen	A3
Gera	B3
Giessen	B3
Göppingen	B4
Görlitz	C3
Goslar	B3
Gotha	B3
Göttingen	B3
Greifswald	C1
Guben	C2
Güstrow	C2
Hagen	A3
Halberstadt	B3

Halle	B3
Hamburg	B2
Hameln	B2
Hamm	A3
Hanau	B3
Hannover	B2
Heidelberg	B4
Heidenheim	B4
Heilbronn	B4
Herne	A3
Hildesheim	B2
Hindelang	B5
Hof	B3
Ingolstadt	B4
Jena	B3
Kaiserslautern	A4
Karlsruhe	A4
Kassel	B3
Kaufbeuren	B5
Kempten	B5
Kiel	B1
Kleve	A3
Koblenz	A3
Krefeld	A3
Kulmbach	B4
Landshut	C4
Leipzig	B3
Leverkusen	A3
Lindau	B5
Lippstadt	B3
Lübeck	B2
Luckenwalde	C2
Ludwigsburg	B4
Ludwigshafen am Rhein	B2
Lüneburg	B2
Lünen	A3
Magdeburg	B2
Mainz	B4
Mannheim	B4
Marburg	B3
Marl	A3
Meissen	C3
Memmingen	B5
Moers	A3
Mönchengladbach	A3
Mülheim an der Ruhr	A3

Munich	B4
Münster	A3
Naumburg	B3
Neubrandenburg	C2
Neumünster	B1
Neunkirchen	A4
Neuss	A3
Neustrelitz	C2
Nienburg	B2
Nordenham	B2
Nordhausen	B3
Nordhorn	A2
Northeim	B3
Nuremberg	B4
Oberammergau	B5
Oberhausen	A3
Offenbach	B3
Oldenburg	B2
Osnabrück	B2
Paderborn	B3
Passau	C4
Pforzheim	B4
Pirmasens	A4
Plauen	B3
Potsdam	C2
Puttgarden	B1
Ratingen	A3
Ravensburg	B5
Recklinghausen	A3
Regensburg	C4
Remagen	A3
Remscheid	A3
Reutlingen	B4
Riesa	C3
Rosenheim	C5
Rostock	C1
Saarbrücken	A4
Salzgitter	B2
Sassnitz	C1
Schleswig	B1
Schwäbisch Gmünd	B4
Schwedt	C2
Schweinfurt	B3
Siegen	B3
Singen	B5
Solingen	A3

Spandau	C2
Speyer	B4
Stendal	B2
Stralsund	C1
Straubing	C4
Stuttgart	B4
Suhl	B3
Trier	A4
Tübingen	B4
Uelzen	B2
Ulm	B4
Weiden	C4
Weimar	B3
Wetzlar	B3
Wiesbaden	B3
Wilhelmshaven	B2
Wismar	B2
Witten	A3
Wittenberg	C3
Wittenberge	B2
Wolfsburg	B2
Worms	B4
Wuppertal	A3
Würzburg	B4
Zittau	C3
Zwickau	C3

Other Features

Ammersee, lake	B4
Baltic, sea	C1
Bavarian Alps, mts.	B5
Bayerischer Wald, mts.	C4
Black, forest	A4
Bohemian, forest	C4
Chiem, lake	C5
Constance, lake	B5
Danube, river	B4
East Frisian, islands	A2
Eifel, plateau	A3
Elbe, river	B2, C3
Ems, river	A3
Erzgebirge, mts.	C3
Fehmarn, island	B1
Fichtelberg, mt.	C3
Fichtelgebirge, mts.	B4
Franconian Jura, mts	B4

Frankenwald, mts.	B3
Fulda, river	B3
Harz, mts.	B3
Havel, river	C2
Helgoland, island	A1
Hunsruck, mts.	A4
Inn, river	C4
Isar, river	C4
Kiel, bay	B1
Lahn, river	B3
Lech, river	B4
Lüneburger Heide, region	B2
Main, river	B4
Main-Danube, canal	B4
Mecklenburg, bay	B1
Mittelland, canal	B2
Mosel, river	A4
Mulde, river	C3
Müritz, lake	C2
Neckar, river	B4
Neisse, river	C3
Nord-Ostsee, canal	B1
North, sea	A1
Northern European, plain	B2
North Frisian, islands	B1
Oberpfälzer Wald, mts.	C4
Odenwald, forest	B4
Oder, river	C2
Oderhaff, lake	C2
Pomeranian, bay	C1
Rhine, river	A3, A4
Rügen, island	C1
Ruhr, river	B3
Saale, river	B3
Saar, river	A4
Salzach, river	C4
Schweriner, lake	B2
Spessart, mts.	B4
Spree, river	C3
Starnberg, lake	B5
Swabian Jura, mts.	B4
Taunus, mts.	B3
Thuringian, forest	B3
Werra, river	B3
Weser, river	B2
Zugspitze, mt.	B5

Czech Republic

⊛ National Capital
• Other City

1:3,637,000

0   25   50 mi
0   25   50 km
Lambert Conformal Conic Projection

Czech Republic

Capital: Prague
Area: 30,449 sq. mi.
78,883 sq. km.
Population: 10,281,000
Largest City: Prague
Language: Czech
Monetary Unit: Koruna

© MapQuest.com, Inc.

Czech Republic:
Map Index

Administrative Regions
Brněský C4
Budějovický B3
Jihlavský B3
Karlovarský A2
Královéhradecký B2
Liberecký B2
Olomoucký C3
Ostravský D3
Prague City B2
Pardubický C3
Plzeňský A3
Středočeský B3
Ústecký A2
Zlínský D3

Cities and Towns
Břeclav C4
Brno C3
České Budějovice B4
Cheb A2
Děčín B2
Frýdek-Místek D3
Havířov D3
Hradec Králové B2
Jihlava B3
Karlovy Vary A2
Karviná D3
Kladno A3
Klatovy A3
Kolín B2
Liberec B2
Most A2
Olomouc C3
Opava C3
Ostrava D3
Pardubice B2
Plzeň A3
Prague, *capital* B2
Přerov C3
Prostějov C3
Strakonice A3
Šumperk C3
Svitavy C3
Tábor B3
Trutnov B2
Ústí nad Labem B2
Zlín D3
Znojmo C4

Other Features
Berounka, *river* A3
Bohemia, *region* A3
Bohemian, *forest* A3
Bohemian-Moravian, *heights* ..B3
Carpathian, *mts.* C4
Dyje, *river* B4
Erzgebirge, *mts.* A2
Labe, *Elbe, river.* B2
Morava, *river* C3
Moravia, *region* C3
Odra, *Oder, river* C3
Sázava, *river* B3
Silesia, *region* B2
Sněžka, *mt.* B2
Sudeten, *mts.* B2
Šumava, *mts.* A3
Vltava, *river* B3

Slovakia

Capital: Bratislava
Area: 18,933 sq. mi.
49,049 sq. km.
Population: 5,396,000
Largest City: Bratislava
Language: Slovak
Monetary Unit: New Koruna

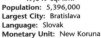

Slovakia:
Map Index

Regions
Banskobystrický C2
Bratislavský A2
Košický C2
Nitriansky B2
Prešovský C2
Trenčiansky A2
Trnavský A2
Žilinský B2

Cities and Towns
Banská Bystrica B2
Bardejov C2
Bratislava, *capital* A2
Humenné C2
Komárno B3
Košice C2
Levice B2
Liptovský Mikuláš B2
Lučenec B2
Martin B2
Michalovce C2
Nitra B2
Nové Zamky B3
Piešťany A2
Poprad C2
Považská Bystrica B2
Prešov C2
Prievidza B2
Ružomberok B2
Spišská Nová Ves C2
Trenčín B2
Trnava A2
Žilina B2
Zvolen B2

Other Features
Biele Karpaty, *mts.* A2
Carpathian, *mts.* A2
Danube, *river* A3
Gerlachovka, *mt.* C2
Hornád, *river* C2
Hron, *river* B2
Ipeľ, *river.* B2
Laborec, *river* C2
Male Karpaty, *mts.* A2
Morava, *river* A2
Ondava, *river* C2
Slaná, *river* B2
Slovenskérudohorie, *mts.* ..C2
Tatra, *range* B2
Váh, *river* A2

Slovakia

⊛ National Capital
• Other City

1:4,353,000

0   25   50   75 mi
0   25   50   75 km
Lambert Conformal Conic Projection

© MapQuest.com, Inc.

Romania:
Map Index

Cities and Towns
Alba Iulia B2
Alexandria C4
Arad A2
Bacău D2
Baia Mare B2
Bîrlad D2
Bistriţa C2
Botoşani D2
Brăila D3
Braşov C3
Bucharest, *capital* D3
Buzău D3
Călăraşi D3
Cernavodă E3
Cluj-Napoca B2
Constanţa E3
Craiova B3
Dej B2
Deva B3
Dorohoi D2
Drobeta-Turnu Severin B3
Făgăraş C3
Feteşti D3
Focşani D3
Galaţi E3
Giurgiu C4
Hunedoara B3
Iaşi D2
Lugoj A3
Luperi A3
Medgidia E3
Mediaş C2
Miercurea Ciuc C2
Oltenţa D3
Oneşti D2
Oradea A2
Petrila B3
Petroşani B3
Piatra Neamţ D2
Piteşti C3
Ploieşti D3
Rădăuţi C2
Reghin C2
Reşiţa A3
Rîmnicu Vîlcea C3
Roman D2
Salonta A2
Satu Mare B2
Sfîntu Gheorghe C3
Sibiu C3
Sighetul Marmaţiei B2

Hungary

1 BÉKÉSCSABA
2 BUDAPEST
3 DEBRECEN
4 DUNAÚJVÁROS
5 EGER
6 GYOR
7 HÓDMEZOVÁSÁRHELY
8 KAPOSVÁR
9 KECSKEMÉT
10 MISKOLC
11 NAGYKANIZSA
12 NYÍREGYHÁZA
13 PÉCS
14 SOPRON
15 SZEGED
16 SZÉKESFEHÉRVÁR
17 SZOLNOK
18 SZOMBATHELY
19 TATABÁNYA
20 VESZPRÉM
21 ZALAEGERSZEG

Hungary

Capital: Budapest
Area: 35,919 sq. mi.
93,054 sq. km.
Population: 10,186,000
Largest City: Budapest
Language: Hungarian
Monetary Unit: Forint

Hungary

⊛ National Capital
• Other City

1:4,187,000

0   40   80 mi
0   40   80   120 km
Lambert Conformal Conic Projection

© MapQuest.com, Inc.

Hungary:
Map Index

Counties
Bács-Kiskun B2
Baranya B3
Békés C2
Békéscsaba C2
Borsod-Abaúj-Zemplén ...C1
Budapest (city) B2
Csongrád C2
Debrecen C2
Dunaújváros B2
Eger C2
Fejér B2
Gyor A2
Gyor-Moson- Sopron A2
Hajdú-Bihar C2
Heves C2

Hódmezovásárhely C2
Jász-Nagykun-Szolnok C2
Kaposvár A2
Kecskemét B2
Komárom-Esztergom B2
Miskolc C1
Nagykanizsa A2
Nógrád B2
Nyíregyháza C2
Pécs B2
Pest B2
Somogy A2
Sopron A2
Szabolcs- Szatmár-Bereg ..C1
Szeged C2
Székesfehérvár B2
Szolnok C2
Szombathely A2
Tatabánya B2

Tolna B2
Vas A2
Veszprém A2
Zala A2
Zalaegerszeg A2

Cities and Towns
Ajka A2
Baja B2
Békéscsaba C2
Budapest, capital B2
Cegléd B2
Debrecen C2
Dunaújváros B2
Eger C2
Érd B2
Esztergom B2
Gyöngyös B2
Gyor A2

Hajdúböszörmény C2
Hódmezovásárhely C2
Jászberény B2
Kaposvár A2
Karcag C2
Kazincbarcika C1
Kecskemét B2
Keszthely A2
Kiskunhalas B2
Komárom B2
Miskolc C1
Mohács B2
Nagykanizsa A2
Nyíregyháza C2
Oroszháza C2
Ózd C1
Paks B2
Pápa A2
Pécs B2

Salgótarján B1
Siófok B2
Sopron A2
Székesfehérvár B2
Szekszárd B2
Szentes C2
Szolnok C2
Szombathely A2
Tatabánya B2
Tokaj C1
Vác B2
Veszprém A2
Zalaegerszeg A2

Other Features
Bakony, mts. A2
Balaton, lake A2
Bükk, mts. C1

Danube, river A2, B2
Drava, river A2
Great Alföld, plain B2
Hernád, river C1
Ipoly, river B1
Kékes, mt. C2
Kiskörei-víztároló, lake .C2
Körös, river C2
Little Alföld, plain A2
Maros, river B2
Mátra, mts. B2
Mecsek, mts. B2
Neusiedler (Fertö), lake .A2
Rába, river A2
Sió, river B2
Tisza, river C2
Zala, river A2

Romania

Capital: Bucharest
Area: 91,699 sq. mi.
267,174 sq. km.
Population: 22,334,000
Largest City: Bucharest
Language: Romanian
Monetary Unit: Leu

Sighisoara C2
Siret D2
Slatina C3
Slobozia D3
Suceava D2
Tecuci D3
Timisoara A3
Tîrgoviste C3
Tirgu Jiu B3
Tirgu-Mures C2
Tirgu Neamt D2
Tirgu Ocna D2
Tulcea E3
Turda B2
Turnu Magurele C4
Vaslui D2
Zalau B2

Other Features
Apuseni, mts. B2
Arges, river C3
Banat, region A3
Bicaz, reservoir D2
Bihor, mts. B2
Bistrita, river C2
Carpathian, mts. B1
Danube, river B3, D3, E3
Dobruja, region E4
Ialomita, river D3
Iron Gate, reservoir B3
Jiu, river B3
Moldavia, region D2
Moldoveanu, mt. B3
Mures, river C3
Mouths of the Danube, delta ..E3
Olt, river C3
Prut, river E2
Razelm, lake E3
Siret, river D2
Somes, river B2
Transylvanian Alps, mts. .B3
Walachia, region B3

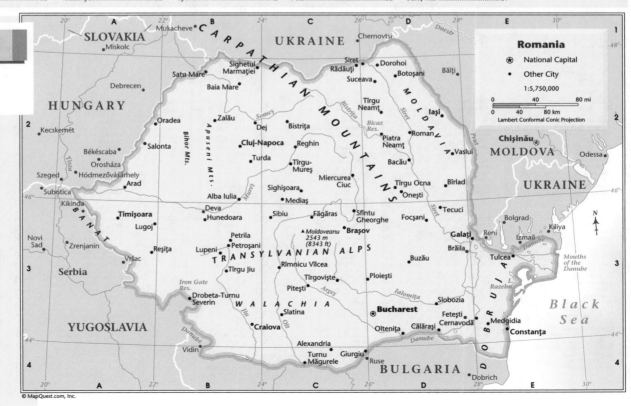

Romania

⊛ National Capital
• Other City

1:5,750,000

0   40   80 mi
0   40   80 km
Lambert Conformal Conic Projection

© MapQuest.com, Inc.

Part of Russia extends onto the continent of Asia.

Russia
⊛ National Capital
• Other City

1:44,857,000

0 250 500 750 mi
0 250 500 750 1000 km
Modified Oblique Conic Conformal Projection

Russia

Capital: Moscow
Area: 6,592,800 sq. mi.
　　　17,079,793 sq. km.
Population: 146,394,000
Largest City: Moscow
Language: Russian
Monetary Unit: Ruble

INTERNAL DIVISIONS
1 ADYGEYA
2 KARACHAYEVO-CHERKESIYA
3 KABARDINO-BALKARIYA
4 NORTH OSSETIA-ALANIYA
5 INGUSHETIYA
6 CHECHNYA
7 MORDOVIYA
8 CHUVASHIYA
9 MARIY-EL
10 TATARSTAN
11 UDMURTIYA
12 KOMI-PERMYAT AUT. OKRUG

© MapQuest.com, Inc.

Russia:
Map Index

Internal Divisions
Adygeya (republic) D5
Aginskiy Buryat (autonomous
　okrug) G4
Altay (republic) F4
Bashkortostan (republic) D4
Buryatiya (republic) G4
Chechnya (republic) D5
Chukotka (autonomous okrug) J3
Chuvashiya (republic) D4
Dagestan (republic) D5
Evenkiya (autonomous okrug) ...F3
Ingushetiya (republic) D5
Kabardino-Balkariya (republic) ..D5
Kalmykiya (republic) D5
Karachayevo-Cherkesiya
　(republic) C3
Kareliya (republic) C3
Khakasiya (republic) F4
Khanty-Mansiy
　(autonomous okrug) E3
Komi (republic) D3
Komi-Permyat
　(autonomous okrug) D3
Koryakiya (autonomous okrug) J3
Mariy-El (republic) D4
Mordoviya (republic) D4
Nenetsiya (autonomous okrug) ..D3
North Ossetia Alaniya (republic) ..D5
Tatarstan (republic) D4
Taymyriya (autonomous okrug) F2
Tyva (republic) F4
Udmurtiya (republic) D4
Ust-Ordynskiy Buryat (autonomous
　okrug) G5
Sakha (Yakutiya) (republic) ..H3
Yamalo-Nenesiya
　(autonomous okrug) E3
Yevrey (autonomous oblast) ...H5

Cities and Towns
Abakan F4
Achinsk F4
Aginskoye G4
Aldan H4
Anadyr J3
Angarsk G4
Apatity C3
Arkhangelsk D3
Astrakhan D4
Barabinsk E4
Barnaul F4
Belomorsk C3
Berezniki D4
Birobizhan H5
Biysk F4
Blagoveshchensk D4
Blagoveshchensk H4
Bodaybo G4
Bratsk G4
Bryansk C4
Cheboksary D4
Chelyabinsk E4
Cherepovets C4
Cherskiy J3
Chita G4
Dikson F2
Dudinka F3
Elista D5
Gorno-Altaysk F4
Groznyy D5
Igarka F3
Inta D3
Irkutsk G4
Ishim E4
Ivanovo D4
Izhevsk D4
Kaliningrad B4
Kamensk-Uralskiy E4
Kansk F4
Kazan D4
Kemerovo F4
Khabarovsk H5
Khanty-Mansiysk E3

Khatanga G2
Kirensk G4
Kirov D4
Kolpashevo F4
Komsomol'sk-na-Amure H4
Kotlas D3
Krasnodar C5
Krasnoyarsk F4
Kudymkar D4
Kurgan E4
Kursk C4
Kyzyl F4
Lensk G3
Lesosibirsk F4
Lipetsk C4
Magadan H4
Magdagachi H4
Magnitogorsk D4
Makhachkala D5
Mirnyy G3
Mogocha G4
Moscow, capital C4
Murmansk C3
Naberezhnyye Chelny D4
Nakhodka H5
Naryan-Mar D3
Nikolayevsk-na-Amure I4
Nizhnevartosk E3
Nizhny Novgorod D4
Nizhny Tagil D4
Nordvik G2
Norilsk F3
Novgorod C4
Novokuznetsk F4
Novosibirsk F4
Okha I4
Okhotsk I4
Omsk E4
Orenburg D4
Orsk D4
Palana J4
Pechora D3
Penza D4
Perm D4

Petropavlovsk-Kamchatskiy I4
Petrozavodsk C3
Pevek J3
Prokopyevsk F4
Provideniya K3
Pskov C4
Rostov-na-Donu C5
Rubtsovsk F4
Ryazan C4
St. Petersburg C4
Salekhard E3
Samara D4
Saransk D4
Saratov D4
Serov E4
Skovorodino H4
Smolensk C4
Sochi C5
Sovetskaya Gavan I5
Stavropol D5
Surgut E3
Susuman I3
Svobodnyy H4
Syktyvkar D3
Tara E4
Tiksi H2
Tobolsk E4
Tolyatti D4
Tomsk F4
Tula C4
Tulun G4
Tura G3
Tynda H4
Tyumen E4
Ufa D4
Ukhta D3
Ulan-Ude G4
Ussuriysk H5
Ust-Ilimsk G4
Ust-Kut G4
Ust-Ordynskiy G4
Verkhoyansk H3
Vilyuysk H3

Vladivostok H5
Volgograd D5
Vologda C4
Vorkuta E3
Voronezh C4
Yakutsk H3
Yaroslavl C4
Yekaterinburg E4
Yoshkar-Ola D4
Yuzhno-Sakhalinsk I5
Zyryanka I3

Other Features
Aldan, river H4
Amur, river H4
Anadyr, gulf K3
Angara, river F4
Azov, sea C5
Baikal, lake G4
Baltic, sea B4
Barents, sea D2
Bering, sea K4
Bering, strait K3
Black, sea C5
Caspian, sea D6
Caucasus, mts. D5
Central Russian, upland C4
Central Siberian, plateau G3
Central, range I4
Chelyuskin, cape G2
Cherskiy, range I3
Chukchi, peninsula K3
Chukchi, range J3
Chukchi, sea K2
Dnepr, river C4
Dzhugdzhur, range H4
East Siberian, sea J2
Franz Josef Land, islands D1
Gyda, peninsula E2
Indigirka, river H3
Irtysh, river E4
Kamchatka, peninsula J4
Kara, sea E2

Kola, peninsula C3
Kolyma, range J3
Kolyma, river I3
Koryak, range J3
Kuril, islands I5
Ladoga, lake C4
Laptev, sea H2
Lena, river H3
Lower Tunguska, river F3
New Siberian, islands I2
North Siberian, lowland G2
Northern Divina, river D3
Northern European, plain C4
Novaya Zemlya, islands D2
Ob, river E3
Oka, river D4
Okhotsk, sea I4
Olenek, river G3
Onega, lake C3
Pechora, river D3
Sakhalin, island I4
Sayan, mts. F4
Severnaya Zemlya, islands F1
Shelikhov, gulf I4
Siberia, region G3
Sikhote Alin, range H4
Stanovoy, range H4
Tatar, strait I4
Taymyr, peninsula F2
Ural, mts. D4
Ural, river D5
Ussuri, river H5
Verkhoyansk, range H3
Vilyuy, river G3
Volga, river D5
West Siberian, plain E3
White, sea C3
Wrangel, island J2
Yablonovyy, range G4
Yamal, peninsula E2
Yenisey, river F3
Zhelaniya, cape E2

Armenia

Capital: Yerevan
Area: 11,500 sq. mi.
29,793 sq. km.
Population: 3,409,000
Largest City: Yerevan
Language: Armenian
Monetary Unit: Dram

Armenia: Map Index

Cities and Towns

Alaverdi	B1
Ararat	B3
Artashat	B3
Artik	A2
Artsvashen	C2
Dilijan	B2
Ejmiatsin	B2
Gavarr	C2
Goris	D3
Gyumri	A2
Hoktemberyan	B2
Hrazdan	B2
Ijevan	C2
Kafan	D3
Kirovakan	B2
Martuni	C2
Meghri	D4
Sisian	D3
Sotk	C2
Stepanavan	B2
Tashir	B1
Vardenis	C2
Vayk	C3
Yerevan, capital	B2

Other Features

Akhuryan, river	A2
Aragats, mt.	B2
Aras, river	B2
Arpa, river	C3
Debed, river	B2
Hrazdan, river	B2
Lesser Caucasus, mts.	B1
Sevan, lake	C2
Vorotan, river	C3

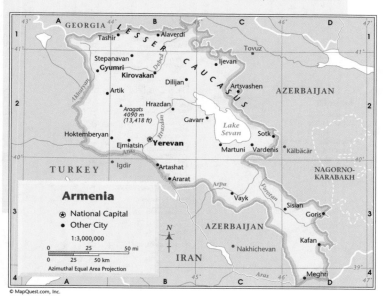

Armenia

⊛ National Capital
• Other City

1:3,000,000

0   25   50 mi
0   25   50 km
Azimuthal Equal Area Projection

Georgia

Capital: Tbilisi
Area: 26,900 sq. mi.
69,689 sq. km.
Population: 5,067,000
Largest City: Tbilisi
Language: Georgian
Monetary Unit: Lari

Georgia: Map Index

Cities and Towns

Akhalkalaki	B4
Akhaltsikhe	B4
Akhmeta	C3
Batumi	A4
Bolnisi	C4
Borjomi	B4
Chiatura	B3
Gagra	A2
Gori	C4
Gudauta	A2
Jvari	B3
Khashuri	B4
Kobuleti	A4
Kutaisi	B3
Lagodekhi	D4
Marneuli	C4
Mtskheta	C4
Ochamchire	A3
Ozurgeti	A3
Poti	A3
Rustavi	C4
Samtredia	B3
Senaki	B3
Sukhumi	A3
Tbilisi, capital	C4
Telavi	C4
Tqvarcheli	A3
Tsiteli-Tsqaro	D4
Tskhinvali	B3
Tsnori	C4
Zestaponi	B3
Zugdidi	A3

Other Features

Abkhazia, autonomous republic	A3
Ajaria, autonomous republic	A4
Alazani, river	C4
Caucasus, mts.	A2
Enguri, river	A3
Iori, river	C4
Lesser Caucasus, mts.	B4
Mqinvartsveri, mt.	C3
Mtkvari, river	C4
Rioni, river	B3
Shkhara, mt.	B3
South Ossetia, region	B3

Azerbaijan

Capital: Baku
Area: 33,400 sq. mi.
86,528 sq. km.
Population: 7,908,000
Largest City: Baku
Language: Azerbaijani
Monetary Unit: Manat

Azerbaijan: Map Index

Cities and Towns

Ağcabädi	B2
Ağdam	B3
Ağstafa	A2
Älät	C3
Äli Bayramli	C3
Astara	C3
Baku, capital	C2
Balakän	B2
Bärdä	B2
Biläsuvar	C3
Gäncä	B2
Göyçay	B2
Kälbäcär	B2
Länkäran	C3
Mingäçevir	B2
Nakhichevan	A3
Quba	C2
Şahbuz	A3
Şäki	B2
Salyan	C3
Sumqayit	C2
Tovuz	A2
Xaçmaz	C2
Xankändi	B3
Yevlax	B2
Zaqatala	B2

Other Features

Abşeron, peninsula	C2
Aras, river	B3
Bazardüzü Daği, mt.	B2
Caucasus, range	A1
Karabakh, canal	B2
Kür, river	A2, C2
Kür-Aras, lowland	B2
Lesser Caucasus, range	A2
Mingäçevir, reservoir	B2
Nagorno-Karabakh, autonomous region	B2
Samur, river	B2
Talish, mts.	C3

Azerbaijan

⊛ National Capital
• Other City

1:5,673,000

0   25   50 mi
0   25   50 km
Azimuthal Equal Area Projection

Estonia:
Map Index

Cities and Towns
Haapsalu B2
Kärdla B1
Keila C1
Kohtla-Järve D1
Kunda C1
Kuressaare B2
Mustvee D2
Narva E1
Paldiski C1
Pärnu C2
Rapla C1
Tallinn, *capital* C1
Tapa C1
Tartu D2
Tõrva C2
Türi C2

Valga D3
Viljandi C2
Virtsu B2
Võru D3

Other Features
Baltic, *sea* A1
Finland, *gulf* C1
Hiiumaa, *island* B2
Irbe, *strait* A3
Munamägi, *mt.* D3
Narva, *river* D1
Pärnu, *river* C2
Pedja, *river* D2
Peipus, *lake* D2
Pskov, *lake* D3
Riga, *gulf* B3
Saaremaa, *island* B2
Võrts Järv, *lake* D2

Estonia
Capital: Tallinn
Area: 17,413 sq. mi.
45,111 sq. km.
Population: 1,409,000
Largest City: Tallinn
Language: Estonian
Monetary Unit: Kroon

Estonia
⊛ National Capital
• Other City
1:7,000,000
0   50   100 mi
0   50   100 km
Lambert Conformal Conic Projection
© MapQuest.com, Inc.

Latvia
Capital: Riga
Area: 24,900 sq. mi.
64,508 sq. km.
Population: 2,354,000
Largest City: Riga
Language: Latvian
Monetary Unit: Lat

Latvia
⊛ National Capital
• Other City
1:7,760,000
0   50   100 mi
0   50   100 km
Conic Equidistant Projection
© MapQuest.com, Inc.

Latvia:
Map Index

Cities and Towns
Aluksne D2
Bauska C2
Cesis C2
Daugavpils D3
Gulbene D2
Jekabpils C2
Jelgava B2
Jurmala B2
Kuldiga A2
Liepaja A2
Limbazi C2
Ogre C2
Pavilosta A2
Rezekne D2
Riga, *capital* C2
Salacgriva C2
Saldus B2
Smiltene C2
Talsi B2
Tukums B2
Valka C2
Valmiera C2
Ventspils A2

Other Features
Baltic, *sea* A2
Burtnieku, *lake* C2
Gaizina, *mt.* C2
Reznas, *lake* D2
Riga, *gulf* B2
Usmas, *lake* B2
Western Dvina, *river* C2

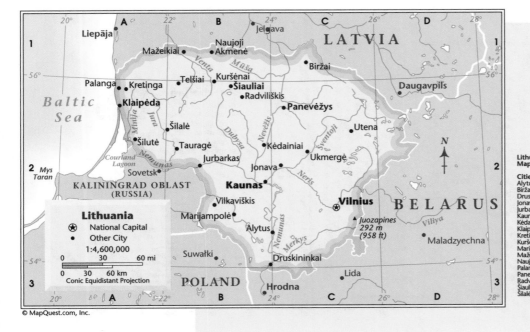

Lithuania
Capital: Vilnius
Area: 25,213 sq. mi.
65,319 sq. km.
Population: 3,585,000
Largest City: Vilnius
Language: Lithuanian
Monetary Unit: Litas

Lithuania
⊛ National Capital
• Other City
1:4,600,000
0   30   60 mi
0   30   60 km
Conic Equidistant Projection

© MapQuest.com, Inc.

Lithuania:
Map Index

Cities and Towns
Alytus C2
Birzai C1
Druskininkai B2
Jonava C2
Jurbarkas B2
Kaunas B2
Kédainiai B2
Klaipéda A2
Kretinga A2
Kuršénai B1
Marijampolé B2
Mažeikiai A2
Naujoji Akmené B1
Palanga A2
Panevézys C2
Radviliškis B2
Šiauliai B2
Šilalé B2

Šiluté A2
Tauragé B2
Telšiai B2
Ukmergé C2
Utena C2
Vilkaviškis B2
Vilnius, *capital* C2

Other Features
Baltic, *sea* A2
Courland, *lagoon* A2
Dubysa, *river* B2
Juozapines, *mt.* C2
Jura, *river* A2
Merkys, *river* C2
Minija, *river* A2
Mūša, *river* B1
Nemunas, *river* A2, C2
Neris, *river* C2
Nevėžis, *river* B2
Šventoji, *river* C2
Venta, *river* B1

Belarus

Capital: Minsk
Area: 80,134 sq. mi.
207,601 sq. km.
Population: 10,402,000
Largest City: Minsk
Languages: Belarussian, Russian
Monetary Unit: Belarus ruble

Belarus: Map Index

Cities and Towns

Asipovichy	D3
Babruysk	D3
Baranavichy	C3
Brest	A3
Homyel	E3
Hrodna	A3
Krychaw	E3
Lida	B3
Mahilyow	E3
Maladzyechna	C2
Mazyr	D3
Minsk, *capital*	C3
Orsha	E2
Pastavy	C2
Pinsk	C3
Polotsk	D2
Rechytsa	E3
Salihorsk	C3
Smilovichi	D3
Smolevichi	D2
Vawkavysk	B3
Vitsyebsk	E2
Zhlobin	D3

Other Features

Bug, *river*	A3
Byarezina, *river*	D3
Byelaruskaya Hrada, *range*	C3
Dnepr, *river*	E3
Dnepr-Bug, *canal*	B3
Dzyarzhynskaya Hara, *mt.*	C3
Nyoman, *river*	B3
Pripyats, *marshes*	C4
Pripyats, *river*	C3
Ptsich, *river*	D3
Sozh, *river*	E3
Western Dvina, *river*	D2

Ukraine: Map Index

Cities and Towns

Balaklava	C4
Belaya Tserkov	C2
Berdyansk	D3
Cherkassy	C2
Chernigov	C1
Chernivtsi	B2
Chornobyl'	C1
Dneprodzerzhinsk	D2
Dnipropetrovsk	D2
Donetsk	D2
Feodosiya	D3

Gorlovka	D2
Ivano-Frankovsk	A2
Izmail	B3
Kachovka	C3
Kerch	D3
Kharkiv	D1
Kherson	C3
Khmelnytskyy	B2
Khust	A2
Kiev, *capital*	C1
Kirovograd	C2
Konotop	C1
Korosten	B1
Kotovsk	B2
Kovel	A1

Kramatorsk	D2
Kremenchug	C2
Kryvyi Rih	C2
Lisichansk	D2
Luhansk	D2
Lutsk	B1
Lviv	A2
Makeyevka	D2
Mariupol	D3
Melitopol	D3
Mogilev Podolskiy	B2
Mykolaiv	C3
Nikopol	C3
Odesa	C3
Pervomaysk	C2

Poltava	C2
Priluki	C1
Rovno	B1
Sevastopol	C4
Shostka	C1
Simferopol	C4
Sumy	C1
Ternopol	B2
Uman	C2
Uzhgorod	A2
Vinnitsa	B2
Yalta	C4
Yevpatoriya	C3
Zaporizhzhia	D2
Zhitomir	B1

Other Features

Azov, *sea*	D3
Black, *sea*	C3
Bug, *river*	A1
Carpathian, *mts.*	A2
Crimean, *mts.*	C4
Crimean, *peninsula*	C4
Desna, *river*	C1
Dneprodzerzhinsk, *reservoir*	C2
Dnieper, *river*	C1,C3
Dniester, *river*	B2
Donets, *basin*	D2
Donets, *river*	D2
Hoverla, *mt.*	A2
Kakhova, *reservoir*	C3

Karkinit, *bay*	C3
Kerch, *strait*	D3
Kiev, *reservoir*	C1
Kremenchug, *reservoir*	C2
Pripyat, *river*	A1
Prut, *river*	B2
Psel, *river*	C1
Sluch, *river*	B1
Southern Bug, *river*	B2
Taganrog, *gulf*	D3
Tisza, *river*	A2
Volyno-Podol'skaya Vozvyshennost, *uplands*	B2
Vorskla, *river*	C1

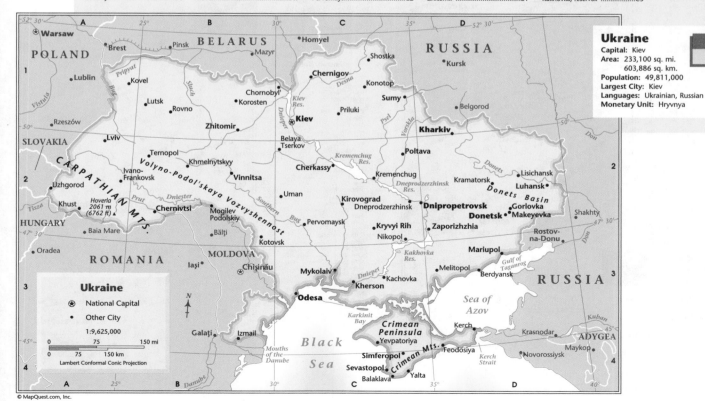

Ukraine

Capital: Kiev
Area: 233,100 sq. mi.
603,886 sq. km.
Population: 49,811,000
Largest City: Kiev
Languages: Ukrainian, Russian
Monetary Unit: Hryvnya

© MapQuest.com, Inc.

Slovenia

Capital: Ljubljana
Area: 7,821 sq. mi.
20,262 sq. km.
Population: 1,971,000
Largest City: Ljubljana
Languages: Slovenian, Serbo-Croatian
Monetary Unit: Tolar

Slovenia: Map Index

Cities and Towns
Celje C2
Idrija B2
Jesenice B2
Kočevje B3
Koper A3
Kranj B2
Krško C3
Ljubljana, *capital* B2
Maribor C2
Murska Sobota D2
Nova Gorica A3
Novo Mesto C3
Postojna B3
Ptuj C2

Other Features
Adriatic, *sea* A3
Drava, *river* C2
Julian Alps, *mts.* A2
Krka, *river* B3
Kupa, *river* B3
Mura, *river* C2
Sava, *river* B2
Savinja, *river* B2
Trieste, *gulf* A3
Triglav, *mt.* A2

© MapQuest.com, Inc.

Croatia

Capital: Zagreb
Area: 21,829 sq. mi.
56,552 sq. km.
Population: 4,677,000
Largest City: Zagreb
Language: Serbo-Croatian
Monetary Unit: Kuna

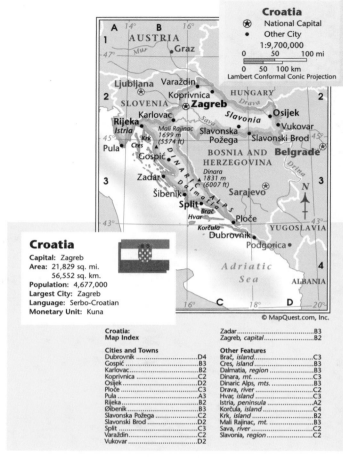

Croatia: Map Index

Cities and Towns
Dubrovnik D4
Gospić B3
Karlovac B2
Koprivnica C2
Osijek D2
Ploče C3
Pula A3
Rijeka B2
Øibenik B3
Slavonska Požega C2
Slavonski Brod D2
Split C3
Varaždin C2
Vukovar D2

Zadar B3
Zagreb, *capital* B2

Other Features
Brač, *island* C3
Cres, *island* B3
Dalmatia, *region* B3
Dinara, *mt.* C3
Dinaric Alps, *mts.* B3
Drava, *river* C2
Hvar, *island* C3
Istria, *peninsula* A2
Korčula, *island* C4
Krk, *island* B2
Mali Rajinac, *mt.* B3
Sava, *river* C2
Slavonia, *region* C2

© MapQuest.com, Inc.

Bosnia and Hercegovina: Map Index

Cities and Towns
Banja Luka B1
Bihać A1
Bijeljina C1
Bosanska Gradiška B1
Bosanska Krupa A1
Brčko B1
Bugojno B1
Derventa B1
Doboj B1
Foča B2
Gacko B2
Goražde B2
Gračanica B1
Jajce B1
Livno B2
Mostar B2
Pale B2
Prijedor A1
Sanski Most A1
Sarajevo, *capital* B2
Srebrenica C1
Teslić B1
Trebinje B2
Tuzla B1
Zavidovići B1
Zenica B1
Zvornik C1

Other Features
Bosna, *river* B1
Dinara, *mt.* A2
Dinaric Alps, *mts.* A1
Drina, *river* C1
Neretva, *river* B2
Sava, *river* B1
Una, *river* A1
Vrbas, *river* B1

© MapQuest.com, Inc.

Bosnia and Herzegovina

Capital: Sarajevo
Area: 19,741 sq. mi.
51,142 sq. km.
Population: 3,483,000
Largest City: Sarajevo
Language: Serbo-Croatian
Monetary Unit: Convertible ruble

F.Y.R. Macedonia

Capital: Skopje
Area: 9,928 sq. mi.
25,720 sq. km.
Population: 2,023,000
Largest City: Skopje
Languages: Macedonian, Albanian, Serbo-Croatian, Turkish
Monetary Unit: Denar

F.Y.R. Macedonia: Map Index

Cities and Towns
Bitola B2
Blatec C2
Debar A2
Gevgelija C2
Kavadarci C2
Kičevo A2
Kočani C2
Kruševo B2
Kumanovo B1
Ohrid A2
Prilep B2
Skopje, *capital* B2
Štip C2
Struga A2
Strumica C2
Tetovo A1
Titov Veles B2

Other Features
Belasica, *mts.* C2
Bregalnica, *river* C2
Crna, *river* B2
Crna Gora, *mts.* B1
Doiran, *lake* C2
Jakupica, *mts.* B2
Korab, *mt.* A2
Kožuf, *mt.* B3
Nidže, *mts.* B3
Ogražden, *mts.* C2
Ohrid, *lake* A3
Prespa, *lake* B3
Treska, *river* B2
Vardar, *river* C2

© MapQuest.com, Inc.

Albania

⊛ National Capital
• Other City

1:3,750,000

0   15   30 mi
0   15   30 km

Lambert Conformal
Conic Projection

YUGOSLAVIA
Montenegro
Serbia
NORTH ALBANIAN ALPS
Lake Scutari
Drin
Bar
Puke
Shkodër
Kosovo
Prizren
Shëngjin
Kukës
Korab 2751 m (9026 ft)
Skopje
Laç
Peshkópi
Krujë
F.Y.R. MACEDONIA
Durrës
Tirana
Erzen
Kavajë
Elbasan
Shkumbin
Lake Ohrid
Lushnjë
Devoll
Bitola
Pogradec
Seman
Fier
Berat
Korçë
Flórina
Osum
Vijosë
Vlorë
Ersekë
Lake Prespa
Gjirokastër
Erikoússa
Othonoi
Sarandë
Mathrákion
Kérkira
GREECE
Adriatic Sea
Strait of Otranto
Ionian Sea
Buene

© MapQuest.com, Inc.

Federal Republic of Yugoslavia

⊛ National Capital
• Other City

1:3,682,000

0   30   60 mi
0   30   60 km

Lambert Conformal Conic Projection

HUNGARY
Pécs
Szeged
Békéscsaba
Subotica
Senta
Kikinda
Sombor
BANAT
VOJVODINA
Timişoara
Osijek
Vrbas
Bečej
Zrenjanin
Drava
Velik
Canal
CROATIA
Bačka Palanka
Novi Sad
Fruška Gora
Vršac
ROMANIA
Danube
Sremska Mitrovica
Sava
Pančevo
Šabac
Belgrade
Smederevo
Požarevac
Drobeta-Turnu Severin
Tuzla
BOSNIA AND HERZEGOVINA
Drina
Valjevo
SERBIA
Velika Morava
Bor
Vidin
Sarajevo
Kragujevac
Goražde
Užice
Čačak
Zapadna Morava
Svetozarevo
Zaječar
Zlatibor
Kraljevo
Priboj
Ibar
Kruševac
Jastrebac
Niš
Pljevlja
Novi Pazar
Kopaonik
Prokuplje
Leskovac
Pirot
Nišava
Durmitor
Tara
MONTENEGRO
Nikšić
Đaravica 2656 m (8714 ft)
Kosovska Mitrovica
Zeta
Beli Drim
Peć
KOSOVO
Pristina
Vranje
Podgorica
N. Albanian Alps
Đakovica
Uroševac
Cetinje
Gulf of Kotor
L. Scutari
Prizren
Šar Planina
Crna Gora
Pernik
BULGARIA
Bar
Shkodër
Skopje
Vardar
ALBANIA
F.Y.R. MACEDONIA
Adriatic Sea
Durrës
Tirana

© MapQuest.com, Inc.

Albania: Map Index

Cities and Towns
Berat A3
Durrës A2
Elbasan B2
Ersekë B3
Fier A3
Gjirokastër B3
Kavajë A2
Korçë B3
Krujë A2
Kukës B1
Laç A2
Lushnjë A3
Peshkopi B2
Pogradec B3
Pukë A1
Sarandë A4
Shëngjin A2
Shkodër A1
Tirana, capital A2
Vlorë A3

Drin, river A1
Erzen, river A2
Ionian, sea A4
Korab, mt. B2
North Albanian Alps, range A1
Ohrid, lake B2
Osum, river B3
Otranto, strait A3
Prespa, lake C3
Scutari, lake A1
Seman, river A3
Shkumbin, river A2
Vijosë, river A3

Albania

Capital: Tirana
Area: 11,100 sq. mi.
          28,756 sq. km.
Population: 3,365,000
Largest City: Tirana
Languages: Albanian, Greek
Monetary Unit: Lek

Other Features
Adriatic, sea A2
Buene, river A2
Devoll, river B3

Yugoslavia: Map Index

Internal Divisions
Kosovo (province) B3
Montenegro (republic) A3
Serbia (republic) B2
Vojvodina (province) A2

Cities and Towns
Bačka Palanka A2
Bar A3
Bečej B2
Belgrade, capital B2
Bor C2
Čačak B3
Cetinje A3
Đakovica B3
Kikinda B2
Kosovska Mitrovica B3
Kragujevac B2
Kraljevo B3
Kruševac B3
Leskovac B3
Nikšić A3
Niš B3
Novi Pazar B3
Novi Sad A2
Pančevo B2
Peć B3
Pirot C3
Pljevlja A3
Podgorica A3

Požarevac B2
Priboj A3
Pristina B3
Prizren B3
Prokuplje B3
Šabac A2
Senta B2
Smederevo B2
Sombor A2
Sremska Mitrovica A2
Subotica A1
Svetozarevo B3
Uroševac B3
Užice A3
Valjevo A2
Vranje B3
Vrbas A2
Vršac B2
Zaječar C3
Zrenjanin B2

Other Features
Adriatic, sea A4
Balkan, mts. C3
Beli Drim, river B3
Crna Gora, mts. A3
Danube, river A2, B2
Đaravica, mt. B3
Dinaric Alps, mts. A3
Drina, river A2
Durmitor, mts. A3
Fruška Gora, mts. A2
Ibar, river B3

Jastrebac, mts. B3
Južna, river B3
Kopaonik, mts. B3
Kotor, gulf A3
Morava, river B3
Nišava, river C3
North Albanian Alps, mts. B3
Šar Planina, mts. B3
Sava, river A2
Scutari, lake A3
Tara, river A3
Tisa, river B2
Velika Morava, river B2
Veliki, canal A2
Zapandna Morava, river A3
Zeta, river A3
Zlatibor, mts. A3

Yugoslavia

Capital: Belgrade
Area: 39,449 sq. mi.
          102,199 sq. km.
Population: 11,207,000
Largest City: Belgrade
Language: Serbo-Croatian
Monetary Unit: New Yugoslav dinar

Moldova

★ National Capital
• Other City

1:4,800,000

0   35   70 mi
0   35   70 km

Lambert Conformal Conic Projection

Moldova

Capital: Chişinău
Area: 13,012 sq. mi.
33,710 sq. km.
Population: 4,461,000
Largest City: Chişinău
Languages: Moldovan, Russian
Monetary Unit: Moldovan leu

Moldova: Map Index

Cities and Towns

Bălţi	A2
Basarabeasca	B2
Bender (Tighina)	B2
Briceni	A1
Cahul	B3
Căuşeni	B2
Chişinău, capital	B2
Comrat	B3
Dubăsari	B2
Fălești	A2
Florești	B2
Leova	B2
Orhei	B2
Rîbniţa	B2
Rîșcani	B2
Soroca	B1
Tiraspol	B2
Ungheni	A2

Other Features

Botna, river	B2
Bugeac, region	B3
Codri, region	A3
Cogalnic, river	B2
Dnestr, river	B2
Ialpug, river	B2
Prut, river	A1, B3
Raut, river	B2

Bulgaria: Map Index

Administrative Regions

Blagoevgrad	B4	Pleven	C2
Burgas	F3	Plovdiv	C3
Dobrich	F2	Primorsko	F3
Gabrovo	D3	Razgrad	E2
Haskovo	D4	Ruse	D2
Jambol	E3	Samokov	B3
Kardzhali	D4	Shumen	E2
Kjustendil	A3	Silistra	F1
Lovech	C3	Sliven	E3
Montana	B2	Smoljan	C4
Pazardzhik	C3	Sofia, capital	B3
Pernik	A3	Stara Zagora	D3
Pleven	C2	Svilengrad	E4
Plovdiv	C3	Svishtov	D2
Razgrad	E2	Targovishte	E2
Ruse	D2	Varna	F2
Shumen	F2	Veliko Tarnovo	D2
Silistra	F2	Vidin	A2
Sliven	E3	Vratsa	B2
Smoljan	C4		
Sofia	B3	**Other Features**	
Sofia City	B3	Arda, river	C4
Stara Zagora	D3	Balkan, mts.	B2
Targovishte	E2	Danube, river	B2
Varna	F2	Golyama Kamchiya, river	E2
Veliko Tarnovo	D2	Iskŭr, river	C2
Vidin	A2	Kamchiya, river	F2
Vraca	B2	Luda Kamchiya, river	E3
		Ludogorie, region	E2
Cities and Towns		Maritsa, river	D3
Asenovgrad	C3	Mesta, river	B4
Aytos	F3	Musala, mt.	B3
Blagoevgrad	B4	Ogosta, river	B2
Burgas	F3	Osŭm, river	C2
Dimitrovgrad	D3	Rhodope, mts.	C4
Dobrich	F2	Rila, mts.	B3
Elkhovo	E3	Sredna Gora, mts.	C3
Gabrovo	D3	Struma, river	A3
Haskovo	D4	Stryama, river	C3
Jambol	E3	Thrace, region	D4
Kardzhali	D4	Thracian, plain	C3
Kazanlŭk	D3	Tundzha, river	E3
Kjustendil	A3	Yantra, river	D2
Kozloduy	B2		
Lom	B2		
Lovech	C2		
Madan	C4		
Montana	B2		
Oryakhovo	B2		
Panagyurishte	C3		
Pazardzhik	C3		
Pernik	B3		
Petrich	B4		

Bulgaria

Capital: Sofia
Area: 42,855 sq. mi.
111,023 sq. km.
Population: 8,195,000
Largest City: Sofia
Language: Bulgarian
Monetary Unit: Lev

Bulgaria

★ National Capital
• Other City

1:3,210,000

0   25   50   75 mi
0   25   50   75 km

Lambert Conformal Conic Projection

Greece

⊛ National Capital

● Other City

1:6,500,000

0 — 75 — 150 mi
0 — 75 — 150 km
Lambert Conformal Conic Projection

Inset map:
Mándra, Akharnaí, Kifisiá, Asprópirgos, Aigáleo Óros, Néa Liósia, Elevsís, Dháfni, Khalándrion, Peristéri, Bay of Elevsís, Keratsínion, Níkaia, Athens, Paianía, Kallithéa, Selínia, Piraiévs, Áyios Dhimítrios, Salamís, Kalamáki, Saronic Gulf, Ellinikón, Glifádha

0 — 2 — 4 mi
0 — 2 — 4 km

Main map labels:
Plovdiv, Skopje, F.Y.R. MACEDONIA, BULGARIA, Edirne, Black Sea, Tirana, ALBANIA, Sérrai, EASTERN MACEDONIA & THRACE, Xánthi, Komotiní, İstanbul, Sea of Marmara, CENTRAL MACEDONIA, Kavála, Thásos, Alexandroúpolis, Bursa, Véroia, Thessaloníki, Thásos, Samothráki, Çanakkale, Kastoría, Kozáni, Khalkidhikí, Mount Áthos, WESTERN MACEDONIA, Kateríni, Olympus 2917 m (9570 ft), Límnos, NORTHERN AEGEAN, Kérkira, Ioánnina, PINDUS MTS., Piniós, Lárisa, Northern Sporades, Lésvos, TURKEY, Kérkira, EPIRUS, Tríkala, THESSALY, Vólos, Aegean Sea, Mitilíni, ITALY, Ionian Sea, Préveza, Lamía, Euboea, Skíros, IONIAN ISLANDS, Agrínion, CENTRAL GREECE, Khalkís, Khíos, İzmir, IthÁki, Mesolóngion, Kifisós, ATTICA, Mediterranean, Kefallinía, Pátrai, Gulf of Corinth, Athens, Ándros, Sámos, Zákinthos, WESTERN GREECE, Corinth, Isthmus of Corinth, Piraiévs, Delos, Ikaría, Árgos, PELOPONNESUS, Aíyina, Mílinos, CYCLADES, DODECANESE, Kalámai, Idhra, Páros, Náxos, Bodrum, Pílos, Sparta, SOUTHERN AEGEAN, Kos, Neápolis, Mílos, Astipálaia, Rhodes, Kíthira, Thíra, Rhodes, Sea of Crete, Kárpathos, Khaniá, Iráklion, CRETE, Crete

© MapQuest.com, Inc.

Greece:
Map Index

Regions
Attica B2
Central Greece B2
Central Macedonia B1
Crete C4
Eastern Macedonia and
  Thrace C1
Epirus B2
Ionian Islands B2
Northern Aegean C2
Peloponnesus B3
Southern Aegean C3
Thessaly B2
Western Greece B3
Western Macedonia B1

Cities and Towns
Agrínion B2
Akharnaí ....Inset
Alexandroúpolis C1
Árgos B3
Asprópirgos ....Inset
Athens, capital ....B3, Inset
Áyios Dhimítrios ....Inset
Corinth B3
Dháfni ....Inset
Elevsís ....Inset
Ellinikón ....Inset
Glifádha ....Inset
Ioánnina B2
Iráklion C4
Kalámai B3

Kalamáki ....Inset
Kallithéa ....Inset
Kastoría B1
Kateríni B1
Kavála C1
Keratsínion ....Inset
Kérkira A2
Khalándrion ....Inset
Khalkís B2
Khaniá B4
Kifisiá ....Inset
Komotiní C1
Kozáni B1
Lamía B2
Lárisa B2
Mándra ....Inset
Mesolóngion B2
Mitilíni C2
Néa Liósia ....Inset
Neápolis B3
Níkaia ....Inset
Paianía ....Inset
Pátrai B2
Peristéri ....Inset
Pílos B3
Piraiévs ....B3, Inset
Préveza B2
Rhodes D3
Selínia ....Inset
Sérrai B1
Sparta B3
Thásos C1
Thessaloníki B1
Tríkala B2
Véroia B1

Vólos B2
Xánthi C1

Other Features
Aegean, sea C2
Aigáleo, mts. ....Inset
Aíyina, island B3
Akhelóös, river B2
Alfíos, river B3
Aliákmon, river B1
Ándros, island C3
Astipálaia, island C3
Áthos, mt. C1
Corinth, gulf B2
Corinth, isthmus B3
Crete, island C4
Crete, sea C4
Cyclades, islands C3
Delos, island C3
Dodecanese, islands C3
Elevsís, bay ....Inset
Euboea, island B2
Idhra, island B3
Ikaría, island C3
Ionian, islands B2
Ionian, sea A2
Itháki, island B2
Kárpathos, island C4
Kefallinía, island B2
Kérkira, island A2
Khalkidhikí, peninsula B1
Khíos, island C2
Kifissós, river B2
Kíthira, island B3
Kos, island C3

Lésvos, island C2
Límnos, island C2
Míkonos, island C3
Mílos, island C3
Náxos, island C3
Northern Sporades, islands ..B2
Olympus, mt. B1
Páros, island C3
Pindus, mts. B2
Piniós, river B2
Prespa, lake B1
Rhodes, island D3
Salamís, island ....Inset
Sámos, island C3
Samothráki, island C1
Saronic, gulf ....Inset
Skíros, island C2
Struma, river B1
Thásos, island C1
Thíra, island C3
Zákinthos, island B3

Greece

Capital: Athens
Area: 50,949 sq. mi.
  131,992 sq. km.
Population: 10,707,000
Largest City: Athens
Language: Greek
Monetary Unit: Drachma

© MapQuest.com, Inc.

Iceland

Capital: Reykjavík
Area: 36,699 sq. mi.
95,075 sq. km.
Population: 273,000
Largest City: Reykjavík
Language: Icelandic
Monetary Unit: New Icelandic króna

Iceland: Map Index

Cities and Towns

Akranes	A2
Akureyri	B2
Dalvík	B2
Eskifjördhur	C2
Hafnarfjördhur	A3
Höfn	C2
Ísafjördhur	A1
Keflavík	A3
Kópavogur	A2
Ólafsvík	A2
Reykjavík, capital	A2
Saudhárkrókur	B2
Siglufjördhur	B1
Thingvellir	A2
Vestmannaeyjar	A3

Other Features

Blanda, river	B2
Breidhafjördhur, fjord	A2
Faxaflói, bay	A2
Greenland, sea	B1
Grímsey, island	B1
Heimaey, island	A3
Hekla, volcano	B3
Horn, cape	A1
Húnaflói, bay	A2
Hvannadalshnúkur, mt.	B3
Hvítá, river	A2
Laki, volcano	A2
Surtsey, island	A3
Vatnajökull, ice cap	B2

Iceland

⊛ National Capital
• Other City

1:10,240,000

0   50   100 mi
0   50   100 km

Lambert Conformal Conic Projection

Norway

Capital: Oslo
Area: 125,050 sq. mi.
323,964 sq. km.
Population: 4,439,000
Largest City: Oslo
Language: Norwegian
Monetary Unit: Norwegian krone

Norway: Map Index

Cities and Towns

Ålesund	B3
Alta	E1
Arendal	B4
Bergen	B3
Bodø	C2
Drammen	C4
Dumbås	B3
Egersund	B4
Florø	A3
Fredrikstad	C4
Gjøvik	C3
Hamar	C3
Hammerfest	E1
Harstad	D2
Haugesund	B4
Kinsarvik	B3
Kirkenes	F2
Kristiansand	B4
Kristiansund	B3
Lakselv	F1
Leikanger	B3
Lillehammer	C3
Mo	C2
Molde	B3
Mosjøen	C2
Moss	C4
Namsos	C3
Narvik	D2
Oslo, capital	C3
Skien	B4
Stavanger	B4
Steinkjer	C3
Tromsø	D2
Trondheim	C3
Vadsø	F1

Other Features

Barents, sea	E1
Boknafjord, fjord	B4
Dovrefjell, mts.	B3
Finnmark, plateau	E2
Glåma, river	C3
Glittertinden, mt.	B3
Hallingdal, valley	B3
Hardangerfjord, fjord	B4
Hardangervidda, plateau	B3
Jotunheimen, mts.	B3
Lofoten, islands	C2
Mjøsa, lake	C3
North, cape	F1
North, sea	A3
Norwegian, sea	A2
Oslofjord, fjord	C4
Skagerrak, strait	B4
Sognafjord, fjord	B3
Tana, river	F1
Trondheimsfjord, fjord	B3
Vesterålen, islands	C2

© MapQuest.com, Inc.

Finland:
Map Index

Internal Divisions

Eastern Finland (province)......C2
Lapland (province)......C1
Oulu (province)......C1
Southern Finland (province)......C2
Western Finland (province)......B2
Central Finland (region)......C2
Central Ostrobothnia (region)..B2
Etelä-Savo (region)......C2
Häme (region)......B2
Itä-Uusimaa (region)......C2
Kainuu (region)......C2
Kymenlaakso (region)......C2
North Karelia (region)......C2
Northern Ostrobothnia
(region)......B2
Ostrobothnia (region)......B2
Päijät Häme (region)......C2
Pirkanmaa (region)......B2
Satakunta (region)......B2
Savo (region)......C2
South Karelia (region)......C2
South Ostrobothnia (region)....B2
South-West Finland (region).....B2
Uusimaa (region)......B2

Cities and Towns

Espoo......B2

Hämeenlinna......B2
Hangö......B3
Helsinki, capital......B2
Hyvinkää......B2
Iisalmi......C2
Imatra......C2
Ivalo......C1
Jakobstad......B2
Jämsä......C2
Joensuu......C2
Jyväskylä......C2
Kajaani......C2
Kemi......B1
Kemijärvi......C1
Kokkola......B2
Kolari......B1
Kotka......C2
Kouvola......C2
Kuopio......C2
Lahti......C2
Lappeenranta......C2
Lieksa......D2
Mariehamn (Maarianhamina)......A2
Mikkeli......C2
Muonio......B1
Oulu......C1
Pori......B2
Raahe......B2
Rauma......B2
Rovaniemi......C1
Salo......B2
Savonlinna......C2

Seinäjoki......B2
Tampere......B2
Tornio......B1
Turku......B2
Vaasa......B2
Vantaa......B2
Varkaus......C2
Ylivieska......B2

Other Features

Åland, islands......B2
Baltic, sea......B3
Bothnia, gulf......B2
Finland, gulf......C3
Haltiatunturi, mt.......B1
Iijoki, river......C1
Inari, lake......C1
Kemijoki, river......C1
Kivi, lake......C2
Lapland, region......C1
Lokka, reservoir......C1
Muoniojoki, river......B1
Näsi, lake......B2
Oulu, lake......C2
Oulujoki, river......C1
Ounasjoki, river......B1
Päijänne, lake......C2
Pielinen, lake......C2
Saimaa, lake......C2
Tenojoki, river......C1
Torniojoki, river......C1
Ylikitka, lake......C1

Finland

★ National Capital
• Other City

1:10,000,000

0   50   100   150 mi
0   50 100 150 200 km
Lambert Conformal Conic Projection

Finland

Capital: Helsinki
Area: 130,559 sq. mi.
    338,236 sq. km.
Population: 5,158,000
Largest City: Helsinki
Languages: Finnish, Swedish
Monetary Unit: Markka, Euro

Sweden

★ National Capital
• Other City

1:11,333,000

0   50   100   150 mi
0   50 100 150 km
Lambert Conformal Conic Projection

Sweden

Capital: Stockholm
Area: 173,732 sq. mi.
    450,083 sq. km.
Population: 8,911,000
Largest City: Stockholm
Language: Swedish
Monetary Unit: Krona

Sweden:
Map Index

Counties

Blekinge......C3
Dalarna......B2
Gävleborg......C2
Gotland......C3
Halland......B3
Jämtland......B2
Jönköping......B3
Kalmar......C3
Kronoberg......B3
Malmöhus......B3
Norrbotten......C1
Örebro......B3
Östergötland......B3
Skåne......B3
Södermanland......C3
Stockholm......C3
Uppsala......C3
Värmland......B3
Västerbotten......C2
Västernorrland......C2

Västmanland......C3
Västra Götaland......B3

Cities and Towns

Borås......B3
Eskilstuna......C3
Falun......C2
Gällivare......D1
Gävle......C2
Göteborg......B3
Halmstad......B3
Haparanda......D1
Härnösand......C2
Helsingborg......B3
Hudiksvall......C2
Jönköping......B3
Kalmar......C3
Karlskrona......C3
Karlstad......B3
Kiruna......D1
Kristianstad......B3
Kristinehamn......B3
Linköping......B3
Luleå......D1
Lund......B3
Malmberget......D1
Malmö......B3
Norrköping......C3
Örebro......B3
Örnsköldsvik......C2
Östersund......B2
Sarjektjakko......C1
Skellefteå......D1
Söderhamn......C2
Stockholm, capital......C3
Sundsvall......C2
Trollhättan......B3
Uddevalla......B3
Umeå......D2
Uppsala......C3

Västerås......C3
Växjö......B3
Visby......C3

Other Features

Ångermanälven, river......C2
Baltic, sea......D2
Bothnia, gulf......D2
Dalälven, river......C2
Faxälven, river......C2
Göta, canal......B3
Gotland, island......C3
Hornavan, lake......C1
Indalsälven, river......B2
Kalixälven, river......D1
Kattegat, strait......B3
Kebnekaise, mt.......C1
Kjölen, mts.......C1
Klarälven, river......B2
Ljusnanälven, river......C2
Luleälven, river......D1
Mälaren, lake......C3
Muonioälven, river......D1
Norra Storfjället, mt.......C1
Öland, island......C3
Øresund, sound......B3
Österdalälven, river......B2
Skagerrak, strait......A3
Skellefteälven, river......D1
Småland, region......B3
Storavan, lake......C1
Storsjön, lake......B2
Torneälven, river......D1
Uddjaur, lake......C1
Umeälven, river......C2
Vänern, lake......B3
Vättern, lake......B3
Vindelälven, river......C2

MAJOR CITIES

Algeria
Algiers	1,483,000
Oran	590,000
Constantine	483,000

Angola
Luanda	(metro) 2,081,000

Benin
Cotonou	402,000
Porto-Novo	144,000

Botswana
Gaborone	183,000

Burkina Faso
Ouagadougou	824,000

Burundi
Bujumbura	235,440

Cameroon
Douala	(metro) 1,320,000
Yaoundé	1,119,000

Cape Verde
Praia	61,000

Central African Republic
Bangui	474,000

Chad
N'Djamena	(metro) 826,000

Comoros
Moroni	(metro) 30,000

Congo, Democratic Republic of the
Kinshasa	3,800,000
Lubumbashi	739,000

Congo, Republic of the
Brazzaville (metro)	1,004,000

Côte d'Ivoire
Abidjan	2,793,000
Yamoussoukro	107,000

Djibouti
Djibouti	(metro) 450,000

Egypt
Cairo	6,789,000
Alexandria	3,328,000
Port Said	470,000
Suez	418,000

Equatorial Guinea
Malabo	38,000

Eritrea
Asmara	358,000

Ethiopia
Addis Ababa	2,085,000

Gabon
Libreville	275,000

The Gambia
Banjul	40,000

Ghana
Accra	(metro) 1,673,000

Guinea
Conakry	(metro) 1,558,000

Guinea-Bissau
Bissau	138,000

Kenya
Nairobi	959,000
Mombasa	401,000

Lesotho
Maseru	109,000

Liberia
Monrovia	(metro) 962,000

Libya
Tripoli	(metro) 1,682,000

Madagascar
Antananarivo	(metro) 876,000

Malawi
Blantyre	332,000
Lilongwe	234,000

Mali
Bamako	810,000

Mauritania
Nouakchott	550,000

Mauritius
Port Louis	146,000

Morocco
Casablanca	2,943,000
Fez	564,000
Rabat	1,220,000

Mozambique
Maputo	(metro) 2,212,000

Namibia
Windhoek	114,000

Niger
Niamey	392,000

Nigeria
Lagos	1,300,000
Ibadan	1,300,000
Abuja	250,000

Rwanda
Kigali	237,000

São Tomé & Príncipe
São Tomé	43,000

Senegal
Dakar	1,641,000

Seychelles
Victoria	(metro) 24,000

Sierra Leone
Freetown	470,000

Somalia
Mogadishu	997,000

South Africa
Cape Town	2,350,000
Johannesburg	1,916,000
Durban	1,137,000
Pretoria	1,080,000
Port Elizabeth	853,000
Bloemfontein	300,000

Sudan
Omdurman	1,271,000
Khartoum	947,000

Swaziland
Mbabane	38,000

Tanzania
Dar es-Salaam	(metro) 1,747,000

Togo
Lomé	600,000

Tunisia
Tunis	674,000

Uganda
Kampala	(metro) 954,000

Western Sahara
el-Aaiún	90,000

Zambia
Lusaka	(metro) 1,317,000

Zimbabwe
Harare	(metro) 1,410,000

International comparability of city population data is limited by various data inconsistencies.

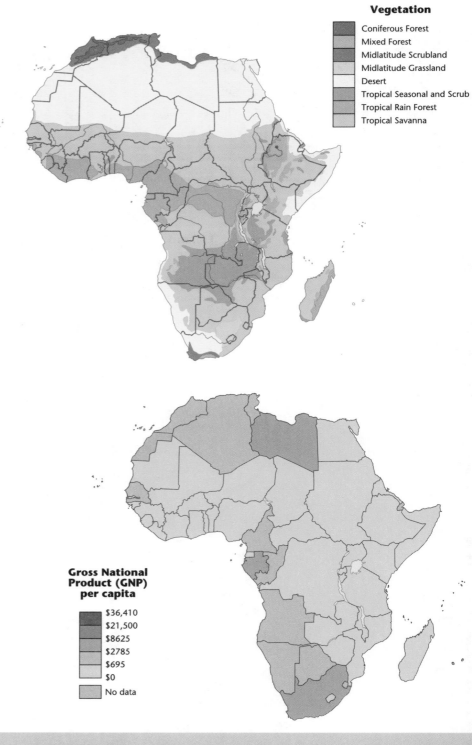

Vegetation

- Coniferous Forest
- Mixed Forest
- Midlatitude Scrubland
- Midlatitude Grassland
- Desert
- Tropical Seasonal and Scrub
- Tropical Rain Forest
- Tropical Savanna

Gross National Product (GNP) per capita

- $36,410
- $21,500
- $8625
- $2785
- $695
- $0
- No data

© MapQuest.com, Inc.

Africa: Population, by nation (in millions)

| NIGERIA 113.8 | EGYPT 67.3 | ETHIOPIA 59.7 | CONGO, DEM.REP. 50.5 | S. AFR. 43.4 | SUDAN 34.5 | TANZ. 31.3 | ALGERIA 31.1 | MOROC. 29.7 | KENYA 28.8 | All other African countries 288.3 |

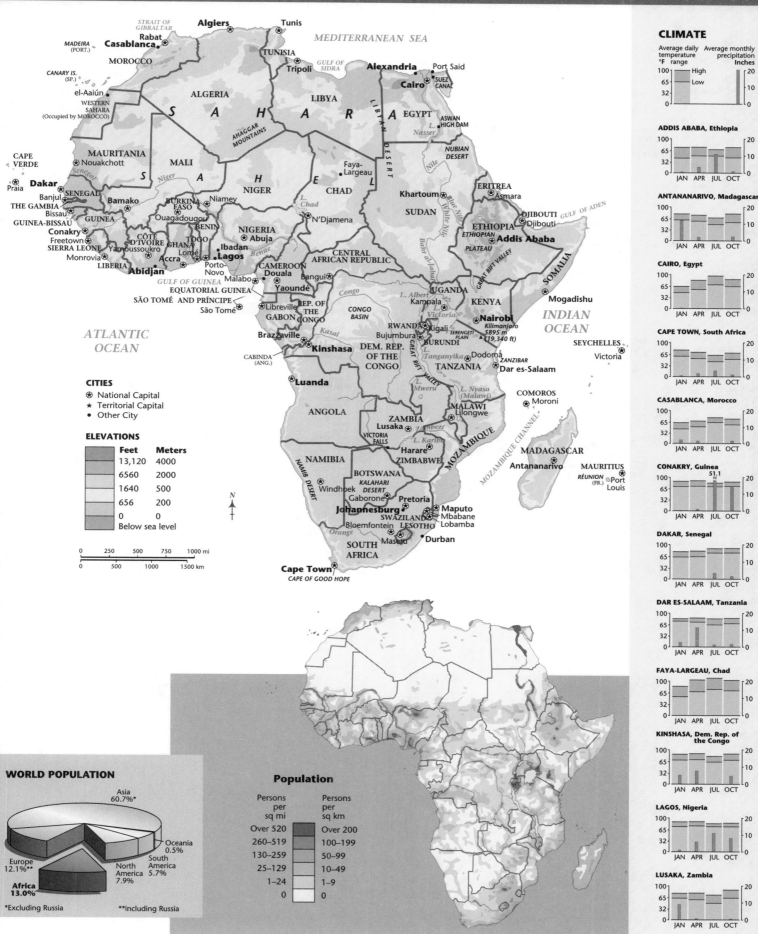

CLIMATE

Average daily temperature °F range

Average monthly precipitation Inches

High
Low

ADDIS ABABA, Ethiopia

JAN APR JUL OCT

ANTANANARIVO, Madagascar

JAN APR JUL OCT

CAIRO, Egypt

JAN APR JUL OCT

CAPE TOWN, South Africa

JAN APR JUL OCT

CASABLANCA, Morocco

JAN APR JUL OCT

CONAKRY, Guinea

51.1

JAN APR JUL OCT

DAKAR, Senegal

JAN APR JUL OCT

DAR ES-SALAAM, Tanzania

JAN APR JUL OCT

FAYA-LARGEAU, Chad

JAN APR JUL OCT

KINSHASA, Dem. Rep. of the Congo

JAN APR JUL OCT

LAGOS, Nigeria

JAN APR JUL OCT

LUSAKA, Zambia

JAN APR JUL OCT

CITIES

⊛ National Capital
★ Territorial Capital
• Other City

ELEVATIONS

Feet	Meters
13,120	4000
6560	2000
1640	500
656	200
0	0
Below sea level	

0 250 500 750 1000 mi
0 500 1000 1500 km

WORLD POPULATION

Asia 60.7%*
Oceania 0.5%
South America 5.7%
North America 7.9%
Europe 12.1%**
Africa 13.0%

*Excluding Russia   **Including Russia

Population

Persons per sq mi	Persons per sq km
Over 520	Over 200
260–519	100–199
130–259	50–99
25–129	10–49
1–24	1–9
0	0

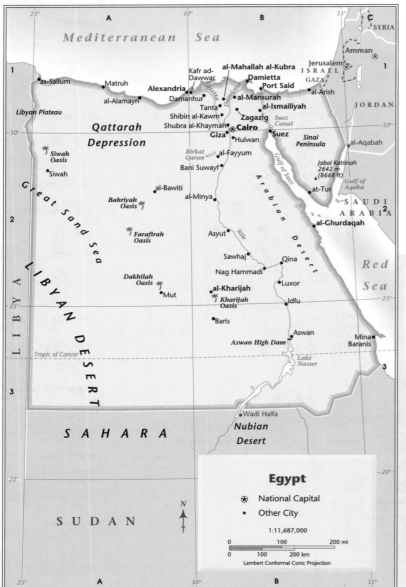

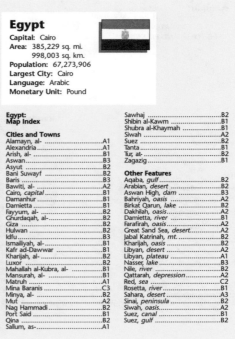

Egypt

Capital: Cairo
Area: 385,229 sq. mi.
998,003 sq. km.
Population: 67,273,906
Largest City: Cairo
Language: Arabic
Monetary Unit: Pound

Egypt:
Map Index

Cities and Towns
Alamayn, al- A1
Alexandria A1
Arish, al- B1
Aswan B3
Asyut B2
Bani Suwayf B2
Baris B3
Bawiti, al- A2
Cairo, *capital* B1
Damanhur B1
Damietta B1
Fayyum, al- B2
Ghurdaqah, al- B2
Giza B1
Hulwan B2
Idfu B2
Ismailiyah, al- B1
Kafr ad-Dawwar B1
Kharijah, al- B2
Luxor B2
Mahallah al-Kubra, al- B1
Mansurah, al- B1
Matruh A1
Mina Baranis C3
Minya, al- B2
Mut A2
Nag Hammadi B2
Port Said B1
Qina B2
Sallum, as- A1

Sawhaj B2
Shibin al-Kawm B1
Shubra al-Khaymah B1
Siwah A2
Suez B1
Tanta B1
Tur, at- B2
Zagazig B1

Other Features
Aqaba, *gulf* B2
Arabian, *desert* B2
Aswan High, *dam* B3
Bahriyah, *oasis* A2
Birkat Qarun, *lake* B2
Dakhilah, *oasis* A2
Damietta, *river* B1
Farafirah, *oasis* A2
Great Sand Sea, *desert* A2
Jabal Katrinah, *mt.* B2
Kharijah, *oasis* B2
Libyan, *desert* A2
Libyan, *plateau* A1
Nasser, *lake* B3
Nile, *river* B2
Qattarah, *depression* A2
Red, *sea* C2
Rosetta, *river* B1
Sahara, *desert* A3
Sinai, *peninsula* B2
Siwah, *oasis* A2
Suez, *canal* B1
Suez, *gulf* B2

Libya

Capital: Tripoli
Area: 679,359 sq. mi.
1,759,997 sq. km.
Population: 4,992,838
Largest City: Tripoli
Language: Arabic
Monetary Unit: Dinar

Libya:
Map Index

Cities and Towns
Ajdabiya D1
Awbari B2
Bani Walid B1
Bayda, al- D1
Benghazi D1
Birak B2
Darnah D1
Ghadamis A1
Gharyan B1
Ghat B3
Jaghbub, al- D2
Jalu D2
Jawf, al- D3
Khums, al- B1
Marj, al- D1
Marsa al-Burayqah C1
Misurata B1
Murzuq B2
Qaryah ash-Sharqiyah, al- B1

Qatrun, al- B3
Sabha B2
Surt C1
Tobruk D1
Tripoli, *capital* B1
Uwaynat, al- B2
Waddan C2
Yafran B1
Zillah C2
Zuwarah B1

Other Features
Bette, *mt.* C3
Cyrenaica, *region* D2
Fezzan, *region* B2
Hamra, al-, *plateau* B1
Haruj al-Aswad, *hills* C2
Jabal Akakus, *mts.* B2
Jabal al-Uwaynat, *mt.* D3
Libyan, *desert* D2
Sahara, *desert* C2
Sidra, *gulf* C1
Tripolitania, *region* B1

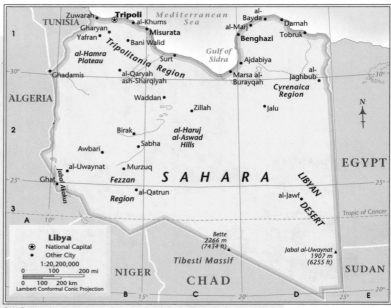

© MapQuest.com, Inc.

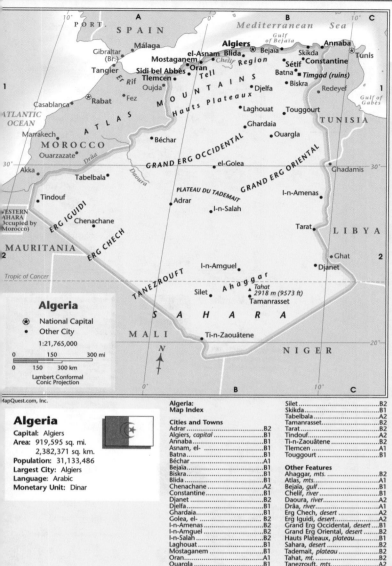

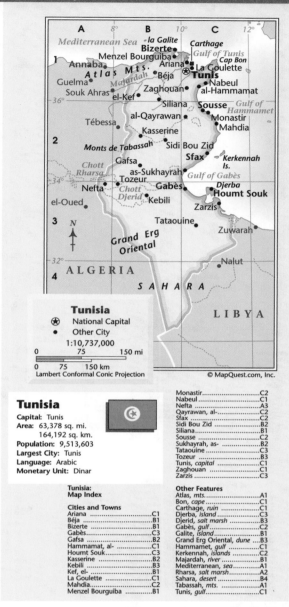

Algeria

Capital: Algiers
Area: 919,595 sq. mi.
2,382,371 sq. km.
Population: 31,133,486
Largest City: Algiers
Language: Arabic
Monetary Unit: Dinar

Algeria: Map Index

Cities and Towns

Adrar	B2
Algiers, *capital*	B1
Annaba	B1
Asnam, el-	B1
Batna	B1
Béchar	A1
Bejaïa	B1
Biskra	B1
Blida	B1
Chenachane	A2
Constantine	B1
Djanet	B2
Djelfa	B1
Ghardaia	B1
Golea, el-	B2
I-n-Amenas	B2
I-n-Amguel	B2
I-n-Salah	B2
Laghouat	B1
Mostaganem	B1
Oran	A1
Ouargla	B1
Sétif	B1
Sidi bel Abbès	A1
Silet	B2
Skikda	B1
Tabelbala	A2
Tamanrasset	B2
Tarat	B2
Tindouf	A2
Ti-n-Zaouâtene	A2
Tlemcen	A1
Touggourt	B1

Other Features

Ahaggar, *mts.*	B2
Atlas, *mts.*	A1
Bejaïa, *gulf*	B1
Chelif, *river*	B1
Daoura, *river*	A2
Drâa, *river*	A1
Erg Chech, *desert*	A2
Erg Iguidi, *desert*	A2
Grand Erg Occidental, *desert*	B1
Grand Erg Oriental, *desert*	B2
Hauts Plateaux, *plateau*	B1
Sahara, *desert*	B2
Tademait, *plateau*	B2
Tahat, *mt.*	B2
Tanezrouft, *mts.*	A2
Tell Region, *region*	B1
Timgad, *ruins*	B1

Tunisia

Capital: Tunis
Area: 63,378 sq. mi.
164,192 sq. km.
Population: 9,513,603
Largest City: Tunis
Language: Arabic
Monetary Unit: Dinar

Tunisia: Map Index

Cities and Towns

Ariana	C1
Béja	B1
Bizerte	B1
Gabès	C3
Gafsa	B2
Hammamat, al-	C1
Houmt Souk	C3
Kasserine	B2
Kebili	B3
Kef, el-	B1
La Goulette	C1
Mahdia	C2
Menzel Bourguiba	B1
Monastir	C2
Nabeul	C1
Nefta	A3
Qayrawan, al-	B2
Sfax	B2
Sidi Bou Zid	B2
Siliana	B1
Sousse	B2
Sukhayrah, as-	B2
Tataouine	C3
Tozeur	B3
Tunis, *capital*	C1
Zaghouan	C1
Zarzis	C3

Other Features

Atlas, *mts.*	A1
Bon, *cape*	C1
Carthage, *ruin*	C1
Djerba, *island*	C3
Djerid, *salt marsh*	B3
Gabès, *gulf*	C2
Galite, *island*	B1
Grand Erg Oriental, *dune*	B3
Hammamet, *gulf*	C1
Kerkennah, *islands*	C2
Majardah, *river*	B1
Mediterranean, *sea*	A1
Rharsa, *salt marsh*	A2
Sahara, *desert*	B4
Tabassah, *mts.*	A1
Tunis, *gulf*	C1

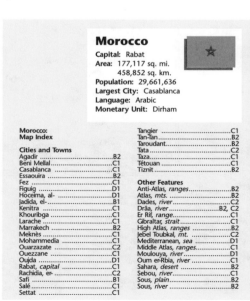

Morocco

Capital: Rabat
Area: 177,117 sq. mi.
458,852 sq. km.
Population: 29,661,636
Largest City: Casablanca
Language: Arabic
Monetary Unit: Dirham

Morocco: Map Index

Cities and Towns

Agadir	B2
Beni Mellal	C1
Casablanca	C1
Essaouira	B2
Fez	C1
Figuig	D1
Hoceima, al-	D1
Jadida, el-	B1
Kenitra	C1
Khouribga	C1
Larache	C1
Marrakech	B2
Meknès	C1
Mohammedia	C1
Ouarzazate	C2
Ouezzane	C1
Oujda	D1
Rabat, *capital*	C1
Rachidia, er-	C2
Safi	B1
Salé	C1
Settat	C1
Tangier	C1
Tan-Tan	B2
Taroudant	B2
Tata	C2
Taza	C1
Tétouan	C1
Tiznit	B2

Other Features

Anti-Atlas, *ranges*	B2
Atlas, *mts.*	C1
Dades, *river*	C2
Drâa, *river*	B2, C2
Er Rif, *range*	C1
Gibraltar, *strait*	C1
High Atlas, *ranges*	B2
Jebel Toubkal, *mt.*	C2
Mediterranean, *sea*	D1
Middle Atlas, *ranges*	C1
Moulouya, *river*	D1
Oum er-Rbia, *river*	C1
Sahara, *desert*	B2
Sebou, *river*	C1
Sous, *plain*	B2
Sous, *river*	B2

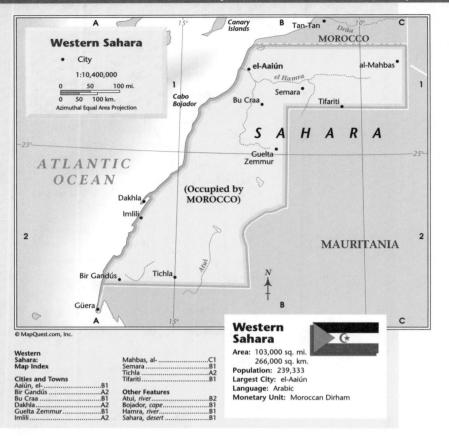

Western Sahara

- City

1:10,400,000

0 50 100 mi.
0 50 100 km.
Azimuthal Equal Area Projection

© MapQuest.com, Inc.

Western Sahara: Map Index

Cities and Towns

Aaiún, el-	B1
Bir Gandús	A2
Bu Craa	B1
Dakhla	A2
Guelta Zemmur	B1
Imlili	A2

Other Features

Mahbas, al-	C1
Semara	B1
Tichla	A2
Tifariti	B1
Atui, river	B2
Bojador, cape	B1
Hamra, river	B1
Sahara, desert	B1

Western Sahara

Area: 103,000 sq. mi.
266,000 sq. km.
Population: 239,333
Largest City: el-Aaiún
Language: Arabic
Monetary Unit: Moroccan Dirham

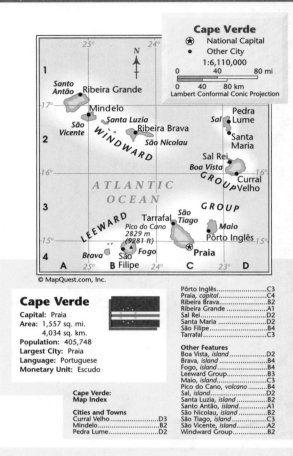

Cape Verde

- National Capital
- Other City

1:6,110,000

0 40 80 mi.
0 40 80 km.
Lambert Conformal Conic Projection

© MapQuest.com, Inc.

Cape Verde

Capital: Praia
Area: 1,557 sq. mi.
4,034 sq. km.
Population: 405,748
Largest City: Praia
Language: Portuguese
Monetary Unit: Escudo

Cape Verde: Map Index

Cities and Towns

Curral Velho	D3
Mindelo	B2
Pedra Lume	D2

Pôrto Inglês	C3
Praia, capital	C4
Ribeira Brava	B2
Ribeira Grande	A1
Sal Rei	D2
Santa Maria	D2
São Filipe	B4
Tarrafal	C3

Other Features

Boa Vista, island	D2
Brava, island	B4
Fogo, island	B4
Leeward Group	B3
Maio, island	C3
Pico do Cano, volcano	B4
Sal, island	D2
Santa Luzia, island	B2
Santo Antão, island	A1
São Nicolau, island	B2
São Tiago, island	C3
São Vicente, island	A2
Windward Group	B2

Mali: Map Index

Cities and Towns

Ansongo	D2
Bafoulabé	A3
Bamako, capital	B3
Bougouni	B3
Bourem	C2
Djenné	C2
Gao	C2
Goundam	C2
Kayes	A3
Kidal	D2
Kita	B3
Koulikoro	B3
Koutiala	B3
Ménaka	D2
Mopti	C3
Niono	B3
Nioro du Sahel	B2

San	C3
Ségou	B3
Sikasso	B3
Taoudenni	C1
Tessalit	D1
Timbuktu	C2

Other Features

Adrar des Iforas, massif	D2
Azaouâd, region	C2
Bani, river	B3
Baoulé, river	B3
Djouf, el-, desert	B1
Erg Chech, desert	C1
Hombori, mts.	C2
Hombori Tondo, mt.	C2
Niger, river	B3
Sahara, desert	C1
Sahel, region	C2
Senegal, river	A3

Mali

Capital: Bamako
Area: 482,077 sq. mi.
1,248,904 sq. km.
Population: 10,429,124
Largest City: Bamako
Language: French
Monetary Unit: Franc

Mauritania

Capital: Nouakchott
Area: 398,000 sq. mi.
1,031,088 sq. km.
Population: 2,581,738
Largest City: Nouakchott
Languages: Arabic, Wolof
Monetary Unit: Ouguiya

Mauritania

- National Capital
- Other City

1:2,350,000

0 150 300 mi.
0 150 300 km.
Lambert Conformal Conic Projection

© MapQuest.com, Inc.

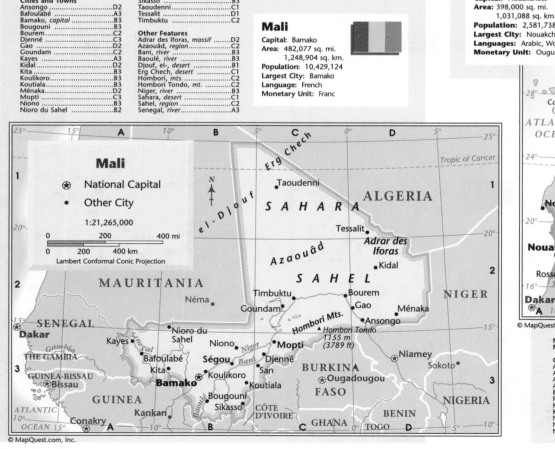

Mali

- National Capital
- Other City

1:21,265,000

0 200 400 mi.
0 200 400 km.
Lambert Conformal Conic Projection

© MapQuest.com, Inc.

Mauritania: Map Index

Cities and Towns

Akjoujt	B3
Aleg	B3
Atâr	B2
Ayoûn el-Atroûs	C3
Bîr Mogreïn	B1
Fdérik	B2
Kaédi	B3
Kiffa	C3
Néma	C3
Nouadhibou	A2
Nouakchott, capital	A3

Ouadane	C2
Rosso	B3
Sélibaby	B4
Tichit	C3
Tidjikdja	C3
Zouîrât	B2

Other Features

Adrar, region	B2
Djouf, el-, desert	C3
Erg Iguidi, desert	D1
Sahara, desert	C1
Senegal, river	B3
Tagânt, region	C3

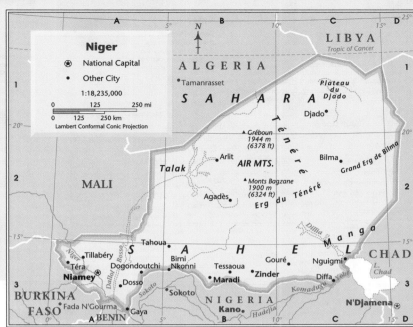

Niger: Map Index

Cities and Towns
Agadès	B2
Arlit	B2
Bilma	C2
Birni Nkonni	B3
Diffa	C3
Djado	C1
Dogondoutchi	A3
Dosso	A3
Gaya	A3
Gouré	C3
Maradi	B3
Nguigmi	C3
Niamey, capital	A3
Tahoua	B3
Téra	A3
Tessaoua	B3
Tillabéry	A3
Zinder	B3

Other Features
Air, mts.	B2
Bagzane, mt.	B2
Chad, lake	C3
Dallol Bosso, river	A3
Dillia, river	C2
Djado, plateau	C1
Erg du Ténéré, desert	B2
Grand Erg de Bilma, desert	C2
Gréboun, mt.	B1
Komadugu Yobe, river	C3
Manga, region	C2
Niger, river	A3
Sahara, desert	A1
Sahel, region	A3
Talak, region	B2
Ténéré, desert	C1

Niger

Capital: Niamey
Area: 497,000 sq. mi.
 1,287,565 sq. km.
Population: 9,962,242
Largest City: Niamey
Language: French
Monetary Unit: CFA franc

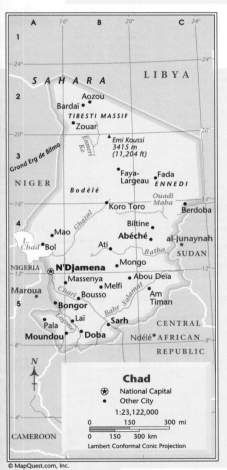

Chad

Capital: N'Djamena
Area: 495,755 sq. mi.
 1,248,339 sq. km.
Population: 7,557,436
Largest City: N'Djamena
Languages: French, Arabic
Monetary Unit: CFA franc

Chad: Map Index

Cities and Towns
Abéché	C4
Abou Deïa	B5
Am Timan	C5
Aozou	B2
Ati	B4
Bardaï	B2
Berdoba	C4
Biltine	C4
Bol	A4
Bongor	B5
Bousso	B5
Doba	B5
Fada	C3
Faya-Largeau	B3
Koro Toro	B4
Laï	B5
Mao	A4
Massenya	B5
Melfi	B4
Mongo	B4
Moundou	A5
N'Djamena, capital	A4
Pala	A5
Sarh	B5
Zouar	B2

Other Features
Bahr Salamat, river	B5
Batha, river	C4
Bodélé, depression	B3
Chad, lake	A4
Chari, river	A5
Emi Koussi, mt.	B3
Ennedi, plateau	C3
Enneri Ke, river	B3
Ghazal, river	B4
Grand Erg de Bilma, desert	A3
Logone, river	A5
Ouadi Maba, river	C4
Sahara, desert	A2
Tibesti, massif	B2

Sudan: Map Index

Cities and Towns
Atbarah	C2
Babanusah	B3
Damazin, ad-	C3
Dunqulah	C1
Fashir, al-	B2
Halaib	D1
Juba	C4
Junaynah, al-	A2
Kaduqli	B3
Kassala	D2
Khartoum, capital	C2
Khartoum North	C2
Khashm al-Qirbah	C2
Kuraymah	C1
Kusti	C2
Malakal	C3
Nuhud, an-	B2
Nyala	B2
Omdurman	C2
Pibor Post	C3
Port Sudan	D1
Qadarif, al-	C2
Rumbek	B3
Sannar	C2
Ubayyid, al-	C2
Wadi Halfa	C1
Wad Madani	C2
Waw	B3
Yambio	B4

Other Features
Akobo, river	C3
Atbarah, river	C2
Bahr al-Arab, river	B3
Bahr al-Ghazal, river	C3
Bahr al-Jabal, river	C3
Blue Nile, river	C2
Kangen, river	C3
Kinyeti, mt.	C4
Libyan, desert	B1
Lol, river	B3
Nasser, lake	C1
Nile, river	C1, C2
Nuba, mts.	B3
Nubian, desert	C1
Red, sea	D1
Red Sea, hills	D1
Sobat, river	C3
Sudd, region	B3
Sue, river	B3
Wadi al-Malik, river	B2
Wadi Howar, river	B2
White Nile, river	C3

Sudan

Capital: Khartoum
Area: 966,757 sq. mi.
 2,530,459 sq. km.
Population: 34,475,690
Largest City: Khartoum
Language: Arabic
Monetary Unit: Pound

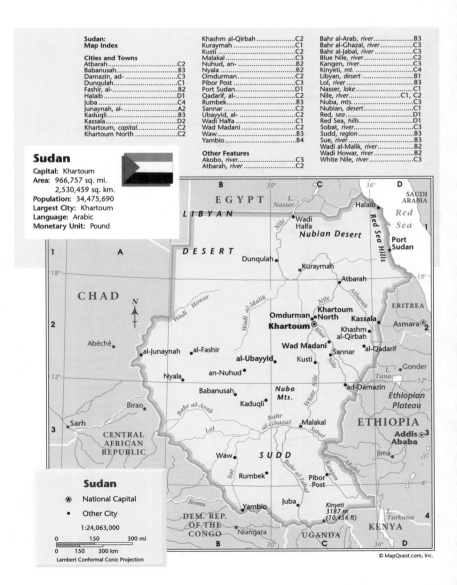

© MapQuest.com, Inc.

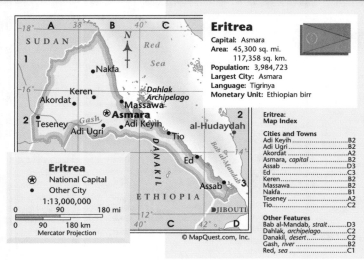

Eritrea

Capital: Asmara
Area: 45,300 sq. mi.
117,358 sq. km.
Population: 3,984,723
Largest City: Asmara
Language: Tigrinya
Monetary Unit: Ethiopian birr

Eritrea
⊛ National Capital
• Other City
1:13,000,000
0   90   180 mi
0   90   180 km
Mercator Projection

Eritrea:
Map Index

Cities and Towns
Adi Keyih B2
Adi Ugri B2
Akordat A2
Asmara, capital B2
Assab D3
Ed C3
Keren B2
Massawa B2
Nakfa B1
Teseney A2
Tio C2

Other Features
Bab al-Mandab, strait D3
Dahlak, archipelago C2
Danakil, desert C2
Gash, river B2
Red, sea C1

© MapQuest.com, Inc.

Djibouti

⊛ National Capital
• Other City
1:5,500,000
0   25   50 mi
0   25   50 km
Transverse Mercator Proj.

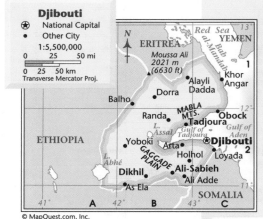

Djibouti:
Map Index

Cities and Towns
Alayli Dadda B1
Ali Adde B2
Ali-Sabieh B2
Arta B2
As Ela B2
Balho B1
Dikhil B2
Djibouti, capital B1
Dorra B1
Holhol B2
Khor Angar C1
Loyada C2
Obock C2
Randa B1
Tadjoura B2
Yoboki B2

Other Features
Abhé, lake A2
Aden, gulf C2
Assal, lake B2
Bab al-Mandab, strait C1
Gaggade, plain B2
Mabla, mts. B1
Moussa Ali, mt. B1
Red, sea C1
Tadjoura, gulf B2

© MapQuest.com, Inc.

Djibouti

Capital: Djibouti
Area: 8,950 sq. mi.
23,187 sq. km.
Population: 447,439
Largest City: Djibouti
Languages: Cushitic languages
Monetary Unit: Franc

Ethiopia
⊛ National Capital
• Other City
1:15,053,000
0   100   200 mi
0   100   200 km
Mercator Projection

Ethiopia

Capital: Addis Ababa
Area: 437,794 sq. mi.
1,134,181 sq. km.
Population: 59,680,383
Largest City: Addis Ababa
Language: Amharic
Monetary Unit: Birr

© MapQuest.com, Inc.

Somalia:
Map Index

Cities and Towns
Baraawe A3
Baydhabo A3
Beledweyne B3
Benderbeyla C2
Berbera B1
Boosaaso B1
Burco B2
Ceerigaabo B1
Dhuusamareeb B2
Eyl B2
Gaalkacyo B2
Garoowe B2
Hargeysa B2
Hobyo B2
Jamaame A3
Jawhar B3
Jilib A3
Kismayu A4
Luuq A3
Marka A3
Mogadishu, capital B3
Qardho B2
Xuddur A3

Other Features
Aden, gulf B1
Gees Gwardafuy, cape C1
Juba, river A3
Nugaal, valley B2
Raas Xaafun, cape C1
Surud Ad, mt. B1
Webi Shabeelle, river B3

Somalia

Capital: Mogadishu
Area: 246,300 sq. mi.
638,083 sq. km.
Population: 7,140,643
Largest City: Mogadishu
Language: Somali, Arabic
Monetary Unit: Shilling

Somalia
⊛ National Capital
• Other City
1:22,100,000
0   150   300 mi
0   150   300 km
Miller Cylindrical Projection

© MapQuest.com, Inc.

Ethiopia:
Map Index

Cities and Towns
Addis Ababa, capital C2
Adwa C1
Arba Minch B3
Asela C3
Asosa B2
Awasa C3
Bahir Dar B2
Debre Birhan C2
Debre Markos B2
Degeh Bur D2
Dese C2
Dire Dawa D2
Goba C3
Gonder B1
Gore B2
Harer D2
Imi D3
Jima B3
Mekele C1
Nazret C3
Negele C3
Nekemte B2
Shewa Gimira B3
Weldiya C2
Werder D3

Other Features
Abaya, lake B3
Abhe, lake C2
Akobo, river A3
Atbara, river B1
Awash, river C2
Baro, river B2
Blue Nile, river B2
Choke, mts. B2
Dawa, river C3
Denakil, desert C1
Dinder, river B1
Ethiopian, plateau C2
Genale, river C3
Great Rift, valley C3
Ogaden, region C3
Omo, river B3
Provisional
Administrative Line D3
Ras Dashen, mt. C1
Tana, lake B1
Tekeze, river B1
Turkana, lake A3
Wabe Gestro, river C3
Wabe Shebele, river C3
Ziway, lake C3

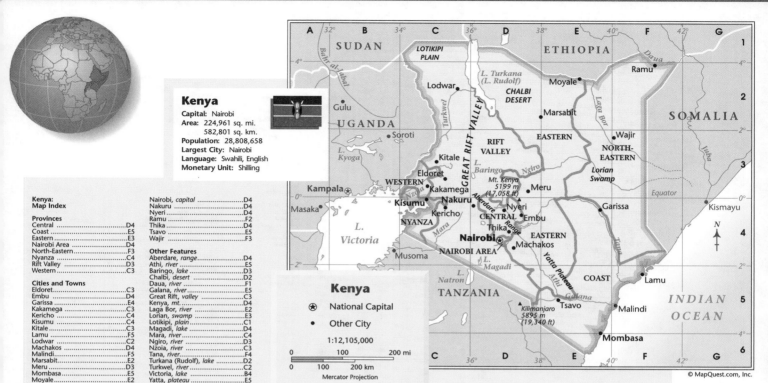

Kenya

Capital: Nairobi
Area: 224,961 sq. mi.
582,801 sq. km.
Population: 28,808,658
Largest City: Nairobi
Language: Swahili, English
Monetary Unit: Shilling

Kenya:
Map Index

Provinces
Central	D4
Coast	E5
Eastern	E3
Nairobi Area	D4
North-Eastern	F3
Nyanza	C4
Rift Valley	D3
Western	C3

Cities and Towns
Eldoret	C3
Embu	D4
Garissa	E4
Kakamega	C3
Kericho	C4
Kisumu	C4
Kitale	C3
Lamu	F5
Lodwar	C2
Machakos	D4
Malindi	F5
Marsabit	E2
Meru	D3
Mombasa	E5
Moyale	E2

Nairobi, *capital*	D4
Nakuru	D4
Nyeri	D4
Ramu	F2
Thika	D4
Tsavo	E5
Wajir	F3

Other Features
Aberdare, *range*	D4
Athi, *river*	E5
Baringo, *lake*	D3
Chalbi, *desert*	D2
Daua, *river*	F1
Galana, *river*	E5
Great Rift, *valley*	C3
Kenya, *mt.*	D4
Laga Bor, *river*	E3
Lorian, *swamp*	E3
Lotikipi, *plain*	C1
Magadi, *lake*	D4
Mara, *river*	C4
Ngiro, *river*	D3
Nzoia, *river*	C3
Tana, *river*	F4
Turkana (Rudolf), *lake*	D2
Turkwel, *river*	C2
Victoria, *lake*	B4
Yatta, *plateau*	E5

Kenya

⊛ National Capital
• Other City

1:12,105,000

0   100   200 mi
0   100   200 km
Mercator Projection

© MapQuest.com, Inc.

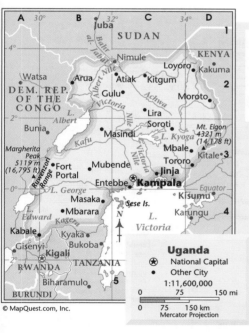

Uganda

Capital: Kampala
Area: 93,070 sq. mi.
241,114 sq. km.
Population: 22,804,973
Largest City: Kampala
Language: English
Monetary Unit: Shilling

Uganda:
Map Index

Cities and Towns
Arua	B2
Atiak	C2
Entebbe	C3
Fort Portal	B3
Gulu	C2
Jinja	C3
Kabale	A4
Kampala, *capital*	C3
Kitgum	C2
Lira	C2
Loyoro	D2
Masaka	B4
Masindi	B3
Mbale	D3
Mbarara	B4
Moroto	D2

Mubende	B3
Soroti	C3
Tororo	D3

Other Features
Achwa, *river*	C2
Albert, *lake*	B3
Albert Nile, *river*	B2
Bahr al-Jabal, *river*	B2
Edward, *lake*	A4
Elgon, *mt.*	D3
George, *lake*	B4
Kafu, *river*	B3
Kagera, *river*	B4
Kyoga, *lake*	C3
Margherita, *peak*	A3
Ruwenzori, *range*	B3
Sese, *islands*	C4
Victoria, *lake*	C4
Victoria Nile, *river*	B2, C3

Uganda

⊛ National Capital
• Other City

1:11,600,000

0   75   150 mi
0   75   150 km
Mercator Projection

© MapQuest.com, Inc.

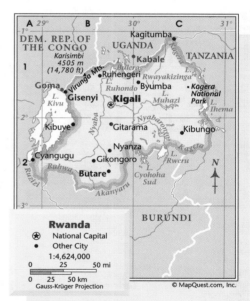

Rwanda

⊛ National Capital
• Other City

1:4,624,000

0   25   50 mi
0   25   50 km
Gauss-Krüger Projection

© MapQuest.com, Inc.

Rwanda

Capital: Kigali
Area: 10,169 sq. mi.
26,345 sq. km.
Population: 8,154,933
Largest City: Kigali
Languages: French, Kinyarwanda
Monetary Unit: Franc

Burundi

⊛ National Capital
• Other City

1:6,548,000

0   50   100 mi
0   50   100 km
Conic Equidistant Projection

© MapQuest.com, Inc.

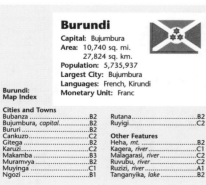

Burundi

Capital: Bujumbura
Area: 10,740 sq. mi.
27,824 sq. km.
Population: 5,735,937
Largest City: Bujumbura
Languages: French, Kirundi
Monetary Unit: Franc

Burundi:
Map Index

Cities and Towns
Bubanza	B2
Bujumbura, *capital*	B2
Bururi	B2
Cankuzo	C2
Gitega	B2
Karuzi	C2
Makamba	B3
Muramvya	B2
Muyinga	C1
Ngozi	B1

Rutana	B2
Ruyigi	C2

Other Features
Heha, *mt.*	B2
Kagera, *river*	C1
Malagarasi, *river*	C2
Ruvubu, *river*	C2
Ruzizi, *river*	A1
Tanganyika, *lake*	B2

Rwanda:
Map Index

Cities and Towns
Butare	B2
Byumba	C1
Cyangugu	A2
Gikongoro	B2
Gisenyi	B1
Gitarama	B2
Kagitumba	C1
Kibungo	C2
Kibuye	B1
Kigali, *capital*	B1
Nyanza	B2
Ruhengeri	B1

Other Features
Akanyaru, *river*	B2

Bulera, *lake*	B1
Cyohoha Sud, *lake*	C2
Ihema, *lake*	C1
Kagera National Park	C1
Kagera, *river*	C1, B1
Karisimbi, *mt.*	B1
Kivu, *lake*	B1
Muhazi, *lake*	C1
Nyaba, *river*	B2
Nyabarongo, *river*	B1
Ruhondo, *lake*	B1
Ruhwa, *river*	B1
Ruzizi, *river*	A2
Rwayakizinga, *lake*	C1
Rweru, *lake*	C2
Virunga, *mts.*	B1

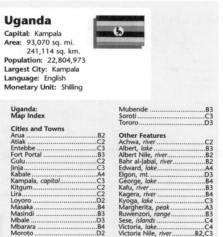

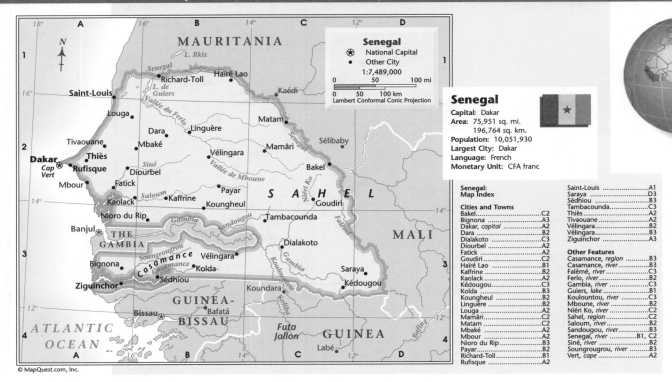

Senegal
Capital: Dakar
Area: 75,951 sq. mi.
  196,764 sq. km.
Population: 10,051,930
Largest City: Dakar
Language: French
Monetary Unit: CFA franc

Senegal:
Map Index

Cities and Towns
Bakel C2
Bignona A3
Dakar, *capital* A2
Dara B2
Dialakoto C3
Diourbel A2
Fatick A2
Goudiri C2
Haïré Lao B1
Kaffrine B2
Kaolack A2
Kédougou C3
Kolda B3
Koungheul B2
Linguère B2
Louga A2
Mamâri C2
Matam C2
Mbaké A2
Mbour A2
Nioro du Rip B3
Payar B2
Richard-Toll B1
Rufisque A2

Saint-Louis A1
Saraya D3
Sédhiou B3
Tambacounda C2
Thiès A2
Tivaouane A2
Vélingara B2
Vélingara B3
Ziguinchor A3

Other Features
Casamance, *region* B3
Casamance, *river* B3
Falémé, *river* C3
Ferlo, *river* B2
Gambia, *river* C3
Guiers, *lake* B1
Koulountou, *river* C3
Mboune, *river* B2
Niéri Ko, *river* C2
Sahel, *region* C2
Saloum, *river* B2
Sandougou, *river* B3
Senegal, *river* B1, C2
Siné, *river* B2
Soungrougrou, *river* B3
Vert, *cape* A2

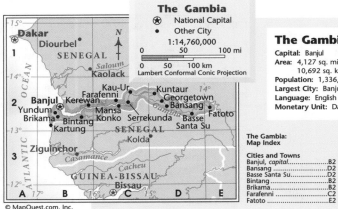

The Gambia
Capital: Banjul
Area: 4,127 sq. mi.
  10,692 sq. km.
Population: 1,336,320
Largest City: Banjul
Language: English
Monetary Unit: Dalasi

The Gambia:
Map Index

Cities and Towns
Banjul, *capital* B2
Bansang D2
Basse Santa Su D2
Bintang B2
Brikama B2
Farafenni C2
Fatoto E2

Georgetown D2
Kartung B2
Kau-Ur C2
Kerewan B2
Kuntaur C2
Mansa Konko C2
Serrekunda C2
Yundum B2

Other Feature
Gambia, *river* D2

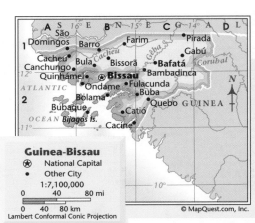

Guinea-Bissau
Capital: Bissau
Area: 13,948 sq. mi.
  36,135 sq. km.
Population: 1,234,555
Largest City: Bissau
Language: Portuguese
Monetary Unit: CFA franc

Guinea-Bissau:
Map Index

Cities and Towns
Bafatá C1
Bambadinca C1
Barro B1
Bissau, *capital* B2
Bissorã B1
Bolama B2
Buba C2
Bubaque B2
Bula B1
Cacheu A1
Cacine B2
Canchungo A1
Catió B2
Farim B1
Fulacunda B2
Gabú C1
Ondame B2
Pirada C1
Quebo C2
Quinhámel B2
São Domingos A1

Other Features
Bijagós, *islands* A2
Cacheu, *river* B1
Corubal, *river* D1
Gêba, *river* C1

Guinea:
Map Index

Cities and Towns
Beyla D3
Conakry, *capital* B3
Coyah B3
Dabola C2
Fria B2
Guéckédou C3
Kailahun C3
Kali C1
Kamsar A2
Kankan D2
Kérouané D3
Kindia B2
Kissidougou C3
Kouroussa D2
Labé B2
Lélouma B2
Macenta D3
Mamou B2
Niagassola D1
Nzérékoré D4
Siguiri D2
Tougué C2
Yomou D4

Other Features
Bafing, *river* C2
Futa Jallon, *plateau* B1
Gambia, *river* C1
Los, *islands* A3
Milo, *river* D3
Niger, *river* D4
Nimba, *mts.* D4
Tinkisso, *river* C2

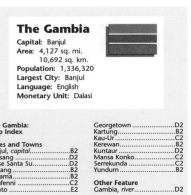

Guinea
Capital: Conakry
Area: 94,926 sq. mi.
  245,922 sq. km.
Population: 7,538,953
Largest City: Conakry
Language: French
Monetary Unit: Guinea franc

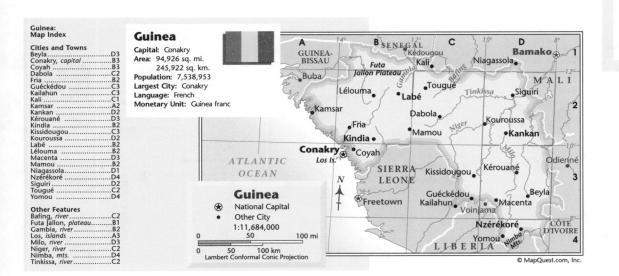

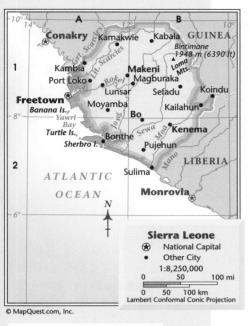

© MapQuest.com, Inc.

Côte d'Ivoire (Ivory Coast)

⊛ National Capital
• Other City

1:9,789,000

0   75   150 mi
0   75   150 km
Lambert Conformal Conic Projection

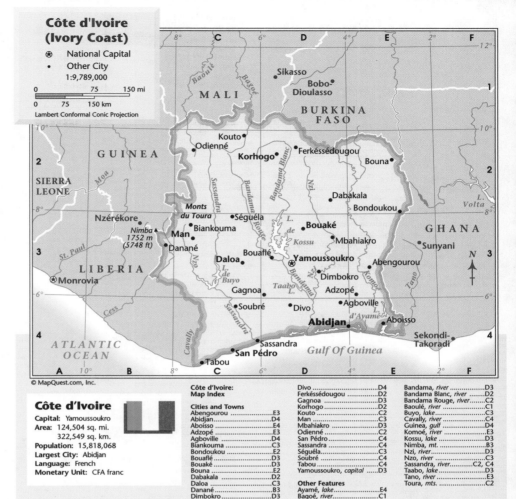

© MapQuest.com, Inc.

Sierra Leone

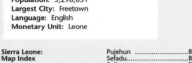

Capital: Freetown
Area: 27,699 sq. mi.
      71,759 sq. km.
Population: 5,296,651
Largest City: Freetown
Language: English
Monetary Unit: Leone

**Sierra Leone:
Map Index**

Cities and Towns

Bo	B2
Bonthe	A2
Freetown, capital	A1
Kabala	B1
Kailahun	B1
Kamakwie	A1
Kambia	A1
Kenema	B2
Koindu	B1
Lunsar	A1
Magburaka	B1
Makeni	B1
Moyamba	A1
Port Loko	A1
Pujehun	B2
Sefadu	B1
Sulima	B2

Other Features

Banana, islands	A1
Bintimane, mt.	B1
Great Scarcies, river	A1
Jong, river	A2
Little Scarcies, river	A1
Loma, mts.	B1
Mano, river	B2
Moa, river	B2
Rokel, river	A1
Sewa, river	B2
Sherbro, island	A2
Turtle, islands	A2
Yawri, bay	A2

Côte d'Ivoire

Capital: Yamoussoukro
Area: 124,504 sq. mi.
      322,549 sq. km.
Population: 15,818,068
Largest City: Abidjan
Language: French
Monetary Unit: CFA franc

**Côte d'Ivoire:
Map Index**

Cities and Towns

Abengourou	E3
Abidjan	D4
Aboisso	E4
Adzopé	D4
Agboville	D4
Biankouma	C3
Bondoukou	E2
Bouaflé	D3
Bouaké	D3
Bouna	E2
Dabakala	D2
Daloa	C3
Danané	B3
Dimbokro	D3

Divo	D4
Ferkéssédougou	D2
Gagnoa	D3
Korhogo	D2
Kouto	C2
Man	C3
Mbahiakro	D3
Odienné	C2
San Pédro	C4
Sassandra	C4
Séguéla	C3
Soubré	C4
Tabou	C4
Yamoussoukro, capital	D3

Other Features

Ayamé, lake	E4
Bagoé, river	C1

Bandama, river	D3
Bandama Blanc, river	D2
Bandama Rouge, river	C2
Baoulé, river	C1
Buyo, lake	C3
Cavally, river	C4
Guinea, gulf	D4
Komoé, river	E3
Kossu, lake	D3
Nimba, mt.	B3
Nzo, river	C3
Sassandra, river	C2, C4
Taabo, lake	D3
Tano, river	E3
Toura, mts.	C2

São Tomé & Príncipe

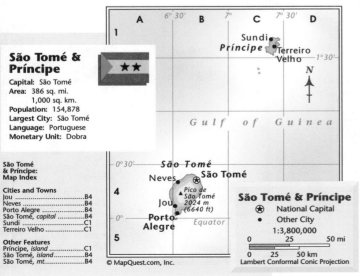

© MapQuest.com, Inc.

Capital: São Tomé
Area: 386 sq. mi.
      1,000 sq. km.
Population: 154,878
Largest City: São Tomé
Language: Portuguese
Monetary Unit: Dobra

**São Tomé
& Príncipe:
Map Index**

Cities and Towns

Jou	B4
Neves	B4
Porto Alegre	B4
São Tomé, capital	B4
Sundi	C1
Terreiro Velho	C1

Other Features

Príncipe, island	C1
São Tomé, island	B4
São Tomé, mt.	B4

São Tomé & Príncipe

⊛ National Capital
• Other City

1:3,800,000

0   25   50 mi
0   25   50 km
Lambert Conformal Conic Projection

Liberia

Capital: Monrovia
Area: 38,250 sq. mi.
      99,093 sq. km.
Population: 2,923,725
Largest City: Monrovia
Language: English
Monetary Unit: Dollar

**Liberia:
Map Index**

Cities and Towns

Buchanan	A3
Gbarnga	B2
Grand Cess	B3
Greenville	B3
Harbel	A2
Harper	C3
Kakata	A2
Monrovia, capital	A2
Nyaake	C3
Plibo	C3
River Cess	B3
Robertsport	A2
Tapeta	B2
Tubmanburg	A2
Voinjama	B1
Yekepa	B2
Zorzor	B2
Zwedru	B2

Other Features

Bomi, hills	A2
Bong, range	A2
Cavalla, river	C3
Cess, river	B3
Dube, river	C3
Makona, river	A1
Mano, river	A2
Mesurado, cape	A2
Moro, river	A2
Nimba, mts.	B2
Palmas, cape	C3
Putu, range	B3
St. Paul, river	A2
Wutivi, mt.	B1

Liberia

⊛ National Capital
• Other City

1:11,221,000

0   60   120 mi
0   60   120 km
Lambert Conformal Conic Projection

© MapQuest.com, Inc.

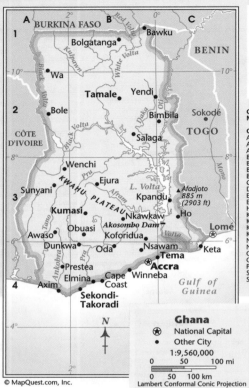

Ghana

Capital: Accra
Area: 92,098 sq. mi.
238,596 sq. km.
Population: 18,887,626
Largest City: Accra
Language: English
Monetary Unit: Cedi

Ghana:
Map Index

Cities and Towns
Accra, capital B4
Awaso A3
Axim A4
Bawku B1
Bimbila C2
Bole A2
Bolgatanga B1
Cape Coast B4
Dunkwa B4
Ejura B3
Elmina B4
Ho C3
Keta C4
Koforidua B3
Kpandu C3
Kumasi B3
Nkawkaw B3
Nsawam B4
Obuasi B3
Oda B4
Prestea A4
Salaga B2
Sekondi-Takoradi B4
Sunyani A3
Tamale B2
Tema C4
Wa A1
Wenchi A3
Winneba B4
Yendi B2

Other Features
Afadjoto, mt. C3
Afram, river B3
Akosombo, dam C3
Ankobra, river A4
Black Volta, river A2
Daka, river B2
Guinea, gulf C3
Kulpawn, river B1
Kwahu, plateau B3
Oti, river C2
Pra, river B4
Pru, river B3
Red Volta, river B1
Tano, river A3
Volta, lake. C3
Volta, river C3
White Volta, river B1

Ghana

⊛ National Capital
● Other City
1:9,560,000

0   50   100 mi
0 50 100 km
Lambert Conformal Conic Projection

© MapQuest.com, Inc.

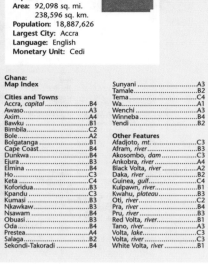

Burkina Faso

⊛ National Capital
● Other City
1:14,785,000

0   100   200 mi
0 100 200 km
Lambert Conformal Conic Projection

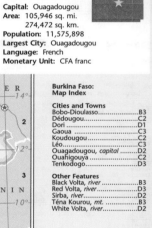

Burkina Faso

Capital: Ouagadougou
Area: 105,946 sq. mi.
274,472 sq. km.
Population: 11,575,898
Largest City: Ouagadougou
Language: French
Monetary Unit: CFA franc

Burkina Faso:
Map Index

Cities and Towns
Bobo-Dioulasso B3
Dédougou C2
Dori D1
Gaoua C3
Koudougou C2
Léo C3
Ouagadougou, capital D2
Ouahigouya C2
Tenkodogo D3

Other Features
Black Volta, river B3
Red Volta, river D2
Sirba, river D2
Téna Kourou, mt. B3
White Volta, river D2

© MapQuest.com, Inc.

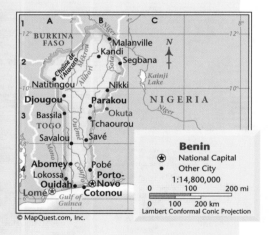

Benin

⊛ National Capital
● Other City
1:14,800,000

0   100   200 mi
0 100 200 km
Lambert Conformal Conic Projection

© MapQuest.com, Inc.

Benin

Capital: Porto-Novo
Area: 43,500 sq. mi.
112,694 sq. km.
Population: 6,305,567
Largest City: Cotonou
Language: French
Monetary Unit: CFA franc

Benin:
Map Index

Cities and Towns
Abomey A4
Bassila A3
Cotonou B4
Djougou A3
Kandi B2
Lokossa A4
Malanville B2
Natitingou A2
Nikki B3
Ouidah B4
Parakou B3
Pobé B4
Porto-Novo, capital B4
Savalou A3
Savé B3
Segbana B2
Tchaourou B3

Other Features
Alibori, river B2
Chaîne de l'Atacora, mts. ...A2
Couffo, river B4
Guinea, gulf A4
Mékrou, river B2
Mono, river A4
Niger, river B1
Ouémé, river B3
Sota, river B2

Togo

Capital: Lomé
Area: 21,925 sq. mi.
56,801 sq. km.
Population: 5,081,413
Largest City: Lomé
Language: French
Monetary Unit: CFA franc

Togo:
Map Index

Cities and Towns
Amlamé B3
Aného B3
Anié B3
Atakpamé B3
Badou B3
Bafilo B2
Bassar B2
Blitta B2
Dapaong B1
Kanté B2
Kara B2
Kpalimé B3
Kpémé B3
Lomé, capital B3
Mango B1
Niamtougou B2
Sokodé B2
Sotouboua B2
Tabligbo B3
Tchamba B2
Tsévié B3

Other Features
Agou, mt. B3
Benin, bight B4
Mono, river B2
Oti, river B1

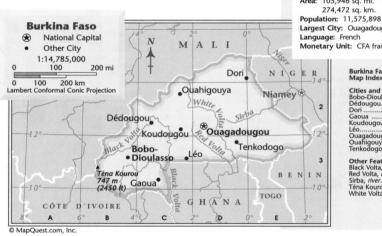

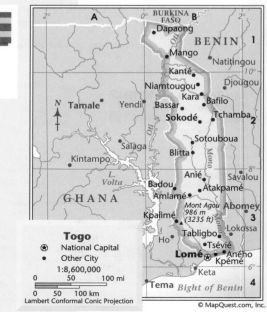

Togo

⊛ National Capital
● Other City
1:8,600,000

0   50   100 mi
0 50 100 km
Lambert Conformal Conic Projection

© MapQuest.com, Inc.

© MapQuest.com, Inc.

Nigeria

⊛ National Capital

• Other City

1:10,667,000

0   100   200 mi

0   100   200 km

Lambert Conformal Conic Projection

Nigeria

Capital: Abuja
Area: 356,669 sq. mi.
    924,013 sq. km.
Population: 113,828,587
Largest City: Lagos
Language: English
Monetary Unit: Naira

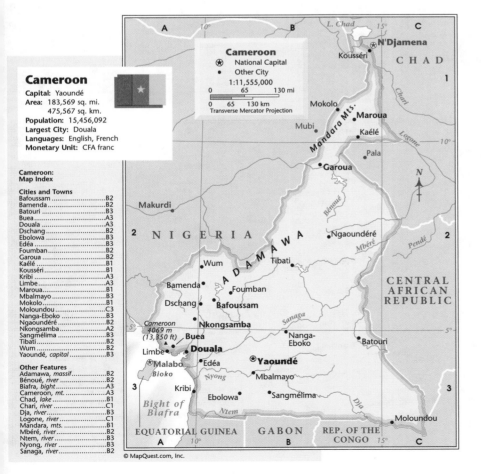

© MapQuest.com, Inc.

Cameroon

⊛ National Capital

• Other City

1:11,555,000

0   65   130 mi

0   65   130 km

Transverse Mercator Projection

Cameroon

Capital: Yaoundé
Area: 183,569 sq. mi.
    475,567 sq. km.
Population: 15,456,092
Largest City: Douala
Languages: English, French
Monetary Unit: CFA franc

Cameroon:
Map Index

Cities and Towns
Bafoussam B2
Bamenda B2
Batouri B3
Buea A3
Douala A3
Dschang B2
Ebolowa B3
Edéa B3
Foumban B2
Garoua B2
Kaélé B1
Kousséri B1
Kribi A3
Limbe A3
Maroua B1
Mbalmayo B3
Mokolo B1
Moloundou C3
Nanga-Eboko B3
Ngaoundéré B2
Nkongsamba B3
Sangmélima B3
Tibati B2
Wum B2
Yaoundé, capital B3

Other Features
Adamawa, massif B2
Bénoué, river B2
Biafra, bight A3
Cameroon, mt. A3
Chari, river B1
Dja, river B3
Logone, river C1
Mandara, mts. B1
Mbéré, river B2
Ntem, river B3
Nyong, river B3
Sanaga, river B2

Nigeria:
Map Index

Cities and Towns
Aba D5
Abakaliki E4
Abeokuta B4
Abuja, capital D3
Ado-Ekiti C4
Afikpo D5
Akure C4
Asaba D4
Awka D4
Azare F2
Bauchi E2
Benin City C4
Bida D3
Birnin Kebbi C1
Biu G2
Bonny D5
Burutu C5
Calabar E5
Damaturu F2
Dutse E2
Ede C4
Enugu D4
Geidam F1
Gombe F2
Gummi C1
Gusau D1
Ibadan B4
Ife C4
Ikeja B4
Ikorodu B4
Ila C3
Ilesha C4
Ilorin C3
Iseyin B4
Iwo C4
Jalingo F3
Jebba C3
Jos E3
Kaduna D2
Kano E1
Katsina D1
Kaura-Namoda D1
Kishi B3
Kontagora C2
Kumo F2
Lafia E3
Lagos B4
Lokoja D4
Maiduguri G2

Makurdi E4
Minna D3
Mubi G2
Mushin B4
Nguru F1
Nsukka D4
Offa C3
Ogbomosho C4
Okene D4
Ondo C4
Onitsha D4
Oron E5
Oshogbo C4
Owerri D5
Oyo B4
Port Harcourt D5
Potiskum F2
Sapele C5
Shaki B3
Sokoto C1
Umuahia D5
Uyo C5
Warri C5
Wukari E4
Yola G3
Zaria D2

Other Features
Adamawa, massif E5
Benin, bight B5
Benue, river E3
Bunsuru, river D1
Chad, lake G1
Cross, river E4
Dimlang, mt. F3
Gongola, river F2
Guinea, gulf B5
Hadejia, river E1
Jos, plateau E2
Ka, river C2
Kaduna, river D2
Kainji, lake C2
Katagum, river E2
Komadugu Gana, river F2
Komadugu Yobe, river F1
Niger, delta C5
Niger, river C2, D5
Oban, hills E5
Ogun, river B3
Osse, river C4
Sokoto, plains C1
Sokoto, river C1
Taraba, river F3

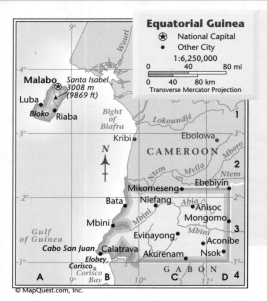

Equatorial Guinea
⊛ National Capital
● Other City
1:6,250,000
0   40   80 mi
0   40   80 km
Transverse Mercator Projection

© MapQuest.com, Inc.

Equatorial Guinea

Capital: Malabo
Area: 10,831 sq. mi.
     28,060 sq. km.
Population: 465,746
Largest City: Malabo
Language: Spanish
Monetary Unit: CFA franc

Equatorial Guinea: Map Index

Cities and Towns
Aconibe C3
Akurenam C3
Añisoc C3
Bata B3
Calatrava B3
Ebebiyín D2
Evinayong C3
Luba A1
Malabo, *capital* A1
Mbini B3
Mikomeseng C2
Mongomo D3

Niefang C3
Nsok D3
Riaba A1

Other Features
Abia, *river* C3
Biafra, *bight* B1
Bioko, *island* A1
Corisco, *bay* B4
Corisco, *island* B4
Elobey, *islands* B3
Guinea, *gulf* A3
Mbini, *river* C3
Mboro, *river* D4
San Juan, *cape* B3
Santa Isabel, *peak* A1

Gabon

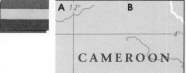

Capital: Libreville
Area: 103,347 sq. mi.
     267,738 sq. km.
Population: 1,225,853
Largest City: Libreville
Language: French
Monetary Unit: CFA franc

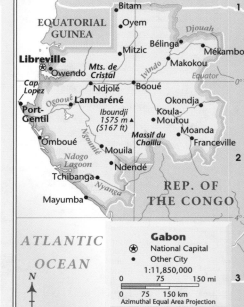

Gabon
⊛ National Capital
● Other City
1:11,850,000
0   75   150 mi
0   75   150 km
Azimuthal Equal Area Projection

© MapQuest.com, Inc.

Gabon: Map Index

Cities and Towns
Bélinga B1
Bitam A1
Booué A2
Franceville B2
Koula-Moutou B2
Lambaréné A2
Libreville, *capital* A1
Makokou B2
Mayumba A2
Mékambo B1
Mitzic A1
Moanda B2
Mouila A2
Ndendé A2
Ndjolé A2

Okondja B2
Omboué A2
Owendo A1
Oyem A1
Port-Gentil A2
Tchibanga A2

Other Features
Chaillu, *mts.* B2
Cristal, *mts.* A1
Djouah, *river* B1
Iboundji, *mt.* A2
Ivindo, *river* B1
Lopez, *cape* A2
Ndogo, *lagoon* A2
Ngounié, *river* A2
Nyanga, *river* A2
Ogooué, *river* A2

Republic of the Congo
⊛ National Capital
● Other City
1:18,000,000
0   100   200 mi
0   100   200 km
Azimuthal Equal Area Projection

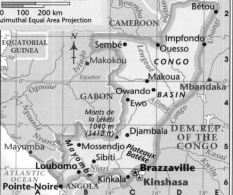

© MapQuest.com, Inc.

Republic of the Congo

Capital: Brazzaville
Area: 132,047 sq. mi.
     342,091 sq. km.
Population: 2,716,814
Largest City: Brazzaville
Language: French
Monetary Unit: CFA franc

Republic of the Congo: Map Index

Cities and Towns
Bétou E2
Brazzaville, *capital* C6
Djambala C5
Ewo C4
Impfondo D3
Kinkala C6
Loubomo B6
Makoua C4
Mossendjo B5
Ouesso D3
Owando C4
Pointe-Noire A6

Sembé C3
Sibiti B5

Other Features
Alima, *river* D4
Batéké, *plateau* C5
Congo, *basin* D3
Congo, *river* D4
Ivindo, *river* B3
Lékéti, *mts.* C5
Lengoué, *river* C3
Mayombé, *massif* B5
Niari, *river* B5
Nyanga, *river* A5
Sangha, *river* D2
Ubangi, *river* E2

Central African Republic (C.A.R.)

Capital: Bangui
Area: 240,324 sq. mi.
     622,601 sq. km.
Population: 3,444,951
Largest City: Bangui
Language: French
Monetary Unit: CFA franc

Central African Republic: Map Index

Cities and Towns
Bambari B2
Bangassou B3
Bangui, *capital* A3
Batangafo A2
Berbérati A3
Birao B1
Bossangoa A2
Bouar A2
Bria B2
Kaga Bandoro A2
Mobaye B3
Ndélé B2
Nola A3
Obo C2
Yalinga B2

Other Features
Chari, *river* A2
Chinko, *river* B2
Gribingui, *river* A2
Kadei, *river* A3
Kotto, *river* B2
Lobaye, *river* A2
Mambéré, *river* A2
Massif des Bongos, *range* B2
Mpoko, *river* A2
Ouaka, *river* B2
Ouarra, *river* C2
Ouham, *river* A2
Pendé, *river* A2
Toussoro, *mt.* B2
Ubangi, *river* A3

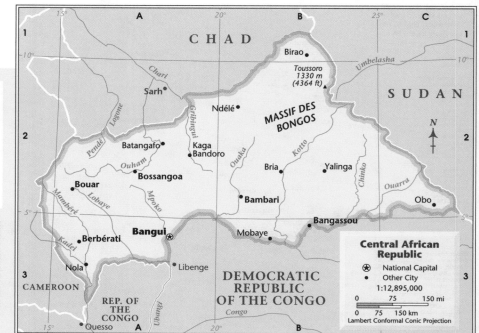

Central African Republic
⊛ National Capital
● Other City
1:12,895,000
0   75   150 mi
0   75   150 km
Lambert Conformal Conic Projection

© MapQuest.com, Inc.

Democratic Republic of the Congo

Capital: Kinshasa
Area: 905,446 sq. mi.
2,345,715 sq. km.
Population: 50,481,305
Largest City: Kinshasa
Language: French
Monetary Unit: Congolese franc

Democratic Republic of the Congo: Map Index

Regions

Bandundu	B2
Bas-Congo	A2
Équateur	B1
Kasai-Occidental	B2
Kasai-Oriental	B2
Katanga	C3
Kinshasa	B2
Maniema	C2
Nord-Kivu	C2
Orientale	C1
Sud-Kivu	C2

Cities and Towns

Banana	A2
Bandundu	B2
Boende	B2
Bolobo	B2
Boma	A2
Bondo	B1
Bukavu	C2
Bumba	B1
Bunia	C1
Buta	C1
Dilolo	B3
Gemena	B1
Goma	C2
Ikela	B2
Ilebo	B2
Inga	A2
Isiro	C1
Kabalo	C2
Kahemba	B2
Kalemie	C2
Kamina	C3
Kananga	B2
Kikwit	B2
Kindu	C2
Kinshasa, capital	A2
Kisangani	C1
Kolwezi	C3
Likasi	C3
Lisala	B1
Lodja	B2
Lubumbashi	C3
Lusambo	B2
Manono	B2
Matadi	A2
Mbandaka	B2
Mbanza-Ngungu	A2
Mbuji-Mayi	B2
Moba	C2
Mwene-Ditu	B2
Tshikapa	B2
Uvira	C2
Watsa	C1
Yangambi	C1

Other Features

Albert, lake	C1
Aruwimi, river	C1
Bomu, river	C1
Congo, river	B1
Congo Basin, region	B1
Edward, lake	C2
Kasai, river	B2
Katanga, plateau	B3
Kivu, lake	C2
Kwa, river	B2
Kwango, river	B2
Lomami, river	C2
Lualaba, river	C3
Luapula, river	C3
Lukuga, river	C2
Luvua, river	C3
Mai-Ndombe, lake	B2
Margherita, peak	C1
Mitumba, mts.	C2
Mweru, lake	C3
Sankuru, river	B2
Tanganyika, lake	C2
Tshuapa, river	B2
Tumba, lake	B2
Ubangi, river	B1
Uele, river	C1
Upemba, lake	C3

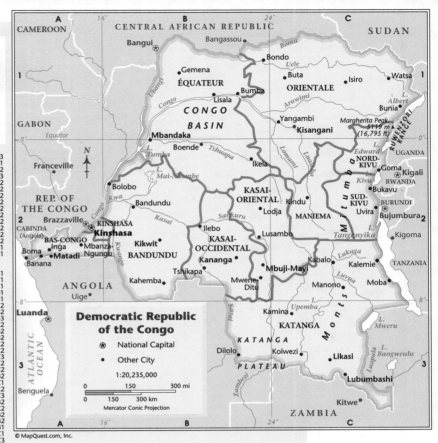

Democratic Republic of the Congo

⊛ National Capital
• Other City

1:20,235,000

| 0 | 150 | 300 mi |
| 0 | 150 | 300 km |

Mercator Conic Projection

© MapQuest.com, Inc.

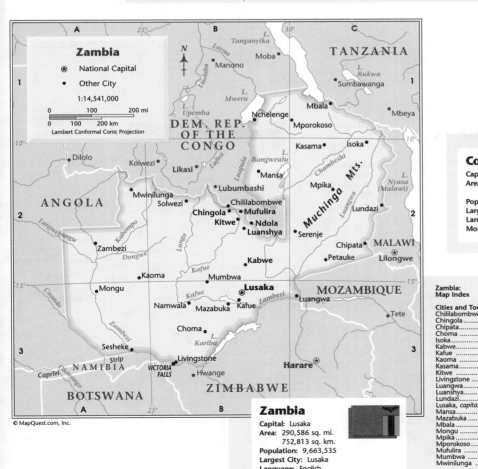

Zambia

⊛ National Capital
• Other City

1:14,541,000

| 0 | 100 | 200 mi |
| 0 | 100 | 200 km |

Lambert Conformal Conic Projection

© MapQuest.com, Inc.

Zambia

Capital: Lusaka
Area: 290,586 sq. mi.
752,813 sq. km.
Population: 9,663,535
Largest City: Lusaka
Language: English
Monetary Unit: Kwacha

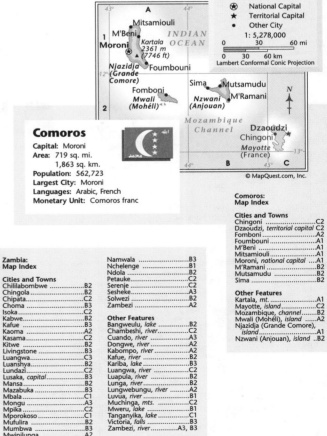

Comoros

⊛ National Capital
★ Territorial Capital
• Other City

1: 5,278,000

| 0 | 30 | 60 mi |
| 0 | 30 | 60 km |

Lambert Conformal Conic Projection

© MapQuest.com, Inc.

Comoros

Capital: Moroni
Area: 719 sq. mi.
1,863 sq. km.
Population: 562,723
Largest City: Moroni
Languages: Arabic, French
Monetary Unit: Comoros franc

Zambia: Map Index

Cities and Towns

Chililabombwe	B2
Chingola	B2
Chipata	C2
Choma	B3
Isoka	C2
Kabwe	B2
Kafue	B3
Kaoma	A2
Kasama	C2
Kitwe	B2
Livingstone	B3
Luangwa	C3
Luanshya	B2
Lundazi	C2
Lusaka, capital	B3
Mansa	B2
Mazabuka	B3
Mbala	C1
Mongu	A3
Mpika	C2
Mporokoso	C1
Mufulira	B2
Mumbwa	B3
Mwinilunga	A2
Namwala	B3
Nchelenge	B1
Ndola	B2
Petauke	C2
Serenje	C2
Sesheke	A3
Solwezi	B2
Zambezi	A2

Other Features

Bangweulu, lake	B2
Chambeshi, river	C2
Cuando, river	A3
Dongwe, river	A2
Kabompo, river	A2
Kafue, river	B3
Kariba, lake	B3
Luangwa, river	C2
Luapula, river	B2
Lunga, river	B2
Lungwebungu, river	A2
Luvua, river	B1
Muchinga, mts.	C2
Mweru, lake	B1
Tanganyika, lake	C1
Victoria, falls	B3
Zambezi, river	A3, B3

Comoros: Map Index

Cities and Towns

Chingoni	C2
Dzaoudzi, territorial capital	C2
Fomboni	A2
Foumbouni	A1
M'Beni	A1
Mitsamiouli	A1
Moroni, national capital	A1
M'Ramani	B2
Mutsamudu	B2
Sima	B2

Other Features

Kartala, mt.	A1
Mayotte, island	C2
Mozambique, channel	B2
Mwali (Mohéli), island	A2
Njazidja (Grande Comore), island	A1
Nzwani (Anjouan), island	B2

Tanzania

⊛ National Capital
● Other City

1:11,000,000

0   100   200 mi
0   100   200 km

Lambert Conformal Conic Projection

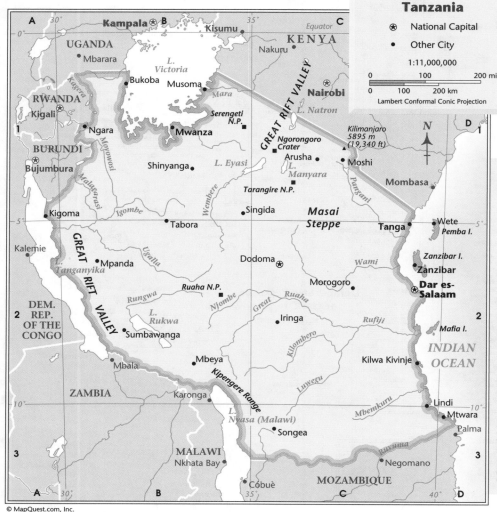

© MapQuest.com, Inc.

Tanzania
Capital: Dar es-Salaam, Dodoma
Area: 364,017 sq. mi.
943,049 sq. km.
Population: 31,270,820
Largest City: Dar es-Salaam
Languages: Swahili, English
Monetary Unit: Shilling

Tanzania:
Map Index

Cities and Towns

Arusha	C1
Bukoba	B1
Dar es-Salaam, *capital*	C2
Dodoma, *capital*	C2
Iringa	C2
Kigoma	A1
Kilwa Kivinje	C2
Lindi	C2
Mbeya	B2
Morogoro	C2
Moshi	C1
Mpanda	B2
Mtwara	D3
Musoma	B1
Mwanza	B1
Ngara	B1
Shinyanga	B1
Singida	B1
Songea	C3
Sumbawanga	B2
Tabora	B2
Tanga	C2
Wete	C1
Zanzibar	C2

Other Features

Eyasi, *lake*	B1
Great Rift, *valley*	B2, C1
Great Ruaha, *river*	C2
Igombe, *river*	B1
Kagera, *river*	B1
Kilimanjaro, *mt.*	C1
Kilombero, *river*	C2
Kipengere, *range*	B2
Luwegu, *river*	C2
Mafia, *island*	C2
Malagarasi, *river*	B1
Manyara, *lake*	C1
Mara, *river*	B1
Masai, *steppe*	C1
Mbemkuru, *river*	C3
Moyowosi, *river*	B1
Natron, *lake*	C1
Ngorongoro, *crater*	C1
Njombe, *river*	B2
Nyasa (Malawi), *lake*	B3
Pangani, *river*	C1
Pemba, *island*	C2
Ruaha Natl. Park	B2
Rufiji, *river*	C2
Rukwa, *lake*	B2
Rungwa, *river*	B2
Ruvuma, *river*	C3
Serengeti Natl. Park	B1
Tanganyika, *lake*	A2
Tarangire Natl. Park	C1
Ugalla, *river*	B2
Victoria, *lake*	B1
Wami, *river*	C2
Wembere, *river*	B1
Zanzibar, *island*	C2

Malawi
Capital: Lilongwe
Area: 45,747 sq. mi.
118,516 sq. km.
Population: 10,000,416
Largest City: Blantyre
Languages: English, Chichewa
Monetary Unit: Kwacha

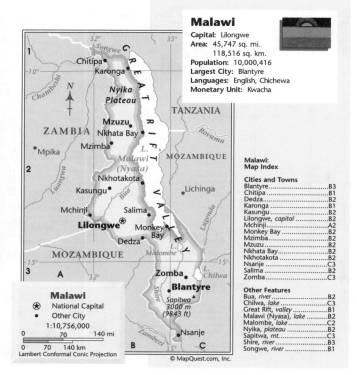

© MapQuest.com, Inc.

Malawi

⊛ National Capital
● Other City

1:10,756,000

0   70   140 mi
0   70   140 km

Lambert Conformal Conic Projection

Malawi:
Map Index

Cities and Towns

Blantyre	B3
Chitipa	B1
Dedza	B2
Karonga	B1
Kasungu	B2
Lilongwe, *capital*	B2
Mchinji	A2
Monkey Bay	B2
Mzimba	B2
Mzuzu	B2
Nkhata Bay	B2
Nkhotakota	B2
Nsanje	C3
Salima	B2
Zomba	C3

Other Features

Bua, *river*	B2
Chilwa, *lake*	C3
Great Rift, *valley*	B1
Malawi (Nyasa), *lake*	B2
Malombe, *lake*	C2
Nyika, *plateau*	B2
Sapitwa, *mt.*	C3
Shire, *river*	B3
Songwe, *river*	B1

Mozambique
Capital: Maputo
Area: 313,661 sq. mi.
812,593 sq. km.
Population: 19,124,335
Largest City: Maputo
Language: Portuguese
Monetary Unit: Metical

Mozambique:
Map Index

Cities and Towns

Angoche	C3
Beira	B3
Chimoio	B3
Chinde	C3
Cuamba	C2
Inhambane	B5
Lichinga	B2
Maputo, *capital*	B5
Moçambique	D2
Moçimboa da Praia	D1
Nacala	D2
Nampula	C2
Pebane	D2
Pemba	D2
Quelimane	C3
Tete	B2
Vilanculos	B4
Xai-Xai	B5

Other Features

Binga, *mt.*	B3
Búzi, *river*	B4
Cabora Bassa, *dam*	B2
Cabora Bassa, *lake*	A2
Changane, *river*	B4
Chilwa, *lake*	C2
Chire, *river*	B3
Lebombo, *mts.*	A4
Limpopo, *river*	B4
Lugenda, *river*	C2
Lúrio, *river*	C2
Mozambique, *channel*	C3
Namuli, *highlands*	C2
Nyasa (Malawi), *lake*	B2
Rovuma, *river*	C1
Save, *river*	B4
Zambezi, *river*	B3

Mozambique

⊛ National Capital
● Other City

1:25,181,000

0   150   300 mi
0   150   300 km

Modified Lambert Conformal Conic Projection

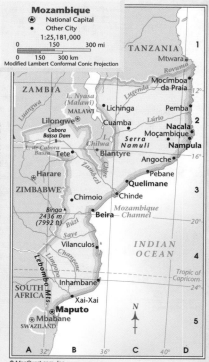

© MapQuest.com, Inc.

Mauritius

⊛ National Capital
• Other City

1:1,635,000

0   10   20 mi

0   10   20 km

Transverse Mercator Projection

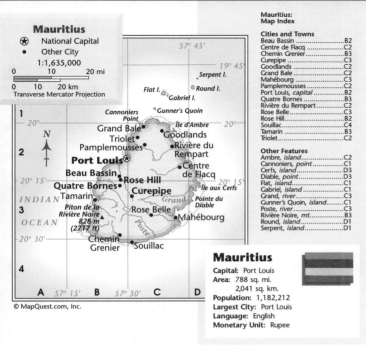

© MapQuest.com, Inc.

Mauritius:
Map Index

Cities and Towns

Beau Bassin	B2
Centre de Flacq	C2
Chemin Grenier	B3
Curepipe	C3
Goodlands	C2
Grand Bale	C2
Mahébourg	C3
Pamplemousses	C2
Port Louis, *capital*	B2
Quatre Bornes	B3
Rivière du Rempart	C2
Rose Belle	C3
Rose Hill	B2
Souillac	C4
Tamarin	B3
Triolet	C2

Other Features

Ambre, *island*	C2
Cannoniers, *point*	C1
Cerfs, *island*	D3
Diable, *point*	D3
Flat, *island*	C1
Gabriel, *island*	C1
Grand, *river*	C3
Gunner's Quoin, *island*	C1
Poste, *river*	C3
Rivière Noire, *mt.*	B3
Round, *island*	D1
Serpent, *island*	D1

Mauritius

Capital: Port Louis
Area: 788 sq. mi.
2,041 sq. km.
Population: 1,182,212
Largest City: Port Louis
Language: English
Monetary Unit: Rupee

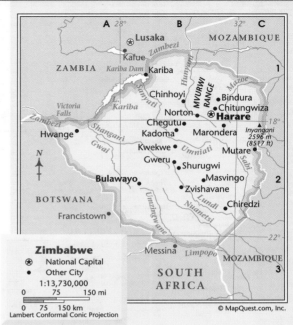

© MapQuest.com, Inc.

Zimbabwe

⊛ National Capital
• Other City

1:13,730,000

0   75   150 mi

0   75   150 km

Lambert Conformal Conic Projection

Zimbabwe

Capital: Harare
Area: 150,872 sq. mi.
390,860 sq. km.
Population: 11,163,160
Largest City: Harare
Language: English
Monetary Unit: Dollar

Zimbabwe:
Map Index

Cities and Towns

Bindura	B1
Bulawayo	B2
Chegutu	B1
Chinhoyi	B1
Chiredzi	B2
Chitungwiza	B2
Gweru	B2
Harare, *capital*	B1
Hwange	A2

Kadoma	B2
Kariba	B1
Kwekwe	B2
Marondera	B2
Masvingo	B2
Mutare	C2
Norton	B1
Shurugwi	B2
Zvishavane	B2

Other Features

Gwai, *river*	A2
Hunyani, *river*	B1
Inyangani, *mt.*	C2
Kariba, *lake*	A1
Limpopo, *river*	B3
Lundi, *river*	B2
Mazoe, *river*	B1
Mvurwi, *range*	B1
Nuanetsi, *river*	B2
Sabi, *river*	C2
Sanyati, *river*	B1
Shangani, *river*	A2
Umniati, *river*	B2
Umzingwani, *river*	B2
Victoria, *falls*	A1
Zambezi, *river*	A1, B1

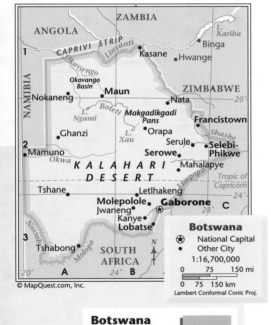

© MapQuest.com, Inc.

Botswana

⊛ National Capital
• Other City

1:16,700,000

0   75   150 mi

0   75   150 km

Lambert Conformal Conic Proj.

Botswana

Capital: Gaborone
Area: 224,607 sq. mi.
581,883 sq. km.
Population: 1,464,167
Largest City: Gaborone
Language: English
Monetary Unit: Pula

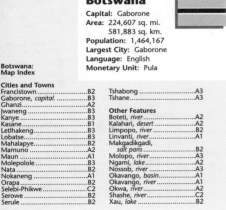

Botswana:
Map Index

Cities and Towns

Francistown	B2	Tshabong	A3
Gaborone, *capital*	B3	Tshane	A3
Ghanzi	A2		
Jwaneng	B3	**Other Features**	
Kanye	B3	Boteti, *river*	A2
Kasane	B1	Kalahari, *desert*	A2
Letlhakeng	B3	Limpopo, *river*	B2
Lobatse	B3	Linvanti, *river*	A1
Mahalapye	B2	Makgadikgadi,	
Mamuno	A2	salt pans	B2
Maun	A1	Molopo, *river*	A3
Molepolole	B3	Ngami, *lake*	A2
Nata	B2	Nossob, *river*	A3
Nokaneng	A1	Okavango, *basin*	A1
Orapa	B2	Okavango, *river*	A1
Selebi-Phikwe	C2	Okwa, *river*	A2
Serowe	B2	Shashe, *river*	C2
Serule	B2	Xau, *lake*	B2

Madagascar

⊛ National Capital
• Other City

1:17,474,000

0   100   200 mi

0   100   200 km

Lambert Conformal Conic Projection

© MapQuest.com, Inc.

Madagascar

Capital: Antananarivo
Area: 226,658 sq. mi.
587,197 sq. km.
Population: 14,873,387
Largest City: Antananarivo
Languages: Malagasy, French
Monetary Unit: Malagasy franc

Madagascar:
Map Index

Cities and Towns

Ambatolampy	B2
Ambatondrazaka	B2
Ambositra	B3
Ampanihy	A3
Andoany	B1
Antalaha	C1
Antananarivo, *capital*	B2
Antsirabe	B2
Antsiranana	B1
Antsohihy	B1
Farafangana	B3
Fianarantsoa	B3
Ihosy	B3
Mahajanga	A2
Maintirano	A2
Manakara	B3
Marovoay	B2
Morombe	A3
Morondava	A3
Toamasina	B2
Tôlanaro	B3

Toliara	A3
Tsiroanomandidy	B2

Other Features

Alaotra, *lake*	B2
Ambre, *cape*	B1
Ankaratra, *mts.*	B2
Bemaraha, *plateau*	A2
Betsiboka, *river*	B2
Kinkony, *lake*	B2
L'Isalo, *mts.*	B3
Mahajamba, *river*	B2
Mangoky, *river*	A3
Maromokotro, *mt.*	B1
Menarandra, *river*	A3
Mozambique, *channel*	A2
Nosy Be, *island*	B1
Nosy Sainte Marie, *island*	B2
Onilahy, *river*	A3
Saint-André, *cape*	A2
Sainte-Marie, *cape*	B4
Sofia, *river*	B2
Tsaratanana, *mts.*	B1
Tsiribihina, *river*	B2

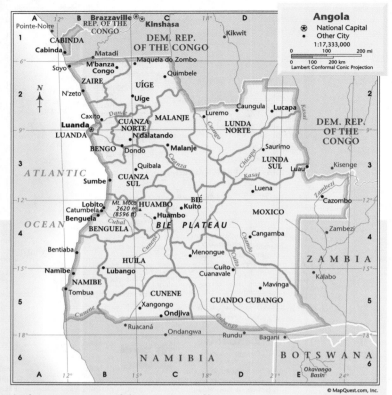

Angola
Capital: Luanda
Area: 481,354 sq. mi.
    1,247,031 sq. km.
Population: 11,177,537
Largest City: Luanda
Language: Portuguese
Monetary Unit: Kwanza

Angola: Map Index

Provinces

Bengo	B3
Benguela	B4
Bié	C4
Cabinda	B1
Cuando Cubango	D5
Cuanza Norte	B2
Cuanza Sul	B3
Cunene	C5
Huambo	B4
Huíla	B4
Luanda	B3
Lunda Norte	D2
Lunda Sul	D3
Malanje	C2
Moxico	D4
Namibe	B5
Uíge	C2
Zaire	B2

Cities and Towns

Benguela	B4
Bentiaba	B4
Cabinda	B1
Cangamba	D4
Catumbela	B4
Caungula	D2
Caxito	B2
Cazombo	E3
Cuíto Cuanavale	D5
Dondo	B3
Huambo	C4
Kuito	C4
Lobito	B4
Luanda, *capital*	B2
Luau	E3
Lubango	B5
Lucapa	D2
Luena	D3
Luremo	C2
Malanje	C3
Maquela do Zombo	C2
Mavinga	D5
M'banza Congo	C4
Menongue	C4
Namibe	B5
N'dalatando	B3
Ondjiva	C5
Quibala	C3
Quimbele	C2
Saurimo	D3
Soyo	B2
Sumbe	B3
Tombua	B5
Uíge	C2
Xangongo	C5

Other Features

Bié, *plateau*	C4
Chicapa, *river*	D3
Cuando, *river*	D4
Cuango, *river*	D2
Cuanza, *river*	C3
Cubal, *river*	B4
Cubango, *river*	D5
Cuíto, *river*	C5
Cunene, *river*	B5, C4
Dande, *river*	B2
Kasai, *river*	D3
Môco, *mt.*	C4
Zambezi, *river*	E3

Seychelles
Capital: Victoria
Area: 176 sq. mi.
    456 sq. km.
Population: 79,164
Largest City: Victoria
Languages: English, French
Monetary Unit: Rupee

Seychelles: Map Index

Cities and Towns

Anse Boileau	Inset
Anse Royale	Inset
Cascade	Inset
De Quincy Village	Inset
Misere	Inset
Port Glaud	Inset
Takamaka	Inset
Victoria, *capital*	Inset

Other Features

Aldabra, *islands*	A2
Amirante, *islands*	B2
Cerf, *island*	Inset
Cosmoledo, *island group*	A2
Farquhar, *island group*	B2
La Digue, *island*	C1
Mahé, *island*	C1, Inset
Mahé, *island group*	B1
Praslin, *island*	C1
St. Anne, *island*	Inset
Silhouette, *island*	C1

Namibia

Capital: Windhoek
Area: 318,146 sq. mi.
    824,212 sq. km.
Population: 1,648,270
Largest City: Windhoek
Language: English, Afrikaans
Monetary Unit: Rand

Namibia: Map Index

Cities and Towns

Bethanien	C4
Gobabis	C2
Grootfontein	C1
Karasburg	C4
Karibib	B2
Katima Mulilo	E1
Keetmanshoop	C4
Khorixas	B2
Lüderitz	B4
Maltahöhe	B3
Mariental	C3
Okahandja	B2
Okakarara	C2
Omaruru	B2
Ondangwa	B1
Opuwo	A1
Oranjemund	B4
Oshakati	B1
Otavi	C1
Otjiwarongo	B2
Outjo	B2
Rehoboth	C3
Rundu	C1
Swakopmund	B2
Tsumeb	C1
Tsumkwe	D1
Walvis Bay	B2
Windhoek, *capital*	C2

Other Features

Auob, *river*	C3
Brandberg, *mt.*	B2
Caprivi, *strip*	D1
Eiseb, *river*	D2
Etosha, *pan*	B1
Fish, *river*	C4
Kalahari, *desert*	C3
Kaoko Veld, *mts.*	A1
Kaukau Veld, *region*	C2
Kunene, *river*	A1
Linyanti, *river*	E1
Namib, *desert*	A1, B3
Nossob, *river*	C3
Okavango, *river*	C1
Omatako, *river*	C1
Orange, *river*	C4
Ruacana, *falls*	B1
Skeleton, *coast*	A1
Ugab, *river*	B2
Zambezi, *river*	E1

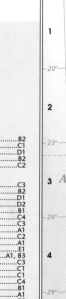

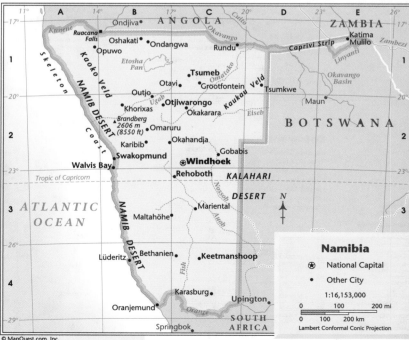

© MapQuest.com, Inc.

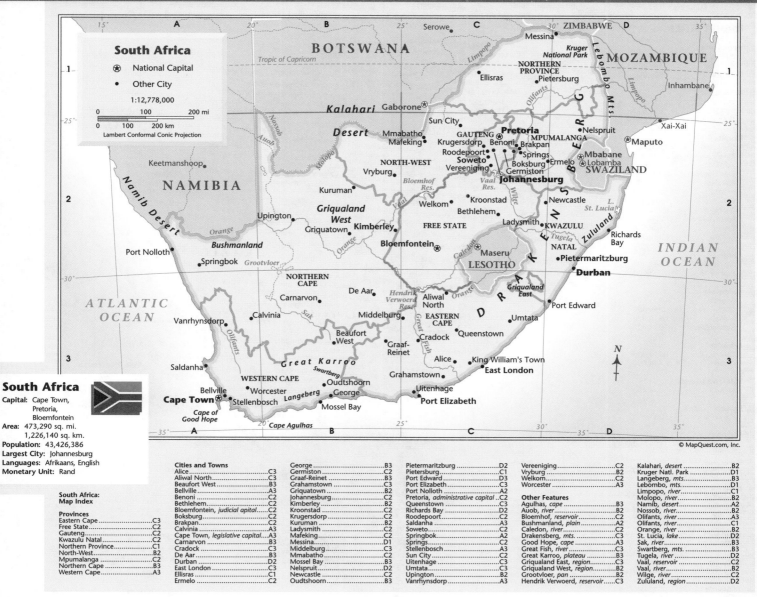

South Africa

Capital: Cape Town,
Pretoria,
Bloemfontein
Area: 473,290 sq. mi.
1,226,140 sq. km.
Population: 43,426,386
Largest City: Johannesburg
Languages: Afrikaans, English
Monetary Unit: Rand

South Africa:
Map Index

Provinces

Eastern Cape	C3
Free State	C2
Gauteng	C2
Kwazulu Natal	C2
Northern Province	C1
North-West	B2
Mpumalanga	C2
Northern Cape	B3
Western Cape	A3

Cities and Towns

Alice	C3
Aliwal North	C3
Beaufort West	B3
Bellville	A3
Benoni	C2
Bethlehem	C2
Bloemfontein, judicial apital	C2
Boksburg	C2
Brakpan	C2
Calvinia	A3
Cape Town, legislative capital	A3
Carnarvon	B3
Cradock	C3
De Aar	B3
Durban	D2
East London	C3
Ellisras	C1
Ermelo	C2

George	B3
Germiston	C2
Graaf-Reinet	B3
Grahamstown	C3
Griquatown	B2
Johannesburg	C2
Kimberley	B2
Kroonstad	C2
Krugersdorp	C2
Kuruman	B2
Ladysmith	C2
Mafeking	C2
Messina	D1
Middelburg	C2
Mmabatho	C2
Mossel Bay	B3
Nelspruit	D2
Newcastle	C2
Oudtshoorn	B3

Pietermaritzburg	D2
Pietersburg	C1
Port Edward	D3
Port Elizabeth	C3
Port Nolloth	A2
Pretoria, administrative capital	C2
Queenstown	C3
Richards Bay	D2
Roodepoort	C2
Saldanha	A3
Soweto	C2
Springbok	A2
Springs	C2
Stellenbosch	A3
Sun City	C2
Uitenhage	C3
Umtata	C3
Upington	B2
Vanrhynsdorp	A3

Vereeniging	C2
Vryburg	B2
Welkom	C2
Worcester	A3

Other Features

Agulhas, cape	B3
Auob, river	B2
Bloemhof, reservoir	C2
Bushmanland, plain	A2
Caledon, river	C2
Drakensberg, mts.	C3
Good Hope, cape	A3
Great Fish, river	C3
Great Karroo, plateau	B3
Griqualand East, region	C3
Griqualand West, region	B2
Grootvloer, pan	B2
Hendrik Verwoerd, reservoir	C3

Kalahari, desert	B2
Kruger Natl. Park	D1
Langeberg, mts.	B3
Lebombo, mts.	D1
Limpopo, river	C1
Molopo, river	B2
Namib, desert	A2
Nossob, river	B2
Olifants, river	A3
Olifants, river	C1
Orange, river	B2
St. Lucia, lake	D2
Sak, river	B3
Swartberg, mts.	B3
Tugela, river	D2
Vaal, reservoir	C2
Vaal, river	B2
Wilge, river	C2
Zululand, region	D2

South Africa

Capital: Cape Town,
Pretoria,
Bloemfontein
Area: 473,290 sq. mi.
1,226,140 sq. km.
Population: 43,426,386
Largest City: Johannesburg
Languages: Afrikaans, English
Monetary Unit: Rand

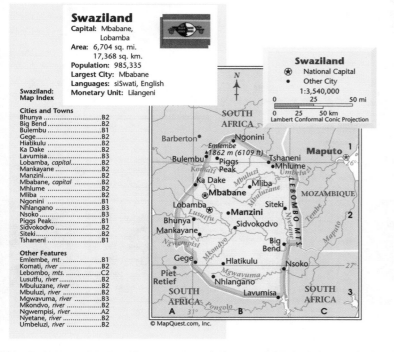

Swaziland

Capital: Mbabane,
Lobamba
Area: 6,704 sq. mi.
17,368 sq. km.
Population: 985,335
Largest City: Mbabane
Languages: siSwati, English
Monetary Unit: Lilangeni

Swaziland:
Map Index

Cities and Towns

Bhunya	B2
Big Bend	B2
Bulembu	B1
Gege	B2
Hlatikulu	B2
Ka Dake	B3
Lavumisa	B3
Lobamba, capital	B2
Mankayane	B2
Manzini	B2
Mbabane, capital	B2
Mhlume	B2
Mliba	B2
Ngonini	B1
Nhlangano	B3
Nsoko	B3
Piggs Peak	B1
Sidvokodvo	B2
Siteki	B2
Tshaneni	B1

Other Features

Emlembe, mt.	B1
Komati, river	B1
Lebombo, mts.	C2
Lusutfu, river	B2
Mbuluzane, river	B2
Mbuluzi, river	B2
Mgwavuma, river	B3
Mkondvo, river	B2
Ngwempisi, river	A2
Nyetane, river	B2
Umbeluzi, river	B2

Swaziland

⊛ National Capital
• Other City
1:3,540,000

Lesotho

Capital: Maseru
Area: 11,716 sq. mi.
30,352 sq. km.
Population: 2,128,950
Largest City: Maseru
Language: English
Monetary Unit: Loti

Lesotho:
Map Index

Cities and Towns

Butha-Buthe	B1
Leribe	B1
Libono	B1
Mafeteng	A2
Maseru, capital	A2
Mohales Hoek	A3
Mokhotlong	C2
Morija	A2
Pitseng	B2
Qachas Nek	B3
Quthing	A3
Roma	A2
Sekake	B2
Teyateyaneng	B2
Thaba-Tseka	B2

Other Features

Caledon, river	A1
Central, range	B2
Drakensberg, mts.	A2
Makhaleng, river	A2
Maloti, mts.	B2
Matsoku, river	B2
Orange, river	A3, B2
Sources, mt.	B1
Thabana Ntlenyana, mt.	C2
Tsedike, river	B3

Lesotho

⊛ National Capital
• Other City
1:5,811,000

MAJOR CITIES

Argentina
Buenos Aires	2,961,000
Córdoba	1,148,000
Rosario	895,000

Bolivia
La Paz	739,000
Santa Cruz	833,000
El Alto	527,000

Brazil
São Paulo	10,018,000
Rio de Janeiro	5,606,000
Salvador	2,263,000
Belo Horizonte	2,097,000
Fortaleza	1,917,000
Brasília	1,738,000
Curitiba	1,409,000
Recife	1,330,000
Pôrto Alegre	1,296,000
Belém	1,168,000
Manaus	1,138,000

Chile
Santiago	4,641,000
Puente Alto	363,000

Colombia
Bogotá	4,945,000
Cali	1,666,000
Medellín	1,630,000
Barranquilla	994,000

Ecuador
Guayaquil	1,974,000
Quito	1,444,000

Falkland Islands
Stanley	1,200

French Guiana
Cayenne	41,000

Guyana
Georgetown	195,000

Paraguay
Asunción	547,000

Peru
Lima	5,682,000
Arequipa	619,000
Trujillo	509,000

Suriname
Paramaribo	216,000

Uruguay
Montevideo	1,303,000

Venezuela
Caracas	3,673,000
Maracaibo	1,221,000
Barquisimeto	954,000
Valencia	911,000

International comparability of city population
data is limited by various data inconsistencies.

CITIES
- ⊗ National Capital
- ★ Territorial Capital
- • Other City

ELEVATIONS

	Feet	Meters
	13,120	4000
	6560	2000
	1640	500
	656	200
	0	0
	Below sea level	

N

0	250	500	750	1000 mi
0	250	500	750	1000	1250	1500 km

South America: Population, by nation (in millions)

BRAZIL 171.9	COLOM. 39.3	ARGEN. 36.7	PERU 26.6	VENEZ. 23.2	All other S. Am. countries 45.6

© MapQuest.com, Inc.

Gross National Product (GNP) per capita

- $36,410
- $21,500
- $8625
- $2785
- $695
- $0
- No data

Vegetation

- Unclassified Highlands
- Deciduous Forest
- Mixed Forest
- Midlatitude Scrubland
- Midlatitude Grassland
- Desert
- Tropical Seasonal and Scrub
- Tropical Rain Forest
- Tropical Savanna

CLIMATE

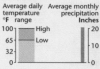

Average daily temperature °F range — High, Low

Average monthly precipitation Inches

ASUNCIÓN, Paraguay

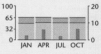

BOGOTÁ, Colombia

BUENOS AIRES, Argentina

CARACAS, Venezuela

CAYENNE, French Guiana

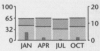

LA PAZ, Bolivia

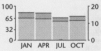

LIMA, Peru

MANAUS, Brazil

PUNTA ARENAS, Chile

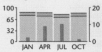

RECIFE, Brazil

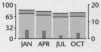

RIO DE JANEIRO, Brazil

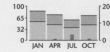

SANTIAGO, Chile

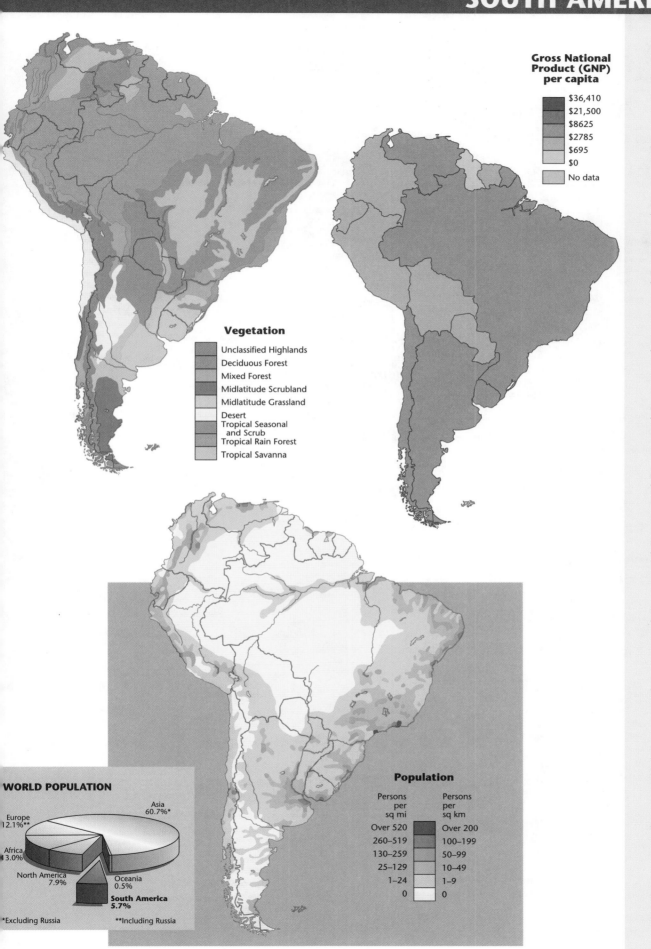

WORLD POPULATION

- Asia 60.7%*
- Europe 12.1%**
- Africa 13.0%
- North America 7.9%
- Oceania 0.5%
- **South America 5.7%**

*Excluding Russia   **Including Russia

Population

Persons per sq mi	Persons per sq km
Over 520	Over 200
260–519	100–199
130–259	50–99
25–129	10–49
1–24	1–9
0	0

Argentina

⊛ National Capital
★ Territorial Capital
● Other City

1:17,760,000

0   200   400 mi
0   200   400 km
Modified Chamberlain Trimetric Projection

© MapQuest.com, Inc.

Argentina

Capital: Buenos Aires
Area: 1,073,518 sq. mi.
      2,781,134 sq. km.
Population: 36,737,664
Largest City: Buenos Aires
Language: Spanish
Monetary Unit: Peso

Argentina:
Map Index

Provinces
Buenos Aires C4
Catamarca B2
Chaco C2
Chubut B5
Córdoba C3
Corrientes D2
Distrito Federal D3
Entre Ríos D3
Formosa D1
Jujuy B1
La Pampa B4
La Rioja B2
Mendoza B3
Misiones E2
Neuquén B4
Río Negro B4
Salta B2
San Juan B3
San Luis B3
Santa Cruz A6
Santa Fe C2
Santiago del Estero C2
Tierra del Fuego B7
Tucumán B2

Cities and Towns
Avellaneda D3
Bahía Blanca C4
Buenos Aires, *capital* D3
Calafate A7
Catamarca B2
Comodoro Rivadavia B6
Concordia D3
Córdoba C3
Corrientes D2
Curuzú Cuatiá D2
Embarcación C1
Esquel A5
Formosa D2
Godoy Cruz B3
Lanús D3

La Plata D4
La Rioja B2
Lomas de Zamora D4
Mar del Plata D4
Mendoza B3
Necochea D4
Neuquén B4
Olavarría C4
Paraná C3
Posadas D2
Presidencia Roque
   Sáenz Peña C2
Puerto Deseado B6
Puerto Santa Cruz B7
Rawson B5
Reconquista C2
Resistencia D2
Río Cuarto C3
Río Gallegos B7
Rosario C3
Salta B1
San Antonio Oeste B5
San Carlos de Bariloche A5
San Francisco C3
San Juan B3
San Luis B3
San Miguel de Tucumán B2
San Nicolás C3
San Rafael B3
San Salvador de Jujuy B1
Santa Fe C3
Santa Rosa C4
Santiago del Estero C2
Tandil D4
Ushuaia B7
Viedma C5
Villa María C3

Other Features
Aconcagua, *mt.* A3
Andes, *mts.* A6–B1
Argentino, *lake* A7
Atuel, *river* B4
Beagle, *channel* B7
Bermejo, *river* C2

Blanca, *bay* C4
Buenos Aires, *lake* A6
Cardiel, *lake* A6
Champaquí, *mt.* C3
Chico, *river* B6
Chubut, *river* A5
Colorado, *river* B4
Córdoba, *range* B3
Desaguadero, *river* B3
Deseado, *river* B6
Domuyo, *volcano* A4
Dungeness, *point* B7
Estados, *island* C7
Fitzroy, *mt.* A6
Gallegos, *river* A7
Gran Chaco, *region* C1
Grande, *bay* B7
Iguaçu, *falls* E2
Iguaçu, *river* E2
Lanín, *volcano* A4
Llullaillaco, *volcano* B1
Magellan, *strait* B7
Mar Chiquita, *lake* C3
Mercedario, *mt* B3
Negro, *river* B4
Ojos del Salado, *mt.* B2
Pampas, *plain* C4
Paraguay, *river* D2
Paraná, *river* D2
Patagonia, *region* A6
Pilcomayo, *river* C1
Plata, Río de la, *estuary* ..D3
Rasa, *point* C5
Salado, *river* B3
Salado, *river* C4
San Antonio, *cape* D4
San Jorge, *gulf* B6
San Martín, *lake* A6
San Matías, *gulf* C5
Santa Cruz, *river* A7
Tres Puntas, *cape* B6
Tupungato, *mt.* B3
Uruguay, *river* D3
Valdés, *peninsula* C5
Viedma, *lake* A6

Paraguay

Paraguay

Capital: Asunción
Area: 157,048 sq. mi.
      406,752 sq. km.
Population: 5,434,095
Largest City: Asunción
Language: Spanish
Monetary Unit: Guarani

Paraguay:
Map Index

Departments
Alto Paraguay C2
Alto Paraná E4
Amambay E3
Asunción D4
Boquerón B2
Caaguazú D4
Caazapá D5
Canendiyú E4
Central D4
Concepción D3
Cordillera D4
Guairá D4
Itapúa E5
Misiones D5
Ñeembucú C5
Paraguarí D5
Presidente Hayes C4
San Pedro D4

Cities and Towns
Abaí E4
Asunción, *capital* D4
Caacupé D4
Caaguazú E4
Caazapá D5
Capitán Pablo Lagerenza B1
Ciudad del Este E4
Concepción D3
Coronel Oviedo D4
Doctor Pedro P. Peña A3
Encarnación E5

Filadelfia B3
Fuerte Olimpo D2
General
   Eugenio A. Garay A2
Mariscal Estigarribia B3
Paraguarí D4
Pedro Juan Caballero E3
Pilar C5
Pozo Colorado C2
Puerto Bahía C2
Puerto Pinasco D3
Salto del Guairá E4
San Juan Bautista D5
San Lorenzo D4
San Pedro D4
Villa Hayes D4
Villarrica D4

Other Features
Acaray, *river* E4
Amambay, *mts.* E3
Apa, *river* D3
Chaco Boreal, *region* B2
Gran Chaco, *region* B3
Iguazú, *falls* E4
Itaipú, *reservoir* E4
Jejuí-Guazú, *river* D4
Montelindo, *river* C3
Paraguay, *river* C2, C5
Paraná, *river* C5, E5
Pilcomayo, *river* B3, C4
Tebicuary, *river* D5
Verde, *river* C3
Ypané, *river* D3
Ypoá, *lake* D4

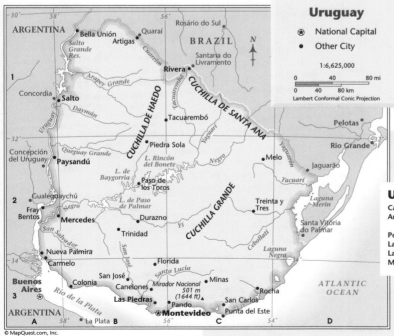

Uruguay

Capital: Montevideo
Area: 68,037 sq. mi.
      176,215 sq. km.
Population: 3,308,523
Largest City: Montevideo
Language: Spanish
Monetary Unit: New peso

Uruguay:
Map Index

Cities and Towns
Artigas B1
Bella Unión B1
Canelones B3
Carmelo A2
Colonia A3
Durazno B2
Florida B3
Fray Bentos A2
Las Piedras B3
Melo C2
Mercedes A2
Minas C3
Montevideo, *capital* B3
Nueva Palmira A2
Pando C3
Paso de los Toros B2
Paysandú A2
Piedra Sola B2
Punta del Este C3
Rivera C1
Rocha C3
Salto B1
San Carlos C3
San José B3
Tacuarembó C1
Treinta y Tres C2
Trinidad B2

Other Features
Arapey Grande, *river* B1
Baygorria, *lake* B2
Cebollatí, *river* C2
Cuareim, *river* B1
Daymán, *river* B1
Grande, *range* C2
Haedo, *range* B2
Merín, *lagoon* D2
Mirador Nacional, *mt.* C3
Negra, *lagoon* D2
Negro, *river* C2
Paso de Palmar, *lake* B2
Plata, *river* B3
Queguay Grande, *river* B2
Rincón del Bonete, *lake* ...B2
Salto Grande, *reservoir* B1
San José, *river* B2
San Salvador, *river* A2
Santa Ana, *river* B3
Santa Lucía, *river* B3
Tacuarembó, *river* C1
Tacuarí, *river* C2
Uruguay, *river* A1
Yaguarí, *river* C1
Yaguarón, *river* D2
Yi, *river* C2

Chile

Capital: Santiago
Area: 292,135 sq. mi.
756,826 sq. km.
Population: 14,973,843
Largest City: Santiago
Language: Spanish
Monetary Unit: Peso

Chile:
Map Index

Regions
Aisén del General Carlos
Ibáñez del Campo B8
Antofagasta C2
Atacama B3
Bío-Bío B6
Coquimbo B4
El Libertador General
Bernardo O'Higgins B4
La Araucanía B6

Cities and Towns
Aguada de Cachinal C2
Aguas Blancas C2
Algarrobo ....Inset

Los Lagos B7
Magallanes y Antártica
Chilena B9
Maule B5, B6
Región Metropolitana B4,
Inset
Tarapacá C1
Valparaíso ....B4, Inset

Altamira C3
Ancud B7
Angol B6
Antofagasta B2
Arica B1
Balmaceda B8
Calama C2
Casablanca ....Inset
Castro B7
Cerro Castillo B9
Chaitén B7
Chañaral B3
Chiapa C1

Chile Chico B8
Chillán B6
Chuquicamata C2
Cochrane B8
Coihaique B8
Colina ....Inset
Collaguasi C2
Concepción B6
Conchalí ....Inset
Constitución B5
Copiapó B3
Coquimbo B3
Curicó B4

El Tabo ....Inset
El Trébol B3
Freirina B3
Gatico B2
Illapel B4
Iquique B2
Lampa ....Inset
La Serena B3
La Unión B7
Lebu B6
Linares B5
Los Andes B4
Los Ángeles B6
Maipú ....Inset
Mamiña C2
Melipilla ....Inset
Ñuñoa ....Inset
Osorno B7
Ovalle B4
Parral B6
Pisagua B1
Porvenir B9
Potrerillos C3
Puente Alto ....Inset
Puerto Aisén B8
Puerto Cisnes B7
Puerto Montt B7
Puerto Natales B7
Puerto Varas B7
Puerto Williams C9
Punta Arenas B9
Punta Delgada B9
Putre C1
Quellón B7
Quillota B4
Quilpué ....Inset
Rancagua B4
Rungue ....Inset
San Antonio ....B4, Inset
San Bernardo ....Inset
San Félix B3
San Fernando B4
San Pedro de Atacama C2
Santa Inés ....Inset
Santiago, capital ......B4, Inset
Socompa C2
Talagante ....Inset
Talca B5
Talcahuano B6
Taltal B3
Temuco B6
Tilomonte C2
Tocopilla B2
Tomé B6
Unión B6
Valdivia B6
Vallenar B3
Valparaíso ....B4, Inset
Victoria B6
Viña del Mar ....B4, Inset

Other Features
Aconcagua, river B4
Ancud, gulf B7
Andes, mts. B8, C4
Atacama, desert C2
Bascuñán, cape B3
Bío-Bío, river B6
Brunswick, peninsula B9
Buenos Aires, lake B8
Campana, island A8
Chiloé, island B7
Chonos, archipelago B7
Cochrane, lake B8
Concepción, bay B6
Copiapó, river B3
Corcovado, gulf B7
Desolación, island B9
Domeyko, mts. C3
Dungeness, point C9
Duque de York, island A9
Elqui, river B3
Fitzroy, mt. B8
Galera, point B6
Horn, cape C9
Hoste, island C9
Imperial, river B6
Lanín, volcano B6
Lengua de Vaca, point B4
Llanquihue, lake B7
Llullaillaco, volcano C2
Loa, river B2
Madre de Dios, island A9
Magdalena, island B7
Magellan, strait B9
Maipo, river ....B4, Inset
Maule, river B5
Navarino, island C9
Occidental, mts. C1
Ojos del Salado, mt. C3
Ollagüe, volcano C2
Penas, gulf B8
Rapel, river B4
Reina Adelaida, archipelago ...B9
San Martín, lake B8
San Valentín, mt. B8
Santa Inés, island B9
Taitao, peninsula A8
Tierra del Fuego, island C9
Toltén, river B6
Wellington, island A8

Peru

Capital: Lima
Area: 496,225 sq. mi.
1,285,216 sq. km.
Population: 26,624,582
Largest City: Lima
Languages: Spanish, Quechua
Monetary Unit: Nuevo Sol

Peru:
Map Index

Cities and Towns

Abancay	C3
Arequipa	C4
Ayacucho	C3
Cajamarca	B2
Callao	B3
Cerro de Pasco	B3
Chachapoyas	B2
Chiclayo	B2
Chimbote	B2
Chincha Alta	B3
Cuzco	C3
Huacho	B3
Huancavelica	B3
Huancayo	B3
Huánuco	B2
Huaraz	B2
Ica	B3
Ilo	C4
Iquitos	C1
Juliaca	C4
La Oroya	B3
Lima, capital	B3
Mollendo	C4
Moquegua	C4

Moyobamba	B2
Nazca	C3
Pacasmayo	B2
Paita	A2
Patavilca	B3
Pisco	B3
Piura	A2
Pucallpa	C2
Puerto Maldonado	D3
Puno	C4
Salaverry	B2
San Juan	B4
Sicuani	C3
Sullana	A1
Tacna	C4
Talara	A1
Tarapoto	B2
Tingo María	B2
Trujillo	B2
Tumbes	A1
Yurimaguas	B2

Other Features

Amazon, river	C1
Andes, mts.	B1, C3
Apurímac, river	C3
Central, mts.	B2
Colca, river	C4

Coropuna, mt.	C4
Guayaquil, gulf	A1
Huallaga, river	B2
Huascarán, mt.	B2
La Montaña, region	C2
Machupicchu, ruins	C3
Madre de Dios, river	C3
Mantaro, river	B3
Marañón, river	B1, B2
Napo, river	C1
Negra, point	A2
Occidental, mts.	B2, C4
Oriental, mts.	B2, C3
Pastaza, river	B1
Purús, river	C2
Putumayo, river	C1
Santiago, river	B1
Sechura, desert	A2
Tambo, river	C3
Tambo, river	C4
Tigre, river	B1
Titicaca, lake	D4
Ucayali, river	C2
Urubamba, river	C3
Vilcabamba, mts.	C3
Yavarí, river	C1

Bolivia:
Map Index

Departments

Beni	A2
Chuquisaca	B4
Cochabamba	A3
La Paz	A3
Oruro	A3
Pando	A2
Potosí	A4
Santa Cruz	B3
Tarija	B4

Cities and Towns

Aiquile	A3
Camiri	B4
Cobija	A2
Cochabamba	A3
Fortín Ravelo	B3
Guaqui	A3
La Paz, capital	A3
Llallagua	A3
Magdalena	B2
Mojos	A3
Montero	B3
Oruro	A3
Potosí	A4
Puerto Suárez	C3
Riberalta	A2
Roboré	C3
San Borja	A2

San Cristóbal	B2
San Ignacio	B3
San José de Chiquitos	B3
San Matías	C3
Santa Ana	B2
Santa Cruz	B3
Santa Rosa del Palmar	B3
Sucre, capital	A3
Tarija	B4
Tarvo	B3
Trinidad	B2
Tupiza	A4
Uyuni	A4
Villazón	A4
Yacuiba	B4

Other Features

Abuná, river	A2
Altiplano, plateau	A3
Beni, river	A2
Chaparé, river	A3
Cordillera Central, mts.	A3
Cordillera Occidental, mts.	A3
Cordillera Oriental, mts.	A3
Cordillera Real, mts.	A3
Desaguadero, river	A3
Gran Chaco, region	B4
Guaporé, river	A2
Ichilo, river	B3
Illampu, mt.	A3
Illimani, mt.	A3

Iténez, river	B2
Madre de Dios, river	A2
Mamoré, river	A2
Ollagüe, volcano	A4
Paraguá, river	B2
Paraguay, river	C4
Pilaya, river	B4
Pilcomayo, river	B3
Poopó, lake	A3
Sajama, mt.	A3
Salar de Uyuni, salt flat	A4
San Luis, lake	B2
San Pablo, river	B3
Titicaca, lake	A3
Yata, river	A2
Yungas, region	A3

Bolivia

Capital: La Paz, Sucre
Area: 424,164 sq. mi.
1,098,871 sq. km.
Population: 7,982,850
Largest City: La Paz
Languages: Spanish, Quechua, Aymara
Monetary Unit: Boliviano

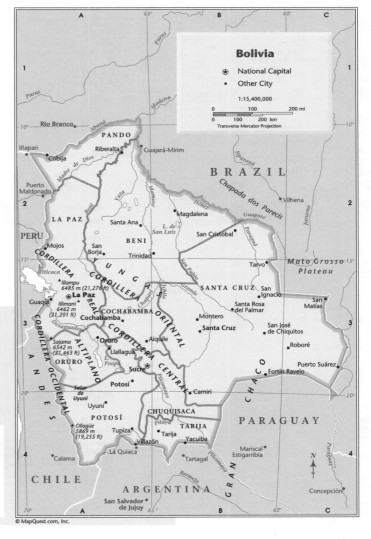

© MapQuest.com, Inc.

Colombia

Capital: Bogotá
Area: 440,831 sq. mi.
1,142,049 sq. km.
Population: 39,309,422
Largest City: Bogotá
Language: Spanish
Monetary Unit: Peso

Colombia: Map Index

Internal Divisions

Amazonas (commisary)	B5
Antioquia (dept.)	B3
Arauca (intendency)	C3
Atlántico (dept.)	B2
Bolívar (dept.)	B2
Boyacá (dept.)	B3
Caldas (dept.)	B3
Capital District	B4
Caquetá (dept.)	B4
Casanare (intendency)	C3
Cauca (dept.)	A4
César (dept.)	B2
Chocó (dept.)	A3
Córdoba (dept.)	B2
Cundinamarca (dept.)	B3
Guainía (commisary)	C4
Guaviare (commissary)	B4
Huila (dept.)	B4
La Guajira (dept.)	B2
Magdalena (dept.)	B2
Meta (dept.)	B4
Nariño (dept.)	A4
Norte de Santander (dept.)	B2
Putumayo (intendency)	A4
Quindío (dept.)	B3
Risaralda (dept.)	B3
San Andrés y Providencia (intendency)	Inset
Santander (dept.)	B3
Sucre (dept.)	B2
Tolima (dept.)	B4
Valle del Cauca (dept.)	A4
Vaupés (commissary)	C4
Vichada (commissary)	C3

Cities and Towns

Arauca	C3
Armenia	B3
Barrancabermeja	B3
Barranquilla	B2
Bogotá, capital	B3
Bucaramanga	B3
Buenaventura	A4
Cali	A4
Cartagena	B2
Cravo Norte	C3
Cúcuta	B3
El Encanto	B5
Florencia	B4
Ibagué	B3
Leticia	C6
Manizales	B3
Medellín	B3
Miraflores	B4
Mitú	C4

Mocoa	A4
Montería	B2
Neiva	B4
Orocué	C3
Palmira	A4
Pasto	A4
Pereira	B3
Popayán	A4
Puerto Carreño	D3
Puerto Inírida	D4
Puerto Leguízamo	B5
Quibdó	A3
Ríohacha	B2
San Felipe	D4
San José del Guaviare	B4
Santa Marta	B2
Sincelejo	B2
Tumaco	A4
Tunja	B3
Turbo	A2
Valledupar	B2
Villavicencio	B3
Vista Hermosa	B4
Yopal	B3

Other Features

Albuquerque, cays	Inset
Amazon, river	C5
Andes, range	A4
Apaporis, river	C4
Atrato, river	A3
Caquetá, river	B5
Cauca, river	B3
Cordillera Central, range	A4
Cordillera Occidental, range	A4
Cordillera Oriental, range	B4
Cristóbal Colón, peak	B2
Gallinas, point	C1
Guainía, river	C4
Guajira, peninsula	C1
Guaviare, river	C4
Huila, mt.	A4
Llanos, prairie	C3
Magdalena, river	B3
Meta, river	C3
Orinoco, river	D3
Patía, river	A4
Providencia, island	Inset
Putumayo, river	B5
Roncador, cay	Inset
San Andrés, island	Inset
San Juan, river	A3
Serranilla, bank	Inset
Sierra Nevada de Santa Marta, mts.	B2
Tolima, mt.	B3
Vaupés, river	B4
Vichada, river	C3

Venezuela: Map Index

Internal Divisions

Amazonas (territory)	C3
Anzoátegui (state)	D2
Apure (state)	C2
Aragua (state)	C2
Barinas (state)	C2
Bolívar (state)	D2
Carabobo (state)	C2
Cojedes (state)	C2
Delta Amacuro (territory)	D2
Dependencias Federales	C1
Distrito Federal	C1
Falcón (state)	B1
Guárico (state)	C2
Lara (state)	B1
Mérida (state)	B2
Miranda (state)	C1
Monagas (state)	D2
Nueva Esparta (state)	D1
Portuguesa (state)	C2
Sucre (state)	D1
Táchira (state)	B2
Trujillo (state)	B2
Yaracuy (state)	C1
Zulia (state)	B2

Cities and Towns

Acarigua	C2
Anaco	D2
Barcelona	D1
Barinas	B2
Barquisimeto	C1
Baruta	C1
Cabimas	B1
Calabozo	C2
Canaima	D2
Caracas, capital	C1
Carora	C1
Carúpano	D1
Ciudad Bolívar	D2
Ciudad Guayana	D2
Coro	C1
Cumaná	D1
El Tigre	D2
Guanare	C2
Güiria	D1
La Asunción	D1
La Guaira Maiquetía	C1
Los Teques	C1
Maiquetía	C1
Maracaibo	B1
Maracay	C2
Maturin	D2
Mérida	B2

Petare	C1
Puerto Ayacucho	C2
Puerto Cabello	C1
Puerto La Cruz	D1
Punto Fijo	B1
San Cristóbal	B2
San Felipe	C1
San Fernando de Apure	C2
San Juan de Los Morros	C2
Santa Elena de Uairén	D3
Trujillo	B2
Tucupita	D2
Valencia	C1
Valera	B2

Other Features

Angel, falls	D2
Apure, river	C2
Arauca, river	C2
Bolívar, mt.	B2
Caroni, river	D2
Casiquiare, river	C3
Caura, river	D2
Cojedes, river	C2
Guri, reservoir	D2
Guiana, highlands	D2
La Tortuga, island	C1
Llanos, plain	B2

Maracaibo, lake	B2
Margarita, island	D1
Mérida, mts.	B2
Meta, river	C2
Neblina, mt.	C3
Negro, river	B3
Orinoco, river	C3, D2
Pacaraima, mts.	D3
Paria, gulf	D1
Parima, mts.	D3
Roraima, mt.	D2
Venezuela, gulf	B1

Venezuela

Capital: Caracas
Area: 352,144 sq. mi.
912,050 sq. km.
Population: 23,203,466
Largest City: Caracas
Language: Spanish
Monetary Unit: Bolívar

© MapQuest.com, Inc.

Ecuador
Capital: Quito
Area: 105,037 sq. mi.
272,117 sq. km.
Population: 12,562,496
Largest City: Guayaquil
Language: Spanish
Monetary Unit: Sucre

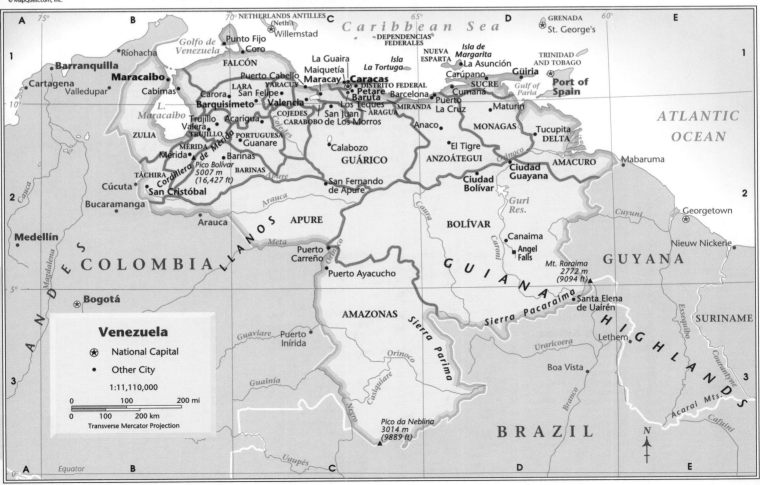

Guyana

Guyana
- National Capital
- Other City

1:10,660,000

0 75 150 mi
0 75 150 km

Transverse Mercator Projection

© MapQuest.com, Inc.

Guyana

Capital: Georgetown
Area: 83,000 sq. mi.
214,969 sq. km.
Population: 705,156
Largest City: Georgetown
Language: English
Monetary Unit: Guyana dollar

Guyana:
Map Index

Cities and Towns
Anna Regina	B2
Apoteri	B4
Bartica	B2
Biloku	B5
Charity	B2
Georgetown, *capital*	B2
Isherton	B4
Lethem	B4
Linden	B3
Mabaruma	B1
Mahdia	B3
Matthews Ridge	A2
New Amsterdam	C2
Suddie	B2

Other Features
Acarai, *mts.*	B5
Barama, *river*	B2
Berbice, *river*	B3
Courantyne, *river*	B3
Cuyuni, *river*	A2
Demerara, *river*	B3
Essequibo, *river*	B3, B5
Kaieteur, *falls*	B3
Kanuku, *mts.*	B4
Mazaruni, *river*	A2
Merume, *mts.*	A2
New, *river*	C4
Pakaraima, *mts.*	A3
Potaro, *river*	B3
Rawa, *river*	B4
Roraima, *mt.*	A3
Takutu, *river*	B4

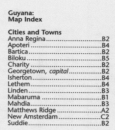

Suriname

Suriname
- National Capital
- Other City

1:9,840,000

0 60 120 mi
0 60 120 km

Conic Equidistant Projection

© MapQuest.com, Inc.

Suriname

Capital: Paramaribo
Area: 63,037 sq. mi.
163,265 sq. km.
Population: 431,156
Largest City: Paramaribo
Language: Dutch
Monetary Unit: Suriname guilder

Suriname:
Map Index

Cities and Towns
Albina	B2
Apetina	B3
Apoera	A2
Benzdorp	B3
Brokopondo	B2
Groningen	B2
Moengo	B2
Nieuw Amsterdam	B2
Nieuw Nickerie	A2
Paramaribo, *capital*	B2
Paranam	B2
Sipaliwini	A3
Totness	A2
Zanderij	B2

Other Features
Coeroeni, *river*	A3
Coppename, *river*	A2
Corantijn, *river*	A2
Ellerts de Haan, *mts.*	A3
Juliana Top, *mt.*	A3
Kabelebo, *river*	A3
Kayser, *mts.*	A3
Lawa, *river*	B2
Litani, *river*	B3
Lucie, *river*	A3
Marowijne, *river*	B2
Nickerie, *river*	A2
Oelemari, *river*	B3
Oranje, *mts.*	B3
Saramacca, *river*	B2
Suriname, *river*	B2
Tapanahoni, *river*	B3
Tumuc-Humac, *mts.*	B3
Wilhelmina, *mts.*	A2
W.J. van Blommestein, *lake*	B2

French Guiana

French Guiana:
Map Index

Cities and Towns
Apatou	A1
Cacao	B1
Camopi	B2
Cayenne, *capital*	B1
Grand Santi	A1
Iracoubo	B1
Kaw	B1
Kourou	B1
Mana	B1
Maripasoula	A2
Ouanary	C1
Régina	B1
Rémire	B1
Saint-Élie	B1
Saint-Georges	C2
Saint-Laurent du Maroni	A1
Saül	B2

Other Features
Camopi, *river*	B2
Devil's, *island*	B1
Lawa, *river*	A2
Litani, *river*	A2
Mana, *river*	B1
Maroni, *river*	A1
Oyapock, *river*	B2
Salut, *islands*	B1
Tampok, *river*	B2
Tumuc-Humac, *mts.*	A2

French Guiana

Capital: Cayenne
Area: 35,135 sq. mi.
91,000 sq. km.
Population: 167,982
Largest City: Cayenne
Language: French
Monetary Unit: French franc

French Guiana
- Territorial Capital
- Other City

1:8,410,000

0 50 100 mi
0 50 100 km

Conic Equidistant Projection

© MapQuest.com, Inc.

Brazil: Map Index

States and Federal District

Acre	A2
Alagoas	E2
Amapá	C1
Amazonas	B2
Bahia	D3
Ceará	E2
Espírito Santo	D3
Federal District	D3
Goiás	D3
Maranhão	D2
Mato Grosso	C3
Mato Grosso do Sul	C4
Minas Gerais	D3
Paraíba	E2
Paraná	C4
Pernambuco	E2
Piauí	D2
Rio de Janeiro	D4, Inset I
Rio Grande do Norte	E2
Rio Grande do Sul	C4
Rondônia	B3
Roraima	B1
Santa Catarina	C4
São Paulo	C4, Inset II
Sergipe	E3
Tocantins	D3

Cities and Towns

Alagoinhas	E3
Altamira	C2
Anápolis	D3
Aracaju	E3
Bacabal	D2
Bauru	D4
Belém	D2
Belford Roxo	Inset I
Belo Horizonte	D3
Boa Vista	B1
Bom Jesus da Lapa	D3
Brasília, capital	D3
Cáceres	C3
Cachimbo	C2
Campina Grande	E2
Campinas	D4
Campo Grande	C4
Campos	D4
Campos Elísios	Inset I
Carapicuíba	Inset II
Corumbá	C3
Cotia	Inset II
Cruzeiro do Sul	A2
Cubatão	Inset II
Cuiabá	C3
Curitiba	D4
Diadema	Inset II
Dourados	C4
Duque de Caxias	Inset I
Feira de Santana	D3
Floriano	D2
Florianópolis	D4
Fortaleza	E2
Foz do Iguaçu	C4
Goiânia	D3
Governador Valadares	D3
Guajara Mirim	B3
Guarujá	Inset II
Guarulhos	Inset II
Ilhéus	E3
Imbariê	Inset I
Imperatriz	D2
Inhomirim	Inset I
Ipiiba	Inset I
Itabira	D3
Itabuna	E3
Itaipu	Inset I
Itajaí	D4
Itapecerica da Serra	Inset II
Itapeva	Inset II
Itaquaquecetuba	Inset II
Jaboatão	E2
Jacare-Acanga	C2
Japeri	Inset I
Jir Paraná	B3
João Pessoa	E2
Joinville	D4
Juàzeiro	D2
Juàzeiro do Norte	E2
Juiz de Fora	D4
Jundiai	D4
Lajes	C4
Londrina	C4
Macapá	C1
Maceió	E2
Majé	Inset I
Manaus	B2
Maraba	D2
Mariana	D3
Mauá	Inset II
Mogi das Cruzes	Inset II
Monjolo	Inset I
Montes Claros	D3
Mozzoro	E2
Natal	E2
Neves	Inset I
Nilópolis	Inset I
Niterói	D4, Inset I
Nova Iguaçu	Inset I
Olinda	E2
Osasco	Inset II
Palmas	D3
Paranaguá	D4
Parnaiba	D2
Passo Fundo	C4
Paulo Afonso	E2
Pelotas	C5
Petrolina	D2
Petrópolis	D4, Inset I
Piracicaba	D4
Poá	Inset II
Pôrto Alegre	C5
Pôrto Velho	B2
Queimados	Inset I
Randonopolis	C3
Recife	E2
Ribeirão Pires	Inset II
Ribeirão Prêto	D4
Rio Branco	B2
Rio de Janeiro	D4, Inset I
Rio Grande	C5
Rio Verde	C3
Salvador	E3
Santa Maria	C4
Santana do Livramento	C5
Santarém	C2
Santo André	Inset II
Santos	D4, Inset II
São Bernardo do Campo	Inset II
São Caetano do Sul	Inset II
São Gonçalo	Inset I
São João de Meriti	Inset I
São José do Rio Prêto	D4
São Luís	D2
São Paulo	D4, Inset II
São Vincente	Inset II
Sobral	D2
Sorocaba	D4
Suzano	Inset II
Taboão da Serra	Inset II
Tefé	B2
Teresina	D2
Tubarão	D4
Uberaba	D3
Uberlândia	D3
Vincente de Carvalho	Inset II
Vitória	D3
Vitória da Conquista	D3
Volta Redonda	D4

Other Features

Acaraí, range	C1
Açúcar, mt.	Inset I
Amazon, basin	B2
Amazon, river	B2
Araguaia, river	C3
Aripuanã, river	C2
Baleia, point	D3
Bandeira, mt.	D3
Billings, reservoir	Inset II
Branco, river	B1
Brazilian, highlands	D3
Caviana, island	D1
Chapada dos Parecis, range	C3
Corcovado, mt.	Inset I
Corumbau, point	E3
Furnas, reservoir	D4
Geral, range	C4
Grande, river	D3
Guandu, river	Inset I
Guaporé, river	B3
Guiana, highlands	B1
Içá, river	B2
Iguaçu, falls	B2
Itaipu, reservoir	C4
Japurá, river	B2
Jari, river	C1
Javari, river	A2
Juruá, river	B2
Juruena, river	C3
Madeira, river	B2
Mantiqueira, range	D4
Mar, range	D4
Marajó, island	D2
Mato Grosso, plateau	C3
Mexiana, island	D1
Neblina, mt.	B1
Negro, river	B2
Órgãos, range	Inset I
Pantanal, lowland	C4
Pará, river	C2
Paraguai, river	C3
Paraná, river	C4
Parima, range	B1
Parnaíba, river	D2
Patos, lagoon	C5
Paulo Afonso, falls	E2
Pedra Açú, mt.	Inset I
Purus, river	B2
Roncador, range	C3
São Francisco, river	D3
Selvas, region	B2
Sobradinho, reservoir	D3
Tapajós, river	C2
Taquari, river	C3
Teles Pires, river	C2
Tietê, river	Inset II
Tocantins, river	D2
Tucuruí, reservoir	D2
Tumucumaque, range	C1
Uruguai, river	C4
Xingu, river	C3

Brazil

Capital: Brasília
Area: 3,286,470 sq. mi.
8,514,171 sq. km.
Population: 171,853,126
Largest City: São Paulo
Language: Portuguese
Monetary Unit: Real

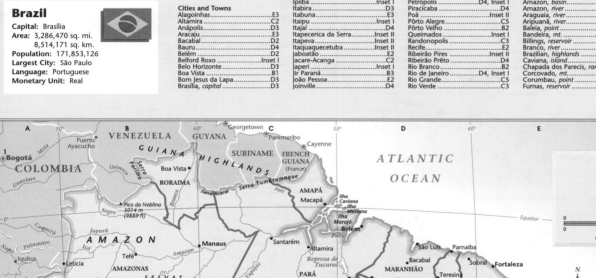

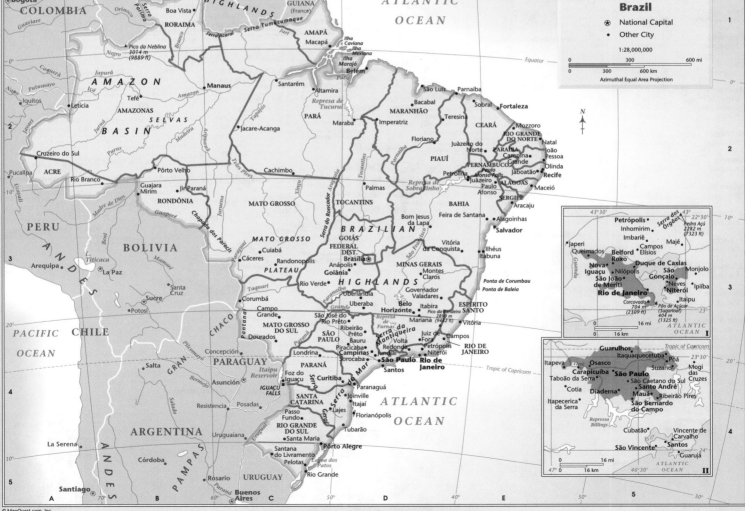

MAJOR CITIES

Antigua & Barbuda
St. Johns 27,000

Bahamas
Nassau 172,000

Barbados
Bridgetown 6,000

Belize
Belize City 45,000
Belmopan 4,000

Canada (metro)
Toronto 4,264,000
Montréal 3,327,000
Vancouver 1,832,000
Ottawa 1,010,000

Costa Rica
San José 324,000

Cuba
Havana 2,185,000

Dominica
Roseau 16,000

Dominican Republic
Santo Domingo 2,135,000

El Salvador (metro)
San Salvador 1,214,000

Grenada
St. George's 30,000

Guatemala (metro)
Guatemala 2,205,000

Haiti
Port-au-Prince 884,000

Honduras (metro)
Tegucigalpa 995,000

Jamaica (metro)
Kingston 587,000

Mexico
Mexico City 8,489,000
Guadalajara 1,633,000
Puebla 1,223,000

Nicaragua (metro)
Managua 1,124,000

Panama
Panamá 465,000

Puerto Rico
San Juan 428,000

St. Kitts & Nevis
Basseterre 15,000

St. Lucia
Castries 45,000

St. Vincent & Grenadines
Kingstown 15,000

Trinidad & Tobago
Port of Spain 43,000

United States (Census 2000)
New York 8,008,000
Los Angeles 3,695,000
Chicago 2,896,000
Houston 1,954,000
Philadelphia 1,518,000
Phoenix 1,321,000
San Diego 1,223,000
Washington, D.C. 572,000

International comparability of city population data is limited by various data inconsistencies.

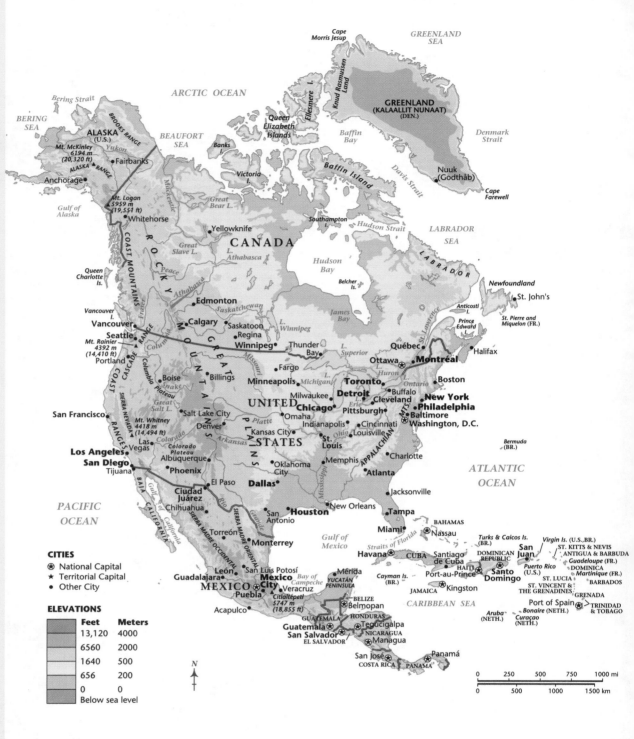

CITIES
⊛ National Capital
★ Territorial Capital
• Other City

ELEVATIONS

Feet	Meters
13,120	4000
6560	2000
1640	500
656	200
0	0
Below sea level	

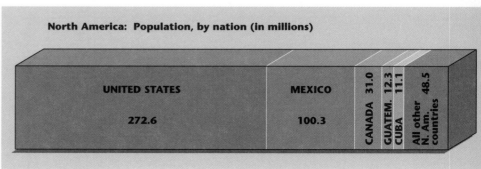

North America: Population, by nation (in millions)

UNITED STATES	MEXICO	CANADA	GUATEM.	CUBA	All other N. Am. countries
272.6	100.3	31.0	12.3	11.1	48.5

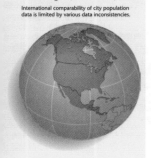

© MapQuest.com, Inc.

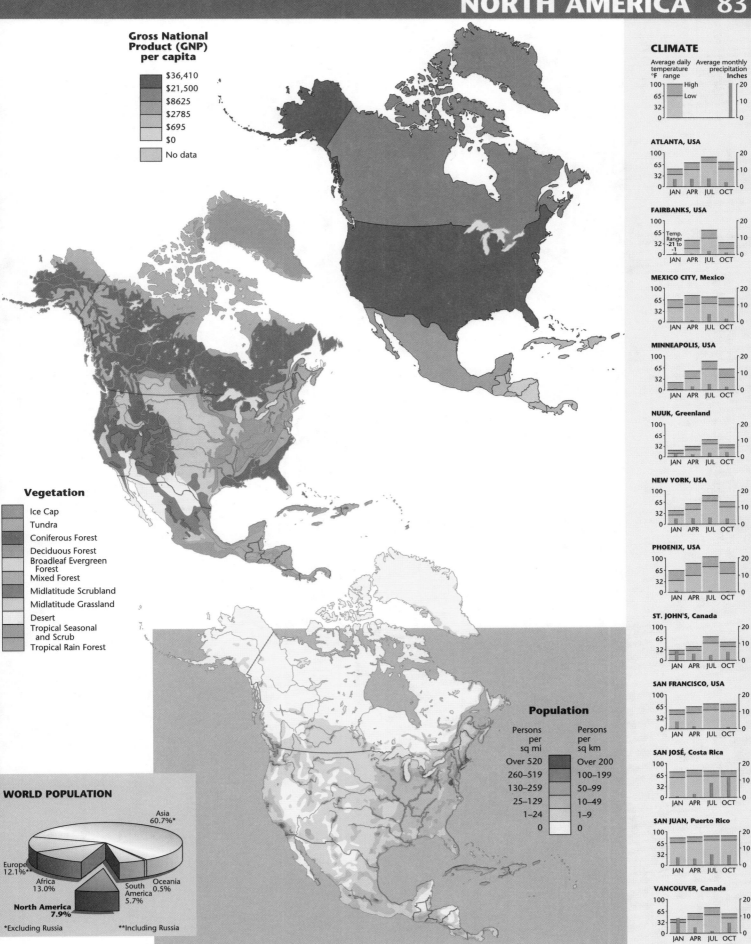

Gross National Product (GNP) per capita

- $36,410
- $21,500
- $8625
- $2785
- $695
- $0
- No data

Vegetation

- Ice Cap
- Tundra
- Coniferous Forest
- Deciduous Forest
- Broadleaf Evergreen Forest
- Mixed Forest
- Midlatitude Scrubland
- Midlatitude Grassland
- Desert
- Tropical Seasonal and Scrub
- Tropical Rain Forest

CLIMATE

Average daily temperature °F range   Average monthly precipitation Inches

- ATLANTA, USA
- FAIRBANKS, USA — Temp. Range -21 to -1
- MEXICO CITY, Mexico
- MINNEAPOLIS, USA
- NUUK, Greenland
- NEW YORK, USA
- PHOENIX, USA
- ST. JOHN'S, Canada
- SAN FRANCISCO, USA
- SAN JOSÉ, Costa Rica
- SAN JUAN, Puerto Rico
- VANCOUVER, Canada

Population

Persons per sq mi	Persons per sq km
Over 520	Over 200
260–519	100–199
130–259	50–99
25–129	10–49
1–24	1–9
0	0

WORLD POPULATION

- Asia 60.7%*
- Europe 12.1%**
- Africa 13.0%
- North America 7.9%
- South America 5.7%
- Oceania 0.5%

*Excluding Russia   **Including Russia

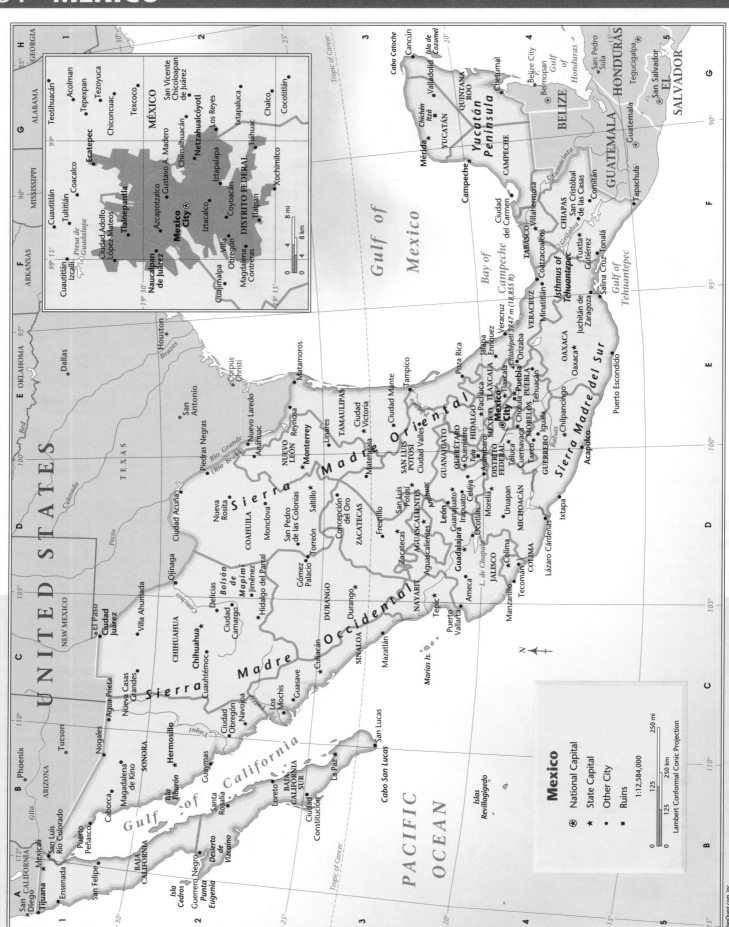

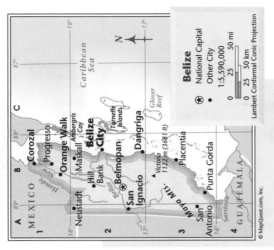

© MapQuest.com, Inc.

Belize

National Capital ⊛
Other City ●

1:5,590,000

0 25 50 mi
0 25 50 km

Lambert Conformal Conic Projection

Belize

Capital: Belmopan
Area: 8,867 sq. mi.
   22,972 sq. km.
Population: 235,789
Largest City: Belize City
Language: English
Monetary Unit: Belize dollar

Belize:
Map Index

Cities and Towns

Belize City	B2
Belmopan, capital	B2
Corozal	B1
Dangriga	B2
Hill Bank	B2
Maskall	B1
Neustadt	A2
Orange Walk	B1
Placentia	B3
Progreso	B1
Punta Gorda	B3
San Antonio	A3
San Ignacio	A2

Other Features

Ambergris Cay, island	C2
Belize, river	B2
Glover, reef	C3
Hondo, river	B1
Maya, mts.	A3
New, river	B1
Sarstoon, river	A4
Turneffe, islands	C2
Victoria, peak	B3

© MapQuest.com, Inc.

Guatemala

National Capital ⊛
Other City ●

1:8,150,000

0 50 100 mi
0 50 100 km

Lambert Conformal Conic Projection

Guatemala

Capital: Guatemala City
Area: 42,042 sq. mi.
   108,917 sq. km.
Population: 12,335,580
Largest City: Guatemala City
Language: Spanish
Monetary Unit: Quetzal

Guatemala:
Map Index

Cities and Towns

Antigua	C5
Champerico	B5
Chinajá	C4
Cobán	C4
Escuintla	C5
Flores	D3
Guatemala City, capital	C5
Huehuetenango	B4
Jutiapa	D5
La Libertad	C3
Mazatenango	B5
Paxbán	C2
Puerto Barrios	E4
Quetzaltenango	B5
Salamá	C4
San José	C5
San Luis	C6
Santo Tomás de Castilla	E4
Tikal	D3
Zacapa	D5

Other Features

Atitlán, lake	B5
Chixoy, river	C4
Honduras, gulf	E3
Izabal, lake	E4
Motagua, river	D4
Pasión, river	C3
Paz, river	C6
Petén-Itzá, lake	D3
San Pedro, river	C2
Sarstún, river	D4
Sierra Madre, mts.	C5
Suchiate, river	A5
Tacaná, volcano	A4
Usumacinta, river	B4
	C3

Mexico

Capital: Mexico City
Area: 756,066 sq. mi.
   1,958,720 sq. km.
Population: 100,294,036
Largest City: Mexico City
Language: Spanish
Monetary Unit: New peso

Mexico:
Map Index

States

Aguascalientes	D3
Baja California	A1
Baja California Sur	B2
Campeche	F4
Chiapas	F4
Chihuahua	C2
Coahuila	D2
Colima	D4
Distrito Federal	E4, Inset
Durango	C3
Guanajuato	D3
Guerrero	D4
Hidalgo	E3
Jalisco	D4
México	E4, Inset
Michoacán	D4
Morelos	Inset
Nayarit	C3
Nuevo León	E2
Oaxaca	E4
Puebla	E4
Querétaro	D3
Quintana Roo	G3
San Luis Potosí	D3
Sinaloa	C3
Sonora	B1
Tabasco	F4
Tamaulipas	E3
Tlaxcala	E4
Veracruz	E4
Yucatán	G3
Zacatecas	D3

Cities and Towns

Acámbaro	D4
Acapulco	E4
Acolman	Inset
Agua Prieta	C1
Aguascalientes, state capital	D3
Ameca	D3
Atzcapotzalco	Inset
Anáhuac	D2
Caborca	B1
Campeche, state capital	F4
Cancún	G3
Celaya	D3
Chalco	Inset
Chetumal, state capital	G4
Chihuahua, state capital	C2
Chilpancingo, state capital	E4
Chalmalhuacán	Inset
Cholula	E4
Ciudad Acuña	D2
Ciudad Adolfo López Mateos	Inset
Ciudad Camargo	C2
Ciudad Constitución	B3
Ciudad del Carmen	F4
Ciudad Mante	E3
Ciudad Obregón	C2
Ciudad Valles	E3
Ciudad Victoria, state capital	E3
Coacalco	Inset
Coatzacoalcos	F4
Colima, state capital	D4
Comitán	F4
Concepción del Oro	D3

Coyoacán	Inset
Cuajimalpa	Inset
Cuauhtémoc	C2
Cuautitlán Izcalli	Inset
Cuernavaca, state capital	E4
Culiacán, state capital	C3
Delicias	C2
Durango, state capital	D3
Ecatepec	Inset
Ensenada	A1
Fresnillo	D3
Gómez Palacio	D2
Guadalajara, state capital	D3
Guanajuato, state capital	D3
Guasave	C2
Guaymas	B2
Guerrero Negro	B2
Gustavo A. Madero	Inset
Hermosillo, state capital	B2
Hidalgo del Parral	C2
Iguala	E4
Irapuato	D3
Ixtapaluca	Inset
Iztacalco	Inset
Iztapalapa	Inset
Jalapa Enríquez, state capital	E4
Jiménez	D2
Juchitán de Zaragoza	F4
La Paz, state capital	B3
Lázaro Cárdenas	D4
León	D3
Linares	E3
Loreto	B2
Los Mochis	C2
Los Reyes	Inset
Magdalena de Kino	B1
Magdalena Contreras	Inset
Manzanillo	D4
Matamoros	E2
Matehuala	D3
Mazatlán	C3
Mérida, state capital	G3
Mexicali, state capital	A1
Mexico City, national capital	E4, Inset
Minatitlán	F4
Monclova	D2
Monterrey, state capital	E2
Morelia, state capital	D4
Naucalpan de Juárez	Inset
Navojoa	C2
Netzahualcóyotl	Inset
Nogales	B1
Nueva Casas Grandes	C1
Nueva Rosita	D2
Nuevo Laredo	E2
Oaxaca, state capital	E4
Ocotlán	D3
Ojinaga	D2
Orizaba	E4
Pachuca, state capital	E3
Piedras Negras	D2
Poza Rica	E3
Puebla, state capital	E4
Puerto Escondido	E4
Puerto Peñasco	B1
Puerto Vallarta	C3
Querétaro, state capital	D3
Reynosa	E2
Salina Cruz	F4
Saltillo, state capital	D3

San Cristóbal de las Casas	F4
San Felipe	B1
San Luis	C2
San Luis Potosí, state capital	D3
San Pedro de las Colonias	D2
Santa Rosalía	B2
San Vicente Chicoloapan de Juárez	Inset
Tampico	E3
Tapachula	F5
Taxco	E4
Tecomán	D4
Tehuacán	E4
Teoloyucan	Inset
Teotihuacán	Inset
Tepexpan	Inset
Tepic, state capital	D3
Texcoco	Inset
Tezoyuca	Inset
Tijuana	A1
Tlalnepantla	Inset
Tláhuac	Inset
Tlalpan	Inset
Tlaxcala, state capital	E4
Toluca, state capital	E4
Tonalá	F4
Torreón	D2
Tultitlán	Inset
Tuxtla Gutiérrez, state capital	F4
Unuapan	D4
Valladolid	G3
Veracruz	E4
Villa Ahumada	C1
Villahermosa, state capital	F4
Villa Obregón	Inset
Xochimilco	Inset
Zacatecas, state capital	D3

Other Features

Anáhuac, depression	D3
Balsas, river	D4
Bolsón de Mapimí, depression	D2
California, gulf	B1
Campeche, bay	F4
Catoche, cape	G3
Cedros, island	A2
Chapala, lake	D3
Chichén Itzá, ruins	G3
Citlaltépetl, mt.	E4
Concho, river	C2
Cozumel, island	G3
Eugenia, point	A2
Fuerte, river	C2
Grijalva, river	F4
Guadalupe, reservoir	Inset
Marías, islands	C3
Pánuco, river	E3
Revillagigedo, islands	B4
Río Grande (Río Bravo), river	D2
San Lucas, cape	B3
Sierra Madre del Sur, mts.	D4
Sierra Madre Occidental, mts.	C2
Sierra Madre Oriental, mts.	D2
Tehuantepec, gulf	F4
Tehuantepec, isthmus	F4
Tiburón, island	B2
Tula, ruins	E3
Vizcaíno, desert	B2
Yaqui, river	C2
Yucatán, peninsula	G4

Honduras

Capital: Tegucigalpa
Area: 43,277 sq. mi.
112,117 sq. km.
Population: 5,997,327
Largest City: Tegucigalpa
Language: Spanish
Monetary Unit: Lempira

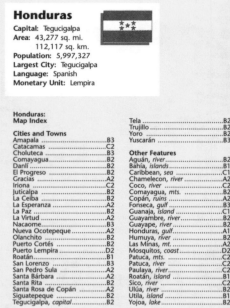

Honduras: Map Index

Cities and Towns

Amapala	B3
Catacamas	C2
Choluteca	B3
Comayagua	B2
Danlí	B2
El Progreso	B2
Gracias	A2
Iriona	C2
Juticalpa	B2
La Ceiba	B2
La Esperanza	A2
La Paz	B2
La Virtud	A2
Nacaome	B3
Nueva Ocotepeque	A2
Olanchito	B2
Puerto Cortés	B2
Puerto Lempira	D2
Roatán	B1
San Lorenzo	B3
San Pedro Sula	A2
Santa Bárbara	A2
Santa Rita	A2
Santa Rosa de Copán	A2
Siguatepeque	B2
Tegucigalpa, capital	B2
Tela	B2
Trujillo	B2
Yoro	B2
Yuscarán	B3

Other Features

Aguán, river	B2
Bahía, islands	B1
Caribbean, sea	C1
Chameleon, river	A2
Coco, river	C2
Comayagua, mts.	B2
Copán, ruins	A2
Fonseca, gulf	B3
Guanaja, island	C1
Guayambre, river	B2
Guayape, river	B2
Honduras, gulf	A1
Humuya, river	B2
Las Mínas, mt.	A2
Mosquitos, coast	D2
Patuca, mts.	C2
Patuca, river	C2
Paulaya, river	C2
Roatán, island	B1
Sico, river	C2
Ulúa, river	B2
Utila, island	B1
Yojoa, lake	B2

© MapQuest.com, Inc.

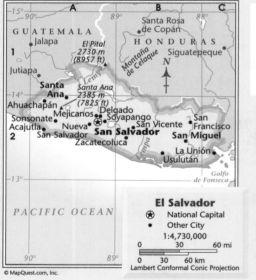

El Salvador

Capital: San Salvador
Area: 8,124 sq. mi.
21,047 sq. km.
Population: 5,839,079
Largest City: San Salvador
Language: Spanish
Monetary Unit: Colón

El Salvador: Map Index

Cities and Towns

Acajutla	A2
Ahuachapán	A2
Delgado	A2
La Unión	C2
Mejicanos	A2
Nueva San Salvador	A2
San Francisco	B2
San Miguel	B2
San Salvador, capital	A2
Santa Ana	A2
San Vicente	B2
Sonsonate	A2
Soyapango	A2
Usulután	B2
Zacatecoluca	B2

Other Features

El Pital, mt.	A1
Fonseca, gulf	C2
Lempa, river	A1, B2
Santa Ana, volcano	A2

© MapQuest.com, Inc.

Costa Rica: Map Index

Cities and Towns

Alajuela	B2
Cartago	C3
Colorado	C2
Golfito	C4
Heredia	B2
La Cruz	A1
Liberia	A2
Limón	C3
Los Chiles	B1
Puerto Jiménez	C4
Puerto Quepos	B3
Puntarenas	B3
San José, capital	B3
Santa Cruz	A2

Other Features

Arenal, lake	B2
Central, range	B2
Chirripó, mt.	C3
Chirripó, river	C2
Coronado, bay	B3
Dulce, gulf	C4
Frio, river	B2
General, river	C3
Grande, river	B3
Guanacaste, range	A2
Irazú, volcano	C3
Nicoya, gulf	B3
Papagayo, gulf	A2
Pirris, river	B3
Reventazón, river	C2
San Carlos, river	B2
San Juan, river	B2
Sarapiquí river	B2
Sixaola, river	C3
Talamanca, range	C3
Tempisque, river	A2

Costa Rica

Capital: San José
Area: 19,730 sq. mi.
51,114 sq. km.
Population: 3,674,490
Largest City: San José
Language: Spanish
Monetary Unit: Colón

© MapQuest.com, Inc.

Nicaragua

Capital: Managua
Area: 50,880 sq. mi.
　131,813 sq. km.
Population: 4,717,132
Largest City: Managua
Language: Spanish
Monetary Unit: Córdoba

Nicaragua:
Map Index

Cities and Towns

Bluefields	C3
Boaco	B2
Bocay	B1
Chinandega	A2
Colonia Nueva Guínea	B3
Corinto	A2
Diriamba	A3
Estelí	A2
Granada	B3
Jinotega	B2
Jinotepe	A3
Juigalpa	B2
La Rosita	B2
León	A2
Managua, *capital*	A2
Masaya	A3
Matagalpa	B2
Nagarote	A2
Ocotal	A2
Prinzapolka	C2
Puerto Cabezas	C1
Puerto Sandino	A2
Rama	B2
Río Blanco	B2
Río Grande	A2
Rivas	B3
San Carlos	B3
San Juan del Norte	C3
San Juan del Sur	B3
Siuna	B2
Somoto	A2
Waspam	C1
Wiwili	B2

Other Features

Bambana, *river*	B2
Bismuna, *lagoon*	C1
Bluefields, *bay*	C3
Bocay, *river*	B2
Chontaleña, *mts.*	B2
Coco, *river*	A2, C1
Cosigüina, *mt.*	A2
Cosigüina, *point*	A2
Dariense, *mts.*	B2
Escondido, *river*	B2
Fonseca, *gulf*	A2
Gracias a Dios, *cape*	C1
Grande de Matagalpa, *river*	B2
Huapí, *mts.*	B2
Isabelia, *mts.*	B2
Kurinwás, *river*	B2
Maíz, *islands*	C2
Managua, *lake*	A2
Mico, *river*	B2
Miskitos, *cays*	C1
Mogotón, *mt.*	A2
Mosquitos, *coast*	C3
Nicaragua, *lake*	B3
Ometepe, *island*	B3
Perlas, *lagoon*	C2
Perlas, *point*	C2
Prinzapolka, *river*	B2
San Juan, *river*	B3
San Juan del Norte, *bay*	C3
Siquia, *river*	B2
Solentiname, *island*	B3
Tipitapa, *river*	A2
Tuma, *river*	B2
Wawa, *river*	B1
Zapatera, *island*	B3

Panama

Capital: Panamá
Area: 29,157 sq. mi.
　75,536 sq. km.
Population: 2,778,526
Largest City: Panamá
Language: Spanish
Monetary Unit: Balboa

Panama:
Map Index

Cities and Towns

Aguadulce	B2
Almirante	A2
Bajo Boquete	A2
Balboa	C2
Bocas del Toro	A2
Changuinola	A2
Chitré	B3
Coclé del Norte	B2
Colón	C2
Cristóbal	C2
David	A2
El Porvenir	C2
La Palma	C2
Las Tablas	B3
Panamá, *capital*	C2
Penonomé	B2
Portobelo	C2
Puerto Armuelles	A2
San Miguelito	C2
Santiago	B2
Yaviza	D2

Other Features

Azuero, *peninsula*	B3
Barú, *volcano*	A2
Bayano, *lake*	C2
Burica, *point*	A2
Chagres, *river*	C2
Chiriquí, *gulf*	A3
Chiriquí, *lagoon*	B2
Chucunaque, *river*	D2
Coiba, *island*	B3
Darién, *mts.*	D2
Gatún, *lake*	C2
Mala, *point*	B3
Manzanillo, *point*	C2
Mosquitos, *gulf*	B2
Panamá, *bay*	C2
Panama, *canal*	C2
Panama, *gulf*	C3
Parita, *bay*	B2
Perlas, *archipelago*	C2
Rey, *island*	C2
San Blas, *mts.*	C2
San Miguel, *gulf*	C2
Tabasará, *mts.*	B2
Tuira, *river*	D2

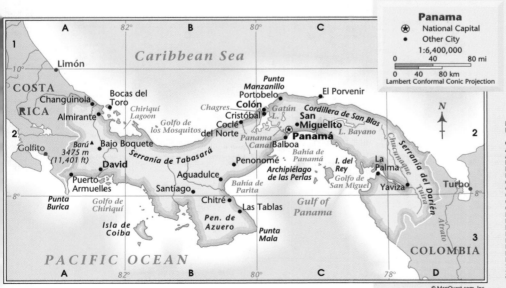

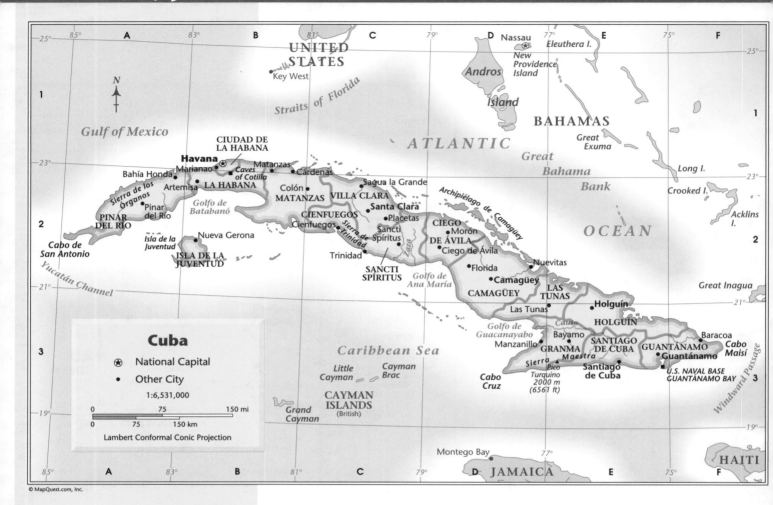

Cuba

⊛ National Capital

• Other City

1:6,531,000

0 — 75 — 150 mi
0 — 75 — 150 km

Lambert Conformal Conic Projection

© MapQuest.com, Inc.

Cuba

Capital: Havana
Area: 42,804 sq. mi.
110,890 sq. km.
Population: 11,096,395
Largest City: Havana
Language: Spanish
Monetary Unit: Peso

Cuba:
Map Index

Provinces
Camagüey D2
Ciego de Ávila D2
Cienfuegos C2
Ciudad de La Habana B1
Granma E3
Guantánamo E3
Holguín E3
Isla de la Juventud
(special municipality) B2
La Habana B1
Las Tunas E2
Matanzas B2
Pinar del Río A2
Sancti Spíritus C2
Santiago de Cuba E3
Villa Clara C2

Cities and Towns
Artemisa B2
Bahía Honda A2
Baracoa F3
Bayamo E3
Camagüey D2
Cárdenas B1
Ciego de Ávila D2
Cienfuegos C2
Colón C2
Florida D2
Guantánamo E3
Havana, capital B1
Holguín E3
Las Tunas E3

Manzanillo D3
Marianao B1
Matanzas B1
Morón D2
Nueva Gerona B2
Nuevitas D2
Pinar del Río A2
Placetas C2
Sagua la Grande C2
Sancti Spíritus C2
Santa Clara C2
Santiago de Cuba E3
Trinidad C2

Other Features
Ana María, gulf D2
Batabanó, gulf B2
Camagüey, archipelago D2
Cauto, river E3
Cotilla, caves B2
Cruz, cape D3
Florida, straits B1
Guacanayabo, gulf D3
Juventud, island B2
Maestra, mts. D3
Maisí, cape F3
Mexico, gulf A1
Órganos, mts. A2
San Antonio, cape A2
Trinidad, mts. C2
Turquino, mt. E3
U.S. Naval Base
Guantánamo Bay E3
Windward, passage F3
Yucatán, channel A2
Zaza, river C2

Jamaica

Capital: Kingston
Area: 4,244 sq. mi.
10,995 sq. km.
Population: 2,652,443
Largest City: Kingston
Language: English
Monetary Unit: Dollar

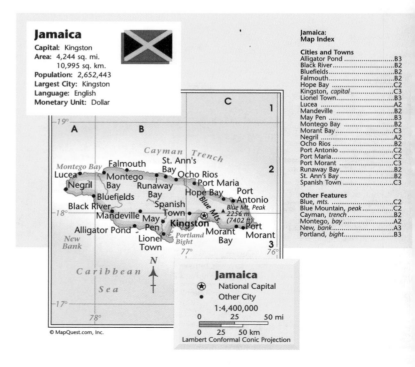

Jamaica

⊛ National Capital

• Other City

1:4,400,000

0 — 25 — 50 mi
0 — 25 — 50 km

Lambert Conformal Conic Projection

© MapQuest.com, Inc.

Jamaica:
Map Index

Cities and Towns
Alligator Pond B3
Black River B2
Bluefields B2
Falmouth B2
Hope Bay C2
Kingston, capital C3
Lionel Town B3
Lucea A2
Mandeville B2
May Pen B3
Montego Bay B2
Morant Bay C3
Negril A2
Ocho Rios B2
Port Antonio C2
Port Maria C2
Port Morant C3
Runaway Bay B2
St. Ann's Bay B2
Spanish Town C3

Other Features
Blue, mts. C2
Blue Mountain, peak C2
Cayman, trench B2
Montego, bay A3
New, bank A3
Portland, bight B3

Bonao B2
Cabrera C1
Comendador A2
Cotuí B1
Dajabón A1
El Macao D2
El Seibo C2
Hato Mayor C2
Higüey D2
Jimaní A2
La Romana D2
La Vega B1
Luperón B1
Mao A1
Miches C2
Moca B1
Monte Cristi A1
Monte Plata C2
Nagua C1
Neiba A2
Oviedo A3
Pedernales A3
Pedro Santana A1
Puerto Plata B1
Sabana de la Mar C1
Sabaneta A1
Salcedo B1
Samaná C1
San Cristóbal B2
San Francisco de Macorís B1
San José de las Matas A1
San Juan A2
San Pedro de Macorís B2
Santiago B1
Santo Domingo, capital B2
Sousúa B1

Dominican Republic:
Map Index

Provinces
Azua B2
Bahoruco A2
Barahona A2
Dajabón A1
Distrito Nacional B2
Duarte C1
El Seibo C2
Espaillat B1
Hato Mayor C2
Independencia A2
La Altagracia D2
La Estrelleta A1
La Romana D2
La Vega B1
María Trinidad Sánchez B1
Monseñor Nouel B2
Monte Cristi A1
Monte Plata C2
Pedernales A3
Peravia B2
Puerto Plata B1
Salcedo B1
Samaná C1
Sánchez Ramírez B1
San Cristóbal B2
San Juan A2
San Pedro de Macorís C2
Santiago B1
Santiago Rodríguez A1
Valverde B1

Cities and Towns
Azua B2
Baní B2
Barahona A2

Other Features
Bahoruco, mts. A2
Beata, cape A3
Beata, island A3
Calderas, bay B2
Camú, river B1
Central, range B2
Cibao, valley A1
Duarte, mt. B1
Engaño, cape D2
Enriquillo, lake A2
Mona, passage D2
Neiba, mts. A2
Ocoa, bay B2
Oriental, range C2
Ozama, river B2
Samaná, bay C1
Samaná, cape C1
Saona, island D2
Septentrional, range B1
Soco, river C2
Yaque del Norte, river A1
Yaque del Sur, river A1
Yuna, river B2

ATLANTIC OCEAN

© MapQuest.com, Inc.

Dominican Republic
Capital: Santo Domingo
Area: 18,704 sq. mi.
    48,456 sq. km.
Population: 8,129,734
Largest City: Santo Domingo
Language: Spanish
Monetary Unit: Peso

Dominican Republic
⊛ National Capital
• Other City
1:3,778,000
0   20   40 mi
0   20   40 km
Transverse Mercator Projection

© MapQuest.com, Inc.

Haiti
⊛ National Capital
• Other City
1:5,593,000
0   30   60 mi
0   30   60 km
Lambert Conformal Conic Projection

Haiti:
Map Index

Departments
Artibonite C1
Centre D1
Grand Anse B2
Nord C1
Nord-Est D1
Nord-Ouest B1
Ouest C2
Sud B2
Sud-Est C2

Cities and Towns
Anse-à-Galets C2
Belle-Anse C2
Cap-Haïtien C1
Dame-Marie A2
Ennery C1
Gonaïves C1
Hinche C1
Jacmel C2
Jérémie A2
Léogâne C2
Les Cayes B2
Miragoâne B2
Mirebalais C2
Port-au-Prince, capital C2
Port-de-Paix B1
Port-Salut B2
Saint-Marc C1

Other Features
Artibonite, river C1
Gonâve, gulf B1
Gonâve, island B2
Gravois, point B3
Pic de la Selle, mt. D2
Port-au-Prince, bay C2
Tortuga, island C1
Vache, island B2
Windward, passage B1

Haiti
Capital: Port-au-Prince
Area: 10,695 sq. mi.
    27,614 sq. km.
Population: 6,884,264
Largest City: Port-au-Prince
Languages: French, Creole
Monetary Unit: Gourde

The Bahamas
Capital: Nassau
Area: 5,382 sq. mi.
    13,943 sq. km.
Population: 283,705
Largest City: Nassau
Languages: English, Creole
Monetary Unit: Dollar

Turks and Caicos Is.
Capital: Grand Turk
Area: 193 sq. mi.
    500 sq. km.
Population: 16,863
Largest City: Grand Turk
Language: English
Monetary Unit: U.S. Dollar

Bahamas and
Turks & Caicos Islands:
Map Index

Bahamas

Cities and Towns
Alice Town B2
Arthur's Town B3
Freeport A2
Kemps Bay B3
Marsh Harbour B2
Matthew Town C4
Nassau, capital B2
Nicholls' Town A2
Sandy Point B2

Other Features
Acklins, island C4
Andros, island A3
Cat, island B3
Crooked, island C4
Crooked Island, passage C4
Eleuthera, island B2
Exuma, sound B3
Grand Bahama, island A2
Great Abaco, island B2
Great Bahama, bank A3

Great Exuma, island B3
Great Inagua, island C4
Harbour, island B2
Little Inagua, island C4
Long, island C3
Mayaguana, island C4
Mayaguana, passage C4
New Providence, island B3
Northeast Providence,
  channel B2
Rum, cay C3
Samana, cay C3
San Salvador, island C3
Water, cays A3

Turks & Caicos Islands

Cities and Towns
Cockburn Harbour D4
Grand Turk, capital D4

Other Features
Ambergris, cay D4
Caicos, islands D4
Grand Turk, island D4
Providenciales, island C4
Salt, cay D4
Turks, islands D4

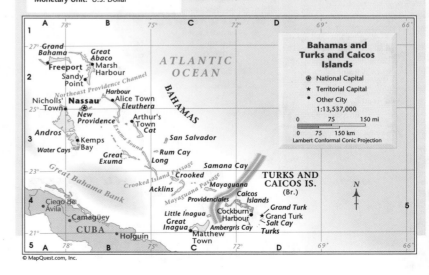

Bahamas and Turks and Caicos Islands
⊛ National Capital
★ Territorial Capital
• Other City
1:13,537,000
0   75   150 mi
0   75   150 km
Lambert Conformal Conic Projection

ATLANTIC OCEAN

© MapQuest.com, Inc.

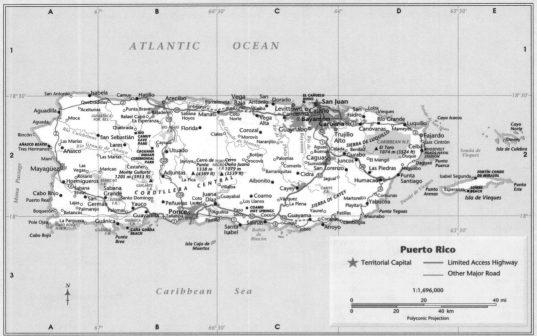

Puerto Rico

Capital: San Juan
Area: 3,492 sq. mi.
9,047 sq. km.
Population: 3,887,652
Largest City: San Juan
Languages: Spanish, English
Monetary Unit: U.S. dollar

Puerto Rico

★ Territorial Capital
— Limited Access Highway
— Other Major Road

1:1,696,000

0   20   40 mi
0   20   40 km

Polyconic Projection

© MapQuest.com, Inc.

Puerto Rico: Map Index

Cities and Towns

Adjuntas	B2
Aguada	A2
Aguadilla	A2
Aguas Buenas	C2
Aguilita	B2
Aibonito	C2
Añasco	A2
Arecibo	B2
Arroyo	C3
Bajadero	B2
Barceloneta	B2
Barranquitas	C2
Bayamón	C2
Cabo Rojo	A2
Caguas	C2
Camuy	B2
Candelaria	C2
Canóvanas	D2
Carolina	C2
Cataño	C2
Cayey	C2
Ceiba	D2
Ceiba	D2
Celada	C2
Ciales	C2
Cidra	C2
Coamo	C2
Coco	C2
Comerío	C2
Coquí	C3
Corazón	C3
Corozal	C2
Coto Laurel	C2
Dorado	C2
Fajardo	D2
Florida	B2
Guánica	B2
Guayama	C3
Guayanilla	B2
Guaynabo	C2
Gurabo	C2
Hatillo	B2
Hormigueros	A2
Humacao	D2
Imbéry	B2
Isabela	A1
Jayuya	B2
Jobos	C3
Juana Díaz	B2
Juncos	C2
Lajas	A2
Lares	A2
Las Piedras	D2
Levittown	D2
Loíza	D2
Luquillo	D2
Manatí	B2
Martorell	D2
Maunabo	D2
Mayagüez	A2
Moca	A2
Naguabo	D2
Pastillo	C3
Patillas	C2
Peñuelas	B2
Ponce	B2
Puerto Real	A2
Punta Santiago	D2
Quebradillas	B2
Río Grande	D2
Sabana Grande	A2
Salinas	C2
San Antonio	C2
San Germán	A2
San Isidro	D2
San Juan, *capital*	C2
San Lorenzo	D2
San Sebastián	B2
Santa Isabel	C3
Santo Domingo	A2
Trujillo Alto	C2
Utuado	B2
Vega Alta	C2
Vega Baja	C2
Vieques	E2
Villalba	B2
Yabucoa	D2
Yauco	B2

Other Features

Añasco, *beach*	A2
Arenas, *point*	C2
Bayamón, *river*	C2
Brea, *point*	B3
Cabo Rojo Natl. Wildlife Refuge	A3
Caguana Indian Ceremonial Park	B2
Caja de Muertos, *island*	C3
Caña Gorda, *beach*	B3
Caribbean, *sea*	B3
Caribbean Natl. Forest	D2
Carite Forest Reserve	C2
Coamo Hot Springs	C2
Cordillera Central, *mts.*	C2
Culebra, *island*	E2
Culebrinas, *river*	A2
Doña Juana, *mt.*	B2
El Cañuelo, *ruins*	C2
El Toro, *mt.*	D2
Este, *point*	E2
Fortín Conde de Mirasol, *fort*	E1
Grande de Añasco, *river*	A2
Grande de Manatí, *river*	B2
Guajataca Forest Reserve	A2
Guánica Forest Reserve	B3
Guilarte, *mt.*	B2
Guilarte Forest Reserve	B2
Icacos, *key*	D2
Jobos, *bay*	C3
La Plata, *river*	C2
Maricao Forest Reserve	A2
Mona, *passage*	A2
Norte, *key*	E2
Puerca, *point*	D2
Punta, *mt.*	B2
Rincón, *bay*	A2
Río Abajo Forest Reserve	B2
Río Camuy Cave Park	B2
Rojo, *cape*	A3
Roosevelt Roads Naval Station	D2
San Juan, *passage*	A2
Sierra de Cayey, *mts.*	C2
Sierra de Luquillo, *mts.*	D2
Sombe, *beach*	E2
Susua Forest Reserve	B2
Toro Negro Forest Reserve	C2
Vieques, *island*	E2
Vieques, *passage*	E2
Vieques, *sound*	D2
Yeguas, *point*	C2

Antigua & Barbuda

⊛ National Capital
● Other City

1:1,480,000

0   10   20 mi
0   10   20 km

Transverse Mercator Projection

© MapQuest.com, Inc.

Antigua and Barbuda

Capital: St. John's
Area: 171 sq. mi.
443 sq. km.
Population: 64,246
Largest City: St. John's
Language: English
Monetary Unit: East Caribbean dollar

Antigua and Barbuda: Map Index

Cities and Towns

Bolands	D5
Cedar Grove	E5
Codrington	E2
Falmouth	E5
Freetown	E5
Old Road	D5
St. John's, *capital*	D5

Other Features

Antigua, *island*	D4
Barbuda, *island*	E3
Boggy, *peak*	D5
Cobb, *cove*	E1
Codrington, *lagoon*	D1
Goat, *point*	D1
Gravenor, *bay*	E2
Palmetto, *point*	D2
Redonda, *island*	A6
Shirley, *cape*	E6
Spanish, *point*	E2
Willoughby, *bay*	E5

Dominica: Map Index

Cities and Towns

Berekua	B4
Castle Bruce	B2
Colihaut	A2
Glanvillia	A2
La Plaine	B3
Laudat	B3
Marigot	B2
Massacre	B3
Pointe Michel	B3
Pont Cassé	B3
Portsmouth	A2
Rosalie	B3
Roseau, *capital*	B3
Saint Joseph	A3
Salibia	B2
Salisbury	A2
Soufrière	B4
Vieille Case	B1
Wesley	B2

Other Features

Boiling, *lake*	B3
Dominica, *passage*	A1
Grand, *bay*	B4
Layou, *river*	B3
Morne Diablotin, *mt.*	B2
Roseau, *river*	B3
Toulaman, *river*	B2

Dominica

Capital: Roseau
Area: 290 sq. mi.
751 sq. km.
Population: 64,881
Largest City: Roseau
Language: English
Monetary Unit: East Caribbean dollar

Dominica

⊛ National Capital
● Other City

1:1,076,000

0   6   12 mi
0   6   12 km

Lambert Conformal Conic Projection

© MapQuest.com, Inc.

St. Kitts & Nevis

⊛ National Capital
● Other City

1:670,000

0   4   8 mi
0   4   8 km

Transverse Mercator Projection

St. Kitts & Nevis: Map Index

Cities and Towns

Basseterre, *capital*	B2
Bath	C3
Cayon	B1
Charlestown	C3
Cotton Ground	C2
Dieppe Bay Town	B1
Fig Tree	C3
Newcastle	C2
Old Road Town	B2
St. Paul's	A1
Sandy Point Town	A1
Zion	C3

Other Features

Great Salt, *pond*	C2
Nag's Head, *cape*	C2
Narrows, *strait*	C2
Nevis, *island*	C3
St. Kitts (St. Christopher), *island*	B2

St. Kitts & Nevis

Capital: Basseterre
Area: 104 sq. mi.
269 sq. km.
Population: 42,838
Largest City: Basseterre
Language: English
Monetary Unit: East Caribbean dollar

© MapQuest.com, Inc.

St. Lucia

Capital: Castries
Area: 238 sq. mi.
617 sq. km.
Population: 154,020
Largest City: Castries
Language: English
Monetary Unit: East Caribbean dollar

St. Lucia:
Map Index

Cities and Towns
Canaries A2
Castries, *capital* B1
Choiseul A3
Dauphin B1
Dennery B2
Desruisseau B3
Grand Anse B1
Gros Islet B1
Laborie B3
La Croix Maingot A2
Micoud B3
Mon Repos B2

Praslin B2
Soufrière A2
Vieux Fort B3

Other Features
Canelles, *river* B3
Cul de Sac, *river* B2
Fond d'Or, *river* B2
Gimie, *mt.* A2
Maria, *islands* B3
Moule à Chique, *cape* B3
Point, *cape* B1
Saint Lucia, *channel* B1
Saint Vincent, *passage* B4
Soufrière, *volcano* A2

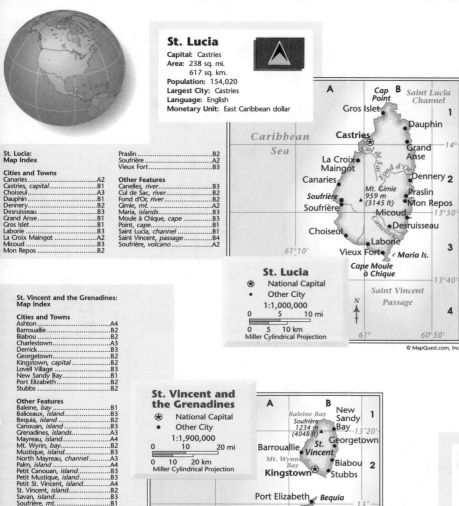

St. Lucia

⊛ National Capital
• Other City
1:1,000,000
0   5   10 mi
0 5 10 km
Miller Cylindrical Projection

© MapQuest.com, Inc.

Barbados

⊛ National Capital
• Other City
1:809,000
0   5   10 mi
0 5 10 km
Azimuthal Equal Area Projection

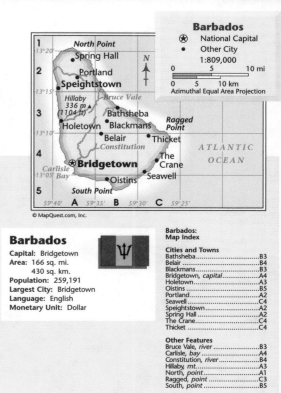

© MapQuest.com, Inc.

Barbados

Capital: Bridgetown
Area: 166 sq. mi.
430 sq. km.
Population: 259,191
Largest City: Bridgetown
Language: English
Monetary Unit: Dollar

Barbados:
Map Index

Cities and Towns
Bathsheba B3
Belair B4
Blackmans B3
Bridgetown, *capital* A4
Holetown A3
Oistins B5
Portland A2
Seawell C4
Speightstown A2
Spring Hall A2
The Crane C4
Thicket C4

Other Features
Bruce Vale, *river* B3
Carlisle, *bay* A4
Constitution, *river* B4
Hillaby, *mt.* A3
North, *point* A1
Ragged, *point* C3
South, *point* B5

St. Vincent and the Grenadines:
Map Index

Cities and Towns
Ashton A4
Barrouallie B2
Biabou B2
Charlestown A3
Derrick B3
Georgetown B2
Kingstown, *capital* B2
Lovell Village B3
New Sandy Bay B1
Port Elizabeth B2
Stubbs B2

Other Features
Baleine, *bay* B1
Baliceaux, *island* B3
Bequia, *island* B2
Canouan, *island* B3
Grenadines, *islands* A3
Mayreau, *island* A4
Mt. Wynn, *bay* B2
Mustique, *island* B3
North Mayreau, *channel* A3
Palm, *island* A4
Petit Canouan, *island* B3
Petit Mustique, *island* B3
Petit St. Vincent, *island* A4
St. Vincent, *island* B2
Savan, *island* B3
Soufrière, *mt.* B1
Tobago, *cays* A4
Union, *island* A4
Windward, *islands* B4

St. Vincent and the Grenadines

⊛ National Capital
• Other City
1:1,900,000
0   10   20 mi
0 10 20 km
Miller Cylindrical Projection

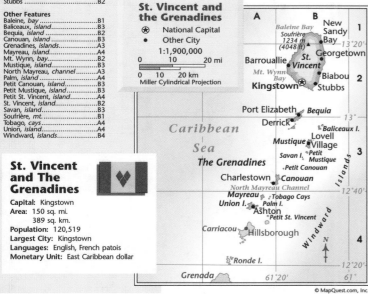

© MapQuest.com, Inc.

St. Vincent and The Grenadines

Capital: Kingstown
Area: 150 sq. mi.
389 sq. km.
Population: 120,519
Largest City: Kingstown
Languages: English, French patois
Monetary Unit: East Caribbean dollar

Trinidad & Tobago

Capital: Port of Spain
Area: 1,980 sq. mi.
5,130 sq. km.
Population: 1,102,096
Largest City: Port of Spain
Language: English
Monetary Unit: Dollar

Trinidad & Tobago:
Map Index

Cities and Towns
Arima A2
Canaan B1
Chaguanas A2

Charlotteville B1
Couva A2
Fullarton A2
Guayaguayare A2
Matelot A2
Moruga A2
Pierreville A2
Plymouth B1
Point Fortin A2
Port of Spain, *capital* A2
Princes Town A2
Rio Claro A2
St. Augustine A2
San Fernando A2
San Francique A2
Sangre Grande A2
Scarborough B1
Siparia A2
Toco B2

Other Features
El Cerro del Aripo, *mt.* A2
Paria, *gulf* A2
Pitch, *lake* A2
Tobago, *island* B1
Trinidad, *island* A2

Trinidad & Tobago

⊛ National Capital
• Other City
1:2,700,000
0   15   30 mi
0 15 30 km
Azimuthal Equal Area Projection

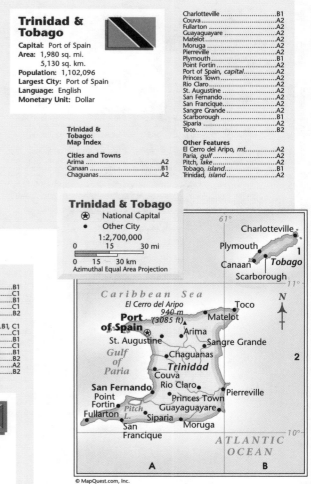

© MapQuest.com, Inc.

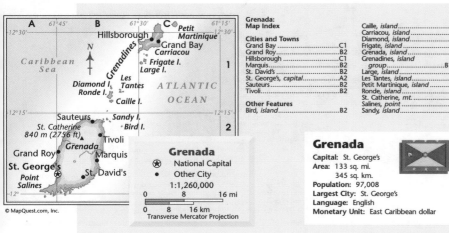

Grenada:
Map Index

Cities and Towns
Grand Bay C1
Grand Roy B2
Hillsborough C1
Marquis B2
St. David's B2
St. George's, *capital* A2
Sauteurs B2
Tivoli B2

Other Features
Bird, *island* B2

Caille, *island* B1
Carriacou, *island* C1
Diamond, *island* B1
Frigate, *island* C1
Grenada, *island* B2
Grenadines, *island group* B1, C1
Large, *island* B2
Les Tantes, *island* C1
Petit Martinique, *island* C1
Ronde, *island* B1
St. Catherine, *mt.* B2
Salines, *point* A2
Sandy, *island* B2

Grenada

⊛ National Capital
• Other City
1:1,260,000
0   8   16 mi
0 8 16 km
Transverse Mercator Projection

© MapQuest.com, Inc.

Grenada

Capital: St. George's
Area: 133 sq. mi.
345 sq. km.
Population: 97,008
Largest City: St. George's
Language: English
Monetary Unit: East Caribbean dollar

Canada

Legend:
- ⊛ National Capital
- ★ Provincial/Territorial Capital
- • Other City

1:30,244,000

Azimuthal Equal Area Projection

750 mi

750 km

0   250   500

ATLANTIC OCEAN

PACIFIC OCEAN

ARCTIC OCEAN

Beaufort Sea

Chukchi Sea

Hudson Bay

Baffin Bay

Davis Strait

Labrador Sea

Denmark Strait

GREENLAND (KALAALLIT NUNAAT) (Denmark)

ICELAND

Alaska (United States)

UNITED STATES

YUKON TERRITORY

NORTHWEST TERRITORIES

NUNAVUT

BRITISH COLUMBIA

ALBERTA

SASKATCHEWAN

MANITOBA

ONTARIO

QUÉBEC

NEWFOUNDLAND

LABRADOR

NEW BRUNSWICK

NOVA SCOTIA

PRINCE EDWARD ISLAND

Ottawa ⊛

Whitehorse ★

Yellowknife ★

Edmonton ★

Regina ★

Winnipeg ★

Toronto ★

Québec ★

Fredericton ★

Halifax ★

Charlottetown ★

St. John's ★

Iqaluit ★

Victoria ★

Mt. Logan 5959 m (19,551 ft)

Mt. St. Elias 5489 m (18,008 ft)

Mt. McKinley 6194 m (20,320 ft)

Mt. Robson 3954 m (12,972 ft)

Mt. Waddington 3994 m (13,704 ft)

ROCKY MOUNTAINS

COAST MOUNTAINS

MACKENZIE MTS.

BROOKS RANGE

CASCADE RANGE

APPALACHIAN MTS.

GREAT PLAINS

ELLESMERE ISLAND

BAFFIN ISLAND

VICTORIA ISLAND

BANKS ISLAND

VANCOUVER ISLAND

QUEEN CHARLOTTE ISLANDS

QUEEN ELIZABETH ISLANDS

© MapQuest.com, Inc.

Canada: Map Index

ALBERTA
Cities and Towns
Banff ... F3
Calgary ... F3
Edmonton, *capital* ... F3
Fort McMurray ... G3
Grande Prairie ... F3
High Level ... F3
Jasper ... F3
Lethbridge ... F4
Medicine Hat ... F4
Peace River ... F3
Red Deer ... F3
Whitecourt ... F3
Other Features
Athabasca, *river* ... F3
Peace, *river* ... F3

BRITISH COLUMBIA
Cities and Towns
Dawson Creek ... E3
Fort Nelson ... E3
Fort St. John ... E3
Kamloops ... E4
Kelowna ... F4
Kitimat ... D3
Masset ... E4
Nanaimo ... E4
Ocean Falls ... E3
Port Hardy ... E3
Prince George ... D3
Prince Rupert ... D3
Trail ... F4
Vancouver ... E4
Victoria, *capital* ... E4
Williams Lake ... E3
Other Features
Coast, *mts.* ... D3
Fraser, *river* ... E3
Queen Charlotte, *islands* ... D3
Robson, *mt.* ... F3

Rocky, *mts.* ... G2
Vancouver, *island* ... J1
Waddington, *mt.* ... F2

MANITOBA
Cities and Towns
Brandon ... H4
Brochet ... G3
Churchill ... H3
Dauphin ... G3
Flin Flon ... G3
Lynn Lake ... H3
Thompson ... H3
Winnipeg, *capital* ... H4
York Factory ... H3
Other Features
Churchill, *river* ... G3
Hudson, *bay* ... J3
Manitoba, *lake* ... H3
Nelson, *river* ... H3
Saskatchewan, *river* ... H3
Southern Indian, *lake* ... H3
Winnipeg, *lake* ... H3
Winnipegosis, *lake* ... G3

NEW BRUNSWICK
Cities and Towns
Fredericton, *capital* ... L4
Moncton ... L4
Saint John ... L4
Other Feature
Fundy, *bay* ... L4

NEWFOUNDLAND
Cities and Towns
Cartwright ... K3
Corner Brook ... K4
Gander ... K4
Grand Falls ... K4
Happy Valley-Goose Bay ... K3
Hebron ... K3
Labrador City ... K3
Marystown ... K4

Nain ... L3
St. John's, *capital* ... M4
Other Features
Cabot, *strait* ... M4
Hamilton, *inlet* ... L3
Labrador, *region* ... L3
Labrador, *gulf* ... L4
St. Lawrence, *gulf* ... L4
Smallwood, *reservoir* ... L3

NORTHWEST TERRITORIES
Cities and Towns
Arviat ... H2
Déline ... E2
Fort McPherson ... D2
Fort Simpson ... E2
Fort Smith ... F2
Hay River ... F2
Inuvik ... D2
Sachs Harbour ... E1
Yellowknife, *capital* ... F2
Other Features
Amundsen, *gulf* ... E1
Banks, *island* ... D1
Beaufort, *sea* ... D1
Fort Smith, *region* ... E2
Great Bear, *lake* ... E2
Great Slave, *lake* ... F2
Inuvik, *region* ... D2
Mackenzie, *gulf* ... D2
Mackenzie, *mts.* ... D2
Mackenzie, *river* ... E2
M'Clure, *strait* ... E1
Melville, *island* ... F1
Prince Patrick, *island* ... E1
Slave, *river* ... F2
Victoria, *island* ... F1
Viscount Melville, *sound* ... F1

NUNAVUT
Cities and Towns
Arctic Bay ... J1
Baker Lake ... H2

Cambridge Bay ... G2
Grise Fiord ... J1
Iqaluit, *capital* ... K2
Kugluktuk ... F2
Pangnirtung ... K1
Pond Inlet ... K1
Rankin Inlet ... H2
Repulse Bay ... J2
Resolute ... H1
Other Features
Amadjuak, *lake* ... K2
Axel Heiberg, *island* ... H1
Back, *river* ... G2
Baffin, *bay* ... L1
Baffin, *island* ... K1
Baffin, *region* ... H2
Baker, *lake* ... H2
Bathurst, *island* ... G1
Belcher, *islands* ... J3
Boothia, *gulf* ... H1
Boothia, *peninsula* ... H1
Brodeur, *peninsula* ... J1
Coats, *island* ... J2
Cumberland, *sound* ... L2
Davis, *strait* ... M2
Devon, *island* ... J1
Dubawnt, *lake* ... G2
Ellesmere, *island* ... K1
Foxe, *basin* ... K2
Foxe, *channel* ... J2
Home, *bay* ... L2
Hudson, *bay* ... J2
Hudson, *strait* ... K2
Jones, *sound* ... J1
Keewatin, *region* ... H2
King William, *island* ... H2
Kitikmeot, *region* ... H2
Mansel, *island* ... J2
M'Clintock, *channel* ... G1
Melville, *island* ... G2
Melville, *peninsula* ... J2
Nettilling, *lake* ... K2
Ottawa, *islands* ... J3
Parry, *channel* ... J1

Prince Charles, *island* ... K2
Prince of Wales, *island* ... H1
Queen Elizabeth, *islands* ... G2
Queen Maud, *gulf* ... G2
Smith, *sound* ... K1
Somerset, *island* ... H1
Southampton, *island* ... J2
Victoria, *island* ... G1

NOVA SCOTIA
Cities and Towns
Halifax, *capital* ... L4
Sydney ... L4
Yarmouth ... L4
Other Features
Cabot, *strait* ... M4
Cape Breton, *island* ... M4
Fundy, *bay* ... L4
Sable, *cape* ... L4

ONTARIO
Cities and Towns
Cornwall ... K4
Fort Frances ... H4
Geraldton ... J4
Hamilton ... J4
Kapuskasing ... J4
Kingston ... K4
Kirkland Lake ... J4
Kitchener ... J4
London ... J4
Moosonee ... J3
Nipigon ... J4
North Bay ... K4
Ottawa, *national capital* ... K4
Peterborough ... K4
Rimouski ... K4
Sarnia ... J4
Sault Ste. Marie ... J4
Sudbury ... J4
Thunder Bay ... J4
Timmins ... J4
Toronto, *capital* ... K4
Windsor ... J4

ALBERTA

Other Features
Anticosti, *island* ... L4
Caniapiscau, *river* ... L3
Feuilles, *river* ... K3
Hudson, *bay* ... J3
Hudson, *strait* ... K2
James, *bay* ... J3
Minto, *lake* ... K3
Mistassini, *lake* ... K3
Ottawa, *river* ... L4
St. Lawrence, *gulf* ... L4
St. Lawrence, *river* ... K4
Ungava, *bay* ... K3
Ungava, *peninsula* ... K2

SASKATCHEWAN
Cities and Towns
Estevan ... G4
La Loche ... G3
Moose Jaw ... G3
Prince Albert ... G3
Regina, *capital* ... G3
Saskatoon ... G3
Uranium City ... G3
Other Features
Athabasca, *lake* ... G3
Churchill, *river* ... G3
Great Plains, *plain* ... G3
Reindeer, *lake* ... G3
Saskatchewan, *river* ... G3
Wollaston, *lake* ... G3

YUKON TERRITORY
Cities and Towns
Dawson ... D2
Faro ... D2
Mayo ... D2
Watson Lake ... E2
Whitehorse, *capital* ... D2
Other Features
Beaufort, *sea* ... D1
Logan, *mt.* ... C2
St. Elias, *mts.* ... C2
Yukon, *river* ... D2

Winisk ... J3

PRINCE EDWARD ISLAND
Cities and Towns
Charlottetown, *capital* ... L4

QUÉBEC
Cities and Towns
Baie-Comeau ... L4
Chibougamau ... K4
Chicoutimi ... K4
Chisasibi ... J3
Gagnon ... K4
Gaspé ... L4
Havre-St.-Pierre ... L4
Inukjuak ... K3
Kuujjuaq ... L3
Matagami ... J4
Montréal ... K4
Port-Cartier ... L4
Puvirnituq ... K3
Québec, *capital* ... K4
Radisson ... K4
Rouyn-Noranda ... K4
Schefferville ... K4
Sept-Îles ... L4
Shawinigan ... K4
Sherbrooke ... K4
Trois-Rivières ... K4
Val-d'Or ... K4
Waskaganish ... K3

Canada
Capital: Ottawa
Area: 3,849,674 sq. mi.
9,973,249 sq. km.
Population: 31,006,347
Largest City: Toronto
Languages: English, French
Monetary Unit: Canadian dollar

New Brunswick
Capital: Fredericton
Area: 28,355 sq. mi.
73,459 sq. km.
Population: 738,133
Largest City: Saint John

Ontario
Capital: Toronto
Area: 412,581 sq. mi.
1,068,863 sq. km.
Population: 10,753,573
Largest City: Toronto

Manitoba
Capital: Winnipeg
Area: 250,947 sq. mi.
650,122 sq. km.
Population: 1,113,898
Largest City: Winnipeg

Nunavut
Capital: Iqaluit
Area: 800,775 sq. mi.
2,074,000 sq. km.
Population: 24,730
Largest City: Iqaluit

Yukon Territory
Capital: Whitehorse
Area: 186,661 sq. mi.
483,578 sq. km.
Population: 30,766
Largest City: Whitehorse

British Columbia
Capital: Victoria
Area: 365,947 sq. mi.
948,049 sq. km.
Population: 3,724,500
Largest City: Vancouver

Nova Scotia
Capital: Halifax
Area: 21,425 sq. mi.
55,505 sq. km.
Population: 909,282
Largest City: Halifax

Saskatchewan
Capital: Regina
Area: 251,866 sq. mi.
652,503 sq. km.
Population: 990,237
Largest City: Saskatoon

Alberta
Capital: Edmonton
Area: 255,287 sq. mi.
661,265 sq. km.
Population: 2,696,826
Largest City: Edmonton

Northwest Territories
Capital: Yellowknife
Area: 520,850 sq. mi.
1,349,000 sq. km.
Population: 39,672
Largest City: Yellowknife

Québec
Capital: Québec
Area: 594,860 sq. mi.
1,541,088 sq. km.
Population: 7,138,795
Largest City: Montréal

Newfoundland
Capital: St. John's
Area: 156,949 sq. mi.
406,604 sq. km.
Population: 551,792
Largest City: St. John's

Prince Edward Island
Capital: Charlottetown
Area: 2,185 sq. mi.
5,661 sq. km.
Population: 134,557
Largest City: Charlottetown

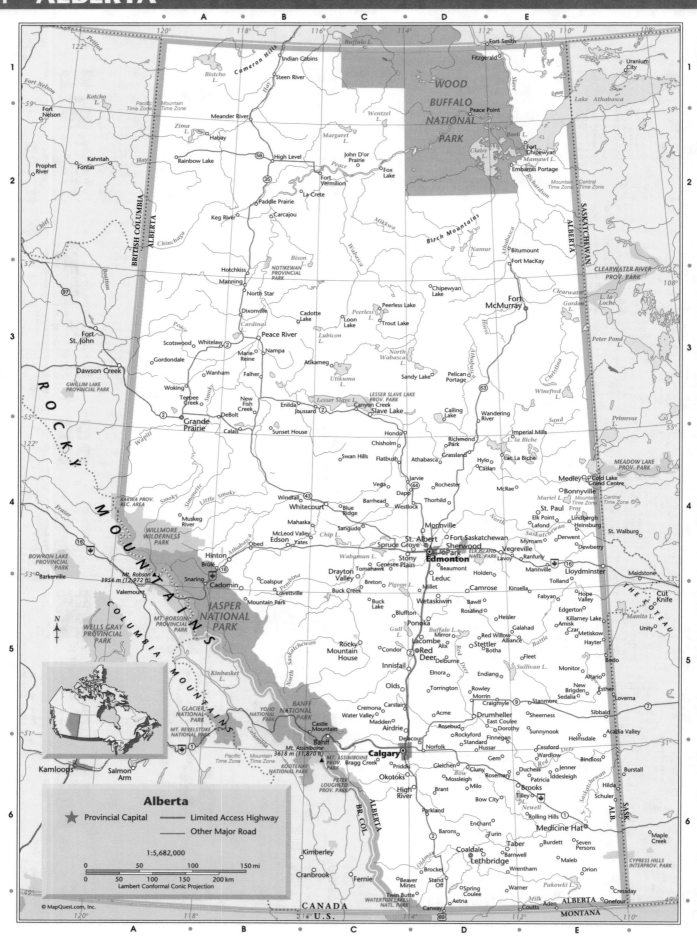

Alberta

★ Provincial Capital   —— Limited Access Highway

                     —— Other Major Road

1:5,682,000

0   50   100   150 mi

0   50   100   150   200 km

Lambert Conformal Conic Projection

© MapQuest.com, Inc.

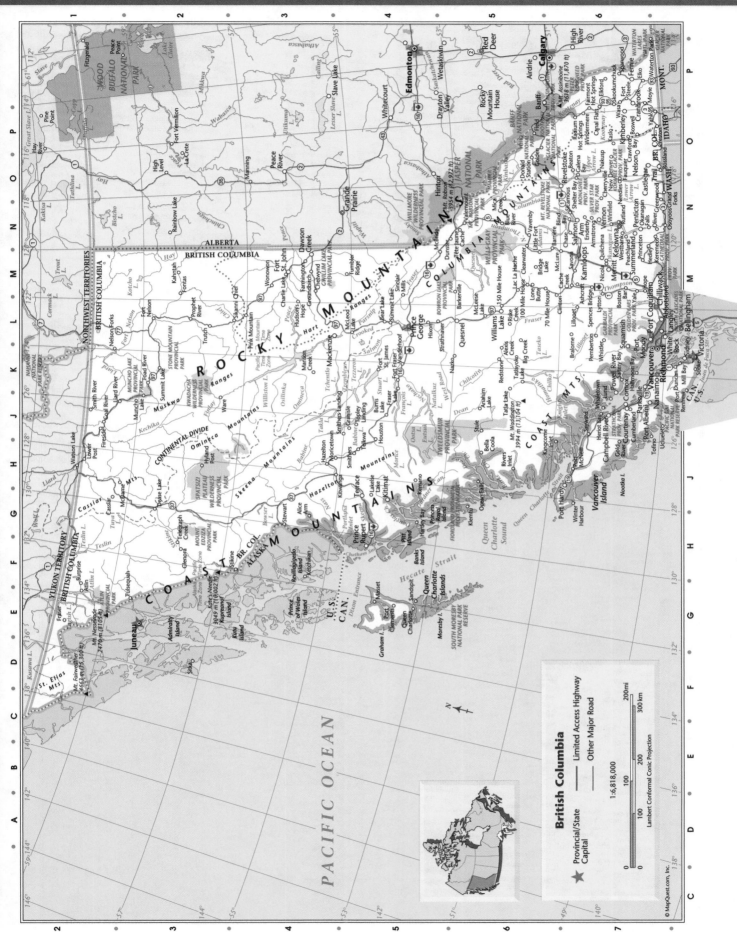

British Columbia

Provincial/State
Capital

Limited Access Highway
Other Major Road

1:6,818,000

Lambert Conformal Conic Projection

PACIFIC OCEAN

©MapQuest.com, Inc.

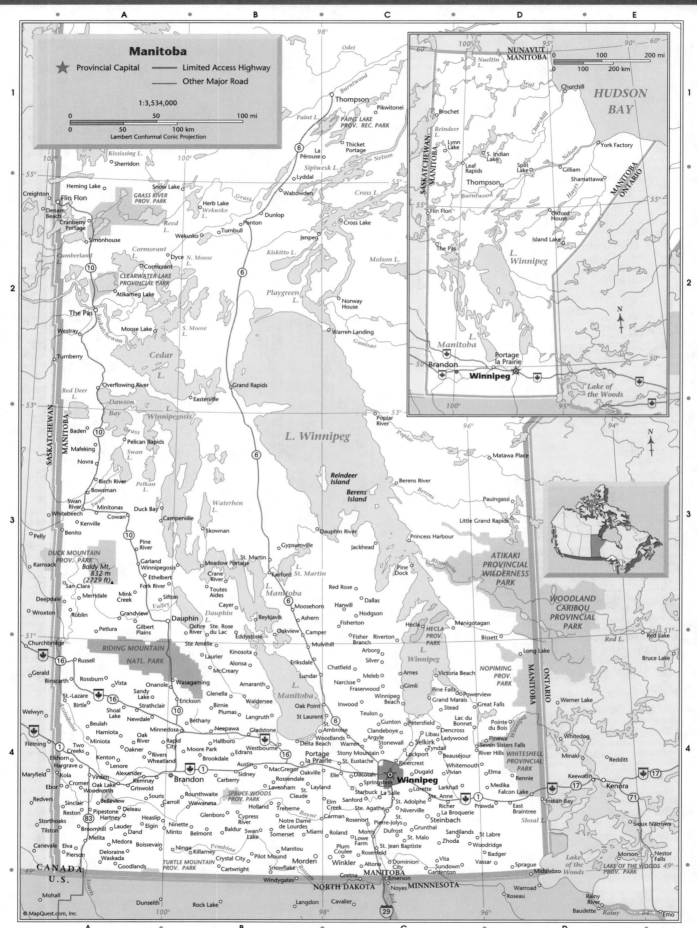

Manitoba

★ Provincial Capital ── Limited Access Highway
── Other Major Road

1:3,534,000

Lambert Conformal Conic Projection

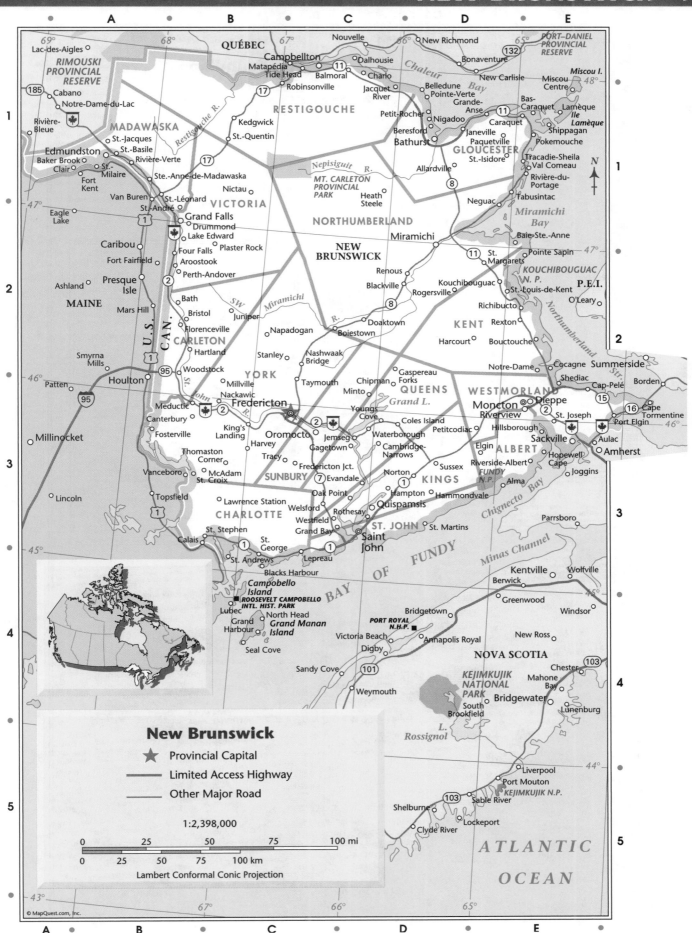

New Brunswick

★ Provincial Capital

━━ Limited Access Highway

── Other Major Road

1:2,398,000

0   25   50   75   100 mi

0   25   50   75   100 km

Lambert Conformal Conic Projection

© MapQuest.com, Inc.

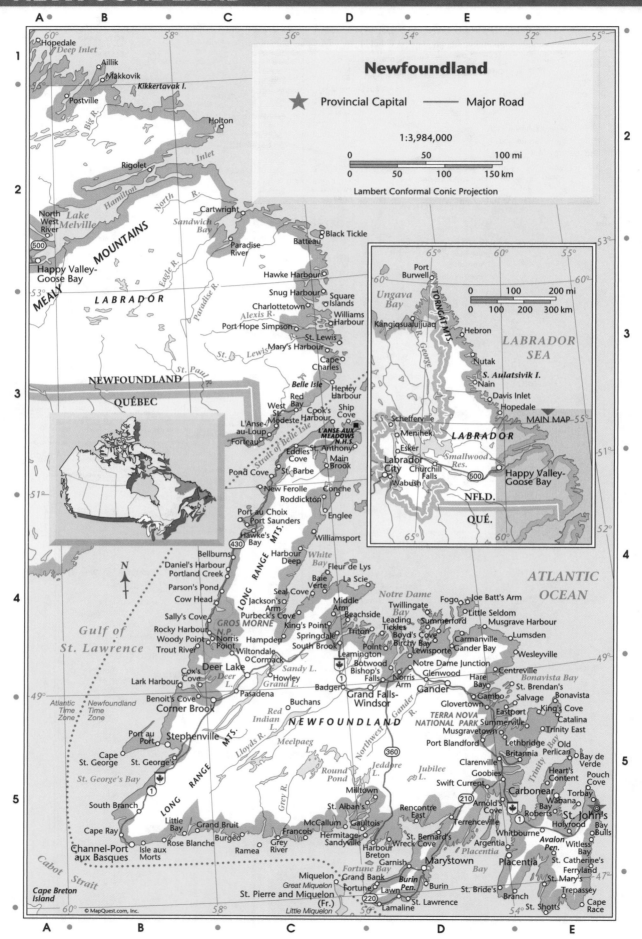

Newfoundland

★ Provincial Capital ——— Major Road

1:3,984,000

0   50   100 mi
0   50   100   150 km

Lambert Conformal Conic Projection

Inset map (Labrador):

LABRADOR SEA

Port Burwell
Ungava Bay
Kangiqsualujjuaq
Hebron
Nutak
S. Aulatsivik I.
Nain
Davis Inlet
Hopedale
MAIN MAP
Schefferville
Menihek
LABRADOR
Esker
Smallwood Res.
Labrador City
Churchill Falls
Wabush
Happy Valley-Goose Bay
NFLD.
QUÉ.

0   100   200 mi
0   100   200   300 km

Main map labels:

Hopedale
Deep Inlet
Aillik
Makkovik
Kikkertavak I.
Postville
Holton
Rigolet
Hamilton Inlet
North West River
Lake Melville
Cartwright
Big R.
North R.
Sandwich Bay
Paradise River
Batteau
Black Tickle
MEALY MOUNTAINS
Happy Valley-Goose Bay
Eagle R.
LABRADOR
Paradise R.
Hawke Harbour
Snug Harbour
Square Islands
Alexis R.
Charlottetown
Williams Harbour
St. Lewis
Port Hope Simpson
St. Lewis
Mary's Harbour
St. Paul R.
Cape Charles
NEWFOUNDLAND
QUÉBEC
Belle Isle
Henley Harbour
Red Bay
Ship Cove
West St. Modeste
Cook's Harbour
L'Anse-au-Loup
Forteau
L'ANSE AUX MEADOWS N.H.S.
St. Anthony
Eddies Cove
Main Brook
Pond Cove
St. Barbe
New Ferolle
Conche
Roddickton
Englee
Port au Choix
Port Saunders
Hawke's Bay
Williamsport
Bellburns
Harbour Deep
White Bay
Daniel's Harbour
Portland Creek
Fleur de Lys
La Scie
Parson's Pond
Baie Verte
Cow Head
Seal Cove
Notre Dame Bay
Fogo
Joe Batt's Arm
Jackson's Arm
Middle Arm
Twillingate
Little Seldom
Sally's Cove
Purbeck's Cove
Beachside
Leading Tickles
Summerford
Musgrave Harbour
Rocky Harbour
King's Point
Triton
Boyd's Cove
Carmanville
Lumsden
GROS MORNE N.P.
Norris Point
Hampden
Springdale
Birchy Bay
Gander Bay
Wesleyville
Woody Point
South Brook
Lewisporte
Trout River
Wiltondale
Leamington
Cormack
Notre Dame Junction
Centreville
Deer Lake
Howley
Botwood
Glenwood
Bonavista Bay
Cox's Cove
Deer L.
Sandy L.
Bishop's Falls
Norris Arm
Hare Bay
St. Brendan's
Lark Harbour
Pasadena
Grand L.
Badger
Gander
Gambo
Salvage
Bonavista
Benoit's Cove
Buchans
Grand Falls-Windsor
Glovertown
Eastport
King's Cove
Corner Brook
Red Indian L.
NEWFOUNDLAND
TERRA NOVA NATIONAL PARK
Summerville
Catalina
Port au Port
Stephenville
Lloyds R.
Meelpaeg L.
Jeddore L.
Musgravetown
Lethbridge
Trinity East
Cape St. George
St. George's
LONG RANGE MTS.
Round Pond
Jubilee L.
Port Blandford
Britannia
Old Perlican
St. George's Bay
Milltown
Clarenville
Bay de Verde
Pouch Cove
South Branch
St. Alban's
Rencontre East
Goobies
Swift Current
Heart's Content
Little Bay
Grand Bruit
McCallum
Gaultois
Terrenceville
Carbonear
Torbay
Cape Ray
Burgeo
Francois
Hermitage
Arnold's Cove
Roberts
Wabana
St. John's
Channel-Port aux Basques
Isle aux Morts
Rose Blanche
Ramea
Grey River
Sandyville
Harbour Breton
Wreck Cove
St. Bernard's
Whitbourne
Holyrood
Bay Bulls
Cape Breton Island
Cabot Strait
Miquelon
Great Miquelon
Grand Bank
Garnish
Marystown
Placentia Bay
Argentia
Placentia
Avalon Pen.
Witless Bay
St. Pierre and Miquelon (Fr.)
Little Miquelon
St. Pierre
Fortune
Lawn
Burin Pen.
Burin
St. Catherine's
Ferryland
St. Mary's
Lamaline
St. Lawrence
St. Bride's
Branch
Trepassey
St. Shotts
Cape Race

Gulf of St. Lawrence

ATLANTIC OCEAN

Atlantic Time Zone | Newfoundland Time Zone

N

© MapQuest.com, Inc.

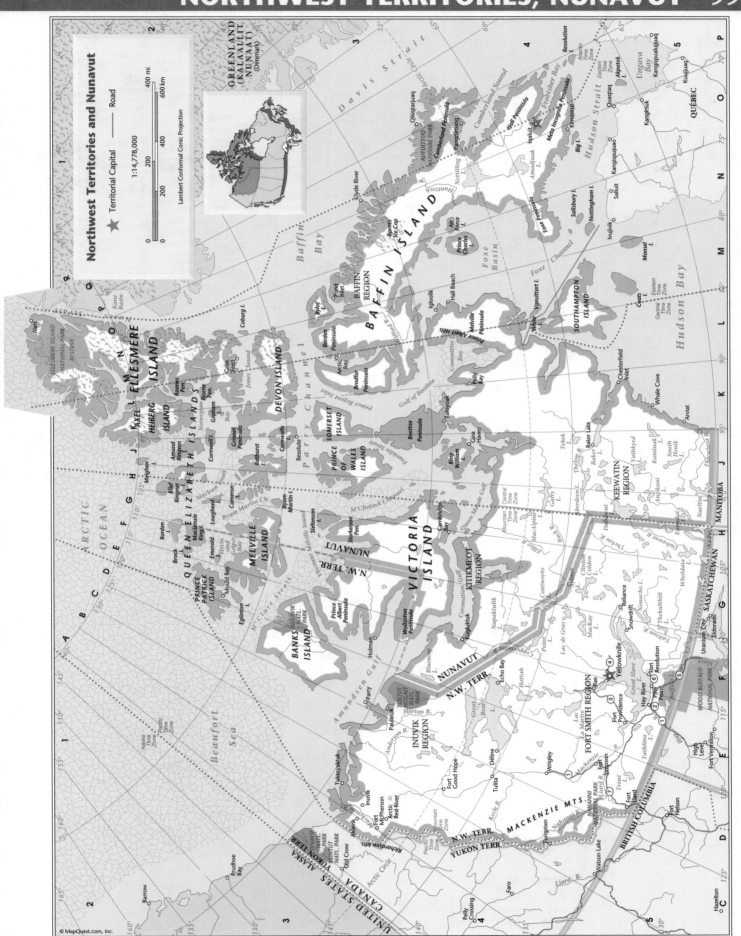

Northwest Territories and Nunavut

★ Territorial Capital
— Road

1:14,778,000

Lambert Conformal Conic Projection

400 mi
600 km

© MapQuest.com, Inc.

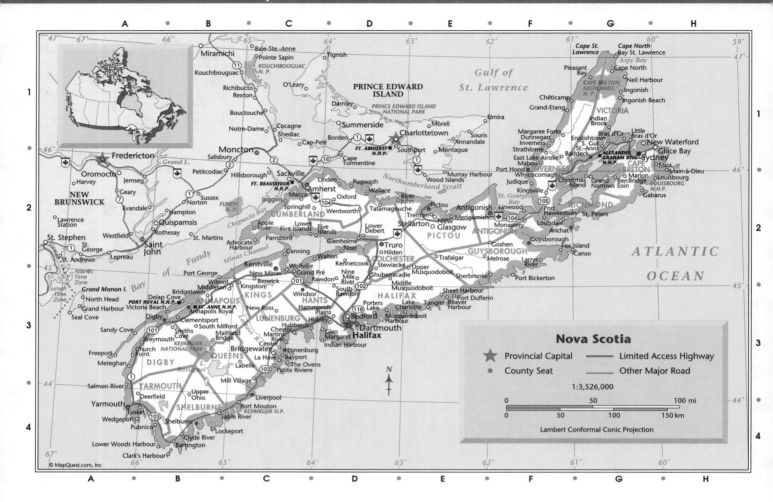

Nova Scotia

⭐ Provincial Capital — Limited Access Highway

● County Seat — Other Major Road

1:3,526,000

0   50   100 mi

0   50   100   150 km

Lambert Conformal Conic Projection

© MapQuest.com, Inc

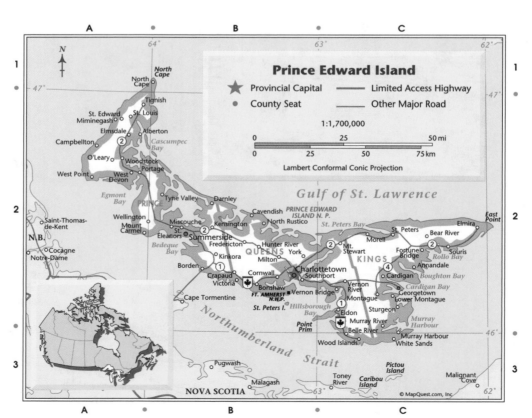

Prince Edward Island

⭐ Provincial Capital — Limited Access Highway

● County Seat — Other Major Road

1:1,700,000

0   25   50 mi

0   25   50   75 km

Lambert Conformal Conic Projection

© MapQuest.com, Inc

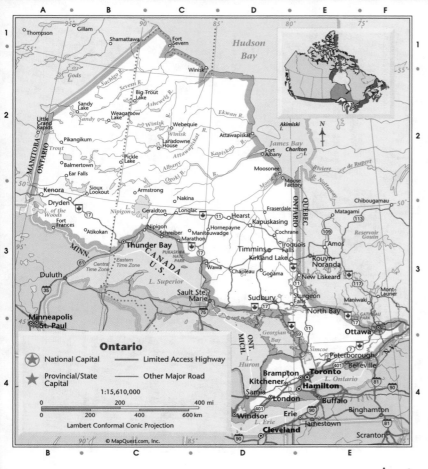

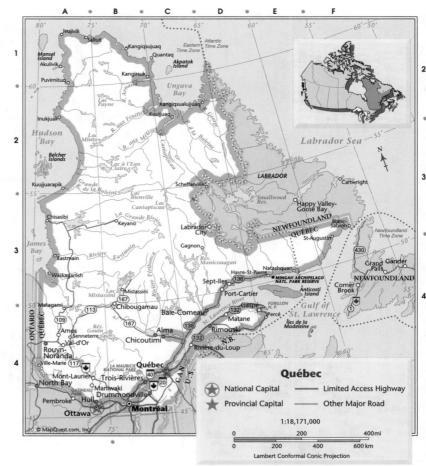

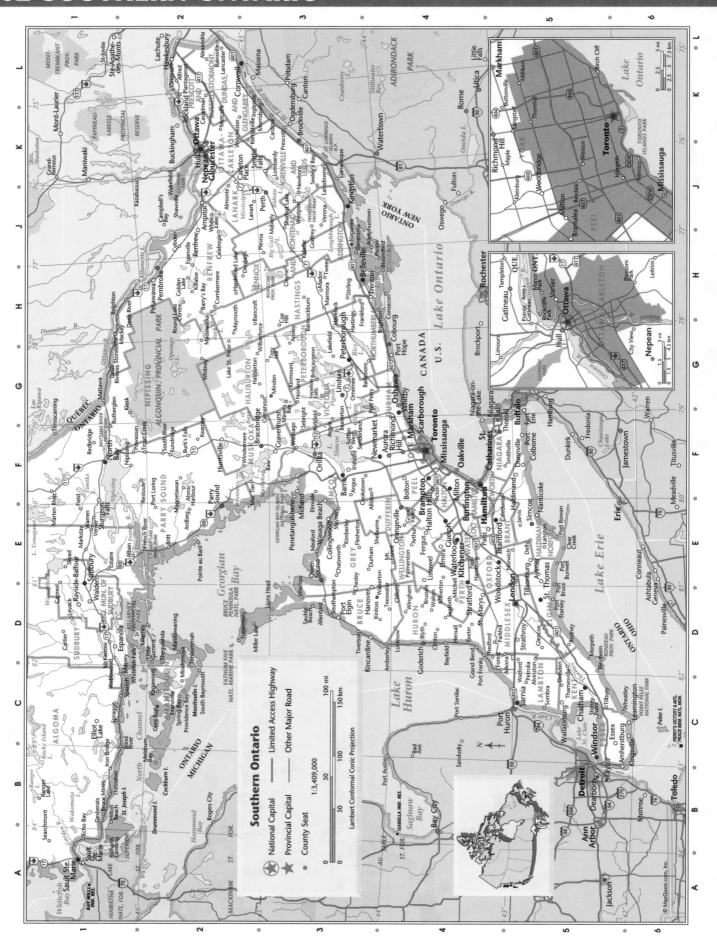

Southern Ontario

— Limited Access Highway
— Other Major Road

★ National Capital
★ Provincial Capital
• County Seat

1:3,409,000

Lambert Conformal Conic Projection

© MapQuest.com, Inc.

Southern Québec

⊛ National Capital
★ Provincial Capital

Limited Access Highway
Other Major Road

1:3,580,000

Lambert Conformal Conic Projection

0   50   100   150 km
0   50   100 mi

Inset (Québec)

Beauport
Charlesbourg
Vanier
Québec
Ste-Foy
Sillery
Lévis
Lauzon
St-Romuald
St-Jean-Chrysostome
Charny
Bernières
St-Rédempteur
Cap-Rouge
L'Ancienne-Lorette
Loretteville
St-Émile
Lac St-Charles

Inset (Montréal)

Repentigny
Terrebonne
Bois-des-Filion
Lorraine
Blainville
Ste-Thérèse
Laval
Île Jésus
Montréal-Nord
St-Léonard
Anjou
Montréal
Outremont
Westmount
Verdun
La Salle
Longueuil
Mont-Royal
St-Lambert
Boucherville
Brossard
St-Hubert
Candiac
Delson
Châteauguay
Kahnawake
Lachine
Dorval
Pointe-Claire
Hampstead
Pierrefonds
St-Laurent
Deux-Montagnes
Ste-Eustache
L'Île Perrot

Main map labels

GASPÉ PENINSULA
FORILLON NAT'L. PARK
QUÉBEC
N.B.
Percé
Chandler
Grande-Rivière
Barachois
Gaspé
Douglastown
Rivière-au-Renard
Cap-aux-Os
L'Anse-à-Valleau
Cloridorme
Grande-Vallée
Murdochville
Mont-St-Pierre
La Martre
Ste-Anne-des-Monts
Cap-Chat
Les Méchins
Gros-Morne
Les Îlets-Caribou
Pointe-des-Monts
Grande-Rivière

GASPÉSIE PROVINCIAL PARK
MATANE PROVINCIAL RESERVE
CHIC-CHOCS PROV. RES.
Miguasha Centre
Caplan
New Richmond
Carleton
Nouvelle
Maria
Escuminac
Pointe-à-la-Croix
Dalhousie
Campbellton
Matapédia
Routhierville
Amqui
Causapscal
Ste-Angèle-de-Mérici
Sayabec
St-Marcellin
MT. CARLETON PROV. PARK
Caraquet

R. Bonaventure
R. Cascapédia
R. Matapédia
Chaleur Bay
Restigouche
Eastern Time Zone
Atlantic Time Zone

Baie-Comeau
Godbout
Franquelin
Pointe-Lebel
Betsiamites
Ragueneau
Chute-aux-Outardes
Colombier
Forestville
Labrieville
Sault-au-Mouton
Les Escoumins
Tadoussac
Rivière-Ste-Marguerite
L'Isle-Verte
Cacouna
Rivière-du-Loup
St-Pascal
St-André
Kamouraska
St-Germain
Mont-Carmel
St-Pacôme
St-Onésime
La Pocatière
St-Jean-Port-Joli
Cap-St-Ignace
Montmagny
St-Pierre
Berthier-sur-Mer
St-Raphaël
St-Vallier
Beaumont
Lévis
Québec

SAGUENAY PROV. PARK
Matane
Mont-Joli
Métis-sur-Mer
Ste-Luce
Rimouski
Le Bic
St-Fabien
Trois-Pistoles
St-Cyprien
St-Hubert
Cabano
Dégelis
St-Marc-du-Lac-Long
Notre-Dame-du-Lac
Edmundston
MAINE
N.B.
ME.
PARKE PROV. RES.
RIMOUSKI PROV. RES.
DUCHÉNIER PROV. RES.
Lac-des-Aigles
Les Escoumins

R. aux Outardes
R. Betsiamites
R. Manicouagan
Rés. Manicouagan Deux
R. Portneuf

Chicoutimi
Jonquière
La Baie
Alma
St-Bruno
Métabetchouan
Chambord
Lac-Bouchette
Roberval
St-Félicien
La Doré
Normandin
Péribonka
Mistassini
Dolbeau
Notre-Dame-de-Lorette
St-Ludger-de-Milot
Péribonka
St-Monique
St-Henri-de-Taillon
St-Ambroise
St-David-de-Falardeau
Ste-Rose-du-Nord
Ste-Félix-d'Otis
Boilleau
Lac St-Jean

LAURENTIDES PROVINCIAL RESERVE
ASHUAPMUSHUAN PROVINCIAL RESERVE
ASSINICA PROV. RESERVE
LACS ALBANEL, MISTASSINI & WACONICHI PROVINCIAL RESERVE
Chibougamau
Chapais

POINTE-TAILLON PROV. PARK
GRANDS-JARDINS PROV. PARK
JACQUES-CARTIER PROV. PARK
Baie-St-Paul
Ste-Agnès
La Malbaie
Clermont
Les Éboulements
St-Tite-des-Caps
St-Siméon
Baie-Ste-Catherine
Pointe-au-Pic
Cap-à-l'Aigle

R. Saguenay
R. Malbaie
R. Jacques-Cartier
Île d'Orléans
Beaupré
Ste-Anne-de-Beaupré
Charlesbourg
Ste-Foy
Charny
Québec
Lévis
Stoneham

Charlesbourg
St-Raymond
Pont-Rouge
Donnacona
Ste-Croix
St-Apollinaire
St-Jacques-de-Leeds
Plessisville
Princeville
Victoriaville
Ste-Croix
Deschaillons
Lotbinière

Ste-Marie
St-Joseph-de-Beauce
Beauceville
St-Georges
La Guadeloupe
St-Zacharie
Lac-Etchemin
St-Camille-de-Lellis
Ste-Justine
Ste-Claire
St-Philémon
St-Prosper

Lac Mégantic
Lac-Mégantic
Nantes
Woburn
Scotstown
Stornoway
La Patrie
St-Ludger
Gould
Weedon
East Angus
Cookshire
Compton
Coaticook
Ayer's Cliff
Magog
Sherbrooke
Windsor
Richmond
Danville
Asbestos
Brompton-ville
Waterloo
Granby
Cowansville
Bedford
St-Albans

MAINE
N.H.
VT.
U.S.
CANADA

St. John R.
Allagash
Wildreness Waterway
Moosehead L.
Chesuncook L.
Flagstaff L.
Old Town
Bangor
Belfast
Waterville
Skowhegan
Rumford
Jackman
Greenville
Kennebec

La Tuque
Rivière-aux-Rats
Grandes-Piles
Grand-Mère
Shawinigan
Grand-Mère
Cap-de-la-Madeleine
Trois-Rivières
Louiseville
St-Michel-des-Saints
St-Gabriel
St-Côme
Notre-Dame-de-la-Merci
Ste-Émélie-de-l'Énergie
Rawdon
Joliette
Berthierville
Sorel
Tracy
Drummondville
St-Hyacinthe
Bécancour
Nicolet
Pierreville
St-François-du-Lac
Baie-du-Febvre
Ste-Eulalie
St-Léonard-d'Aston

RÉS. FAUN. MASTIGOUCHE
RÉSERVE DU ST-MAURICE
ST-MAURICE PROVINCIAL RESERVE
LA MAURICIE NAT'L. PARK
MATTAWIN PROVINCIAL RESERVE
ROUGE-MATTAWIN PROVINCIAL RESERVE
MONT-TREMBLANT PROVINCIAL RESERVE
PAPINEAU-LABELLE PROV. RES.

Parent
Manouane
Réservoir Gouin
Lac Kempt
Lac Mitchinamécus
Lac Taureau

Ste-Agathe-des-Monts
St-Jovite
Mont-Tremblant
St-Donat
L'Ascension
Labelle
La Conception
Ste-Véronique
Nominingue
Mont-Laurier
Ferme-Neuve
Lac-du-Cerf
Val-des-Bois
Notre-Dame-du-Laus
Lac-Nominingue
Ferme-Neuve
Maniwaki
Grand-Remous
Chénéville
St-André-Avellin
Notre-Dame-de-la-Salette
Montebello
Papineauville
Thurso
Buckingham

Montréal
Laval
Repentigny
Terrebonne
Mascouche
L'Assomption
Joliette
St-Jérôme
St-Sauveur
Lachute
Mirabel
St-Eustache
Vaudreuil
Dorion
Rigaud
Hawkesbury
Ste-Anne-de-Bellevue
Pointe-Claire
St-Rémi
Châteauguay
Salaberry-de-Valleyfield
Huntingdon
Beauharnois
St-Jean-sur-Richelieu
Iberville
Chambly
Marieville
Farnham
Contrecœur
Varennes
Boucherville
Longueuil
Beloeil
St-Antoine
St-Denis
St-Hilaire

QUÉ.
ONT.
N.Y.
VT.
CAN.
U.S.
Massena
Malone
Cornwall
Ottawa
Hull
Gatineau
Aylmer
Plattsburgh
St. Albans
Burlington
L. Champlain
Lac Memphrémagog

R. Gatineau
R. du Lièvre
R. Rouge
R. du Nord
R. Richelieu
R. St-François
R. Yamaska
Réservoir Baskatong
RÉS. PAPINEAU-LABELLE PROV. RES.

© MapQuest.com, Inc.

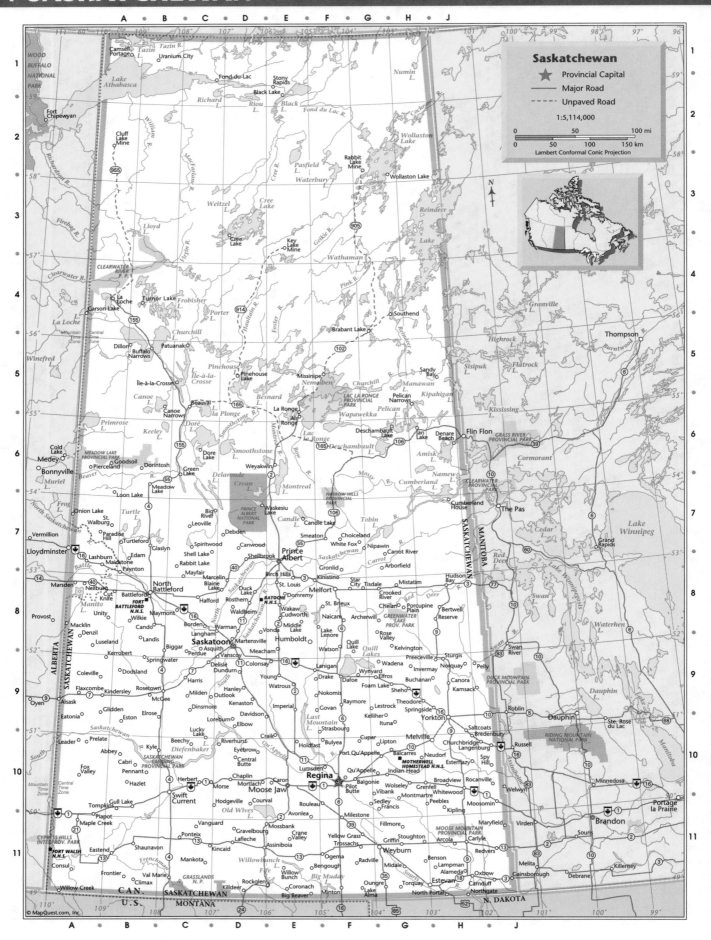

Saskatchewan

★ Provincial Capital
— Major Road
‑‑‑ Unpaved Road

1:5,114,000

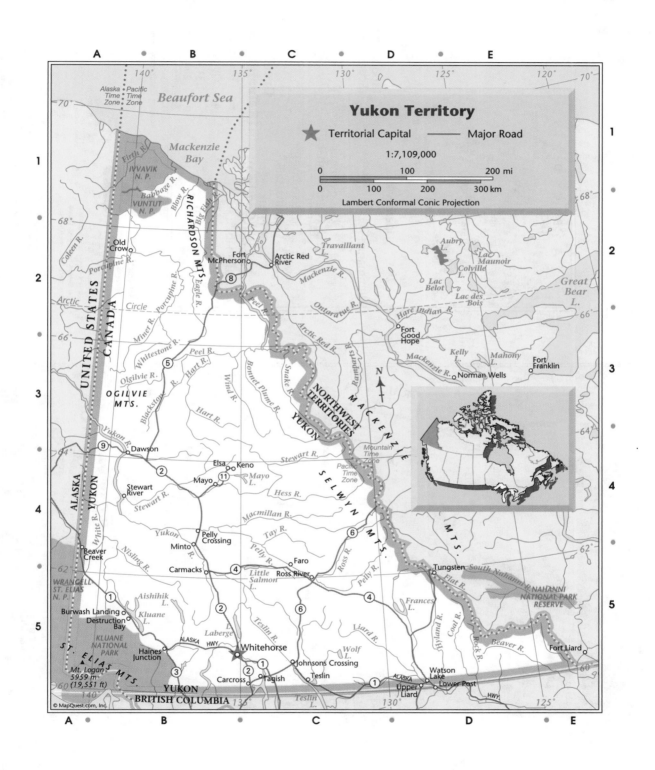

Yukon Territory

★ Territorial Capital — Major Road

1:7,109,000

0   100   200 mi

0   100   200   300 km

Lambert Conformal Conic Projection

Beaufort Sea

Mackenzie Bay

IVVAVIK N.P.

VUNTUT N.P.

RICHARDSON MTS

Old Crow

Fort McPherson

Arctic Red River

Travaillant L.

Aubry L.

Lac Maunoir

Lac Colville

Lac Belot

Lac des Bois

Great Bear L.

Arctic Circle

Fort Good Hope

Kelly L.

Mahony L.

Fort Franklin

Norman Wells

Mackenzie R.

OGILVIE MTS.

NORTHWEST TERRITORIES

YUKON

Dawson

Elsa   Keno

Mayo

Mayo L.

Stewart R.

Mountain Time Zone

Pacific Time Zone

SELWYN MTS.

Stewart River

Hess R.

Macmillan R.

Pelly Crossing

Minto

Carmacks

Tay R.

Faro

Ross River

Little Salmon L.

Ross R.

Pelly R.

Tungsten

South Nahanni R.

NAHANNI NATIONAL PARK RESERVE

Beaver Creek

Frances L.

Fort Liard

Burwash Landing

Destruction Bay

KLUANE NATIONAL PARK

Aishihik L.

Kluane L.

L. Laberge

Teslin R.

Wolf L.

Liard R.

Beaver R.

Haines Junction

Whitehorse

Johnsons Crossing

Teslin

Watson Lake

Lower Post

ST. ELIAS MTS.

Mt. Logan 5959 m (19,551 ft)

Carcross

Tagish

Upper Liard

ALASKA HWY

YUKON

BRITISH COLUMBIA

WRANGELL ST. ELIAS N.P.

ALASKA

UNITED STATES

CANADA

Alaska Time Zone   Pacific Time Zone

© MapQuest.com, Inc.

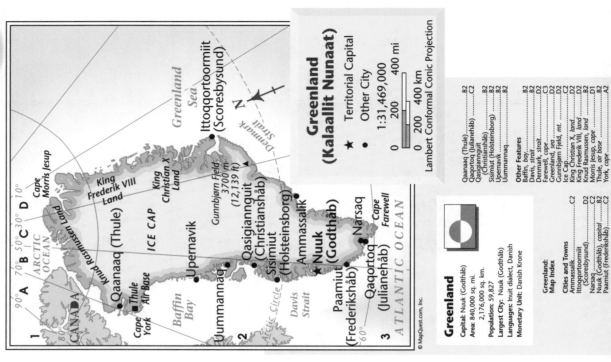

Greenland (Kalaallit Nunaat)

★ Territorial Capital
● Other City

1:31,469,000

0   200   400 km
0   200   400 mi

Lambert Conformal Conic Projection

Greenland

Capital: Nuuk (Godthåb)
Area: 840,000 sq. mi.
    2,176,000 sq. km.
Population: 59,827
Largest City: Nuuk (Godthåb)
Languages: Inuit dialect, Danish
Monetary Unit: Danish Krone

Greenland:
Map Index

Qaanaaq (Thule)	B2
Qaqortoq (Julianehåb)	C2
Qasigiannguit (Christianshåb)	B2
Sisimiut (Holsteinsborg)	B2
Upernavik	B2
Uummannaq	B2

Other Features

Baffin, bay	B2
Davis, strait	B2
Denmark, strait	C3
Farewell, cape	D2
Greenland, sea	D2
Gunnbjørn Field, mt.	C2
Ice Cap	C2
King Christian X, land	D2
King Frederik VIII, land	D2
Knud Rasmussen, land	B2
Morris Jesup, cape	D1
Thule, air base	B2
York, cape	A2

Cities and Towns

Ammassalik	C2
Ittoqqortoormiit (Scoresbysund)	D2
Narsaq	C2
Nuuk (Godthåb), capital	C2
Paamiut (Frederikshåb)	C2

© MapQuest.com, Inc.

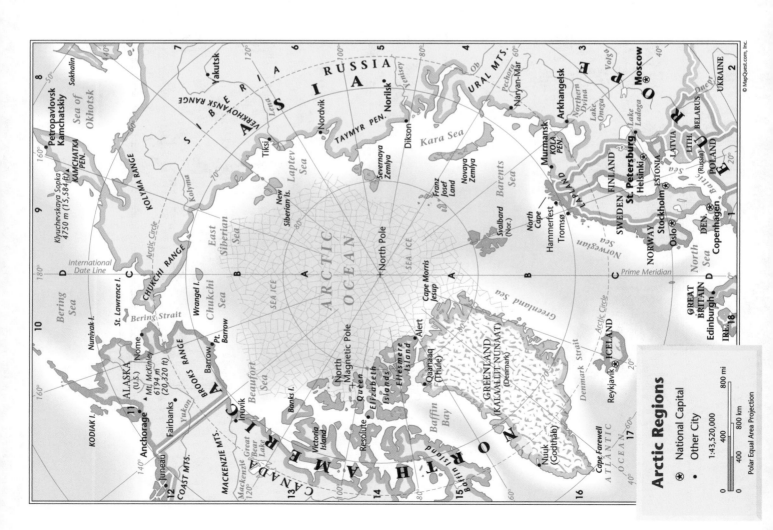

Arctic Regions

⊛ National Capital
● Other City

1:43,520,000

0   400   800 km
0   400   800 mi

Polar Equal Area Projection

© MapQuest.com, Inc.

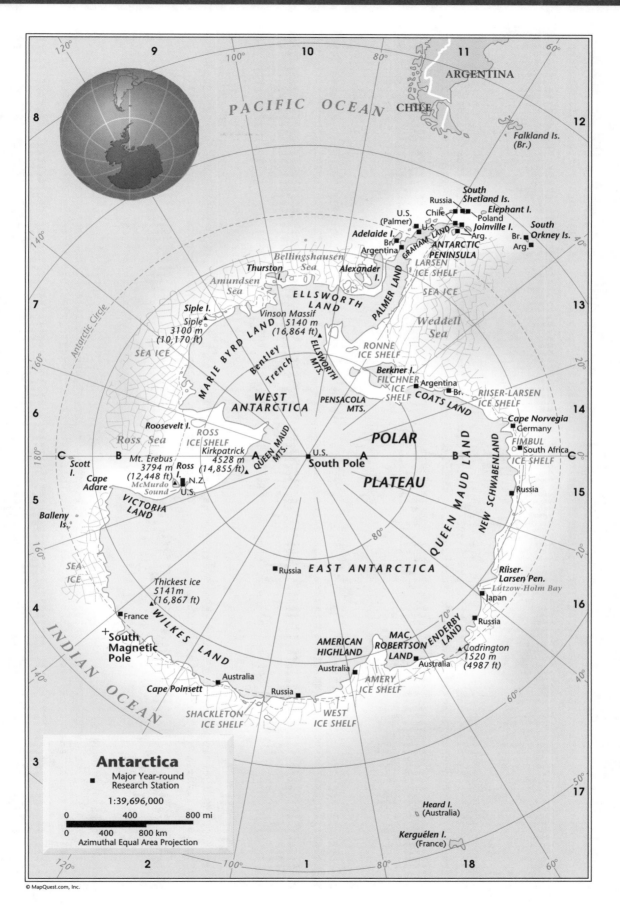

PACIFIC OCEAN

ARGENTINA

CHILE

Falkland Is.
(Br.)

South Shetland Is.
Russia
U.S. (Palmer)
Chile
Poland
Elephant I.
Joinville I.
Arg.
Adelaide I.
Br.
U.S.
GRAHAM LAND
Br. **South Orkney Is.**
Arg.
Argentina
ANTARCTIC PENINSULA

Bellingshausen Sea
Thurston I.
Alexander I.
LARSEN ICE SHELF
Amundsen Sea
ELLSWORTH LAND
PALMER LAND
SEA ICE
Siple I.
Siple
3100 m
(10,170 ft)
Weddell Sea
Vinson Massif
5140 m
(16,864 ft)
SEA ICE
MARIE BYRD LAND
ELLSWORTH MTS.
RONNE ICE SHELF
Berkner I.
FILCHNER ICE SHELF
Argentina
Br.
RIISER-LARSEN ICE SHELF
Bentley Trench
WEST ANTARCTICA
PENSACOLA MTS.
COATS LAND

Roosevelt I.
ROSS ICE SHELF
Ross Sea
Cape Norvegia
Germany
QUEEN MAUD MTS.
FIMBUL ICE SHELF
South Africa
Scott I.
B
Mt. Erebus
3794 m
(12,448 ft)
Ross I.
Kirkpatrick
4528 m
(14,855 ft)
U.S.
South Pole
POLAR PLATEAU
QUEEN MAUD LAND
NEW SCHWABENLAND
Russia
Cape Adare
N.Z.
McMurdo Sound
U.S.
A
A
B
C
VICTORIA LAND
Balleny Is.
SEA ICE
Russia
EAST ANTARCTICA
Russia
Riiser-Larsen Pen.
Lützow-Holm Bay
Japan
Thickest ice
5141m
(16,867 ft)
Russia
France
✝ **South Magnetic Pole**
WILKES LAND
AMERICAN HIGHLAND
MAC. ROBERTSON LAND
ENDERBY LAND
Codrington
1520 m
(4987 ft)
Australia
Australia
Australia
Australia
AMERY ICE SHELF
Cape Poinsett
Russia
SHACKLETON ICE SHELF
WEST ICE SHELF
INDIAN OCEAN

Heard I.
(Australia)

Kerguélen I.
(France)

Antarctica

■ Major Year-round Research Station

1:39,696,000

0   400   800 mi
0 400 800 km
Azimuthal Equal Area Projection

A

Key Page
Aachen A3 40
Aaiún, el- B1 58
Aalst C2 33
Aarau C1 35
Aare, *river* B1, B2 35
Aba D5 65
Abadan B3 22
Abaí E4 75
Abakaliki E4 65
Abakan D6 44
Abancay C3 77
Abaya, *lake* B3 60
Abbeville C1 34
Abbey B10 104
Abbotsford L6 95
Abdali B1 24
Abéché C4 59
Abemama, *island* A1 17
Abengourou E3 63
Åbenrå B3 32
Abeokuta B4 65
Aberdeen Inset 10
Aberdeen C1 30
Aberdeen, *lake* H4 99
Aberdeen, S. Dak. D1 126
Aberystwyth B3 30
Abha B2 24
Abhe, *lake* C2 60
Abia, *river* C3 66
Abidjan D4 63
Abilene, Tex. D2 126
Abkhazia, autonomous republic A3 45
Aboisso E4 63
Abomey A4 64
Abou Deïa B5 59
Abrantes A3 36
Abruzzi C2 38
Abşeron, *peninsula* C2 45
Abu Dhabi, *capital* C2 25
Abu Kamal B2 27
Abuja, *capital* D3 65
Abuná, *river* A2 77
Acadia Valley E5 94
Acajutla A2 86
Acámbaro D4 84
Acapulco E4 84
Acarai, *mts.* B5 80
Acaray, *river* E4 75
Acarigua C2 79
Accra, *capital* B4 64
Achill, *island* A2 31
Achinsk D6 44
Achwa, *river* C2 61
Acklins, *island* C4 89
Acme D5 94
Acolman Inset 84
Aconcagua, *mt.* A3 74
Aconcagua, *river* B4 76
Aconibe C3 66
Acquaviva A1 39
Acre A2 81
Acre (Akko) B1 26
Acton E4 102
Acton Vale D6 103
Açúcar, *mt.* Inset I 81
Adamawa, *massif* B2, E5 65
Adams, *lake* N5 95
Adana C3 27
Adapazarı B2 27
Adare, *cape* B5 107
Addis Ababa, *capital* C2 60
Addu, *atoll* A5 19
Adelaide, *island* C11 107
Adelaide, S.A., *capital* C3, Inset II 14
Aden B2 25
Aden E6 94
Aden, *gulf* B1, C2 60
Adi Keyih B2 60
Adi Ugri B2 60
Adige, *river* B1 38
Adirondack, *mts.*, N.Y. F1 126
Adjuntas B2 90
Admiralty, *islands* A2 15
Ado-Ekiti C4 65
Adolphustown H3 102
Adour, *river* B5 34
Adrar B2 57
Adrar des Iforas, *massif* D2 58
Adriatic, *sea* C2 38
Advocate Harbour C2 100
Adwa C1 60
Adygeya, republic E4 44
Adzopé E3 63
Aegean, *sea* C2 51
Ærø, *island* C4 32
Aetna D6 94
Afadjoto, *mt.* C3 64
Afghanistan 22
Afikpo D5 65
Afram, *river* B3 64
Afyon B2 27
Agadès B2 59
Agadir B2 57
Agartala F4 20
Agboville D4 63
Ağcabädi B2 45
Ağdam B3 45
Agen C4 34
Aginskiy Buryat, autonomous okrug D7 44
Aginskoye D7 44
Agou, *mt.* B3 64
Agra C3 20
Ağri E2 27
Agrigento C3 38
Agrínion B2 51
Ağstafa A2 45
Agua Prieta C1 84
Aguada A2 90
Aguadilla A2 90
Aguadulce B2 87
Aguán, *river* B2 86
Aguarico, *river* C3 79
Aguas Blancas C2 76
Aguas Buenas C2 90
Aguascalientes, *state capital* D3 84
Águilas F4 37
Aguilita B2 90
Agung, *mt.* C2 13
Agusan, *river* C4 12
Ahmadabad B4 20
Ahmadi, al- C2 24
Ahmic Harbour F2 102
Ahuachapán A2 86
Ahvaz B3 22
Ahwar B2 25
Aibonito C2 90
Aigáleo, *mts.* Inset 51
Ailinglapalap, *island* B2 16
Aillik B1 98
Ailuk, *island* B1 16
Aiquile A3 77
Air Force, *island* O3 99
Air Ronge E5 104
Aïr, *mts.* B2 59
Airdrie C5 94
Aishihik, *lake* B5 105
Aisne, *river* D2 34
Aiwo A2 16
Aix-en-Provence D5 34
Aix-les-Bains D4 34
Aíyina, *island* B3 51
Aizawl F4 20
Aizuwakamatsu C2 8
Ajaccio Inset I 34
Ajaria, autonomous republic A4 45
Ajdabiya D1 56
Ajka A2 43
Ajman C2 25
Ajmer B3 20
Akanyaru, *river* B2 61
Akashi B3 8
Akhalkalaki B4 45
Akhaltsikhe B4 45
Akharnaí Inset 51
Akhelóös, *river* B2 51
Akhmeta C3 45
Akhuryan, *river* A2 45
Akita D2 8
Akjoujt B3 58
Aklavik A3 99
Akobo, *river* A3 60
Akola C4 20
Akordat A2 60
Akosombo, *dam* C3 64
Akpatok, *island* P4 99
Akranes A2 52
Akron, Ohio E1 126
Aksaray C2 27
Aksu B1 10
Akulivik A1 101
Akure C4 65
Akurenam C3 66
Akureyri B2 52
Akuseki, *island* A4 8
Alabama E2 126
Alagoas E2 81
Alagoinhas E3 81
Alajuela B2 86
Alakol, *lake* E2 23
Alamayn, al- A1 56
Alameda H11 104
Alampur Inset II 20
Åland, *islands* B2 53
Alanya C3 27
Alarcón, *reservoir* E3 37
Alaska Inset I 126
Alaska, *gulf*, Alaska Inset I 126
Alaska, *range*, Alaska Inset I 126
Älät C3 45
Alaverdi B2 45
Alay, *mts.* B1, C3 23
Alayli Dadda B1 60
Alazani, *river* C4 45
Alba Iulia B2 43
Albacete F3 37
Alban E1 102
Albania 49
Albany, *capital*, N.Y. F1 126
Albany, Ga. E2 126
Albany, *river* C2 101
Albany, W.A. A3 14
Albert Nile, *river* B2 61
Albert, *canal* C1 33
Albert, *lake* B3 61
Alberton A2 100
Albi C5 34
Albina B2 80
Alboran, *sea* E4 37
Ålborg B1 32
Ålborg, *bay* C2 32
Albuquerque, *cays* Inset 78
Albuquerque, N. Mex. C2 126
Albury, N.S.W. D3 14
Alcalá de Henares Inset II 37
Alcañiz F2 37
Alcántara, *reservoir* C3 37
Alcázar de San Juan E3 37
Alcira F3 37
Alcobendas Inset II 37
Alcorcón E2, Inset II 37
Alcoy F3 37
Aldabra, *islands* A2 70
Aldan D8 44
Aldan, *river* D8 44
Alderney, *island* Inset II 30
Aleg B3 58
Alençon C2 34
Alert Q1 99
Alès D4 34
Alessandria B1 38
Ålesund B3 52
Aleutian *islands*, Alaska Inset I 126
Alexander A4 96
Alexander, *island* B11 107
Alexandra A4 15
Alexandria C4 43
Alexandria A1 56
Alexandria L2 102
Alexandria, La. D2 126
Alexandroúpolis C1 51
Alexis Creek L5 95
Alexis, *river* C3 98
Alfíos, *river* B3 51
Alfred L2 102
Algarrobo Inset 76
Algarve, *region* A4 36
Algeciras D4 37
Algeria 57
Alghero B2 38
Algiers, *capital* B1 57
Ali Adde B2 60
Äli Bayramli C3 45
Ali-Sabieh B2 60
Aliákmon, *river* B1 51
Alibori, *river* B2 64
Alicante F3 37
Alice C3 71
Alice Arm H3 95
Alice Springs, N.T. C2 14
Alice Town B2 89
Aligarh C3 20
Alima, *river* D4 66
Aliwal North C3 71
Alix D5 94
Alkmaar B2 32
Allahabad D3 20
Allardville D1 97
Allen, *lake* B1 31
Allenford D3 102
Allentown, Pa. F1 126
Alleppey (Alappuzah) C7 20
Alliance E5 94
Allier, *river* C3 34
Alligator Pond B3 88
Alliston F3 102
Allumette, *lake* H2 102
Alma E3 97
Alma E3 103
Almada A3 36
Almadén D3 37
Almansa F3 37
Almaty (Alma-Ata) D2 23
Almendralejo C3 37
Almelo D2 32
Almendra, *reservoir* C2 37
Almería E4 37
Almirante A2 87
Almonte J2 102
Alonsa B4 96
Alor Setar A1 13
Alor, *island* D2 13
Alotau B3 15
Alpena, Mich. E1 126
Alps, *mts.* 29
Alsace D2 34
Alsask A9 104
Alta E1 52
Altai, *mts.* B1 10
Altamira C2 81
Altamira C3 76
Altario E5 94
Altay B1 10
Altay B2 11
Altay, republic F4 44
Altdorf C2 35
Altiplano, *plateau* A3 77
Altona C4 96
Altun, *range* B2 10
Aluksne D2 46
Alvinston D5 102
Alytus C2 46
Alzette, *river* B2 33
Am Timan C5 59
Amadjuak, *lake* O4 99
Amadora A3 36
Amagasaki B3 8
Amahai D2 13
Amakusa, *islands* A3 8
Amambay, *mts.* E3 75
Amami, *island* Inset II 8
Amapá C1 81
Amapala B3 86
Amarah, al- C2 24
Amaranth B4 96
Amarillo, Tex. C2 126
Amasya C2 27
Amazon, *basin* B2 81
Amazon, *river* B2 81
Amazonas B2 81
Ambato B3 79
Ambatolampy B2 69
Ambatondrazaka B2 69
Amberg B4 40
Ambergris Cay, *island* C2 85
Ambergris, *cay* D4 89
Amberley D3 102
Ambon D2 13
Ambositra B3 69
Ambre, *cape* B1 69
Ambrym, *island* C3 18
Amdanga Inset II 20
Ameca D3 84
Ameland, *island* C1 32
American Samoa 18
Amersfoort C2 32
Amery Ice Shelf, *glacier* C18 107
Amherst C2 100
Amherstburg B5 102
Amiens C2 34
Amindivi, *islands* B6 20
Amirante, *islands* B2 70
Amisk E5 94
Amisk, *lake* H6 104
Amlamé B3 64
Amman, *capital* A2 26
Ammassalik C2 106
Ammersee, *lake* B4 40
Amos A4 101
Ampanihy A3 69
Amparai C4 19
Amqui J3 103
Amran A1 25
Amravati C4 20
Amritsar B2 20
Amsterdam, *capital* B2 32
Amstetten D2 39
Amu Darya, *river* B1, D2 22
Amund Ringnes, *island* J1 99
Amundsen, *gulf* C2 99
Amundsen, *sea* B9 107
Amur, *river* D8 44
Amyun A1 26
Ana María, *gulf* D2 88
Anabar C1 16
Anaco D2 79
Anadyr C10 44
Anadyr, *gulf* C11 44
Anahim Lake K5 95
Anáhuac D2 84
Anápolis D3 81
Añasco A2 90
Añasco, *beach* A2 90
Anatolia, *region* B2 27
Anatom, *island* C5 18
Anchorage, Alaska Inset I 126
Ancona C2 38
Ancud B7 76
Ancud, *gulf* B7 76
Andalusia D4 37
Andaman, *islands* F6 20
Andaman, *sea* B3 12
Anderlecht C2 33
Anderson, *river* C3 99
Andes, *mts.* 73
Andheri Inset I 20
Andizhan D2 23
Andoany B1 69
Andong C4 9
Andorra 36
Andorra la Vella, *capital* B2 36
Andreas, *cape* C1 27
Ándros, *island* A3 89
Ándros, *island* C3 51
Androth, *island* B6 20
Aného B3 64
Anelghowhat C5 18
Anetan B1 16
Aneto, *mt.* G1 37
Angara, *river* D6 44
Angarsk D7 44
Angaur B4 17
Angel, *falls* D2 79
Angeles B3 12
Ångermanälven, *river* C2 53
Angers B3 34
Angikuni, *lake* H4 99
Angkor Thom, *ruins* B2 11
Angkor Wat, *ruins* B2 11
Anglesey, *island* B3 30
Angoche C3 68
Angol B6 76
Angola 70
Angoulême C4 34
Angus F3 102
Anholt, *island* C2 32
Anhui E2 10
Anibare B2 16
Anié B3 64
Añisoc C3 66
Anjou J5 103
Anju A3 9
Ankang D2 10
Ankara, *capital* C2 27
Ankaratra, *mts.* B2 69
Ankobra, *river* A4 64
Ann Arbor, Mich. E1 126
Anna Regina B2 80
Annaba B1 57
Annam, *mts.* A2 11
Annandale C2 100
Annapolis Royal B3 100
Annapolis, *capital*, Md. F2 126
Annapurna, *mt.* B2 19
Annecy D4 34
Anqing E2 10
Ansbach B4 40
Anse Boileau Inset 70
Anse Royale Inset 70
Anse-à-Galets C2 89
Anshan F1 10
Ansongo D2 58
Antalaha C1 69
Antalya B3 27
Antalya, *gulf* B3 27
Antananarivo, *capital* B2 69
Antarctic, *peninsula* C12 107
Antarctica 107
Antequera D4 37
Anti-Atlas, *ranges* B2 57
Anti-Lebanon, *mts.* B1 26
Anticosti, *island* D4 101
Antigonish F2 100
Antigua C5 85
Antigua, *island* D4 90
Antigua and Barbuda 90
Antioch (Antakya) D3 27
Antofagasta B2 76
Antrim, *mts.* A2 30
Antsirabe B2 69
Antsiranana B1 69
Antsohihy B1 69
Antwerp C1 33
Anuradhapura B3 19
Anyang E2 10
Anyang B4 9
Anyos B2 36
Aoa C1 18
Aoba, *island* B2 18
Aomori D1 8
Aoral, *mt.* C3 11
Aosta A1 38
Aozou B2 59
Apa, *river* D3 75
Apaporis, *river* C4 78
Apatity C3 44
Apatou A1 80
Apeldoorn C2 32
Apennines, *range* B1 38
Apetina B3 80
Api, *mt.* A2 19
Apia, *capital* C2 18
Apo, *volcano* C5 12
Apoera A2 80
Apolima, *island* B2 18
Apolima, *strait* B2 18
Apoteri B4 80
Appalachian, *mts.* E2 126
Apple River C2 100
Apsley G3 102
Apulia C2 38
Apure, *river* C2 79
Apurímac, *river* C3 77
Apuseni, *mts.* B2 43
Aqaba, *gulf* A3, B3 26
Aqabah, al- A3 26
Aqtau B2 23
Aqtobe B1 23
Aquileia C1 38
Aquitaine B4 34
Ara D3 20
Arabah, al-, *river* A2, B2 26
Arabian, *desert* B2 56
Arabian, *sea* A5, Inset I 20
Aracaju E3 81
Arcachon B4 34
Arad A2 43
Aradah B3 25
Arafura, *sea* E2 13
Aragats, *mt.* B2 45
Aragón F2 37
Araguaia, *river* C3 81
Arak B3 22
Arakabesan, *island* B3 17
Arakan Yoma, *mts.* B2 12
Aral C2 23
Aral, *sea* A2, B2 23
Aran, *islands* B2 31
Aranda de Duero E2 37
Aranjuez E2 37
Aranyaprathet C3 12
Arapey Grande, *river* B1 75
Ararat B3 45
Ararat (Ağri Daği), *mt.* F2 27
Aras, *river* E2 27
Arauca C3 78
Arauca, *river* C2 79
Aravalli, *range* B3 20
Arawa B2 15
Arba Minch B3 60
Arborfield G7 104
Arborg C4 96
Archerwill G8 104
Arcola H11 104
Arctic Bay L2 99
Arctic Red River B3 99
Arda, *river* C4 50
Ardabil B2 22
Ardara B1 31
Ardbeg E2 102
Ardennes, *plateau* D2 33
Ardennes, *region* D1 34
Arecibo B2 90
Arekalong, *peninsula* C2 17
Arenal, *lake* B2 86
Arenas, *point* D2 90
Arendal B4 52
Arequipa C4 77
Arezzo B2 38
Argenteuil Inset II 34
Argentia D5 98
Argentina 74
Argentino, *lake* A7 74
Argeş, *river* C3 43
Arghandab, *river* B2 22
Argonne, *forest* D2 34
Árgos B3 51
Argyle C4 96
Argyle F3 102
Århus C2 32
Ari, *atoll* A3 19
Ariana C1 57
Arica B1 76
Arichat F2 100
Arima A2 91
Arinsal A2 36
Aripuanã, *river* C2 81
Arish, al- B1 56
Arizona B2 126
Arkansas D2 126
Arkansas, *river* D2 126
Arkhangelsk C4 44
Arklow C2 31
Arkona D4 102
Arles D5 34
Arlit B2 59
Arlon D3 33
Armagh A2 30
Armenia 45
Armenia B3 78
Armidale, N.S.W. E3 14
Armstrong N6 95
Armstrong C2 101
Arnaud, *river* B2 101
Arnes C4 96
Arnhem C3 32
Arnhem Land, *region* C1 14
Arnhem, *cape* C1 14
Arno, *island* C2 16
Arno, *river* B2 38
Arnold's Cove D5 98
Arnprior J2 102
Arnsberg B3 40
Aroostook B2 97
Arorae, *island* C2 17
Arpa, *river* C3 45
Arpajon Inset II 34
Arqalyq C1 23
Arran, *island* B2 30
Arras C1 34
Arroyo C3 90
Arta B2 60
Artashat B3 45
Artemisa B2 88
Arthur E4 102
Arthur's Town B3 89
Artibonite, *river* C1 89
Artigas B1 75
Artik A2 45
Artsvashen C2 45
Artvin E2 27
Aru, *islands* E2 13
Arua B2 61
Aruba, *island* C2 82
Arun, *river* D2 19
Arusha C1 68
Aruvi, *river* B3 19
Aruwimi, *river* C1 67
Arvayheer C2 11
As Ela B2 60
Asaba D4 65
Asadabad C2 22
Asahi Dake, *mt.* Inset I 8
Asahikawa Inset I 8
Asama, *mt.* C2 8
Asansol E4 20
Asau A2 18
Asbestos E6 103
Ascoli Piceno C2 38
Asela C3 60
Asenovgrad C3 50
Ashburton B3 15
Ashburton, *river* A2 14
Ashcroft M6 95
Ashdod B2 26
Ashern B3 96
Asheville, N.C. E2 126
Asheweig, *river* C2 101
Ashgabat, *capital* C3 22
Ashikaga C2 8
Ashizuri, *cape* B3 8
Ashmore and Cartier, *islands* B1 14
Ashqelon B2 26
Ashton A4 91
Ashuapmushuan, *river* C2 103
Asinara, *island* B2 38
Asipovichy D3 47
Asir, *region* B2 24
Askar B1 25
Asmara, *capital* B2 60
Asnam, el- B1 57
Aso, *mt.* A3 8
Asosa B2 60
Aspiring, *mt.* A3 15
Asprópirgos Inset 51
Asquith C8 104
Assab D3 60
Assal, *lake* B2 60
Assen D2 32
Assiniboia D11 104
Assiniboine, *mt.* P6 95
Assiniboine, *river* A4 96
Astana (Akmola), *capital* D1 23
Astara C3 45
Asti B1 38
Astipálaia, *island* C3 51
Astorga C1 37
Astrakhan E4 44
Astrolabe, *reefs* C2 18
Asturias C1 37
Asunción, *capital* D4 75
Aswan B3 56
Aswan High, *dam* B3 56
Asyut B2 56
At-Bashy D2 23
Atacama, *desert* C2 76
Atakpamé B3 64
Ataq B2 25
Atâr B2 58
Atatürk, *reservoir* D3 27
Atbara, *river* B1 60
Atbarah C2 59
Atbarah, *river* C2 59
Atbasar C1 23
Ath B2 33
Athabasca D4 94
Athabasca, *lake* A1 104
Athabasca, *river* B4, D3, E2 94
Athens, *capital* B3, Inset 51
Athens, Ga. E2 126
Athi, *river* E5 61
Athlone C2 31
Áthos, *mt.* C1 51
Ati B4 59
Atiak C2 61
Atikameg C3 94
Atikameg Lake A2 96
Atikokan B3 101
Atitlán, *lake* B5 85
Atlanta, *capital*, Ga. E2 126
Atlantic City, N.J. F2 126
Atlas, *mts.* A1, B2 57
Atlin F1 95
Atlin, *lake* F1 95
Atrai, *river* B4 21
Atrak, *river* D2 22
Atrato, *river* A3 78
Attapu D4 11
Attawapiskat D2 101
Attawapiskat, *river* C2 101
Atuel, *river* B4 74
Atyrau B2 23
Aua C1 18
Aube, *river* D3 34
Auch C5 34
Auckland B2 15
Augsburg B4 40
Augusta, *capital*, Maine G1 126
Augusta, Ga. E2 126
Auki B1 16
Aulac E3 97
Aunuu, *island* C1 18
Auob, *river* C3 70
Aur, *island* C2 16
Aurangabad C5 20
Aurillac C4 34
Aurora F3 102
Ausa, *river* C1 39
Austin B4 96
Austin, *capital*, Tex. D2 126
Australia 14
Australian Alps, *mts.* D3 14
Australian Capital Territory D3 14
Austria 39
Auvergne C4 34
Auxerre C3 34
Avalon, *peninsula* E5 98
Aveiro A2 36
Avellaneda D3 74
Avellino C2 38
Aviemore B1 30
Avignon D5 34
Ávila D2 37
Avilés D1 37
Avon, *islands* A2 18
Avon, *river* C3 30
Avonlea E10 104
Awaji B3 8

Name	Key	Page
Awaji, *island*	B3	8
Awasa	C3	60
Awash, *river*	C2	60
Awaso	A3	64
Awbari	B2	56
Awjilah	D4	65
Awwali, *river*	A2	26
Axel Heiberg, *island*	K1	99
Axim	A4	64
Ayacucho	C3	77
Ayagöz	E2	23
Aydin	A3	27
Ayer Chawan, *island*	A1	13
Ayer's Cliff	D6	103
Áyios Dhimítrios	Inset	51
Aylesbury	Inset III	30
Aylmer	E5	102
Aylmer	A6	103
Aylmer, *lake*	G4	99
Aylmer, *lake*	E6	103
Ayn, al-	C3	25
Ayoûn el-Atroûs	C3	58
Ayr	B2	30
Aytos	F3	50
Azaouâd, *region*	C2	58
Azare	F2	65
Azaz	A1	27
Azcapotzalco	Inset	84
Azerbaijan		45
Azerbaijan, *region*	B2	22
Azogues	B4	79
Azores, *islands*		5
Azov, *sea*	D3	47
Azraq ash-Shishan	B2	26
Azua	B2	89
Azuero, *peninsula*	B3	87

B

Name	Key	Page
Ba, *river*	B3	11
Baalbek	B1	26
Bab al-Mandab, *strait*	C1	60
Babahoyo	B3	79
Babanusah	B3	59
Babar, *island*	D2	13
Babbage, *river*	B1	105
Babda	A2	26
Babelthuap, *island*	C3	17
Babine, *lake*	J4	95
Babine, *river*	J3	95
Babruysk	D3	47
Babu Bheri	Inset II	20
Babuyan, *channel*	B2	12
Babuyan, *islands*	B2	12
Babylon, *ruins*	B2	24
Bac Lieu	A5	11
Bacabal	D2	81
Bacău	D2	43
Back, *river*	H3	99
Bačka Palanka	A2	49
Bacolod	B4	12
Bad Ems	A3	40
Bad Ischl	C3	39
Bad Kreuznach	A4	40
Bad Reichenhall	C5	40
Badajoz	C3	37
Badalona	H2	37
Badanah	B1	24
Badas	A2	13
Baddeck	G1	100
Baden	C1	35
Baden	E2	39
Baden	A3	96
Baden-Baden	A4	40
Baden-Württemberg	B4	40
Badger	D4	96
Badger	C5	98
Badou	B3	64
Bafatá	C1	62
Baffin	L1	92
Baffin, *island*	M2	99
Baffin, *region*	N2	99
Bafilo	B2	64
Bafing, *river*	C2	62
Bafoulabé	A3	58
Bafoussam	B2	65
Baghdad, *capital*	B1	24
Baghlan	B1	22
Baglung	C2	19
Bagoé, *river*	C1	63
Baguio	B2	12
Bagzane, *mt.*	B2	59
Bahamas		89
Bahawalpur	D4	21
Bahia	D3	81
Bahía Blanca	C4	74
Bahía Honda	A2	88
Bahía, *islands*	B1	86
Bahir Dar	B2	60
Bahoruco, *mts.*	A2	89
Bahr al-Arab, *river*	B3	59
Bahr al-Ghazal, *river*	C3	59
Bahr al-Jabal, *river*	C3	59
Bahr Salamat, *river*	B5	59
Bahrain		25
Bahrain, *gulf*	A2	25
Baia Mare	B2	43
Baicheng	F1	10
Baidyabati	Inset II	20
Baie Verte	C4	98
Baie-Comeau	H2	103
Baie-des-Sables	J3	103
Baie-St-Paul	F4	103
Baie-Ste-Anne	E1	97
Baie-Ste-Catherine	G3	103
Bailieboro	G3	102
Bainsville	L2	102
Bair	B2	26
Baiti	B1	16
Baja	A2	43
Baja California	A1	84
Baja California Sur	B2	84
Bajadero	B2	90
Bajo Boquete	A2	87
Bakel	C2	62
Baker Brook	A1	97
Baker Lake	J4	99
Bakersfield, Calif.	B2	126

Name	Key	Page
Bakhardok	C2	22
Bakhtaran	B3	22
Bakhtiari, *region*	B3	22
Bakony, *mts.*	A2	43
Baku, *capital*	C2	45
Bala	F2	102
Bala, *lake*	B3	30
Balabac, *island*	A5	12
Balabac, *strait*	A5	12
Balakän	B2	45
Balaklava	C4	47
Balaton, *lake*	A2	43
Balbina	C2	87
Balcarres	G10	104
Baldur	B4	96
Baldy, *mt.*	A3	96
Balearic, *islands*	G3	37
Balearic, *sea*	G2	37
Baleine, *river*	C2	101
Balgonie	F10	104
Balhaf	B2	25
Balho	B1	60
Bali, *island*	C2	13
Baliceaux, *island*	B3	91
Balikesir	A2	27
Balikpapan	C2	13
Balkan, *mts.*	B2	50
Balkh	B1	22
Balkhash	D2	23
Balkhash, *lake*	D2	23
Ballarat, Vic.	D3	14
Ballancourt-sur-Essonne	Inset II	34
Balleny, *islands*	C5	107
Ballerup	D3	32
Ballina	B1	31
Bally	Inset II	20
Ballymena	A2	30
Balmaceda	B8	76
Balmoral	C1	97
Balmertown	B2	101
Balsas, *river*	E4	84
Bălţi	A2	50
Baltic, *sea*		29
Baltimore, Md.	F2	126
Baluchistan, *region*	E4	22
Balykchy	E1	23
Balzers	B2	33
Bam	D4	22
Bamako, *capital*	B3	58
Bamangachi	Inset II	20
Bambadinca	C1	62
Bambana, *river*	B2	87
Bambari	B2	66
Bamberg	B4	40
Bamenda	B2	65
Bamian	B2	22
Bamingui	B2	66
Ban Houayxay	A1	11
Ban Phai	C2	11
Banaba, *island*	A2	17
Banana	A2	67
Bananga	F7	20
Banat, *region*	A3	43
Banbury	C3	30
Bancroft	H2	102
Banda Aceh	A1	13
Banda, *sea*	D2	13
Bandama Blanc, *river*	D2	63
Bandama Rouge, *river*	C2	63
Bandama, *river*	D3	63
Bandar Beheshti	E4	22
Bandar Lampung	B2	13
Bandar Seri Begawan, *capital*	B2	13
Bandar-e Abbas	D4	22
Bandar-e Anzali	B2	22
Bandar-e Bushehr	C4	22
Bandar-e Khomeyni	B3	22
Bandar-e Torkeman	C2	22
Bandeira, *mt.*	D4	81
Bandera	Inset I	20
Bandundu	B3	67
Bandung	B2	13
Banff	C5	94
Bangalore	C6	20
Bangar	C2	13
Bangassou	B3	66
Banggi, *island*	D1	13
Banghiang, *river*	C3	11
Bangka, *island*	B2	13
Bangkok, *capital*	B3	12
Bangladesh		21
Bangor	B2	30
Bangor	B3	30
Bangor, Maine	G1	126
Bangui, *capital*	A3	66
Bangweulu, *lake*	B2	67
Bani Suwayf	B2	56
Bani Walid	B1	56
Bani, *river*	B3	58
Baniyas	A2	27
Banja Luka	B1	48
Banjarmasin	C2	13
Banjul, *capital*	B2	62
Banks, *island*	G4	95
Banks, *island*	D2	99
Banks, *islands*	B1	18
Banks, *peninsula*	B3	15
Bann, *river*	A2	30
Bannockburn	H3	102
Bansang	D2	62
Bansbaria	Inset II	20
Banská Bystrica	B2	42
Bantry	B3	31
Bantry, *bay*	B3	31
Baoding	E2	10
Baoshan	C3	10
Baotou	E1	10
Baoulé, *river*	B3	58
Baquba	B2	24
Baquerizo Moreno	Inset	79
Bar	A3	49
Bar-le-Duc	D2	34
Baraawe	A3	60
Barabinsk	D5	44
Baracaldo	E1	37
Barachois	M3	103

Name	Key	Page
Baracoa	F3	88
Barahona	A2	89
Barak Barak	B2	22
Barakpur	Inset II	20
Baram, *river*	B2	13
Barama, *river*	B2	80
Baranagar	Inset II	20
Baranavichy	C3	47
Barasat	Inset II	20
Barbados		91
Barbuda, *island*	E3	90
Barcelona	D1	79
Barcelona	H2	37
Barceloneta	B2	90
Bärdä	B2	45
Bardaï	B2	59
Bardejov	C2	42
Bareilly	C3	20
Barents, *sea*	B3	44
Bargachia	Inset II	20
Bari	D2	38
Baril, *lake*	E2	94
Barinas	B2	79
Barind, *region*	B4	21
Baris	B3	56
Barisal	D6	21
Bark, *lake*	H2	102
Barkerville	M4	95
Barkly, *tableland*	C1	14
Barletta	D2	38
Barnaul	D6	44
Barnes, *ice cap*	O3	99
Barnsley	C3	30
Barnstaple	B3	30
Barnwell	D6	94
Baro, *river*	B2	60
Barons	D6	94
Barquisimeto	C1	79
Barra, *island*	A2	30
Barrancabermeja	B3	78
Barranquilla	B2	78
Barranquitas	C2	90
Barreiro	A3	36
Barrhead	C4	94
Barrie	F3	102
Barrière	M5	95
Barrington	B4	100
Barrow	B1	62
Barrouallie	B2	91
Barrow, Alaska	Inset I	126
Barrow, *river*	C2	31
Barrow-in-Furness	B2	30
Barry's Bay	H2	102
Bartang, *river*	B1	23
Bartica	B2	80
Barú, *volcano*	A1	87
Baruun-Urt	C2	11
Bas-Caraquet	E1	97
Basarabeasca	B2	50
Basel	B1	35
Bashi, *channel*	B5	12
Basilan	B5	12
Basilan, *island*	B5	12
Basildon	Inset III	30
Basilicata	C2	38
Basque Country	E1	37
Basra	B2	24
Bass Rock, *islet*	C2	30
Bass, *strait*	D3	14
Bassar	B2	64
Basse Santa Su	D2	62
Basse-Normandie	B2	34
Bassein	B3	12
Basseterre, *capital*	B2	90
Bassila	A3	64
Bastia	Inset I	34
Bastogne	D2	33
Bata	A3	66
Bataan, *peninsula*	B3	12
Batabanó, *gulf*	B2	88
Batan, *islands*	B1	12
Batang	C3	10
Batang Duri	B2	13
Batangafo	A2	66
Batangas	B3	12
Batdambang	B2	11
Bate, *bay*	Inset IV	14
Batéké, *plateau*	C5	66
Bath	C3	90
Bath	C3	30
Bath	C3	97
Batha, *river*	C4	59
Bathsheba	B3	34
Bathurst	D1	97
Bathurst, *capital*	J1	99
Batin, Wadi al-, *river*	A2	24
Batinah, al-, *region*	C1	25
Batman	E3	27
Baton Rouge, *capital*, La.	D2	126
Batouri	B3	65
Batroun, al-	A1	26
Battambang	D2	98
Batticaloa	C4	19
Battle, *river*	A7	104
Battleford	B8	104
Batu Pahat	B2	13
Batumi	A4	45
Baubau	D2	13
Bauchi	E2	65
Bauru	D4	81
Bauska	C3	46
Bautzen	C3	40
Bavarian Alps, *mts.*	B5	40
Bawiti, al-	B2	56
Bawku	B1	64
Bawlf	D5	94
Bay Bulls	E5	98
Bay de Verde	E5	98
Bay Roberts	E5	98
Bay St. Lawrence	G1	100
Bayamo	E3	88
Bayamón	C2	90
Bayamón, *river*	C2	90
Bayan Har, *range*	C2	10

Name	Key	Page
Bayanhongor	C2	11
Bayda, al-	B1	25
Bayda, al-	D1	56
Baydhabo	A3	60
Bayerischer Wald, *mts.*	C4	40
Bayeux	B2	34
Baygorria, *lake*	B2	75
Baykal, *lake*	D7	44
Bayonne	B5	34
Bayport	C3	100
Bayramaly	D3	22
Bayreuth	B4	40
Bays, *lake*	F2	102
Bazardüzü Daği, *mt.*	B2	45
Bazin, *river*	A4	103
Beachside	D4	98
Beagle, *channel*	B7	74
Bear Lake	L4	95
Bear River	C2	100
Beata, *cape*	A3	89
Beata, *island*	A3	89
Beaton	O6	95
Beauceville	F5	103
Beaufort West	B3	71
Beaufort, *sea*	B1	105
Beaulac	E6	103
Beaumont	D4	94
Beaumont, Tex.	D2	126
Beaupré	F4	103
Beauséjour	C2	96
Beauvais	C2	34
Beaver Creek	A4	105
Beaver Harbour	E3	100
Beaver Hill, *lake*	D2	96
Beaver Mines	C6	94
Beaver, *river*	A6	104
Beaver, *river*	D5	105
Beaverton	F3	102
Beavercour	D5	103
Bécancour	D5	103
Bečej	B2	49
Bedaque, *bay*	B2	100
Bedford	C3	100
Bedford	D3	30
Bedford	D6	103
Bedok	B1	13
Beechy	C10	104
Beersheba	A2	26
Behala	Inset II	20
Bei'an	F1	10
Beijing, *capital*	E2	10
Beira	B3	68
Beirut, *capital*	A2	26
Beja	B3	36
Béja	B1	57
Bejaïa	B1	57
Bejaïa, *gulf*	B1	57
Bekaa, *valley*	A2	26
Békéscsaba	C2	43
Bela	A2	21
Belapurpada	Inset I	20
Belarus		47
Belasica, *mts.*	C2	48
Belaya Tserkov	C2	47
Beledweyne	B3	60
Belém	D2	81
Bélep, *islands*	C2	18
Belfast	B2	30
Belford Roxo	Inset I	81
Belfort	D3	34
Belfort, *gap*	D3	34
Belgium		33
Belgrade, *capital*	B2	49
Beli Drim, *river*	B3	49
Belitung, *island*	B2	13
Belize		85
Belize City	B2	85
Belize, *river*	B2	85
Bell Isle, *strait*	C4	98
Belle-Anse	C2	89
Belle, *island*	C3	98
Belledune	D1	97
Belleoram	C4	98
Belleview	A4	96
Belleville	H3	102
Bellingham, Wash.	A1	126
Bellingshausen, *sea*	B10	107
Bellinzona	D2	35
Bello	A1	78
Bellona, *island*	A1	16
Belluno	C1	38
Bellville	A3	71
Belmont	B4	96
Belmopan, *capital*	B2	85
Belo Horizonte	D3	81
Beloeil	C6	103
Belomorsk	C3	44
Belomaraha, *plateau*	A2	69
Bemidji, Minn.	D1	126
Ben Eoin	G2	100
Ben Nevis, *mt.*	B2	30
Benavente	C2	37
Bend, Oreg.	A1	126
Bender (Tighina)	B2	50
Benderbeyla	C2	60
Bendigo, Vic.	D3	14
Benevento	C2	38
Benghazi	D1	56
Bengkulu	B2	13
Bengbu	E2	10
Bengough	E11	104
Benguela	B4	70
Bení Mellal	C1	57

Name	Key	Page
Beni, *river*	C2	11
Benidorm	F3	37
Benin		64
Benin City	C4	65
Benin, *bight*	B5	65
Benito	A3	96
Benoit's Cove	B5	98
Benoni	C2	71
Bénoué, *river*	B3	65
Benson	G11	104
Bentiaba	B4	70
Benue, *river*	E3	65
Benxi	F1	10
Benzdorp	B3	80
Beqa, *island*	B3	17
Bequia, *island*	B2	91
Berat	A3	49
Berbera	B1	60
Berbérati	A3	66
Berbice, *river*	B3	80
Berdoba	C4	59
Berdyansk	D3	47
Berekua	B4	90
Berens River	C3	96
Berens, *island*	C3	96
Berens, *river*	C3	96
Beresford	D1	97
Berezniki	D4	44
Bergamo	B1	38
Bergen op Zoom	B3	32
Bergerac	C4	34
Bergisch Gladbach	A3	40
Bering, *sea*	Inset I	126
Bering, *strait*	C11	44
Berkner, *island*	B12	107
Berlin, *capital*	C2	40
Bermejo, *river*	C2	74
Bermuda, *island*		82
Bern, *capital*	B2	35
Bernburg	B3	40
Bernese Alps, *mts.*	B2	35
Bernières	K6	103
Berounka, *river*	A3	42
Bertwell	H8	104
Berwick	C2	100
Berwick-upon-Tweed	C2	30
Besançon	D3	34
Beskid, *mts.*	D4	41
Besnard, *lake*	D5	104
Besor, *river*	B2	26
Bethanien	C4	70
Bethany	B4	96
Bethel, Alaska	Inset I	126
Bethierville	C5	103
Bethlehem	C2	71
Béticos, *mts.*	E4	37
Bétou	E2	66
Betsiamites	H3	103
Betsiamites, *river*	G2	103
Betsiboka, *river*	B2	69
Bette, *mt.*	C3	56
Beulah	A4	96
Beyla	D3	62
Beyneu	C2	23
Beyşehir, *lake*	B3	27
Béziers	C5	34
Bhadrakh	E2	20
Bhadreswar	Inset II	20
Bhagalpur	E3	20
Bhairahawa	B2	19
Bhaktapur	C2	19
Bhamapur	D5	20
Bhamo	C1	12
Bhandup	Inset I	20
Bharatpur	C3	20
Bhatapara	D4	20
Bhatpara	Inset II	20
Bhavnagar	B4	20
Bhawanipur	Inset I	20
Bheri, *river*	B2	19
Bhima, *river*	C5	20
Bhimpur	Inset II	20
Bhiwandi	Inset I	20
Bhopal	C4	20
Bhubaneswar	E4	20
Bhuj	A4	20
Bhunya	B2	71
Bhutan		19
Biabou	B2	91
Biafra, *bight*	A3	65
Biak, *island*	E2	13
Biała Podlaska	F2	41
Białkouma	C3	63
Biarritz	B5	34
Bicaz, *reservoir*	D2	43
Biche, *lake*	E4	94
Bida	D3	65
Biel	B1	35
Biel, *lake*	B1	35
Bielefeld	A2	40
Bielsko-Biała	D4	41
Bien Hoa	B4	11
Bienville, *lake*	C2	101
Big Beaver	E11	104
Big Bend	B2	71
Big Creek	L5	95
Big Fish, *river*	B1	105
Big Gull, *lake*	J3	102
Big Muddy, *lake*	F11	104
Big River	C7	104
Big Trout Lake	C2	101
Big, *island*	O4	99
Big, *river*	B2	98
Biggar	C8	104
Bignona	A3	62
Bigstone, *river*	D1	96
Bihać	A1	48
Bihar	E3	20
Bijagós, *islands*	A2	62
Bijeljina	C1	48
Bikaner	B3	20
Bikar, *island*	C1	16
Bikini, *island*	B1	16

Name	Key	Page
Bilaspur	D4	20
Biläsuvar	C3	45
Bilauktaung, *range*	B3, C3	12
Bilbao	E1	37
Billings, Mont.	C1	126
Billings, *reservoir*	Inset II	81
Bilma	C2	59
Biloku	B5	80
Biloxi, Miss.	E2	126
Biltine	C4	59
Bimbila	C2	64
Binche	C2	33
Bindloss	E6	94
Bindura	B1	69
Binga, *mt.*	B3	68
Bingen	A4	40
Binscarth	A4	96
Bint Jubayl	A2	26
Bintang	B2	62
Bintimane, *mt.*	B1	63
Bío-Bío, *river*	B6	76
Bioko, *island*	A1	66
Bir Gandús	A2	58
Bîr Morgrein	C1	58
Birak	B2	56
Birao	B1	66
Biratnagar	D3	19
Birch Cliff	K5	102
Birch Hills	E7	104
Birch River	A3	96
Birch, *mts.*	D2	94
Birchy Bay	D4	98
Bird, *island*	B2	91
Birendranagar	B2	19
Birganj	C2	19
Birjand	D3	22
Birkat Qarun, *lake*	B2	56
Birkenhead	B3	30
Birkirkara	B2	36
Bîrlad	D2	43
Birmingham	C3	30
Birmingham, Ala.	E2	126
Birni Nkonni	B3	59
Birnin Kebbi	C1	65
Birobizhan	E8	44
Birtle	A4	96
Biržai	C1	46
Birzebbuga	B3	36
Biscay, *bay*	B4	34
Bishkek, *capital*	D1	23
Bishnupur	Inset II	20
Bishop's Falls	D4	98
Biskra	B1	57
Bislig	C4	12
Bismarck, *archipelago*	A2	15
Bismarck, *capital*, N. Dak.	C1	126
Bismarck, *range*	A2	15
Bismarck, *sea*	A2	15
Bismuna, *lagoon*	C1	87
Bison, *lake*	B2	94
Bissau, *capital*	B2	62
Bissett	D3	96
Bissorä	B1	62
Bistcho, *lake*	A1	94
Bistriţa	C2	43
Bistriţa, *river*	C2	43
Bitam	A1	66
Bitola	B2	48
Bitumount	E2	94
Biu	G2	65
Biwa, *lake*	B3	8
Biysk	D6	44
Bizard, *island*	H5	103
Bizerte	B1	57
Bjorne, *peninsula*	L1	99
Black (Da), *river*	A2	11
Black Country, *region*	C3	30
Black Lake	E1	104
Black River	B2	88
Black Tickle	D2	98
Black Volta, *river*	A2, B3	64
Black, *forest*	A4	40
Black, *hills*, S. Dak.	C1	126
Black, *lake*	E1	104
Black, *sea*		29
Blackburn	B3	30
Blackmans	B3	91
Blackpool	C3	30
Blacks Harbour	C3	97
Blackstone, *river*	B3	105
Blackville	D2	97
Blackwater, *river*	B2, C1	31
Blagoevgrad	B4	50
Blagoveshchensk	D4	44
Blagoveshchensk	D8	44
Blaine Lake	D8	104
Blainville	H5	103
Blanc, *mt.*	D4	34
Blanc, *reservoir*	C4	103
Blanc-Sablon	E3	101
Blanca, *bay*	C4	74
Blanda, *river*	B2	52
Blantyre	B3	68
Blarney	B3	31
Blatec	C2	48
Blenheim	B3	102
Blenheim	D5	102
Blida	B1	57
Bligh Water, *sound*	B2	17
Blind Bay	N6	95
Blind River	C1	102
Blitta	B2	64
Bloemfontein, *judicial capital*	C2	71
Blois	B3	34
Bloodvein, *river*	C3	96
Bloomfield	H4	102
Bloomington, Ind.	E2	126
Blossom Park	H6	102
Blow, *river*	B1	105
Blue Mountain, *peak*	C3	88
Blue Nile, *river*	C2	59
Blue Ridge	C4	94
Blue River	N5	95
Blue, *mts.*	E3	14
Blue, *mts.*		29
Bluefields	B2	88
Bluefields	C3	87

Key Page
Bluenose, *lake* E3 99
Bluffton C5 94
Blyth D4 102
Bo B2 63
Bo Hai, *gulf* E2 10
Boa Vista B1 81
Boa Vista, *island* D2 58
Boaco B2 87
Bobcaygeon G3 102
Bobo-Dioulasso B3 64
Bocas del Toro A2 87
Bocay B1 87
Bocay, *river* B2 87
Bocholt A3 40
Bochum A3 40
Bodaybo D7 44
Bodo E5 94
Bodø C2 52
Boende B2 67
Boggeragh, *mts.* B2 31
Boggy, *peak* D5 90
Bogor B2 13
Bogotá, *capital* B3 78
Bogra C4 21
Bohemia, *region* A3 42
Bohemian, *forest* A3 42
Bohemian-Moravian, *heights* B3 42
Bohol, *island* C4 12
Bohol, *sea* C4 12
Boiestown C2 97
Boilleau F3 103
Bois-des-Filion H5 103
Boise, *capital*, Idaho B1 126
Boissevain A4 96
Boknafjord, *fjord* B4 52
Boksburg C2 71
Bol A4 59
Bolama B2 62
Bolands D5 90
Bole A2 64
Bolgatanga B1 64
Bolívar, *mt.* B2 79
Bolivia 77
Bolligen B2 35
Bolnisi C4 45
Bolobo B2 67
Bologna B1 38
Bolovens, *plateau* D4 11
Bolsena, *lake* B2 38
Bolsón de Mapimí, *depression* D2 84
Bolton C3 30
Bolton F4 102
Bolu B2 27
Bolzano B1 38
Bom Jesus da Lapa D3 81
Boma A2 67
Bombay B5, Inset I 20
Bomu, *river* C1 67
Bon Pays, *region* B2 33
Bon, *cape* C1 57
Bonaire, *island* 82
Bonao B2 89
Bonaventure L3 103
Bonaventure, *river* L3 103
Bonavista E5 98
Bonavista, *bay* E5 98
Bondo B1 67
Bondoukou E2 63
Bondy Inset II 34
Bongor A5 59
Bonin, *islands* Inset III 8
Bonn A3 40
Bonnet Plume, *river* C3 105
Bonny D5 65
Bonnyville E4 94
Bonshaw B2 100
Bonthe A2 63
Bööntsagaan, *lake* B2 11
Boosaaso B1 60
Boothia, *gulf* K2 99
Boothia, *peninsula* K2 99
Booué A2 66
Bor C2 49
Borås B3 53
Bordeaux B4 34
Borden B2 100
Borden C8 104
Borden, *island* F1 99
Borden, *peninsula* M2 99
Borđoy, *island* Inset 32
Borgo Maggiore B1 39
Borivli Inset I 20
Borjomi B4 45
Borneo, *island* C1 13
Bornholm, *island* E3 32
Bosanska Gradiška B1 48
Bosanska Krupa A1 48
Bosna, *river* B1 48
Bosnia & Hercegovina 48
Boso, *peninsula* D3 8
Bosporus, *strait* B2 27
Bossangoa A2 66
Bosten, *lake* B1 10
Boston C3 30
Boston Bar M6 95
Boston, *capital*, Mass. F1 126
Boswell O6 95
Botany, *bay* Inset IV 14
Boteti, *river* A2 69
Botha D5 94
Bothnia, *gulf* B2, D2 53
Botna, *river* B2 50
Botoşani D2 43
Botrange, *mt.* E2 33
Botswana 69
Botte Donato, *mt.* D3 38
Bottrop A3 40
Botwood D4 98
Bouaflé D3 63
Bouaké D3 63
Bouar A2 66
Boucherville J5 103
Bouctouche E2 97
Bougainville, *island* B2 15
Boughton, *bay* C2 100
Bougouni B3 58
Boulder, Colo. C2 126
Boulogne-Billancourt Inset II 34
Boulogne-sur-Mer C1 34
Bouna E2 63
Bourail C2 18
Bourem C2 58
Bourg-en-Bresse D3 34
Bourges C3 34
Bourgogne C3 34
Bourke, N.S.W. D3 14
Bournemouth C4 30
Bousso B5 59
Bow City D6 94
Bow, *river* D6 94
Bow, *river* E6 104
Bowen, Qld. D2 14
Bowling Green, Ky. E2 126
Bowser, *lake* H3 95
Bowsman A3 96
Boyd's Cove D4 98
Boyne, *river* C2 31
Boyne, *river* B4 96
Bozeman, Mont. B1 126
Brabant Lake G4 104
Brač, *island* C3 48
Bracciano, *lake* C2 38
Bracebridge F2 102
Bradford C3 30
Braga A2 36
Bragança B2 36
Bragg Creek C6 94
Brahmanbaria E5 21
Brahmaputra, *river* F3 20
Brăila D3 43
Braintree Inset III 30
Brakpan C2 71
Bralorne L6 95
Bramalea H5 102
Brampton F4 102
Branch E5 98
Branco, *river* B1 81
Brandberg, *mt.* B2 70
Brandenburg C2 40
Brandon B4, C2 96
Brant D6 94
Brantford E4 102
Bras d'Or G1 100
Brasília, *capital* D3 81
Braşov C3 43
Bratislava, *capital* A2 42
Bratsk D7 44
Braunau C2 39
Brava, *coast* H2 37
Brava, *island* B4 58
Brazil 81
Brazilian, *highlands* D3 81
Brazzaville, *capital* C6 66
Brčko B1 48
Brea, *point* B3 90
Břeclav C4 42
Brecon Beacons, *mts.* B3 30
Breda B3 32
Bredenbury H10 104
Bregalnica, *river* C2 48
Breidhafjördhur, *fjord* A2 52
Bremen B2 40
Bremerhaven B2 40
Brenner, *pass* B3 39
Brentwood Inset III 30
Brescia B1 38
Brest A3 47
Brest A2 34
Bretagne B2 34
Breton C4 94
Bria B2 66
Briançon D4 34
Briceni A1 50
Bridge Lake M5 95
Bridgeport, Conn. F1 126
Bridgetown B3 100
Bridgetown, *capital* A4 91
Bridgewater C3 100
Brienzersee, *lake* B2 35
Brighton C4 30
Brighton H3 102
Brikama B2 62
Brindisi D2 38
Brisbane, Qld., *capital* E2, Inset III 14
Brisbane, *river* Inset III 14
Bristol C3 30
Bristol B2 97
Bristol, *channel* B3 30
Britannia E5 98
Britt E2 102
Brive-la-Gaillarde C4 34
Brno C3 42
Broadview H10 104
Brochet C1 96
Brock, *island* F1 99
Brocket D6 94
Brockville K3 102
Brodfur, *peninsula* L2 99
Broken Hill, N.S.W. D3 14
Brokopondo B2 80
Brolin C3 30
Bromptonville E6 103
Brookdale B4 96
Brooks E6 94
Brooks *range*, Alaska Inset I 126
Broome, W.A. B1 14
Broomhill A4 96
Brossard J6 103
Brownsville, Tex. D3 126
Bruce Mines B1 102
Bruce Peninsula N.P. D2 102
Brugge B1 33
Brugge-Ghent, *canal* B1 33
Brûlé B4 94
Brunei 13
Brunei, *bay* C1 13
Brunei, *river* B2 13
Brunswick B2 40
Brunswick, Ga. E2 126
Brunswick, *peninsula* B9 76
Brussels D4 102
Brussels, *capital* C2 33
Bryan, Tex. D2 126
Bryansk D3 44
Bsharri B1 26
Bu Craa B1 58
Bua, *river* B2 68
Buada B2 16
Buala A1 16
Buba C2 62
Bubanza B2 61
Bubaque B2 62
Bubiyan, *island* C2 24
Bucaramanga B3 78
Buchanan A3 63
Buchanan H9 104
Buchans C5 98
Bucharest, *capital* D3 43
Buck Creek C4 94
Buck Lake C5 94
Buckingham A6 103
Budapest, *capital* B2 43
Buea A3 65
Buenaventura A4 78
Buendía, *reservoir* E2 37
Buene, *river* A2 49
Buenos Aires, *capital* D3 74
Buenos Aires, *lake* A6 74
Buffalo Narrows B5 104
Buffalo, *lake* D5 94
Buffalo, *lake* E4 99
Buffalo, N.Y. F1 126
Bug, *river* E2, F3 41
Bugeac, *region* B3 50
Bugojno B1 48
Buhayrat al-Asad, *lake* B1 27
Buj-Buj Inset II 20
Bujumbura, *capital* B2 61
Buka, *island* B2 15
Bukavu C2 67
Bukhara B3 23
Bukit Pagon, *mt.* C3 13
Bukit Panjang B1 13
Bukit Timah B1 13
Bükk, *mts.* C1 43
Bukoba B1 68
Bula B1 62
Bulawayo B2 69
Bulembu B1 71
Bulgan C2 11
Bulgaria 50
Bulle B2 35
Bulyea F10 104
Bumba B1 67
Bunbury, W.A. A3 14
Bundaberg, Qld. E2 14
Bungo, *channel* B3 8
Bunia C1 67
Bunsuru, *river* D1 65
Buon Me Thuot B4 11
Buqayq C1 24
Buraydah B1 24
Burco B2 60
Burdekin, *river* D1 14
Burdett E6 94
Burdur, *lake* B3 27
Burdwan E4 20
Büren B3 40
Burgas F3 50
Burgeo C5 98
Burgos E1 37
Burhanpur C4 20
Burica, *point* A2 87
Burin D5 98
Burin, *peninsula* D5 98
Buriram C3 12
Burk's Falls F2 102
Burke, *channel* J5 95
Burkina Faso 64
Burlington F4 102
Burlington, Vt. F1 126
Burma (Myanmar) 12
Burnley C3 30
Burns Lake K4 95
Burntwood, *lake* A1 96
Burntwood, *river* B1, C1, D2 96
Bursa B2 27
Burtnieku, *lake* C2 46
Buru, *island* D2 13
Burundi 61
Bururi B2 61
Burutu C5 65
Burwash Landing B5 105
Bury C3 30
Bury St. Edmunds D3 30
Buryatiya, *republic* D7 44
Bushmanland, *plain* A2 71
Buta C1 67
Butare B2 61
Bute, *island* B2 30
Butha-Buthe B1 71
Butte, Mont. B1 126
Buttonville K5 102
Butuan C4 12
Butwal B2 19
Buurgplaatz, *mt.* B1 33
Buxton C3 30
Buyant-Uhaa D3 11
Buyo, *lake* C3 63
Büyük Menderes, *lake* A3 27
Buzău D3 43
Búzi, *river* B4 68
Büzmeyin C2 22
Byam Martin, *channel* G1 99
Byam Martin, *island* H1 99
Byarezina, *river* D3 47
Byblos, *ruins* A1 26
Bydgoszcz C2 41
Byelaruskaya Hrada, *range* C3 47
Bylot, *island* N2 99
Bytom D3 41
Byumba C1 61

C

Ca Mau A5 11
Ca, *river* A2 11
Caacupé D4 75
Caaguazú E4 75
Caazapá D5 75
Cabanatuan B3 12
Cabano H4 103
Cabimas B1 79
Cabinda B1 70
Cabo Rojo A2 90
Cabora Bassa, *dam* B2 68
Cabora Bassa, *lake* A2 68
Caborca B1 84
Cabrera C1 89
Cabrera, *island* H3 37
Cabri B10 104
Čačak B3 49
Cacao B1 80
Cáceres C3 81
Cáceres C3 37
Cache Creek M6 95
Cacheu A1 62
Cacheu, *river* B1 62
Cachimbo C2 81
Cacine B2 62
Cacouna G4 103
Cadiz B4 12
Cádiz C4 37
Cádiz, *gulf* C4 37
Cadomin B4 94
Cadotte Lake B3 94
Caen B2 34
Caerleon C3 30
Caernarfon B3 30
Cagayan de Oro C4 12
Cagayan Sulu, *island* A5 12
Cagayan, *islands* B4 12
Cagayan, *river* B2 12
Cagliari B3 38
Cagliari, *gulf* B3 38
Caguas C2 90
Caha, *mts.* B3 31
Cahors C4 34
Cahul B3 50
Caicos, *islands* D4 89
Caidasm da Rainha A3 36
Caille, *island* B1 91
Cairns, Qld. D1 14
Cairo, *capital* B1 56
Cairo, Ill. E2 126
Caja de Muertos, *island* B3 90
Cajamarca B2 77
Calabar E5 65
Calabogie J2 102
Calabozo C2 79
Calabria D3 38
Calafate A7 74
Calais C1 34
Calais B3 94
Calais B3 97
Calama C2 76
Calamian, *islands* A3 12
Calapan B3 12
Călăraşi D3 43
Calatayud F2 37
Calatrava B3 66
Calbayog C3 12
Calcutta E4, Inset II 20
Caledon, *river* A1, C2 71
Caledonia F4 102
Calgary C5 94
Cali A4 78
California B2 126
California, *gulf* B1 84
Callao B3 77
Calling Lake D3 94
Caltanissetta C3 38
Calvi Inset I 34
Calvinia A3 71
Cam Ranh B4 11
Camagüey D2 88
Camagüey, *archipelago* D2 88
Camberley Inset III 30
Cambodia 11
Cambrai C1 34
Cambrian, *mts.* B3 30
Cambridge D3 30
Cambridge Bay G3 99
Cambridge-Narrows D3 97
Cameron, *hills* B1 94
Cameron, *island* H1 99
Cameroon 65
Cameroon, *mt.* A3 65
Camiri B4 77
Camopi B2 80
Camopi, *river* B2 80
Campana, *island* A8 76
Campania C2 38
Campbell River K6 95
Campbellton C1 97
Campbellton A2 100
Campbellton K4 103
Campbelltown, N.S.W. Inset IV 14
Campbelltown, S.A. Inset II 14
Campbeltown B2 30
Campeche, *bay* F4 84
Campeche, *state capital* F4 84
Camper B3 96
Camperville A3 96
Campina Grande E2 81
Campinas D4 81
Campo Grande C4 81
Campobasso C2 38
Campobello, *island* C4 97
Campos D4 81
Campos Elísios Inset I 81
Camrose D4 94
Camsell Portage A1 104
Camú, *river* B1 89
Camuy B2 90
Can Tho A4 11
Caña Gorda, *beach* B3 90
Canaan B1 91
Canada 92
Canaima D2 79
Çanakkale A2 27
Canal Flats P6 95
Canaray, *islands* Inset I 37
Canaries A2 91
Canary, *islands* 55
Canaveral, *cape*, Fla. E3 126
Canberra, A.C.T., *natl. capital* D3 14
Canchungo A1 62
Cancún G3 84
Candelaria C2 90
Candiac J6 103
Candle Lake E7 104
Cando B8 104
Canelles, *river* B3 91
Canelones B3 75
Cangamba D4 70
Cangzhou E2 10
Caniapiscau, *lake* C3 101
Caniapiscau, *river* C3 101
Çankırı C2 27
Cankuzo C2 61
Cannes D5 34
Canning C2 100
Canning, *river* Inset I 14
Canoe Narrows B5 104
Canoe, *lake* B5 104
Canora H9 104
Canossa B1 38
Canouan, *island* B3 91
Canóvanas D2 90
Canso G2 100
Cantabria D1 37
Cantábrica, *mts.* C1 37
Canterbury D3 30
Canterbury B3 97
Canterbury, *bight* B3 15
Canterbury, *plains* B3 15
Canton, *island* B2 17
Canwood D7 104
Canyon Creek C3 94
Cao Bang B1 11
Cap-aux-Os M3 103
Cap-Chat K2 103
Cap-de-la-Madeleine D5 103
Cap-Haïtien C1 89
Cap-Pelé E2 97
Cap-Rouge K6 103
Cap-St-Ignace F4 103
Cape Charles D3 98
Cape Coast B4 64
Cape Girardeau, Mo. E2 126
Cape North G1 100
Cape Race E5 98
Cape Ray B5 98
Cape St. George B5 98
Cape Tormentine E2 97
Cape Town, *legislative capital* A3 71
Cape Verde 58
Cape York, *peninsula* D1 14
Capitán Pablo Lagerenza B1 75
Caplan L3 103
Caprara, *point* B2 38
Capreol D1 102
Capri, *island* C2 38
Capua C2 38
Caquetá, *river* B5 78
Car Nicobar, *island* F7 20
Caracas, *capital* C1 79
Caramoan, *peninsula* B3 12
Carapicuíba Inset II 81
Caraquet E1 97
Carberry B4 96
Carbonara, *cape* B3 38
Carbonear E5 98
Carbonia B3 38
Carcajou B2 94
Carcassonne C5 34
Carcross C5 105
Cardamom, *mts.* A3 11
Cárdenas B1 88
Cardiel, *lake* A6 74
Cardiff B3 30
Cardigan C2 100
Cardigan, *bay* B3 30
Cardigan, *bay* C2 100
Cardinal K3 102
Cardinal, *lake* B3 94
Caribbean, *sea* 82
Carievale A4 96
Carleton K3 103
Carleton Place J2 102
Carlingford C1 31
Carlingford, *lake* C1 31
Carlisle C2 30
Carlisle, *bay* A4 91
Carlow C2 31
Carlsbad, N. Mex. C2 126
Carlyle H11 104
Carmacks B4 105
Carman B4 96
Carmanville D4 98
Carmarthen B3 30
Carmelo A2 75
Carnac B3 34
Carnarvon B3 71
Carnarvon G2 102
Carnarvon, W.A. A2 14
Carnduff J11 104
Carnic Alps, *range* C4 39
Carnsore, *point* C2 31
Carolina D2 90
Caroline, *island* D2 17
Caroline, *islands* B2 15
Caron E10 104
Caroni, *river* D2 79
Carora C1 79
Carpathian, *mts.* 43
Carpentaria, *gulf* C1 14
Carrantuohill, *mt.* B3 31
Carriacou, *island* C1 91
Carrick-on-Shannon B2 31
Carroll A4 96
Carrot River G7 104
Carson City, *capital*, Nev. B2 126
Carstairs C5 94
Cartagena B2 78
Cartagena F4 37
Cartago C3 86
Carthage, *ruin* C1 57
Cartier D1 102
Cartwright B4 96
Cartwright C2 98
Carúpano D1 79
Carvoeiro, *cape* A3 36
Carway D6 94
Casa Grande, Ariz. B2 126
Casablanca Inset 76
Casablanca C1 57
Casamance, *region* B3 62
Casamance, *river* B3 62
Cascade Inset 70
Cascade, *range* A1 126
Cascapedia, *river* K3 103
Cascumpec, *bay* B2 100
Caserta C2 38
Cashel C2 31
Casiquiare, *river* C3 79
Caslan D4 94
Casper, Wyo. C1 126
Caspian, *depression* B2 23
Caspian, *sea* 7
Casselman K2 102
Cassiar H1 95
Cassiar, *mts.* G1 95
Castel Gandolfo C2 38
Castellón de la Plana F3 37
Castelo Branco B3 36
Castile and León D1, E1 37
Castile-la Mancha E3 37
Castle Bruce B2 90
Castle Mountain C5 94
Castlebar B2 31
Castlegar O6 95
Castries, *capital* B1 91
Castro B7 76
Cat, *island* B3 89
Catacamas C2 86
Catalina E5 98
Catalonia G2 37
Catamarca B2 74
Catanduanes, *island* C3 12
Catania C3 38
Cataño C2 90
Catanzaro D3 38
Catió B2 62
Catoche, *cape* G3 84
Catumbela B4 70
Cauca, *river* B3 78
Caucasus, *mts.* A1, A2 45
Caungula D2 70
Caura, *river* D2 79
Causapscal J3 103
Căuşeni B2 50
Cauto, *river* E3 88
Cauvery, *river* C6 20
Cavalla, *river* C3 63
Cavally, *river* C4 63
Cavan C2 31
Cavendish B2 100
Caviana, *island* D1 81
Caxito B2 70
Cayambe, *mt.* C3 79
Cayenne, *capital* B1 80
Cayer B3 96
Cayey C2 90
Cayman, *trench* B2 88
Cayman, *islands* 82
Cayon B1 90
Cazombo E3 70
Ceará E2 81
Cebollatí, *river* C2 75
Cebu B4 12
Cebu, *island* B4 12
Cedar City, Utah B2 126
Cedar Grove E5 90
Cedar Rapids, Iowa D1 126
Cedar, *lake* A2 96
Cedros, *island* A2 84
Ceduna, S.A. C3 14
Ceerigaabo B1 60
Cefalù C3 38
Cegléd B2 43
Ceiba C2 90
Ceiba D2 90
Celada D2 90
Celaya D3 84
Celebes (Sulawesi), *island* D2 13
Celebes, *sea* D1 13
Celje C2 48
Celtic, *sea* B3 31
Central African Republic 66
Central Butte D10 104
Central Makran, *range* B4 21
Central Siberian, *plateau* C7 44
Centre C3 34
Centre C3 100
Centre de Flacq C2 69
Centreville E4 98
Ceram, *island* D2 13
Ceram, *sea* D2 13
Cerf, *island* Inset 70
Cernavodă E3 43
Cerro Castillo B9 76
Cerro de Pasco B3 77
Cervati, *mt.* C2 38
Cesis C2 46
České Budějovice B4 42
Cess, *river* B3 63
Cessford E6 94
Cetinje A3 49
Ceuta D5 37
Cévennes, *mts.* C4 34
Ceyhan, *river* D3 27
Chachapoyas B2 77
Chaco Boreal, *region* B2 75
Chad 59
Chad, *lake* A4, C3 59
Chaeryŏng, *river* A3 9
Chagai, *hills* B4 21
Chaghcharan B2 22
Chagres, *river* C2 87
Chaguanas A2 91
Chaitén B7 76
Chaiyaphum C3 12
Chalco Inset 84
Chaleur, *bay* D1 97
Chalna C6 21
Châlons-sur-Marne D2 34
Chambal, *river* C3 20
Chambéry D4 34
Chambeshi, *river* C2 67
Chambord D3 103
Chamelecon, *river* A2 86
Chamonix-Mont-Blanc D4 34
Champagne Castle, *mt.* C2 71
Champagne-Ardenne D2 34
Champaquí, *mt.* C3 74
Champasak C4 11
Champerico B5 85

	Key	Page
Champlain	D5	103
Chañaral	B3	76
Chança, river	B4	36
Chandannagar	Inset II	20
Chandigarh	C2	20
Chandler	M3	103
Chandpur	D5	21
Chandrapur	C5	20
Chang (Yangtze), river	D2, E2	10
Changane, river	B4	68
Changchun	F1	10
Changde	E3	10
Changhua	B1	9
Changi	B1	13
Changjin	B2	9
Changjin, river	B2	9
Changsha	E3	10
Changuinola	A2	87
Changyŏn	A3	9
Changzhi	E2	10
Changzhou	F2	10
Channel Islands, Calif.	A2	126
Chantilly	C2	34
Chao Phraya, river	B3	12
Chapada dos Parecis, range	C3	81
Chaparé, river	A3	77
Chapleau	D3	101
Chaplin	D10	104
Chardzhou	D2	22
Charente, river	B4	34
Chari, river	A5	59
Charikar	B1	22
Charity	B2	80
Charleroi	C2	33
Charles	A1	96
Charlesbourg	E5, Inset	103
Charleston, capital, W. Va.	E2	126
Charleston, S.C.	F2	126
Charlestown	C3	90
Charlestown	A3	91
Charleville Mézières	D2	34
Charleville, Qld.	D2	14
Charlie Lake	M3	95
Charlo	C1	97
Charlotte, N.C.	E2	126
Charlottetown	C3	98
Charlottetown	B2	100
Charlotteville	B1	91
Charny	E5, K6	103
Charters Towers, Qld.	D2	14
Chartres	C2	34
Chase	N6	95
Châteauguay	C6, H6	103
Châteauroux	C3	34
Châtellerault	C3	34
Chatfield	C4	96
Chatham	Inset III	30
Chatham	C5	102
Chatham, sound	G4	95
Chatkal, river	B2	23
Chatsworth	E3	102
Chattanooga, Tenn.	E2	126
Chau Doc	A4	11
Chaumont	D2	34
Chaves	B2	36
Cheb	A2	42
Cheboksary	D4	44
Chechŏn	C4	9
Chechnya, republic	E4	44
Cheduba, island	B2	12
Chegutu	B2	69
Cheju	Inset	9
Cheju, island	Inset	9
Cheju, strait	Inset	9
Chek Keng	Inset	10
Chelan	G8	104
Cheleken	A2	22
Chelif, river	B1	57
Chelles	Inset II	34
Chełm	F3	41
Chelmsford	D3, Inset III	30
Cheltenham	C3	30
Chelyabinsk	D5	44
Chelyuskin, cape	B7	44
Chembur	Inset I	20
Chemin Grenier	B3	69
Chemnitz	C3	40
Chenab, river	D3	21
Chenachane	Inset I	20
Chénéville	A6	103
Chengde	E1	10
Chengdu	D2	10
Chennai (Madras)	D6	20
Cherbourg	B2	34
Cherepovets	D3	44
Cherkassy	C2	47
Chernigov	C1	47
Chernivtsi	B2	47
Cherrapunji	F3	20
Cherryville	N6	95
Cherskiy	C10	44
Cherskiy, range	C8	44
Chesapeake, bay	F2	126
Chesley	D3	102
Chester	C3	30
Chester	C3	100
Chesterfield	C3	30
Chesterfield Inlet	K4	99
Chesterfield, islands	A2	18
Cheticamp	G1	100
Chetumal, state capital	G4	84
Chetwynd	M3	95
Cheviot, hills	C2	30
Chevreuse	Inset II	34
Cheyenne, capital, Wyo.	C1	126
Chhukha	C2	19
Chi, river	C2	12
Chiai	B2	9
Chiang Mai	B2	12
Chiang Rai	B2	12
Chiapa	C1	76
Chiapas	F4	84
Chiatura	B3	45
Chiba	D3	8
Chibougamau	B2	103
Chibougamau, lake	B2	103
Chicago, Ill.	E1	126
Chicapa, river	D3	70
Chichén Itzá, ruins	G3	84
Chichester	C4	30
Chichi, island	Inset III	8
Chiclayo	B2	77
Chico	B6	74
Chiconcuac	Inset	84
Chicoutimi	E3	103
Chief, river	L2	95
Chiem, lake	C5	40
Chiesanuova	B2	39
Chieti	C2	38
Chifeng	E1	10
Chignecto, bay	C2	100
Chihuahua, state capital	C2	84
Chilaw	A5	19
Chile		76
Chile Chico	B8	76
Chililabombwe	B2	67
Chilko, lake	K5	95
Chillán	B6	76
Chilliwack	M6	95
Chiloé, island	B7	76
Chilung	C5	9
Chilwa, lake	B2, C3	68
Chimalhuacán	Inset	84
Chimay	C2	33
Chimborazo, mt.	B3	79
Chimbote	B2	77
Chimoio	B2	68
Chin, hills	B2	12
China		10
Chinajá	C4	85
Chinandega	A2	87
Chincha Alta	B3	77
Chinchaga, river	A3	94
Chinde	C3	68
Chindwin, river	B1	12
Chingola	B2	67
Chingoni	C2	68
Chinhae	C5	9
Chinhoyi	B1	69
Chiniot	D3	21
Chinju	C5	9
Chinko, river	B2	66
Chioggia	C1	38
Chip, lake	C4	94
Chipata	C2	67
Chipewyan Lake	D3	94
Chipman	C2	97
Chira, river	A5	77
Chirchiq, river	C2	23
Chire, river	B3	68
Chiredzi	B2	69
Chiriquí, gulf	A3	87
Chiriquí, lagoon	A3	87
Chirner	Inset I	20
Chirripó, mt.	C3	86
Chirripó, river	C2	86
Chisasibi	A3	101
Chisholm	C4	94
Chişinău, capital	B2	50
Chita	D7	44
Chitipa	B1	68
Chitose	Inset I	8
Chitral	D2	21
Chitré	B3	87
Chittagong	E6	21
Chitungwiza	B1	69
Chixoy, river	C4	85
Choa Chu Kang	A1	13
Choiceland	F7	104
Choiseul	A3	91
Choiseul, island	A1	16
Choisy-le Roi	Inset II	34
Chojnice	C2	41
Choke, mts.	B2	60
Cholet	B3	34
Cholpon-Ata	E1	23
Cholula	E4	84
Choluteca	B3	86
Choma	B3	67
Chomo Lhari, mt.	A1	19
Chon Buri	B3	12
Chone	A3	79
Chŏngch'ŏn, river	A3	9
Chŏngjin	C2	9
Chŏngju	B4	9
Chŏngju	A3	9
Chongqing	D3	10
Chonju	B5	9
Chonos, archipelago	B7	76
Chontaleña, mts.	B2	87
Chornobyl'	C1	47
Chorzów	D3	41
Choshui, river	B2	9
Choybalsan	D2	11
Christchurch	B3	15
Christina, river	E3	94
Christmas Island	G2	100
Chu, river	D1	23
Chubut, river	A5	74
Chucunaque, river	D2	87
Chugoku, mts.	B3	8
Chukchi, peninsula	C11	44
Chukchi, range	C10	44
Chukchi, sea	B11	44
Chukotka, autonomous okrug	C10	44
Chumphon	B4	12
Chunan	B1	9
Chung Hau	Inset	10
Chungho	B1	9
Ch'ungju	B4	9
Chungli	B1	9
Chungqing, Ind. Mun.	D3	10
Chungyang, range	C3	9
Chuquicamata	C2	76
Chur	D2	35
Church Point	A3	100
Churchbridge	A4	96
Churchbridge	J10	104
Churchill	D1	96
Churchill Falls	D3	98
Churchill, river	B4	104
Churchill, river	D1	96
Churia, mts.	B2	19
Chute-aux-Outardes	H2	103
Chuuk, islands	C2	15
Chuvashiya, republic	D4	44
Ciales	C2	90
Cibao, valley	A1	89
Cicia, island	C2	17
Cidra	C2	90
Ciechanów	E2	41
Ciego de Ávila	D2	88
Cienfuegos	C2	88
Cieza	F3	37
Cijara, reservoir	D3	37
Cikobia, island	C1	17
Cilacap	B2	13
Cilician Gates, pass	C3	27
Cimone, mt.	B1	38
Cincinnati, Ohio	E2	126
Cirebon	B2	13
Citlaltépetl, mt.	E4	84
City View	G6	102
Ciudad Acuña	D2	84
Ciudad Bolívar	D2	79
Ciudad Camargo	C2	84
Ciudad Constitución	B3	84
Ciudad del Carmen	F4	84
Ciudad del Este	E4	75
Ciudad Guayana	D2	79
Ciudad Juárez	C1	84
Ciudad Mante	E3	84
Ciudad Obregón	C2	84
Ciudad Real	E3	37
Ciudad Rodrigo	C2	37
Ciudad Valles	E3	84
Ciudad Victoria, state capital	E3	84
Ciudadela	H2	37
Civitavecchia	B2	38
Clair	A1	97
Claire, lake	D2	94
Clandeboye	C4	96
Clara	C2	31
Clarenville	D5	98
Clark's Harbour	B4	100
Clarksville, Tenn.	E2	126
Clear Creek	E5	102
Clear, cape	B3	31
Clearwater	M5	95
Clearwater, river	E3	94
Clementsport	B3	100
Clermont	F4	103
Clermont-Ferrand	C4	34
Clervaux	B1	33
Clerve, river	B1	33
Cleveland, Ohio	E1	126
Clifden	A2	31
Clifford	E4	102
Climax	B11	104
Clinton	M5	95
Clinton	D4	102
Clinton Colden, lake	G4	99
Cloncurry, Qld.	D2	14
Clonmel	C2	31
Cloridorme	M2	103
Clovis, N. Mex.	C2	126
Cloyne	H3	102
Cluff Lake Mine	A2	104
Cluj-Napoca	B3	43
Cluny	D3	34
Cluny	D6	94
Clutha, river	A4	15
Clyde River	B4	100
Clyde River	P2	99
Clyde, estuary	B2	30
Clyde, river	B2	30
Clydebank	B2	30
Coacalco	Inset	84
Coahuila	D2	84
Coal River	J1	95
Coal, river	D5	105
Coaldale	D6	94
Coalspur	B4	94
Coamo	C2	90
Coast, mts.	F2, J5	95
Coast, ranges	A1, A2	126
Coaticook	E6	103
Coats Land, region	B13	107
Coats, island	M4	99
Coatzacoalcos	F4	84
Cobán	C4	85
Cobden	J2	102
Cóbh	B3	31
Cobham, river	D2	96
Cobija	A2	77
Cobourg	G4	102
Coburg	B3	40
Coburg, island	N1	99
Cocagne	E2	97
Cochabamba	A3	77
Cochin (Kochi)	C7	20
Cochrane	D3	101
Cochrane	B8	76
Cochrane, lake	B8	76
Cochrane, river	H2	104
Cockburn Harbour	D4	89
Cockburn, island	B2	102
Coclé del Norte	B2	87
Coco	C2	90
Coco, islands	B3	12
Coco, river	A2, C1	87
Cocos, islands		5
Cocotitlán	Inset	84
Cod, cape, Mass.	G1	126
Codri, region	A3	50
Codrington	E2	90
Codrington, mt.	C17	107
Cody, Wyo.	C1	126
Coe Hill	H3	102
Coeroeni, river	A3	80
Coeur d'Alene, Idaho	B1	126
Cogalnic, river	B2	50
Cognac	B4	34
Coiba, island	B3	87
Coihaique	B8	76
Coimbatore	C6	20
Coimbra	A2	36
Cojedes, river	C2	79
Colca, river	C4	77
Colchester	D3	30
Cold Lake	E4	94
Coleraine	A2	30
Coles Island	D3	97
Coleville	A9	104
Colihaut	A2	90
Colima, state capital	D4	84
Colina	Inset	76
Coll, island	A2	30
Collaguasi	C2	76
Collingwood	B3	15
Collingwood	E3	102
Colmar	D2	34
Colombia		78
Colombier	H3	103
Colombo, capital	A5	19
Colón	C2	87
Colón	C2	88
Colonia	A2	15
Colonia	B3	75
Colonia Nueva Guinea	B3	87
Colonsay	E9	104
Colonsay, island	A2	30
Colorado	C2	86
Colorado	C2	126
Colorado Springs, Colo.	C2	126
Colorado, plateau	B2	126
Colorado, river	B4	74
Colorado, river	B4	126
Columbia, capital, S.C.	E2	126
Columbia, mts.	M4	95
Columbia, plateau	B1	126
Columbia, river	B1	126
Columbus, capital, Ohio	E2	126
Columbus, Ga.	E2	126
Coma Pedrosa, mt.	A1	36
Comayagua	B2	86
Comayagua, mts.	B2	86
Combermere	H2	102
Comendador	A2	89
Comerío	C2	90
Comilla	E5	21
Comino, island	B1	36
Cominotto, island	B1	36
Comitán	F4	84
Committee, bay	L3	99
Como	B1	38
Como, lake	B1	38
Comodoro Rivadavia	B6	74
Comorin, cape	C7	20
Comoros		67
Comox	K6	95
Compiègne	C2	34
Compton	E6	103
Comrat	B2	50
Con Son, islands	B5	11
Conakry, capital	B3	62
Concepción	B6	76
Concepción	D3	75
Concepción del Oro	D3	84
Conchalí	Inset	76
Conche	D4	98
Conchos, river	C2	84
Concord, capital, N.H.	F1	126
Concordia	D3	74
Condor	C5	94
Congo, Dem Rep of		67
Congo, Rep of		66
Congo, basin	D3	66
Congo, river	D4	66
Congo, river	B1	67
Conn, lake	B1	31
Connecticut	F1	126
Connemara, region	B2	31
Consecon	H4	102
Constance	B5	40
Constance (Bodensee), lake	D1	35
Constanţa	E3	43
Constantine	B1	57
Constitución	B6	76
Consul	A11	104
Contrecoeur	C6	103
Contwoyto, lake	G3	99
Conwy	B3	30
Coober Pedy, S.A.	C2	14
Cook, mts.	B3	15
Cook, strait	B3	15
Cookshire	E6	103
Cookstown	F3	102
Coos Bay, Oreg.	A1	126
Copán, ruins	A2	86
Copenhagen, capital	D3	32
Copiapó	B3	76
Copiapó, river	B3	76
Coppename, river	A2	80
Coppermine, river	F3	99
Coquí	C3	90
Coquimbo	B3	76
Coral, sea	E1	14
Corantijn, river	A2	80
Corazón	A2	87
Corbeil-Essonnes	Inset II	34
Corcovado, gulf	B7	76
Corcovado, mt.	Inset I	81
Córdoba	C3	74
Córdoba	D4	37
Córdoba, range	B3	74
Corinth	B3	51
Corinth, gulf	B2	51
Corinth, isthmus	B3	51
Corinto	A2	87
Corisco, bay	A6	66
Corisco, island	B4	66
Cork	B3	31
Cormack	C4	98
Cormoran, reef	B2	17
Cormorant	A2	96
Cormorant, lake	A2	96
Cornélia de Llogregat	G2	37
Corner Brook	C5	98
Corno, mt.	C2	38
Cornwall	L2	102
Cornwall	L2	102
Cornwall, island	K1	99
Cornwallis, island	J1	99
Coro	C1	79
Coromandel, peninsula	C2	15
Coronach	E11	104
Coronado, bay	B3	86
Coronation, gulf	F3	99
Coronel Oviedo	D4	75
Coropuna, mt.	C4	77
Corozal	B1	85
Corozal	C2	90
Corpus Christi, Tex.	D3	126
Corregidor, island	B3	12
Corrib, lake	B2	31
Corrientes	D2	74
Corse	Inset I	34
Corsica, island	Inset I	34
Cortina d'Ampezzo	C1	38
Cortona	B2	38
Çoruh, river	E2	27
Çorum	C2	27
Corumbá	C3	81
Corumbau, point	E3	81
Corvallis, Oreg.	A1	126
Cosenza	D3	38
Coslada	Inset II	37
Cosmoledo, island group	A2	70
Costa Rica		86
Cotabato	C5	12
Côte d'Ivoire		63
Cotentin, peninsula	B2	34
Cotia	Inset II	81
Coto Laurel	B2	90
Cotonou	B4	64
Cotopaxi, mt.	B3	79
Cotswold, hills	C3	30
Cottbus	C3	40
Cotton Ground	C2	90
Cotuí	B2	89
Coubert	Inset II	34
Couffo, river	B4	64
Courantyne, river	B3	80
Courland, lagoon	A2	46
Courtenay	K6	95
Courval	D10	104
Coutts	E6	94
Couva	A2	91
Coventry	C3	30
Covilhã	B2	36
Cow Head	C4	98
Cowan	A3	96
Cowansville	D6	103
Cowes	C4	30
Cox's Bazar	E7	21
Cox's Cove	B4	98
Coyah	B3	62
Coyoacán	Inset	84
Cozumel, island	G3	84
Cracow	C3	71
Cradock	D5	94
Craigmyle	D5	94
Craik	E9	104
Craiova	B3	43
Cranberry Portage	A2	96
Cranbrook	P6	95
Crane River	B2	96
Crane Valley	E11	104
Crapaud	B2	100
Cravo Norte	C3	78
Crawford Bay	O6	95
Crawley	Inset III	30
Crean, lake	D6	104
Cree Lake	D3	104
Cree, river	E2	104
Cremona	B1	38
Cremona	C5	94
Cres, island	B3	48
Cressday	E6	94
Creston	O6	95
Crete, island	C4	51
Crete, sea	C4	51
Créteil	Inset II	34
Crewe	C3	30
Crimean, mts.	C4	47
Crimean, peninsula	C3	47
Cristal, mts.	A1	66
Cristóbal	C2	87
Cristóbal Colón, peak	B2	78
Crna Gora, mts.	B3	49
Crna, river	B2	48
Croatia		48
Crocker, range	D2	13
Cromer	A4	96
Crooked River	G8	104
Crooked, island	C4	89
Crooked, river	L4	95
Cross Lake	C2	96
Cross, river	E4	65
Crotone	D3	38
Cruz, cape	D3	88
Cruzeiro do Sul	A2	81
Crystal City	B4	96
Cu Lao Thu, island	B4	11
Cuajimalpa	Inset	84
Cuamba	D4	70
Cuando, river	D4	70
Cuango, river	D2	70
Cuanza, river	C3	70
Cuareim, river	B1	75
Cuauhtémoc	C2	84
Cuautitlán	Inset	84
Cuautitlán Izcalli	Inset	84
Cuba		88
Cubal, river	B4	70
Cubango, river	D5	70
Cubatão	Inset II	81
Cúcuta	B3	78
Cuddalore	C6	20
Cudworth	E8	104
Cuenca	B4	79
Cuenca	E2	37
Cuernavaca, state capital	E4	84
Cuiabá	C3	81
Cuito Cuanavale	D5	70
Cuito, river	D4	70
Cukorova, region	C3	27
Culebra, island	E2	90
Culebrinas, river	A2	90
Culiacán, state capital	C3	84
Cumaná	D1	79
Cumberland	K6	95
Cumberland House	H7	104
Cumberland, lake	H6	104
Cumberland, peninsula	P3	99
Cumberland, sound	P3	99
Cumbrian, mts.	B2	30
Cunene, river	B5, C4	70
Cuneo	A1	38
Cupar	B2	30
Cupar	F10	104
Curaçao, island		82
Curaray, river	C3	79
Curepipe	C3	69
Curicó	B4	76
Curitiba	D4	81
Curral Velho	D3	58
Curuzú Cuatiá	D2	74
Cut Knife	A8	104
Cuttack	E4	20
Cuxhaven	B2	40
Cuyo, islands	B4	12
Cuyuni, river	A2	80
Cuzco	C3	77
Cyangugu	A2	61
Cyclades, islands	C3	51
Cypress River	B4	96
Cyprus		27
Czar	E5	94
Czech Republic		42
Częstochowa	D3	41

D

	Key	Page
Da Lat	B4	11
Da Nang	B3	11
Dabakala	D2	63
Dabola	C2	62
Dachang	D3	10
Dachau	B4	40
Dacotah	C4	96
Dades, river	C2	57
Dadu	C4	21
Dafoe	F9	104
Dagestan, republic	E4	44
Dagupan	B2	12
Dahlak, archipelago	C2	60
Dahna, ad-, desert	B1	24
Dahuk	B1	24
Dajabón	A1	89
Daka, river	B2	64
Dakar, capital	A2	62
Dakhla	A2	58
Đakovica	B3	49
Dalälven, river	C2	53
Dalandzadgad	C3	11
Dalhousie	C1	97
Dalhousie	K3	103
Dali	D2	10
Dalian	F2	10
Dallas	C3	96
Dallas, Tex.	D2	126
Dallol Bosso, river	A3	59
Dalmatia, region	B3	48
Daloa	C3	63
Dalvík	B2	52
Daly, river	C1	14
Daman	B4	20
Damanhur	B1	56
Damascus, capital	A3	27
Damaturu	F2	65
Damavand, mt.	C2	22
Damazin, ad-	C3	59
Dame-Marie	A2	89
Damietta	B1	56
Damietta, river	B1	56
Dammam, ad-	C1	24
Dammartin-en-Goële	Inset II	34
Dampier, W.A.	A2	14
Damur, ad-	A2	26
Danakil, desert	C2	60
Danané	B3	63
Dand	A4	96
Dande, river	B2	70
Dandeldhura	A2	19
Dandong	F1	10
Dangara	A1	23
Dangme, river	C2	19
Dangrek, mts.	C3	12
Dangriga	B2	85
Daniel's Harbour	C4	98
Danjiangkou	E2	10
Danlí	B2	86
Danube, river		29
Danville	D6	103
Danville, Va.	F2	126
Dao Phu Quoc, island	A4	11
Dapaong	B1	64
Dapp	D4	94
Daqing	F1	10
Dar es-Salaam, capital	C2	68
Dara	A3	27
Dara	B2	62
Đaravica, mt.	B3	49
Darbhanga	E3	20
Darhan	C2	11
Darién, mts.	D2	87
Dariense, mts.	B2	87
Darjiling	E3	20
Darling, range	A3	14
Darling, river	D3	14
Darlington	C2	30
Darłowo	C1	41
Darmstadt	B4	40
Darnah	D1	56
Darnley	B2	100
Dartmoor, plateau	B4	30
Dartmouth	D3	100
Daru	A2	15
Darwin, N.T., capital	C1	14
Dashhowuz	C2	22
Dasht-e Kavir, desert	D3	22
Dasht-e Lut, desert	D2	22
Datong	E1	10
Daua, river	F1	61
Daugavpils	B3	46
Daule, river	B3	79
Dauphin	B1	96
Dauphin North	A3	96
Dauphin River	B3	96
Dauphin, lake	B3	96
Davao	C5	12
Davao, gulf	C5	12

	Key	Page
Davenport, Iowa	D1	126
David	A2	87
Davidson	D9	104
Davis Inlet	E3	98
Davis, *strait*	M2	92
Davos	D2	35
Dawa, *river*	C3	60
Dawhat as-Salwa, *bay*	B3	25
Dawkah	B2	25
Dawna, *range*	B2	12
Dawson	B3	105
Dawson Creek	M3	95
Dawson, *bay*	A2	96
Daymán, *river*	B1	75
Dayr az-Zawr	B2	27
Dayton, Ohio	E2	126
Daytona Beach, Fla.	E3	126
De Aar	B3	71
De Quincy Village	Inset	70
Dead Sea, *lake*	A2	26
Dead, *sea*	B2	26
Dean, *channel*	J5	95
Dean, *river*	K5	95
Dease Lake	G2	95
Death, *valley*, Calif.	B2	126
Deauville	C2	34
Debar	A2	48
Debden	D7	104
Debed, *river*	B2	45
DeBolt	A3	94
Debre Birhan	C2	60
Debre Markos	B2	60
Debrecen	C2	43
Decatur, Ill.	E2	126
Deccan, *plateau*	C5	20
Děčín	B2	42
Dédougou	C2	64
Dedza	B2	68
Dee, *river*	B3, C1	30
Deep River	H1	102
Deep, *inlet*	B1	98
Deepdale	A3	96
Deer Lake	C4	98
Deerfield	A4	100
Degeh Bur	D2	60
Dégelis	H4	103
Dehiwala-Mt. Lavinia	A5	19
Dehra Dun	C2	20
Dej	B2	43
Del Rio, Tex.	C3	126
Delacour	D5	94
Delap Cove	B3	100
Delaronde, *lake*	C6	104
Delaware	F2	126
Delburne	D5	94
Deleau	A4	96
Delft	B2	32
Delft, *island*	A2	19
Delfzijl	D1	32
Delgado	A2	86
Delhi	C3	20
Delhi	E5	102
Delicias	C2	84
Déline	D3	99
Delisle	C9	104
Deloraine	A4	96
Delos, *island*	C3	51
Delson	J6	103
Delta Beach	B4	96
Demerara, *river*	B3	80
Den Helder	B2	32
Denakil, *desert*	C1	60
Denare Beach	H6	104
Denbigh	H2	102
Dencross	C4	96
Dender, *river*	B2	33
Denigomodu	A2	16
Denmark		32
Denmark, *strait*	D2	106
Dennery	B2	91
Denpasar	C2	13
D'Entrecasteaux, *islands*	B2	15
D'Entrecasteaux, *reefs*	C1	18
Denver, *capital*, Colo.	C2	126
Denzil	A8	104
Dera Ghazi Khan	D3	21
Dera Ismail Khan	D3	21
Derby	C3	30
Derg, *lake*	B2	31
Derrick	B3	91
Derventa	B1	48
Derwent	E4	94
Des Moines, *capital*, Iowa	D1	126
Desaguadero, *river*	B2	74
Desaguadero, *river*	A3	77
Desberats	B1	102
Deschaillons	D5	103
Deschambault Lake	G6	104
Dese	C2	60
Deseado, *river*	B6	74
Deseronto	H3	102
Desna, *river*	C1	47
Desolación, *island*	B9	76
Desruisseau	B3	91
Dessau	C3	40
Destruction Bay	B5	105
Detmold	B3	40
Detroit, Mich.	E1	126
Deux Rivieres	G1	102
Deux-Montagnes	H5	103
Deva	B3	43
Deventer	D2	32
Devil's, *island*	B1	80
Devoll, *river*	B3	49
Devon, *island*	L1	99
Devonport, Tas.	D4	14
Dewberry	E4	94
Dezful	B3	22
Dháfni	Inset	51
Dhahran	C1	24
Dhaka, *capital*	D5	21
Dhamar	A2	25
Dhangarhi	A2	19
Dhankuta	D2	19
Dharan	D3	19
Dhaulagiri, *mt.*	B2	19
Dhofar, *region*	B3	25
Dhulagarh	Inset II	20
Dhuusamareeb	B2	60
Diadema	Inset II	81
Dialakoto	C3	62
Diamond, *island*	B1	91
Dibrugarh	F3	20
Diefenbaker, *lake*	C10	104
Diekirch	B2	33
Dien Bien Phu	A2	11
Dieppe	C2	34
Dieppe	E2	97
Dieppe Bay Town	B1	90
Diffa	C3	59
Differdange	A2	33
Digby	B3	100
Digne	D4	34
Digul, *river*	E2	13
Dijon	D3	34
Dikhil	B2	60
Dikson	B6	44
Dili	D2	13
Dilijan	B2	45
Dillon	B5	104
Dilolo	B3	67
Dimbokro	D3	63
Dimitrovgrad	D3	50
Dimlang, *mt.*	F3	65
Dimona	B2	26
Dinagat, *island*	C4	12
Dinajpur	B3	21
Dinant	C2	33
Dinara, *mt.*	A2, C3	48
Dinaric Alps, *mts.*	A1, B3	48
Dinder, *river*	B1	60
Dingle	A2	31
Dingle, *bay*	A2	31
Dingli	B2	36
Dinsmore	C9	104
Diourbel	A2	62
Dipolog	B4	12
Dire Dawa	D2	60
Diriamba	A3	87
Dispur	F3	20
Diu	B4	20
Diuata, *mts.*	C4	12
Divo	D4	63
Divriği	D2	27
Diwaniyah, ad-	C2	24
Dixon Entrance, *channel*	F4	95
Dixonville	B3	94
Diyala, *river*	C2	24
Diyarbakır	E3	27
Dja, *river*	B3	65
Djado	C1	59
Djambala	C5	66
Djanet	B2	57
Djelfa	B1	57
Djenné	C3	58
Djerba, *island*	C3	57
Djibouti		60
Djibouti, *capital*	C2	60
Djouah, *river*	B1	66
Djouf, el-, *desert*	B1, C3	58
Djougou	A3	64
Dnepr-Bug, *canal*	B3	47
Dneprodzerzhinsk	C2	47
Dnieper, *river*	C1, E3	47
Dniester, *river*	B2	47
Dnipropetrovsk	D2	47
Doaktown	C2	97
Doba	B5	59
Doboj	B1	48
Dobrich	F2	50
Dobruja, *region*	E3	43
Doctor Pedro P. Peña	A3	75
Dodecanese, *islands*	C3	51
Dodge City, Kans.	C2	126
Dodoma, *capital*	C2	68
Dodsland	B9	104
Doetinchem	D3	32
Dogo, *island*	B2	8
Dogondoutchi	A3	59
Doha, *capital*	D3	25
Doiran, *lake*	C2	48
Dolbeau	D3	103
Dôle	D3	34
Dolomites, *range*	B1	38
Domagnano	B1	39
Domeyko, *mts.*	C3	76
Dominica		90
Dominica, *passage*	A1	90
Dominican Republic		89
Dominion City	C4	96
Domont	Inset II	34
Domremy	E8	104
Domuyo, *volcano*	A4	74
Don Benito	D3	37
Doña Juana, *mt.*	C2	90
Donald Station	O5	95
Doncaster	C3	30
Dondo	B3	70
Donegal	B1	31
Donegal, *bay*	B1	31
Donets, *basin*	D2	47
Donetsk	D2	47
Dong Hoi	B3	11
Dong Nai, *river*	B4	11
Dongting, *lake*	E3	10
Dongwe, *river*	A2	67
Donnacona	E5	103
Dor, *lake*	C6	104
Dorado	C2	90
Dorchester	C4	30
Dordogne, *river*	C4	34
Dordrecht	B3	32
Dore Lake	C6	104
Dörgön, *lake*	B2	11
Dori	D1	64
Dorintosh	B6	104
Dorking	Inset III	30
Dornoch	B1	30
Dorohoi	D2	43
Dorothy	D5	94
Dorra	B1	60
Dortmund	A3	40
Dorval	H6	103
Dos Hermanas	D4	37
Dosquet	E5	103
Dosso	A3	59
Dothan, Ala.	E2	126
Douai	C1	34
Douala	A3	65
Doubs, *river*	A1	35
Douglas	B2	30
Douglas, *channel*	H4	95
Douglastown	M3	103
Dourados	C4	81
Douro, *river*	B2	36
Dover	D3	30
Dover, *capital*, Del.	F2	126
Dover, *strait*	D4	30
Dovrefjell, *mts.*	B3	52
Dozen, *island*	B2	8
Drâa, *river*	A1, B2, C2	57
Draguignan	D5	34
Drake	E9	104
Drakensberg, *mts.*	B3, C3	71
Drammen	C4	52
Drava, *river*	A2	43
Drayton Valley	C4	94
Dresden	C3	40
Dresden	C5	102
Dreux	C2	34
Drin, *river*	A1	49
Drina, *river*	A2	49
Drobeta-Turnu Severin	B3	43
Drogheda	C2	31
Drumheller	D5	94
Drummond	B2	97
Drummondville	D6	103
Druskininkai	B2	46
Dryden	B3	101
Dschang	B2	65
Duars, *plain*	A3	19
Duarte, *mt.*	B1	89
Dubai	C2	25
Dubăsari	B2	50
Dubawnt, *lake*	H4	99
Dubawnt, *river*	H4	99
Dubbo, N.S.W.	D3	14
Dube, *river*	C3	63
Dublin, *capital*	C2	31
Dubrovnik	D4	48
Dubuque, Iowa	D1	126
Dubysa, *river*	B2	46
Duchess	E6	94
Duck Bay	A3	96
Duck Lake	D8	104
Dudelange	B2	33
Dudinka	C6	44
Dudley	C3	30
Duero, *river*	D2	37
Dufourspitze, *mt.*	B3	35
Dufrost	C4	96
Dugald	C4	96
Duisburg	A3	40
Dukhan	B3	25
Dulce, *gulf*	C4	86
Duluth, Minn.	D1	126
Dum-Dum	Inset II	20
Duma	A1	26
Dumaguete	B4	12
Dumbås	B3	52
Dumfries	B2	30
Dumjor	Inset II	20
Dún Laoghaire	C2	31
Dunaújváros	B2	43
Duncan	L7	95
Duncansby, *cape*	B1	30
Dund-Us	B2	11
Dundalk	C2	31
Dundee	C2	30
Dundurn	D9	104
Dunedin	B4	15
Dunfermline	B2	30
Dungarvan	C2	31
Dunkirk (Dunkerque)	C1	34
Dunkwa	B4	64
Dunlop	B2	96
Dunnegan	F1	100
Dunnville	F5	102
Dunqulah	C1	59
Dunsinane, *mt.*	B2	30
Dunstable	Inset III	30
Dunster	N4	95
Duqm	C2	25
Duque de Caxias	Inset I	81
Duque de York, *island*	A9	76
Durance, *river*	D5	34
Durango, Colo.	C2	126
Durango, *state capital*	D3	84
Durazno	B2	75
Durban	D2	71
Durham	C2	30
Durham	E3	102
Durham, N.C.	F2	126
Durmitor, *mts.*	A3	49
Durrës	A2	49
Dushanbe, *capital*	A1	23
Düsseldorf	A3	40
Dutse	E2	65
Dyce	A2	96
Dyje, *river*	B4	42
Dzaoudzi, territorial *capital*	C2	67
Dzavhan, *river*	B2	11
Dzhugdzhur, *range*	D8	44
Dzungaria, *desert basin*	B1	10
Dzyarzhynskaya Hara, *mt.*	C3	47

E

	Key	Page
Eagle, *river*	B2	98
Eagle, *river*	B2	105
Ear Falls	B2	101
East Angus	E6	103
East Antarctica	B1	107
East Braintree	D4	96
East China, *sea*		7
East Coast Bays	B2	15
East Coulee	D5	94
East Frisian, *islands*	A2	40
East Lake Ainslie	F1	100
East London	C3	71
East Point	C2	100
East Siberian, *sea*	B10	44
East York	K5	102
East, *cape*	C2	15
Eastbourne	D4	30
Eastend	B11	104
Eastern Ghats, *mts.*	C6	20
Easterville	B2	96
Eastmain	A3	101
Eastmain, *river*	B3	101
Eastport	E5	98
Eatonia	A9	104
Eau Claire, Wis.	D1	126
Eauripik, *atoll*	B2	15
Ebebiyín	D2	66
Eberswalde	C2	40
Ebolowa	B3	65
Ebon, *island*	B3	16
Ebor	A4	96
Ebro, *river*	F1	37
Ecatepec	Inset	84
Echo Bay	E3	99
Echo Bay	A1	102
Echternach	B2	33
Écija	D4	37
Ecuador		79
Ed	C3	60
Edam	C2	32
Edam	B7	104
Eddies Cove	C3	98
Eddystone	B3	96
Ede	C4	65
Ede	C2	32
Edéa	B3	65
Edgerton	E5	94
Edinburgh	B2	30
Edirne	A2	27
Edmonton, *capital*	D4	94
Edmundston	A1	97
Edmundston	H4	103
Édouard, *lake*	D4	103
Edrans	B4	96
Edson	B4	94
Edward, *lake*	A4	61
Edwards *plateau*, Tex.	C2	126
Eems, *river*	D1	32
Éfaté, *island*	C3	18
Egadi, *islands*	C3	38
Eganville	H2	102
Eger	C2	43
Egersund	B4	52
Eglinton, *island*	E1	99
Egmont, *bay*	A2	100
Egmont, *cape*	B2	15
Egmont, *mt.*	B2	15
Eğridir, *lake*	B2	27
Egypt		56
Eifel, *plateau*	A3	40
Eigg, *island*	A2	30
Eindhoven	C3	32
Einsiedeln	C1	35
Eiseb, *river*	D2	70
Eisenach	B3	40
Eisenhüttenstadt	C2	40
Eisleben	B3	40
Ejmiatsin	B2	45
Ejura	B3	64
Ekibastuz	D1	23
Ekwan, *river*	D2	101
El Cañuelo, *ruins*	C2	90
El Cerro del Aripo, *mt.*	A2	91
El Encanto	B5	78
El Ferrol	B1	37
El Macao	D2	89
El Paso, Tex.	C2	126
El Pital, *mt.*	A1	86
El Porvenir	C2	87
El Progreso	B2	86
El Salvador		86
El Seibo	C2	89
El Serrat	B1	36
El Tabo	Inset	76
El Tigre	D2	79
El Toro, *mt.*	D2	90
El Trebolar	Inset	76
Elat	B3	26
Elâziğ	D2	27
Elba, *island*	B2	38
Elbasan	B2	49
Elbe, *river*	B2, C3	40
Elbert *mt.*, Colo.	C2	126
Elbląg	D1	41
Elbow	D9	104
Elburz, *mts.*	C2	22
Elche	F3	37
Eldon	C2	100
Eldoret	C3	61
Elephant, *island*	C12	107
Elephanta, *island*	Inset I	20
Eleuthera, *island*	B2	89
Elevsís	Inset	51
Elfros	G9	104
Elgin	B1	30
Elgin	A4	96
Elgin	D3	97
Elgon, *mt.*	D3	61
Eli Malk, *island*	B3	17
Elie	C4	96
Elista	E4	44
Elk	F2	41
Elk Point	E4	94
Elkford	P6	95
Elkhorn	A4	96
Elkhovo	E3	50
Elko	P6	95
Elko, Nev.	B1	126
Ellef Ringnes, *island*	H1	99
Ellerts de Haan, *mts.*	A3	80
Ellesmere, *island*	M1	99
Ellice, *river*	G3	99
Ellinikón	Inset	51
Elliot Lake	C1	102
Ellisras	C1	71
Ellsworth Land, *region*	B10	107
Ellsworth, *mts.*	B10	107
Elm Creek	C4	96
Elma	D4	96
Elmina	B4	64
Elmira	C2	100
Elmira	E4	102
Elmsdale	A2	100
Elmvale	F3	102
Elnora	D5	94
Elqui, *river*	B3	76
Elrose	B9	104
Elsa	B4	105
Elva	A4	96
Elvas	B3	36
Ely	D3	30
Ely, Nev.	B2	126
Embarcación	C1	74
Embarras Portage	E2	94
Embi	B2	23
Embu	D4	61
Emden	A2	40
Emerald, *island*	F1	99
Emerald, Qld.	D2	14
Emerson	C4	96
Emi Koussi, *mt.*	B3	59
Emilia-Romagna	B1	38
Emlembe, *mt.*	B1	71
Emmeloord	C2	32
Emmen	D2	32
Emporia, Kans.	D2	126
Ems, *river*	A2	40
Encarnación	E5	75
Enchant	D6	94
Ende	D2	13
Enderbury, *island*	B2	17
Enderby	N6	95
Enderby Land, *region*	C17	107
Endiang	D5	94
Enewetak, *island*	A1	16
Engadine, *valley*	D2	35
Engaño, *cape*	D2	89
Enggano, *island*	B2	13
Englee	C4	98
English, *channel*	C4	30
Englishtown	G1	100
Enguri, *river*	A3	45
Enid, Okla.	D2	126
Enilda	B3	94
Enna	C3	38
Ennadai, *lake*	H4	99
Ennery	C1	89
Ennis	B2	31
Ennistymon	B2	31
Enns, *river*	D3	39
Enriquillo, *lake*	A2	89
Enschede	D2	32
Ensenada	A1	84
Ensenguly	A3	22
Entebbe	C3	61
Enugu	D4	65
Épi, *island*	C3	18
Épinal	D2	34
Episkopi	A2	27
Epsom	Inset III	30
Equatorial, *channel*	A5	19
Equatorial Guinea		66
Er Rif, *range*	C1	57
Erciyes Daği, *mt.*	C2	27
Érd	B2	43
Erdenet	C2	11
Erebus, *mt.*	B5	107
Erenhot	E1	10
Erfurt	B3	40
Erg Chech, *desert*	C1	58
Erg Iguidi, *desert*	D1	58
Erickson	B4	96
Erie, *lake*	E5	102
Erie, Pa.	E1	126
Eriksdale	B4	96
Erimo, *cape*	Inset I	8
Eritrea		60
Erlangen	B4	40
Ermelo	C2	71
Erne, *river*	A2	30
Errigal, *mt.*	B1	31
Erromango, *island*	C4	18
Ersekë	B3	49
Erzen, *river*	A2	49
Erzgebirge, *mts.*	C3	40
Erzincan	D2	27
Erzurum	E2	27
Esbjerg	B3	32
Esch-sur-Alzette	A2	33
Eschen	B1	33
Escondido, *river*	B2	87
Escuintla	C5	85
Escuminac	K3	103
Esfahan	C3	22
Esil	C1	23
Esker	D3	98
Eskifjördhur	C2	52
Eskilstuna	C3	53
Eskimo Point	K4	99
Eskişehir	B2	27
Esla, *river*	D2	37
Esmeraldas	B2	79
Espanola	D1	102
Española, *island*	Inset	79
Esperance, W.A.	B3	14
Espichel, *cape*	A3	36
Espírito Santo	D3	81
Espiritu Santo, *island*	B2	18
Espoo	B2	53
Esquel	A5	74
Essaouira	B2	57
Essen	A3	40
Essequibo, *river*	B3, B5	80
Essex	C5	102
Esslingen	B4	40
Estados, *island*	C7	74
Estaire	E1	102
Estany d'Engolasters, *lake*	B2	36
Este, *point*	E2	90
Estelí	A2	87
Esterhazy	H10	104
Estevan	G11	104
Esther	E5	94
Eston	B9	104
Estonia		46
Estoril	A3	36
Estrela, *mts.*	B2	36
Esztergom	B2	43
Etchemin, *river*	L6	103
Ethelbert	A3	96
Ethiopia		60
Ethiopia, *plateau*	C2	60
Etna, *mt.*	C3	38
Etobicoke	J5	102
Etosha, *pan*	B1	70
Etrechy	Inset II	34
Etrek, *river*	B3	22
Ettelbruck	B2	33
'Eua, *island*	C4	17
Euboea, *island*	B2	51
Eugene, Oreg.	A1	126
Eugenia, *point*	A2	84
Euphrates, *river*	C2	24
Eureka, Calif.	A1	126
Eutsuk, *lake*	J4	95
Evandale	C3	97
Evansville	C2	102
Evansville, Ind.	E2	126
Evenkiya, autonomous okrug	C6	44
Everest, *mt.*	C2	19
Everett, Wash.	A1	126
Evinayong	C3	66
Évora	B3	36
Évreux	C2	34
Évry	Inset II	34
Ewa	B1	16
Ewell	Inset III	30
Ewo	C4	66
Exeter	B4	30
Exeter	D4	102
Exmoor, *plateau*	B3	30
Extremadura	C3	37
Exuma, *sound*	B3	89
Eyasi, *lake*	B1	68
Eyebrow	D10	104
Eyl	B2	60
Eyre, *lake*	C2	14
Eyre, *peninsula*	C3	14
Eysturoy, *island*	Inset	32

F

	Key	Page
Fabyan	E5	94
Fada	C3	59
Fadiffolu, *atoll*	A2	19
Faenza	B1	38
Faeroe, *islands*	Inset	32
Fagamalo	B1	18
Făgăras	C3	43
Fagasa	B1	18
Fagatogo	B1	18
Fair, *island*	Inset I	30
Fairbanks, Alaska	Inset I	126
Fairford	B3	96
Fairmont Hot Springs	P6	95
Fairweather, *mt.*	D1	95
Faisalabad	D3	21
Faizabad	D3	20
Fajardo	D2	90
Fakfak	E2	13
Falciano	C1	39
Falcon Lake	D4	96
Falelatai	B2	18
Falelima	A2	18
Falémé, *river*	C3	62
Faleniu	B1	18
Fălești	A2	50
Falher	B3	94
Falkland, *islands*	C7	74
Fallujah, al-	B2	24
Falmouth	B2	88
Falmouth	E5	90
False Divi, *point*	D5	20
Falster, *island*	D4	32
Falun	C2	53
Famagusta	B1	27
Fan Si Pan, *mt.*	A1	11
Fangliao	B2	9
Fanø, *island*	B3	32
Farafangana	B3	69
Farafenni	C2	62
Farah	A2	22
Farah, *river*	A2	22
Faraulep, *atoll*	B2	15
Farewell, *cape*	B3	15
Farewell, *cape*	C3	106
Farghona	D2	23
Fargo, N. Dak.	D1	126
Faridpur	C5	21
Farim	B1	62
Farmington	M3	95
Farmington, N. Mex.	C2	126
Farnham	Inset III	30
Faro	B4	36
Faro	C4	105
Farquhar, *island group*	B2	70
Farrellton	A6	103
Fashir, al-	B2	59
Fatick	A2	62
Fatoto	E2	62
Fauquier	N6	95
Faxaflói, *bay*	A2	52
Faxälven, *river*	C2	53
Faya-Largeau	B3	59
Faylakah, *island*	C2	24
Fayyum, al-	B2	56
Fdérik	B2	58
Fehmarn, *island*	B1	40
Fehmarn, *strait*	C4	32
Feira de Santana	E3	81
Feldkirch	A3	39
Felidu, *atoll*	A3	19
Felixstowe	D3	30
Fen, *river*	E2	10
Fenelon Falls	G3	102
Fengshan	B2	9
Fengyüan	B1	9
Feni, *islands*	B2	15
Fens, *region*	D3	30
Feodosiya	D3	47
Fergana, *valley*	D2	23
Fergus	E4	102
Ferkéssédougou	D2	63
Ferlo, *river*	B2	62
Ferme-Neuve	A5	103
Fernandina, *island*	Inset	79
Fernie	P6	95
Ferrara	B1	38
Ferryland	E5	98
Fethiye	B3	27
Feuilles, *river*	B2	101
Feyzabad	C1	22
Fez	C1	57
Fianarantsoa	B3	69
Fichtelberg, *mt.*	C3	40

Key Page
Fichtelgebirge, *mts.* B4 40
Field O5 95
Field E1 102
Fier A3 49
Fife, *lake* E11 104
Fig Tree C3 90
Figueira da Foz A2 36
Figueres H1 37
Figuig D1 57
Fiji 17
Filadelfia B3 75
Filchner Ice Shelf *glacier* B12 107
Filfla, *island* B3 36
Fillmore G11 104
Fimbul Ice Shelf, *glacier* B14 107
Finisterre, *cape* B1 37
Finland 53
Finland, *gulf* C3 53
Finlay, *river* J2 95
Finn, *river* C1 31
Finnegan D5 94
Finnmark, *plateau* E2 52
Fireside J1 95
Firth, *river* A1 105
Fish, *river* C4 70
Fisher Branch C3 96
Fisherton C3 96
Fishguard B3 30
Fitzgerald E1 94
Fitzroy, *mt.* B8 76
Fitzroy, *river* B1 14
Five Islands C2 100
Flagstaff, Ariz. B2 126
Flat, *island* C1 69
Flatbush C4 94
Flaxcombe A9 104
Fleet E5 94
Fleetwood C3 30
Fleming A4 96
Flensburg B1 40
Flesherton E3 102
Fleur de Lys C4 98
Flevoland, *polder* C2 32
Flin Flon A2, C2 96
Flinders, *range* C3 14
Flinders, *river* D1 14
Flint, *island* D3 17
Flint, Mich. E1 126
Flodden Field, *plain* C2 30
Florence B2 38
Florence, S.C. F2 126
Florenceville B2 97
Florencia B4 78
Flores D3 85
Flores, *island* D2 13
Flores, *sea* C2 13
Floreşti B2 50
Floriano D2 81
Florianópolis D4 81
Florida B3 75
Florida D2 88
Florida B2 90
Florida E3 126
Florida Keys, Fla. E3 126
Florida, *straits* B1 88
Florø A3 52
Fly, *river* A2 15
Foam Lake G9 104
Foča B2 48
Focşani D3 43
Foggia C2 38
Fogo D4 98
Fogo, *island* B4 58
Foix C5 34
Folkestone D3 30
Fomboni A2 67
Fond du Lac, *river* F2 104
Fond-du-Lac C1 104
Fonseca, *gulf* B3, C2 86
Fontainebleau C2 34
Fontas M2 95
Fontvieille A2 35
Fonuafo'ou (Falcon), *island* B3 17
Fonualei, *island* C2 17
Forest D4 102
Forestville G3 103
Fork River A3 96
Forlì C1 38
Formentera, *island* G3 37
Formosa D2 74
Fort Albany D2 101
Fort Chipewyan E2 94
Fort Collins, Colo. C1 126
Fort Erie G5 102
Fort Frances B3 101
Fort Fraser K4 95
Fort Good Hope C3 99
Fort Lauderdale, Fla. E3 126
Fort Liard D4 99
Fort MacKay E2 94
Fort McMurray E3 94
Fort McPherson B3 99
Fort Myers, Fla. E3 126
Fort Nelson L2 95
Fort Nelson, *river* L1 95
Fort Norman C4 99
Fort Portal B3 61
Fort Providence E4 99
Fort Qu'Appelle G10 104
Fort Resolution F4 99
Fort Saskatchewan D4 94
Fort Severn C1 101
Fort Simpson D4 99
Fort Smith, Ark. D2 126
Fort Smith, *region* E4 99
Fort St. James K4 95
Fort St. John M3 95
Fort Steele P6 95
Fort Stockton, Tex. C2 126
Fort Vermilion C2 94
Fort Wayne, Ind. E1 126
Fort William B2 30
Fort Worth, Tex. D2 126
Fortaleza E2 81
Forteau C3 98
Forth, *estuary* C2 30
Forth, *river* B2 30

Key Page
Fortín Conde de Mirasol, *fort* E2 90
Fortín Ravelo B3 77
Fortune D5 98
Fortune Bridge C2 100
Fortune, *bay* D5 98
Foster, *river* E4 104
Fosterville B3 97
Foumban B2 65
Foumbouni A1 67
Four Falls B2 97
Foveaux, *strait* A4 15
Fox Island F2 100
Fox Lake C2 94
Fox Valley A10 104
Foxe, *basin* N3 99
Foxe, *channel* M3 99
Foxe, *peninsula* N4 99
Foyle, *inlet* C1 31
Foyle, *lake* A2 30
Foyle, *river* A2 30
Foz do Iguaçu C4 81
France 34
Frances, *lake* D5 105
Franceville B2 66
Franche-Comté D3 34
Francis G10 104
Francistown B2 69
Francois C5 98
François, *lake* K4 95
Franconian Jura, *mts.* B4 40
Frankenwald, *mts.* B3 40
Frankford H3 102
Frankfort, *capital*, Ky. E2 126
Frankfurt am Main B3 40
Frankfurt an der Oder C2 40
Franklin, *strait* J2 99
Franquelin J2 103
Franz Josef Land, *islands* A4 44
Fraser E1 95
Fraser Lake K4 95
Fraser, *river* L5, M4 95
Fraserburgh C1 30
Fraserdale D2 101
Fraserwood C4 96
Fray Bentos A2 75
Fredericia B3 32
Fredericton C3 97
Fredericton B2 100
Fredericton Jct. C3 97
Frederiksberg D3 32
Frederikshavn C1 32
Fredrikstad C4 52
Freeport A2 89
Freeport A3 100
Freetown E5 90
Freetown, *capital* A1 63
Freiberg C3 40
Freiburg A5 40
Freirina B3 76
Fréjus D5 34
Fremantle, W.A. A3, Inset I 14
French Guiana 80
French River E1 102
Frenchman, *river* B11 104
Fresnillo D3 84
Fresno, Calif. B2 126
Fria B2 62
Fribourg B2 35
Friedrichshafen B5 40
Frigate, *island* C1 91
Frisches Haff, *bay* D1 41
Friuli-Venezia Giulia C1 38
Frobisher, *lake* C4 104
Frog, *lake* E4 94
Frome, *lake* D2 14
Frontier B11 104
Frosinone C2 38
Fruška Gora, *mts.* A2 49
Frutigen B2 35
Frýdek-Místek D3 42
Fua'amotu B4 17
Fuenlabrada Inset II 37
Fuerte Olimpo D2 75
Fuerte, *river* C2 84
Fuerteventura, *island* Inset I 37
Fuhayhil, al- C2 24
Fujayrah, al- D2 25
Fuji, *mt.* C3 8
Fujian E3 10
Fujisawa C3 8
Fukue A3 8
Fukue, *island* A3 8
Fukui C2 8
Fukuoka A3 8
Fukushima D2 8
Fukuyama B3 8
Fulacunda B2 62
Fuladi, *mt.* B2 22
Fulda B3 40
Fulda, *river* B3 40
Fullarton A2 91
Funabashi D3 8
Funafuti, *capital* C2 16
Funafuti, *island* C3 16
Fundy, *bay* A3 100
Furnas, *reservoir* D4 81
Fürstenfeld E3 39
Fürth B4 40
Fushun F1 10
Futa Jallon, *plateau* B1 62
Futuna, *island* C4 18
Fuxin F1 10
Fuzhou E3 10
Fyn, *island* C3 32

G

Gaalkacyo B2 60
Gabarus G2 100
Gabès C3 57
Gabès, *gulf* C2 57
Gaborone, *capital* B3 69
Gabon 66
Gabriel, *island* C1 69
Gabrovo D3 50
Gabú C1 62
Gacko B2 48

Key Page
Gaeta C2 38
Gafsa B2 57
Gagetown C3 97
Gagnoa D3 63
Gagnon C3 101
Gagra A2 45
Gainesville, Fla. E3 126
Gainsborough J11 104
Gairdner, *lake* C3 14
Gaizina, *mt.* C2 46
Galahad E5 94
Galana, *river* E5 61
Galápagos, *islands* Inset 79
Galaţi E3 43
Galena Bay O6 95
Galicia C1 37
Galilee, *region* B1 26
Galle B5 19
Gallegos, *river* A7 74
Gallinas, *point* C1 78
Gällivare D1 53
Galoa B3 17
Galveston, Tex. D3 126
Galway B2 31
Galway, *bay* B2 31
Gam, *river* A1 11
Gambia, The 62
Gambia, *river* B2, C3, D2 62
Gambo D5 98
Gamprin B1 33
Gan, *river* E3 10
Gananoque J3 102
Gäncä B2 45
Gander D5 98
Gander Bay D4 98
Gandhinagar B4 20
Ganganagar B3 20
Ganges, *river* E3 20
Gangtok E3 20
Gansu C1, D2 10
Ganzhou E3 10
Gao D2 58
Gaoua C3 64
Gap D4 34
Garabil, *plateau* D3 22
Garabogazköl, *lake* A2 22
Garda, *lake* B1 38
Garden Hill D2 96
Garden Reach Inset II 20
Garden, *island* Inset I 20
Garden, *river* A1 102
Gardenton C4 96
Gardez B2 22
Gardner, *canal* H4 95
Gardner, *island* B2 17
Garissa E4 61
Garland A3 96
Garmisch-Partenkirchen B5 40
Garnish D5 98
Garonne, *river* C4 34
Garoowe B2 60
Garoua B2 65
Garry, *lake* H3 99
Garson Lake A4 104
Garulia Inset II 20
Gary, Ind. E1 126
Gascoyne *river* A2 14
Gash, *river* B2 60
Gaspé M3 103
Gaspé, *peninsula* L3 103
Gaspereau Forks D2 97
Gatal, *cape* E4 37
Gateshead C2 30
Gatico B2 76
Gatineau A6 103
Gatineau Park A6 103
Gatineau, *river* A4, A5 103
Gatún, *lake* C2 87
Gau, *island* B3 17
Gauhati F3 20
Gaultois D5 98
Gavarr C2 45
Gävle C2 53
Gaya E4 20
Gaya A3 59
Gazanjyk B2 22
Gazelle, *peninsula* B2 15
Gaziantep D3 27
Gbarnga B2 63
Gdańsk D1 41
Gdańsk, *gulf* D1 41
Gdynia D1 41
Gêba, *river* C1 62
Geelong, Vic. D3 14
Gege B2 71
Geidam F1 65
Geikie, *river* F3 104
Gejiu D3 10
Gela C3 38
Gelibolu (Gallipoli) A2 27
Gelsenkirchen A3 40
Gem D6 94
Gembloux C2 33
Gemena B1 67
General Eugenio A. Garay A2 75
General Santos C5 12
General, *river* C3 86
Genesee C4 94
Geneva A2 35
Geneva, *lake* A2 35
Genk D2 33
Gennargentu, *mts.* B2 38
Genoa B1 38
Genoa, *gulf* B1 38
Gentilly Inset II 34
Gentofte D3 32
George B3 71
George Town A2 13
George, *river* C2 101
Georgetown B2 91
Georgetown D2 62
Georgetown C2 100
Georgetown, *capital* B2 80
Georgia 45
Georgia E2 126
Georgian, *bay* E2 102
Gera C3 40
Geral, *range* C4 81

Key Page
Gerald A4 96
Geraldton C3 101
Geraldton, W.A. A2 14
Gerlachovka, *mt.* C2 42
Germany 40
Germiston C2 71
Gerona H2 37
Getafe E2, Inset II 37
Gevgelija C2 48
Geylegphug B3 19
Ghabah C2 25
Ghadamis A1 56
Ghaghara, *river* D3 20
Ghana 64
Ghanzi A2 69
Ghardaia B1 57
Gharyan B1 56
Ghat B3 56
Ghatkopar Inset I 20
Ghaydah, al- C1 25
Ghazal, *river* B4 59
Ghazni B2 22
Ghent B1 33
Ghurdaqah, al- B2 56
Giant's Causeway, *headland* A2 30
Gibraltar 36
Gibraltar, *strait* D5 37
Gibson, *desert* B2 14
Giessen B3 40
Gifford, *river* M2 99
Gifu C3 8
Giglio, *island* B2 38
Gijón D1 37
Gikongoro B2 61
Gilbert Plains A3 96
Gilbert, *islands* A1 17
Gilbert, *river* D1 14
Gilgit E2 21
Gilliam D1 96
Gillingham D3 30
Gimie, *mt.* A2 91
Gimli C4 96
Giresun D2 27
Gironde, *river* B4 34
Gisborne C2 15
Gisenyi B1 61
Gitarama B2 61
Gitega B2 61
Giurgiu C4 43
Giza B2 56
Gizo A1 16
Gjirokastër B3 49
Gjoa Haven J3 99
Gjøvik C3 52
Glace Bay H1 100
Gladstone B4 96
Gladstone, Qld. E2 14
Glåma, *river* C3 52
Glanvillia A2 90
Glasgow B2 30
Glasgow, Mont. C1 126
Glaslyn B7 104
Glastonbury C3 30
Gleichen D6 94
Glen Margaret D3 100
Glenboro B4 96
Glencoe D5 102
Glenella B4 96
Glenholme D2 100
Glenora G2 95
Glenwood D5 98
Glidden A9 104
Glifádha Inset 51
Glittertinden, *mt.* B3 52
Gliwice D3 41
Głogów C3 41
Gloucester C3 30
Gloucester K2 102
Glover, *reef* C3 85
Glovertown D5 98
Gmünd D2 39
Goba C3 60
Gobabis C2 70
Gobi, *desert* D1 10
Godavari, *river* C5 20
Godbout J2 103
Goderich D4 102
Godfrey J3 102
Godoy Cruz B3 74
Gods, *lake* D2 96
Gogama D3 101
Goiânia D3 81
Goiás D3 81
Golan Heights, *occ. terr.* A3 27
Gold Coast, Qld. E2 14
Gold River J6 95
Golden O5 95
Golden Lake H2 102
Golea, el- B2 57
Golfito C4 86
Golmud C2 10
Golyama Kamchiya, *river* E2 50
Goma C2 67
Gombe F2 65
Gomera, *island* Inset I 37
Gómez Palacio D2 84
Gonaïves C1 89
Gonâve, *gulf* B1 89
Gonâve, *island* B2 89
Gonder B1 60
Gongola, *river* F2 65
Goobies E5 98
Good Hope, *cape* A3 71
Goodlands C2 69
Goodlands A4 96
Goodsoil A6 104
Göppingen B4 40
Gorakhpur D3 20
Goražde B2 48
Gordon, *lake* E3 94
Gordondale A3 94
Gore B2 60
Gore Bay C2 102
Gori C4 45
Goris D3 45
Gorizia C1 38
Görlitz C3 40
Gorlovka D2 47

Key Page
Gorno-Altay, republic D6 44
Gorno-Altaysk D6 44
Goroka A2 15
Gorontalo D1 13
Gorzów Wielkopolski B2 41
Gosford, N.S.W. E3 14
Goshen F2 100
Goslar B3 40
Gospić B3 48
Gosport C4 30
Göta, *canal* B3 53
Göteborg och Bohus B3 53
Gotha B3 40
Gotland, *island* C3 53
Gotsu B3 8
Göttingen B3 40
Gouda B2 32
Goudiri C2 62
Gouin, *reservoir* B3 103
Goundam C2 58
Gouré C3 59
Govan E9 104
Governador Valadares D3 81
Gowd-e Zereh, *lake* A3 22
Göyçay B2 45
Gozo, *island* A1 36
Graaf-Reinet B3 71
Gračanica B1 48
Gracias A2 86
Grafton, N.S.W. E2 14
Graham Land, *region* C11 107
Graham, *island* F4 95
Graham, *island* K1 99
Grahamstown C3 71
Grampian, *mts.* B2 30
Gran Canaria, *island* Inset I 37
Gran Chaco, *region* B3 75
Granada B3 87
Granada E4 37
Granby D6 103
Grand Anse B1 91
Grand Bahama, *island* A2 89
Grand Bale C2 69
Grand Bank D5 98
Grand Bay C1 91
Grand Bay C3 97
Grand Bend D4 102
Grand Bruit B5 98
Grand Canyon, Ariz. B2 126
Grand Centre E4 94
Grand Cess B3 63
Grand Erg Occidental, *desert* B1 57
Grand Erg Oriental, *desert* B2 57
Grand Falls B1 97
Grand Falls-Windsor D5 98
Grand Forks N6 95
Grand Forks, N. Dak. D1 126
Grand Island, Nebr. D1 126
Grand Junction, Colo. C2 126
Grand Manan, *island* C4 97
Grand Marais C4 96
Grand Narrows G2 100
Grand Pré C2 100
Grand Rapids B2 96
Grand Rapids, Mich. E1 126
Grand Roy B2 91
Grand Santi A1 80
Grand Turk, *capital* D4 89
Grand Turk, *island* D4 89
Grand Valley E4 102
Grand, *canal* C2 31
Grand, *harbor* C2 36
Grand, *lake* D2 97
Grand, *lake* C4 98
Grand, *river* C3 69
Grand-Etang F1 100
Grand-Mère D5 103
Grand-Remous A5 103
Grande Baleine, *river* A2 101
Grande de Añasco, *river* A2 90
Grande de Manatí, *river* C2 90
Grande de Matagalpa, *river* B2 87
Grande Prairie A3 94
Grande, *bay* B7 74
Grande, *range* C2 75
Grande, *river* B3 77
Grande, *river* D3 81
Grande, *river* B3 86
Grande-Anse D1 97
Grande-Rivière M3 103
Grande-Vallée M2 103
Grândola A3 36
Grandview A3 96
Granisle J4 95
Grantham C3 30
Granville Lake A1 96
Gras, *lake* F4 99
Grass, *river* A3, B2 96
Grassland D4 94
Grauspitz, *mt.* B2 33
Gravelbourg D11 104
Gravenhurst F3 102
Gravesend Inset III 30
Gravois, *point* B3 89
Graz D3 39
Great Abaco, *island* B2 89
Great Alföld, *plain* B2 43
Great Artesian, *basin* D2 14
Great Australian, *bight* B3 14
Great Bahama, bank B4 89
Great Barrier, *island* C2 15
Great Barrier, *reef* D1 14
Great *basin*, Nev. B2 126
Great Bear, *lake* D3 99
Great Britain 30
Great Dividing, *range* D1, D3 14
Great Exuma, *island* B3 89
Great Falls C4 96
Great Falls, Mont. B1 126
Great Fish, *river* C3 71
Great Inagua, *island* C4 89
Great Indian, *desert* B3 20
Great Karroo, *plateau* B3 71
Great Nicobar, *island* F7 20
Great Rift, *valley* 55
Great Ruaha, *river* C2 68
Great Salt, *lake*, Utah B1 126

Key Page
Great Sand Sea, *desert* A2 56
Great Sandy, *desert* B2 14
Great Scarcies, *river* A1 63
Great Sea, *reef* B1 17
Great Slave, *lake* F4 99
Great Victoria, *desert* B2 14
Great Wall of China D2 10
Great Yarmouth D3 30
Great Zab, *river* B1 24
Great, *plains* C1 126
Greater Hinggan, *range* F1 10
Greater Sunda, *islands* B2 13
Gréboun, *mt.* B1 59
Gredos, *mts.* D2 37
Greece 51
Greeley, Colo. C1 126
Greely, *fjord* L1 99
Green Bay, Wis. E1 126
Green Lake C6 104
Green, *islands* B2 15
Greenland 106
Greenland, *sea* D2 106
Greenock B2 30
Greensboro, N.C. F2 126
Greenville B3 63
Greenville, S.C. E2 126
Greenwood N6 95
Greifswald C1 40
Grenå C2 32
Grenada 91
Grenada, *island* B2 91
Grenadines, *islands* A3, B1, C1 91
Grenfell H10 104
Grenoble D4 34
Gretna C4 96
Greve D3 32
Grevenmacher B2 33
Grey River C5 98
Grey, *range* D2 14
Greymouth B3 15
Gribingui, *river* A2 66
Griffin G11 104
Griffith, N.S.W. D3 14
Grijalva, *river* F4 84
Grimsby C3 30
Grimsey, *island* B1 52
Grinnell, *peninsula* J1 99
Griqualand East, *region* C3 71
Griqualand West, *region* B2 71
Griquatown B2 71
Grise Fiord M1 99
Griswold A4 96
Groningen B2 80
Groningen D1 32
Gronlid F7 104
Groote Eylandt, *island* C1 14
Grootfontein C1 70
Grootvloer, *pan* B2 71
Gros Islet B1 91
Gros Morne Natl. Park C4 98
Gros-Morne L2 103
Grosseto B2 38
Grossglockner, *mt.* C3 39
Groundbirch M3 95
Groznyy E4 44
Grudziądz D2 41
Grunthal C4 96
Guacanayabo, *gulf* D3 88
Guadalajara E2 37
Guadalajara, *state capital* D3 84
Guadalcanal, *island* A1 16
Guadalquivir, *river* D4 37
Guadalupe, *reservoir* Inset 84
Guadarrama, *mts.* D2 37
Guadeloupe, *island* 82
Guadiana, *river* C3 37
Guaillabamba, *river* B2 79
Guainía, *river* C4 78
Guajara Mirim B3 81
Guajira, *peninsula* C1 78
Guam, *island* 5
Guanacaste, *range* A2 86
Guanaja, *island* C1 86
Guanajuato, *state capital* D3 84
Guanare C2 79
Guandu, *river* Inset I 81
Guangdong E3 10
Guangxi Zhuang D3 10
Guangzhou E3 10
Guánica B3 90
Guantánamo E3 88
Guaporé, *river* B3 81
Guaqui A3 77
Guaranda B3 79
Guarda B2 36
Guarujá Inset II 81
Guarulhos Inset II 81
Guasave C2 84
Guatemala 85
Guatemala City, *capital* C5 85
Guaviare, *river* C4 78
Guayaguayare A2 91
Guayama C3 90
Guayambre, *river* B2 86
Guayanilla B2 90
Guayape, *river* B2 86
Guayaquil B4 79
Guayaquil, *gulf* A4 79
Guayas, *river* B4 79
Guaymas B2 84
Guaynabo C2 90
Guben C3 40
Gudauta A2 45
Gudenå, *river* B2 32
Guecho E1 37
Guéckédou C3 62
Guelph E4 102
Guelta Zemmur B1 58
Guéret C3 34
Guernica Y Luno E1 37
Guernsey, *island* Inset II 30
Guerrero D4 84
Guerrero Negro B2 84
Guiana, *highlands* D2 79
Guiers, *lake* B1 62
Guilarte, *mt.* B2 90
Guildford C3 30
Guilin E3 10

Key Page

Guimarães ...A2 36
Guinea ...62
Guinea, gulf ...62
Guinea-Bissau ...62
Güiria ...D1 79
Guiyang ...D3 10
Guizhou ...D3 10
Gujranwala ...E3 21
Gujrat ...E3 21
Gulbarga ...C5 20
Gulbene ...D2 46
Gulf Coastal, plain ...D3 126
Gulistan ...C2 23
Gull Lake ...B10 104
Gull, lake ...C5 94
Gulu ...C2 61
Gumdag ...B2 22
Gummi ...C1 65
Gunisao, river ...C2 96
Gunnbjørn Fjeld, mt. ...D2 106
Gunton ...C4 96
Guntur ...D5 20
Gurabo ...D2 90
Guri, reservoir ...D2 79
Gusau ...D1 65
Gushgy ...D3 22
Gushgy, river ...D3 22
Gushikawa ...Inset II 8
Gustavo A. Madero ...Inset 84
Güstrow ...C2 40
Guyana ...80
Guysborough ...F2 100
Gwadar ...B5 21
Gwai, river ...A2 69
Gwalior ...C3 20
Gweru ...B2 69
Gyda, peninsula ...B5 44
Gympie, Qld. ...E2 14
Gyöngyös ...B2 43
Győr ...A2 43
Gypsumville ...B3 96
Gyumri ...A2 45
Gyzylarbat ...B2 22

H

Ha Giang ...A1 11
Ha'apai, island group ...B3 17
Haapsalu ...B2 46
Haarlem ...B2 32
Habarut ...C1 25
Habay ...A4 94
Haboro ...Inset I 8
Hachijo, island ...C3 8
Hachinohe ...D1 8
Hachioji ...C3 8
Haddummati, atoll ...A4 19
Hadejia, river ...E1 65
Hadera ...B1 26
Haderslev ...B3 32
Hadhramaut, district ...B1 25
Hadithah, al- ...B2 24
Haedo, range ...B2 75
Haeju ...A3 9
Hafford ...C8 104
Hafnarfjördhur ...A3 52
Hagen ...A3 40
Hague, cape ...B2 34
Haha, island ...Inset III 8
Haifa ...B1 26
Haifa, bay ...B1 26
Haikou ...E4 10
Hail ...B1 24
Hailar ...E1 10
Hainan ...D4 10
Haines Junction ...B5 105
Haiphong ...B2 11
Hairé Lao ...B1 62
Haiti ...89
Hajdúböszörmény ...C2 43
Haji Ibrahim, mt. ...B1 24
Hajjah ...A1 25
Haka ...B2 12
Hakodate ...D1, Inset I 8
Halab (Aleppo) ...A1 27
Halaib ...D1 59
Halba ...B1 26
Halberstadt ...B3 40
Haldimand ...F5 102
Halfmoon Bay ...L6 95
Haliburton ...G2 102
Halifax ...D3 30
Halifax, capital ...D4 102
Halil, river ...D4 22
Halisahar ...Inset II 20
Hall Beach ...M3 99
Hall, peninsula ...P4 99
Halla-san, mt. ...Inset 9
Hallboro ...B4 96
Halle ...C2 33
Halle ...B3 40
Hallingdal, valley ...B3 52
Halmahera, island ...D1 13
Halmstad ...B3 53
Haltiatunturi, mt ...B1 53
Halton Hills ...F4 102
Hamadan ...B3 22
Hamah ...A2 27
Hamamatsu ...C3 8
Hamar ...C3 52
Hambantota ...C5 19
Hamburg ...B2 40
Hämeenlinna ...B2 53
Hameln ...B2 40
Hamersley, range ...A2 14
Hamgyŏng, mts. ...C2 9
Hamhŭng ...B3 9
Hami ...C1 10
Hamilton ...C2 15
Hamilton ...B2 30
Hamilton ...F4 102
Hamilton, inlet ...B2 98
Hamiota ...A4 96
Hamm ...A3 40
Hammamat, al- ...C1 57
Hammamet, gulf ...C1 57
Hammerfest ...E1 52
Hammonds Plains ...D3 100
Hammondvale ...D3 97

Key Page

Hampden ...C4 98
Hampstead ...J5 103
Hampton ...D3 97
Hamun-e Jaz Murian, lake ...D4 22
Hamun-e Saberi, lake ...A2 22
Han, river ...E2 10
Han, river ...B4 9
Hanau ...B3 40
Handan ...E2 10
Hangayn, mts. ...B2 11
Hangö ...B3 53
Hangzhou ...F2 10
Hanley ...D9 104
Hannibal, Mo. ...D2 126
Hannover ...B2 40
Hanoi, capital ...A2 11
Hanover ...D3 102
Hantzsch, river ...O3 99
Hanzhong ...D2 10
Haora ...E4, Inset II 20
Haparanda ...D1 53
Happy Valley-Goose Bay ...A2, E4 98
Har Us, lake ...B2 11
Harad ...C1 24
Harare, capital ...B1 69
Harbel ...A2 63
Harbin ...F1 10
Harbour Breton ...D5 98
Harbour Deep ...C4 98
Harbour, island ...B2 89
Harcourt ...D2 97
Hardangerfjord, fjord ...B4 52
Hardangervidda, plateau ...B3 52
Hardwood Lake ...H2 102
Hare Bay ...D5 98
Harer ...D2 60
Hargeysa ...A2 60
Hargrave ...A4 96
Harirud, river ...A2 22
Härnösand ...C2 53
Harper ...C3 63
Harris ...C9 104
Harrisburg, capital, Pa. ...F1 126
Harrogate ...C2 30
Harstad ...D2 52
Hart, ranges ...L3 95
Hart, river ...B3 105
Hartford, capital, Conn. ...F1 126
Hartland ...B2 97
Hartley Bay ...H4 95
Hartney ...A4 96
Harvey ...C3 97
Harwill ...C3 96
Harz, mts. ...B3 40
Hasa, al-, region ...C1 24
Hasakah, al- ...B1 27
Hashtadan, region ...A1 22
Haslemere ...Inset III 30
Hasselt ...D2 33
Hastings ...C2 15
Hastings ...D4 30
Hastings ...H3 102
Hat Yai ...B5 12
Hatillo ...B2 90
Hato Mayor ...C2 89
Hatteras cape, N.C. ...F2 126
Hattiesburg, Miss. ...E2 126
Haugesund ...B4 52
Haultain, river ...D4 104
Haute-Normandie ...C2 34
Havana, capital ...B1 88
Havel, river ...C2 40
Havelock ...H3 102
Havířov ...D3 42
Havre, Mont. ...C1 126
Havre-St-Pierre ...D3 101
Hawaii ...Inset II 126
Hawaii island, Hawaii ...Inset II 126
Hawalli ...C2 24
Hawar, islands ...B2 25
Hawea, lake ...A3 15
Hawf ...C1 25
Hawick ...C2 30
Hawke Harbour ...D2 98
Hawke's Bay ...C4 98
Hawke, bay ...C2 15
Hawkesbury ...L2 102
Hay River ...E4 99
Hay, river ...A2, B1 94
Hayes, river ...D1, D2 96
Hayma ...C2 25
Hayter ...E5 94
Hazelton ...J3 95
Hazelton, mts. ...H3 95
Hazlet ...B10 104
Hazm, al- ...A1 25
Hearst ...D3 101
Heart's Content ...E5 98
Heaslip ...A4 96
Heath Steele ...C1 97
Hebei ...E2 10
Hebrides, sea ...A1 30
Hebron ...E3 98
Hecate, strait ...G4 95
Hecla ...C3 96
Hecla and Griper, bay ...F1 99
Hedley ...M6 95
Heerenveen ...C2 32
Heerlen ...C4 32
Hefei ...E2 10
Hegang ...G1 10
Heha, mt. ...B2 61
Heidelberg ...B4 40
Heidenheim ...B4 40
Heilbronn ...B4 40
Heilong (Amur), river ...F1 10
Heilongjiang ...F1 10
Heimaey, island ...A3 52
Heinola ...C2 53
Heinsburg ...E4 94
Heisler ...D5 94
Hekla, volcano ...B3 52
Hel ...D1 41
Helen, reef ...Inset 17
Helena, capital, Mont. ...B1 126
Helgoland, island ...A1 40
Hellín ...F3 37
Helmand, river ...A2 22
Helmsdale ...E5 94

Key Page

Helsingborg ...B3 53
Helsingør ...D2 32
Helsinki, capital ...B2 53
Heming Lake ...A2 96
Henan ...E2 10
Henashi, cape ...C1 8
Hengch'un ...B2 9
Hengelo ...D2 32
Hengyang ...E3 10
Henley Harbour ...D3 98
Hensall ...D4 102
Henzada ...B3 12
Herat ...A2 22
Herb Lake ...B2 96
Herbert ...C10 104
Heredia ...B2 86
Hereford ...C3 30
Heriot Bay ...K6 95
Hermitage-Sandyville ...D5 98
Hermon, mt. ...A3 27
Hermosillo, state capital ...B2 84
Hernád, river ...C1 43
Herne ...A3 40
Herning ...B2 32
Hertford ...Inset III 30
Herzliyya ...B1 26
Hess, river ...C4 105
Hesse ...B3 40
Hetauda ...C2 19
Hiatikulu ...B2 71
Hibbing, Minn. ...D1 126
Hicks Bay ...C2 15
Hidaka, mts. ...Inset I 8
Hidalgo ...E3 84
Hidalgo del Parral ...C2 84
Hieflau ...D3 39
Hierro, island ...Inset I 37
Higashiosaka ...B3 8
High Atlas, ranges ...B2 57
High Level ...B2 94
High River ...D6 94
High Tatra, mts. ...D4 42
High Wycombe ...Inset III 30
Highrock ...A1 96
Highrock, lake ...A1 96
Higüey ...D2 89
Hiiumaa, island ...B2 46
Hijaz, al-, region ...A1 24
Hilda ...E6 94
Hilden ...D2 100
Hildesheim ...B2 40
Hill Bank ...B2 85
Hillaby, mt. ...A3 91
Hillah, al- ...B2 24
Hillerød ...D3 32
Hillsborough ...C1 91
Hillsborough ...E3 97
Hillsborough, bay ...C2 100
Hilo, Hawaii ...Inset II 126
Hilton Beach ...B1 102
Hilversum ...C2 32
Himalayas, mts. ...7
Himeji ...B3 8
Hinche ...C1 89
Hindelang ...B5 40
Hindu Kush, range ...B1 22
Hino, cape ...B3 8
Hinton ...B4 94
Hirakata ...B3 8
Hirakud, reservoir ...D4 20
Hirara ...Inset II 8
Hirmil, al- ...B1 26
Hirosake ...D1 8
Hiroshima ...B3 8
Hirtshals ...B1 32
Hisabpur ...Inset II 20
Hitachi ...D2 8
Hixon ...L4 95
Hjørring ...B1 32
Hkakabo Razi, mt. ...C1 12
Ho ...C3 64
Ho Chi Minh City ...B4 11
Hoa Binh ...A2 11
Hobart, Tas., capital ...D4 14
Hobsons, bay ...Inset V 14
Hobyo ...B2 60
Hoceima, al- ...D1 57
Hodgeville ...D10 104
Hodgson ...C3 96
Hódmezővásárhely ...C2 43
Hoeryŏng ...C1 9
Hof ...B3 40
Höfn ...C2 52
Hohe Tauern, mts. ...C3 39
Hohhot ...E1 10
Hokkaido, island ...D1, Inset I 8
Hoktemberyan ...B2 45
Holbæk ...C3 32
Holden ...D4 94
Holdfast ...E10 104
Holetown ...A3 91
Holguín ...E3 88
Holhol ...B2 60
Holland ...B4 96
Holman ...E2 99
Holon ...B1 26
Holstebro ...B2 32
Holton ...C2 98
Holyhead ...B3 30
Holyrood ...E5 98
Holywood ...C2 30
Homathko, river ...K5 95
Hombori Tondo, mt. ...C2 58
Hombori, mts. ...C2 58
Homer, Alaska ...Inset I 126
Homo, bay ...B2 18
Homs ...A2 27
Homyel ...E3 47
Hon Gai ...B2 11
Hondo ...C3 9
Hondo ...D3 94
Honduras ...86
Honduras, gulf ...A1 86
Hong Kong, S.A.R. ...E3 10
Hong Kong, island ...Inset 10
Hongze, lake ...E2 10
Honiara, capital ...A1 16
Honolulu, capital,
  Hawaii ...Inset II 126

Key Page

Honshu, island ...C2 8
Hoogeveen ...D2 32
Hoorn ...C2 32
Hope ...M6 95
Hope Bay ...C2 88
Hope Valley ...E5 94
Hopedale ...A1 98
Hopedale ...E3 98
Hopewell Cape ...E3 97
Horgen ...C1 35
Hormigueros ...A2 90
Hormuz, strait ...D4 22
Horn, cape ...C9 76
Horn, cape ...A1 52
Hornád, river ...C2 42
Hornavan, lake ...C1 53
Hornepayne ...D3 101
Horsburgh, atoll ...A2 19
Horse, river ...D3 94
Horsens ...B3 32
Horton, river ...D3 99
Hospitalet ...H2 37
Hot Springs, Ark. ...D2 126
Hotan ...A2 10
Hotchkiss ...B2 94
Hottah, lake ...E3 99
Houghton, Mich. ...E1 126
Houmt Souk ...C3 57
Houston ...J4 95
Houston, Tex. ...D3 126
Hovd, river ...B2 11
Hove ...C4 30
Hoveria, mt. ...A2 47
Hövsgöl, lake ...C1 11
Howley ...C4 98
Hoy, island ...Inset I 30
Hradec Králové ...B2 42
Hrazdan ...B2 45
Hrazdan, river ...B2 45
Hrodna ...A3 47
Hron, river ...B2 42
Hsinchu ...B1 9
Hsinchuang ...B1 9
Hsintien ...B1 9
Hsinying ...B2 9
Hua Hin ...B3 12
Huacho ...B3 77
Huai, river ...E2 10
Huainan ...E2 10
Hualien ...B2 9
Huallaga, river ...B2 77
Huambo ...C4 70
Huancavelica ...B3 77
Huancayo ...B3 77
Huang (Yellow), river ...D2, E2 10
Huánuco ...B3 77
Huapí, mts. ...B2 87
Huaraz ...B2 77
Huascarán, mt. ...B2 77
Hubbards ...C3 100
Hubei ...E2 10
Hubli-Dharwar ...C5 20
Hubley ...D3 100
Hudaydah, al- ...A2 25
Huddersfield ...C3 30
Hudiksvall ...C2 53
Hudson Bay ...H8 104
Hudson's Hope ...M3 95
Hudson, bay ...J3 92
Hudson, strait ...O4 99
Hue ...B3 11
Huehuetenango ...B4 85
Huelva ...C4 37
Huesca ...F1 37
Hufuf, al- ...C1 24
Hugli, river ...Inset II 20
Hugli-Chunchura ...Inset II 20
Hüichŏn ...B2 9
Huila, mt. ...A4 78
Hüksan Chedo, islands ...A5 9
Hull ...A6 103
Hulun, lake ...E1 10
Hulwan ...B2 56
Humacao ...D2 90
Humber, river ...D3 30
Humboldt ...E8 104
Humenné ...C2 42
Humuya, river ...B2 86
Húnaflói, bay ...A2 52
Hunan ...E3 10
Hunedoara ...B3 43
Hungary ...43
Hŭngnam ...B3 9
Hünsruck, mts. ...A4 40
Hunter River ...B2 100
Huntington, W. Va. ...E2 126
Huntsville ...F2 102
Huntsville, Ala. ...E2 126
Hunyani, river ...B1 69
Huon, islands ...B1 18
Huon, peninsula ...A2 15
Huron, lake ...E1 126
Hussar ...D5 94
Hutchinson, Kans. ...D2 126
Hvannadalshnúkur, mt. ...B3 52
Hvar, island ...C3 48
Hvíta, river ...A2 52
Hwange ...A2 69
Hyargas, lake ...B2 11
Hyderabad ...C5 20
Hyderabad ...C5 21
Hyesan ...C2 9
Hyland Post ...H2 95
Hyland, river ...D5 105
Hylo ...D4 94
Hyvinkää ...B2 53

I

Ialomiţa, river ...D3 43
Ialpug, river ...B2 50
Iaşi ...D2 43
Ibadan ...B4 65
Ibagué ...B3 78
Ibar, river ...B2 49
Ibaraki ...B3 8
Ibarra ...B2 79
Ibb ...A2 25

Key Page

Ibérico, mts. ...F2 37
Ibiza ...G4 37
Ibiza, island ...G3 37
Iboundji, mt. ...A2 66
Ibrahim, river ...A1 26
Ibri ...C1 25
Ica ...B3 77
Içá, river ...B2 81
Icacos, key ...D2 90
Ice Cap ...C2 106
Iceland ...52
Ichŏn ...B3 9
Ichihara ...D3 8
Ichikawa ...C3 8
Ichilo, river ...B3 77
Ichinomiya ...C3 8
Idaho ...B1 126
Idaho Falls, Idaho ...B1 126
Iddesleigh ...E6 94
Idfu ...B3 56
Idhra, island ...B3 51
Idlib ...A2 27
Idrija ...B2 48
Ife ...C4 65
Igarka ...C6 44
Igloolik ...M3 99
Igombe, river ...B1 68
Iguaçu, falls ...C4 81
Iguaçu, river ...E2 74
Iguala ...E4 84
Iguazú, falls ...E4 75
Ih Bogd Uul, mt. ...C3 11
Ihavandiffulu, atoll ...A1 19
Ihosy ...B3 69
Ilan ...B1 9
Iijoki, river ...C1 53
Iisalmi ...C2 53
Ijevan ...B2 45
Ijssel, river ...D2 32
Ijsselmeer, sea ...C2 32
Ijuw ...C2 16
Ikaría, island ...C3 51
Ikeja ...B4 65
Ikela ...B2 67
Iki, island ...A3 8
Ikorodu ...B4 65
Ila ...C4 65
Ilam ...B3 22
Ilam ...E2 10
Île-à-la-Crosse ...C5 104
Île-de-France ...C2 34
Ilebo ...C4 65
Ilesha ...C4 65
Ilford ...D1 96
Ilhéus ...E3 81
Ili, river ...D2 23
Iligan ...C4 12
Illampu, mt. ...A3 77
Illapel ...B4 76
Illimani, mt. ...A3 77
Illinois ...E1 126
Ilo ...C4 77
Iloilo ...B4 12
Ilorin ...C3 65
Imatra ...C2 53
Imbarié ...Inset I 81
Imbé ...B2 90
Imeni Ismail Samani, peak. ...B3 23
Imi ...D3 60
Imjin, river ...B3 9
Imlili ...A2 58
Imperatriz ...D2 81
Imperial ...E9 104
Imperial Mills ...E4 94
Imperial, river ...B6 76
Impfondo ...D3 66
Imphal ...F4 20
Inari, lake ...C1 53
Inch'ŏn ...B4 9
Incles, river ...C1 36
Indalsälven, river ...B2 53
India ...20
Indian Bay ...D4 96
Indian Brook ...G1 100
Indian Cabins ...B1 94
Indian Harbour ...D3 100
Indian Head ...G10 104
Indiana ...E1 126
Indianapolis, capital, Ind. ...E2 126
Indigirka, river ...C9 44
Indispensable, reefs ...B2 16
Indonesia ...13
Indore ...C4 20
Indus, river ...C4, E2 21
Ingleside ...K3 102
Ingolstadt ...B4 40
Ingonish ...G1 100
Ingonish Beach ...G1 100
Ingushetiya, republic ...E4 44
Inhambane ...B5 68
Inhomirim ...Inset I 81
Inland, sea ...B3 8
Inn, river ...B3, C2 39
Inner Hebrides, islands ...A2 30
Inner Mongolia ...E1 10
Innisfail ...D5 94
Innisfil ...F3 102
Innsbruck ...B3 39
Inta ...C5 44
Interlaken ...B3 35
International Falls, Minn. ...D1 126
Inthanon, mt. ...B2 12
Inukjuak ...A2 101
Inuvik ...B3 99
Inuvik, region ...B3 105
Invercargill ...A4 15
Invermay ...G9 104
Inverness ...B1 30
Inverness ...F1 100
Inwood ...C4 96
Inyangani, mt. ...C2 69
Ioánnina ...B2 51
Ionian, islands ...B2 51
Ionian, sea ...B3 51
Iori, river ...C4 45
Iowa ...D1 126
Ipel', river ...B2 42
Ipiíba ...Inset I 81
Ipoh ...A2 13

Key Page

Ipoly, river ...B1 43
Ipswich ...D3 30
Iqaluit, capital, Nunavut ...P4 99
Iquique ...C1 76
Iquitos ...C1 77
Iracoubo ...B1 80
Iráklion ...C4 51
Iran ...22
Iranshahr ...E4 22
Irapuato ...D3 84
Iraq ...24
Irazú, volcano ...C3 86
Irbe, strait ...A3 46
Irbid ...A1 26
Irbil ...B1 24
Ireland ...31
Iri ...B5 9
Irian Jaya, region ...E2 13
Iringa ...C2 68
Iriomote, island ...Inset II 8
Iriona ...C2 86
Irish, sea ...B3 30
Irkutsk ...D7 44
Iron Bridge ...B1 102
Iron Gate Reservoir ...B3 43
Iroquois Falls ...D3 101
Irrawaddy, river ...B2 12
Irtysh, river ...D1 23
Irtysh, river ...D5 44
Isabela ...A1 90
Isabela, island ...Inset 79
Isabela, mts. ...B2 87
Ísafjördhur ...A1 52
Isangel ...C4 18
Isar, river ...C4 40
Ischia, island ...C2 38
Ise ...C3 8
Ise, bay ...C3 8
Isère, river ...D4 34
Isernia ...C2 38
Iseyin ...B4 65
Isherton ...B4 80
Ishigaki, island ...Inset II 8
Ishikari, river ...Inset I 8
Ishim ...D5 44
Ishim, river ...C1 23
Ishinomaki ...D2 8
Ishinomaki, bay ...D2 8
Ishizuchi, mt. ...B3 8
Isiro ...C1 67
İskenderun ...D3 27
Iskŭr, river ...C2 50
Islamabad, capital ...D3 21
Island Lake ...D2 96
Island, lake ...D2 96
Islay, island ...A2 30
Isle aux Morts ...B5 98
Islington ...J6 102
Ismailiyah, al- ...B1 56
Isoka ...C2 67
Isparta ...B3 27
Israel ...26
İstanbul ...B2 27
Istria, peninsula ...A2 48
Italy ...38
İzmir ...A2 27
İznit ...D3 81
Itabuna ...E3 81
Itaipu ...Inset I 81
Itaipú, reservoir ...D4 81
Itajaí ...D4 81
Itanagar ...F3 20
Itapecerica da Serra ...Inset II 81
Itapeva ...Inset II 81
Itaquaquecetuba ...Inset II 81
Iténez, river ...B2 77
Itháki, island ...B2 51
Ittoqqortoormiit
  (Scoresbysund) ...D2 106
Ituna ...G9 104
Ivalo ...C1 53
Ivano-Frankivsk ...A2 47
Ivanovo ...D3 44
Ivindo, river ...B1 66
Ivujivik ...A1 101
Iwaki ...D2 8
Iwakuni ...B3 8
Iwo ...C4 65
Iwo Jima, island ...Inset III 8
Ixelles ...C2 33
Ixtapa ...D4 84
Ixtapaluca ...Inset 84
Izabal, lake ...E4 85
Izhevsk ...D4 44
Izki ...C1 25
Izmail ...B3 47
Iztacalco ...Inset 84
Iztapalapa ...Inset 84
Izu, islands ...C3 8
Izu, peninsula ...C3 8
Izuhara ...A3 8

J

Jabal al-Akhdar, al-, mts. ...C1 25
Jabal al-Uwaynat, mt. ...D3 59
Jabal an-Nabi Shuayb, mt. ...A1 25
Jabal an-Nusayriyah, mts. ...A2 27
Jabal Katrinah, mt. ...B2 56
Jabal Ramm, mt. ...A3 26
Jabal Tuwayq, mts. ...B2 24
Jabal Zuqar, island ...A2 25
Jabalpur ...C4 20
Jaboatão ...E2 81
Jacare-Acanga ...C2 81
Jackhead ...C3 96
Jackson's Arm ...C4 98
Jackson, capital, Miss. ...D2 126
Jackson, port ...Inset IV 14
Jackson, Wyo. ...B1 126
Jacksonville, Fla. ...E2 126
Jacmel ...C2 89
Jacques-Cartier, river ...E4 103
Jacquet River ...C1 97
Jadabpur ...Inset II 20
Jadida, el- ...B1 57
Jaén ...D4 37
Jaffna ...B2 19

	Key	Page
Jafr, al-	B2	26
Jagdalpur	D5	20
Jaghbub, al-	D2	56
Jahrah, al-	B2	24
Jamaica		**88**
Jaipur	C3	20
Jajpurhat	B3	21
Jajce	B1	48
Jakarta, *capital*	B2	13
Jakobstad	B3	53
Jakupica, *mts.*	B2	48
Jalal-Abad	A3	23
Jalalabad	C2	22
Jalapa Enríquez, *state capital*	E4	84
Jalingo	F3	65
Jalisco	D4	84
Jalu	D2	56
Jaluit, *island*	B2	16
Jamaame	A3	60
Jamalpur	C4	21
Jambi	B2	13
James, *bay*	J3	92
Jammu	B2	20
Jamnagar	B4	20
Jampur	Inset II	20
Jämsä	C2	53
Jamshedpur	E4	20
Jamuna, *river*	C4	21
Jan Lake	H6	104
Jan Mayen, *island*		5
Janai	Inset II	20
Janakpur	C3	19
Janeville	D1	97
Jangy-Bazar	B2	23
Japan		**8**
Japan, *sea*	B2	8
Japanese Alps, *mts.*	C3	8
Japeri	Inset I	81
Japurá, *river*	B2	81
Jarama, *river*	Inset II	37
Jarash	A1	26
Jari, *river*	C1	81
Jarvie	D4	94
Jarvis	E5	102
Jask	D4	22
Jastrebac, *mts.*	B3	49
Jászberény	B2	43
Java, *island*	C2	13
Java, *sea*	C2	13
Javari, *river*	A2	81
Jawf, al-	A1	24
Jawf, al-	D3	56
Jawhar	B3	60
Jaya, *mt.*	E2	13
Jayapura	F2	13
Jayuya	B2	90
Jazirah, al-, *region*	B1	27
Jazzin	A2	26
Jebba	C3	65
Jebel Toubkal, *mt.*	C2	57
Jeddah	A2	24
Jeddore, *lake*	D5	98
Jefferson City, *capital, Mo.*	D2	126
Jejuí-Guazú, *river*	D4	75
Jejur	Inset II	20
Jekabpils	C2	46
Jelenia Góra	B3	41
Jelgava	B2	46
Jemseg	C3	97
Jena	B3	40
Jengish Chokusu, *mt.*	G1	23
Jenner	E6	94
Jenpeg	B2	96
Jérémie	A2	89
Jerez de la Frontera	C4	37
Jersey, *island*	Inset II	30
Jerudong	B2	13
Jerusalem, *capital*	B2	26
Jesenice	B2	48
Jessore	C5	21
Jésus, *island*	J5	103
Jetait	A1	96
Jhang Sadar	D3	21
Jhansi	C3	20
Jhelum	D3	21
Jhelum, *river*	D3	21
Ji'an	E3	10
Jiamusi	G1	10
Jiangsu	E2	10
Jiangxi	E3	10
Jiddah, *island*	A1	25
Jihlava	B3	42
Jilib	A3	60
Jilin	F1	10
Jilin	F1	10
Jima	B3	60
Jimaní	A2	89
Jiménez	D2	84
Jinan	E2	10
Jingdezhen	E3	10
Jining	E2	10
Jinja	C3	61
Jinotega	B2	87
Jinotepe	A3	87
Jinsha (Yangtze), *river*	C2	10
Jinzhou	F1	10
Jipijapa	A3	79
Jiparaná, *river*	B3	81
Jirgatol	B3	23
Jiu, *river*	B3	43
Jiujiang	E3	10
Jixi	G1	10
Jizan	B2	24
Jizzakh	C2	23
João Pessoa	E2	81
Jobos	C3	90
Jodhpur	B3	20
Joe Batt's Arm	D4	98
Joensuu	C2	53
Joetsu	C2	8
Joggins	C2	100
Johannesburg	C2	71
John D'or Prairie	B3	94
Johnsons Crossing	C5	105
Johor Baharu	B2	13
Johor, *strait*	B2	13
Joinville	D4	81
Joinville, *island*	C12	107

	Key	Page
Joka	Inset II	20
Joliet, Ill.	E1	126
Joliette	C5	103
Jolo	B5	12
Jolo, *island*	B5	12
Jonava	C2	46
Jones, *sound*	L1	99
Jonesboro, Ark.	D2	126
Jong, *river*	A2	63
Jönköping	B3	53
Jonquière	E3	103
Joplin, Mo.	D2	126
Jordan		**26**
Jordan, *river*	A2	26
Jos	E3	65
Jos, *plateau*	E2	65
Jotunheimen, *mts.*	B3	52
Joussard	B4	94
Juan de Fuca, *strait*	L7	95
Juana Díaz	B2	90
Juàzeiro	D2	81
Juàzeiro do Norte	E2	81
Juba	C4	59
Juba, *river*	A3	60
Jubail	A1	26
Jubayl	C1	24
Jubayl, al-	C1	24
Jubilee, *lake*	D5	98
Júcar, *river*	F3	37
Juchitán de Zaragoza	F4	84
Judique	F2	100
Juigalpa	B2	87
Juiz de Fora	D4	81
Juliaca	C4	77
Julian Alps, *mts.*	A2	48
Juliana Top, *mt.*	A3	80
Jullundur	C2	20
Jumayliyah, al-	C2	25
Jumla	B2	19
Junagadh	B4	20
Juncos	D2	90
Jundiai	D4	81
Juneau, *capital, Alaska*	Inset I	126
Jungfrau, *mt.*	B2	35
Juniper	B2	97
Juniyah	A2	26
Juozapines, *mt.*	C2	46
Jura, *island*	B2	30
Jura, *mts.*	A2	35
Jura, *river*	A2	46
Jurbarkas	B2	46
Jurmala	A1	46
Jurong	A1	13
Juruá, *river*	B2	81
Juruena, *river*	C3	81
Jutiapa	D5	85
Juticalpa	B2	86
Jutland, *peninsula*	B3	32
Juventud, *island*	B2	88
Južna, *river*	B3	49
Jvari	B3	45
Jwaneng	B3	69
Jyväskylä	C2	53

K

	Key	Page
K2 (Godwin Austen), *mt.*	A2	10
Ka Dake	B2	71
Ka, *river*	C2	65
Kabala	B1	63
Kabale	A4	61
Kabalo	C2	67
Kabardino-Balkariya, *republic*	E4	44
Kabelebo, *river*	A2	80
Kabompo, *river*	A2	67
Kabul, *capital*	B2	22
Kabul, *river*	B2	22
Kabwe	B2	67
Kachovka	C3	47
Kadavu, *island*	B3	17
Kadei, *river*	A3	66
Kadoma	D2	69
Kaduna	D2	65
Kaduna, *river*	D2	65
Kaduqli	B3	59
Kaédi	B3	58
Kaélé	B1	65
Kaeo	B2	15
Kaesŏng	B4	9
Kafan	D3	45
Kaffrine	B2	62
Kafr ad-Dawwar	B1	56
Kafu, *river*	B3	61
Kafue	B3	67
Kafue, *river*	B3	67
Kaga Bandoro	A2	66
Kagawong	C2	102
Kagera, *river*	B4, C1, C2	61
Kagitumba	C1	61
Kagoshima	A4	8
Kahayan, *river*	C2	13
Kahemba	B2	67
Kahnawake	H6	103
Kahntah	M2	95
Kahoolawe *island, Hawaii*	Inset II	126
Kai, *islands*	E2	13
Kaieteur, *falls*	B3	80
Kaifeng	E2	10
Kaikoura	B3	15
Kailahun	C3	62
Kailahun	B1	63
Kainji, *lake*	C2	65
Kaiserslautern	A4	40
Kaitaia	B1	15
Kajaani	C2	53
Kakamega	C3	61
Kakata	A2	63
Kakeroma, *island*	Inset II	8
Kakhovka, *reservoir*	C3	47
Kakinada	D5	20
Kaladar	H3	102
Kalahari, *desert*	A2	69
Kalámai	B3	51
Kalamáki	Inset	51
Kälbäcär	B2	45
Kalemie	C2	67

	Key	Page
Kalgoorlie-Boulder, W.A.	B3	14
Kali	C1	62
Kali, *river*	B2	19
Kaliningrad	D3	44
Kalimantan, *region*	C2	13
Kalixälven, *river*	D1	53
Kallithéa	Inset	51
Kalmar	C3	53
Kalmykiya, *republic*	E4	44
Kalpeni, *island*	B7	20
Kalu, *river*	B5	19
Kalundborg	C3	32
Kalutara	A5	19
Kalwa	Inset I	20
Kamakwie	A1	63
Kaman	Inset I	20
Kaman, *island*	A1	20
Kamaran, *island*	A1	25
Kamarhati	Inset II	20
Kambia	A1	63
Kamchatka, *peninsula*	D10	44
Kamchiya, *river*	F2	50
Kamensk-Uralsky	D5	44
Kamet, *mt.*	C2	20
Kamina	C3	67
Kaminak, *lake*	J4	99
Kamloops	M6	95
Kampala, *capital*	C3	61
Kampong Cham	D4	11
Kampong Chhnang	C3	11
Kampong Saom	B5	11
Kampong Thum	C3	11
Kampot	C5	11
Kamsack	J9	104
Kamsar	A2	62
Kamui, *cape*	Inset I	8
Kananga	B2	67
Kanazawa	C2	8
Kanchenjunga, *mt.*	D2	19
Kanchipuram	C6	20
Kanchrapara	Inset II	20
Kandi	B2	64
Kandy	B4	19
Kane, *basin*	P1	99
Kangaroo, *island*	C3	14
Kangen, *river*	C3	59
Kanggye	B2	9
Kanghwa, *bay*	A4	9
Kangiqsualujjuaq	C2	101
Kangiqsujuaq	B1	101
Kangirsuk	B1	101
Kangnŭng	C4	9
Kangshan	B2	9
Kankan	D2	62
Kano	E1	65
Kanpur	D3	20
Kansaripara	Inset II	20
Kansas	D2	126
Kansas City, Kans.	D2	126
Kansas City, Mo.	D2	126
Kansay	A1	23
Kansk	D6	44
Kanté	B2	64
Kanuku, *mts.*	B4	80
Kanye	B3	69
Kaohsiung	B2	9
Kaoko Veld, *mts.*	A1	70
Kaolack	A2	62
Kaoma	A2	67
Kaop'ing, *river*	B2	9
Kapfenberg	D3	39
Kapingamarangi, *atoll*	C2	15
Kapiskau, *river*	D2	101
Kaposvár	A2	43
Kapuskasing	D3	101
Kara, *sea*	B5	44
Kara-Kum, *canal*	D3	22
Kara-Kum, *desert*	C2	22
Kara-Say	F2	23
Karabakh, *canal*	B2	45
Karachayevo-Cherkesiya, *republic*	E4	44
Karachi	C5	21
Karaj	C2	22
Karak, al-	A2	26
Karakol	F1	23
Karakoram, *range*	C1	20
Karaman	C3	27
Karasburg	C4	70
Karawanken, *range*	D4	39
Karbala	B2	24
Karcag	C2	43
Kardiva, *channel*	A2	19
Kärdla	B1	46
Kareliya, *republic*	C3	44
Kariba	B1	69
Kariba, *lake*	A1	69
Karibib	B2	70
Karisimbi, *mt.*	B1	61
Karkar, *island*	A2	15
Karkinit, *bay*	C3	47
Karlovac	B2	48
Karlovy Vary	A2	42
Karlskrona	C3	53
Karlsruhe	B4	40
Karlstad	B3	53
Karnali, *river*	B2	19
Karnaphuli, *reservoir*	F6	21
Karnaphuli, *river*	E6	21
Karonga	B1	68
Karpas, *peninsula*	C1	27
Kárpathos, *island*	C4	51
Kars	E2	27
Kartala, *mt.*	A1	67
Kartung	A3	62
Karun, *river*	B3	22
Karuzi	C2	61
Karviná	D3	42
Kasai, *river*	C2	67
Kasama	B1	69
Kasane	B1	69
Kasba, *lake*	H4	99
Kashan	C2	22
Kashi	A2	10
Kashiwa	Inset II	8
Kasinathpur	Inset II	20
Kaslo	O6	95
Kassala	D2	59
Kassel	B3	40

	Key	Page
Kasserine	B2	57
Kastamonu	C2	27
Kastoria	B1	51
Kastrup	D3	32
Kasugai	C3	8
Kasungu	B2	68
Kasur	E3	21
Katagum, *river*	E2	65
Katanga, *plateau*	B3	67
Katerini	B1	51
Kate's Needle, *mt.*	F2	95
Katherine, N.T.	C1	14
Kathgodam	C3	20
Kathiawar, *peninsula*	B4	20
Kathmandu, *capital*	C2	19
Katowice	D3	41
Katrine, *lake*	B2	30
Katsina	D1	65
Kattegat, *strait*	C2	32
Kau-Ur	C2	62
Kauai Island, Hawaii	Inset II	126
Kaufbeuren	B5	40
Kaukau Veld, *region*	C2	70
Kaunas	B2	46
Kaura-Namoda	D1	65
Kavadarci	B3	49
Kavajë	A2	49
Kavála	C1	51
Kavaratti, *island*	B6	20
Kavieng	B2	15
Kavir-e Namak, *desert*	D3	22
Kaw	B1	80
Kawagoe	C3	8
Kawaguchi	C3	8
Kawasaki	C3	8
Kawhia	B2	15
Kawthaung	C4	12
Kayangel, *islands*	C1	17
Kayes	A3	58
Kayser, *mts.*	A3	80
Kayseri	C2	27
Kazakh Upland, *region*	C2	23
Kazakhstan		**23**
Kazan	D4	44
Kazanlŭk	D3	50
Kazincbarcika	C1	43
Kearney	F2	102
Kearney, Nebr.	D1	126
Keban, *reservoir*	D2	27
Kebili	B3	57
Kebir, *river*	B1	26
Kebnekaise, *mt.*	C1	53
Kechika, *river*	J2	95
Kecskemét	B2	43
Kédainiai	B2	46
Kedgwick	B1	97
Kediri	C2	13
Kédougou	C3	62
Keele	C4	99
Keeley, *lake*	B6	104
Keetmanshoop	C4	70
Keewatin, *region*	J4	99
Kef, el-	B1	57
Kefallinía, *island*	B2	51
Keflavík	A3	52
Keg River	B2	94
Keila	C1	46
Kékes, *mt.*	C2	43
Kelang	A2	13
Kelani, *river*	B4	19
Keliher	G9	104
Kelowna	N6	95
Kelsey	C1	96
Keluang	B2	13
Kelvington	G8	104
Kemano	J4	95
Kemerovo	D6	44
Kemi	B1	53
Kemijärvi	C1	53
Kemijoki, *river*	C1	53
Kemnay	A4	96
Kempenland, *region*	D1	33
Kemps Bay	B3	89
Kempt, *lake*	B4	103
Kempten	B5	40
Kemptville	K2	102
Kenaston	D9	104
Kendal	C2	30
Kendari	D2	13
Kenema	B2	63
Keng Tung	C2	12
Kenilworth	C3	30
Kenitra	C1	57
Kennetcook	D2	100
Keno	B4	105
Kenora	B3	101
Kensington	A4	96
Kenton	A4	96
Kentucky	E2	126
Kentville	C2	100
Kenya, *mt.*	C1	61
Kenya		**61**
Kenya, *mt.*	D4	61
Keokradong, *mt.*	F7	21
Kerang Nyatan	B3	13
Keratsinion	Inset	51
Kerch	D3	47
Kerch, *strait*	D3	47
Kerema	B2	15
Keremeos	N6	95
Keren	B2	60
Kerewan	B2	62
Kerguelen, *islands*		5
Kericho	C4	61
Kerinci, *mt.*	B2	13
Kerkennah, *islands*	C2	57
Kerki	D3	22
Kérkira	A2	51
Kérkira, *island*	A2	51
Kerman	D3	22
Kerman, *region*	D4	22
Kérouané	D3	62
Kerrobert	A9	104
Kerulen, *river*	D2	11
Keszthely	A2	43
Keta	C4	64
Ketchikan, Alaska	Inset I	126
Key Lake Mine	E3	104
Key West, Fla.	E3	126

	Key	Page
Keyano	B3	101
Khabarovsk	E8	44
Khabur, *river*	B1	27
Khakasiya, *republic*	D6	44
Khalándrion	Inset	51
Khalkhidhikí, *peninsula*	B1	51
Khalkís	B2	51
Khaluf	C2	25
Khambhât, *gulf*	B4	20
Khamis Mushayt	B2	24
Khan-Tengri, *mt.*	F2	23
Khanaqin	C2	24
Khania	B4	51
Khanka, *lake*	G1	10
Khanty-Mansiya, *autonomous okrug*	C5	44
Khanty-Mansiysk	C5	44
Kharagpur	E4	20
Kharg, *island*	C4	22
Kharijah, al-	B2	56
Kharijah, *oasis*	B2	56
Kharj, al-	B1	24
Kharkiv	D1	47
Khartoum North	C2	59
Khartoum, *capital*	C2	59
Khashm al-Qirbah	C2	59
Khashuri	B4	45
Khasi, *hills*	F3	20
Khaskovo	D4	50
Khatanga	B7	44
Khawr, al-	C2	25
Kherson	C2	47
Khíos, *island*	C2	51
Khiran, al-	C2	24
Khmelnytskyy	B2	47
Khojak, *pass*	C2	22
Khon Kaen	C2	12
Khor Angar	C1	60
Khorasan, *region*	D2	22
Khorat, *plateau*	C2	12
Khorixas	B2	70
Khorramabad	B2	22
Khorramshahr	B3	22
Khorugh	C2	23
Khouribga	C1	57
Khowst	C2	22
Khudzhand	A1	23
Khujayli	A2	23
Khulna	C6	21
Khums, al-	B1	56
Khuriya Muriya, *islands*	C3	25
Khust	A2	47
Khuzestan, *region*	A2	22
Khvoy	A2	22
Khyber, *pass*	C2	22
Kibungo	C2	61
Kibuye	A2	61
Kičevo	A2	48
Kidal	D2	58
Kidderminster	C3	30
Kiel	B1	40
Kiel, *bay*	B1	40
Kielce	E3	41
Kiev, *capital*	C1	47
Kiev, *reservoir*	C1	47
Kiffa	C3	58
Kifisiá	Inset	51
Kifissós, *river*	B2	51
Kigali, *capital*	B1	61
Kigoma	A1	68
Kii, *channel*	B3	8
Kii, *peninsula*	B3	8
Kikinda	B2	48
Kikkertavak, *island*	B2	98
Kikwit	B2	67
Kilchu	C2	9
Kildare	C2	31
Kilimanjaro, *mt.*	C1	68
Kilinochchi	C2	19
Kilkee	B2	31
Kilkenny	C2	31
Killala, *bay*	B1	31
Killaloe	H2	102
Killarney	B2	31
Killarney	B4	96
Killarney	D1	102
Killarney Lake	E5	94
Killdeer	D11	104
Killeen, Tex.	D2	126
Kilmarnock	B2	30
Kilombero, *river*	C2	68
Kilwa Kivinje	C2	68
Kimbe	B2	15
Kimberley	O6	95
Kimberley	B2	71
Kimberley	E3	102
Kimberley, *plateau*	B1	14
Kimch'aek	C2	9
Kimch'ŏn	C4	9
Kinabalu, *mt.*	D1	13
Kinabatangan, *river*	D2	13
Kinbasket, *lake*	N5	95
Kinbasket, *lake*	O5	95
Kincaid	C11	104
Kincardine	D3	102
Kindersley	A9	104
Kindia	B2	62
Kindu	C2	67
King Leopold, *range*	B1	14
King William, *island*	J3	99
King's Cove	E5	98
King's Lynn	D3	30
King's Point	D4	98
Kingcome Inlet	J6	95
Kingman, Ariz.	C3	126
Kingston	C3	100
Kingston	J3	102
Kingston upon Hull	C3	30
Kingston upon Thames	Inset III	30
Kingston, *capital*	C3	88
Kingstown, *capital*	B2	91
Kingsville	F2	100
Kinistino	E8	104
Kinkala	B2	66
Kinkora	B2	100
Kinloss	D3	102

	Key	Page
Kinmount	G3	102
Kinnairds, *cape*	C1	30
Kinosota	B4	96
Kinsarvik	B3	52
Kinsella	E5	94
Kinshasa, *capital*	A2	67
Kinyeti, *mt.*	C4	59
Kioa, *island*	C2	17
Kiosk	G1	102
Kipengere, *range*	B2	68
Kipling	H10	104
Kirakira	B2	16
Kirensk	D7	44
Kiribati		**17**
Kırıkkale	C2	27
Kiritimati (Christmas), *island*	D1	17
Kirkcaldy	B2	30
Kirkenes	F2	52
Kirkfield	G3	102
Kirkland Lake	D3	101
Kirkpatrick, *mt.*	A5	107
Kirkuk	B1	24
Kirkwall	Inset	30
Kirov	D4	44
Kirovakan	B2	45
Kirovograd	C2	47
Kirşehir	C2	27
Kirthar, *range*	C4	21
Kiruna	D1	53
Kisangani	C1	67
Kishi	B3	65
Kiskitto, *lake*	B2	96
Kiskörei-víztároló, *lake*	C2	43
Kiskunhalas	B2	43
Kismayo	A4	60
Kissidougou	C3	62
Kississing, *lake*	A1	96
Kisumu	C4	61
Kita	B2	58
Kita, *island*	Inset III	8
Kitakami, *river*	D2	8
Kitakyushu	A3	8
Kitale	C3	61
Kitami	Inset I	8
Kitami, *mts.*	Inset I	8
Kitchener	E4	102
Kitgum	C2	61
Kíthira, *island*	B3	51
Kitikmeot, *region*	G3	99
Kitimat	H4	95
Kitwanga	H3	95
Kitwe	B2	67
Kivi, *lake*	C2	53
Kivu, *lake*	B1	61
Kızıl Irmak, *river*	C2	27
Kjølen, *mts.*	C1	53
Kladno	A2	42
Klagenfurt	D4	39
Klaipėda	A2	46
Klamath Falls, Oreg.	A1	126
Klarälven, *river*	B2	53
Klatovy	A3	42
Kleinburg	J5	102
Klemtu	H5	95
Kleve	A3	40
Kloulklubed	B3	17
Kluane, *lake*	B5	105
Knee, *lake*	D1	96
Knight, *inlet*	K6	95
Knockboy, *mt.*	B3	31
Knokke	B1	33
Knoxville, Tenn.	E2	126
Ko Chang, *island*	C3	12
Ko Kut, *island*	C4	12
Ko Phangan, *island*	B4	12
Ko Samui, *island*	B4	12
Ko Tarutao, *island*	B5	12
Kobe	B3	8
Koblenz	A3	40
Kobuleti	A4	45
Kočani	C2	48
Kočevje	B3	48
Kochi	B3	8
Kodiak, Alaska	Inset I	126
Kofarnihon, *river*	A2	23
Köflach	D3	39
Koforidua	B3	64
Kofu	C3	8
Køge	D3	32
Kohima	F3	20
Kohtla-Järve	D1	46
Koindu	B1	63
Koje-do, *island*	C5	9
Kokkina	A1	27
Kokkola	B2	53
Kokshetau	C1	23
Kola	A4	96
Kola, *peninsula*	C3	44
Kolari	B1	53
Kolda	B3	62
Kolding	B3	32
Kolhapur	B5	20
Kolín	B2	42
Kolkata (Calcutta)	E4, Inset II	20
Kołobrzeg	B1	41
Kolpashevo	D6	44
Kolshet	Inset I	20
Kolumadulu, *atoll*	A3	19
Kolwezi	C3	67
Kolyma, *range*	C10	44
Kolyma, *river*	C9	44
Komadugu Gana, *river*	F2	65
Komadugu Yobe, *river*	F1	65
Komárno	B2	42
Komárom	B2	43
Komati, *river*	B2	71
Komatsu	C2	8
Komi, *republic*	C4	44
Komi-Permyat, *autonomous okrug*	D4	44
Komoé, *river*	E3	63
Komotiní	C1	51
Komsomolsk-na-Amure	D8	44
Konar, *river*	D2	21
Konduz	B1	22
Konduz, *river*	B1	22
Koné	C2	18
Kong, *river*	D4	11

Name	Key	Page
Konibodom	B1	23
Konin	D2	41
Konnagar	Inset II	20
Konotop	C1	47
Kontagora	C2	65
Kontum	B3	11
Konya	C3	27
Kootenay, lake	O6	95
Kootenay, river	P6	95
Kopaonik, mts.	B3	49
Kópavogur	A2	52
Koper	A3	48
Kopet, mts.	B2, D2	22
Koprivnica	C2	48
Korab, mt.	B2	49
Korab, mt.	A2	48
Korçë	B3	49
Korčula, island	C4	48
Korea, bay	A3	9
Korea, strait	C5	9
Korhogo	D2	63
Koriyama	D2	8
Korla	B1	10
Koro Toro	B4	59
Koro, island	B2	17
Koro, sea	B2	17
Koror, capital	B3	17
Koror, island	C3	17
Korosten	B1	47
Kortrijk	B2	33
Koryak, range	C10	44
Koryakiya, autonomous okrug	C10	44
Kosŏng	C3	9
Kos, island	C3	51
Kosciusko, mt.	D3	14
Koshigaya	C3	8
Koshiki, islands	A4	8
Košice	C2	42
Kosovo, province	B3	49
Kosrae	D2	15
Kosrae, island	D2	15
Kossol, passage	C2	17
Kossol, reef	C2	17
Kossu, lake	D3	63
Koszalin	C1	41
Kota	C3	20
Kota Baharu	B1	13
Kota Kinabalu	D2	13
Kotcho, lake	M1	95
Kotka	C2	53
Kotlas	C4	44
Kotor, gulf	A3	49
Kotovsk	B2	47
Kotto, river	B2	66
Kouchibouguac	D2	97
Koudougou	C2	64
Koula-Moutou	B2	66
Koulikoro	B3	58
Koulountou, river	C3	62
Koumac	C2	18
Koungheul	B2	62
Kourou	B1	80
Kouroussa	D2	62
Kousséri	B1	65
Koutiala	B3	58
Kouto	C2	63
Kouvola	C2	53
Kovel	A1	47
Kowŏn	B3	9
Kowloon	Inset	10
Kowt-e Ashrow	B2	22
Kozáni	B1	51
Kozhikode	C6	20
Kozloduy	B2	50
Kozu, island	C3	8
Kožuf, mts.	C2	48
Kpalimé	B3	64
Kpandu	C3	64
Kpémé	B3	64
Kra, isthmus	B4	12
Kracheh	E3	11
Kragujevac	B2	49
Krakatau, island	B2	13
Kraków	D3	41
Kraljevo	B3	49
Kramatorsk	D2	47
Kranj	A2	48
Kranji	B1	13
Krasnodar	E3	44
Krasnoyarsk	D6	44
Krefeld	A3	40
Kremenchug	C2	47
Kretinga	A2	46
Kribi	A3	65
Krishna, river	C5	20
Kristiansand	B4	52
Kristianstad	B3	53
Kristiansund	B3	52
Kristinehamn	B3	53
Krk, island	B3	48
Krka, river	B3	48
Krong Kaoh Kong	A4	11
Kroonstad	C2	71
Krosnow	E4	41
Krško	C3	48
Krugersdorp	C2	71
Kruję	A2	49
Kruševac	B3	49
Kruševo	B2	48
Krychaw	E3	47
Kryvyi Rih	C2	47
Kuala Abang	B2	13
Kuala Belait	A2	13
Kuala Lumpur, capital	A2	13
Kuala Terengganu	B2	13
Kuantan	B2	13
Kuching	C3	13
Kuchino, island	A4	8
Kudymkar	D4	44
Kufstein	B3	99
Kugluktuk	C4	96
Kuito	C4	70
Kukës	B1	49
Kul, river	D4	22
Kula Kangri, mt.	B1	19
Kuldiga	A2	46
Kulmbach	B3	40
Kulob	A2	23
Kulpawn, river	B1	64
Kum, river	B4	9
Kumamoto	A3	8
Kumanovo	B1	48
Kumasi	B3	64
Kume, island	Inset II	8
Kumo	F2	65
Kunda	D1	46
Kunene, river	A1	70
Kunlun, mts.	B2	10
Kunming	D3	10
Kunsan	B5	9
Kuntaur	D2	62
Kuopio	C2	53
Kupa, river	B3	48
Kupang	D3	13
Kür, river	A2, C2	45
Kür-Aras, lowland	B2	45
Kura, river	E2	27
Kurashiki	B3	8
Kuraymah	C1	59
Kürdzhali	D4	50
Kure	B3	8
Kuressaare	B2	46
Kurgan	D5	44
Kuril, islands	E9	44
Kurinwás, river	B2	87
Kurla	Inset I	20
Kursk	D3	44
Kuru, river	C2	19
Kuruman	B2	71
Kurume	A3	8
Kurunegala	B4	19
Kushiro	Inset I	8
Kushtia	C5	21
Kusŏng	A3	9
Kusti	C2	59
Kut, al-	C2	24
Kütahya	B2	27
Kutaisi	B3	45
Kutch, gulf	A4	20
Kutno	D2	41
Kuujjuaq	C2	101
Kuujjuarapik	A2	101
Kuwait		24
Kuwait, bay	B2	24
Kuwait, capital	B2	24
Kwa, river	B2	67
Kwahu, plateau	B3	64
Kwajalein, island	B2	16
Kwangju	B5	9
Kwango, river	B2	67
Kwekwe	B2	69
Kyaukpyu	B2	12
Kyle	B10	104
Kyle of Lochalsh	B1	30
Kyoga, lake	C3	61
Kyŏngju	C5	9
Kyoto	B3	8
Kyrenia	B1	27
Kyrgyzstan		23
Kyrenia, range	B1	27
Kyushu, island	A3	8
Kyustendil	A3	50
Kyzyl	D6	44
Kyzyl-Kyya	C2	23
Kyzyl-Suu, river	C3	23
Kyzylkum, desert	B2	23

L

Name	Key	Page
La Asunción	D1	79
La Baie	F3	103
La Broquerie	C4	96
La Ceiba	B2	86
La Chaux-de-Fonds	A1	35
La Coma, river	B1	36
La Conception	B5	103
La Condamine	B1	35
La Coruña	B1	37
La Crete	B2	94
La Croix Maingot	A2	91
La Crosse, Wis.	D1	126
La Cruz	A1	86
La Digue, island	C1	70
La Doré	D3	103
La Esperanza	A2	86
La Goulette	C1	57
La Grande, river	B3	101
La Guadeloupe	F6	103
La Guaira Maiquetía	C1	79
La Have	C3	100
La Laguna	Inset I	37
La Libertad	A4	79
La Libertad	C3	85
La Loche	A4	104
La Louvière	C2	33
La Malbaie	F4	103
La Martre	K2	103
La Martre, lake	E4	99
La Montaña, region	C2	77
La Oroya	B3	77
La Palma	C2	87
La Palma, island	Inset I	37
La Paz	B2	86
La Paz, capital	A3	77
La Paz, state capital	B3	84
La Pérouse	B1	96
La Pérouse, strait	Inset I	8
La Plaine	B3	90
La Plata	D4	74
La Plata, river	C2	90
La Plonge, lake	C5	104
La Pocatière	F4	103
La Prairie	J6	103
La Rioja	B2	74
La Rioja	E1	37
La Rochelle	B3	34
La Roda	D2	89
La Romana	D2	89
La Ronge	E5	104
La Ronge, lake	E6	104
La Rosita	B2	87
La Salle	J6	103
La Scie	D4	98
La Serena	B3	76
La Spezia	B1	38
La Tortuga, island	C1	79
La Tuque	D4	103
La Unión	B7	76
La Unión	C2	86
La Vega	B1	89
La Virtud	A2	86
La-Roche-sur-Yon	B3	34
Labasa	B2	17
Labé	B2	62
Labe (Elbe), river	B2	42
Labelle	C3	100
Laberge, lake	B5	105
Labi	A3	13
Laborec, river	C2	42
Laborie	B3	91
Labrador City	D3	98
Labrieville	G2	103
Labu	C2	13
Labuan, island	D2	13
Laç	A2	49
Lac du Bonnet	C4	96
Lac La Biche	E4	94
Lac La Hache	M5	95
Lac Mégantic	F6	103
Lac-aux-Sables	D5	103
Lac-Bouchette	D3	103
Lac-des-Aigles	H4	103
Lac-des-Îles	A5	103
Lac-Édouard	D4	103
Lac-Etchemin	F5	103
Lac-Nominingue	A5	103
Lac-Saguay	A5	103
Laccadive, islands	B6	20
Lachenaie	J5	103
Lachine	H6	103
Lachute	B6	103
Lacombe	D5	94
Ladhiqiyah, al- (Latakia)	A2	27
Ladoga, lake	C3	44
Ladysmith	C2	71
Ladywood	C4	96
Lae	A2	15
Lae, island	B2	16
Laem, mt.	B3	12
Læsø, island	C1	32
Lafayette, La.	D2	126
Lafia	E3	65
Lafleche	D11	104
Lafond	E4	94
Laghouat	B1	57
Lagodekhi	D4	45
Lagos	B4	65
Lagos	A4	36
Laguna de Bay, lake	B3	12
Lahave, river	C3	100
Lahij	A2	25
Lahn, river	B3	40
Lahore	E3	21
Lahti	C2	53
Laï	B5	59
Lairg	B1	30
Lajas	A2	90
Lajes	C4	81
Lakatoro	B3	18
Lake Alma	F11	104
Lake Charlotte	E3	100
Lake Edward	B2	97
Lake Harbour	O4	99
Lake Lenore	F8	104
Lake St. Peter	G2	102
Lake, district	B2	30
Lakeba, island	C3	17
Lakeba, passage	C3	17
Lakefield	G3	102
Lakelse Lake	H4	95
Lakhpat	A4	20
Laki, volcano	B2	52
Lakselv	F1	52
Lalitpur	C2	19
Lamaline	D5	98
Lamap	B3	18
Lambaréné	A2	66
Lambton	E6	103
Lamèque	E1	97
Lamèque, island	E1	97
Lami	B3	17
Lamía	B2	51
Lammermuir, hills	C2	30
Lamon, bay	B3	12
Lampa	Inset	77
Lampang	B2	12
Lampeter	B3	30
Lampman	H11	104
Lamu	F5	61
Lan, river	A1	11
Lanai island, Hawaii	Inset II	126
Lanark	J2	102
Lancaster	C2	30
Lancaster	L2	102
L'Ancienne-Lorette	K5	103
Land's End, promontory	B4	30
Lander, Wyo.	C1	126
Landes, region	B5	34
Landis	B8	104
Landshut	C4	40
Lang Son	B2	11
Langeburg, mts.	B3	71
Langeland, island	C4	32
Langenburg	J10	104
Langham	D8	104
Langkawi, island	A1	13
Langley	L6	95
Langruth	B4	96
Langstaff	K5	102
Langton	E5	102
Languedoc-Roussillon	C5	34
Lanigan	E9	104
Lanín, volcano	A4	74
Länkäran	B2	45
L'Annonciation	B5	103
Lansdowne	J3	102
Lansdowne House	C2	101
L'Anse-à-Valleau	M2	103
L'Anse-au-Loup	C3	98
L'Anse-aux-Gascons	M3	103
L'Anse-St-Jean	F3	103
Lansing, capital, Mich.	E1	126
Lantau, island	Inset	10
Lanús	D3	74
Lanzarote, island	Inset I	37
Lanzhou	D2	10
Lao Cai	A1	11
Laoag	B2	12
Laoang	C3	12
Laon	C2	34
Laos		11
Lapithos	B1	27
Lapland, region	B1	53
Lappeenranta	C2	53
Laptev, sea	B8	44
L'Aquila	C2	38
Larache	C1	57
Laramie, Wyo.	C1	126
Laredo, Tex.	D3	126
Lares	B2	90
Larestan, region	C4	22
Large, island	C1	91
Lárisa	B2	51
Lark Harbour	B4	98
Larkana	C4	21
Larkhall	C4	96
Larnaca	B2	27
Larne	B2	30
Larochette	F2	100
Larrys River	F2	100
Larsen Ice Shelf, glacier	C12	107
Las Cruces, N. Mex.	C2	126
Las Minas, mt.	A2	86
Las Palmas	Inset I	37
Las Piedras	D2	90
Las Piedras	B3	75
Las Tablas	B3	87
Las Tunas	E3	88
Las Vegas, N. Mex.	C2	126
Las Vegas, Nev.	B2	126
L'Ascension	B5	103
Lashburn	A7	104
Lashio	C2	12
Lashkar Gah	A2	22
Last Mountain, lake	E9	104
Latacunga	B3	79
Late, island	C2	17
Latina	C2	38
Latium	C2	38
Lau, island group	C2	17
Laucala, island	C2	17
Laudat	B3	90
Lauder	A4	96
Launceston	B4	30
Launceston, Tas.	D4	14
Laurie River	A1	96
Laurier	B4	96
Lausanne	A2	35
Lautoka	A2	17
Laval	B2	34
Laval	C6, J5	103
Lavenham	B4	96
Lavoy	E4	94
Lavumisa	B3	71
Lawa, river	A2, B2	80
Lawn	D5	98
Lawrence Station	B3	97
Lawton, Okla.	D2	126
Layland	B4	96
Layou, river	B3	90
Lázaro Cárdenas	D4	84
Le Bic	H3	103
Le Creusot	D3	34
Le Havre	C2	34
Le Mans	C2	34
Le Puy	C4	34
Leader	A10	104
Leading Tickles	D4	98
Leaf Rapids	D1	96
Leamington	C5	102
Lebanon		26
Lebanon, mts.	B1	26
Lebombo, mts.	C2, D1	71
Lebu	B6	76
Lecce	D2	38
Lech	B3	39
Lech, river	B4	40
Leduc	D4	94
Lee, river	B3	31
Leeds	C3	30
Leeuwarden	C1	32
Leeuwin, cape	A3	14
Leeward Group	A1	27
Lefka	A1	27
Lefkoniko	B1	27
Leganés	Inset II	37
Legazpi	B3	12
Legnica	C3	41
Leicester	C3	30
Leichhardt, river	D1	14
Leiden	B2	32
Leie, river	B3	33
Leikanger	B3	52
Leipzig	C3	40
Leiria	A3	36
Leitrim	H6	102
Leixões	A2	36
Lékéti, mts.	C5	66
Lélouma	B2	62
Lelystad	C2	32
Lempa river	A1, B2	86
Lena, river	C8	44
Leneinsk	C2	23
Lenghu	C2	10
Lengoué, river	C3	66
Lenore	A4	96
Lens	C1	34
Lensk	C7	44
Léo	C3	64
Leoben	D3	39
Léogâne	C2	89
León	B3	84
León	A2	87
León	D1	37
Leonora	B2	14
Leova	B2	50
Leoville	C7	104
Lepontine Alps, mts.	C2	35
Lepreau	C3	97
Lepsi	D2	23
Leribe	B1	71
Lérida	A3	37
Lerwick	Inset I	30
Les Cayes	B2	89
Les Éboulements	F4	103
Les Escaldes	B2	36
Les Escoumins	G3	103
Les Islets-Caribou	J2	103
Les Méchins	K3	103
Les Tantes, island	B1	91
Les Ulis	Inset II	34
Leskovac	B3	49
Lesosibirsk	D6	44
Lesotho		71
Lesser Caucasus, mts.	A2, B4	45
Lesser Hinggan, range	F1	10
Lesser Slave, lake	C3	94
Lesser Sunda, islands	C2	13
Lestrock	G9	104
Lésvos, island	C3	51
Leszno	C3	41
Lethbridge	D6	94
Lethbridge	E5	98
Lethem	B4	80
Leticia	C6	78
Letlhakeng	C1	31
Letterkenny	C2	33
Leuven	B2	33
Levack	D1	102
Levallois-Perret	Inset II	34
Leveque, cape	B1	14
Leverkusen	A3	40
Levice	B2	42
Lévis	E5, L6	103
Levittown	C2	90
Lewes	D4	30
Lewis, island	A1	30
Lewisporte	D4	98
Lewiston, Idaho	B1	126
Lewiston, Maine	F1	126
Lexington, Ky.	E2	126
Leyte, island	C4	12
Lhasa	C3	10
Lhobrak, river	C2	19
Lhuntshi	C2	19
Lianyungang	E2	10
Liao, river	F1	10
Liaoning	F1	10
Liaoyang	F1	10
Liaoyuan	F1	10
Liard River	J1	95
Liard, river	K1	95
Libau	C4	96
Liberec	B2	42
Liberia	A2	86
Liberia		63
Liberia	B2	86
Libono	A2	71
Libreville, capital	A1	66
Libya		56
Libyan, desert	A2, D2	56
Lichfield	C3	30
Lichinga	B2	68
Lida	B3	47
Liechtenstein		33
Liège	D2	33
Lieksa	D2	53
Lienz	C4	39
Liepāja	A2	46
Lièvre, river	A5	103
Lifford	C1	31
Lifou, island	C3	18
Lifuka, island	C3	17
Liguria	B1	38
Ligurian, sea	B2	38
Lihir, group	D4	104
Likasi	C3	67
Likiep, island	B1	16
Lille	C1	34
Lille, strait	B3	32
Lillehammer	C3	52
Lillooet	M6	95
Lillooet, river	L6	95
Lilongwe, capital	B2	68
Lima, capital	B3	77
Lima, river	A2	36
Limassol	B2	27
Limbazi	C2	46
Limbe	A3	65
Limburg	D2	33
Limerick	B2	31
Limfjorden, channel	B2	32
Límnos, island	C2	51
Limoges	C4	34
Limón	C6	78
Limón	B3	86
Limours	Inset II	34
Limousin	C4	34
Limpopo, river	C1	71
Linares	E3	84
Linares	B5	76
Linares	E3	37
Lincoln	C3	30
Lincoln, capital, Nebr.	D1	126
Lindau	B5	40
Lindbergh	D5	94
Linden	B3	80
Linden	D2	100
Lindi	C2	68
Lindsay	G3	102
Line, islands	D1	17
Lingayen, gulf	B2	12
Lingga, island	B2	13
Lingshi	C2	19
Linguère	B2	62
Linköping	B2	53
Linhe	D2	10
Linière	K5	103
Linvanti, river	A1	69
Linwood	F2	100
Linz	D2	39
Lion, gulf	D5	34
Lionel Town	B3	88
Lions Head	D3	102
Lipa	B3	12
Lipari, islands	C3	38
Lipetsk	B2	44
Lippstadt	B3	40
Lipton	G10	104
Liptovský Mikuláš	B2	42
Lira	C2	61
Lisala	B1	67
L'Isalo, mts.	B3	69
Lisbon, capital	A3	36
Lisichansk	D2	47
L'Isle-Adam	Inset II	34
L'Isle-Verte	G3	103
Lismore, N.S.W.	E2	14
Listowel	E4	102
Litani, river		
Litani, river	A2, B3	80
Lithuania		46
Little Alföld, plain	A2	43
Little Andaman, island	F6	20
Little Bay	B5	98
Little Bras d'Or	G1	100
Little Current	D2	102
Little Fort	M5	95
Little Grand Rapids	D3	96
Little Inagua, island	C4	89
Little Rock, capital, Ark.	D2	126
Little Salmon, lake	C4	105
Little Scarcies, river	A1	63
Little Seldom	D6	94
Little Smoky, river	A4	94
Little St. Bernard, pass	D4	34
Little Zab, river	B1	24
Liuzhou	D3	10
Liverpool	C3	30
Liverpool	C3	100
Liverpool, bay	B3	67
Livingstone	B3	67
Livno	B2	48
Livorno	B2	38
Ljubljana, capital	B2	48
Ljusnanälven, river	B2	53
Llallagua	A3	77
Llandrindod Wells	B3	30
Llanos, plain	C3	78
Llanos, prairie	C3	78
Llanquihue, lake	B7	76
Lleyn, peninsula	B3	30
Llorts	B1	36
Lloyd, lake	B3	104
Lloydminster	E4	94
Lloydminster	A7	104
Lloyds, river	C5	98
Lullaillaco, volcano	B1	74
Lo Wu	Inset	10
Lo, river	A1	11
Loa, river	B2	76
Lobamba, capital	B2	71
Lobatse	B2	71
Lobaye, river	A2	66
Lobito	B4	70
Locarno	C2	35
Lockeport	C4	100
Lockport	C4	96
Lod (Lydda)	B2	25
Lodja	B2	67
Lodwar	B2	61
Łódź	D3	41
Loei	C2	12
Loess, plateau	D2	10
Lofoten, islands	C2	52
Logan, mt.	A5	105
Logan, river	Inset II	14
Logan, Utah	B1	126
Logone, river	A5	59
Logroño	E1	37
Loi-kaw	C2	12
Loire, river	C3	34
Loíza	C2	90
Loja	B4	79
Loja	D4	37
Lokka, reservoir	C1	53
Lokoja	C4	65
Lokossa	A4	64
Lol, river	C3	59
Lolland, island	C4	32
Lom	B2	50
Lomami, river	C2	67
Lomas de Zamora	D4	74
Lomawai	A3	17
Lombardy	B1	38
Lombardy	J3	102
Lombok, island	C2	13
Lomé, capital	B3	64
Lomond, lake	B2	30
Łomża	F2	41
London	C3	30
London, capital	C3, Inset III	30
Londonderry	A2	30
Londrina	C4	81
Lone Butte	M5	95
Long Beach, Calif.	B2	126
Long island, N.Y.	F1	126
Long Lake	C3	94
Long Range, mts.	B5, C4	98
Long Xuyen	A4	11
Long, island	C3	89
Longford	C3	31
Longlac	C3	101
Longreach, Qld.	D2	14
Longueuil	J5	103
Longview, Tex.	D2	126
Loon Lake	C3	94
Loon Lake	A6	104
Loop Head, cape	B2	31
Lop Buri	B3	12
Lop, lake	C1	10
Lorca	F4	37
Loreburn	D9	104
Lorengau	A2	15
Loreto	B2	84
Lorette	C4	96
Loretteville	K5	103
Lorient	B3	34
Lorne, estuary	B2	30
Lorraine	D2	34
Lorraine	H5	103
Los Andes	B4	76
Los Ángeles	B6	76
Los Angeles, Calif.	B2	126
Los Chiles	B1	86
Los Mochis	C2	84
Los Reyes	Inset	84
Los Teques	C1	79
Lot, river	C4	34

Key Page
Louang Namtha A1 11
Loubomo B6 66
Louga A2 62
Lough Erne, *lake* A2 30
Loughborough, *lake* J3 102
Lougheed, *island* G1 99
Louisbourg H2 100
Louisdale F2 100
Louiseville D5 103
Louisiade, *archipelago* B3 15
Louisiana D2 126
Louisville, Ky. E2 126
Lourdes B5 34
Louri C2 19
Louvres Inset II 34
Lovech C2 50
Lovell Village B3 91
Lovettville B4 94
Lowe Farm C4 96
Lower Arrow, *lake* N6 95
Lower Debert D2 100
Lower Five Islands C2 100
Lower Hutt B3 15
Lower Montague C2 100
Lower Post H1 95
Lower Saxony B2 40
Lower Tunguska, *river* C6 44
Lower Woods Harbour B4 100
Lowestoft D3 30
Loyada C2 60
Loyalty, *islands* C2 18
Loyoro D2 61
Lualaba, *river* C2 67
Luanda, *capital* B2 70
Luang Prabang B2 11
Luang Prabang, *range* A3 11
Luang, *mt.* B4 12
Luangwa C3 67
Luangwa, *river* C3 67
Luanshya B2 67
Luapula, *river* B2, C3 67
Luau E3 70
Luba A1 66
Lubango B5 70
Lubbock, Tex. C2 126
Lübeck B2 40
Lubicon, *lake* C3 94
Lublin F3 41
Lubumbashi C3 67
Lucapa D2 70
Lucca B2 38
Lucea A2 88
Lucena B3 12
Lucena D4 37
Lučenec B2 42
Lucern, *lake* C2 35
Lucerne C1 35
Lucie, *river* A3 80
Luckenwalde C2 40
Lucknow D3 20
Lucknow D4 102
Lucky Lake C9 104
Luda Kamchiya, *river* E3 50
Lüderitz B4 70
Ludhiana C2 20
Ludogorie, *region* E2 50
Ludwigsburg B4 40
Ludwigshafen am Rhein B4 40
Luena D3 70
Lugano C3 35
Lugano, *lake* C3 35
Luganville B2 18
Lugenda, *river* C2 68
Lugo C1 37
Lugoj A3 43
Luhansk D2 47
Lukuga, *river* C2 67
Luleå D1 53
Luleälven, *river* D1 53
Lumphat F2 11
Lumsden E4 98
Lumsden F10 104
Lumut A2 13
Lund B3 53
Lund K6 95
Lundar B4 96
Lundazi C2 67
Lundi, *river* B2 69
Lüneburg B2 40
Lünen A3 40
Lunenburg C3 100
Lunga, *river* B2 67
Lungwebungu, *river* A2 67
Lunsar A1 63
Luoyang E2 10
Lupeni B3 43
Luperón B1 89
Luquillo D2 90
Luremo C2 70
Lúrio, *river* C2 68
Lusaka, *capital* B3 67
Lusambo B2 67
Luseland A8 104
Lushnjë A3 49
Lusutfu, *river* B2 71
Luton C3 30
Lutsk B1 47
Lützow-Holm, *bay* C16 107
Luuq A3 60
Luvua, *river* B1, C2 67
Luwegu, *river* C2 68
Luxembourg 33
Luxembourg, *capital* B2 33
Luxor B2 56
Luzarches Inset II 34
Luzhou D3 10
Luzon, *island* B3 12
Luzon, *strait* B2 12
Lviv A2 47
Lyddal B1 96
Lyme, *bay* C4 30
Lynn Lake C1 96
Lyon D4 34
Lytton M6 95

M

Ma, *river* A2 11
Maan A2 26
Key Page
Maas, *river* C3, D3 32
Maastricht C4 32
Mabaruma B1 80
Maberly J3 102
Mabou F1 100
Mac Tier F2 102
MacAlpine, *lake* H3 99
Macao, S.A.R. E3 10
Macapá C1 81
Macas B4 79
Maccan C2 100
Macdonnell, *ranges* C2 14
Macedonia, F.Y.R. 48
Maceió E2 81
Macenta D3 62
Macerata C2 38
Macfarlane, *river* C2 104
Macgregor B4 96
Machakos D4 61
Machala B4 79
Machida C3 8
Machupicchu, *ruins* C3 77
MacKay, *lake* F4 99
Mackay, Qld. D2 14
Mackenzie L3 95
Mackenzie King, *island* F1 99
Mackenzie, *bay* B1 105
Mackenzie, *mts.* C4 99
Mackenzie, *river* B3, D4 99
Mackey H1 102
Macklin A8 104
Maclean, *strait* G1 99
Macmillan, *river* C4 105
Mâcon D3 34
Macon, Ga. E2 126
Madaba A2 26
Madagascar 69
Madan C4 50
Madang A2 15
Madawaska G2 102
Madden C5 94
Madeira, *island* 55
Madeira, *river* B2 81
Madhumati, *river* C5 21
Madhupur Tract, *region* D4 21
Madinat ath-Thawrah B2 27
Madison, *capital*, Wis. E1 126
Madiun C2 13
Madoc H3 102
Madre de Dios, *island* A9 76
Madre de Dios, *river* A2, C3 77
Madrid, *capital* E2, Inset II 37
Madriu, *river* B3 36
Madura, *island* C2 13
Madurai C7 20
Maebashi C2 8
Maestra, *mts.* D3 88
Maéwo, *island* C2 18
Mafeking A3 96
Mafeteng A2 71
Mafia, *island* C2 68
Mafikeng C2 71
Mafra A3 36
Mafraq, al- B1 26
Magdalena de Kino B1 84
Magadan D9 44
Magburaka B1 63
Magdagachi D8 44
Magdalena B2 77
Magdalena Contreras Inset 84
Magdalena, *island* B7 76
Magdalena, *river* B3 78
Magdeburg B2 40
Magelang C2 13
Magellan, *strait* B9 76
Maggiore, *lake* B1 38
Magnetawan F2 102
Magnitogorsk D4 44
Magog D6 103
Mahabharat, *range* B2 19
Mahajamba, *river* B2 69
Mahajanga B2 69
Mahalapye B2 69
Mahallah al-Kubra, al- B1 56
Mahanadi, *river* D4 20
Mahaska C4 94
Mahbas, al- C1 58
Mahdia B3 80
Mahdia C2 57
Mahé, *island* C1, Inset 70
Mahébourg C3 69
Mahilyow E3 47
Mahim, *bay* Inset I 20
Mahón J3 37
Mai-Ndombe, *lake* B2 67
Maidstone D3 30
Maidstone A7 104
Maiduguri G2 65
Main Brook C3 98
Main, *river* B4 40
Main-à-Dieu H1 100
Main-Danube, *canal* B4 40
Maine G1 126
Mainland, *island* Inset I 30
Maintirano A2 69
Mainz B4 40
Maio, *island* C3 58
Maipo, *river* B4, Inset 76
Maipú Inset 76
Maisí, *cape* F3 88
Maisons-Laffitte Inset II 34
Maitland Bridge B3 100
Maíz, *islands* C2 87
Maizuru B3 8
Majardah, *river* B1 57
Majé Inset I 81
Majorca, *island* H3 37
Majuro, *capital* C2 16
Majuro, *island* C2 16
Makamba B3 61
Makassar, *strait* C2 13
Makeni B1 63
Makeyevka D2 47
Makhachkala E4 44
Makhaleng, *river* A2 71
Makin, *island* A1 17
Makkovik B1 98
Makokou B1 66
Makona, *river* A1 63
Key Page
Makoua C4 66
Makran Coast, *range* B5 21
Makung A2 9
Makurdi E4 65
Malabar, *coast* B6 20
Malabo, *capital* A1 66
Malacca, *strait* A1, A2 13
Malad Inset I 20
Maladzyechna C2 47
Málaga D4 37
Malagarasi, *river* B1 68
Malaita, *island* B1 16
Malakal C3 59
Malakula, *island* B3 18
Malang C2 13
Malanje C3 70
Malanville B2 64
Mälaren, *lake* C3 53
Malatya D2 27
Malawi 68
Malay, *peninsula* A1 13
Malaysia 13
Malbaie, *river* F4 103
Malbun B2 33
Malcolm, *atoll* A1 19
Malden, *island* D2 17
Maldives 19
Male Karpaty, *mts.* A2 42
Male, *atoll* A2 19
Male, *capital* A2 19
Maleb E6 94
Malegaon B4 20
Mali 58
Mali Rajinac, *mt.* B3 48
Malindi F5 61
Mallaig B1 30
Mallow B2 31
Malmberget D1 53
Malmédy E2 33
Malmö B3 53
Maloelap, *island* C2 16
Malombe, *lake* C2 68
Maloti, *mts.* B2 71
Malta 36
Maltahöhe B3 70
Malton J5 102
Mamâri C2 62
Mamawi, *lake* E2 94
Mambéré, *river* A2 66
Mamburao B3 12
Mamiña C2 76
Mamoré, *river* A2 77
Mamou B2 62
Mamry, *lake* E1 41
Mamtalah, al- B2 25
Mamuno A2 69
Man C3 63
Mana B1 80
Mana, *river* B1 80
Manado D1 13
Managua, *capital* A2 87
Managua, *lake* A2 87
Manakara B3 69
Manama, *capital* B1 25
Manatí B2 90
Manaus C2 81
Manawan, *lake* G5 104
Manbij A1 27
Manchester C3 30
Manchester, N.H. F1 126
Manchurian, *plain* F1 10
Mand, *river* C4 22
Mandalay C2 12
Mandalgov C2 11
Mandara, *mts.* B1 65
Mandaue B4 12
Mandeville B2 88
Mándra Inset 51
Mandurah, W.A. A3 14
Manfredonia C2 38
Manga, *region* C2 59
Mangalore B6 20
Mango B1 64
Mangoky, *river* A3 69
Manicouagan, *reservoir* C3 101
Manicougan Deux, *reservoir* H2 103
Manigotagan C3 96
Manila, *bay* B3 12
Manila, *capital* B3 12
Manisa A2 27
Manito, *lake* A8 104
Manitoba, *lake* B3, B4, D2 96
Manitou B4 96
Manitoulin, *island* C2 102
Manitouwadge C3 101
Manitowaning D2 102
Maniwaki A5 103
Manizales B3 78
Mankato, Minn. D1 126
Mankayane B2 71
Mankota C11 104
Mankulam B2 19
Mannar A3 19
Mannar, *gulf* C7 20
Mannar, *island* A2 19
Mannheim B4 40
Manning B3 94
Mannville E4 94
Mano, *river* A2, B2 63
Manokwari E2 13
Manono C2 67
Manono, *island* B2 18
Manor Park H5 102
Manori, *point* Inset I 20
Manouane B4 103
Manpŏ B2 9
Mansa B2 67
Mansa Konko C2 62
Mansel, *island* M4 99
Manson Creek K3 95
Mansurah, al- B1 56
Manta A3 79
Manta, *bay* A3 79
Mantaro, *river* B3 77
Mantiqueira, *range* D4 81
Mantova B1 38
Mantua (Mantova) B1 38
Manukau B2 15
Key Page
Manus, *island* A2 15
Manyara, *lake* C1 68
Manzanillo D3 88
Manzanillo D4 84
Manzini B2 71
Mao A1 89
Mao A4 59
Maple J5 102
Maple Creek A11 104
Maputo, *capital* B5 68
Maquela do Zombo C2 70
Mar Chiquita, *lake* C3 74
Mar del Plata D4 74
Mar, *range* D4 81
Mara, *river* C4 61
Maraba D2 81
Maracaibo B1 79
Maracaibo, *lake* B2 79
Maracay C1 79
Maradi B3 59
Marajó, *island* D2 81
Marakei, *island* A1 17
Maramasike, *island* B1 16
Maranhão D2 81
Marano, *river* C1 39
Marañón, *river* B1, B2 77
Maras D3 27
Marathon C3 101
Marbella D4 37
Marburg B3 40
Marcelin D8 104
Marche C2 38
Marchena, *island* Inset 79
Mardan D2 21
Mardin E3 27
Maré, *island* D2 18
Maremma, *region* B2 38
Margaree Forks F1 100
Margaret, *lake* C2 94
Margarita, *island* D1 79
Margate D3 30
Margherita, *peak* A3 61
Maria L3 103
Mariana, *islands* B3 91
Mariana D3 81
Marianao B1 88
Marías, *islands* C3 84
Marib B1 25
Maribor C2 48
Marie Byrd Land, *region* B8 107
Marie-Reine B3 94
Mariehamn (Maarianhamina) A2 53
Mariental C3 70
Marigot B2 90
Marijampolė B2 46
Marinduque, *island* B3 12
Marino C2 18
Marion Bridge G2 100
Maripasoula A2 80
Mariscal Estigarribia B3 75
Maritime Alps, *range* D4 34
Maritsa, *river* D3 50
Mariupol D3 47
Mariy El, *republic* D4 44
Marj Uyun A2 26
Marj, al- D1 56
Marka A3 60
Markham F4, K5 102
Markham, *river* A2 15
Markstay E1 102
Marl A3 40
Marmara, *sea* B2 27
Marmora H3 102
Marne, *river* C2, Inset II 34
Marneuli C4 45
Maromokotro, *mt.* B1 69
Marondera B2 69
Maroni, *river* A1 80
Maros, *river* C2 43
Maroua B1 65
Marovoay B2 69
Marowijne, *river* B2 80
Marquette, Mich. E1 126
Marquis B2 91
Marrakech B2 57
Marsa al-Burayqah C1 56
Marsabit E2 61
Marsala C3 38
Marsaxlokk, *bay* C3 36
Marsden A8 104
Marseille D5 34
Marsh Harbour B2 89
Marshall Is. 16
Marsoui L2 103
Martaban, *gulf* C3 12
Marten River F1 102
Martensville D8 104
Martin B2 42
Martinique, *island* 82
Martins River C3 100
Martorell D2 90
Martuni C2 45
Mary C3 22
Mary's Harbour D3 98
Maryborough, Qld. E2 14
Maryfield A4 96
Maryfield J11 104
Maryland F2 126
Marystown D5 98
Masada, *ruins* B2 26
Masai, steppe C1 68
Masaka B4 61
Masan C5 9
Masaya A3 87
Masbate B3 12
Masbate, *island* B3 12
Mascouche C6 103
Maseru, *capital* A2 71
Masfut D2 25
Mashhad D2 22
Masindi B3 61
Masirah, *gulf* C2 25
Masirah, *island* C2 25
Mask, *lake* B2 31
Maskall B2 85
Massachusetts F1 126
Massacre B3 90
Massawa B2 60
Key Page
Massenya B5 59
Masset F4 95
Massey C1 102
Massif Central, *plateau* C4 34
Massif des Bongos, *range* B2 66
Massy Inset II 34
Masuda A3 8
Masvingo B2 69
Mat, *river* B2 49
Matadi A2 67
Matagalpa B2 87
Matagami A4 101
Matale B4 19
Matam C2 62
Matamoros E2 84
Matane J3 103
Matanzas B1 88
Matapédia C1 97
Matapédia K4 103
Matara B6 19
Mataram C2 13
Mataró H2 37
Matautu C2 18
Matawa Place D3 96
Matehuala D3 84
Matelot A2 91
Matera D2 38
Mathura C3 20
Matlock C3 30
Mato Grosso C3 81
Mato Grosso do Sul C4 81
Mato Grosso, *plateau* C3 81
Mátra, *mts.* B2 43
Matrah C1 25
Matruh A1 56
Matsoku, *river* B2 71
Matsudo C3 8
Matsue B3 8
Matsumae D1, Inset I 8
Matsumoto C2 8
Matsuyama B3 8
Mattawa G1 102
Mattawin, *river* C5 103
Matterhorn, *mt.* B3 35
Matthew Town C4 89
Matthews Ridge A2 80
Mauá Inset II 81
Maui, *island*, Hawaii Inset II 126
Maule, *river* B5 76
Maumturk, *mts.* B2 31
Maun A2 69
Mauna Loa, *mt.*, Hawaii Inset II 126
Maunabo D2 90
Mauren B1 33
Maurepas Inset II 34
Mauritania 58
Mauritius 69
Mavinga D5 70
May Pen B3 88
Maya, *mts.* A3 85
Mayaguana, *island* C4 89
Mayaguana, *passage* C4 89
Mayagüez A2 90
Maydi A1 25
Mayfair C7 104
Maymont C8 104
Maymyo C2 12
Maynooth C2 31
Maynooth H2 102
Mayo B4 105
Mayo, *lake* C4 105
Mayombé, *massif* B5 66
Mayon, *volcano* B3 12
Mayotte, *island* C2 67
Mayreau, *island* A4 91
Mayumba A2 66
Mazabuka B3 67
Mazandaran, *region* C2 22
Mazar-e Sharif B1 22
Mazaruni, *river* A2 80
Mazatenango B5 85
Mazatlán C3 84
Mažeikiai B1 46
Mazoe, *river* B1 69
Mazyr D3 47
Mbabane, *capital* B2 71
Mbahiakro D3 63
Mbaké A2 62
Mbala C1 67
Mbale D3 61
Mbalmayo B3 65
Mbandaka B2 67
M'banza Congo B2 70
Mbanza-Ngungu B2 67
Mbarara B4 61
Mbemkuru, *river* C3 68
M'Beni A1 67
Mbéré, *river* B2 65
Mbeya B2 68
Mbini B3 66
Mbini, *river* C3 66
Mboro, *river* D4 66
Mboune, *river* B2 62
Mbour A2 62
Mbuji-Mayi B2 67
Mbuluzane, *river* B2 71
Mbuluzi, *river* B2 71
McAdam B3 97
McAllen, Tex. D3 126
McBride M4 95
McCallum C5 98
McCreary B4 96
McDame H1 95
McGee B9 104
Mchinji A2 68
McKerrow D1 102
McKinley *mt.*, Alaska Inset I 126
McLeese Lake L5 95
McLeod Lake L4 95
McLeod Valley C4 94
M'Clintock, *channel* H2 99
M'Clure, *strait* D2 99
McLure M5 95
McMurdo, *sound* B5 107
McRae E4 94
Meacham E8 104
Meadow Lake B6 104
Meadow Portage B3 96
Meaford E3 102
Key Page
Mealy, *mts.* A3 98
Meander River B1 94
Mecca A2 24
Mechelen C1 33
Mecklenburg, *bay* B1 40
Mecklenburg-Western Pomerania C2 40
Mecsek, *mts.* B2 43
Medan A1 13
Medellín B3 78
Medford, Oreg. A1 126
Medgidia E3 43
Mediaș C2 43
Medicine Hat E6 94
Medika D4 96
Medina A1 24
Medina del Campo D2 37
Medit B2 13
Mediterranean, *sea* 29
Medley E4 94
Medora A4 96
Meductic B3 97
Meelpaeg, *lake* C5 98
Meerut C3 20
Meghna, *river* D5 21
Meghri D4 45
Meighen, *island* J1 99
Meiktila B2 12
Meissen C3 40
Mejicanos A2 86
Mékambo B1 66
Mekele C1 60
Mékinac, *lake* D4 103
Meknès C1 57
Mekong, *delta* B5 11
Mekong, *river* A1, A4, C4, D3 11
Mékrou, *river* B2 64
Melaka B2 13
Melbourne, Fla. E3 126
Melbourne, Vic., *capital* D3 14
Meldrum Bay B2 102
Meleb C4 96
Melekeok C3 17
Mélèzes, *river* B2 101
Melfi B5 59
Melfort F8 104
Melipilla Inset 76
Melita A4 96
Melitopol D3 47
Mellieha B2 36
Mellieha, *bay* B2 36
Melo C2 75
Melrose E2 100
Melun Inset II 34
Melville H10 104
Melville, *island* C1 14
Melville, *island* F1 99
Melville, *lake* B2 98
Melville, *peninsula* M3 99
Memmingen B5 40
Memphis, Tenn. D2 126
Memphrémagog, *lake* D6 103
Menai, *strait* B3 30
Ménaka D2 58
Mende C4 34
Mendoza B3 74
Meneng B3 16
Menihek D3 98
Mennecy Inset II 34
Menongue C4 70
Mentawai, *islands* A2 13
Menzel Bourguiba B1 57
Meppel D2 32
Mequinenza, *lake* F2 37
Merano B1 38
Merauke F2 13
Mercedario, *mt* B3 74
Mercedes A2 75
Mergui C3 12
Mergui, *archipelago* C4 12
Mérida B2 79
Mérida C3 37
Mérida, *mts.* B2 79
Mérida, *state capital* G3 84
Meridian, Miss. E2 126
Merigomish E2 100
Merín, *lagoon* D2 75
Merir, *island* Inset 17
Merkys, *river* C2 46
Meron, *mt.* B1 26
Merredin, W.A. A3 14
Merrick, *mt.* B2 30
Merridale A3 96
Merritt M6 95
Mersch B2 33
Mersey, *river* C3 30
Mersin C3 27
Merthyr Tydfil B3 30
Meru D3 61
Merume, *mts.* A2 80
Mesaoria, *plain* B1 27
Meseta, *plateau* D3 37
Mesolóngion B2 51
Mesopotamia, *region* B2 24
Messina D1 71
Messina C3 38
Messina, *strait* C3 38
Mesta, *river* B4 50
Meta Incognita, *peninsula* P4 99
Meta, *river* C3 78
Métabetchouan E3 103
Metcalfe K2 102
Meteghan A3 100
Métis-sur-Mer J3 103
Metiskow E5 94
Metz D2 34
Meulan Inset II 34
Meuse, *river* D2 33
Mexiana, *island* D1 81
Mexicali, *state capital* A1 84
Mexico 84
Mexico City, *national capital* E4, Inset 84
Mexico, *gulf* 82
Meymaneh A1 22
Meyungs B3 17
Mgwavuma, *river* B3 71
Mhlume B2 71
Miami B4 96

Key Page

Miami, Fla. E3 126
Mianwali D3 21
Miaoli B1 9
Mica Creek N5 95
Michalovce C2 42
Miches C2 89
Michigan E1 126
Michigan, lake E1 126
Michoacán D4 84
Mico, river B2 87
Micoud B3 91
Micronesia 15
Midale G11 104
Middelburg C3 71
Middelburg A3 32
Middle Andaman, island F6 20
Middle Arm C4 98
Middle Atlas, ranges C1 57
Middle Lake E8 104
Middle Musquodoboit D2 100
Middlebro D4 96
Middlesbrough C2 30
Middleton B3 100
Midi-Pyrénées C5 34
Midland F3 102
Midland, Tex. C2 126
Midlands, region C3 30
Miercurea Ciuc C2 43
Mieres D1 37
Mikkeli C2 53
Mikkwa, river C2 94
Mikomeseng C2 66
Mikonos, island C3 51
Mikura, island C3 8
Miladummadulu, atoll A1 19
Milagro B4 79
Milan B1 38
Milden C9 104
Mildura, Vic. D3 14
Miles City, Mont. C1 126
Milestone F10 104
Milford Haven B3 30
Milford Sound A3 15
Milh, lake B2 24
Mili, island C2 16
Milk, river E6 94
Mill Bay L7 95
Mill Village C3 100
Miller Lake D2 102
Millet D4 94
Milliken K5 102
Milltown D5 98
Millville B2 97
Milne, bay B3 15
Milo D6 94
Milo, river C3 62
Mílos, island C3 51
Milton B2 100
Milton F4 102
Milverton E4 102
Milwaukee, Wis. E1 126
Mimico J6 102
Miminegash A2 100
Mina Baranis C3 56
Mina Salman B1 25
Minami, island ....Inset III 8
Minas C3 75
Minas Gerais D3 81
Minas, channel C2 100
Minatitlán F4 84
Minch, strait B1 30
Mindanao, island C5 12
Mindelo B2 58
Mindemoya C2 102
Minden G3 102
Mindoro, island B3 12
Mindoro, strait B3 12
Miner's Bay G3 102
Miner, river B3 105
Mingaçevir B2 45
Mingaçevir, reservoir B2 45
Minho, river A1 36
Minicoy, island B7 20
Minija, river A2 46
Miniota A4 96
Minitonas A3 96
Mink Creek A3 96
Minna D3 65
Minneapolis, Minn. D1 126
Minnedosa B4 96
Minnesota D1 126
Miño, river C1 37
Minorca, island H2 37
Minot, N. Dak. C1 126
Minsk, capital C3 47
Minto B4 96
Minto C2 97
Minto B4 105
Minto, lake B3 101
Minton F11 104
Minya, al- B2 56
Miquelon, island M4 92
Mira H1 100
Mirabel B6 103
Mirador Nacional, mt. C3 75
Miraflores B4 78
Miragoâne B2 89
Miramichi D1 97
Miramichi, bay E1 97
Miranda de Ebro E1 37
Mirbat B3 25
Mirebalais C2 89
Miri D2 13
Mirnyy C7 44
Mirpur Khas C3 21
Mirror D5 94
Miscou, island E1 97
Miscouche B2 100
Misery, mt. B1 90
Miskolc E1 43
Misool, island E2 13
Missinipe F5 104
Mississauga F4, J6 102
Mississippi J2 102
Mississippi, lake J2 102
Mississippi, river D1 126
Missoula, Mont. B1 126
Missouri D2 126

Missouri, river D1 126
Mistassibi, river D1 103
Mistassini D3 103
Mistassini, lake B3 101
Mistassini, river D2 103
Mistatim G8 104
Mistelbach E2 39
Misurata C1 56
Mitchell D4 102
Mitchell, mt., N.C. E2 126
Mitchell, river D1 14
Mitchinamécus, lake A4 103
Mitilíni C2 51
Mito D2 8
Mitsamiouli A1 67
Mittelland, canal B2 40
Mitú C4 78
Mitzic A1 66
Miyake, island C3 8
Miyako D2 8
Miyako, island ....Inset II 8
Miyakonojo A4 8
Miyazaki A4 8
Mizen Head, cape B3 31
Mizo, hills F4 20
Mizpe Ramon B2 26
Mjøsa, lake C3 52
Mkondvo, river B2 71
Mliba B2 71
Mmabatho C2 71
Mo C2 52
Moa, island D2 13
Moa, river B2 63
Moab, Utah C2 126
Moala, island group B3 17
Moanda B2 66
Moba C2 67
Mobaye B3 66
Mobile, Ala. E2 126
Moca B1 89
Moca A2 90
Moçambique D2 68
Mocha, (Mukha, al-) A2 25
Mocímboa da Praia D1 68
Môco, mt. C4 70
Mocoa A4 78
Modena B1 38
Moengo B2 80
Moers A3 40
Mogadishu, capital B3 60
Mogami, river D2 8
Mogi das Cruzes ....Inset II 81
Mogilev Podolskiy B2 47
Mogocha D7 44
Mogotón, mt. A2 87
Mohács B3 43
Mohales Hoek A3 71
Mohammedia C1 57
Moher, cliffs B2 31
Mohinora D2 8
Moi C4 78
Mojave, desert, Calif. B2 126
Mojos A2 77
Mokhotlong C2 71
Mokolo B1 65
Mokpŏ B5 9
Mold B3 30
Moldavia, region D2 43
Moldova 50
Moldoveanu, mt. C3 43
Molepolole B3 69
Molise C2 38
Mollendo C4 77
Molokai island, Hawaii ....Inset II 126
Molopo, river B2 71
Moloundou C3 65
Molson, lake C2 96
Molucca, sea D2 13
Moluccas, islands D2 13
Mombasa E5 61
Mombetsu ....Inset I 8
Mon Repos B2 91
Mon, island D4 32
Monaco 35
Monaco, capital B1 35
Monaghan C1 31
Monaghan F2 100
Monastery C2 57
Monastir C2 57
Mönchengladbach A3 40
Monclova D2 84
Moncton E2 97
Mondego, cape A2 36
Mondego, river B2 36
Monforte C1 37
Mongo B4 59
Mongolia 11
Mongolian, plateau C2 11
Mongomo D3 66
Mongu A3 67
Monitor E5 94
Monjolo ....Inset I 81
Monkey Bay B2 68
Mono, river A4, B2 64
Monopoli D2 38
Monrovia, capital A2 63
Mons B2 33
Mont-Carmel G4 103
Mont-Joli H3 103
Mont-Laurier A5 103
Mont-Royal J5 103
Mont-St-Pierre L2 103
Mont-Tremblant-Village B5 103
Montague C2 100
Montalto, mt. D3 38
Montana B2 50
Montana B1 126
Montargis C2 34
Montauban C4 34
Monte Carlo B1 35
Monte Cristi A1 89
Monte Plata B2 89
Montebello B6 103
Montecristo, island B2 38
Montegiardino B2 39
Montego Bay B2 88
Montélimar D4 34
Montelindo, river C3 75

Montenegro, republic A3 49
Montepulciano B2 38
Monterey, Calif. A2 126
Montería B2 78
Montero B3 77
Montes Claros D3 81
Montevideo, capital B3 75
Montgomery, capital, Ala. ...D2 126
Montluçon C3 34
Montmagny F5 103
Montmartre G10 104
Montpelier, capital, Vt. F1 126
Montpellier C5 34
Montréal C6, J5 103
Montréal, island J5 103
Montreal, lake E6 104
Montreal, river E6 104
Montreuil ....Inset 34
Montreux A2 35
Montrose C2 30
Monywa B2 12
Monza B1 38
Moore Park B4 96
Moose Factory D2 101
Moose Jaw E10 104
Moose Lake A2 96
Moose, river D2 101
Moosehorn B3 96
Moosomin J10 104
Moosonee D2 101
Mopti C3 58
Moquegua C4 77
Moradabad C3 20
Morant Bay C3 88
Moratuwa A5 19
Morava, river A2, C3 42
Morava, river B2 49
Moravia, region C3 42
Moray, estuary B1 30
Morden B4 96
Mordoviya, republic E4 44
Moree, N.S.W. D2 14
Morehead A2 15
Morelia, state capital D4 84
Morell C2 100
Morelos E4 84
Morena, river D3 37
Moresby, island F5 95
Moreton, bay ....Inset III 14
Morgan City, La. D3 126
Morges A2 35
Morghab, river A1 22
Morghob B1 23
Morghob, river B1 23
Morice, lake J4 95
Moricetown J3 95
Morija A2 71
Morinville D4 94
Morioka D2 8
Morlaix B2 34
Morne Diablotin, mt. B2 90
Moro, gulf B5 12
Moro, river A2 63
Morocco 57
Morogoro C2 68
Morombe A3 69
Morón D2 88
Morón C2 11
Morón de la Frontera D4 37
Morondava A3 69
Morondon C2 78
Morpeth D5 102
Morphou A1 27
Morrin D5 94
Morris C4 96
Morrisburg K3 102
Mors, island B2 32
Morse C10 104
Mortlach D10 104
Mortlock, islands C2 15
Moruga A2 91
Moscow, capital D3 44
Mosel, river A4 40
Moselle, river D2 34
Moshi C1 68
Mosjøen C2 52
Mosquitos, coast C3 87
Moss C4 52
Mossbank E11 104
Mossel Bay B3 71
Mossendjo B5 66
Mossleigh D6 94
Mossy, river F6 104
Most A2 42
Mostaganem B1 57
Mostar B2 48
Móstoles ....Inset II 37
Mosul B1 24
Motagua, river D4 85
Motherwell B2 30
Mouila A2 66
Mould Bay E1 99
Moule à Chique, cape B3 91
Moulmein C3 12
Moulouya, river D1 57
Moundou B5 59
Mount Carmel A2 100
Mt. Forest E4 102
Mount Gambier, S.A. D3 14
Mount Hagen A2 15
Mount Isa, Qld. C2 14
Mt. Stewart C2 100
Mountain Park B5 94
Moura B3 36
Mourne, mts. A2 30
Mouscron B2 33
Moussa Ali, mt. B1 60
Mouths of the Danube, delta E3 43
Mouths of the Ganges, delta C7 21
Mouths of the Indus, delta ..E2 21
Moyale C2 61
Moyamba A1 63
Moyie P6 95
Moyobamba B2 77

Moyowosi, river B1 68
Mozambique 68
Mozambique, channel 55
Mozzoro E2 81
Mpanda B2 68
Mpika C2 67
Mpoko, river A2 66
Mporokoso C1 67
M'Ramani B2 67
Mtkvari, river C4 45
Mtskheta C4 45
Mtwara D3 68
Muang Khammouan C3 11
Muang Không C4 11
Muang Khôngxédôn C4 11
Muang Paklay A2 11
Muang Pakxan B2 11
Muang Vangviang B2 11
Muang Xaignabouri A2 11
Muang Xay A1 11
Muang Xépôn D3 11
Muang Xon B1 11
Muar B2 13
Muara C1 13
Mubende B3 61
Mubi G2 65
Muchinga, mts. C2 67
Mudanjiang F1 10
Mudawwarah, al- B3 26
Mufulira B2 67
Muğla B3 27
Muharraq, al-, island B1 25
Mühlhausen B3 40
Mui Bai Bung, point A5 11
Mukalla, al- B2 25
Muko, island ....Inset III 8
Mulaku, atoll A3 19
Mulde, river C3 40
Mulhacén, mt. E4 37
Mülheim an der Ruhr A3 40
Mulhouse D3 34
Mull, island A2 30
Mullaittivu B2 19
Mullingar C2 31
Multan D3 21
Mulund ....Inset I 20
Mulvihill B4 96
Mumbai (Bombay) ....B5, Inset I 20
Mumbai (Bombay), harbor ....Inset I 20
Mumbra ....Inset I 20
Mumbwa B3 67
Mun, river C3 12
Muna, island D2 13
Munamägi, mt. D3 46
Muncho Lake K2 95
Munich B4 40
Munsan B4 9
Münster A3 40
Munster, province B2 31
Muonio B1 53
Muonioälven, river D1 53
Muoniojoki, river B1 53
Mur, river D3 39
Mura, river C2 48
Muramvya B2 61
Murat, river E2 27
Murchison, river A2 14
Murcia F4 37
Murdochville L3 103
Mureş, river B2 43
Murgab, river D3 22
Muriel, lake E4 94
Murilo, atoll C2 15
Müritz, lake C2 40
Murmansk C3 44
Muroran ....D1, Inset I 8
Muroto, cape B3 8
Murray Harbour C3 100
Murray River C2 100
Murray, harbour C2 100
Murray, lake A2 15
Murray, river D3 14
Murrumbidgee, river D3 14
Murska Sobota D2 48
Mürz, river D3 39
Murzuq B2 56
Muş E2 27
Mûša, river B1 46
Musala, mt. B3 50
Musan C1 9
Muscat, capital C1 25
Musgrave Harbour E4 99
Musgrave, ranges C2 14
Musgravetown E5 98
Mushin B4 65
Muskeg River A4 94
Muskegon, Mich. E1 126
Muskogee, Okla. D2 126
Muskoka, lake F2 102
Muskwa, ranges J2 95
Musoma B1 68
Musquodoboit Harbour D3 100
Mussau, island A2 15
Mustang B3 91
Mustique, island B3 91
Mustvee D2 46
Musu-dan, point C2 9
Mut D1 8
Mutare C2 69
Mutsamudu B2 67
Mutsu D1 8
Muyinga C1 61
Muyun Kum, desert D2 23
Muzaffarabad D2 21
Muynoq A2 23
Mwali (Mohéli), island A2 67
Mwanza B1 68
Mwene-Ditu C2 67
Mweru, lake B1, C3 65
Mwinilunga A2 67
My Tho B4 11
Myanmar (Burma) 12
Myingyan B2 12
Myitkyina C1 12
Mykolaïv C2 47
Mymensingh D4 21
Myrnam E4 94

Mysore C6 20
Mzimba B2 68
Mzuzu B2 68

N

N'dalatando B3 70
N'Djamena, capital A4 59
N'zeto A1 70
Naas C2 31
Nabatiyah at-Tahta, an- A2 26
Naberezhnyye Chelny D4 44
Nabeul C1 57
Nabk, an- A2 27
Nabouwalu B2 17
Nacala D2 68
Nacaome B3 86
Nackawic B3 97
Nadi A2 17
Nadi, bay A2 17
Nadur B1 36
Naduri B2 17
Næstved C3 32
Nafud, an-, desert B1 24
Nag Hammadi B2 56
Naga B3 12
Naga, hills F3 20
Nagano C2 8
Nagaoka C2 8
Nagarote A2 87
Nagasaki A3 8
Nagorno-Karabakh, autonomous region A2 45
Nagoya C3 8
Nagpur C4 20
Nagua C1 89
Naguabo D2 90
Nagykanizsa A2 43
Naha ....Inset II 8
Nahanni, river C4 99
Nahariyya B1 26
Naicam F8 104
Naihati ....Inset II 20
Nain E3 98
Nairobi, capital D4 61
Najaf, an- B2 24
Najd, region B1 24
Najin D1 9
Najran B2 24
Nakadori, island A4 8
Nakano, island A4 8
Nakfa B1 60
Nakhichevan A3 45
Nakhodka E8 44
Nakhon Phanom C2 12
Nakhon Ratchasima C3 12
Nakhon Sawan B3 12
Nakhon Si Thammarat B4 12
Nakina C2 101
Nakodu B2 17
Nakskov C4 32
Naktong, river C5 9
Nakuru D4 61
Nakusp O6 95
Nal, river B4 21
Nalikul ....Inset II 20
Nam Dinh B2 11
Nam Ngum, reservoir B2 11
Nam Tok B3 12
Namangan E2 23
Namew, lake H6 104
Namib, desert A1, B3 70
Namibe B5 70
Namibia 70
Namoluk, atoll C2 15
Namonuito, atoll C2 15
Nampŏ A3 9
Nampa B3 94
Nampula C2 68
Namsos C2 52
Namu, island B2 16
Namuli, highlands C2 33
Namur C2 33
Namur, lake B3 94
Namwala B3 67
Nan B2 12
Nan Ling, mts. E3 10
Nan, river B2 12
Nanaimo L6 95
Nanchang E3 10
Nanchong D2 10
Nancy D2 34
Nanda Devi, mt. C2 20
Nanded C5 20
Nanga Parbat, mt. E2 21
Nanga-Eboko B2 65
Nangi ....Inset II 20
Nangnim-sanmaek, mts. B3 9
Nanjing E2 10
Nanning D3 10
Nanole ....Inset I 20
Nantou B1 9
Nanterre ....Inset II 34
Nantes B3 34
Nanticoke E5 102
Nanumanga, island B1 16
Nanumea, island B1 16
Nanyang E2 10
Nao, cape G3 37
Napadogan C2 97
Napaktulik, lake F3 99
Napanee J3 102
Napier C2 15
Naples C2 38
Naples, bay C2 38
Napo, river C1 77
Nara B3 8
Nara, canal C4 21
Narathiwat B4 12
Narayanganj D5 21
Narayani, river C3 19
Narbonne C5 34
Narcisse C4 96
Nares, strait O1 99
Narew, river E2 41
Narmada, river C4 20
Narrogin, W.A. A3 14
Narrows, river C2 90
Narsaq C2 106

Narva E1 46
Narva, river D1 46
Narvik D2 52
Naryan-Mar C4 44
Naryn E2 23
Naryn, river E2 23
Nashshash, an- C3 25
Nashville, capital, Tenn. E2 126
Nashwaak Bridge C2 97
Näsi, lake B2 53
Nasik B4 20
Nasiriyah, an- C2 24
Nass, river H3 95
Nassau, capital B2 89
Nasser, lake B2 56
Nata B2 69
Natal B2 81
Natalkuz, lake K4 95
Natashquan D3 101
Natitingou A2 64
Natron, lake C1 68
Natuna Besar, island B1 13
Naucalpan de Juárez ....Inset 84
Naujoji Akmenė B1 46
Naumburg B3 40
Nauru 16
Navabad A1 23
Navarino, island C9 76
Navarra F1 37
Navojoa C2 84
Navua B3 17
Navua, river A3 17
Nawabshah C4 21
Nawoiy C2 23
Náxos, island C3 51
Nayarit C3 84
Nazareth B1 26
Nazca C3 77
Naze ....Inset II 8
Nazko L5 95
Nazret C2 60
Nchelenge B1 67
Ndélé B2 66
Ndendé A2 66
Ndjolé A2 66
Ndola B2 67
Néa Liósia ....Inset 51
Neagh, lake A2 30
Neápolis B3 51
Nebitdag B2 22
Neblina, mt. B1 81
Nebraska D1 126
Nechako, river K4 95
Neckar, river B4 40
Necochea D4 74
Neder Rijn, river C3 32
Nee Soon B1 13
Needles N6 95
Neepawa B4 96
Nefta A3 57
Negele C3 60
Negev, region B2 26
Negombo A4 19
Negra, lagoon D2 75
Negra, point A2 77
Negril A4 88
Negro, river B4 74
Negro, river C2 75
Negros, island B4 12
Neguac D1 97
Neiafu C2 17
Neiba A2 89
Neiba, mts. A2 89
Neijiang D3 10
Neil Harbour G1 100
Neilburg A8 104
Neisse, river C3 40
Neiva B4 78
Nekemte C2 60
Nellore C6 20
Nelson B3 15
Nelson O6 95
Nelson Forks L1 95
Nelson House B1 96
Nelson, river C1, D1 96
Nelspruit D2 71
Néma D3 58
Nemeiben, lake E5 104
Nemunas, river A2, C2 46
Nemuro ....Inset I 8
Nemuro, strait ....Inset I 8
Nenagh B2 31
Nendo, island C2 16
Nenetsiya, autonomous okrug C4 44
Nepal 19
Nepalganj B2 19
Nepean C6, K2 102
Nepisiguit, river C1 97
Neretva, river B2 48
Neris, river C2 46
Ness, lake B1 30
Nesselrode, mt. E1 95
Nestaocano, river C2 103
Netanya B1 26
Netherlands 32
Nettilling, lake O3 99
Netzahualcóyotl ....Inset 84
Neubrandenburg C2 40
Neuchâtel A2 35
Neuchâtel, lake A2 35
Neudorf G10 104
Neufchâteau D3 33
Neumünster B1 40
Neunkirchen A4 40
Neuquén B4 74
Neusiedler, lake E3 39
Neuss A3 40
Neustadt A2 85
Neustrelitz C2 40
Nevada B2 126
Nevada, mts. E4 37
Nevers C3 34
Neves ....Inset I 81
Nevėžis, river B2 46
Nevis, island C3 90
New Amsterdam B2 80

Key Page

New Brigden E5 94
New Britain, island B2 15
New Caledonia, island C2 18
New Carlisle L4 103
New Delhi, capital C3 20
New Denver O6 95
New England, range E3 14
New Ferrolle C4 98
New Fish Creek B3 94
New Georgia Group, islands A1 16
New Glasgow E2 100
New Guinea, island A2 15
New Hamburg E4 102
New Hampshire F1 126
New Hanover, island B2 15
New Haven, Conn. F1 126
New Ireland, island B2 15
New Jersey F1 126
New Kowloon .... Inset 10
New Liskeard E3 101
New Mexico C2 126
New Minas C2 100
New Orleans, La. D3 126
New Plymouth B2 15
New Providence, island B3 89
New Richmond L3 103
New Ross C3 100
New Sandy Bay B1 91
New Schwabenland, region B16 107
New Siberian, islands B9 44
New South Wales D3 14
New Territories, island .... Inset 10
New Waterford G1 100
New Waterway, channel B3 32
New York F1 126
New York, N.Y. F1 126
New Zealand 15
New, river C4 80
New, river B1 85
Newark, N.J. F1 126
Newboro J3 102
Newcastle C2 90
Newcastle C2 71
Newcastle upon Tyne C2 30
Newcastle, N.S.W. E3 14
Newcastle-under-Lyme C3 30
Newdale A4 96
Newell, lake E6 94
Newman, W.A. A2 14
Newmarket D3 30
Newmarket F3 102
Newport C3 30
Newport News, Va. F2 126
Newquay B4 30
Newry A2 30
Newtown St. Boswells C2 30
Neyagawa B3 8
Neyshabur D2 22
Ngami, lake A2 69
Ngaoundéré B2 65
Ngara B1 68
Ngaramasch B4 17
Ngauruhoe, mt. C2 15
Ngerkeel B3 17
Ngemelis, islands C2 17
Ngermechau C2 17
Ngetbong C2 17
Ngiro, river D3 61
Ngoc Linh, mt. B3 11
Ngonini B1 71
Ngorongoro, crater C1 68
Ngounié, river A2 66
Ngozi B1 61
Nguigmi C3 59
Ngulu, atoll A2 15
Nguru F1 65
Ngwempisi, river A2 71
Nha Trang B4 11
Nhlangano B3 71
Niagara Falls F4 102
Niagara-on-the-Lake F4 102
Niagassola D1 62
Niamey, capital A3 59
Niamtougou B2 64
Niari, river B5 66
Nias, island A1 13
Nibok B2 16
Nicaragua 87
Nicaragua, lake B3 87
Nice D5 34
Nicholls' Town A2 89
Nickerie, river A2 80
Nicobar, islands F7 20
Nicola M6 95
Nicolet D5 103
Nicosia, capital B1 27
Nicoya, gulf B3 86
Nictau B1 97
Nidže, mts. B3 48
Niedere Tauern, range D3 39
Niefang C3 66
Nienburg B2 40
Niéri Ko, river C2 62
Nieuw Amsterdam B2 80
Nieuw Nickerie A2 80
Nigadoo D1 97
Niğde C3 27
Niger 59
Niger, delta C5 65
Niger, river B3 58
Nigeria 65
Nii, island C2 8
Niigata C2 8
Niihama B3 8
Niihau, island, Hawaii .... Inset II 126
Nijmegen C3 32
Nikaia .... Inset 51
Nikki B3 64
Nikko C2 8
Nikolayevsk-na-Amure D9 44
Nikopol C2 47
Nikšić A3 49
Nilandu, atoll A2 19
Nile, river B2 56
Nilgiri, hills C6 20
Nilópolis .... Inset I 81
Nimba, mt. B3 63

Key Page

Nimba, mts. B2 63
Nîmes D5 34
Nine Mile River D2 100
Ninette B4 96
Ninga B4 96
Ningbo F3 10
Ningxia Hui D2 10
Ninigo, group A2 15
Niono B3 58
Nioro du Rip B3 62
Nioro du Sahel B3 58
Niort B3 34
Nipawin F7 104
Nipigon C3 101
Nipigon, lake C3 101
Nipissing F1 102
Nipissing, lake F1 102
Niš B3 49
Nisāva, river C3 49
Nishino, island .... Inset III 8
Nishinomiya B3 8
Nisling, river B4 105
Niterói .... D4, Inset I 81
Nitra B2 42
Niuafobu, island B1 17
Niuatoputapu, island C1 17
Niulakita, island C4 16
Niutao, island B2 16
Niverville C4 96
Nizamabad C5 20
Nizhnevartosk D4 44
Nizhny Novgorod D4 44
Nizhny Tagil D4 44
Njazidja (Grande Comore), island A1 67
Njombe, river B2 68
Nkawkaw B3 64
Nkhata Bay B2 68
Nkhotakota B2 68
Nkongsamba A2 65
Noakhali E6 21
Nobeoka A3 8
Noel D2 100
Nogales B1 84
Nogales, Ariz. B2 126
Nojima, cape B4 21
Nok Kundi B4 21
Nokaneng A1 69
Nokomis E9 104
Nola A3 66
Nome, Alaska .... Inset I 126
Nonacho, lake G4 99
Nong Khai C2 12
Nonsan B4 9
Nonthaburi B3 12
Nootka, island J6 95
Norak A1 23
Nord-Ostsee, canal B1 40
Nord-Pas-de-Calais C1 34
Nordenham B2 40
Nordhausen B3 40
Nordhorn A2 40
Nordvik B7 44
Norfolk D5 94
Norfolk, Va. F2 126
Norilsk C6 44
Norland G3 102
Normandin D3 103
Normandie B3 34
Norquay H9 104
Norra Storfjället, mt. C1 53
Norris Arm D4 98
Norris Point C4 98
Norrköping C3 53
Norte, key E2 90
N. Albanian Alps, mts. A1, B3 49
North Andaman, island F6 20
North Battleford B8 104
North Bay F1 102
North Cape B1 100
North Carolina F2 126
North China, plain E2 10
North Comino, channel B1 36
North Dakota C1 126
North Downs, hills C3 30
North Frisian, islands B4 32
North Holland, canal B2 32
North Korea 9
North Magnetic Pole B13 106
North Malosmadulu, atoll A2 19
N. Moose, lake B2 96
North Ossetiya, republic E4 44
North Platte, Nebr. C1 126
North Portal H11 104
North Rhine-Westphalia A3 40
North Rustico B2 100
North Saskatchewan, river D8 104
North Sea, canal B2 32
North Shields C2 30
North Siberian, lowland B6 44
North Star B3 94
North Taranaki, bight B2 15
N. Thompson, river N5 95
North Uist, island A1 30
North Wabasca, lake D3 94
North West River A2 98
North West, cape A2 14
North York K5 102
North, cape F1 52
North, channel A2 30
North, channel B1 102
North, island B2 15
North, river B2 98
North, sea 29
Northallerton C2 30
Northampton C3 30
Northeast, polder C2 32
Northeim B3 40
Northern Divina, river C4 44
Northern European, plain B2 40
Northern Sporades, islands B2 51
Northern Territory C2 14
Northgate H11 104
Northumberland, strait .. B3, D2 100
Northwest Gander, river D5 98
Norton D3 97
Norvegia, cape B14 107
Norway 52
Norway House C2 96
Norwegian, bay K1 99

Key Page

Norwegian, sea A2 63
Norwich D3 30
Norwich E4 102
Nossob, river C3 70
Nosy Be, island B1 69
Nosy Sainte Marie, island B2 69
Noteć, river C2, D2 41
Noto, peninsula C2 8
Notre Dame de Lourdes B4 96
Notre Dame Junction D4 98
Notre Dame, bay D4 98
Notre-Dame E2 97
Notre-Dame-de-la-Merci B5 103
Notre-Dame-de-la-Salette A6 103
Notre-Dame-de-Lorette D2 103
Notre-Dame-du-Bon-Conseil D5 103
Notre-Dame-du-Lac H4 103
Notre-Dame-du-Laus A5 103
Nottingham C3 30
Nottingham, island N4 99
Nouadhibou A2 58
Nouakchott, capital A3 58
Nouméa, capital C2 18
Nouvelle K3 103
Nova Gorica A3 48
Nova Iguaçu .... Inset I 81
Novara B1 38
Novaya Zemlya, islands B4 44
Nové Zamky B3 42
Novgorod D3 44
Novi Pazar B3 49
Novi Sad A2 49
Novo Mesto C3 48
Novokuznetsk D6 44
Novosibirsk D6 44
Novra A2 48
Nowshak, mt. D2 21
Nowy Sącz E4 41
Nsanje C3 68
Nsawam B4 64
Nsok D3 66
Nsoko B3 71
Nsukka C4 65
Ntem, river B3 65
Nu'ulua, island D3 18
Nu'utele, island D3 18
Nuba, mts. C3 59
Nubian, desert C1 59
Nueltin, lake J4 99
Nueva Casas Grandes C1 84
Nueva Gerona B2 88
Nueva Loja C2 79
Nueva Ocotepeque A2 86
Nueva Palmira A2 75
Nueva Rosita D2 84
Nueva San Salvador A2 86
Nuevitas D2 88
Nuevo Laredo E2 84
Nuevo León D2 84
Nuevo Rocafuerte D3 79
Nuguria, islands B2 15
Nuhud, an- C2 59
Nui, island B2 16
Nuku'alofa, capital B4 17
Nukufetau, island C2 16
Nukulaelae, island C2 16
Nukuoro, atoll C2 15
Nukus A2 23
Nullarbor, plain B3 14
Numazu C3 8
Ñuñoa .... Inset 76
Nuoro B2 38
Nuremberg B4 40
Nutak E3 98
Nuuk (Godthåb), capital B2 106
Nuuuli B1 18
Nuwara Eliya B5 19
Nyaake C3 63
Nyaba, river B2 61
Nyala B2 59
Nyanga, river A2 66
Nyanza B2 61
Nyasa (Malawi), lake .. B2, B3 68
Nyborg C3 32
Nyeri D4 61
Nyetane, river B2 71
Nyika, plateau B2 68
Nyíregyháza C2 43
Nykøbing C4 32
Nyoman, river B3 47
Nyong, river B3 65
Nysa C3 41
Nzérékoré D4 62
Nzi, river D3 63
Nzoia, river C3 61
Nzwani (Anjouan), island B2 67

Key Page

O

O'Leary A2 100
Oahu, island, Hawaii .... Inset II 126
Oak Lake A4 96
Oak Point C4 96
Oak Point C3 97
Oak River A4 96
Oakland, Calif. A2 126
Oakner A4 96
Oakview A3 96
Oakville A4 96
Oakville F4 102
Oamaru B4 15
Oaxaca, state capital E4 84
Ob, river C5 44
Oban B2 30
Obed B4 94
Oberammergau B5 40
Oberhausen A3 40
Oberpfälzer Wald, mts. C4 40
Obi, island D2 13
Obihiro .... Inset I 8
Obo C2 66
Obock C2 60
Obuasi B3 64
Occidental, mts. B2, C4 77
Ocean Falls J5 95
Ochamchire A3 45
Ochil, hills B2 30
Ocho Rios B2 88
Ochre River B3 96
Ocoa, bay B2 89
Ocotal A2 87
Ocotlán D3 84
Oda B4 64
Odei, river C1 96
Odemira A4 36
Odense C3 32
Odense, fjord C3 32
Odenwald, forest B4 40
Oder, river B2, C3 41
Oderhaff, lake C2 40
Odesa C3 47
Odessa, Tex. C2 126
Odienné C2 63
Oeiras A3 36
Oelemari, river B3 80
Offa C3 65
Offenbach B3 40
Ofu, island A1 18
Ogaden, region D3 60
Ogbomosho C3 65
Ogden, Utah B1 126
Ogema F11 104
Ogilvie, mts. B3 105
Oglio, river B1 38
Ogoki, river C2 101
Ogooué, river A2 66
Ogosta, river B2 50
Ogražden, mts. C2 48
Ogre C2 46
Ogun, river B3 65
Ohio E1 126
Ohio, river E2 126
Ohonua C4 17
Ohrid A2 48
Ohrid, lake A2 49
Øibenik B2 48
Oise, river .... C2, Inset II 34
Oistins B5 91
Oita A3 8
Ojinaga D2 84
Ojos del Salado, mt. B2 74
Oka, river D4 44
Okahandja B2 70
Okakarara C2 70
Okanagan Falls N6 95
Okanagan, lake N6 95
Okavango, basin A1 69
Okavango, river A1 69
Okayama B3 8
Okeechobee, lake, Fla. E3 126
Okene D4 65
Okha D9 44
Okhotsk D9 44
Okhotsk, sea D9 44
Oki, islands B2 8
Okinawa, island .... Inset II 8
Okino Erabu, island .... Inset II 8
Oklahoma D2 126
Oklahoma City, capital, Okla. D2 126
Okondja B2 66
Okotoks C6 94
Okushiri, island .... C1, Inset I 8
Okwa, river A2 69
Ólafsvík A2 52
Olanchito B2 86
Öland, island C3 53
Olavarría C4 74
Olbia B2 38
Old Brahmaputra, river C4 21
Old Crow B2 105
Old Perlican E5 98
Old Road D5 90
Old Road Town B2 90
Old Wives, lake D10 104
Oldenburg B2 40
Oldham C3 30
Oldman, river D6 94
Olds C5 94
Olenek, river C7 44
Oléron, island B4 34
Olgilvie, river B3 105
Ólgiy A2 11
Olifants, river A3, C1 71
Olinda E2 81
Oliver N6 95
Ollagüe, volcano C2 76
Ollei C2 17
Olmaliq C2 23
Olomouc C3 42
Olongapo B3 12
Olosega, island A1 18
Olsztyn E2 41
Olt, river C3 43
Olteniţa D3 43
Olympia, capital, Wash. A1 126
Olympus mt., Wash. A1 126
Olympus, mt. B1 51
Omagh A2 30
Omaha, beach B2 34
Omaha, Nebr. D1 126
Oman 25
Oman, gulf C1, D2 25
Omaruru B2 70
Omatako, river C1 70
Omboué A2 66
Omdurman C2 59
Omemee G3 102
Ometepe, island B3 87
Omineca, mts. J2 95
Omineca, river K3 95
Omiya C3 8
Omo, river B2 60
Omsk D5 44
Omuta A3 8
Onamole B4 96
Ondame B4 96
Ondangwa B1 70
Ondara, river C5 70
Ondjiva C5 70
Ondo C4 65
Ondörhaan D2 11
Onefour E6 94

Key Page

Onega, lake C3 44
Oneşti D2 43
Ongjin A4 9
Ongole C5 20
Onilahy, river A3 69
Onion Lake A7 104
Onitsha D4 65
Ono, island B3 17
Onon, river C2, D3 30
Onota, island A2 17
Onsŏng C1 9
Ontario, lake K4 92
Ontong Java, island A1 16
Oostende A1 33
Oostende-Brugge, canal B1 33
Oosterschelde, channel A3 32
Ootsa, lake J4 95
Opava C3 42
Opeongo, lake G2 102
Opole C3 41
Oporto (Porto) A2 36
Opuwo A1 70
Oqsu, river C2 23
Oradea A2 43
Oral B1 23
Oran A1 57
Orange Walk B1 85
Orange, N.S.W. D3 14
Orange, river A3, B2 71
Orangeville E4 102
Oranje, mts. B2 15
Oranjemund B4 70
Orapa B2 69
Ordino B2 36
Ordu D2 27
Örebro C3 53
Oregon A1 126
Orellana, lake D3 37
Orenburg D4 44
Orense C1 37
Øresund, sound D3 32
Órganos, mts. A2 88
Órgãos, range .... Inset I 81
Orhei B2 50
Orhon, river C2 11
Oriental, mts. B2, C3 77
Oriental, range C2 89
Orillia F3 102
Orinoco, river C3, D2 79
Orion E6 94
Oristano B3 38
Orizaba E4 84
Orkney, islands .... Inset I 30
Orlando, Fla. E3 126
Orléans C3 34
Orléans, island F5, L5 103
Ormoc C4 12
Orne, river B2 34
Örnsköldsvik C2 53
Orocué C3 78
Oroluk, atoll C2 15
Oromocto C3 97
Oron E5 65
Orontes, river A2 27
Orosháza C2 43
Orrefors C3 53
Orsha E2 47
Orsk D4 44
Ortegal, cape C1 37
Orumiyeh (Urmia) A2 22
Oruro A3 77
Oryakhovo B2 50
Os, river A3 36
Osaka B3 8
Osasco .... Inset II 81
Osh C2 23
Oshakati B1 70
Oshawa G4 102
Oshima, peninsula .. D1, Inset I 8
Oshogbo C4 65
Osijek D2 48
Osilinka, river K3 95
Öskemen (Ust-Kamenogorsk) E1 23
Oslo, capital C3 53
Oslofjord, fjord C4 52
Osnabrück B2 40
Osorno B7 76
Osoyoos N6 95
Oss C3 32
Osse, river C4 65
Österdalälven, river B2 53
Östersund B2 53
Ostrava D3 42
Ostrołęka E2 41
Osum, river B3 49
Osumi, islands A4 8
Osumi, peninsula A4 8
Osumi, strait A4 8
Osŭm, river C3 50
Otaru .... Inset I 8
Otavalo B2 79
Otavi C1 70
Oti, river B1, C2 64
Otjiwarongo B2 70
Otranto D2 38
Otranto, strait A3 49
Otsu B3 8
Ottawa H5, K2 102
Ottawa, river G1, G5 H5, K2 102
Otterburne C2 32
Ötztal Alps, range B4 39
Ou, mts. D2 8
Ou, river B1 11
Ouadane B2 58
Ouagadougou, capital D2 64
Ouahigouya B2 64
Ouaka, river B2 66
Ouanary C1 80
Ouargla B1 57
Ouarra, river C2 66
Ouarzazate C2 57
Oudtshoorn B3 71
Ouéssé B3 64
Ouesso B1 66
Ouezzane C1 57
Ouham, river B2 66
Ouidah B4 64
Oujda D1 57

Key Page

Oulu C1 53
Oulu, lake C2 53
Oulujoki, river C2 53
Oum er-Rbia, river C1 57
Ounasjoki, river B1 53
Oungre G11 104
Our, river B1 33
Ourthe, river D2 33
Ouse, river C2, D3 30
Outarde, river H2 103
Outer Hebrides, islands A1 30
Outjo C9 104
Outlook C9 104
Ouvéa, island C2 18
Ovalau, island B2 17
Ovalle B4 76
Overflakkee, island B3 32
Overflowing River A2 96
Oviedo A3 89
Oviedo D1 37
Owando C4 66
Owen Sound E3 102
Owen Stanley, range A2 15
Owendo A1 66
Owensboro, Ky. E2 126
Owerri D5 65
Oxbow H11 104
Oxford C3 30
Oxford D2 96
Oxford House D1, D2 96
Oxford, lake D2 96
Oyapock, river B2 80
Oyem A1 66
Oyo B4 65
Ozama, river B2 89
Ozark, plateau D2 126
Ózd C1 43
Özgön C2 23
Ozoir-la-Ferrière .... Inset II 34
Ozurgeti A4 45

P

Pa-an C3 12
Paamiut (Frederikshåb) C2 106
Pabna C4 21
Pacaraima, mts. D3 79
Pacasmayo B2 77
Pachuca, state capital E3 84
Padang B2 13
Paddle Prairie B2 94
Paderborn B3 40
Padma, river D5 21
Padua (Padova) B1 38
Paektu-san, mt. C2 9
Pagadian B5 12
Pago Pago, capital B1 18
Pahang, river B2 13
Paianía .... Inset 51
Päijänne, lake C2 53
Paint, lake B1 96
Paisley B2 30
Paita A2 77
Pakaraima, mts. A3 80
Pakistan 21
Pakowki, lake E6 94
Paks B2 43
Pakse C4 11
Pala A5 59
Palaiseau .... Inset II 34
Palana D10 44
Palanga A2 46
Palangkaraya C2 13
Palau 17
Palawan, island A4 12
Paldiski C1 46
Pale B2 48
Palembang B2 13
Palencia D1 37
Palermo C2 38
Palikir, capital C2 15
Palk, strait C7 20
Palliser, cape C3 15
Palm, island A4 91
Palma H3 37
Palmas C2 15
Palmer Land, region B11 107
Palmerston E4 102
Palmerston North C3 15
Palmira A4 78
Palmyra, ruins B2 27
Palos, cape F4 37
Palu C2 13
Pamirs, mts. B2 23
Pamirs, region A2 10
Pampas, plain C4 74
Pamplemousses C2 69
Pamplona F1 37
Panagyurishte C3 50
Panaji B5 20
Panama 87
Panama, canal C2 87
Panamá, capital C3 87
Panama, gulf C3 87
Panay, gulf B4 12
Panay, island B4 12
PanΔevo B2 49
Panch'iao B1 9
Pandan, strait A2 13
Pandaruan, river C2 13
Pando C3 75
Panevėžys C2 46
Pangani, river C1 68
Pangkalpinang B2 13
Pangnirtung Q3 99
Panihati .... Inset II 20
Panj A2 23
Panj, river A2 23
Panjakent A1 23
Panjgur B4 21
P'anmunjŏm B4 9
Pantanal, lowland C4 81
Pantelleria, island C3 38
Pánuco, river E3 84
Panzhihua D3 10
Pápa A2 43
Papagayo, gulf A2 86
Paphos A2 27
Papua, gulf A2 15

	Key	Page
Papua New Guinea		15
Paquetville	D1	97
Pará	C2	81
Pará, river	C2	81
Paradise Hill	A7	104
Paradise River		98
Paraguá, river	B2	77
Paraguai, river	C3	81
Paraguarí	D4	75
Paraguay		75
Paraguay, river	C2, C5	75
Paraíba	E2	81
Parakou	B3	64
Paramaribo, capital	B2	80
Paraná	C3	74
Paraná	C4	81
Paraná, river	D2	74
Paranaguá	D4	81
Paranam	B2	80
Pardubice	B2	42
Parent	B4	103
Parepare	C2	13
Paria, gulf	D1	79
Parima, range	B1	81
Paris, capital	C2, Inset II	34
Paris	E4	102
Parkhill	D4	102
Parkland	D6	94
Parksville	K6	95
Parma	B1	38
Parnaíba	D2	81
Parnaíba, river	D2	81
Pärnu	C2	46
Pärnu, river	C2	46
Paro	A2	19
Paropamisus, range	A2	22
Páros, island	C3	51
Parral	B6	76
Parrsboro	C2	100
Parry	D2	99
Parry Sound	E2	102
Parry, channel	J2	99
Parsnip, river	L4	95
Parson's Pond	C4	98
Pas de la Casa	C2	36
Pasadena	C5	98
Pasfield, lake	E2	104
Pasión, river	C3	85
Paso de los Toros	B2	75
Paso de Palmar, lake	B2	75
Passau	C4	40
Passero, cape	C3	38
Passo Fundo	C4	81
Pastavy	C2	47
Pastaza, river	B1	77
Pastillo	C3	90
Pasto	A4	78
Patagonia, region	A6	74
Patavilca	B3	77
Paterson, N.J.	F1	126
Patía, river	A4	78
Patiala	C2	20
Patillas	C2	90
Patna	E3	20
Patos, lagoon	C5	81
Pátrai	B2	51
Patricia	E6	94
Pattani	B5	12
Patuakhali	D6	21
Patuanak	C5	104
Patuca, mts.	C2	86
Patuca, river	C2	86
Pau	B5	34
Pauingassi	D3	96
Paulatuk	D3	99
Paulaya, river	C2	86
Paulo Afonso	E2	81
Pavaiai	B2	18
Pavia	B1	38
Pavilosta	A2	46
Pavlodar	D1	23
Paxbán	C2	85
Payar	B2	62
Paye	Inset	20
Payne, lake	B2	101
Paynton	B7	104
Pays De La Loire	B3	34
Paysandú	A2	75
Paz, river	C6	85
Pazardzhik	C3	50
Peace Point	D1	94
Peace River		94
Peace, river	A3, C2	94
Peachland	N6	95
Pebane	C3	68
Pe~	B3	49
Pechora	C4	44
Pechora, river	C4	44
Pécs	B2	43
Pedernales	A2	89
Pedja, river	D2	46
Pedra Açú, mt.	Inset I	81
Pedra Lume	D2	58
Pedro Juan Caballero	E3	75
Pedro Santana	A1	89
Peebles	H10	104
Peel, river	B3, C2	105
Peerless Lake	C3	94
Pegasus, bay	B3	15
Pegu	C3	12
Peipus, lake	D2	46
Pekalongan	B2	13
Pekanbaru	B1	13
Pelee, island	C6	102
Peleliu, island	B4	17
Peleng, island	D2	13
Pelican Narrows	H5	104
Pelican Portage	D3	94
Pelican Rapids	A3	96
Pelican, lake	G5	104
Pelkan, lake	A3	96
Pelly	J9	104
Pelly Bay	L3	99
Pelly Crossing	B4	105
Pelly, river	C4, C5	105
Pelotas	C5	81
Pematangsiantar	A1	13
Pemba	D2	68
Pemba, island	C2	68

	Key	Page
Pemberton	L6	95
Pembina, river	B4	94
Pembina, river	B4	96
Pembroke	B3	30
Pembroke	H2	102
Penas, gulf	B8	76
Pendé, river	A2	66
Pendleton, Oreg.	B1	126
Penetanguishene	F3	102
P'enghu (Pescadores), islands	A2	9
Peniche	A3	36
Peninsular Malaysia, region	B2	13
Pennant	B10	104
Pennine Alps, mts.	B2	35
Pennines, mts.	C2	30
Pennsylvania	F1	126
Penonomé	B2	87
Penrith	C2	30
Pensacola, Fla.	E2	126
Pensacola, mts.	A11	107
Pentecost, island	C2	18
Penticton	N6	95
Peñuelas	B2	90
Penza	D4	44
Penzance	B4	30
Peoria, Ill.	E1	126
Perak, river	A2	13
Percé	M3	103
Perdue	C8	104
Pereira	B3	78
Péribonca, river	B3	101
Péribonka	D3	103
Périgueux	C4	34
Perim, island	A2	25
Peristéri	Inset	51
Perlas, archipelago	C2	87
Perlas, lagoon	C2	87
Perm	D4	44
Pernambuco	E2	81
Pernik	B3	50
Perpignan	C5	34
Perrot, island	G6	103
Persian, gulf	C1, C2, C3	24
Perth	B2	30
Perth	J3	102
Perth, W.A., capital	A3, Inset I	14
Perth-Andover	B2	97
Peru		77
Perugia	C2	38
Pervomaysk	C2	47
Pesaro	C2	38
Pescadores, channel	A2	9
Pescara	C2	38
Peshawar	D3	21
Peshkopi	B2	49
Petah Tiqwa	B1	26
Petare	C1	79
Petauke	C2	67
Petawawa	H2	102
Petén-Itzá, lake	D3	85
Peterborough	C3	30
Peterborough	G3	102
Peterhead	C1	30
Petersfield	C4	96
Petit Canouan, island	B3	91
Petit Martinique, island	C1	91
Petit Mustique, island	B3	91
Petit St. Vincent, island	A4	91
Petit-Rocher	D1	97
Petitcodiac	D3	97
Petite Riviere	C3	100
Petlura	A3	96
Petra, ruins	A2	26
Petrich	B4	50
Petrila	B3	43
Petrolia	C5	102
Petrólina	D2	81
Petropavl	C1	23
Petropavlovsk-Kamchatskiy	D9	102
Petrópolis	D4, Inset I	81
Petro∑ani	B3	43
Petrozavodsk	C3	44
Pevek	C10	23
Peyia	A2	27
Pforzheim	B4	40
Phan Rang	B4	11
Phan Thiet	B4	11
Phatthalung	B5	12
Phayao	B2	12
Phetchabun	B2	12
Phetchabun, range	B3	12
Phetchaburi	B3	12
Phichit	B2	12
Philadelphia, Pa.	F2	126
Philippine, sea	C3	12
Philippine, sea	B2	17
Philippines		12
Phitsanulok	B2	12
Phnom Penh, capital	C4	11
Phnum Tbeng Meanchey	C2	11
Phoenix, capital, Ariz.	B2	126
Phoenix, island	B2	17
Phoenix, islands	B1	11
Phôngsali	B1	11
Phou Bia, mt.	B2	11
Phra Nakhon Si Ayutthaya	B3	12
Phuket	B5	12
Phumi Samraong	B1	11
Phuntsholing	A3	19
Pianosa, island	B2	38
Piapot	A10	104
Piatra Neamc	D2	43
Piauí	D2	81
Piave, river	C1	38
Pibor Post	C3	59
Pic de la Selle, mt.	D2	89
Picardie	C2	34
Pickle Lake	B2	101
Pico do Cano, volcano	B4	58
Picton	H3	102
Pictou	E2	100
Pidurutalagala, mt.	B4	19
Piedmont	A1	38
Piedra Sola	B2	75
Piedras Negras	D2	84
Pielinen, lake	C2	53
Pierceland	A6	104
Pierre, capital, S. Dak.	C1	126

	Key	Page
Pierrefonds	G5	103
Pierreville	A2	91
Pierson	A4	96
Pie%t'any	A2	42
Pietermaritzburg	D2	71
Pietersburg	C1	71
Pigeon, lake	C4	94
Pigeon, lake	G3	102
Piggs Peak	B1	71
Pikangikum	B2	101
Pikes peak, Colo.	C2	126
Pikwitonei	C1	96
Pi{a	C2	41
Pilar	C5	75
Pilaya, river	B4	77
Pilcomayo, river	B3, C4	75
Pilica, river	E3	41
Pílos	B3	51
Pilot Butte	F10	104
Pilot Mound	B4	96
Pinang, island	A2	13
Pinar del Río	A2	88
Pinawa	D4	96
Pindus, mts.	B2	51
Pine Bluff, Ark.	D2	126
Pine Dock	C3	96
Pine Falls	C4	96
Pine Point	F4	99
Pine River	A3	96
Pinehouse Lake	D5	104
Pines, island	D2	18
Ping, river	B2	12
P'ingtung	B2	9
Pingxiang	E3	10
Piniós, river	B2	51
Pink Mountain	L2	95
Pink, river	F4	104
Pinsk	C3	47
Pinta, island	Inset	79
Piotrków Trybunalski	D3	41
Pipestone	A4	96
Pipmuacan, reservoir	F2	103
Piracicaba	D4	81
Pirada	C1	62
Piraiévs	B3, Inset	51
Pirmasens	A4	40
Pirot	C3	49
Pirris, river	B3	86
Pisa	B2	38
Pisagua	B1	76
Pisco	B3	77
Pistoia	B2	38
Pite∑ti	C3	43
Pitlochry	B2	30
Pitseng	B2	71
Pitt, island	H4	95
Pittsburgh, Pa.	E1	126
Piura	A2	77
Placentia	B3	85
Placentia	D5	98
Placentia, bay	D5	98
Placenza	B1	38
Placetas	C2	88
Planken	B1	33
Plantagenet	K2	102
Plasencia	C2	37
Plaster Rock	B2	97
Plata, Río de la, estuary	D3	74
Plata, river	B3	75
Platte, river, Nebr.	C1	126
Plauen	C3	40
Playgreen, lake	B2	96
Pleasant Bay	G1	100
Pleiku	B4	11
Plenty, bay	C2	15
Plessisville	E5	103
Pleven	C2	50
Plevna	J3	102
Plibo	C3	63
Pljevlja	A3	49
Plo∆e	C3	48
Ploie∑ti	D3	43
Plovdiv	C3	50
Plum Coulee	C4	96
Plumas	B4	96
Plymouth	B1	91
Plymouth	B4	30
Plze√	A3	42
Po, river	A1, B1	38
Poá	Inset II	81
Pobé	B4	64
Pocatello, Idaho	B1	126
Podgorica	A3	49
Pogradec	B3	49
P'ohang	C4	9
Pohnpei, island	D2	15
Point Fortin	A2	91
Point Leamington	D4	98
Point Pedro	B2	19
Point Prim	B2	100
Point, lake	F3	99
Pointe au Baril	E2	102
Pointe du Bois	D4	96
Pointe Michel	B3	90
Pointe Sapin	D2	97
Pointe-a-la-Croix	K3	103
Pointe-Claire	H6	103
Pointe-des-Monts	J2	103
Pointe-Lebel	H2	103
Pointe-Noire	A6	66
Pointe-Verte	D1	97
Poisson Blanc, reservoir	A6	103
Poissy	Inset II	34
Poitiers	C3	34
Poitou-Charentes	C3	34
Pokemouche	E1	97
Pokhara	B2	19
Poland		41
Polar, plateau	A14	107
Polba	Inset II	20
Polis	A1	27
Polonnaruwa	C4	19
Polotsk	C2	47
Poltava	D2	47
Poltimore	A6	103
Pomeranian, bay	C1	40
Ponce	B2	90

	Key	Page
Pond Cove	C3	98
Pond Inlet	N2	99
Pondicherry	C6	20
Ponferrada	C1	37
Ponoka	D5	94
Pont Cassé	B3	90
Pont-Rouge	E5	103
Pontchartrain	Inset II	34
Ponteix	C11	104
Pontevedra	B1	37
Pontianak	B2	13
Pontic, mts.	D2	27
Pontine, islands	C2	38
Pontine, marshes	C2	38
Pontoise	Inset II	34
Ponton	B2	96
Poole	C4	30
Poopó, lake	A3	77
Popayán	A4	78
Poperinge	A2	33
Poplar River	C3	96
Popomanaseu, mt.	B1	16
Popondetta	B2	15
Poprad	C2	42
Porcupine Plain	G8	104
Porcupine, river	B2	105
Pori	B2	53
Port Alberni	K6	95
Port Antonio	C2	88
Port au Choix	C4	98
Port au Port	B5	98
Port Augusta, S.A.	C3	14
Port Bickerton	F2	100
Port Blair	F6	20
Port Blandford	D5	98
Port Bruce	E5	102
Port Burwell	D3	98
Port Burwell	E5	102
Port Clements	F4	95
Port Colborne	F5	102
Port Coquitlam	L6	95
Port Dufferin	E3	100
Port Elgin	E3	97
Port Elgin	D3	102
Port Elizabeth	B2	71
Port Elizabeth	A4	91
Port Franks	D4	102
Port George		71
Port Glaud	Inset	70
Port Harcourt	D5	65
Port Hardy	J6	95
Port Hawkesbury	F2	100
Port Hedland, W.A.	A2	14
Port Hood	F1	100
Port Hope	G4	102
Port Hope Simpson	C3	98
Port Laoise	C2	31
Port Lincoln, S.A.	C3	14
Port Loko	A1	63
Port Loring	E2	102
Port Louis, capital	B2	69
Port Macquarie, N.S.W.	E3	14
Port Maria	C2	88
Port McNeill	J6	95
Port Moody	L6	95
Port Morant	D4	88
Port Moresby, capital	A2	15
Port Mouton	C4	100
Port Nolloth	A2	71
Port Perry	G3	102
Port Phillip, bay	Inset V	14
Port Pirie, S.A.	C3	14
Port Renfrew	K7	95
Port Rowan	E5	102
Port Said	B1	56
Port Saunders	C4	98
Port Stanley	D5	102
Port Sudan	D1	59
Port Talbot	B3	30
Port-au-Prince, bay	C2	89
Port-au-Prince, capital	C{ock	89
Port-Cartier	C3	101
Port-de-Paix	C1	89
Port-Gentil	A2	66
Port-Salut	A2	89
Portadown	A2	30
Portage	A2	90
Portage la Prairie	B4, D2	96
Portalegre	B3	36
Porter, lake	C4	104
Porth Edward	D3	71
Portimão	A4	36
Portland	A2	91
Portland Creek	C4	98
Portland, bight	B3	88
Portland, inlet	G4	95
Portland, Maine	F1	126
Portland, Oreg.	A1	126
Portneuf, river	G3	103
Porto Alegre	B4	63
Pôrto Alegre	C5	81
Pôrto Inglês	C3	58
Pôrto Velho	B2	81
Porto-Novo, capital	B4	64
Porto-Vecchio	Inset I	34
Portobelo	C2	87
Portoviejo	A3	79
Portree	A1	30
Portsmouth	C4	90
Portsmouth	A2	90
Portsmouth, Va.	F2	126
Portugal		36
Porvenir	B9	76
Posadas	D2	74
Poste, river	C3	34
Postojna	B3	48
Postville	D3	98
Potaro, river	B3	80
Potenza	C2	38
Poti	A3	45
Potiskum	F2	65
Potnarvin	C4	18
Potosí	C3	77
Potrerillos	C3	76
Potsdam	C2	40
Pottuvil	C5	19
Pouch Cove	E5	98

	Key	Page
Poutasi	C3	18
Pouthisat	B3	11
Pova∢ská Bystrica	B2	42
Powassan	F1	102
Powell River	K6	95
Powerview	C4	96
Poyang, lake	E3	10
Poza Rica	E3	84
Po∝arevac	B2	49
Poznań	C2	41
Pozo Colorado	C3	75
Pra, river	B4	64
Prachuap Khiri Khan	B4	12
Prague, capital	B2	42
Praia, capital	B2	58
Praslin	C1	70
Praslin, island	B2	91
Prato	B2	38
Prawda	B4	96
Preeceville	H9	104
Prelate	A10	104
Preparis, island	B3	12
Prescott	K3	102
Prescott, Ariz.	B2	126
Presidencia Roque Sáenz Peña	C2	74
Pre%ov	C2	42
Prespa, lake	B3	48
Presque Isle, Maine	G1	126
Prestea	A4	64
Preston	C3	30
Pretoria, administrative capital	C2	71
Préveza	B2	51
Prey Veng	D4	11
Priboj	A3	49
Priddis	C6	94
Prievidza	B2	42
Prijedor	A1	48
Prilep	B3	48
Priluki	C1	47
Primorsko	F3	50
Primrose, lake	A6	104
Prince Albert	E7	104
Prince Albert, hills	L3	99
Prince Albert, peninsula	E2	99
Prince Charles, island	N3	99
Prince George	L4	95
Prince of Wales, island	J2	99
Prince Patrick, island	E1	99
Prince Regent, inlet	K2	99
Prince Rupert	G4	95
Princes Town	A2	91
Princess Harbour	C3	96
Princess Margriet, canal	C1	32
Princess Royal, island	H4	95
Princeton	M6	95
Princeville	E5	103
Príncipe, island	C1	63
Prinzapolka	C2	87
Prinzapolka, river	C2	87
Pripyats, marshes	C4	47
Pripyats, river	B3	47
Pri%tina	B3	49
Privas	D4	34
Prizren	B3	49
Progresso	B1	85
Prokopyevsk	D6	44
Prokuplje	B3	49
Prome	B2	12
Prophet River	L4	95
Prost~jov	C3	42
Provence-Alpes-Côte-d'Azur	D4	34
Providence Bay	C2	102
Providence, capital, R.I.	F1	126
Providencia, island	Inset	78
Providenciales, island	C4	89
Provideniya	C11	44
Provo, Utah	B1	126
Pru, river	B3	64
Prut, river	B2	47
Przemyśl	F4	41
Psel, river	C1	47
Pskov	D3	44
Pskov, lake	D3	47
Ptsich, river	D3	47
Ptuj	C3	22
Pu'apu'a	B2	18
Pubnico	C2	100
Pucallpa	B2	77
Puck	D1	41
Puebla, state capital	E4	84
Pueblo, Colo.	C2	126
Puente Alto	Inset	76
Puerca, point	D2	90
Puerto Aisén	B8	76
Puerto Armuelles	A2	87
Puerto Ayacucho	C2	79
Puerto Bahía	D3	77
Puerto Barrios	E4	85
Puerto Bolívar	B4	79
Puerto Cabello	C1	79
Puerto Cabezas	C1	87
Puerto Carreño	D2	78
Puerto Cisnes	B7	76
Puerto Cortés	B6	74
Puerto Deseado	B6	74
Puerto Escondido	B5	84
Puerto Inírida	D4	78
Puerto Jiménez	B2	86
Puerto Leguízamo	B5	78
Puerto Lempira	D2	86
Puerto Maldonado	D3	77
Puerto Montt	B7	76
Puerto Natales	B9	76
Puerto Peñasco	B1	84
Puerto Pinasco	D3	75
Puerto Plata	B1	89
Puerto Princesa	A4	12
Puerto Real		90
Puerto Rico		90
Puerto Quepos	A2	87
Puerto Sandino	A2	87
Puerto Santa Cruz	C3	74
Puerto Suárez	C3	77
Puerto Vallarta	C3	84
Puerto Varas	B7	76
Puerto Williams	C9	76

	Key	Page
Puertollano	D3	37
Puglia	C2	38
Pugwash	D2	100
Pujehun	B2	63
Pukatawagan	A1	96
Pukch'Ing	C2	9
Pukë	A1	49
Pula	A3	48
Pulangi, river	C5	12
Pu{awy	E3	41
Pulo Anna, island	Inset	17
Pulusuk, island	B2	15
Puná, island	A4	79
Punakha	A2	19
Pune	B5	20
Punggol	B1	13
P'ungsan	C2	9
Puno	C4	77
Punta, mt.	B2	90
Punta Arenas	B9	76
Punta del Este	C3	75
Punta Delgada	B9	76
Punta Gorda	B3	85
Punta Santiago	D2	90
Puntarenas	B3	86
Punto Fijo	B1	79
Purari, river	A2	15
Purbeck's Cove	C4	98
Purus, river	B2	81
Pusan	C5	9
Putao	C1	12
Putre	C1	76
Puttalam	A3	19
Puttgarden	B1	40
Putumayo, river	B5	78
Puvirnituq	A1	101
Puyo	C3	79
Puysegur, point	A4	15
Pyandzh, river	B1	23
P'yŏngang	B3	9
P'yŏngsng	B3	9
P'yŏngan	B3	9
P'yŏngyang, capital	A3	9
Pyrenees, range	C5	34

Q

	Key	Page
Qaanaaq (Thule)	B2	106
Qachas Nek	B3	71
Qadarif, al-	C2	59
Qaidam, basin	C2	10
Qalat	B2	22
Qalat Bishah	B2	24
Qaleh-ye Now	A2	22
Qaleh-ye Panjeh	C1	22
Qamea, island	C2	17
Qamishli, al-	B1	27
Qandahar	B2	22
Qaqortoq (Julianehåb)	C2	106
Qaraghandy (Karaganda)	D2	23
Qardho	C2	60
Qareh, river	B2	22
Qarokul, lake	B1	23
Qarshi	C2	23
Qaryah ash-Sharqiyah, al-	B1	56
Qasigiannguit (Christianshåb)	B2	106
Qasr as-Sabiyah	C2	24
Qatar		25
Qatranah, al-	B3	56
Qattarah, depression	A2	56
Qayrawan, al-	C2	57
Qayyarah, al-	B1	24
Qazvin	B2	22
Qelelevu, island	C2	17
Qeshm, island	D4	22
Qilian, range	C2	10
Qin Ling, mts.	D2	10
Qina	B2	56
Qingdao	F2	10
Qinghai	C2	10
Qinghai, lake	C2	10
Qinhuangdao	E2	10
Qiqihar	F1	10
Qiryat Gat	B2	26
Qiryat Shemona	B1	26
Qishn	C3	25
Qom	C3	22
Qormi	B2	36
Qostanay	C1	23
Qu'Appelle	G10	104
Qu'Appelle, river	D10	104
Quang Ngai	B3	11
Quantaq	C1	101
Quanzhou	E3	10
Quatre Bornes	B3	69
Quba	C2	45
Qubayyat, al-	B1	26
Québec, capital	E5, L6	103
Quebo	C2	62
Quebradillas	B2	90
Queen Charlotte	F4	95
Queen Charlotte, islands	G4	95
Queen Charlotte, sound	H5	95
Queen Charlotte, strait	H5	95
Queen Elizabeth, islands	J1	99
Queen Maud Land, region	B16	107
Queen Maud, mts.	A5	107
Queen Maude, gulf	H3	99
Queensland	D2	14
Queenstown	B1	13
Queenstown	A3	15
Queenstown	C3	71
Queenstown, Tas.	D4	14
Queguay Grande, river	B2	75
Queimados	Inset I	81
Quelimane	C3	68
Quellón	B7	76
Queluz	A3	36
Querétaro, state capital	D3	84
Quesnel	L5	95
Quesnel, lake	M5	95
Quetta	C3	21
Quetzaltenango	B5	85
Quevedo	B3	79
Quezon City	B2	12
Qui Nhon	B4	11
Quibala	C2	70

Key Page

Quibdó A3 78
Quilchena M6 95
Quill Lake F8 104
Quill, lakes F8 104
Quillota B4 76
Quilpué ....Inset 76
Quimbele C2 70
Quimper A2 34
Quinhámel B2 62
Quintana Roo G4 85
Quispamsis D3 97
Quito, capital B3 79
Qunaytirah, al- A3 27
Qunfudhah, al- B2 24
Qunghirot A2 23
Quqon D2 23
Qurghonteppa A2 23
Qurnat as-Sawda, mt. B1 26
Quthing A3 71
Qyzylorda C2 23

R

Raahe B2 53
Raanes, peninsula L1 99
Raba, river C2 13
Rába, river A2 43
Rabat B2 36
Rabat, capital C1 57
Rabaul B2 15
Rabbit Lake C7 104
Rabbit Lake Mine G2 104
Rabi, island C2 17
Rach Gia A4 11
Rachidia, er- C2 57
Racine, Wis. E1 126
Radium Hot Springs O6 95
Radom E3 41
Radviliškis B2 46
Radville F11 104
Rae E4 99
Rafha B1 24
Rafter A1 96
Ragged, point C3 91
Ragueneau H2 103
Ragusa C3 38
Rahimyar Khan D4 21
Rainier mt., Wash. A1 126
Raipur D4 20
Rajang, river C2 13
Rajbiraj C3 19
Rajkot B4 20
Rajpur ....Inset II 20
Rajshahi B4 21
Raleigh, capital, N.C. F2 126
Ralik, island chain A1 16
Rama B2 87
Ramadi, ar- B2 24
Ramanbati ....Inset II 20
Ramat Gan B1 26
Ramea C5 98
Ramla B2 26
Ramon, mt. B2 26
Ramree, island B2 12
Ramtha, ar- B1 26
Ramu F2 61
Ramu, river A2 15
Rancagua B4 76
Rance, river B2 34
Ranchi E4 20
Randa C2 32
Randers C2 32
Randonópolis C3 81
Ranfurly E4 94
Rangamati F6 21
Ranger Lake B1 102
Rangitikei, river C2 15
Rangpur C3 21
Ranong B4 12
Rapel, river B4 76
Rapid City A4 99
Rapid City, S. Dak. C1 126
Rapla C1 46
Rapti, river B2 19
Raqqah, ar- B2 27
Ras al-Khafji C1 24
Ras al-Khaymah C2 25
Ras an-Naqb A2 26
Ras Dashen, mt. C1 60
Ras Musandam, cape C1 25
Ras Tanura C1 24
Rasa, point C5 74
Rashayya A2 26
Rasht B2 22
Ratak, island chain B1 16
Ratchaburi B3 12
Rathlin, island A2 30
Ratingen A3 40
Ratnapura B5 19
Raukumara, range C2 15
Rauma B2 53
Raurkela D4 20
Raut, river B2 50
Ravenna C1 38
Ravensburg B5 40
Ravenna, river D3 21
Rawalpindi D3 21
Rawdatyan, ar- B2 24
Rawdon D2 100
Rawson B5 74
Raymore F9 104
Rayong B3 12
Rayside-Balfour D1 102
Raz, point A3 34
Razelm, lake A3 104
Razgrad E2 50
Ré, island B3 34
Reading C3 30
Rebun, island ....Inset I 8
Rechytsa E3 47
Recife E2 81
Recklinghausen A3 40
Reconquista D2 74
Red (Hong), river A2 11
Red Bay C3 98

Red Deer D5 94
Red Deer, lake A2 96
Red Deer, river D5, E6 94
Red Indian, lake C5 98
Red Rose C3 96
Red Sucker, lake E2 96
Red Volta, river B1, B3 64
Red Willow D5 94
Red, river C4 96
Red, sea A1 24
Redange A2 33
Redbridge F1 102
Redding, Calif. A1 126
Redonda, island A6 90
Redstone L5 95
Redvers A4 96
Redvers J11 104
Ree, lake B2 31
Reed, lake A2 96
Regensburg C4 40
Reggio di Calabria C3 38
Reggio nell'Emilia B1 38
Reghin C2 43
Regina F10 104
Régina B1 80
Registan, region A2 22
Rehoboth C3 70
Rehovot B2 26
Reigate ....Inset III 30
Reims D2 34
Reina Adelaida, archipelago B9 76
Reindeer, island C3 96
Reindeer, lake H3 104
Reindeer, river G4 104
Reinosa D1 37
Reliance G4 99
Remagen A3 40
Remich B2 33
Rémire B1 80
Remscheid A3 40
Rencontre East D5 98
Renfrew J2 102
Rennell, island B2 16
Rennes B2 34
Rennie D4 96
Reno, Nev. B2 126
Renous D2 97
Repentigny K5 103
Reserve H8 104
Resistencia D2 74
Reșița A3 43
Resolute J2 99
Resolution, island P4 99
Restigouche, river B1 97
Reston A4 96
Restoule F1 102
Réunion, island C3 77
Reus G2 37
Reuss, river C2 35
Reutlingen B4 40
Revelstoke N6 95
Reventazón, river C3 86
Revillagigedo, islands B4 84
Rexdale J5 102
Rexton E2 97
Rey, island C2 87
Reykjavik B3 96
Reykjavík, capital A2 52
Reynosa E2 84
Rezekne D2 46
Reznas, lake D2 46
Rhaetian Alps, mts. D2 35
Rharsa, salt marsh C2 57
Rhine, canal B1, B3 33
Rhine, river A3, A4 40
Rhineland-Palatinate A4 40
Rhode Island F1 126
Rhodes D3 51
Rhodes, island D3 51
Rhodope, mts. C4 50
Rhondda B3 30
Rhône, river D4 34
Rhône-Alpes D4 34
Rhum, island A1 30
Riaba A1 66
Ribe B3 32
Ribeira Brava B2 58
Ribeira Grande A1 58
Ribeirão Pires ....Inset II 81
Ribeirão Prêto D4 81
Riberalta A2 77
Ribnica B2 50
Rice, lake G3 102
Richard, lake C1 104
Richard-Toll B1 62
Richards Bay D2 71
Richards Landing A1 102
Richardson, mts. B1 105
Richardson, river E2 94
Richelieu, river C6 103
Richer C4 96
Richibucto E2 97
Richmond L6 95
Richmond D6 103
Richmond Hill F4, K5 102
Richmond Park C5 103
Richmond, capital, Va. F2 126
Ricobayo, reservoir D2 37
Rida A2 25
Rideau, lake J3 102
Rideau, river H6 102
Riesa C3 40
Rieti C2 38
Riga, capital C2 46
Riga, gulf B2, B3 46
Rigolet B2 98
Riiser-Larsen Ice Shelf, glacier B14 107
Riiser-Larsen, peninsula C16 107
Rijeka A2 43
Rila, mts. B3 50
Rimini C1 38
Rîmnicu Vîlcea C3 43
Rimouski H3 103
Rincón, bay C3 90
Rincón del Bonete, lake C3 75
Ringkøbing B2 32
Río Blanco B2 87

Rio Branco B2 81
Rio Claro A2 91
Río Cuarto C3 74
Rio de Janeiro ....D4, Inset I 81
Río Gallegos B7 74
Río Grande C5 74
Río Grande D2 90
Río Grande A2 87
Rio Grande (Río Bravo), river D2 84
Rio Grande do Norte E2 81
Rio Grande do Sul C4 81
Rio Verde C3 81
Riobamba B3 79
Ríohacha B2 78
Rioni, river B3 45
Riou, lake D1 104
Rîșcani A2 50
Rishiri, island ....Inset I 8
Rishra ....Inset II 20
Riske Creek L5 95
Ritchies, archipelago F6 20
Rivas B3 87
River Cess B3 63
River Hills C4 96
River John D2 100
Rivercrest C4 96
Riverhurst D10 104
Rivers A4 96
Rivers Inlet J5 95
Riverside, Calif. B2 126
Riverside-Albert E3 97
Riverton C3 96
Riverview E2 97
Rivière Bleue G4 103
Rivière du Loup C4 101
Rivière du Rempart C2 69
Rivière Noire, mt. B3 69
Rivière-à-Pierre D4 103
Rivière-au-Renard M3 103
Rivière-aux-Rats D4 103
Rivière-du-Loup G4 103
Rivière-du-Portage E1 97
Rivière-Matawin D5 103
Rivière-Ste-Marguerite G3 103
Rivière-Verte A1 97
Riyadh, capital B1 24
Riyaq B2 26
Roanne D3 34
Roanoke, Va. F2 126
Roatán B1 86
Roatán, island B1 86
Robertsport A2 63
Roberval D3 103
Robinsonville C1 97
Roblin A3 96
Roboré C3 77
Robson, mt. N4 95
Roca, cape A3 36
Rocanville J10 104
Rocha C3 75
Rochdale C3 30
Rochefort B4 34
Rochester, Minn. D1 126
Rochester, N.Y. F1 126
Rock Island D6 103
Rock, river D5 105
Rockcliffe Park H5 102
Rockford, Ill. E1 126
Rockglen E11 104
Rockhampton, Qld. E2 14
Rockland K2 102
Rocky Harbour C4 98
Rocky Island, lake B1 102
Rocky Mountain House C5 94
Rocky, mts. 82
Rockyford D5 94
Roddickton C4 98
Rodez C4 34
Rodney D5 102
Roermond D3 32
Roeselare B2 33
Rogersville D2 97
Roi, island B1 16
Roi Et C2 12
Rojo, cape A3 90
Rokel, river A1 63
Roland C4 96
Rolling Hills E6 94
Rollo, bay C2 100
Rolphton H1 102
Roma A2 71
Roma, Qld. D2 14
Roman D2 43
Romania 43
Rome, capital C2 38
Rømø, island A3 32
Roncador, cay ....Inset 78
Roncador, range C3 81
Ronde, island B1 91
Rondônia B3 81
Rongelap, island B1 16
Rongerik, island B1 16
Rønne E3 32
Ronne Ice Shelf, glacier B11 107
Roodeport D2 22
Roosevelt, island B6 107
Roosevelt Campobello Intl. Hist. Park C4 97
Roper, river C1 14
Roraima B1 81
Roraima, mt. A3 81
Rosa, mt. A3 36
Rosalie B3 90
Rosalind D5 94
Rosario C3 74
Roscommon C2 31
Roscrea C2 31
Rose Belle C2 69
Rose Blanche B5 98
Rose Hill B2 69
Rose Valley G8 104
Rose, island A3 18
Roseau, capital B3 90
Roseau, river A4 96
Rosebud D5 94
Rosemary D6 94

Rosenfeld C4 96
Rosenheim C5 40
Rosenort C4 96
Rosetown B9 104
Ross Ice Shelf, glacier A6 107
Ross River C4 105
Ross, island B5 107
Ross, sea B6 107
Rosseau, lake F2 102
Rossendale B4 96
Rossignol, lake B3 100
Rossland O6 95
Rosslare C2 31
Rosso B3 58
Rosthern D8 104
Rostock C1 40
Rostov-na-Donu E3 44
Roswell, N. Mex. C2 126
Rotherham C3 30
Rothesay D3 97
Roto C2 15
Rotorua C2 15
Rotterdam B3 32
Roubaix C1 34
Rouen C2 34
Rouleau F10 104
Round Lake Centre H2 102
Round, island D1 69
Round, pond C5 98
Rounthwaite B4 96
Rouyn-Noranda A4 101
Rovaniemi C1 53
Rovigo B1 38
Rovno B1 47
Rovuma, river C1 68
Rowley D5 94
Roxas B4 12
Royal, canal C2 31
Ruacana, falls A1 70
Ruahine, range C2 15
Ruapehu, mt. C2 15
Rub al-Khali (Empty Quarter), desert C2 24
Rubtsovsk D6 44
Ruda Śląska D3 41
Rudnyy C1 23
Rufiji, river C2 68
Rufisque A2 62
Rügen, island C1 40
Ruggell B1 33
Ruhengeri B1 61
Ruhr, river B3 40
Rukwa, lake B2 68
Rum, cay B2 89
Rumbek B3 59
Runaway Bay B2 88
Rundu C1 70
Rungna ....Inset 76
Rungwa, river B2 68
Rupel, river C1 33
Ruse D2 50
Russell A4 96
Russia 44
Rustavi C4 45
Rutana B2 61
Ruteng D2 13
Rutherglen F1 102
Rutland N6 95
Ruvubu, river C2 61
Ruvuma, river C1 68
Ruways, ar- B2, C1 25
Ruwenzori, range B2 61
Ruyigi C2 61
Ruzizi, river A1, A2 61
Ružomberok B2 42
Rwanda 61
Rweru, lake C2 61
Ryazan D3 44
Rybnik D3 41
Ryotsu C2 8
Rysy, mt. E4 41
Ryukyu, islands ....A4, Inset II 8
Rzeszów F3 41

S

's Hertogenbosch C3 32
Saale, river B3 40
Saar, river A4 40
Saarbrücken A4 40
Saaremaa, island B2 46
Saarland A4 40
Sab Abar A3 27
Šabac A2 49
Sabadell H2 37
Sabana de la Mar C1 89
Sabana Grande B2 90
Sabaneta A1 89
Sabha B2 56
Sable cape, Fla. E3 126
Sable River B4 100
Sabzevar D2 22
Sachigo, river B2 101
Sackville E3 97
Sacramento, capital, Calif. A2 126
Sadah A1 25
Sado, island C2 8
Sado, river A3 36
Safata, bay A3 18
Safed Koh, range D3 21
Safi B1 57
Safotu B1 18
Saga B2 8
Sagaing B2 12
Sagami, bay C3 8
Sagamihara C3 8
Saginaw, Mich. E1 126
Sagua la Grande C2 88
Saguenay, river F3 103
Sagunto F3 37
Sahara, desert 55
Saharanpur Panipat C3 20
≠ahbuz A3 45

Sahel, region 55
Sahiwal D3 21
Sai Kung ....Inset 10
Saidpur B3 21
Saimaa, lake C2 53
St. Adolphe C4 96
St. Alban's ....C3, Inset III 30
St. Albans B5 107
St. Albert D4 94
St-Alexis-des-Monts C5 103
St. Ambroise E3 103
St. Ambroise B4 96
St.-André B1 97
St. André C4 103
St. Andrews C2 30
St. Andrews B3 97
St-Angèle-de-Mérici J3 103
St. Ann's Bay B2 88
St. Anne, island ....Inset 70
St. Anthony D3 98
St-Antoine C6 103
St-Apollinaire E5 103
St-Augustin E3 101
St. Augustine A2 91
St. Augustine, Fla. E3 126
St. Barbe C3 98
St.-Basile A1 97
St. Bernard's D5 98
St. Brendan's E5 98
St. Bride's D5 98
St-Brieuc B2 34
St-Bruno F8 104
St-Camille-de-Lellis E5 103
St. Catharines F4 102
St. Catherine's E5 98
St. Catherine, mt. B2 91
St-Charles, lake K5 103
St. Clair, lake C5 102
St. Clair, river C5 102
St. Claude B4 96
Saint-Cloud ....Inset II 34
St. Cloud, Minn. D1 126
St-Côme C5 103
St-Constant J6 103
St. Croix B3 97
St-Cyprien H4 103
St-David-de-Falardeau E3 103
St. David's B3 91
St. David's B3 30
Saint-Denis ....Inset II 34
St-Dizier D2 34
St-Donat B5 103
St. Edward A2 100
St. Eleanors B2 100
St. Elias, mts. A5 105
St-Élie B1 80
St-Émile K5 103
Saint-Étienne C4 34
St. Eustache C4 96
St-Eustache H5 103
St-Fabien H3 103
St-Fabien-de-Panet F5 103
St-Félicien E3 103
St-Félix-d'Otis F3 103
St-François, lake E6 103
St-François, river E5 103
St.-Gédéon F6 103
St. George A2 100
St. George's B5 98
St. George's, bay B5 98
St. George's, capital A2 91
St. George's, channel B2 15
Saint George's, channel C3 31
St. George, Utah B2 126
St. Georges, bay F2 100
St-Georges F5 103
Saint-Georges C2 80
Saint-Germain F5 103
Saint-Germain-en-Laye ....Inset II 34
St. Gotthard, pass C2 35
St. Gotthard, tunnel C2 35
St. Helens C3 30
St-Henri-de-Taillon E3 103
St-Hubert J6 103
St-Hyacinthe D6 103
St-Ignace-du-Lac C5 103
St.-Isidore D1 97
St-Jacques A1 97
St-Jacques-de-Leeds E5 103
St. Jean, lake D3 103
St. Jean Baptiste C4 96
St-Jean-Chrysostome L6 103
St-Jean-de-Matha C5 103
St-Jean-Port-Joli F4 103
St-Jean-sur-Richelieu C6 103
St-Jérôme B6 103
Saint John C3 97
St. John, river B2 97
St. John's E5 98
St. John's, capital D5 98
Saint Joseph A3 90
St. Joseph E2 97
St. Joseph, lake B2 102
St. Joseph, Mo. D2 126
St-Joseph-de-Beauce F5 103
St. Kitts (St. Christopher), island B2 90
St. Kitts and Nevis 90
St. Labre C4 96
St-Lambert J5 103
St. Laurent C4 96
St-Laurent J5 103
Saint-Laurent du Maroni A1 80
St. Lawrence D5 98
St. Lawrence, cape G1 100
St. Lawrence, gulf L4 92
St. Lawrence, river K4 92
St. Lawrence Islands N.P. J3 102
St-Lazare A4 96
St.-Léonard B1 97
St.-Léonard J5 103
St. Lewis D3 98
St. Lewis, river C3 98
Saint-Lô B2 34
Saint-Louis A1 62
St. Louis A2 100
St. Louis E8 104

St. Louis, Mo. D2 126
St-Louis, lake H6 103
St.-Louis-de-Kent E2 97
St.-Louis-de-Kent E2 97
St. Lucia 91
St-Ludger F6 103
St. Ludger-de-Milot E3 103
St. Malo C4 96
St.-Malo E6 103
Saint-Malo B2 34
Saint-Malo, gulf B2 34
Saint-Marc C1 89
St-Marc-du-Lac-Long H4 103
St-Marcel F5 103
St-Marcellin H3 103
St. Margarets D2 97
St. Martin B3 96
St. Martin, lake B3 96
St. Martins D3 97
St. Mary's E5 98
St. Marys D4 102
St-Maurice, river C4 103
St-Michel F5 103
St-Michel-des-Saints C5 103
St.-Milaire A1 97
St. Moritz D2 35
St-Nazaire B3 34
St-Nicolas E5 103
St-Pacôme G4 103
St-Pamphile G5 103
St-Pascal G4 103
St. Paul, capital, Minn. D1 126
St. Paul, river A2 63
St. Paul, river C4 103
St. Paul's A1 90
Saint Paul's, bay G2 36
St. Peters G2 100
St. Peters C2 100
St. Peters, bay C2 100
St. Peters, island D3 44
St. Petersburg D3 44
St. Petersburg, Fla. E3 126
St-Philémon F5 103
St. Pierre, island M4 92
St-Pierre-Jolys C4 96
St-Quentin B1 97
St-Raphaël F5 103
St-Rédempteur K6 103
St-Rémi-d'Amherst B5 103
St-Romuald L6 103
St. Shotts E5 98
St-Siméon G4 103
St. Stephen B3 97
St. Thomas D5 102
St-Tite-des-Caps F4 103
St-Vallier L6 103
Saint Vincent, passage B4 91
St. Vincent, gulf ....Inset II 14
St. Vincent and the Grenadines 91
St. Walburg A7 104
St-Zacharie F5 103
Ste-Agathe-des-Monts B5 103
Ste-Amélie B4 96
Ste-Anne-des-Monts K2 103
Ste-Anne-du-Lac A5 103
Ste-Apolline F5 103
Ste-Claire E5 103
Ste-Croix E5 103
Ste-Eulalie D5 103
Ste-Foy E5, K6 103
Ste-Luce H3 103
Ste-Marie E5 103
Ste-Monique E3 103
Ste-Rose-du-Nord F3 103
Ste-Thérèse H5 103
Ste-Véronique A5 103
Ste. Agathe B4 96
Ste. Anne C4 96
Ste. Rose du Lac B3 96
Ste.-Anne-de-Madawaska A1 97
Saintes B4 34
Sajama, mt. A3 77
Sak, river B3 71
Sakai B3 8
Sakarya, river B2 27
Sakha (Yakutiya), republic C8 44
Sakhalin, island I4 44
≠aki B2 45
Sakishima, islands ....Inset II 8
Sakon Nakhon C2 12
Sal Rei B2 58
Sal, island D2 58
Sala'ilua A2 18
Salaberry-de-Valleyfield B6 103
Salacgriva C2 46
Salado, river B3, C2 74
Salaga B2 64
Salahiyah A2 27
Salalah B3 25
Salamá C4 85
Salamanca D2 37
Salamís, island ....Inset 51
Salar de Uyuni, salt flat A4 77
Salaverry B2 77
Salcedo B1 89
Saldanha A3 71
Saldus B2 46
Salé C1 57
Salekhard C5 44
Salelologa B2 18
Salem C2 20
Salem, capital, Oreg. A1 126
Salerno C2 38
Salerno, gulf C2 38
Salford B3 30
Salgótarján B1 43
Salibia B2 90
Salihorsk C3 47
Salima B2 68
Salina Cruz E4 84
Salina, Kans. D2 126
Salinas C3 90
Salines, point A2 91
Salisbury C3 30
Salisbury C3 30

Name	Key	Page
Salisbury, island	N4	99
Salluit	A1	101
Sallum, as-	A1	56
Sally's Cove	C4	98
Salmon Arm	N6	95
Salmon River	A3	100
Salmon, Idaho	B1	126
Salmon, river	L4	95
Salo	B2	53
Salonta	A2	43
Saloum, river	B2	62
Salsette, island	Inset I	20
Salt Lake City, capital, Utah	B1	126
Salt Water, lake	B1	20
Salt, as-	A1	26
Salt, cay	D4	89
Salta	B1	74
Saltcoats	H9	104
Saltery Bay	K6	95
Saltillo, state capital	D2	84
Salto	B1	75
Salto del Guairá	E4	75
Salut, islands	B1	80
Salvador	E3	81
Salvage	E5	98
Salween, river	C2	10
Salyan	C3	45
Salzach, river	C3	39
Salzburg	C3	39
Salzburg Alps, range	C3	39
Salzgitter	B2	40
Samaná	C1	89
Samaná, bay	C1	89
Samaná, cape	C1	89
Samana, cay	C3	89
Samangan	B1	22
Samar, island	C4	12
Samar, sea	C3	12
Samara	D4	44
Samarian, hills	B1	26
Samarinda	C2	13
Samarqand	C3	23
Samarra	B2	24
Samawah, as-	C2	24
Sambalpur	D4	20
Sambre, river	C2	33
Samch'ŏk	C4	9
Samina, river	B2	33
Samoa		18
Samokov	B3	50
Sámos, island	C3	51
Samothráki, island	C1	51
Samsø, island	C3	32
Samsø, strait	C3	32
Samsonvale, lake	Inset III	14
Samsun	D2	27
Samtredia	B3	45
Samur, river	B2	45
San	C3	58
San Andrés, island	Inset	78
San Angelo, Tex.	C2	126
San Antonio	B4, Inset	76
San Antonio	A3	85
San Antonio	C2	90
San Antonio Oeste	B5	74
San Antonio, cape	D4	74
San Antonio, cape	A2	88
San Antonio, Tex.	D3	126
San Baudilio de Llobregat	G2	37
San Bernardino, Calif.	B2	126
San Bernardo	Inset	76
San Blas, mts.	C2	87
San Borja	A2	77
San Carlos	B4	12
San Carlos	C3	75
San Carlos	B3	87
San Carlos de Bariloche	A5	74
San Carlos, river	B2	86
San Clara	A3	96
San Cristóbal	B2	77
San Cristóbal	B2	79
San Cristóbal	B2	89
San Cristóbal de las Casas	F4	84
San Cristóbal, island	B2	16
San Cristóbal, island	Inset	79
San Diego, Calif.	B2	126
San Felipe	D4	78
San Felipe	B1	84
San Félix	B3	76
San Fernando	B2	12
San Fernando	C4	37
San Fernando	B4	76
San Fernando	A2	91
San Fernando de Apure	C2	79
San Francique	A2	91
San Francisco	C3	74
San Francisco	B2	86
San Francisco de Macorís	B1	89
San Francisco, Calif.	A2	126
San Germán	A2	90
San Gimignano	B2	38
San Ignacio	B3	77
San Ignacio	A2	85
San Isidro	D2	90
San Jorge, gulf	B6	74
San José	B3	75
San José	C6	85
San José	B3	77
San José de Chiquitos	B3	77
San José de las Matas	A1	89
San José del Guaviare	B4	78
San Jose, Calif.	A2	126
San José, capital	B3	86
San José, river	B3	74
San Juan	B3	74
San Juan	B4	77
San Juan	A2	89
San Juan, capital	C2	90
San Juan, passage	D2	90
San Juan Bautista	D5	75
San Juan de Los Morros	C2	79
San Juan del Norte	C3	86
San Juan del Norte, bay	C3	87
San Juan del Sur	B3	87
San Juan, river	A3	78
San Juan, river	B3	87
San Lorenzo	D4	75
San Lorenzo	B2	79
San Lorenzo	B3	86
San Lorenzo	D2	90
San Lorenzo, cape	A3	79
San Lucas	C3	84
San Lucas, cape	B3	84
San Luis	B3	74
San Luis	D3	85
San Luis Potosí, state capital	D3	84
San Luis Río Colorado	B1	84
San Luis, lake	B2	77
San Marino		39
San Marino, capital	B1	39
San Marino, river	A1	39
San Martín, lake	A6	74
San Matías	C5	74
San Matías, gulf	C5	74
San Miguel	B2	86
San Miguel de Tucumán	B2	74
San Miguelito	C2	87
San Nicolás	C3	74
San Pablo	B3	12
San Pablo, river	B3	77
San Pawl il-Bahar	B2	36
San Pedro	D4	75
San Pédro	C4	63
San Pedro de Atacama	C2	76
San Pedro de las Colonias	D4	84
San Pedro de Macorís	C2	89
San Pedro Sula	A2	86
San Pedro, river	C2	85
San Pietro, island	B3	38
San Rafael	B3	74
San Remo	A2	38
San Salvador de Jujuy	B1	74
San Salvador, capital	B2	86
San Salvador, island	Inset	79
San Salvador, island	C3	89
San Salvador, river	A2	75
San Sebastián	F1	37
San Sebastián	B2	90
San Severo	C2	38
San Valentín, mt.	B8	76
San Vicente	B2	86
San Vito, cape	C3	38
San, river	E2	11
San, river	F3	41
Sanaa, capital	A1	25
Sanaga, river	B2	65
Sanandaj	B2	22
Sanaw	C1	25
Sancti Spíritus	C2	88
Sand, river	E3	94
Sandakan	C2	13
Sanday, island	Inset I	30
Sandilands	C4	96
Sandougou, river	B3	62
Sandoy, island	Inset	32
Sandspit	G4	95
Sandur	Inset	32
Sandwich, bay	C2	98
Sandy Bay	H5	104
Sandy Cove	A3	100
Sandy Lake	D3	94
Sandy Lake	A4	96
Sandy Lake	B2	101
Sandy Point	B2	89
Sandy Point Town	A1	90
Sandy, island	B2	18
Sandy, island	B2	91
Sandy, lake	C4	98
Sanford	C4	96
Sangha, river	D2	66
Sangmélima	B3	65
Sangre Grande	A2	91
Sangro, river	C2	38
Sangudo	C4	94
Sankosh, river	B2	19
Sankrail	Inset II	20
Sankt Gallen	D1	35
Sankt Pölten	D2	39
Sankuru, river	C2	67
Sannar	C2	59
Sanski Most	A1	48
Sant Julià de Lòria	A3	36
Sant'Antioco, island	B3	38
Santa Ana	A2	77
Santa Ana	A2	86
Santa Ana, range	C1	75
Santa Ana, volcano	A2	86
Santa Bárbara	A2	86
Santa Barbara, Calif.	B2	126
Santa Catarina	C4	81
Santa Clara	C2	88
Santa Coloma de Gramanet	H2	37
Santa Cruz	B3	77
Santa Cruz	A2	86
Santa Cruz de Tenerife	Inset I	37
Santa Cruz, island	Inset	79
Santa Cruz, islands	C2	16
Santa Cruz, river	A7	74
Santa Elena de Uairén	D3	79
Santa Elena, point	A4	79
Santa Fe	C3	74
Santa Fe, N. Mex.	C2	126
Santa Inés	Inset	76
Santa Inés, island	B9	76
Santa Isabel	C3	90
Santa Isabel, island	A1	16
Santa Isabel, peak	A1	66
Santa Lucía, river	B3	75
Santa Luzia, island	B2	58
Santa Maria	D2	58
Santa Maria	C4	81
Santa Maria di Leuca, cape	D3	38
Santa María, island	B3	18
Santa María, island	Inset	79
Santa Marta	B2	78
Santa Rita	B2	79
Santa Rosa	C4	74
Santa Rosa	B4	74
Santa Rosa de Copán	A2	86
Santa Rosa del Palmar	B3	77
Santa Rosalía	B2	84
Santana do Livramento	C5	81
Santander	E1	37
Santarém	C2	81
Santarém	B3	36
Santiago	B1	89
Santiago	B1	37
Santiago de Compostela	B1	37
Santiago de Cuba	E3	88
Santiago del Estero	C2	74
Santiago, capital	B4, Inset	75
Santiago, river	B1	77
Santo André	Inset II	81
Santo Antão, island	A1	58
Santo Domingo de los Colorados	B3	79
Santo Domingo, capital	C2	89
Santo Tomás de Castilla	E4	85
Santos	D4, Inset II	81
Sanyati, river	B1	69
São Bernardo do Campo	Inset II	81
São Caetano do Sul	Inset II	81
São Domingos	A1	62
São Filipe	B4	58
São Francisco, river	D2	81
São Gonçalo	Inset I	81
São João de Meriti	Inset I	81
São José do Rio Prêto	D4	81
São Luís	D2	81
São Nicolau, island	B2	58
São Paulo	D4, Inset II	81
São Tiago, island	C3	58
São Tomé, capital	B4	63
São Tomé, island	B4	63
São Tomé, river	B4	63
São Tomé and Príncipe		63
São Vicente, cape	A4	36
São Vicente, island	A2	58
São Vincente	Inset II	81
Saona, island	D2	89
Saône, river	D3	34
Sapele	C5	65
Sapitwa, mt.	B3	68
Sapporo	Inset I	8
Sar, passage	B3	17
Sar-e Pol	B1	22
Sara Buri	B3	12
Sarajevo, capital	B2	48
Saramacca, river	B2	80
Sarandë	A4	49
Saransk	D4	44
Sarapiquí river	B2	86
Sarasota, Fla.	E3	126
Saratov	D4	44
Saravan	D4	11
Sarawak, state	C2	13
Saraya	D3	62
Sarbhang	B3	19
Sarcelles	Inset II	34
Sarda, river	A2	19
Sardinia, island	B2	38
Sargodha	D3	21
Sarh	B5	59
Sari	C2	22
Sariwŏn	A3	9
Sarjektjakko	C1	53
Sark, island	Inset II	30
Sarnia	C5	102
Saronic, gulf	Inset	51
Šar Planina, mts.	B3	49
Sarstoon, river	A4	85
Sarstún, river	D4	85
Sary Tash	C3	23
Sarygamysh Koli, lake	B2	22
Saryshaghan	D2	23
Sasamungga	A1	16
Sasaram	D4	20
Sasebo	A3	8
Saskatchewan, river	G3	92
Saskatoon	D8	104
Sassandra	C4	63
Sassandra, river	C2, C4	63
Sassari	B2	38
Sassnitz	C1	40
Sata, cape	A4	8
Satna	C4	20
Satpura, range	C4	20
Satsuma, peninsula	A4	8
Sattahip	B3	12
Satu Mare	B2	43
Sauble Beach	D3	102
Saudhárkrókur	B2	52
Saudi Arabia		24
Saül	B2	80
Sault Ste. Marie	A1	102
Sault Ste. Marie, Mich.	E1	126
Sault-au-Mouton	G3	103
Saumur	B3	34
Saurimo	D3	70
Sauteurs	B2	91
Sava, river	B1, B2, C2	48
Savai'i, island	A2	18
Savalou	A3	64
Savan, island	B3	91
Savannah, Ga.	E2	126
Savannakhet	C3	11
Savé	B3	64
Savigny-sur-Orge	Inset II	34
Savinja, river	B2	48
Savona	B1	38
Savonlinna	C2	53
Savu, sea	D2	13
Sawda, mt.	B2	24
Sawhaj	B2	56
Sawqirah	C2	25
Sawqirah, bay	C2	25
Saxony	C3	40
Saxony-Anhalt	B3	40
Sayabec	J3	103
Sayan, mts.	D6	44
Sayhut	C1	25
Sayward	K6	95
Saywun	B1	25
Sázava, river	B3	42
Scafell Pike, mt.	B2	30
Scarborough	C2	30
Scarborough	B1	91
Scarborough	F4, L5	102
Schaan	B2	33
Schaerbeek	Inset II	33
Schaffhausen	C1	35
Schefferville	D3	101
Schefferville	C3	101
Schelde, river	C1	33
Schellenberg	B1	33
Scheveningen	B2	32
Schiedam	B3	32
Schiermonnikoog, island	D1	32
Schleswig	B1	40
Schleswig-Holstein	B2	40
Schouwen, island	A3	32
Schreiber	C3	101
Schuler	E6	94
Schwäbisch Gmünd	B4	40
Schwedt	C2	40
Schweinfurt	B3	40
Schwerin	B2	40
Schweriner, lake	B2	40
Schwyz	C1	35
Scilly, islands	A4	30
Scone	B1	30
Sconser	A1	30
Scotstown	E6	103
Scotswood	A3	94
Scott, island	C5	107
Scottsbluff, Nebr.	C1	126
Scugog, lake	G3	102
Scunthorpe	C3	30
Scutari, lake	A1, A3	49
Szczecinek	C2	41
Seaforth	D4	102
Seal Cove	C4	98
Seal, river	D1	96
Searchmont	A1	102
Seattle, Wash.	A1	126
Seawell	C4	91
Sebright	F3	102
Sechura, desert	A2	77
Seda, river	B3	36
Sedalia	E5	94
Sedan	D2	34
Séddhiou	B3	62
Sedley	F10	104
Seeley's Bay	J3	102
Sefadu	B1	63
Segbana	B2	64
Ségou	B3	58
Segovia	D2	37
Séguéla	C3	63
Segura, river	E3	37
Seinäjoki	B2	53
Seine, river	C2, Inset II	34
Sekake	B2	71
Sekondi-Takoradi	B4	64
Selebi-Phikwe	C2	69
Selenge Mörön, river	C2	11
Sélibaby	A3	62
Selínia	Inset	51
Selkirk	C4	96
Selvas, region	B2	81
Selwyn, mts.	C4	105
Seman, river	A3	49
Semara	B1	58
Semarang	C2	13
Sembawang	B1	13
Sembé	C3	66
Semeru, mt.	C2	13
Semey (Semipalatinsk)	E1	23
Semmering, pass	D3	39
Semois, river	D3	33
Sempach	C1	35
Sen, river	D2	11
Senaki	B1	45
Sendai	D2	8
Senegal		62
Senegal, river	B1, C2	62
Senkaku, islands	Inset II	8
Senmonorom	F3	11
Senne, river	C2	33
Senneterre	A4	101
Senta	B2	48
Seoul, capital	B4	9
Sepik, river	A2	15
Sept-Îles	C3	101
Septentrional, range	A1	89
Serangoon	B1	13
Serbia, republic	B2	49
Seremban	A2	13
Serenje	C2	67
Sergipe	E3	81
Serov	D5	44
Serowe	B2	69
Serpent, island	D1	69
Sérrai	B1	51
Serranilla, bank	Inset	78
Serravalle	B1	39
Serrekunda	C2	62
Serule	B2	69
Sese, islands	C4	61
Sesheke	A3	67
Seti, river	A2	19
Sétif	B1	57
Settat	C1	57
Setúbal	A3	36
Setúbal, bay	A3	36
Sevan, lake	C2	45
Sevastopol	C4	47
Seven Persons	E6	94
Seven Sisters Falls	D4	96
Severn, river	C3	30
Severn, river	C2	30
Severnaya Zemlya, islands	A6	44
Seville	C3	37
Sevran	Inset II	34
Sèvres	Inset II	34
Sewa, river	B2	63
Seward, Alaska	Inset I	126
Seychelles		70
Sfax	C2	57
Sfîntu Gheorghe	C3	43
Sha Tin	Inset	10
Shaanxi	D2	10
Shabwah	B2	25
Shache	A2	10
Shackleton Ice Shelf, glacier	C2	107
Shahr-e Kord	C3	22
Shahrud	D2	22
Shaki	A2	64
Shalqar	B2	23
Sham, ash-	C1	24
Shamgong	B2	19
Shamattawa	E2	96
Shan, plateau	C2	12
Shanchung	B1	9
Shandong	E2	10
Shangani, river	A2	69
Shanghai	F2	10
Shannon	B2	31
Shannon, river	B2	31
Shantou	E3	10
Shanxi	F3	10
Shaoguan	E3	10
Shaoxing	F3	10
Shaoyang	E3	10
Sharbot Lake	J3	102
Sharjah	C2	25
Shashe, river	C2	69
Shashi	E2	10
Shatt al-Arab, river	C2	24
Shaunavon	B11	104
Shawinigan	D5	103
Sheberghan	B1	22
Shediac	E2	97
Sheerness	E5	94
Sheet Harbour	E3	100
Sheffield	C3	30
Sheguianda	D2	102
Sheho	G9	104
Shek Pik	Inset	10
Shelburne	B4	100
Shelburne	E3	102
Shelikhov, gulf	C9	44
Shell Lake	C7	104
Shellbrook	D7	104
Shelter Bay	N6	95
Shēngjin	A2	49
Shenyang	F1	10
Sherbro, island	A2	63
Sherbrooke	E2	100
Sherbrooke	E6	103
Sheridan, Wyo.	C1	126
Sherridon	A1	96
Sherwood Park	D4	94
Shetland, islands	Inset	30
Sheva	Inset I	20
Shewa Gimira	B3	60
Shibar, pass	B2	22
Shibin al-Kawm	B1	56
Shijiazhuang	E2	10
Shikarpur	C4	21
Shikoku, island	B3	8
Shillong	F3	20
Shimizu	C3	8
Shimonoseki	A3	8
Shimonoseki, strait	A3	8
Shinano, river	C2	8
Shindand	A2	22
Shiono, cape	B3	8
Ship Cove	D3	98
Shippagan	E1	97
Shirane, mt.	C2	8
Shiraz	C4	22
Shire, river	B3	68
Shiretoko, cape	Inset I	8
Shizuoka	C3	8
Shkhara, mt.	B3	45
Shkodër	A1	49
Shkumbin, river	A2	49
Shoal Lake	A4	96
Sholapur	C5	20
Shostka	C1	47
Shreveport, La.	D2	126
Shrewsbury	C3	30
Shrirampur	Inset II	20
Shubenacadie	D2	100
Shubra al-Khaymah	B1	56
Shumen	E2	50
Shurugwi	B2	69
Shwebo	B2	12
Shymkent (Chimkent)	C2	23
Siahan, range	B4	21
Sialkot	D3	21
Siargao, island	C4	12
Šiauliai	B2	46
Sibbald	E5	94
Siberia, region	C7	44
Siberut, island	A2	13
Sibiti	B5	66
Sibiu	C3	43
Sibu	C2	13
Sibuyan, island	B3	12
Sibuyan, sea	B3	12
Sicamous	N6	95
Sichuan	D2	10
Sicily, island	C3	38
Sicily, strait	B3	38
Sico, river	C2	86
Sicuani	C3	77
Sidi bel Abbès	A1	57
Sidi Bou Zid	B2	57
Sidlaw, hills	B2	30
Sidney	B2	30
Sidney	B4	96
Sidon (Sayda)	A2	26
Sidra, gulf	C1	56
Sidvokodvo	B2	71
Siedlce	F2	41
Siegen	B3	40
Siempang	E1	11
Siemreab	B2	11
Siena	B2	38
Sieradz	D3	41
Sierra de Cayey, mts.	C2	90
Sierra de Loquillo, mts.	D2	90
Sierra Leone		63
Sierra Madre, mts.	C2	89
Sierra Madre, mts.	C5	85
Sierra Nevada de Santa Marta, mts.	B2	78
Sierra Nevada, mts., Calif.	A2	126
Sifton	A3	96
Siggiewi	B2	36
Sighetul Marmaţiei	B2	43
Sighişoara	C2	43
Siglufjördhur	B1	52
Siguatepeque	B2	86
Siguiri	D2	62
Siirt	E3	27
Sikanni Chief	L2	95
Sikasso	B3	58
Sikhote Alin, range	E8	44
Sikkim (state)	E3	20
Silay	B4	12
Silesia, region	C3	41
Silet	B2	57
Silgarhi	B2	19
Silhouette, island	C1	70
Siliana	B1	57
Silifke	C3	27
Silisili, mt.	B2	18
Silistra	F1	50
Silkeborg	B2	32
Sillery	K6	103
Šilutė	A2	46
Silvassi	B4	20
Silver	C4	96
Silver City, N. Mex.	C2	126
Sima	B2	67
Simcoe, lake	E4	101
Simeulue, island	A1	13
Simferopol	C4	47
Simikot	B1	19
Simla	C2	20
Simon, lake	A6	103
Simonette, river	A4	94
Simonhouse	A2	96
Simpson, desert	C2	14
Sinai, peninsula	B2	56
Sinaloa	C3	84
Sincelejo	B2	78
Sinclair	A4	96
Sinclair Mills	M4	95
Sindhuli Garhi	C2	19
Siné, river	B2	62
Sines	A4	36
Singapore		13
Singapore, capital	B1	13
Singapore, island	B1	13
Singapore, strait	B2	13
Singen	B5	40
Singida	B1	68
Singur	Inset II	20
Sinope	C2	27
Sinp'o	C2	9
Sint-Niklaas	C1	33
Sint-Truiden	D2	33
Sinŭiju	A2	9
Sió, river	B2	43
Siófok	B2	43
Sion	B2	35
Sioux City, Iowa	D1	126
Sioux Falls, S. Dak.	D1	126
Sioux Lookout	B2	101
Sipaliwini	A3	80
Siparia	A2	91
Siping	F1	10
Sipiwesk, lake	C1	96
Siple, island	B8	107
Siple, mt.	B7	107
Siquia, river	B2	87
Sirajganj	C4	21
Sirba, river	D2	64
Siret	D2	43
Siret, river	D2	43
Sirjan	D4	22
Sisaket	C3	12
Sisian	D3	45
Sisimiut (Holsteinsborg)	B2	106
Sisophon	B2	11
Siteki	B2	71
Sitka, Alaska	Inset I	126
Sittang, river	C2	12
Sittard	C4	32
Sittwe	B2	12
Siuna	B2	87
Sivas	D2	27
Sixaola, river	C3	86
Sjælland, island	C3	32
Skagen	C1	32
Skagerrak, strait	A3	53
Skaw, cape	C1	32
Skead	E1	102
Skeena, mts.	H4	95
Skeena, river	H4	95
Skeleton, coast	A1	70
Skellefteå	D2	53
Skellefteälven, river	C1	53
Skien	B4	52
Skierniewice	E3	41
Skikda	B1	57
Skíros, island	C2	51
Skive	B2	32
Skjern, river	B2	32
Skookumchuck	P6	95
Skopje, capital	B2	48
Skovorodino	D8	44
Skownan	B3	96
Skye, island	A1	30
Slagelse	C3	32
Slaná, river	C3	43
Slatina	C3	43
Slave Lake	C3	94
Slave, river	F2	92
Slavonia, region	C2	48
Slavonska Požega	C2	48
Slavonski Brod	D2	48
Sliema	C2	36
Slieve Donard, mt.	B2	31
Sligo	B1	31
Sliven	E3	50
Slobozia	D2	43
Slough	Inset III	30
Slovakia		42
Slovenia		48
Slovenskérudohorie, mts.	B2	42
Sluch', river	B1	47
Słupsk	C1	41
Småland, region	B3	53
Smallwood, reservoir	C2	101
Smeaton	F7	104
Smederevo	B2	48
Smilovichi	D3	47
Smiltene	C2	46
Smith River	J1	95
Smithers	J3	95
Smithers Landing	J3	95
Smiths Cove	B3	100

Name	Key	Page
Smiths Falls	J3	102
Smithville	F4	102
Smoky, river	A3, A4	94
Smolensk	D3	44
Smolevichi	D2	47
Smolyan	C4	50
Smoothstone, lake	D6	104
Smoothstone, river	D4	104
Snake, river	C3	105
Snake, river	B1	126
Snaring	A4	94
Sneek	C1	32
Sn¬«ka, mt.	B2	42
¿niardwy, lake	E2	41
Snow Lake	A2	96
Snowdon, mt.	B3	30
Snowdrift	F4	99
Snowflake	B4	96
Snug Harbour	D3	98
Snuol	E3	11
Soan-kundo, islands	B5	9
Sobaek, mts.	B5	9
Sobat, river	C3	59
Sobradinho, reservoir	D3	81
Sobral	D2	81
Soc Trang	A5	11
Sochi	E3	44
Socompa	C2	76
Socorro, N. Mex.	C2	126
Socotra, island	C2	25
Söderhamn	C2	53
Sofia, capital	B2	50
Sofia, river	B2	69
Sognafjord, fjord	B3	52
Soissons	C2	34
Sljos!n, bay	A3	9
Sokch'o	C3	9
Sokodé	C2	64
Sokoto	C1	65
Sokoto, plains	C1	65
Sokoto, river	C1	65
Sol, coast	D4	37
Sola	B1	18
Soldeu	B2	36
Solihull	C3	30
Solingen	A3	40
Solomon Is.		16
Solomon, sea	B2	15
Solosolo	C2	18
Solway, estuary	B2	30
Solwezi	B2	67
Somalia		60
Sombe, beach	E2	90
Sombor	A2	49
Sombra	C5	102
Somerset	B4	96
Somerset, island	K2	99
SomeΣ, river	B2	43
Somme, river	C2	34
Somoto	A2	87
Son La	A2	11
Son, river	D4	20
Sonarpur	Inset II	20
Sønderborg	B4	32
Sondrio	B1	38
Songea	C3	68
Songhua, river	F1	10
Songkhla	B5	12
Songköl	D2	23
S!ngnam	B4	9
Songnim	A3	9
Songwe, river	B1	68
Sonora	B1	84
Sonsonate	A2	86
Sonsoral, island	Inset	14
Sooke	L7	95
Sopron	A2	43
Sor, river	B3	36
Sorel	C5	103
Soria	E2	37
Sorø	C3	32
Soroca	B1	50
Sorocaba	D4	81
Sorong	E2	13
Soroti	C3	61
Sorraia, river	A3	36
Sorrento	C2	38
Sosnowiec	D3	41
Soso, bay	B3	17
Sota, river	B2	64
Sotk	C2	45
Sotouboua	B2	64
Soubré	C4	63
Soufrière	B4	90
Soufrière	A1	91
Soufrière, mt.	B1	91
Soufrière, volcano	A1	91
Souillac	C4	69
Soungrougrou, river	B3	62
Sources, mt.	B1	71
Souris	A4	96
Souris	C2	100
Souris, river	G11	104
Sous, plain	B2	57
Sous, river	B2	57
Sousúa	B1	89
South Africa		71
South Andaman, island	F6	20
S. Aulatsivik, island	D3	98
South Australia	C2	14
South Baymouth	C2	102
South Bend, Ind.	E1	126
South Branch	B5	98
South Brook	C4	98
South Carolina	E2	126
South China, sea	E4, Inset	10
South Comino, channel	B2	36
South Dakota	C1	126
South Dum-Dum	Inset	20
South Georgia, island		4
S. Gut St.-Anns	C2	100
South Henik, lake	J4	99
S. Indian Lake	D1	96
South Korea		9
South Magnetic Pole	C3	107
South Male, atoll	A3	19
South Malosmadulu, atoll	A2	19
South Milford	B3	100
S. Moose, lake	B2	96
South Orkney, islands	C12	107
South Ossetia, region	B3	45
South Pole	A17	107
South Rawdon	D3	100
South River	F2	102
South Ronaldsay, island	Inset I	30
South Saskatchewan, river	D8	104
South Shetland, islands	C12	107
South Shields	C2	30
South Taranaki, bight	B2	15
South Uist, island	A1	30
South West, cape	A4	15
South, island	A3	15
Southampton	C4	30
Southampton	D3	102
Southampton, island	L4	99
Southend	G4	104
Southend-on-Sea	D3	30
Southern Alps, mts.	A3	15
Southern Bug, river	B2	47
Southern Uplands, mts.	B2	30
Southland, plains	A4	15
Southport	C3	30
Southport	B2	100
Soweto	C2	71
Soyapango	A2	86
Soyo	B2	70
Sozh, river	E3	47
Spa	D2	33
Spain		37
Spanish	C1	102
Spanish Town	C3	88
Sparta	B3	51
Spartanburg, S.C.	E2	126
Spartivento, cape	D3	38
Sparwood	P6	95
Speightstown	A2	91
Spence Bay	K3	99
Spencer, gulf	C3	14
Spences Bridge	M6	95
Sperrin, mts.	A2	30
Spessart, mts.	B4	40
Spey, river	B1	30
Speyer	B4	40
Spiritwood	C7	104
Spi%ská Nová Ves	C2	42
Spithead, channel	C4	30
Split	B3	48
Split Lake	D1	96
Splügen, pass	D2	35
Spokane, Wash.	B1	126
Spoleto	C2	38
Spragge	C1	102
Sprague	D4	96
Spree, river	C3	40
Spring Bay	C2	102
Spring Coulee	D6	94
Spring Hall	A2	91
Springbok	A2	71
Springdale	C4	98
Springfield, capital, Ill.	E2	126
Springfield, Mass.	F1	126
Springfield, Mo.	D2	126
Springhill	C2	100
Springs	C2	71
Springside	H9	104
Springstein	C4	96
Springwater	B9	104
Spruce Grove	D4	94
Spy Hill	J10	104
Squamish	L6	95
Square Islands	D3	98
Sre Ambel	B4	11
Srebrenica	C1	48
Sredna Gora, mts.	C3	50
Sremska Mitrovica	A2	49
Sreng, river	B2	11
Sri Jayawardenepura, capital	A5	19
Sri Lanka		19
Srinagar	B2	20
Stafford	C3	30
Stand Off	D6	94
Standard	D5	94
Stanley	C4	90
Stanmore	E5	94
Stanovoy, range	D8	44
Star City	F8	104
Stara Zagora	D3	50
Starbuck	C4	96
Starbuck, island	L4	5
Starnberg, lake	B5	40
Start, point	B4	30
Staubbach, falls	B2	35
Stavanger	A4	52
Stavropol	E4	44
Stayner	E3	102
Stead	C4	96
Steen River	B1	94
Stefanson, island	G2	99
Steinbach	C4	96
Steinkjer	C3	52
Stellarton	F2	102
Stellenbosch	A3	71
Stendal	B2	40
Stepanavan	B2	45
Stephenville	D5	94
Stettler	D5	94
Stevenage	Inset III	30
Stevenson, lake	C3	96
Stewart	H3	95
Stewart River	B4	105
Stewart, island	A4	15
Stewart, river	B4, C1	105
Stewiacke	D2	100
Steyr	D2	39
Stikine	G3	95
Stikine, river	G3	95
Stirling	B2	30
Stirling	H3	102
>tip	C2	48
Stockerau	C2	39
Stockholm, capital	C3	53
Stoeng Treng	D2	11
Stoke-on-Trent	C3	30
Stonecliffe	H1	102
Stoneham	E4	103
Stonewall	C4	96
Stoney Point	C4	102
Stony Mountain	C4	96
Stony Plain	D4	94
Stony Rapids	E1	104
Storå, river	B2	53
Storavan, lake	C1	53
Store, strait	C3	32
Storkerson, peninsula	G2	99
Stornoway	A1	30
Stornoway	E6	103
Storsjön, lake	B2	53
Storthoaks	A4	96
Stoughton	G11	104
Strakonice	A3	42
Stralsund	C1	40
Strangford	B2	30
Stranraer	A3	30
Strasbourg	D2	34
Strasbourg	F9	104
Stratford	D4	102
Stratford	E6	103
Stratford-upon-Avon	C3	30
Strathclair	A4	96
Strathlorne	F1	100
Strathnaver	A4	96
Strathroy	D5	102
Straubing	C4	40
Streymoy, island	Inset	32
Stromboli, island	C3	38
Stronsay, island	Inset I	30
Struga	A2	48
Struma, river	A3	50
Strumica	C2	48
Stryama, river	C3	50
Stuart, lake	K4	95
Stubbs	B2	91
Stuie	J5	95
Sturgeon	C2	100
Sturgeon Falls	D3	101
Sturgis	H9	104
Stuttgart	B4	40
Subotica	A1	49
Suceava	D2	43
Suchiate, river	A5	85
Sucre, capital	A3	77
Sudan		59
Sudbury	E1	102
Sudd, region	B3	59
Suddie	B2	80
Sudeten, mts.	B3	41
Sudirman, range	E2	13
Su...uroy, island	Inset	32
Sue, river	B3	59
Suez	B1	56
Suez, canal	B1	56
Suez, gulf	B2	56
Sugandha	Inset II	20
Suhar	C1	25
Sühbaatar	C1	11
Suhl	B3	40
Suir, river	C2	31
Suita	B3	8
Sukabumi	B2	13
Sukang	B3	13
Sukhnah, as-	B2	27
Sukhothai	B2	12
Sukhumi	A3	45
Sukkur	C4	21
Sula, islands	D2	13
Sulaiman, range	C4	21
Sulaybikhat, as-	B2	24
Sulaymaniyah, as-	C1	24
Sulayyil, as-	B2	24
Sulima	A3	63
Sullana	A1	77
Sullivan, lake	C4	94
Sulu, archipelago	B5	12
Sulu, sea	A4	12
Sülüktü	A3	23
Sumatra, island	B2	13
Sumava, mts.	A3	42
Sumba, island	D2	13
Sumbar, river	B2	22
Sumbawa, island	C2	13
Sumbawanga	B2	68
Sumbe	B3	70
Summerford	D4	98
Summerland	N6	95
Summerside	B2	100
Summerville	C4	98
Summit Lake	K2	95
Summit Lake	L4	95
>umperk	C3	42
Sumqayit	C1	45
Sumy	C1	47
Sun City	C2	71
Sun Kosi, river	C2	19
Sunch'!n	B5	9
Sundarbans, region	C7	21
Sunderland	B2	30
Sunderland	F3	102
Sundi	C1	63
Sundown	C4	96
Sundridge	F2	102
Sundsvall	C2	53
Sunnynook	E5	94
Sunset House	B3	94
Sunyani	A3	64
Sup'ung, reservoir	A2	9
Superior, lake	J4	92
Superior, Wis.	D1	126
Sur	C1	25
Sur (Tyre)	A2	26
Surab	C4	21
Surabaya	C2	13
Surakarta	C2	13
Surat	B4	20
Surat Thani	B4	12
Sûre, river	A2, B2	33
Surgut	C5	44
Surigao	C3	12
Surin	C3	12
Suriname		80
Suriname, river	B3	80
Surkhob, river	B1	23
Surma, river	E3	21
Surprise	F1	95
Surt	C1	56
Surtsey, island	A3	52
Surud Ad, mt.	B1	60
Sussex	D3	97
Sutton West	F3	102
Sutlej, river	D4	21
Suva, capital	B3	17
Suva{ki	A4	19
Suwano-, island	A4	8
Suwar, as-	B2	27
Suwaqorghan	D2	23
Suwar{ki	F1	41
Suw!n	B4	9
Suzano	Inset II	81
Suzhou	F2	10
Svalbard, islands		5
Svay Rieng	D4	11
Svendborg	C3	32
ventoji, river	C2	46
Svetozarevo	B3	49
Svilengrad	E4	50
Svishtov	D2	50
Svitavy	C3	42
Svobodnyy	D8	44
Swabian Jura, mts.	B4	40
Swains, island	A1	18
Swakopmund	B2	70
Swan Hills	C4	94
Swan Lake	A3	96
Swan River	A3	96
Swan, river	A3	96
Swan, river	Inset I	14
Swansea	B3	30
Swaziland		71
Sweden		53
Swift Current	D5	98
Swift Current	C10	104
Swindon	C3	30
Swords	C2	31
Sydney	G1	100
Sydney, island	B2	17
Sydney, N.S.W., capital	E3, Inset IV	14
Syktyvkar	C4	44
Sylhet	E4	21
Syracuse (Siracusa)	C3	38
Syracuse, N.Y.	F1	126
Syrdarya, river	A1, C2	23
Syria		27
Syrian, desert	B1	26
Szczecin	B2	41
Szeged	C2	43
Székesfehérvár	B2	43
Szekszárd	B2	43
Szentes	C2	43
Szombathely	A2	43

T

Name	Key	Page
Taabo, lake	D3	63
Tabar, islands	B2	15
Tabasará, mts.	C2	87
Tabasco	F4	84
Tabelbala	A2	57
Taber	D6	94
Tablas, island	B3	12
Tabligbo	B4	64
Taboão da Serra	Inset II	81
Tábor	B3	42
Tabora	B2	68
Tabou	C4	63
Tabriz	B2	22
Tabuaeran, island	D1	17
Tabuk	A1	24
Tabusintac	D1	97
Tabwemasana, mt.	B2	18
Tacaná, volcano	A4	85
Tacloban	B4	12
Tacna	A1	77
Tacoma, Wash.	A1	126
Tacuarembó	C1	75
Tacuarembó, river	C1	75
Tacuarí, river	D2	75
Tadjoura	B2	60
Tadmur	B2	27
Tadoussac	G3	103
Taebaek-Sanmaek, mts.	C3	9
Taedong, river	B3	9
Tafahi, island	C1	17
Tafilah, at-	A2	26
Taganrog, gulf	D3	47
Tagish	C2	105
Tagish, lake	E1	95
Tagula, island	B3	15
Tagus, river	C3	37
Tahan, mt.	B2	13
Tahat, mt.	C2	57
Tahoua	B3	59
Tai, lake	F2	10
Ta'an	E2	10
T'aichung	B1	9
Taif, at-	B2	24
T'ainan	B2	9
Taipei, capital	B1	9
Taiping	A8	76
T'aitung	B2	9
Taiwan		10
Taiwan, strait	E3	10
Taiyuan	E2	10
Taizz	A2	25
Tajikistan		23
Tajumulco, volcano	B4	85
Tak	B2	12
Taka, island	B1	16
Takamaka	Inset	70
Takamatsu	B3	8
Takara, island	A4	8
Takatsuki	B3	8
Takev	B3	11
Takipy	A1	96
Takla Makan, desert	B2	10
Takla, lake	K3	95
Takua Pa	B4	12
Takutu, river	B1	80
Talagante	Inset	76
Talak, region	B2	59
Talamanca, range	C3	86
Talara	A1	77
Talas	C1	23
Talaud, islands	D1	13
Talavera de la Reina	D3	37
Talca	B5	76
Talcahuano	B6	76
Taldyqorghan	D2	23
Talish, mts.	C3	45
Tall Afar	B1	24
Tallahassee, capital, Fla.	E2	126
Tallinn, capital	B1	46
Taloqan	B1	22
Talsi	B2	46
Taltal	A3	76
Taltson, river	F4	99
Tamale	B2	64
Tamanrasset	B2	57
Tamarin	B3	69
Tamaulipas	E3	84
Tambacounda	C3	62
Tambo, river	C3, C4	77
Tâmega, river	B2	36
Tampa, Fla.	E3	126
Tampere	B2	53
Tampico	E3	84
Tampines	B1	13
Tampok, river	B2	80
Tamsagbulag	D2	11
Tamu	B1	12
Tamworth, N.S.W.	E3	14
Tan-Tan	B2	57
Tana, lake	B1	60
Tana, river	F4	61
Tana, river	F1	52
Tanabe	B3	8
Tanch'!n	C2	9
Tandil	D4	74
Tanega, island	A4	8
Tanen, range	B2	12
Tanezrouft, mts.	A2	57
Tanga	C2	68
Tanga, islands	B2	15
Tangail	C4	21
Tanganyika, lake	A2	68
Tanggula, range	C2	10
Tangier	C1	57
Tangier	E3	100
Tangshan	E2	10
Tanimbar, islands	E2	13
Tanjungpinang	B1	13
Tanna, island	C4	18
Tano, river	A3	64
Tanshui	B1	9
Tanta	B1	56
Tanzania		68
Taongi, island	B1	16
Taoudenni	C1	58
T'aoyüan	B1	9
Tapa	A1	46
Tapachula	F5	84
Tapajós, river	C2	81
Tapanahoni, river	B3	80
Tapeta	B2	63
Taquari, river	C3	81
Tara	D5	44
Tara, river	A3	49
Taraba, river	F3	65
Tarakan	C1	13
Taranto	D2	38
Taranto, gulf	D2	38
Tarapoto	B2	77
Tararua, range	C3	15
Tarat	B2	57
Tarawa, capital	A1	17
Tarbes	C5	34
Taree, N.S.W.	E3	14
Tarif	B2	25
Tarija	B4	77
Tarim, river	B1	10
Tarin Kowt	B2	22
Tarnobrzeg	E3	41
Tarnów	E4	41
Taroudant	B2	57
Tarragona	G2	37
Tarrasa	G2	37
Tarsus	C3	27
Tartu	D2	46
Tartus	A2	27
Tarvo	B3	77
Taseko, lake	L5	95
Tash Kömür	C2	23
Tashigang	C2	19
Tashir	B1	45
Tashkent, capital	C2	23
Tasikmalaya	B2	13
Tasman, bay	B3	15
Tasman, sea		14
Tasmania	D4	14
Tata	B2	43
Tatabánya	B2	43
Tatamagouche	D2	100
Tataouine	C3	57
Tatar, strait	D9	44
Tatarstan, republic	C4	44
Tathlina, lake	E4	99
Tatla Lake	K5	95
Tatlayoko Lake	K5	95
Tau, island	A1	18
Taumarunui	C2	15
Taung	B2	71
Taunggyi	C2	12
Taunton	C5	9
Taunus, mts.	B3	40
Taupo	C2	15
Taupo, lake	C2	15
Tauranga	C2	15
Taureau, reservoir	C5	103
Taurus, mts.	B3	27
Tavan Bogd Uul, mt.	A2	11
Taverny	Inset II	34
Taveuni, island	C2	17
Tavoy	C3	12
Tavoy, point	C3	12
Tawau	D2	13
Tawi Tawi, island	A5	12
Taxco	E4	84
Tay Ninh	B4	11
Tay, estuary	C2	30
Tay, lake	B2	30
Tay, river	B2	30
Tay, river	C4	105
Taymouth	C2	97
Taymyr, peninsula	B6	44
Taymyriya, autonomous okrug	B6	44
Taza	C1	57
Tazin, lake	A1	104
Tazin, river	B1	104
Tbilisi, capital	C4	45
Tchamba	B2	64
Tchaourou	B2	64
Tchentlo, lake	K3	95
Tchibanga	A2	66
Te Anau, lake	A4	15
Tebicuary, river	D5	75
Tecomán	D4	84
Tecuci	D3	43
Tedzhen	C3	22
Tedzhen, river	C3	22
Teepee Creek	A3	94
Tees, river	C2	30
Teeswater	D3	102
Tefé	B2	81
Tegal	B2	13
Tegucigalpa, capital	B2	86
Tehek, lake	J4	99
Tehkummah	D2	102
Tehran, capital	C2	22
Tehuacán	E4	84
Tehuantepec, gulf	E4	84
Tehuantepec, isthmus	F4	84
Teifi, river	B3	30
Tekapo, lake	B3	15
Tekeze, river	B1	60
Tekirdaæ	A2	27
Tekong, island	C1	13
Tel Aviv-Jaffa	B1	26
Tela	B2	86
Telavi	Inset I	37
Telde	Inset I	37
Telegraph Creek	G2	95
Teles Pires, river	C2	81
Telford	C3	30
Telkwa	J4	95
Telok Anson	A2	13
Tel%iai	B2	46
Tema	C4	64
Temagami, lake	E1	102
Temburong, river	C2	13
Temirtau	D1	23
Tempisque, river	A2	86
Temuco	B6	76
Tena	C3	79
Ténéré, desert	C1	59
Tenerife, island	Inset I	37
Tengiz, lake	C1	23
Tenkodogo	D3	64
Tennant Creek, N.T.	C1	14
Tennessee	E2	126
Tennessee, river	E2	126
Tenojoki, river	C1	53
Tenryu, river	C3	8
Teotihuacán	Inset	84
Tepexpan	Inset	84
Tepic, state capital	D3	84
Téra	A3	59
Terai, region	A2, C2	19
Teraina, island	D1	17
Teramo	C2	38
Teresina	D2	81
Tereul	F2	37
Termiz	C3	23
Termoli	D2	38
Ternate	D1	13
Terni	C2	38
Ternopil	B2	47
Terrace	H4	95
Terre Haute, Ind.	E2	126
Terrebonne	J5	103
Terreiro Velho	C1	63
Terrenceville	D5	98
Terschelling, island	C1	32
Teseney	A2	60
Teshio, river	Inset I	8
Tesiyn, river	B2	11
Tesli~	B1	48
Teslin	C5	105
Teslin, lake	C5	105
Teslin, river	C5	105
Tessalit	D1	58
Tessaoua	B3	59
Testa del Gargano, point	D2	38
Tête Jaune Cache	N5	95
Tétouan	C1	57
Tetovo	A1	48
Teulada, cape	B3	38
Teulon	C4	96
Tewkesbury	C3	30
Texas	D2	126
Texcoco	Inset	84
Texel, island	B1	32
Teyateyaneng	B2	71
Tezontepec	Inset	84
Tezzeron, lake	K4	95
Thaba-Tseka	B2	71
Thabana Ntlenyana, mt.	C2	71
Thai Nguyen	A2	11
Thailand		12
Thailand, gulf	B4, C4	12
Thames, river	C3, Inset III	30
Thamesville	D5	102
Thane	Inset I	20
Thanh Hoa	A2	11
Thanjavur	C6	20

Name	Key	Page
Thar, desert	C4	21
Thásos	C1	51
Thásos, island	C1	51
The Crane	C4	91
The Hague	B2	Hague
The Ovens	C3	100
The Pas	A2, C2	96
Thedford	D4	102
Thekulthili, lake	C1	99
Thelon, river	H4, J4	99
Theodore	H9	104
Thessalon	B1	102
Thetford	D3	30
Thetford Mines	E5	103
Thicket	C4	91
Thicket Portage	C1	96
Thiès	A2	62
Thika	D4	61
Thimphu, capital	A2	19
Thingvellir	A2	52
Thio	C2	18
Thíra, island	C3	51
Thisted	B2	32
Thlewiaza, river	J4	99
Tholen, island	B3	32
Thomaston Corner	B3	97
Thompson	C1, D2	96
Thompson, river	M6	95
Thong Hoe	A1	13
Thorhild	D4	94
Thornhill	K5	102
Thorold	F4	102
Thrace, region	D4	50
Thracian, plain	C3	50
Three Kings, islands	B1	15
Thule, air base	B2	106
Thun	B2	35
Thunder Bay	C3	101
Thunersee, lake	B2	35
Thuringia	B3	40
Thuringian, forest	B3	40
Thurso	B1	30
Thurston, island	B9	107
Ti'avea	D2	18
Ti-n-Zaouâtene	B2	57
Tiáhuac	Inset	84
Tianjin	E2	10
Tibati	B2	65
Tiber, river	C2	38
Tiberias	B1	26
Tiberias (Galilee), lake	A1, B1	26
Tibesti, massif	B2	59
Tibet (Xizang)	B2	10
Tibet, plateau	B2	10
Tiburón, island	B2	84
Tichit	C3	58
Tichla	A2	58
Ticino, river	C2	35
Tide Head	C1	97
Tidjikdja	C3	58
Tien Shan, range	A1	10
Tierra del Fuego, island	C9	76
Tietê, river	Inset II	81
Tignish	A2	100
Tigre, river	B1	77
Tigris, river	B1	24
Tijuana	A1	84
Tikal	D2	85
Tikrit	B2	24
Tiksi	B8	44
Tiladummati, atoll	A1	19
Tilburg	C3	32
Tilbury	C5	102
Tilley	E6	94
Tillabéry	A3	59
Tilomonte	C2	76
Tilson	A4	96
Timaru	B3	15
Timbuktu	C2	58
Timgad, ruins	B1	57
Timişoara	A3	43
Timmins	D3	101
Timor, island	D2	13
Timor, sea	B1	14
Tindouf	A2	57
Tingo María	B2	77
Tinkissa, river	C2	62
Tio	C2	60
Tipitapa, river	A2	87
Tipperary	B2	31
Tirana, capital	A2	49
Tiraspol	B2	50
Tiree, island	A2	30
Tîrgovişte	C3	43
Tîrgu Jiu	B3	43
Tîrgu-Mureş	C2	43
Tîrgu Neamœ	D2	43
Tîrgu Ocna	D2	43
Tirich Mir, mt.	D2	21
Tirso, river	B2	38
Tiruchchirappalli	C6	20
Tisa, river	B2	49
Tisdale	F8	104
Tista, river	C2	21
Tisza, river	C2	43
Titagarh	Inset II	20
Titano, mt.	B1	39
Titicaca, lake	A3, D4	77
Titov Veles	B2	48
Titova Mitrovica	B3	49
Tivaouane	A2	62
Tiverton	B4	30
Tiverton	D3	102
Tivoli	B2	91
Tiznit	B2	57
Tlaipan	Inset	84
Tlalnepantla	Inset	84
Tlaxcala, state capital	E4	84
Tlemcen	A1	57
Toa Payoh	B1	13
Toad River	K2	95
Toamasina	B2	69
Toba Kakar, range	C3	21
Tobago, cays	A4	91
Tobago, island	B1	91
Tobermory	D2	102
Tobi, island	Inset	17
Tobin, lake	G7	104
Tobol, river	C1	23
Tobolsk	D5	44
Tobruk	D1	56
Tocantins	D3	81
Tocantins, river	D2	81
Toco	B2	91
Tocopilla	B2	76
Tocorozawa	C3	8
Tofino	K6	95
Tofua, island	B3	17
Togo		64
Tokachi, river	Inset I	8
Tokara, islands	A4	8
Tokat	D2	27
Tĺkchĺk-kundo, islands	A4	9
Tokmok	D1	23
Tokorozawa	C3	8
Toktogul	C2	23
Toku, island	C2	17
Tokushima	B3	8
Tokuno, island	Inset II	8
Tokuyama	A3	8
Tokyo, capital	C3	8
Tôlanaro	B3	69
Toledo	D3	37
Toledo, mts.	D3	37
Toledo, Ohio	E1	126
Toliara	A3	69
Tolima, mt.	B3	78
Tolland	E4	94
Toltén, river	B6	76
Toluca, state capital	E4	84
Tolyatti	D4	44
Tom Price, W.A.	A2	14
Tomahawk	C1	94
Tomakomai	Inset I	8
Tomanivi, mt.	B2	17
Tombua	B5	70
Tomé	B6	76
Tomelloso	E3	37
Tomiko, lake	F1	102
Tompkins	B10	104
Tomsk	D6	44
Tonalá	F4	84
Tonbridge	Inset III	8
Tone, river	C2	8
Tonga		17
Tongariro, mt.	C2	15
Tongatapu, island	B4	17
Tonghua	F1	10
Tongjos!n, bay	B3	9
Tongliao	F1	10
Tongsa	B2	19
Tongsa, river	B2	19
Tonkin, gulf	E3	11
Tonle Sap, lake	B2,C3	11
Tonle Sap, river	B2	11
Toowoomba, Qld.	E2	14
Topeka, Kans.	D2	126
Topley Landing	J4	95
Torbay	B4	30
Torbay	E5	98
Torghay, plateau	C1	23
Tormes, river	D2	37
Tornealven, river	D1	53
Torngat, mts.	D3	98
Tornio	B1	53
Torniojoki, river	B1	53
Toronto, capital	F4, K5	102
Tororo	D3	61
Torquay	G11	104
Torre del Greco	C2	38
Torrejón de Ardoz	Inset	37
Torrelavega	D1	37
Torrens, lake	C2	11
Torrens, river	Inset II	14
Torrente	F3	37
Torreón	D2	84
Torres, islands	B1	18
Torres, strait	D1	14
Torrington	D5	94
Tórshavn	Inset	32
Tortosa	G2	37
Tortosa, cape	G2	37
Tortuga, island	C1	89
Toruł	D2	41
Tôrva	C2	46
Tory Hill	G3	102
Totness	A2	80
Tottori	B3	8
Touggourt	B1	57
Tougué	C2	62
Toulaman, river	B2	90
Touliu	B2	9
Toulon	D5	34
Toulouse	C5	34
Toungoo	C2	12
Toura, mts.	C2	63
Tourcoing	C1	34
Tournai	B2	33
Tours	C3	34
Toussoro, mt.	B2	66
Toutes Aides	B3	96
Tovuz	A2	45
Towada, lake	D1	8
Townsville, Qld.	D1	14
Toxkan, river	E2	23
Toyama	C2	8
Toyama, bay	C2	8
Toyohashi	C3	8
Toyonaka	B2	8
Toyota	C3	8
Tozeur	B3	57
Tqvarcheli	A3	45
Trabzon	D2	27
Tracadie-Sheila	E1	97
Tracy	C3	34
Tracy	C5	103
Trafalgar	E2	100
Trail	O6	95
Tralee	B2	31
Trang	B5	12
Transantarctic, mts.	B4	107
Transylvanian Alps, mts.	C3	43
Trapani	A1	38
Trasimeno, lake	C3	38
Trat	C3	12
Traun, river	D2	39
Traverse City, Mich.	E1	126
Trebinje	B2	48
Treherne	B4	96
Treinta y Tres	C2	75
Trembleur, lake	K4	95
Trenche, river	C3	103
Trenín	B2	42
Trent, river	C3	30
Trentino-Alto Adige	B1	38
Trenton	B1	38
Trenton	E2	100
Trenton, capital, N.J.	F1	126
Trepassey	E5	98
Tres Puntas, cape	B6	74
Treska, river	B2	48
Treviso	C1	38
Trier	A4	40
Triesen	B2	33
Triesenberg	B2	33
Trieste	C1	38
Trieste, gulf	A3	48
Triglav, mt.	A2	48
Tríkala	B2	51
Trim	C2	31
Trincomalee	C3	19
Trinidad	B2	77
Trinidad	B2	75
Trinidad	B2	91
Trinidad, island	A2	91
Trinidad, mts.	C2	85
Trinidad and Tobago		91
Trinity East	E5	98
Trinity, bay	E5	98
Triolet	C2	69
Tripoli (Tarabulus)	A1	26
Tripoli, capital	B1	56
Tripolitania, region	B1	56
Triton	D4	98
Trivandrum (Thiruvananthapuram)	C7	20
Trnava	A2	42
Trobriand, islands	B2	15
Trois-Pistoles	G3	103
Trois-Rivières	D5	103
Troisvierges	B1	33
Trollhättan	B3	53
Trombay	Inset I	20
Tromsø	D2	52
Trondheim	C3	52
Trondheimsfjord, fjord	B3	52
Trongisvágur	Inset	32
Tro÷ödos, mts.	A2	27
Trossachs	F11	104
Trout Creek	F1	102
Trout Lake	C3	94
Trout River	B4	98
Trout, lake	D4	99
Trout, lake	D4	99
Trouville	C2	34
Trowbridge	C3	30
Troyes	D2	34
Trujillo	B2	79
Trujillo	D2	37
Trujillo	B2	86
Trujillo Alto	C2	90
Truro	B4	100
Truro	D2	100
Trutch	L2	95
Trutnov	B2	42
Tsaratanana, mts.	B1	69
Tsavo	E5	61
Tsedike, river	B3	71
Tsengwen, river	B2	9
Tsetserleg	C2	11
Tsévié	B3	64
Tshabong	A3	69
Tshane	A3	69
Tshaneni	B1	71
Tshikapa	B2	67
Tshuapa, river	B2	67
Tsiribihina, river	B2	69
Tsiroanomandidy	B2	69
Tsiteli-Tsqaro	D4	45
Tskhinvali	B3	45
Tsnori	C4	45
Tsu, island	A3	8
Tsuen Wan	Inset	10
Tsugaru, strait	D1, Inset I	8
Tsumeb	C1	70
Tsumkwe	D1	70
Tsuruga	C3	8
Tsuruoka	C2	8
Tuam	B2	31
Tuas	A1	13
Tuasivi	B2	18
Tubarão	D4	81
Tübingen	B4	40
Tubmanburg	A2	63
Tucson, Ariz.	B2	126
Tucumcari, N. Mex.	C2	126
Tucupita	D2	79
Tucuruí, reservoir	D2	81
Tuen Mun	Inset	10
Tugela, river	D2	71
Tuguegarao	B2	12
Tuira, river	D2	87
Tuktoyaktuk	B3	99
Tuktut Nogait N.P.	D3	99
Tukums	B2	46
Tula	D3	44
Tula, ruins	D3	84
Tulcán	C2	79
Tulcea	D3	43
Tullamore	C2	31
Tulsa, Okla.	D2	126
Tulsequah	F2	95
Tulsipur	C3	19
Tultitlán	Inset	84
Tulun	D7	44
Tuma, river	B2	87
Tumaco	A4	78
Tumba, lake	B2	67
Tumbes	A1	77
Tumbler Ridge	M3	95
Tumen, river	C1	9
Tumuc-Humac, mts.	A2, B3	80
Tumucumaque, range	C1	81
Tunbridge Wells	D3	30
Tundzha, river	E3	50
Tungsten	C4	99
Tunis, capital	C1	57
Tunis, gulf	C1	57
Tunisia		57
Tunja	B3	78
Tupelo, Miss.	E2	126
Tupiza	A4	77
Tupungato, mt.	B3	74
Tur, at-	B2	56
Tura	C7	44
Tura, lowland	A2	23
Turan, lowland	A2	23
Turangi	A1	24
Turbat	A2	78
Turbo	B2	43
Turda	B2	43
Turfan, depression	C1	10
Turin	A1	38
Turin	D6	94
Turkana (Rudolf), lake	D2	61
Turkeston, mts.	A1	23
Turkey		27
Turkmenbashi	A2	22
Turkmenistan		22
Turks and Caicos Islands		89
Turks, islands	D4	89
Turku	B2	53
Turkwel, river	C2	61
Turnberry	A2	96
Turnbull	B2	9
Turneffe, islands	C2	85
Turnhout	C1	33
Turnor Lake	B4	104
Turnu Mœgurele	C4	43
Turquino, mt.	E3	88
Tursunzoda	A1	23
Turtle, lake	B7	104
Turtleford	B7	104
Tuscaloosa, Ala.	E2	126
Tuscany	D2	38
Tusket	B4	100
Tuticorin	C7	20
Tutong	B2	13
Tutong, river	A2	13
Tutuila, island	AI, C2	18
Tuul, river	C2	11
Tuvalu		16
Tuxtla Gutiérrez, state capital	F4	84
Tuy Hoa	B4	11
Tuya, lake	G1	95
Tuz, lake	C2	27
Tuzla	B1	48
Tweed	H3	102
Tweed, river	C2	30
Twillingate	D4	98
Twin Butte	D6	94
Twin Falls, Idaho	B1	126
Two Creeks	A4	96
Tychy	D3	41
Tynda	D8	44
Tyndall	C4	96
Tyne Valley	B2	100
Tyne, river	C2	30
Tyrrhenian, sea	B2	38
Tyumen	D5	44
Tyva, republic	D6	44
Tywi, river	B3	30

U

Name	Key	Page
Uaboe	B1	16
Ubangi, river	B1	67
Ubayyid, al-	C2	59
Ube	A3	8
Ubeda	E3	37
Úbeda	E3	37
Uberaba	D3	81
Uberlândia	D3	81
Ubin, island	B1	13
Ubon Ratchathani	C3	12
Ucayali, river	C2	77
Uccle	C2	33
Uchiura, bay	Inset I	8
Uchquduq	B2	23
Ucluelet	K7	95
Udaipur	B4	20
Uddevalla	B3	53
Uddjaur, lake	C1	53
Udine	C1	38
Udmurtiya, republic	D4	44
Udon Thani	C2	12
Udu, point	C2	17
Uele, river	C1	67
Uelzen	B2	40
Ufa	D4	44
Uga, river	B2	9
Ugalla, river	B2	68
Uganda		61
Uíge	B2	70
Uitenhage	B3	71
Ujae, island	B2	16
Ujelang, island	A2	16
Ujjain	C4	20
Ujung Pandang	C2	13
Ukhta	C4	44
Ukmerg>	B2	46
Ukraine		47
Ulaan-Uul	D2	11
Ulaanbaatar, capital	C2	11
Ulaangom	B2	11
Ulan-Ude	D7	44
Ulansuhai, lake	D1	10
Ulchin	C4	9
Ulhas, river	Inset I	20
Uliastay	B2	11
Ulithi, atoll	A1	15
Ull»ng-do, island	D4	9
Ullapool	B1	30
Ulm	B4	40
Ulsan	C5	9
Ulster, province	C1	31
Ulu DaÆ (Mt. Olympus), mt.	B2	27
Ulúa, river	B2	86
Ulubria	Inset II	20
Uluru (Ayers Rock)	C2	14
Uman	C2	47
Umbeluzi, river	B2	71
Umboi, island	A2	15
Umbria	C2	38
Umeå	D2	53
Umeälven, river	C2	53
Umm al-Qaywayn	C2	25
Umm Bab	B2	25
Umm Qasr	C2	24
Umm Said (Musayid)	D4	25
Umniati, river	B2	69
Umtata	C3	71
Umuahia	D5	65
Umzingwani, river	B2	69
Una, river	A1	48
Unayzah	B1	24
Ungava, bay	L3	92
Ungheni	A2	50
Union	C2	76
Union, island	A4	91
United Arab Emirates		25
United States		126
Unity	A8	104
Unst, island	Inset I	30
Upemba, lake	C3	67
Upernavik	B2	106
Upington	B2	71
Upolu, island	C2	18
Upper Arrow, lake	O6	95
Upper Liard	D5	105
Upper Lough Erne, lake	A3	31
Upper Musquodoboit	E2	100
Upper Ohio	B4	100
Uppsala	C3	53
Ural, mts.	D4	44
Ural, river	B2	23
Uranium City	B1	104
Urawa	C3	8
Urganch	B2	23
Uran	Inset I	20
Urmia, lake	B2	24
Uro%evac	B3	49
Uruapan	D4	84
Urubamba, river	C3	77
Uruguai, river	C4	81
Uruguay		75
Uruguay, river	D3	74
Urukthapel, island	B3	17
Ürümqi	B1	10
Usak	B2	27
Ushuaia	C9	76
Usk, river	C3	30
Üsküdar	B2	27
Usmas, lake	B2	46
Ussuri, river	E8	44
Ussuriysk	E8	44
Ust-Ilimsk	D7	44
Ust-Kamchatsk	D10	44
Ust-Kut	D7	44
Ust-Ordynskiy Buryat, autonomous okrug	D7	44
Ust-Ordynskiy	D7	44
Uster	C1	35
Ústí nad Labem	B2	42
Ustica, island	B2	38
Ustka	C1	41
Ustyurt, plateau	A2, B2	23
Usulután	B2	86
Usumacinta, river	B2	84
Utah	B2	126
Utah, beach	B2	34
Utan	Inset I	20
Utena	C2	46
Utikuma, lake	C3	94
Utila, island	B1	86
Utrecht	C2	32
Utsunomiya	C3	8
Uttaradit	B2	12
Utuado	B2	90
Utupua, island	C2	16
Uummannaq	B2	106
Uvira	C2	67
Uvs, lake	B1	11
Uwajima	B3	8
Uwaynat, al-	D5	65
Uyo	D5	65
Uyuni	A4	77
Uzbekistan		23
Uzhhorod	A2	47
U÷ice	A3	49

V

Name	Key	Page
Vaal, reservoir	C2	71
Vaal, river	B2	71
Vaalserberg, mt.	D4	32
Vaasa	B2	53
Vác	B2	43
Vache, island	B2	89
Vadodara	B4	20
Vadsø	F1	52
Vaduz, capital	B2	33
Vágar, island	Inset	32
Váh, river	A1	23
Vahsh, river	A1	23
Vaitupu, island	C2	16
Vakhan, region	C1	22
Val Comeau	B1	97
Val Marie	C11	104
Val-d'Or	A4	101
Val-des-Bois	A6	103
Valcourt	D6	103
Valdecaño	D2	37
Valdepeñas	E3	37
Valdés, peninsula	C5	74
Valdivia	B6	76
Valemount	N5	95
Valence	D4	34
Valencia	D4	34
Valencia	F3	37
Valencia	C1	79
Valencia, gulf	G3	37
Valenciennes	C1	34
Valera	B2	79
Valga	D3	46
Valira d'Orient	B2	36
Valira, river	B2	36
Valjevo	B2	49
Valka	C2	46
Valladolid	G3	84
Valladolid	D2	37
Valle d'Aosta	A1	38
Valledupar	B3	78
Valledupar	B2	78
Valletta, capital	C2	36
Valley, river	A3	96
Valmiera	B2	46
Valparaíso	B4, Inset	76
Van	E2	27
Van, lake	E2	27
Vancouver	L6	95
Vancouver, island	J6	95
Vanderhoof	K4	95
Vänern, lake	B3	53
Vanguard	C11	104
Vanier	H5	102
Vanier	L5	103
Vanikolo, islands	A2	15
Vanimo	A2	15
Vanrhynsdorp	A3	71
Vanscoy	D8	104
Vansittart, island	M3	99
Vantaa	B2	53
Vanua Balavu, island	C2	17
Vanua Lava, island	B1	18
Vanua Levu, island	B2	17
Vanuatu		18
Varanasi	D3	20
Vara«din	C2	48
Vardar, river	C2	48
Varde, river	B2	32
Vardenis	C2	45
Varkaus	C2	53
Varna	F2	50
Vasai	Inset I	20
Vasai, creek	Inset I	20
Vaslui	D2	43
Vassar	D4	96
Västerås	C3	53
Vatican City		39
Vatnajökull, ice cap	B2	52
Vättern, lake	B3	53
Vatu Lele, island	A3	17
Vaudreuil	C6	103
Vaupés, river	B4	78
Vava'u, island	C2	17
Vavenby	N5	95
Vavuniya	B3	19
Vawkavysk	B3	47
Växjö	B3	53
Vayk	C2	45
Vega	C4	94
Vega Alta	C2	90
Vega Baja	C2	90
Vegreville	D4	94
Veimandu, channel	A3	19
Vejle	B3	32
Velika Morava, river	B2	49
Veliki, canal	A2	49
Veliko T»rnovo	D2	50
Vélingara	B2	62
Vélingara	B3	62
Vella Lavella, island	A1	16
Vellore	C6	20
Veneto	B1	38
Venezuela		79
Venezuela, gulf	B1	79
Venice	C1	38
Venice, gulf	C1	38
Venlo	D3	32
Venta, river	A2	46
Ventimiglia	A2	38
Ventspils	A2	46
Veracruz	E4	84
Vercelli	A2	38
Verde, river	C3	75
Verdun	D2	34
Verdun	J6	103
Vereeniging	C2	71
Verkhoyansk	C8	44
Verkhoyansk, range	C8	44
Vermillion, river	C4	103
Vermont	F1	126
Vernal, Utah	C1	126
Verner	E1	102
Vernon	N6	95
Vernon Bridge	C2	100
Vernon River	C2	100
Véroia	B1	51
Verona	A2	38
Verona	J3	102
Versailles	C2, Inset II	34
Vert, cape	A2	62
Verviers	D2	33
Vesoul	D3	34
Vesterålen, islands	C2	52
Vestmanna	Inset	32
Vestmannaeyjar	A3	52
Vesuvius, volcano	C2	38
Veszprém	A2	43
Vetauua, island	C1	17
Viana do Castelo	A2	36
Vianden	B2	33
Vibank	G10	104
Viborg	B3	32
Vicenza	A1	38
Vich	H2	37
Vichada, river	C3	78
Vichy	C3	34
Victoria	D3	14
Victoria	B6	76
Victoria	A1	38
Victoria	B2	100
Victoria Beach	B3	96
Victoria Beach	B3	100
Victoria Land, region	B5	107
Victoria Nile, river	C3	61
Victoria, capital	Inset	70
Victoria, capital	L7	95
Victoria, falls	B1	69
Victoria, island	F2	99
Victoria, lake	B4, C4	61
Victoria, peak	B3	85
Victoria, Tex.	D3	126
Victoriaville	C4	61
Vidin	A2	50
Viedma	C5	74

Name	Key	Page
Viedma, lake	A6	74
Vieille Case	A1	90
Vienna, capital	E2	39
Vienne	C3	34
Vienne, river	C3	34
Vientiane, capital	B3	11
Vieques	D2	90
Vieques, island	E2	90
Vieques, passage	D2	90
Vieques, sound	E2	90
Vierzon	C2	34
Viet Tri	A2	11
Vietnam		11
Vieux Fort	B3	91
Vigan	B2	12
Vignemale, mt.	B5	34
Vigo	B1	37
Vijayawada	D5	20
Vijosë, river	A3	49
Vila do Conde	A2	36
Vila Nova de Gaia	A2	36
Vila Real	B2	36
Vila Real de Santo Antonio	B4	36
Vila, capital	C3	18
Vilaine, river	B3	34
Vilanculos	B4	68
Vilcabamba, mts.	C3	77
Viljandi	C2	46
Vilkavi%kis	B2	46
Villa Ahumada	C1	84
Villa Hayes	D4	75
Villa María	C3	74
Villa Obregón	Inset	84
Villach	C4	39
Villahermosa, state capital	F4	84
Villalba	C2	90
Villarreal de los Infantes	F3	37
Villarrica	C3	75
Villavicencio	B3	78
Villazón	A4	77
Ville-Marie	A4	101
Villeneuve-Saint-Georges	Inset II	34
Villeroy	E5	103
Vilnius, capital	C2	46
Vilyuy, river	C7	44
Vilyuysk	C8	44
Viña del Mar	B4, Inset	76
Vincennes	Inset II	34
Vincente de Carvalho	Inset II	81
Vinces, river	B3	79
Vindelälven, river	C2	53
Vindhya, range	C4	20
Vinh	A2	11
Vinnitsa	B2	47
Vinson Massif, mt.	B10	107
Virden	A4	96
Virgin, river	C3	104
Virgin, islands		82
Virginia	F2	126
Virtsu	B2	46
Virunga, mts.	B1	61
Visakhapatnam	D5	20
Visayan, islands	B4	12
Visayan, sea	B4	12
Visby	C3	53
Viscount Melville, sound	F2	99
Viseu	B2	36
Vista	A4	96
Vista Hermosa	B4	78
Vistula, river	D2, E3	41
Vita	C4	96
Viterbo	C2	38
Viti Levu, island	A2	17
Vitoria	E1	37
Vitória	D4	81
Vitória da Conquista	D3	81
Vitsyebsk	E2	47
Vivian	C4	96
Vizcaíno, desert	B2	84
Vlaardingen	B3	32
Vladivostok	E8	44
Vlieland, island	B1	32
Vlissingen	A3	32
Vlorë	A3	49
Vltava, river	B3	42
Vöcklabruck	C2	39
Voinjama	B2	63
Vojvodina, province	A2	49
Volcano, islands	Inset III	8
Volga, river	E4	44
Volgograd	E4	44
Vologda	D3	44
Vólos	B2	51
Volta Redonda	D4	81
Volta, lake	C3	64
Volta, river	C3	64
Vonda	D8	104
Vorkuta	C5	44
Voronezh	D3	44
Vorotan, river	C3	45
Vorskla, river	C1	47
Võrts Järv, lake	D2	46
Võru	D3	46
Vosges, mts.	D2	34
Vostok, island	D3	17
Vranje	B3	49
Vratsa	B2	50
Vrbas	A2	49
Vrbas, river	B1	48
Vr%ac	B2	49
Vryburg	B2	71
Vukovar	A2	49
Vunaniu, bay	A3	17
Vung Tau-Con Dao	B4	11
Vunisea	B3	17

W

Name	Key	Page
Wa	A1	64
Waal, river	C3	32
Wabag	A2	15
Wabamun, lake	C4	94
Wabana	E5	98
Wabasca	C2	94
Wabe Gestro, river	C3	60
Wabe Shebele, river	D3	60
Wabowden	B2	96
Wabush	D4	98
Waco, Tex.	D2	126
Wad Madani	C2	59
Waddan	C2	56
Waddenzee, sound	C1	32
Waddington, mt.	K5	95
Wadena	G9	104
Wadi al-Malik, river	B2	59
Wadi as-Sirhan, depression	B2	26
Wadi Halfa	C1	59
Wafrah, al-	B3	24
Wagga Wagga, N.S.W.	D3	14
Waigeo, island	E2	13
Waikato, river	C2	15
Waimamaku	B1	15
Waingapu	D2	13
Wairau, river	B3	15
Waitaki, river	B3	15
Wajh, al-	A1	24
Wajir	F3	61
Wakasa, bay	B3	8
Wakaw	E8	104
Wakayama	B3	8
Wakefield	C3	30
Wakkanai	Inset I	8
Wakomata, lake	B1	102
Wakrah, al-	B3	25
Walachia, region	B3	43
Walbrzych	C3	41
Walcheren, island	A3	32
Walden	D1	102
Waldersee	B4	96
Waldheim	D8	104
Walensee, lake	D1	35
Walkerton	D3	102
Wallace	D2	100
Wallaceburg	C5	102
Wallsall	C3	30
Walton	C2	100
Walton	D4	102
Walvis Bay	B2	70
Wami, river	C2	68
Wanaka, lake	A3	15
Wanapitei, lake	E1	102
Wandering River	D3	94
Wando	B5	9
Wanganui	C2	15
Wanham	A3	94
Wapawekka, lake	F5	104
Wapawsik	B1	96
Wapiti, river	A4	94
Warangal	C5	20
Warbah, island	C1	24
Wardlow	E6	94
Ware	K2	95
Warman	D8	104
Warner	D6	94
Warren	C4	96
Warren	E1	102
Warren Landing	C2	96
Warri	C5	65
Warrington	C3	30
Warrnambool, Vic.	B3	14
Warsaw, capital	E2	41
Warta, river	B2, C2	41
Warwick	C3	30
Wasa	P6	95
Wasaga Beach	F3	102
Wasagaming	B4	96
Washago	F3	102
Washington	A1	126
Washington, cape	A3	17
Washington, capital, D.C.	F2	126
Waskada	A4	96
Waskaganish	A3	101
Waskesiu Lake	D7	104
Waspam	C1	87
Water Valley	C5	94
Water, cays	A3	89
Waterborough	C3	97
Waterbury, lake	F2	104
Waterford	C2	31
Waterhen, lake	B3	96
Waterloo	E4	102
Waterloo	D6	103
Watertown, N.Y.	F1	126
Watford	Inset III	30
Watford	D5	102
Wathaman, lake	G3	104
Watrous	E9	104
Watsa	C1	67
Watson	F8	104
Watson Lake	D5	105
Wau	A2	15
Wavre	C3	33
Waw	B3	59
Wawa	D3	101
Wawa, river	B1	87
Wawanesa	B4	96
Weagamow Lake	B2	101
Webbwood	D1	102
Webequie	C2	101
Webi Shabeelle, river	B3	60
Weddell, sea	B12	107
Wedgeport	A4	100
Weert	C3	32
Wei, river	D2	10
Weiden	C4	40
Weifang	E2	10
Weimar	B3	40
Weipa, Qld.	D1	14
Weitzel, lake	D3	104
Wekusko	B2	96
Wekusko, lake	B2	96
Weldiya	C2	60
Welkom	C2	71
Wellington	A2	100
Wellington, capital	B3	15
Wellington, island	A8	76
Wels	C2	39
Welsford	C3	97
Welshpool	B3	30
Welwyn	A4	96
Wembere, river	B1	68
Wenchi	A3	64
Weno	C2	15
Weno, island	D3	15
Wenshan	D3	10
Wentworth	A2	100
Wentzel, lake	C1	94
Wenzhou	F3	10
Werder	D3	60
Werra, river	B3	40
Weser, river	B2	40
Wesley	B2	90
Wesleyville	E4	98
West Antarctica	A8	107
West Devon	A2	100
West Frisian, islands	B1	32
West Ice Shelf, glacier	C1	107
West Palm Beach, Fla.	E3	126
West Point	A2	100
West Road, river	K4	95
West Siberian, plain	C5	44
West St. Modeste	C3	98
West Virginia	E2	126
Westbank	N6	95
Westbourne	B4	96
Western Australia	B2	14
Western Dvina, river	C2	46
Western Ghats, mts.	B5	20
Western Sahara		58
Western, channel	C5	9
Westerschelde, channel	A3	32
Westfield	C3	97
Westlock	D4	94
Westminster	Inset III	30
Weston	J5	102
Westport	B3	15
Westport	B2	31
Westport	J3	102
Westray	A2	96
Westray, island	Inset I	30
Wetar, island	D2	13
Wetaskiwin	D5	94
Wete	C1	68
Wetzlar	B3	40
Wewak	A1	15
Wexford	C2	31
Weyakwin	E6	104
Weyburn	G11	104
Weymouth	A3	100
Whakatane	C2	15
Whale Cove	K4	99
Whaletown	K6	95
Whangarei	B2	15
Wheatland	A4	96
Wheatley	C5	102
Wheeling, W. Va.	E1	126
Whistler	L6	95
Whitbourne	E5	98
Whitby	G4	102
White Fox	F7	104
White Lake	J2	102
White Nile, river	C3	59
White Rock	L6	95
White Sands	C3	94
White Volta, river	B1, D2	64
White, bay	C4	98
White, island	L3	99
White, river	A4	105
White, sea	C3	44
Whitecourt	C4	94
Whitefish Falls	D1	102
Whitefish, bay	A1	102
Whitehaven	B2	30
Whitehorse	C5	105
Whitelaw	A3	94
Whiteman, range	A2	15
Whitemouth	D4	96
Whitestone, river	B3	105
Whitewood	H10	104
Whitney	C2	102
Whitney mt., Calif.	B2	126
Wholdaia, lake	H4	99
Whyalla, S.A.	C3	14
Whycocomagh	F2	100
Wiarton	D3	102
Wichita Falls, Tex.	D2	126
Wichita, Kans.	D2	126
Wick	B1	30
Wicklow	C2	31
Wicklow Head, cape	D2	31
Wicklow, mts.	C2	31
Wiener Neustadt	E3	39
Wieprz, river	F3	41
Wiesbaden	B3	40
Wigan	C3	30
Wight, island	C4	30
Wilberforce	G2	102
Wilge, river	C2	71
Wilhelm, mt.	A2	15
Wilhelmina, canal	B3	32
Wilhelmina, mts.	A2	80
Wilhelmshaven	B2	40
Wilkes Land, region	B8	107
Wilkie	B8	104
William, river	B2	104
Williams Harbour	D3	98
Williams Lake	L5	95
Williamsport	C4	98
Williston, N.D.	C1	126
Willow Bunch	E11	104
Willow Creek	A11	104
Willowbunch, lake	E11	104
Wilmington, Del.	F2	126
Wilmington, N.C.	F2	126
Wilmot	B3	100
Wiltondale	C4	98
Wiltz	A2	33
Winchester	C3	30
Winchester	K2	102
Wind, river	B3	105
Windermere	O6	95
Windermere	F2	102
Windfall	B4	94
Windhoek, capital	C2	70
Windsor	Inset III	30
Windsor	C3	100
Windsor	D6	103
Windward Group	B2	58
Windward, islands	B4	91
Windward, passage	F3	88
Winefred, lake	E3	94
Winfield	N6	95
Wingham	D4	102
Winisk	C1	101
Winisk, lake	C2	101
Winisk, river	C2	101
Winkler	C4	96
Winneba	B4	64
Winnemucca, Nev.	B1	126
Winnipeg	C4, D2	96
Winnipeg Beach	C4	96
Winnipeg, lake	B3, C4, D2	96
Winnipegosis	B3	96
Winnipegosis, lake	A3	96
Winslow, Ariz.	B2	126
Winston-Salem, N.C.	E2	126
Winter Harbour	H6	95
Winterthur	C1	35
Wisconsin	D1	126
Wismar	B2	40
Witless Bay	E5	98
Witten	A3	40
Wittenberg	C3	40
Wittenberge	B2	40
Witu, island	A2	15
Wiwili	B2	87
W{adys{awowo	D1	41
W{oc{awek	D2	41
Woburn	F6	103
Wodzis{aw ¿l}ski	D3	41
Woking	A3	94
Wolf, lake	C5	105
Wolfsberg	D4	39
Wolfsburg	B2	40
Wolfville	C2	100
Wollaston Lake	G2	104
Wollaston, lake	H2	104
Wollaston, peninsula	E3	99
Wollongong, N.S.W.	G10	104
Wolseley	G10	104
Wolverhampton	C3	30
Wong, river	A2	19
Wonowon	M3	95
W%nsan	B3	9
Wood Islands	C3	100
Woodbridge	J5	102
Woodlands	B1	13
Woodlands	C4	96
Woodlark (Muyua), island	B2	15
Woodnorth	A4	96
Woodridge	C4	96
Woods, lake	B3	101
Woodstock	B2	97
Woodstock	A2	100
Woodstock	A4	102
Woody Point	C4	98
Woomera, S.A.	C3	14
Worcester	C3	30
Worcester	A3	71
Worcester, Mass.	F1	126
Worms	B4	40
Wotho, island	B1	16
Wotje, island	B2	16
Wrangel, island	B10	44
Wrath, cape	B1	30
Wreck Cove	D5	98
Wrentham	D6	94
Wrigley	D4	99
Wroc{aw	C3	41
Wuhan	E2	10
Wuhu	E2	10
Wukari	E4	65
Wum	B2	65
Wuppertal	A3	40
Würzburg	B4	40
Wutivi, mt.	B1	63
Wuwei	D2	10
Wuxi	F2	10
Wuzhong	D2	10
Wuzhou	E3	10
Wye, river	C3	30
Wyndham, W.A.	B1	14
Wynyard	F9	104
Wyoming	C1	126

X

Name	Key	Page
Xaçmaz	C2	45
Xai-Xai	B5	68
Xam Nua	C1	11
Xangongo	C5	70
Xankändi	B3	45
Xánthi	C1	51
Xau, lake	B2	69
Xi'an	D2	10
Xi, river	E3	10
Xiamen	E3	10
Xiangfan	E2	10
Xiangkhoang	B2	11
Xiangtan	E3	10
Xigaze	B3	10
Xingu, river	C3	81
Xining	D2	10
Xinjiang Uygur	B1	10
Xinxiang	E2	10
Xinyang	E2	10
Xochimilco	Inset	84
Xuddur	A3	60
Xuzhou	E2	10

Y

Name	Key	Page
Ya'an	D2	10
Yablonovyy, range	D7	44
Yabucoa	D2	90
Yacuiba	B4	77
Yafran	B1	56
Yaguarí, river	C1	75
Yaguarón, river	D2	75
Yahk	O6	95
Yakima, Wash.	A1	126
Yaku, island	A4	8
Yakutsk	C8	44
Yala	B5	12
Yale	M6	95
Yalinga	C2	66
Yalu, river	C4	47
Yamagata	D2	8
Yamaguchi	A3	8
Yamal, peninsula	C5	44
Yamalo-Nenesiya, autonomous okrug	C5	44
Yambio	B4	120
Yambol	E3	50
Yamoussoukro, capital	D3	63
Yampi, sound	B1	14
Yamuna, river	C3	20
Yan, river	B3	19
Yanbu al-Bahr	A1	24
Yangambi	C1	67
Yangd{k	B3	16
Yangon (Rangoon), capital	C3	12
Yangquan	E2	10
Yangtze, river	C2, D2	10
Yangzhou	E2	10
Yanji	F1	10
Yantai	F2	10
Yantra, river	D2	50
Yao	B3	8
Yaoundé, capital	B3	65
Yap, islands	A2	15
Yapen, island	E2	13
Yaque del Norte, river	A1	89
Yaque del Sur, river	A2	89
Yaqui, river	C2	84
Yare, river	D3	30
Yaren, capital	B3	16
Yariga, mt.	C2	8
Yarmouth	A4	100
Yaroslavl	D3	44
Yasawa, island group	A2	17
Yasuj	C3	22
Yata, river	A2	77
Yates	B4	94
Yatsushiro	A3	8
Yauco	B2	90
Yavarí, river	C1	77
Yaviza	D2	87
Yazd	C3	22
Yazd, region	C3	22
Ybbs, river	D2	39
Ye	C3	12
Yeboah	C3	30
Yecla	F3	37
Yeguas, point	D2	90
Yekaterinburg	D5	44
Yekepa	B2	63
Yell, island	Inset I	30
Yellow Grass	F11	104
Yellow, sea	F2	10
Yellowknife, capital	F4	99
Yemen		25
Yen Bai	A2	11
Yendi	B2	64
Yenisey, river	C6	44
Yeovil	C4	30
Yerevan, capital	B2	45
Yesilhrmak, river	D2	27
Yeu, island	B3	34
Yevlax	B2	45
Yevpatoriya	C3	47
Yevrey, autonomous oblast	E8	44
Yevulun, plain	B1	26
Yi, river	C2	75
Yialousa	C1	27
Yibin	D3	10
Yichang	E2	10
Yichun	F1	10
Yin Shan, mts.	E1	10
Yinchuan	D2	10
Yingkou	F1	10
Yining	B1	10
Ylikitka, lake	C1	53
Ylivieska	B2	53
Yoboki	B2	60
Yogyakarta	C2	13
Yojoa, lake	B2	86
Yokkaichi	C3	8
Yokohama	C3	8
Yokosuka	C3	8
Yola	G3	65
Yom, river	B2	12
Yomou	D4	62
Yonago	B3	8
Yonaguni, island	Inset II	8
Yonne, river	C2	34
Yopal	B3	78
York	C3	30
York	B2	100
York	K5	102
York Factory	E1	96
York, cape	D1	14
Yorkton	H9	104
Yoro	B2	86
Yoshino, river	B3	8
Yoshkar-Ola	D4	44
Y!su	B5	9
Yotvata	B2	26
Youghal	C3	31
Young	E9	104
Youngs Cove	D2	97
Ypané, river	D4	75
Ypoá, lake	D5	75
Ypres	A2	33
Ysyk-Köl, lake	E1	23
Yü Shan, mt.	B2	9
Yuan, river	D3	10
Yubari	Inset I	8
Yucatán, channel	A2	88
Yucatán, peninsula	D2	88
Yuen Long	Inset	10
Yueyang	E3	10
Yugoslavia		49
Yukon, river	D2	92
Yuma, Ariz.	B2	126
Yumen	C2	10
Yuna, river	B2	89
Yundum	B2	62
Yungas, region	A3	77
Yungho	B1	9
Yunnan	C3	10
Yurimaguas	B2	79
Yuscarán	B3	86
Yushu	C2	10
Yuzhno-Sakhalinsk	E9	44
Yverdon	A2	35

Z

Name	Key	Page
Zabbar	C2	36
Zabid	A2	25
Zabol	E3	22
Zabrze	D3	41
Zacapa	D5	85
Zacatecas, state capital	D3	84
Zacatecoluca	B2	86
Zadar	B3	48
Zafra	C3	37
Zagazig	B1	56
Zaghouan	C1	57
Zagreb, capital	B2	48
Zagros, mts.	B3	22
Zahedan	E4	22
Zahlah	A2	26
Zaječar	C3	49
Zákinthos, island	B3	51
Zakopane	D4	41
Zala, river	A2	43
Zalaegerszeg	A2	43
ZalCu	B2	43
Zambales, mts.	B3	12
Zambezi	C2	67
Zambezi, river	A3, B3	67
Zambia		67
Zamboanga	B5	12
Zamboanga, peninsula	B5	12
Zamora	D2	37
Zamora	B5	79
Zamora, river	B4	79
Zamoj~	F3	41
Zanderij	B2	80
Zanjan	B2	22
Zanzibar	C2	68
Zao, mt.	D2	8
Zapadna Morava, river	B3	49
Zapatera, island	B3	87
Zaporizhzhia	D2	47
Zaqatala	B2	45
Zarafobod	A1	23
Zarafshon	A2	23
Zaragoza	F2	37
Zaranj	A2	22
Zareh Sharan	B2	22
Zaria	D2	65
Zarqa, az-	B1	26
Zarzis	C3	57
Zavidovi~i	B1	48
Zaysan	E2	23
Zaysan, lake	E2	23
Zebbug	A1	36
Zeebrugge	B1	33
Zefat	B1	26
Zenica	B1	48
Zeravshan, mts.	A1	23
Zeravshan, river	A1, B2	23
Zermatt	B2	35
Zestaponi	A3	49
Zeta, river	A3	49
Zevulun, plain	B1	26
Zêzere, river	A3	36
Zhambyl (Dzhambul)	D2	23
Zhangjiakou	E1	10
Zhangye	D2	10
Zhanjiang	E3	10
Zhejiang	E3	10
Zhelaniya, cape	B5	44
Zhengzhou	E2	10
Zhenjiang	E2	10
Zhezqazgham	C2	23
Zhitomir	B1	47
Zhlobin	D3	47
Zhob, river	C3	21
Zhoda	C4	96
Zhu, river	E3	10
Zhuzhou	E3	10
Zibo	E2	10
Zielona Góra	B3	41
Zigong	D3	10
Ziguinchor	A3	62
%ilina	B2	42
Zillah	C2	56
Zillertal Alps, range	B3	39
Zima, lake	A2	94
Zimbabwe		69
Zinder	B3	59
Zion	C3	90
Zittau	C3	40
Ziway, lake	C3	60
Zlatibor, mts.	A3	49
Zlín	C3	42
Znojmo	C4	42
Zomba	C3	68
Zonguldak	B2	27
Zorzor	B2	63
Zouar	B2	59
Zouîrât	B2	58
Zrenjanin	B2	49
Zug	C1	35
Zugdidi	A3	45
Zugspitze, mt.	B5	40
Zuid-Willemsvaart, canal	C3	32
Zújar, reservoir	D3	37
Zululand, region	D2	71
Zunyi	D3	10
Zürich	C1	35
Zürichsee, lake	C1	35
Zurrieq	B2	36
Zuwarah	B1	56
Zvishavane	B2	69
Zvolen	C1	42
Zvornik	C1	48
Zwedru	B2	63
Zwickau	C3	40
Zwolle	D2	32
Zyryanka	C9	44
Zaanstad	B2	32

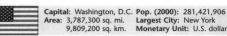

Capital: Washington, D.C. **Pop. (2000):** 281,421,906
Area: 3,787,300 sq. mi. **Largest City:** New York
9,809,200 sq. km. **Monetary Unit:** U.S. dollar

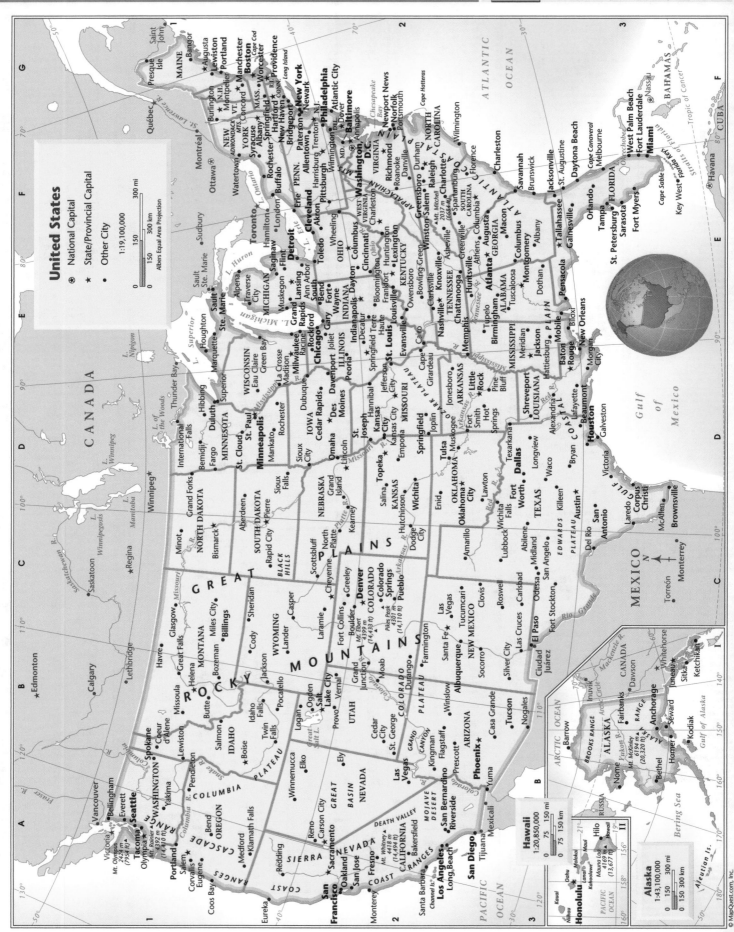

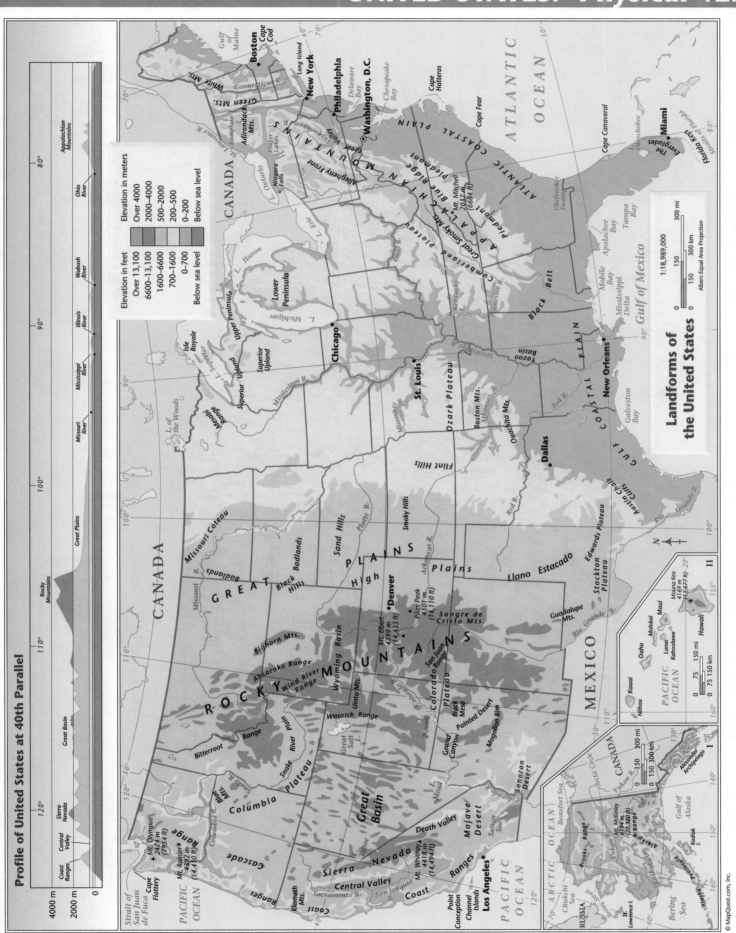

Profile of United States at 40th Parallel

4000 m
2000 m
0

Coast Ranges
Sierra Nevada
Central Valley
Great Basin
Rocky Mountains
Great Plains
Appalachian Mountains

120° 110° 100° 90° 80°

Missouri River
Mississippi River
Wabash River
Illinois River
Ohio River

Elevation in meters
Over 4000
2000–4000
500–2000
200–500
0–200
Below sea level

Elevation in feet
Over 13,100
6600–13,100
1600–6600
700–1600
0–700
Below sea level

CANADA

Gulf of Maine
Cape Cod
Boston
White Mts.
Green Mts.
Connecticut R.
Adirondack Mts.
L. Champlain
Finger Lakes
Long Island
New York
Philadelphia
Delaware Bay
Chesapeake Bay
⊛ **Washington, D.C.**
Cape Hatteras
Cape Fear
ATLANTIC OCEAN
30°
40°
70°
A P P A L A C H I A N   M O U N T A I N S
Allegheny Front
Great Valley
Blue Ridge
Piedmont
Great Smoky Mts.
Mt. Mitchell 2037 m (6684 ft)
Piedmont
ATLANTIC COASTAL PLAIN
Cape Canaveral
L. Okeechobee
Miami
The Everglades
Florida Keys
Straits of Florida
80°

L. Ontario
L. Erie
L. Huron
Niagara Falls
Lower Peninsula
L. Michigan
Upper Peninsula
Isle Royale
L. Superior
Superior Upland
Mesabi Range
L. of the Woods
Superior Upland
Mississippi R.
Chicago
90°
Cumberland Plateau
Kentucky R.
Tennessee R.
Black Belt
Mississippi R.
Yazoo Basin
GULF COASTAL PLAIN
Red R.
New Orleans
Mobile Bay
Apalachee Bay
Tampa Bay
Gulf of Mexico
90°
1:18,989,000
Albers Equal Area Projection
0   150   300 mi
0   150   300 km

Landforms of the United States

CANADA
Missouri R.
Missouri Coteau
Badlands
Black Hills
Badlands
G R E A T   P L A I N S
Sand Hills
Smoky Hills
Flint Hills
Platte R.
High Plains
Plains
Denver
Pikes Peak 4301 m (14,110 ft)
Arkansas R.
Sangre de Cristo Mts.
Llano Estacado
Stockton Plateau
Edwards Plateau
Guadalupe Mts.
Rio Grande R.
Austin Chalk Cliffs
Galveston Bay
Dallas
Ouachita Mts.
Boston Mts.
Arkansas R.
Ozark Plateau
St. Louis
Missouri R.

Bighorn Mts.
Absaroka Range
Wind River Range
Wyoming Basin
Uinta Mts.
Mt. Elbert 4399 m (14,433 ft)
Colorado Plateau
San Juan Range
R O C K Y   M O U N T A I N S
Green R.
Colorado R.
Black Mesa
Grand Canyon
Painted Desert
Mogollon Rim
Wasatch Range
Great Salt L.
Snake River Plain
Columbia Plateau
Bitterroot Range
Blue Mts.
Snake R.
Cascade Range
Columbia R.
Great Basin
L. Mead
Death Valley
Mojave Desert
Salton Sea
Sonoran Desert
Colorado R.
MEXICO
110°

PACIFIC OCEAN
120°
Strait of Juan de Fuca
Cape Flattery
Mt. Olympus 2424 m (7954 ft)
Mt. Rainier 4392 m (14,410 ft)
Klamath Mts.
Coast Ranges
Point Conception
Channel Islands
Los Angeles
Sierra Nevada
Mt. Whitney 4418 m (14,494 ft)
Central Valley
Sacramento R.
San Joaquin R.
Coast Ranges
120°

N

II
PACIFIC OCEAN
Kauai
Niihau
Oahu
Molokai
Lanai
Maui
Kahoolawe
Mauna Kea 4169 m (13,677 ft)
Hawaii
Mauna Loa
20°
160° 155°
0   75   150 mi
0   75   150 km

I
ARCTIC OCEAN
Arctic Circle
Beaufort Sea
Chukchi Sea
Brooks Range
RUSSIA
Bering Sea
St. Lawrence I.
Yukon R.
Mt. McKinley 6194 m (20,320 ft)
Alaska Range
Gulf of Alaska
Kodiak I.
Alaska Peninsula
Alexander Archipelago
CANADA
70°
60°
160° 150° 140° 130°
0   150   300 mi
0   150   300 km

© MapQuest.com, Inc.

Capital: Montgomery	**Pop. (2000):** 4,447,100
Area: 52,400 sq. mi. 135,800 sq. km.	**Largest City:** Birmingham 242,820

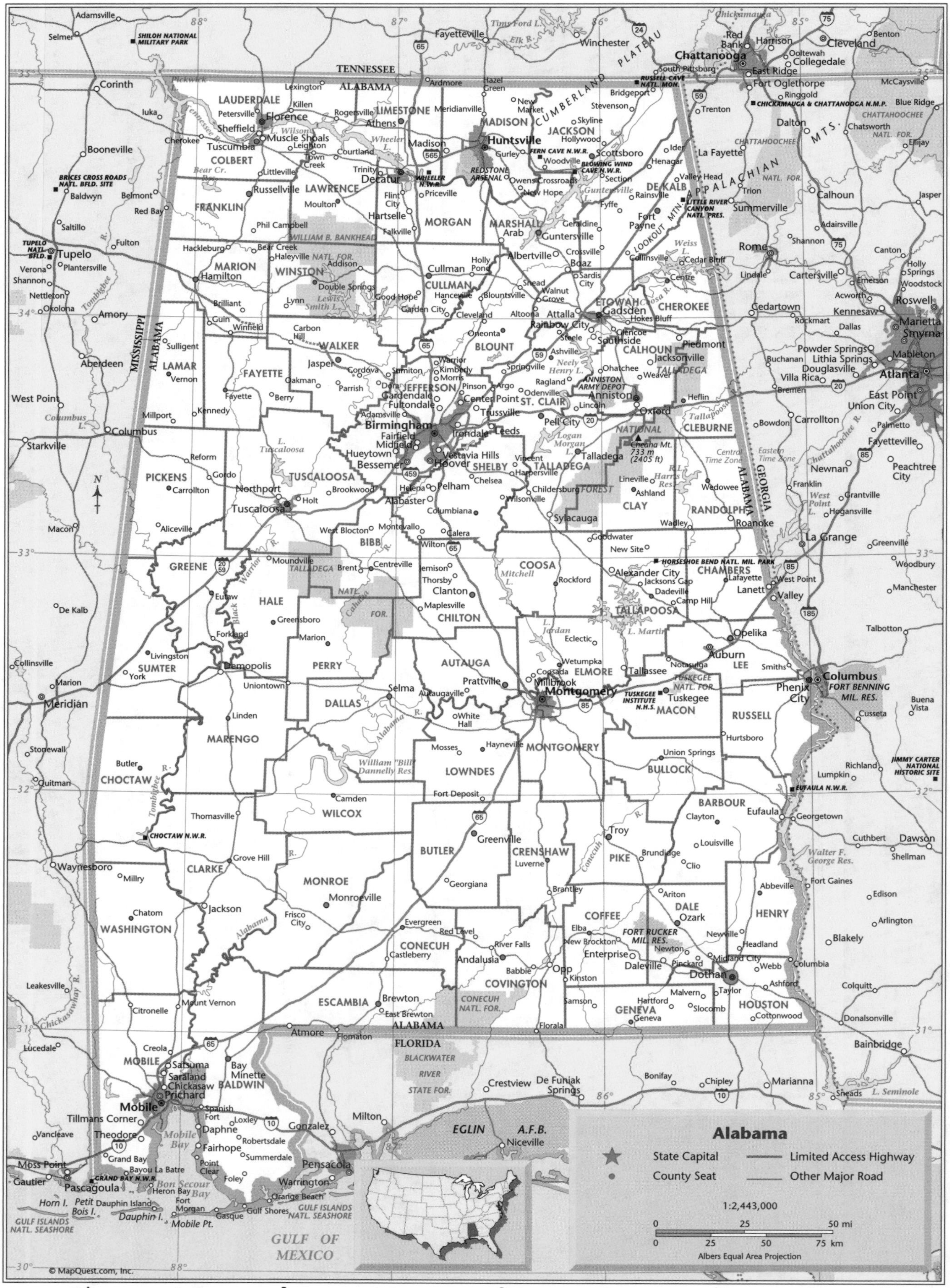

TENNESSEE

ALABAMA

MISSISSIPPI

GEORGIA

FLORIDA

GULF OF MEXICO

CUMBERLAND PLATEAU

APPALACHIAN MTS.

Counties and places (selected labels):

Adamsville, Selmer, Corinth, Iuka, Booneville, Tupelo, Verona, Shannon, Nettleton, Okolona, Amory, Aberdeen, West Point, Starkville, Columbus, Macon, Meridian, Waynesboro, Quitman, Stonewall, Leakesville, Lucedale, Moss Point, Gautier, Pascagoula

Adamsville, Selmer, Shiloh National Military Park, Lexington, Killen, Rogersville, Athens, Ardmore, Fayetteville, Winchester, Red Bank, Harrison, Cleveland, Benton, Collegedale, Chattanooga, East Ridge, Fort Oglethorpe, McCaysville, Blue Ridge

LAUDERDALE, LIMESTONE, MADISON, JACKSON, DE KALB, COLBERT, FRANKLIN, LAWRENCE, MORGAN, MARSHALL, CHEROKEE, ETOWAH, MARION, WINSTON, CULLMAN, BLOUNT, CALHOUN, CLEBURNE, LAMAR, FAYETTE, WALKER, ST. CLAIR, TALLADEGA, CLAY, RANDOLPH, PICKENS, TUSCALOOSA, JEFFERSON, SHELBY, COOSA, CHAMBERS, GREENE, HALE, BIBB, CHILTON, TALLAPOOSA, LEE, SUMTER, PERRY, AUTAUGA, ELMORE, MACON, RUSSELL, MARENGO, DALLAS, LOWNDES, MONTGOMERY, BULLOCK, BARBOUR, CHOCTAW, WILCOX, BUTLER, CRENSHAW, PIKE, DALE, HENRY, CLARKE, MONROE, COFFEE, COVINGTON, GENEVA, HOUSTON, WASHINGTON, CONECUH, ESCAMBIA, MOBILE, BALDWIN

Florence, Sheffield, Muscle Shoals, Tuscumbia, Decatur, Huntsville, Scottsboro, Fort Payne, Rome, Russellville, Moulton, Hartselle, Cullman, Guntersville, Albertville, Boaz, Gadsden, Attalla, Anniston, Oxford, Jasper, Birmingham, Bessemer, Hoover, Vestavia Hills, Pell City, Talladega, Sylacauga, Tuscaloosa, Northport, Centreville, Clanton, Alexander City, Opelika, Auburn, Columbus, Phenix City, Demopolis, Selma, Prattville, Montgomery, Tuskegee, Eufaula, Thomasville, Greenville, Troy, Clayton, Monroeville, Evergreen, Andalusia, Enterprise, Ozark, Dothan, Geneva, Brewton, Atmore, Mobile, Prichard, Daphne, Fairhope, Foley, Gulf Shores, Dauphin I.

Montgomery (State Capital)

Cheaha Mt. 733 m (2405 ft)

Alabama

★ State Capital — Limited Access Highway
• County Seat — Other Major Road

1:2,443,000

0 — 25 — 50 mi
0 — 25 — 50 — 75 km

Albers Equal Area Projection

© MapQuest.com, Inc.

Capital: Juneau
Area: 656,400 sq. mi.
1,700,000 sq. km.
Pop. (2000): 626,932
Largest City: Anchorage
260,283

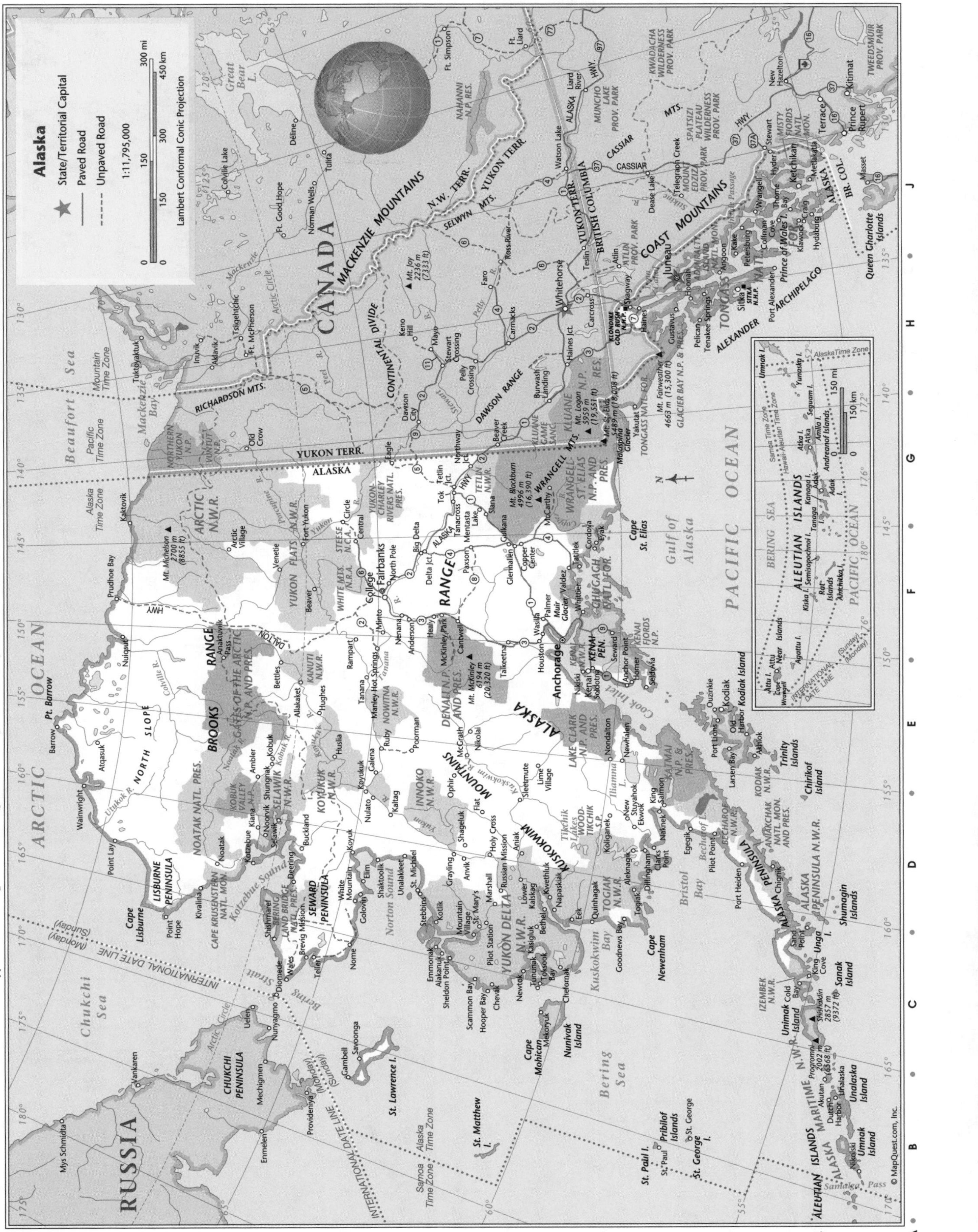

Alaska

★ State/Territorial Capital
— Paved Road
- - - Unpaved Road

300 mi — 450 km

1:11,795,000

Lambert Conformal Conic Projection

RUSSIA

CANADA

ARCTIC OCEAN

Beaufort Sea

Chukchi Sea

Bering Sea

PACIFIC OCEAN

Gulf of Alaska

BROOKS RANGE

ALASKA RANGE

MACKENZIE MOUNTAINS

COAST MOUNTAINS

WRANGELL-ST. ELIAS N.P. AND PRES.

DENALI N.P. AND PRES.

Mt. McKinley 6194 m (20,320 ft)

Anchorage

Fairbanks

Juneau

Barrow

Nome

Valdez

Kodiak Island

ALEUTIAN ISLANDS

Bristol Bay

Norton Sound

Kotzebue Sound

Cook Inlet

NORTH SLOPE

SEWARD PENINSULA

ALASKA PENINSULA

KENAI PEN.

YUKON TERR.

BRITISH COLUMBIA

N.W. TERR.

INTERNATIONAL DATE LINE

Arctic Circle

© MapQuest.com, Inc.

Capital: Phoenix
Area: 114,000 sq. mi.
295,300 sq. km.
Pop. (2000): 5,130,632
Largest City: Phoenix
1,321,045

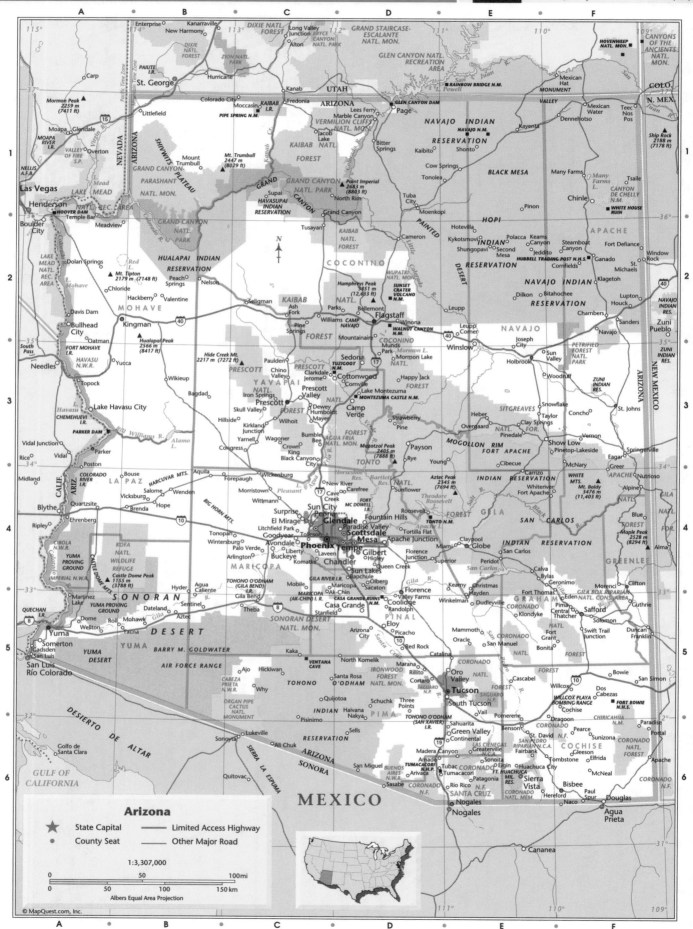

Arizona

★ State Capital —— Limited Access Highway
• County Seat —— Other Major Road

1:3,307,000

0   50   100mi
0   50   100   150 km

Albers Equal Area Projection

© MapQuest.com, Inc.

Capital: Little Rock
Area: 53,200 sq. mi.
137,700 sq. km.
Pop. (2000): 2,673,400
Largest City: Little Rock
183,133

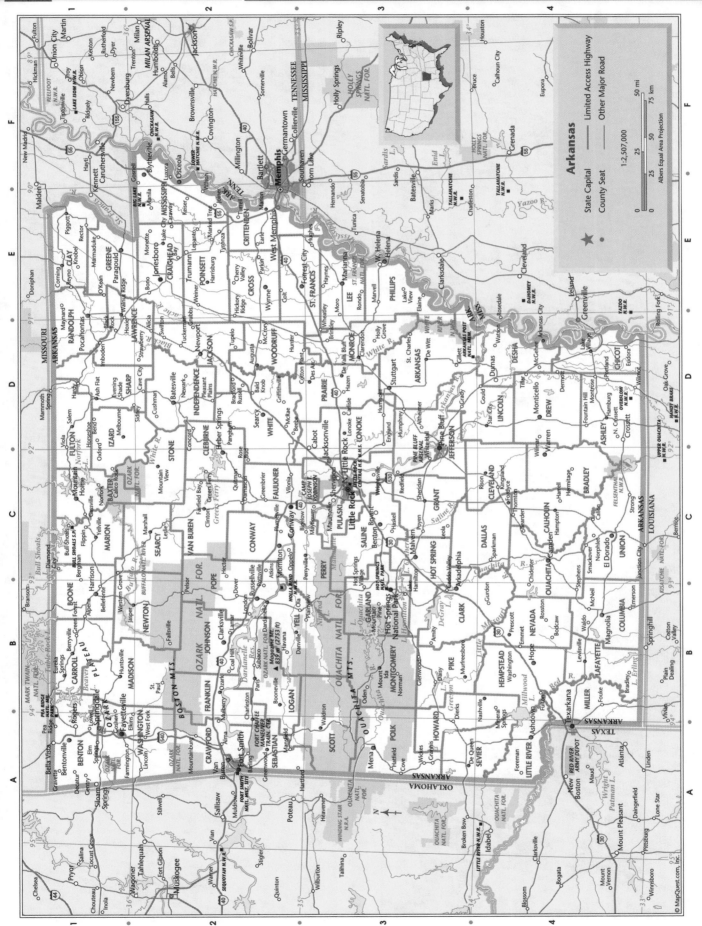

Arkansas

★ State Capital
• County Seat

— Limited Access Highway
— Other Major Road

1:2,507,000

50 mi
75 km

Albers Equal Area Projection

© MapQuest.com, Inc.

Capital: Sacramento
Area: 163,700 sq. mi.
424,000 sq. km.
Pop. (2000): 33,871,648
Largest City: Los Angeles
3,694,820

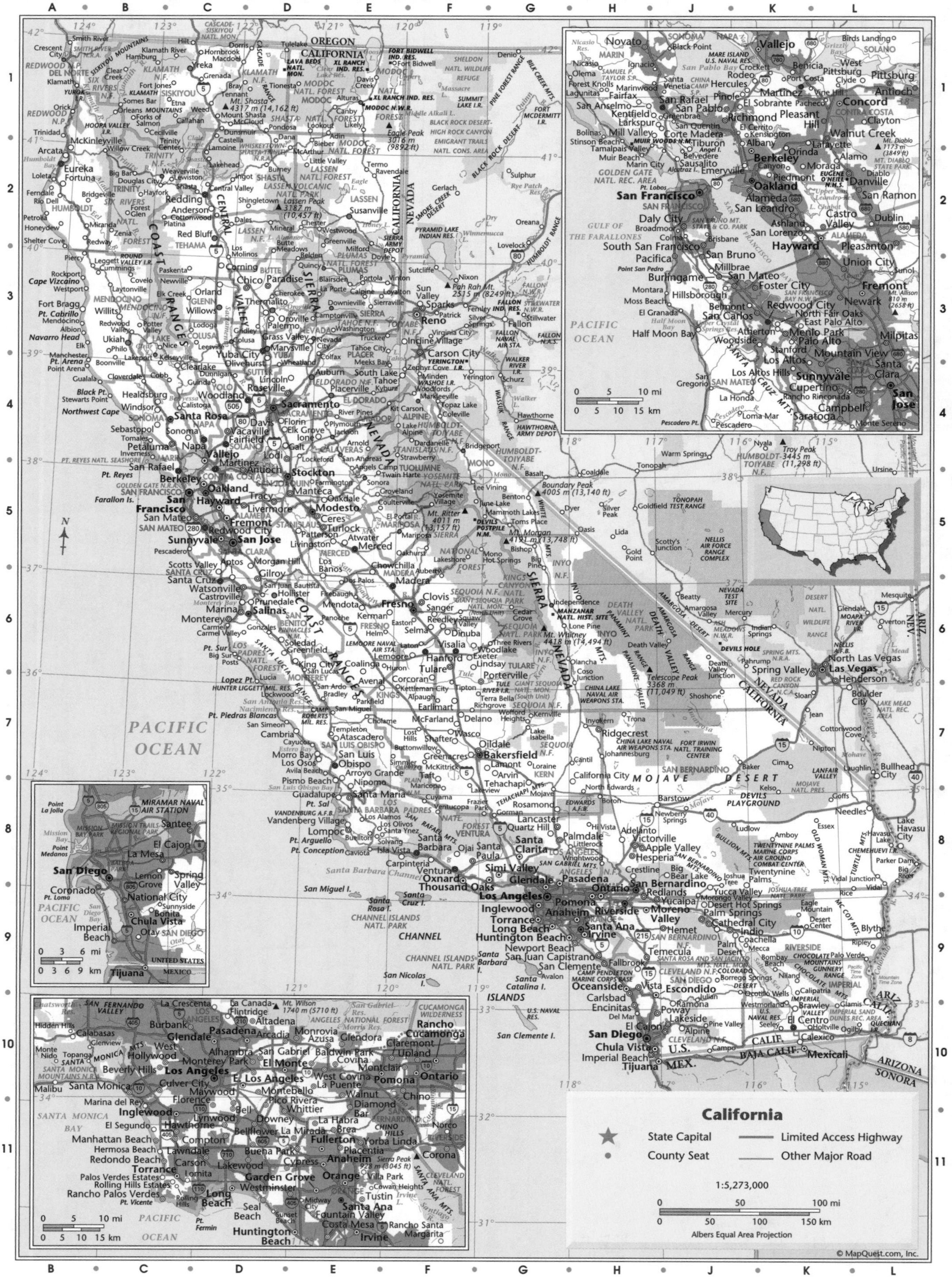

California

★ State Capital
• County Seat
—— Limited Access Highway
—— Other Major Road

1:5,273,000

0   50   100 mi
0   50 100 150 km

Albers Equal Area Projection

© MapQuest.com, Inc.

Capital: Denver	Pop. (2000): 4,301,261
Area: 104,100 sq. mi.	Largest City: Denver
269,600 sq. km.	554,636

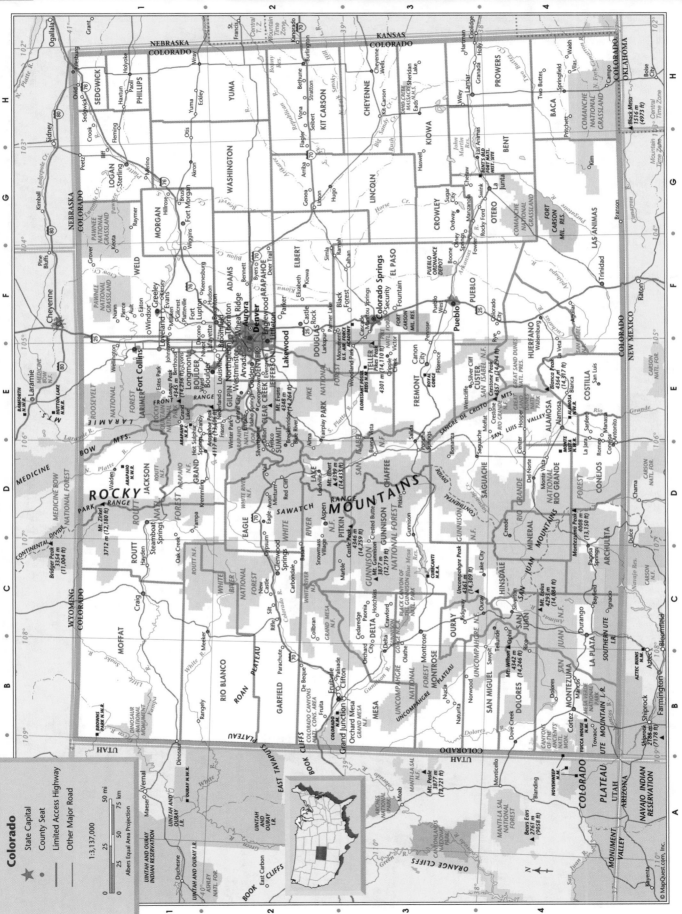

Colorado
★ State Capital
• County Seat
━━ Limited Access Highway
━━ Other Major Road

1:3,137,000

Albers Equal Area Projection

© MapQuest.com, Inc.

Capital: Hartford
Area: 5,500 sq. mi.
14,400 sq. km.
Pop. (2000): 3,405,565
Largest City: Bridgeport
139,529

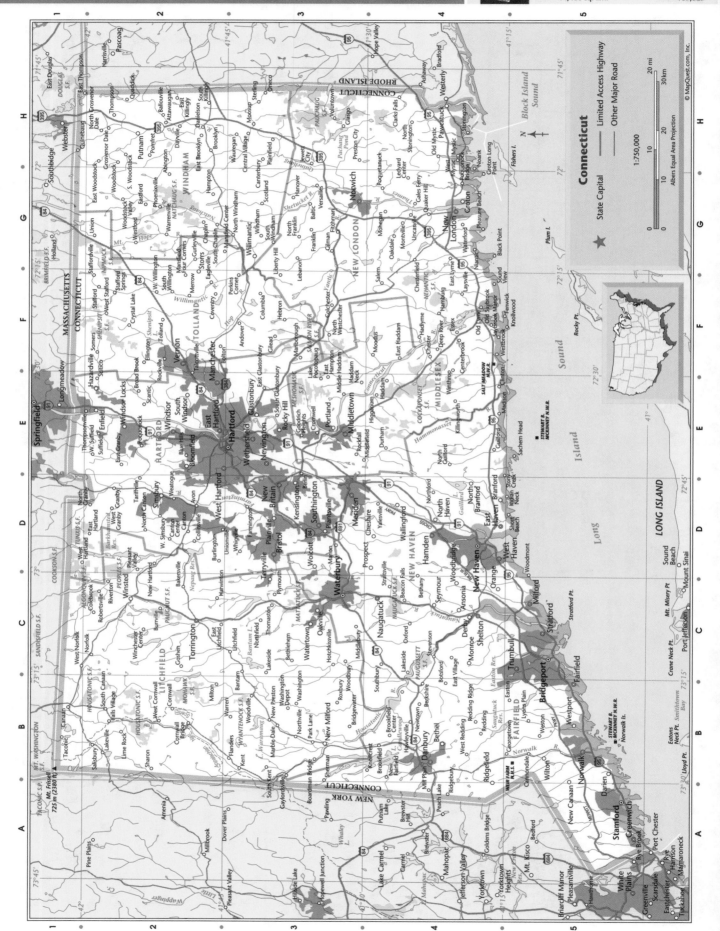

Connecticut

★ State Capital
━━ Limited Access Highway
━━ Other Major Road

1:750,000
Albers Equal Area Projection

© MapQuest.com, Inc.

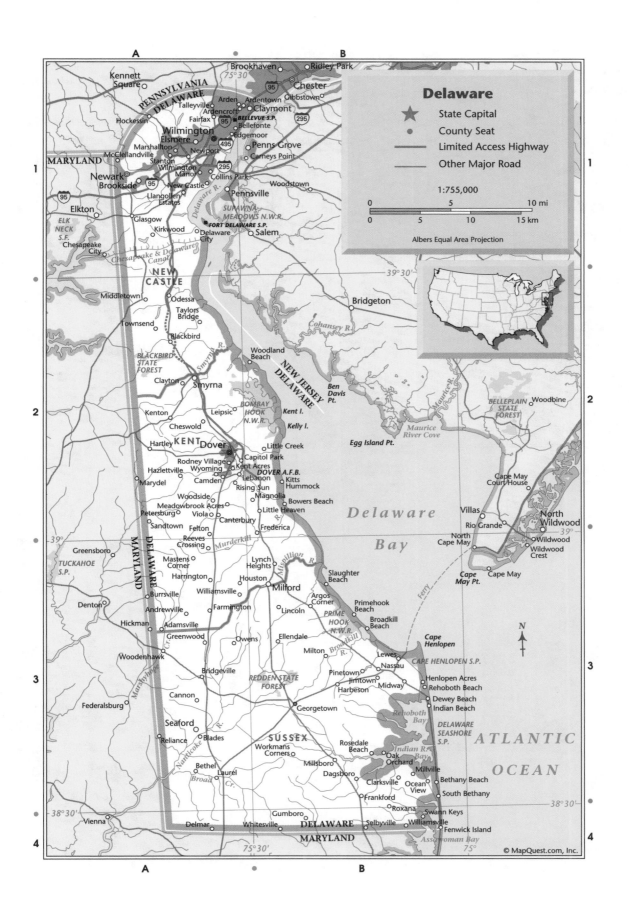

Delaware

★ State Capital
● County Seat
── Limited Access Highway
── Other Major Road

1:755,000

| 0 | 5 | 10 mi |
| 0 | 5 | 10 | 15 km |

Albers Equal Area Projection

© MapQuest.com, Inc.

Capital: Tallahassee | **Pop. (2000):** 15,982,378
Area: 65,800 sq. mi. | **Largest City:** Jacksonville
170,300 sq. km. | 735,617

Florida

★ State Capital
• County Seat
── Limited Access Highway
── Other Major Road

1:3,135,000

0   25   50 mi
0   25   50   75 km
Albers Equal Area Projection

© MapQuest.com, Inc.

Capital: Atlanta	Pop. (2000): 8,186,453
Area: 59,400 sq. mi.	Largest City: Atlanta
153,900 sq. km.	416,474

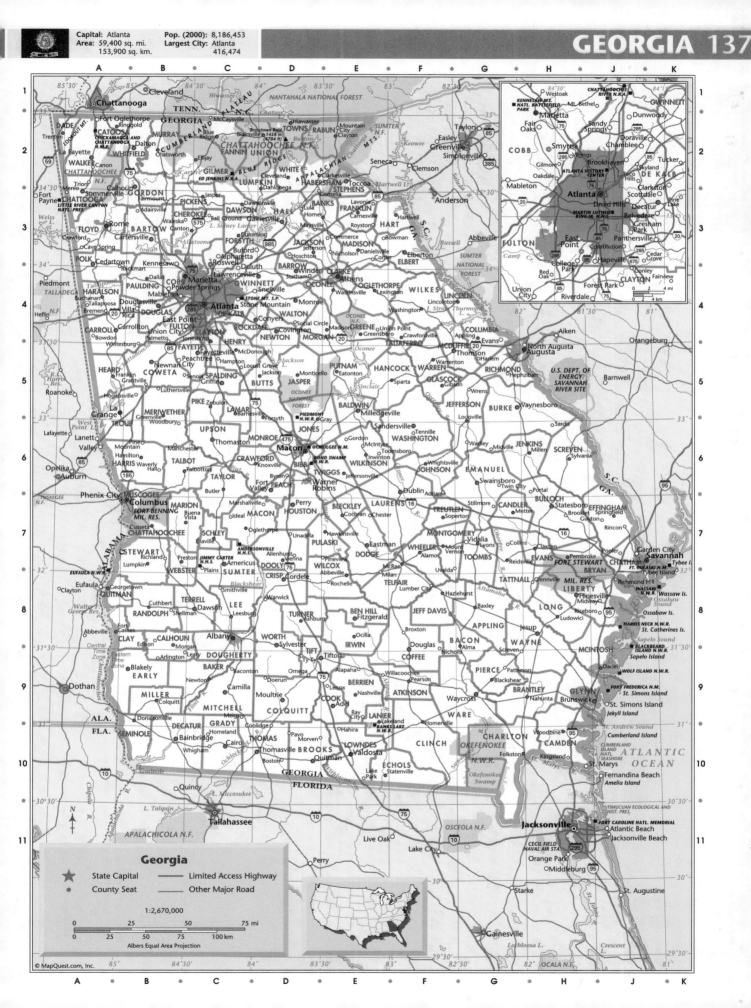

Georgia

★ State Capital ── Limited Access Highway
● County Seat ── Other Major Road

1:2,670,000

0 25 50 75 mi
0 25 50 75 100 km
Albers Equal Area Projection

© MapQuest.com, Inc.

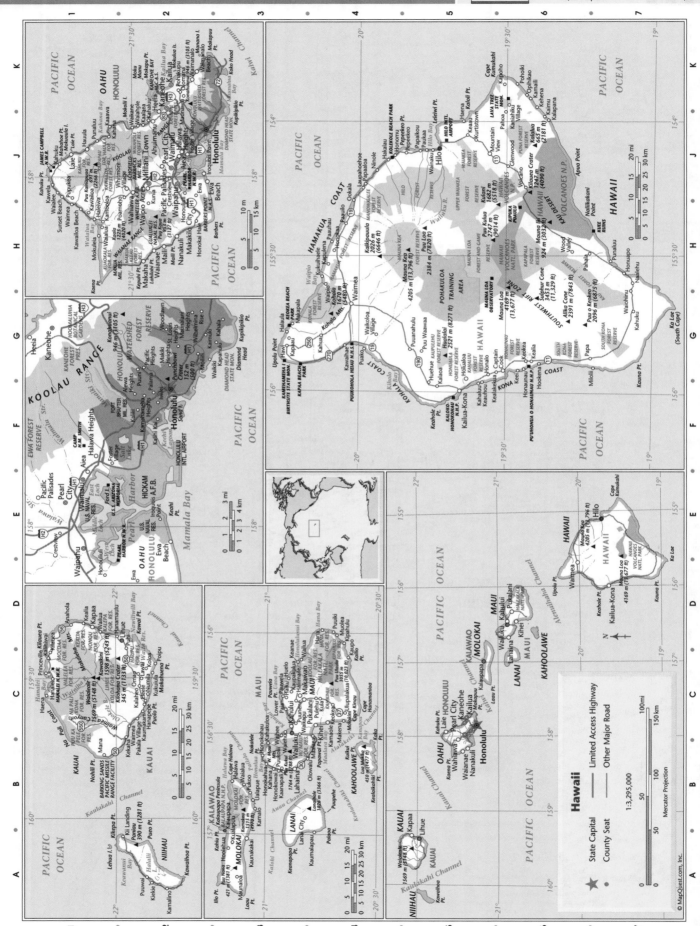

Capital: Honolulu
Area: 10,900 sq. mi.
28,300 sq. km.
Pop. (2000): 1,211,537
Largest City: Honolulu
371,657

Hawaii

State Capital ★
County Seat •

Limited Access Highway
Other Major Road

1:3,295,000

Mercator Projection

© MapQuest.com, Inc.

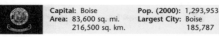

Capital: Boise
Area: 83,600 sq. mi.
216,500 sq. km.
Pop. (2000): 1,293,953
Largest City: Boise
185,787

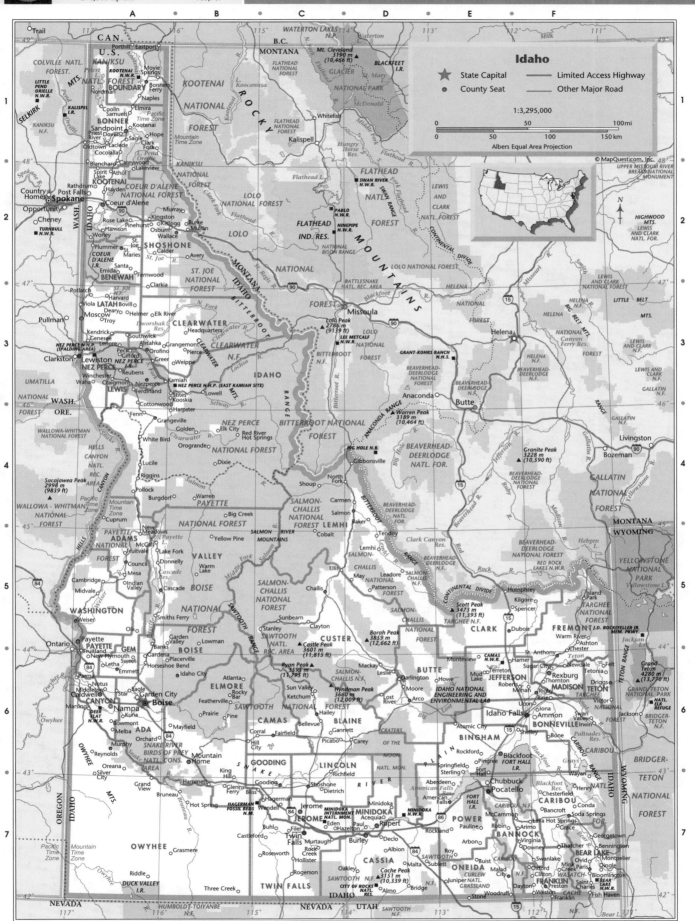

Capital: Springfield
Area: 57,900 sq. mi.
150,000 sq. km.

Pop. (2000): 12,419,293
Largest City: Chicago
2,896,016

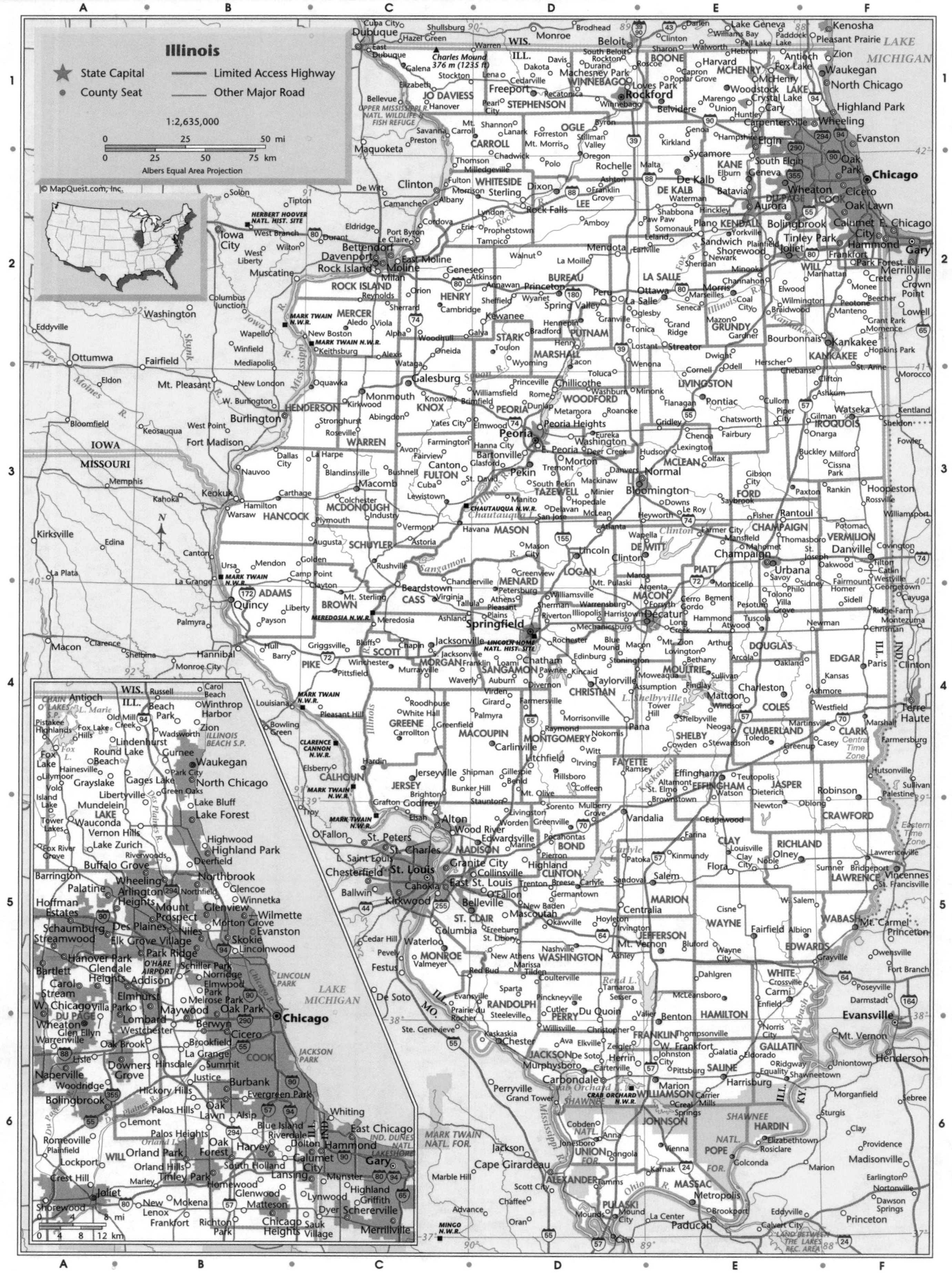

ILLINOIS

Illinois

★ State Capital — Limited Access Highway
• County Seat — Other Major Road

1:2,635,000

0   25   50 mi
0   25   50   75 km

Albers Equal Area Projection

© MapQuest.com, Inc.

HERBERT HOOVER NATL. HIST. SITE

Capital: Indianapolis
Area: 36,400 sq. mi.
94,300 sq. km.
Pop. (2000): 6,080,485
Largest City: Indianapolis
791,926

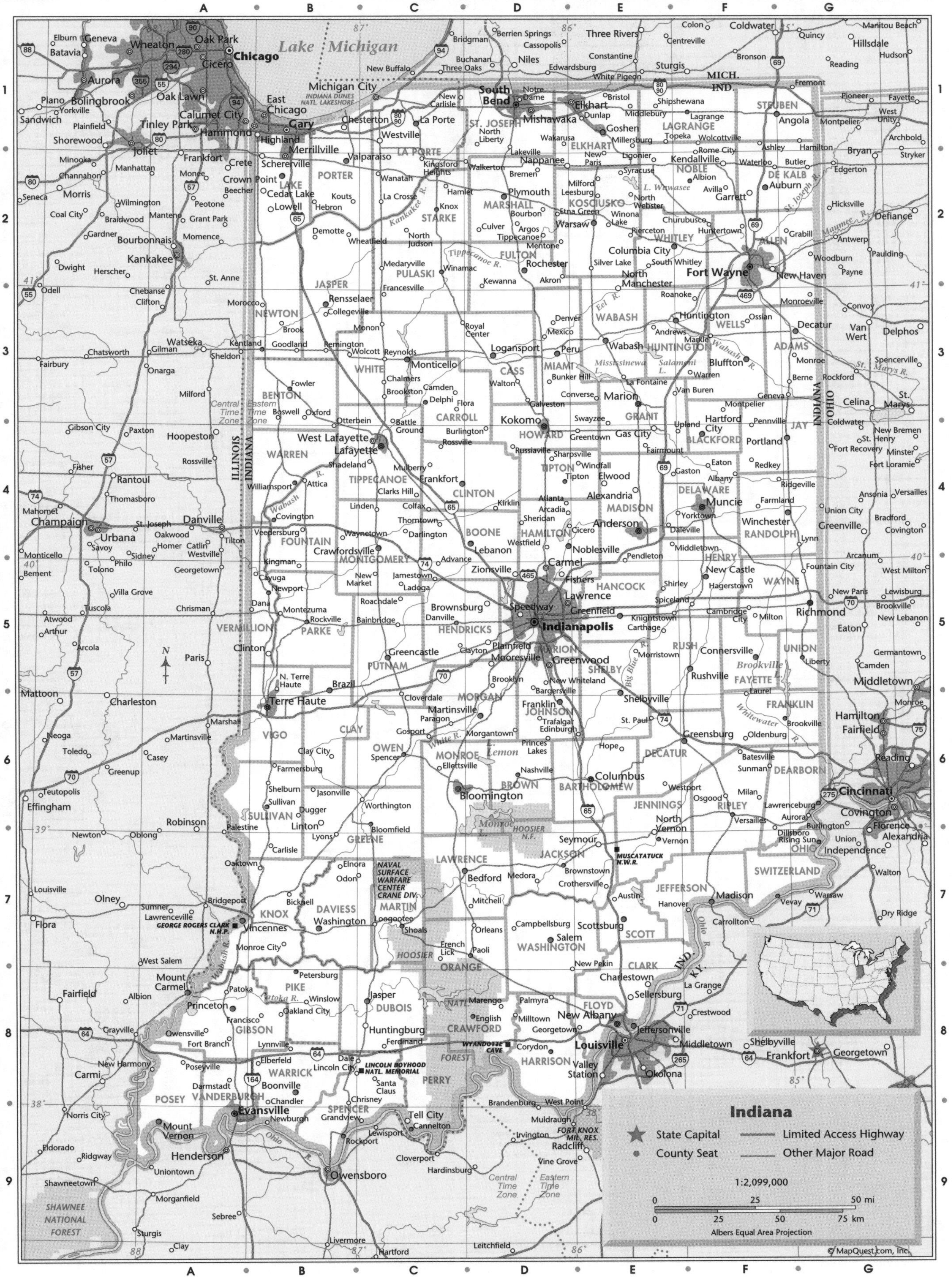

Lake Michigan

Indiana

★ State Capital   —— Limited Access Highway
● County Seat   —— Other Major Road

1:2,099,000

0   25   50 mi
0 25 50 75 km

Albers Equal Area Projection

© MapQuest.com, Inc.

Capital: Des Moines
Area: 56,300 sq. mi.
145,800 sq. km.
Pop. (2000): 2,926,324
Largest City: Des Moines
198,682

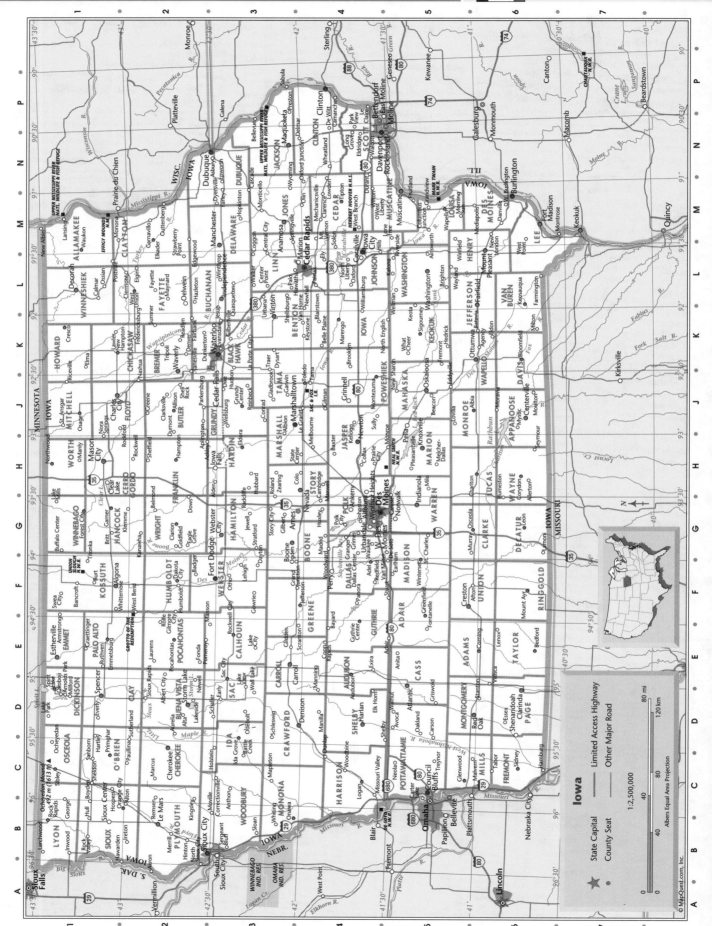

Iowa

Limited Access Highway
Other Major Road

1:2,500,000

State Capital
County Seat

© MapQuest.com, Inc.
Albers Equal Area Projection

80 mi
120 km

Capital: Topeka
Area: 82,300 sq. mi.
213,100 sq. km.
Pop. (2000): 2,688,418
Largest City: Wichita 344,284

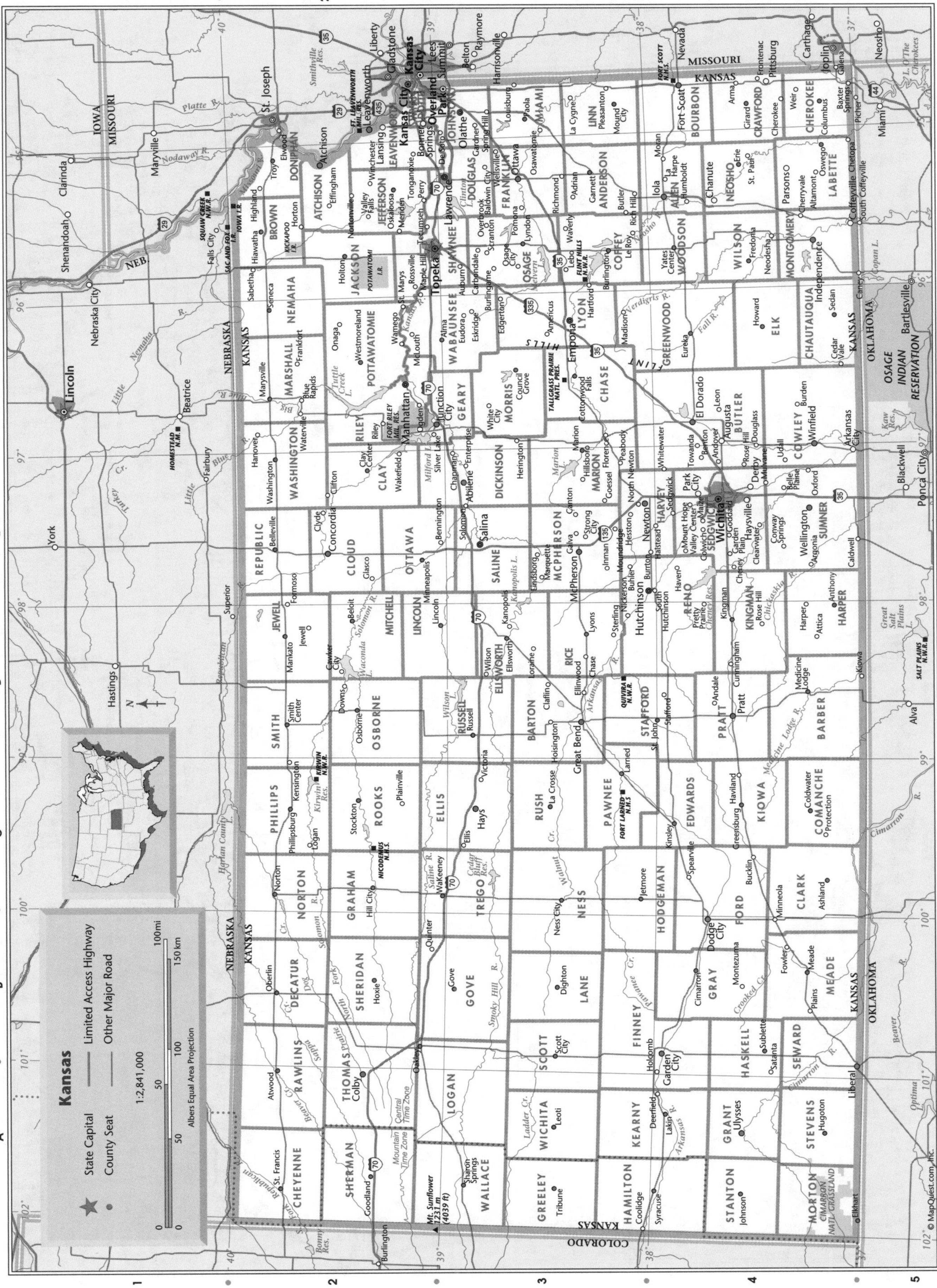

KANSAS

Kansas

1:2,841,000

Albers Equal Area Projection

Legend:
— Limited Access Highway
— Other Major Road
★ State Capital
• County Seat

0 50 100 mi
0 50 100 150 km

Central Time Zone
Mountain Time Zone

Surrounding states/labels: IOWA, MISSOURI, NEBRASKA, COLORADO, OKLAHOMA, KANSAS

Counties: CHEYENNE, RAWLINS, DECATUR, NORTON, PHILLIPS, SMITH, JEWELL, REPUBLIC, WASHINGTON, MARSHALL, NEMAHA, BROWN, DONIPHAN, ATCHISON, SHERMAN, THOMAS, SHERIDAN, GRAHAM, ROOKS, OSBORNE, MITCHELL, CLOUD, CLAY, RILEY, POTTAWATOMIE, JACKSON, WALLACE, LOGAN, GOVE, TREGO, ELLIS, RUSSELL, LINCOLN, OTTAWA, DICKINSON, GEARY, WABAUNSEE, SHAWNEE, JEFFERSON, LEAVENWORTH, WYANDOTTE, JOHNSON, DOUGLAS, GREELEY, WICHITA, SCOTT, LANE, NESS, RUSH, BARTON, ELLSWORTH, SALINE, MCPHERSON, MARION, CHASE, LYON, OSAGE, FRANKLIN, MIAMI, HAMILTON, KEARNY, FINNEY, HODGEMAN, PAWNEE, STAFFORD, RICE, RENO, HARVEY, BUTLER, GREENWOOD, WOODSON, ALLEN, BOURBON, LINN, STANTON, GRANT, HASKELL, GRAY, FORD, EDWARDS, KIOWA, PRATT, KINGMAN, SEDGWICK, ELK, WILSON, NEOSHO, CRAWFORD, MORTON, STEVENS, SEWARD, MEADE, CLARK, COMANCHE, BARBER, HARPER, SUMNER, COWLEY, CHAUTAUQUA, MONTGOMERY, LABETTE, CHEROKEE

Cities: Topeka, Wichita, Kansas City, Overland Park, Olathe, Lawrence, Lincoln, St. Joseph, Salina, Hutchinson, Dodge City, Garden City, Liberal, Hays, Manhattan, Junction City, Emporia, El Dorado, Newton, McPherson, Great Bend, Pittsburg, Coffeyville, Independence, Arkansas City, Winfield, Parsons, Chanute, Iola, Fort Scott, Ottawa, Atchison, Leavenworth, Goodland, Colby, Oakley, Concordia, Beloit, Belleville, Marysville, Seneca, Hiawatha, Holton

MapQuest.com, Inc.

Capital: Frankfort **Pop. (2000):** 4,041,769
Area: 40,400 sq. mi. **Largest City:** Lexington
104,700 sq. km. 260,512

Kentucky

Limited Access Highway
Other Major Road

★ State Capital
● County Seat

50 mi
0 25
0 25 50 75 km

1:2,252,000
Albers Equal Area Projection

©MapQuest.com, Inc.

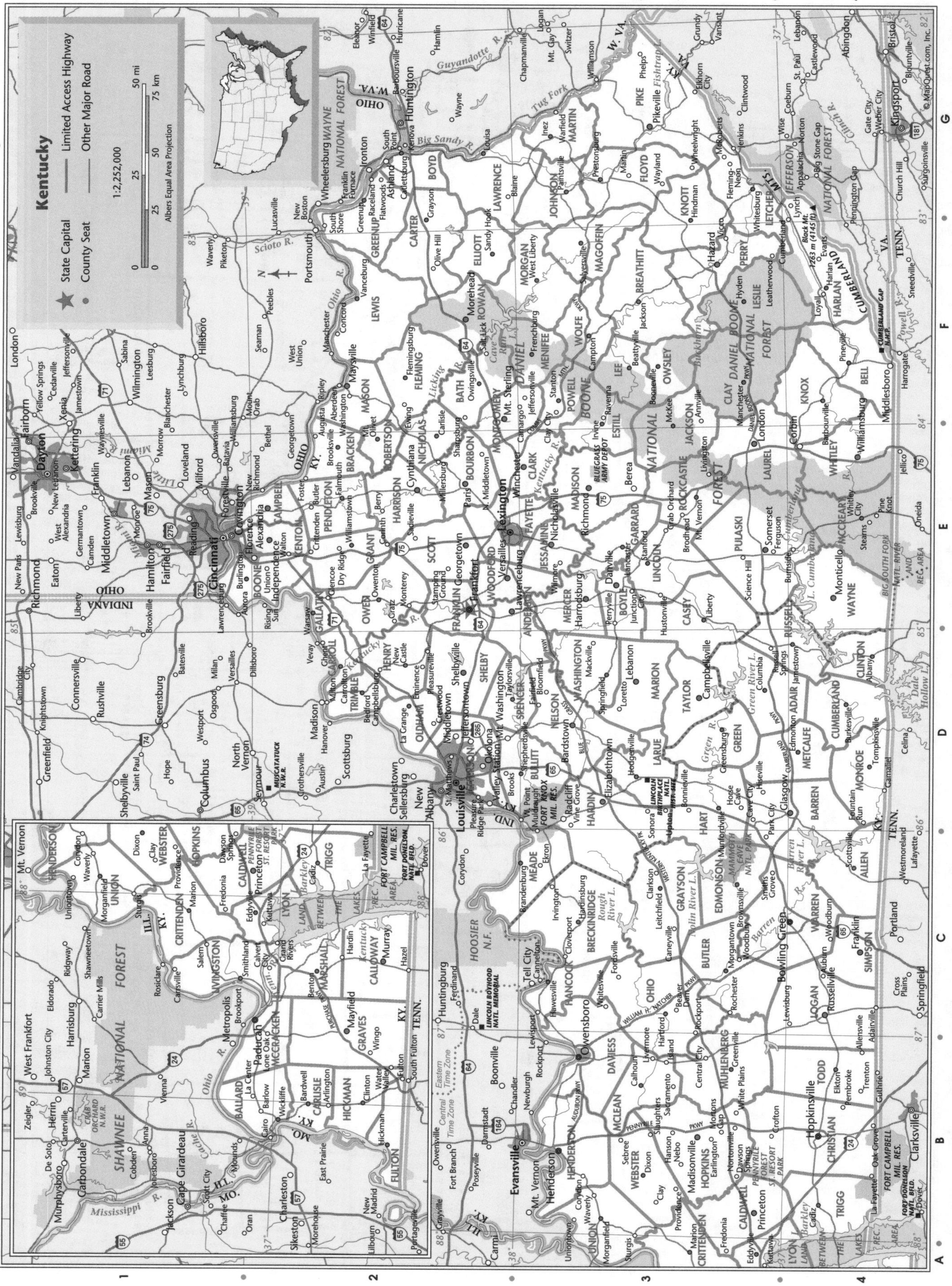

Capital:	Baton Rouge	Pop. (2000):	4,468,976
Area:	51,800 sq. mi.	Largest City:	New Orleans
	134,300 sq. km.		484,674

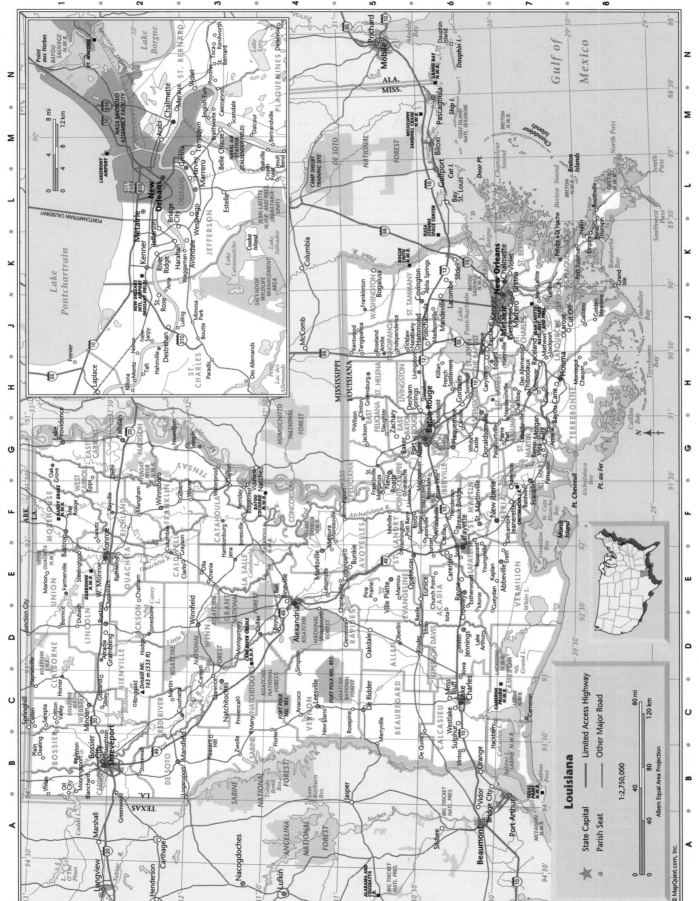

Louisiana

★ State Capital
● Parish Seat
— Limited Access Highway
— Other Major Road

1:2,750,000

Albers Equal Area Projection

© MapQuest.com, Inc.

Capital: Augusta
Area: 35,400 sq. mi.
91,700 sq. km.
Pop. (2000): 1,274,923
Largest City: Portland
64,249

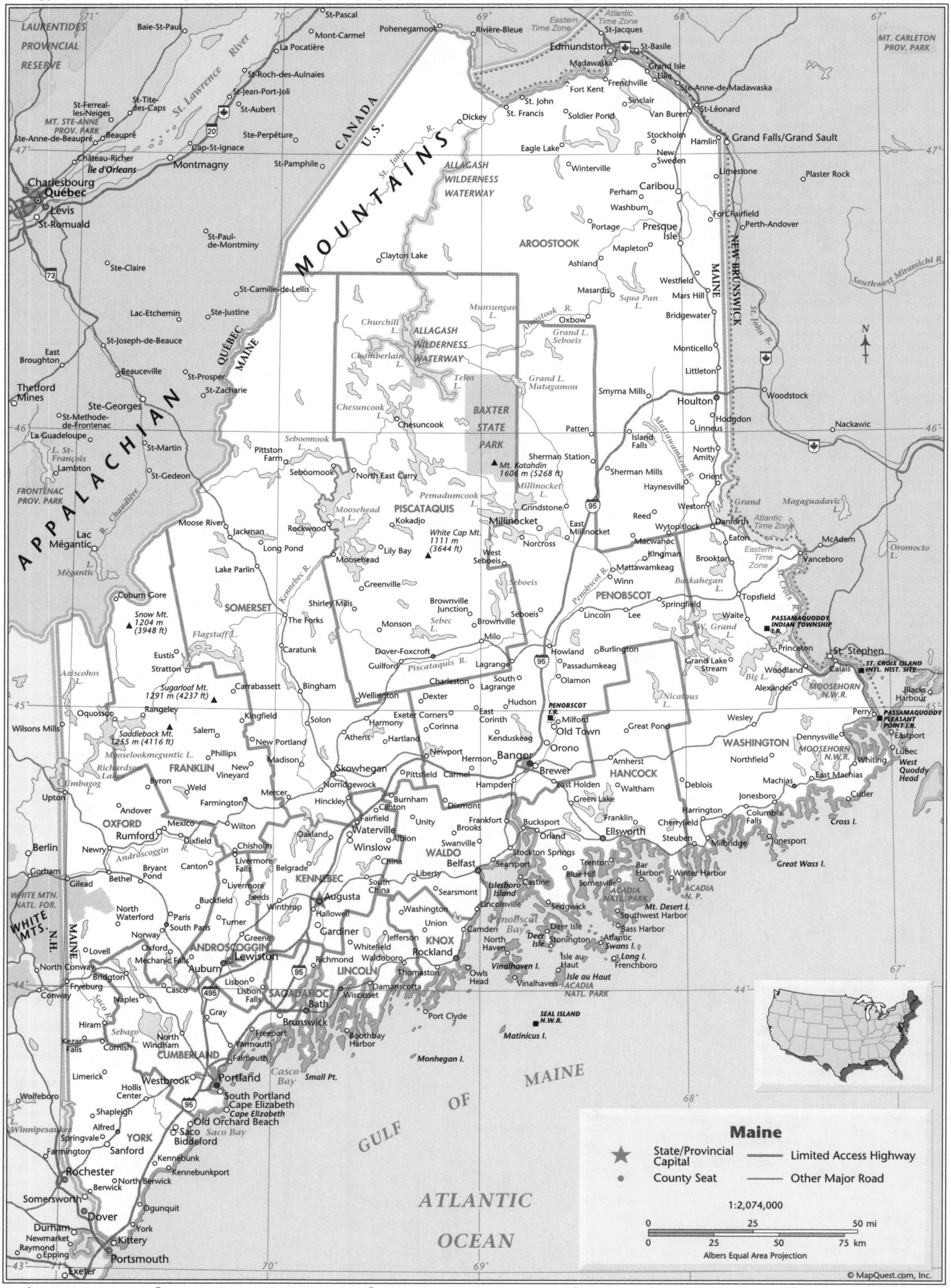

ATLANTIC OCEAN

GULF OF MAINE

CANADA
U.S.

QUÉBEC
MAINE

NEW BRUNSWICK

N.H.

APPALACHIAN MOUNTAINS

ALLAGASH WILDERNESS WATERWAY

AROOSTOOK

PISCATAQUIS

PENOBSCOT

SOMERSET

FRANKLIN

OXFORD

KENNEBEC

WALDO

KNOX

LINCOLN

HANCOCK

WASHINGTON

ANDROSCOGGIN

SAGADAHOC

CUMBERLAND

YORK

BAXTER STATE PARK

ACADIA NATL. PARK

Mt. Katahdin 1606 m (5268 ft)
White Cap Mt. 1111 m (3644 ft)
Snow Mt. 1204 m (3948 ft)
Sugarloaf Mt. 1291 m (4237 ft)
Saddleback Mt. 1255 m (4116 ft)
Mt. Carleton

Maine

★ State/Provincial Capital
● County Seat
— Limited Access Highway
— Other Major Road

1:2,074,000

0   25   50 mi
0   25   50   75 km

Albers Equal Area Projection

© MapQuest.com, Inc.

Capital: Annapolis
Area: 12,400 sq. mi.
32,100 sq. km.
Pop. (2000): 5,296,486
Largest City: Baltimore
651,154

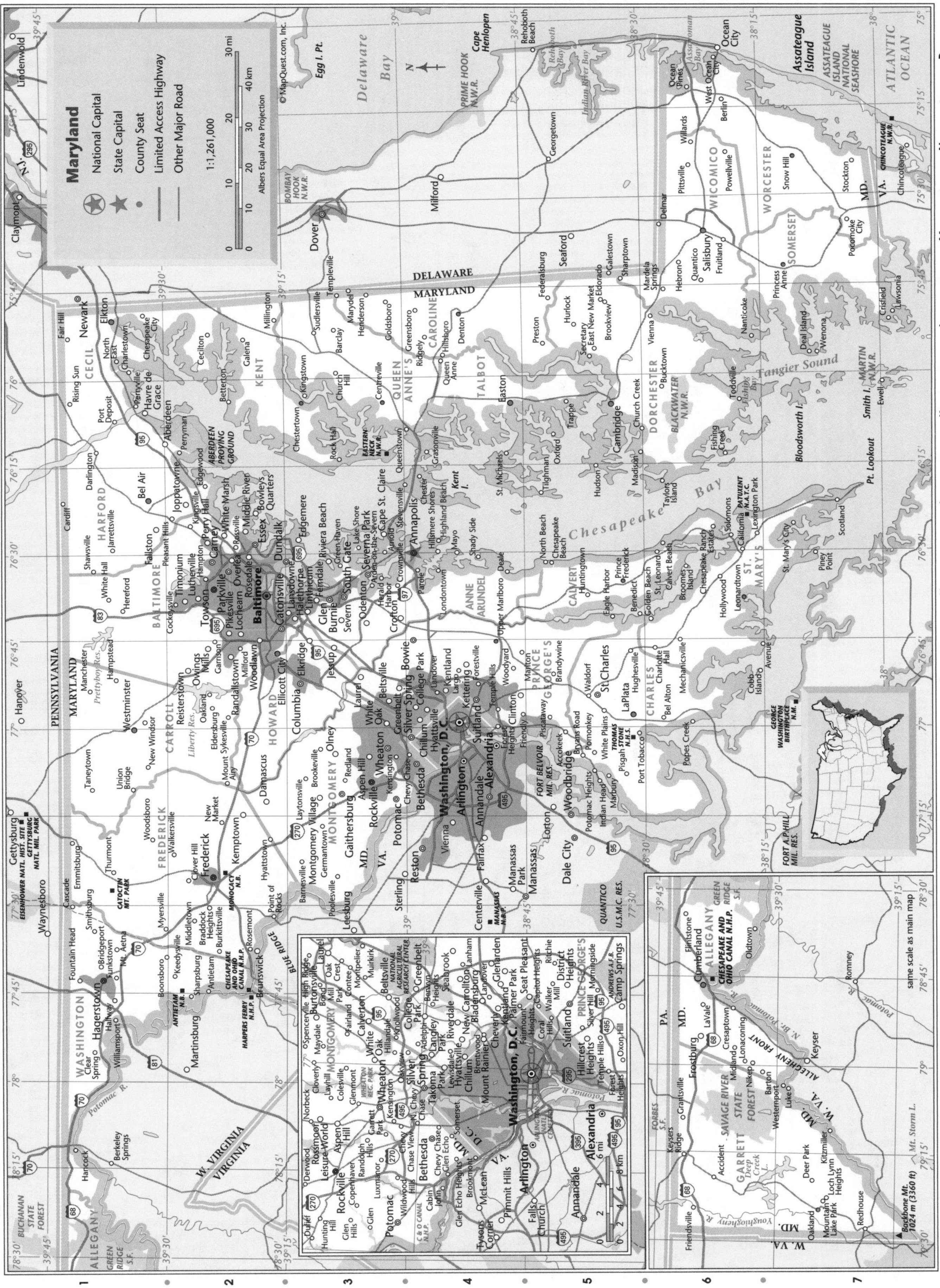

Maryland

- ⊛ National Capital
- ★ State Capital
- • County Seat
- Limited Access Highway
- Other Major Road

1:1,261,000

Albers Equal Area Projection

© MapQuest.com, Inc.

same scale as main map

Capital: Boston
Area: 10,600 sq. mi.
27,300 sq. km.
Pop. (2000): 6,349,097
Largest City: Boston
589,141

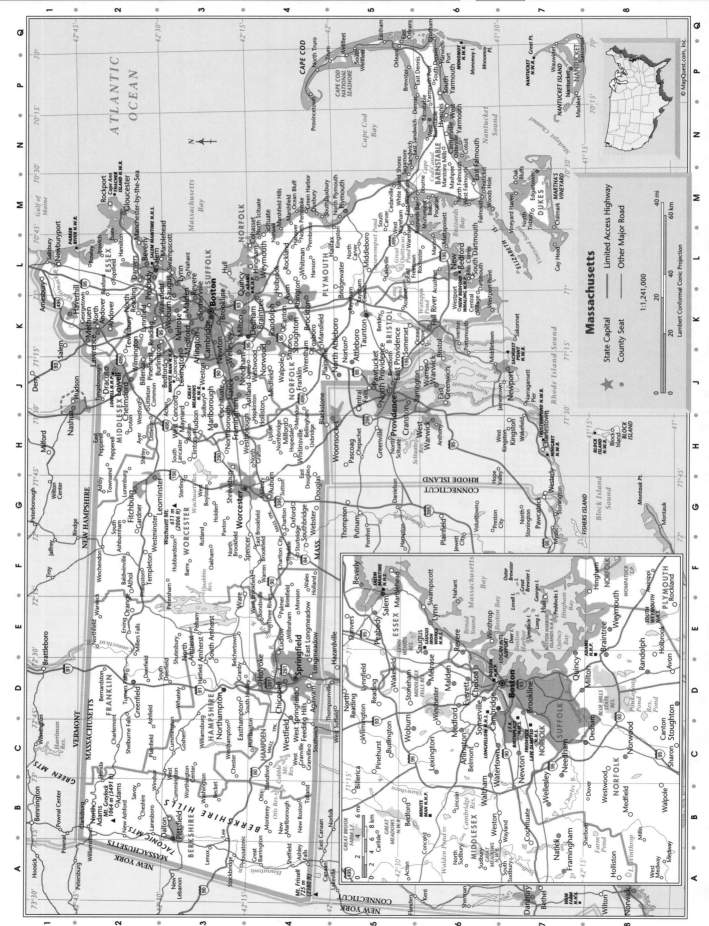

Massachusetts

★ State Capital
● County Seat

— Limited Access Highway
— Other Major Road

1:1,241,000

Lambert Conformal Conic Projection

© MapQuest.com, Inc.

ATLANTIC OCEAN

Gulf of Maine

Massachusetts Bay

Cape Cod Bay

CAPE COD

CAPE COD NATIONAL SEASHORE

Nantucket Sound

MARTHA'S VINEYARD

NANTUCKET

NEW HAMPSHIRE

VERMONT

NEW YORK

CONNECTICUT

RHODE ISLAND

Rhode Island Sound

Block Island Sound

BERKSHIRE HILLS

TACONIC MTS.

GREEN MTS.

Boston

Worcester

Springfield

Providence

Capital: Lansing
Area: 96,700 sq. mi.
250,500 sq. km.
Pop. (2000): 9,938,444
Largest City: Detroit 951,270

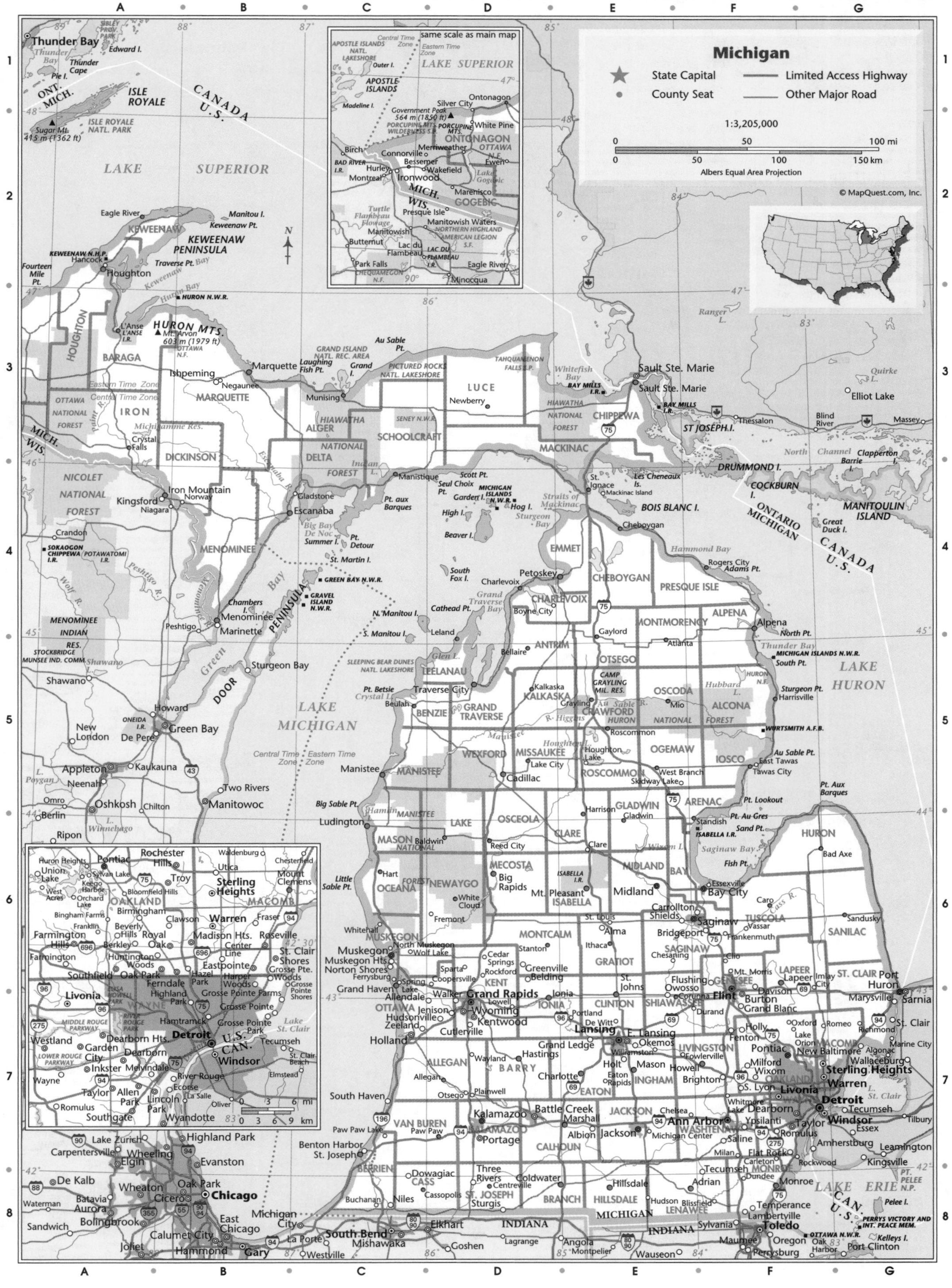

Michigan

★ State Capital
• County Seat
— Limited Access Highway
— Other Major Road

1:3,205,000

0   50   100 mi
0   50   100   150 km

Albers Equal Area Projection

© MapQuest.com, Inc.

Capital: St. Paul
Area: 86,900 sq. mi.
225,200 sq. km.
Pop. (2000): 4,919,479
Largest City: Minneapolis
382,618

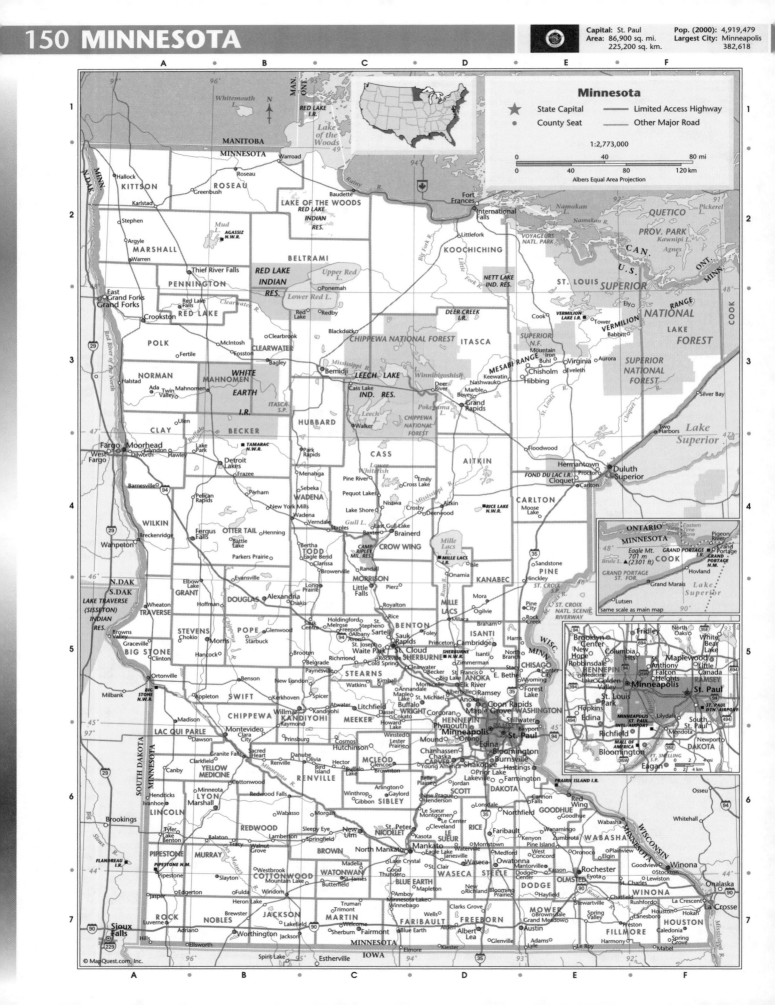

Minnesota

★ State Capital — Limited Access Highway
• County Seat — Other Major Road

1:2,773,000

0   40   80 mi
0   40   80   120 km

Albers Equal Area Projection

© MapQuest.com, Inc.

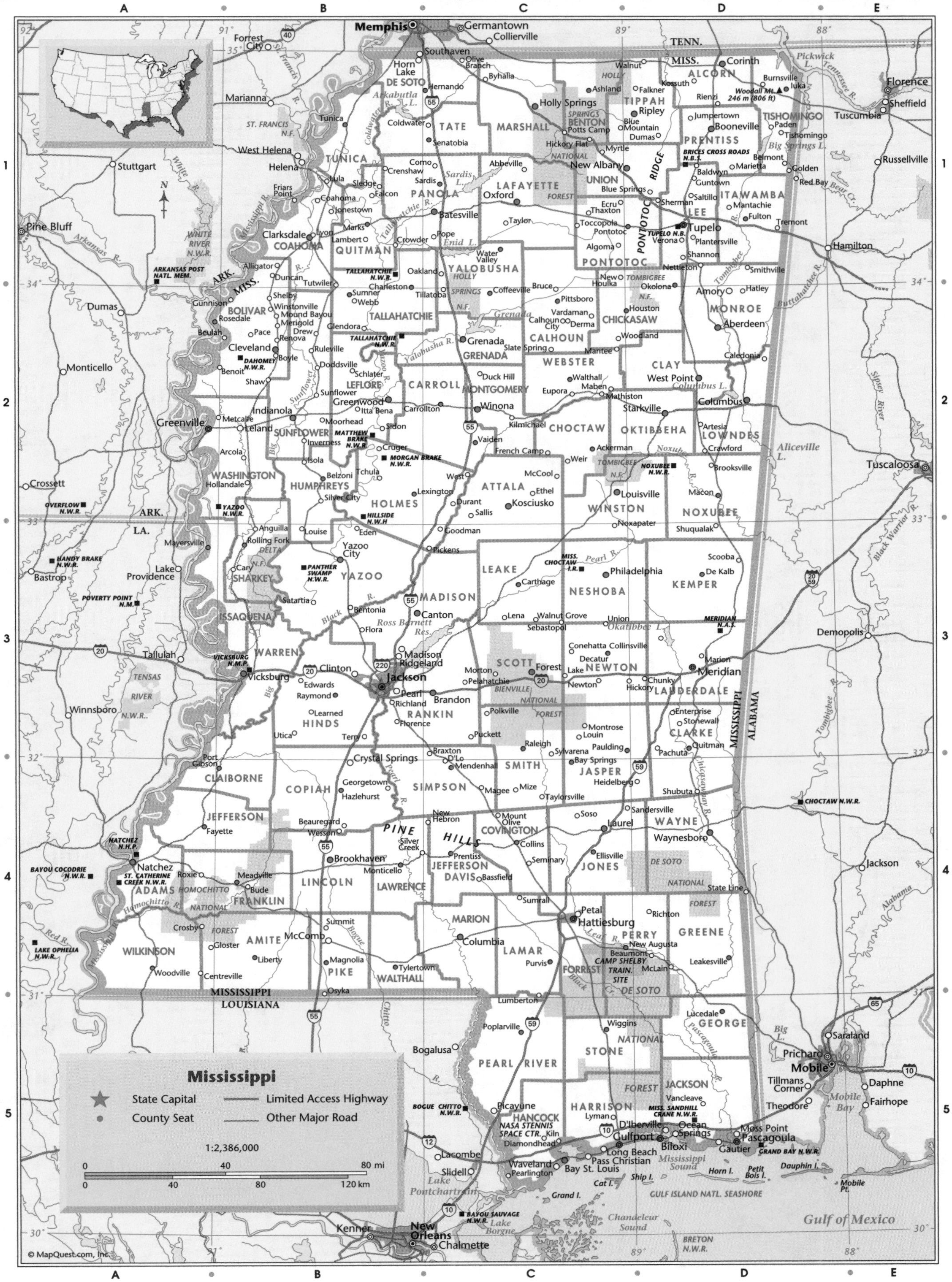

Capital: Jackson
Area: 48,400 sq. mi. 125,400 sq. km.
Pop. (2000): 2,844,658
Largest City: Jackson 184,256

Legend

Mississippi

★ State Capital
• County Seat
— Limited Access Highway
— Other Major Road

1:2,386,000

0   40   80 mi
0   40   80   120 km

© MapQuest.com, Inc.

County names (selected): DE SOTO, TUNICA, TATE, MARSHALL, BENTON, TIPPAH, ALCORN, TISHOMINGO, PANOLA, LAFAYETTE, UNION, PONTOTOC, PRENTISS, LEE, ITAWAMBA, COAHOMA, QUITMAN, YALOBUSHA, CALHOUN, CHICKASAW, MONROE, BOLIVAR, TALLAHATCHIE, GRENADA, WEBSTER, CLAY, LEFLORE, CARROLL, MONTGOMERY, CHOCTAW, OKTIBBEHA, LOWNDES, SUNFLOWER, HUMPHREYS, HOLMES, ATTALA, WINSTON, NOXUBEE, WASHINGTON, SHARKEY, ISSAQUENA, YAZOO, MADISON, LEAKE, NESHOBA, KEMPER, WARREN, HINDS, RANKIN, SCOTT, NEWTON, LAUDERDALE, CLAIBORNE, COPIAH, SIMPSON, SMITH, JASPER, CLARKE, JEFFERSON, ADAMS, FRANKLIN, LINCOLN, LAWRENCE, COVINGTON, JONES, WAYNE, FRANKLIN, WILKINSON, AMITE, PIKE, WALTHALL, MARION, LAMAR, FORREST, PERRY, GREENE, PEARL RIVER, STONE, GEORGE, HANCOCK, HARRISON, JACKSON, PINE HILLS, JEFFERSON DAVIS

Cities/towns (selected): Memphis, Germantown, Collierville, Southaven, Horn Lake, Olive Branch, Byhalia, Corinth, Burnsville, Iuka, Florence, Sheffield, Tuscumbia, Hernando, Holly Springs, Ashland, Walnut, Kossuth, Rienzi, Coldwater, Senatobia, Abbeville, Oxford, New Albany, Ripley, Booneville, Guntown, Russellville, Batesville, Taylor, Pontotoc, Tupelo, Fulton, Tremont, Hamilton, Clarksdale, Marks, Water Valley, Houston, Amory, Aberdeen, Cleveland, Greenwood, Indianola, Grenada, Starkville, Columbus, Tuscaloosa, Greenville, Yazoo City, Canton, Philadelphia, Meridian, Demopolis, Vicksburg, Jackson, Brandon, Forest, Newton, Natchez, Brookhaven, Hattiesburg, Laurel, Waynesboro, McComb, Columbia, Picayune, Gulfport, Biloxi, Pascagoula, Mobile, New Orleans

Bordering states/features: TENN., MISS., ARK., LA., ALABAMA, LOUISIANA, Gulf of Mexico, Mississippi Sound, Mobile Bay, Lake Pontchartrain

Capital: Jefferson City
Area: 69,700 sq. mi.
180,500 sq. km.
Pop. (2000): 5,595,211
Largest City: Kansas City
441,545

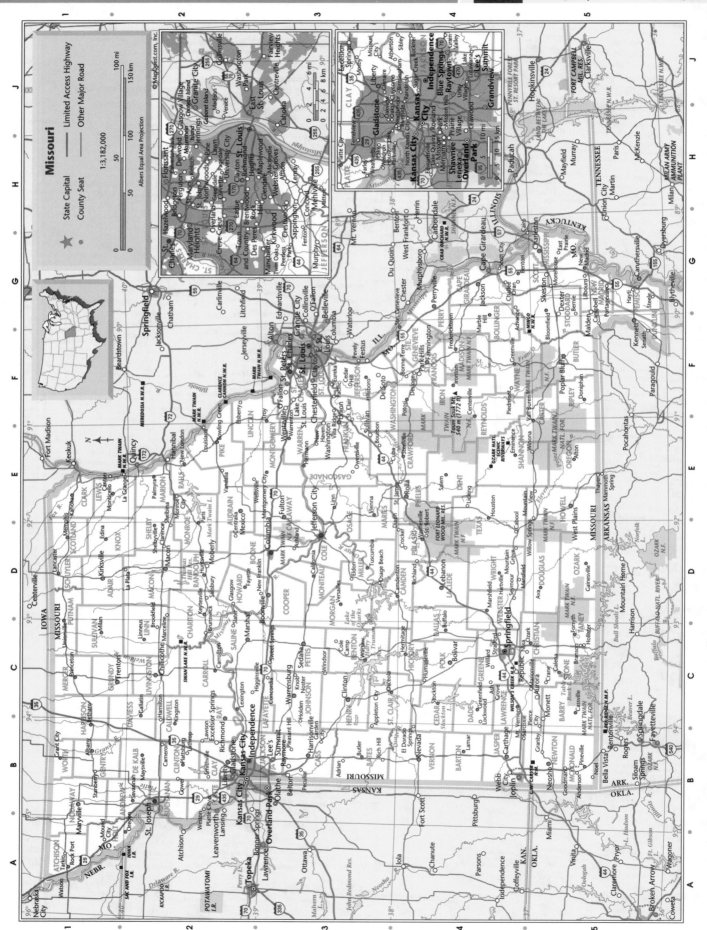

Capital: Helena	Pop. (2000): 902,195
Area: 147,000 sq. mi.	Largest City: Billings
380,800 sq. km.	89,847

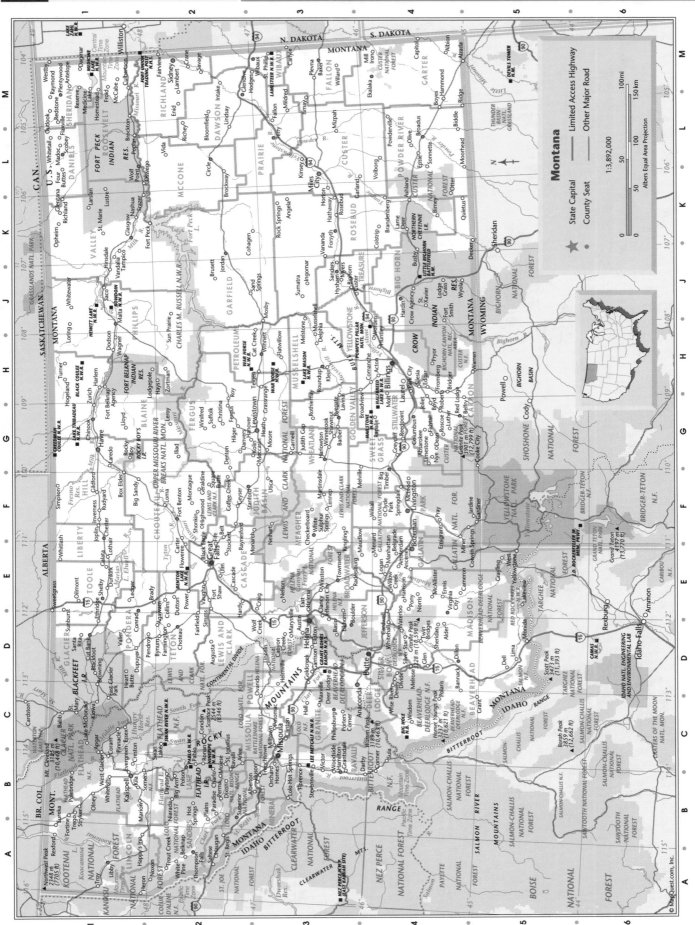

Montana

1:3,892,000

★ State Capital
• County Seat

— Limited Access Highway
— Other Major Road

Albers Equal Area Projection

Capital: Lincoln
Area: 77,400 sq. mi.
200,300 sq. km.
Pop. (2000): 1,711,263
Largest City: Omaha
390,007

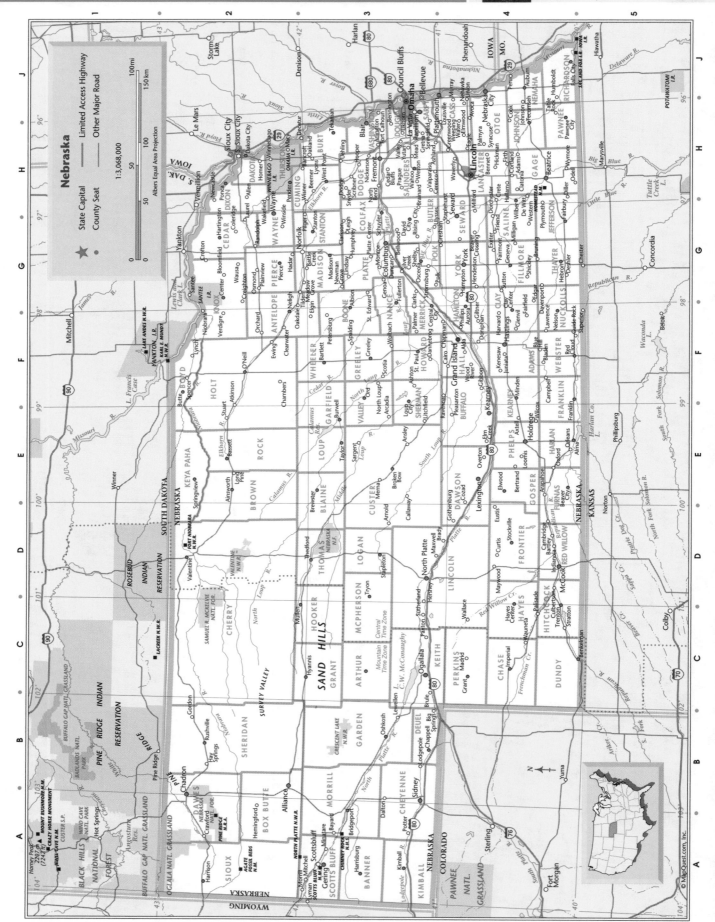

Nebraska

Limited Access Highway
Other Major Road

★ State Capital
● County Seat

1:3,068,000

Albers Equal Area Projection

Capital: Carson City
Area: 110,600 sq. mi.
286,400 sq. km.
Pop. (2000): 1,998,257
Largest City: Las Vegas
478,434

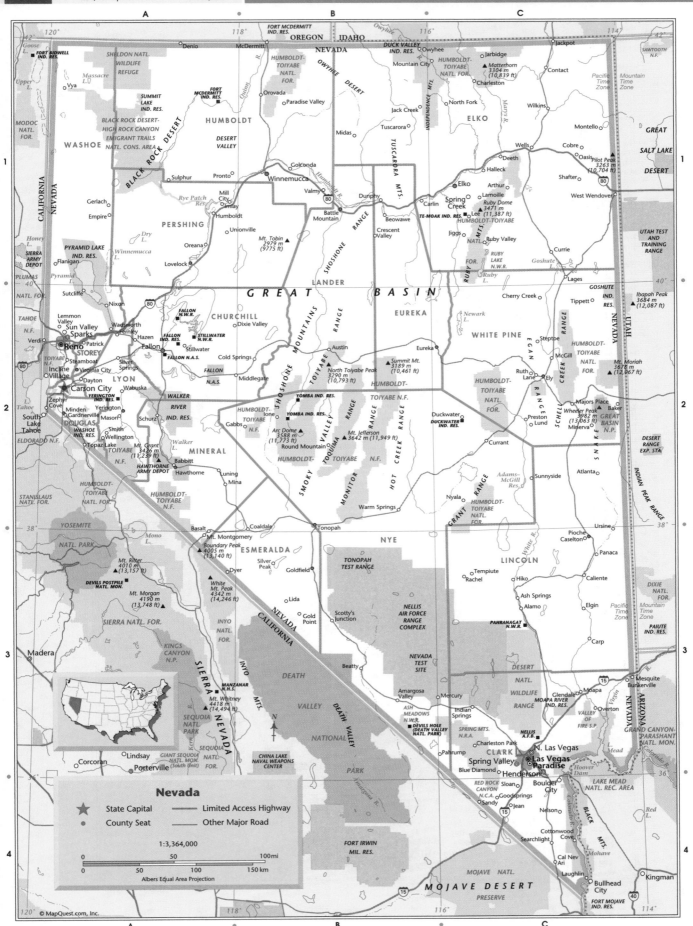

Nevada

★ State Capital
• County Seat
— Limited Access Highway
— Other Major Road

1:3,364,000

0   50   100mi
0   50   100   150km

Albers Equal Area Projection

© MapQuest.com, Inc.

Capital: Concord
Area: 9,400 sq. mi.
24,200 sq. km.
Pop. (2000): 1,235,786
Largest City: Manchester
107,006

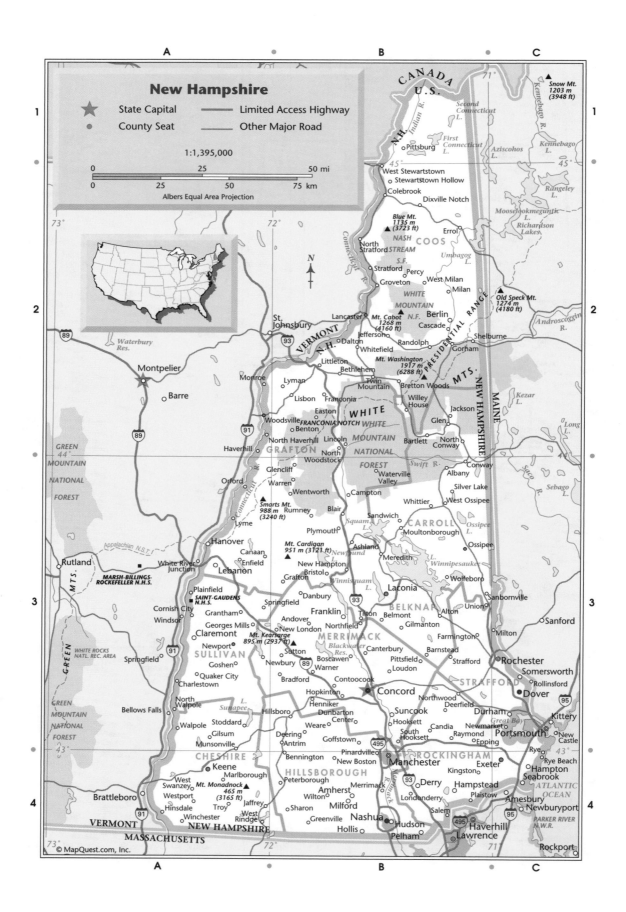

New Hampshire

★ State Capital
● County Seat
— Limited Access Highway
— Other Major Road

1:1,395,000

| 0 | 25 | 50 mi |
| 0 | 25 | 50 | 75 km |

Albers Equal Area Projection

© MapQuest.com, Inc.

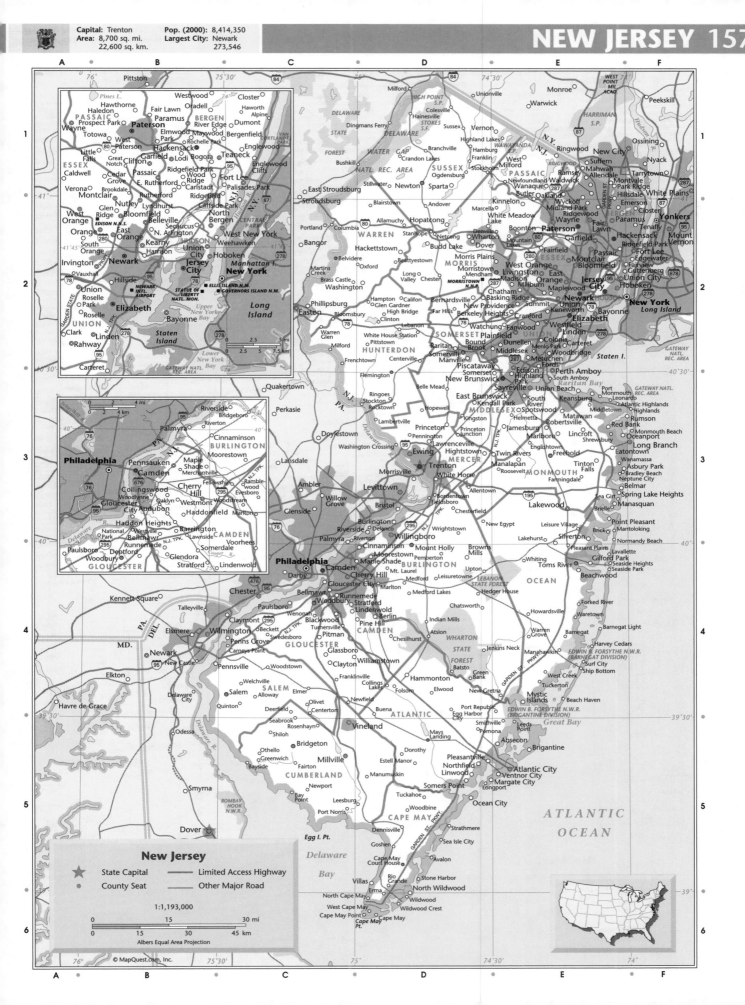

Capital: Trenton
Area: 8,700 sq. mi.
22,600 sq. km.
Pop. (2000): 8,414,350
Largest City: Newark
273,546

New Jersey

★ State Capital
● County Seat
— Limited Access Highway
— Other Major Road

1:1,193,000

0 15 30 mi
0 15 30 45 km

Albers Equal Area Projection

© MapQuest.com, Inc.

Capital: Santa Fe
Area: 121,600 sq. mi. / 314,900 sq. km.
Pop. (2000): 1,819,046
Largest City: Albuquerque 448,607

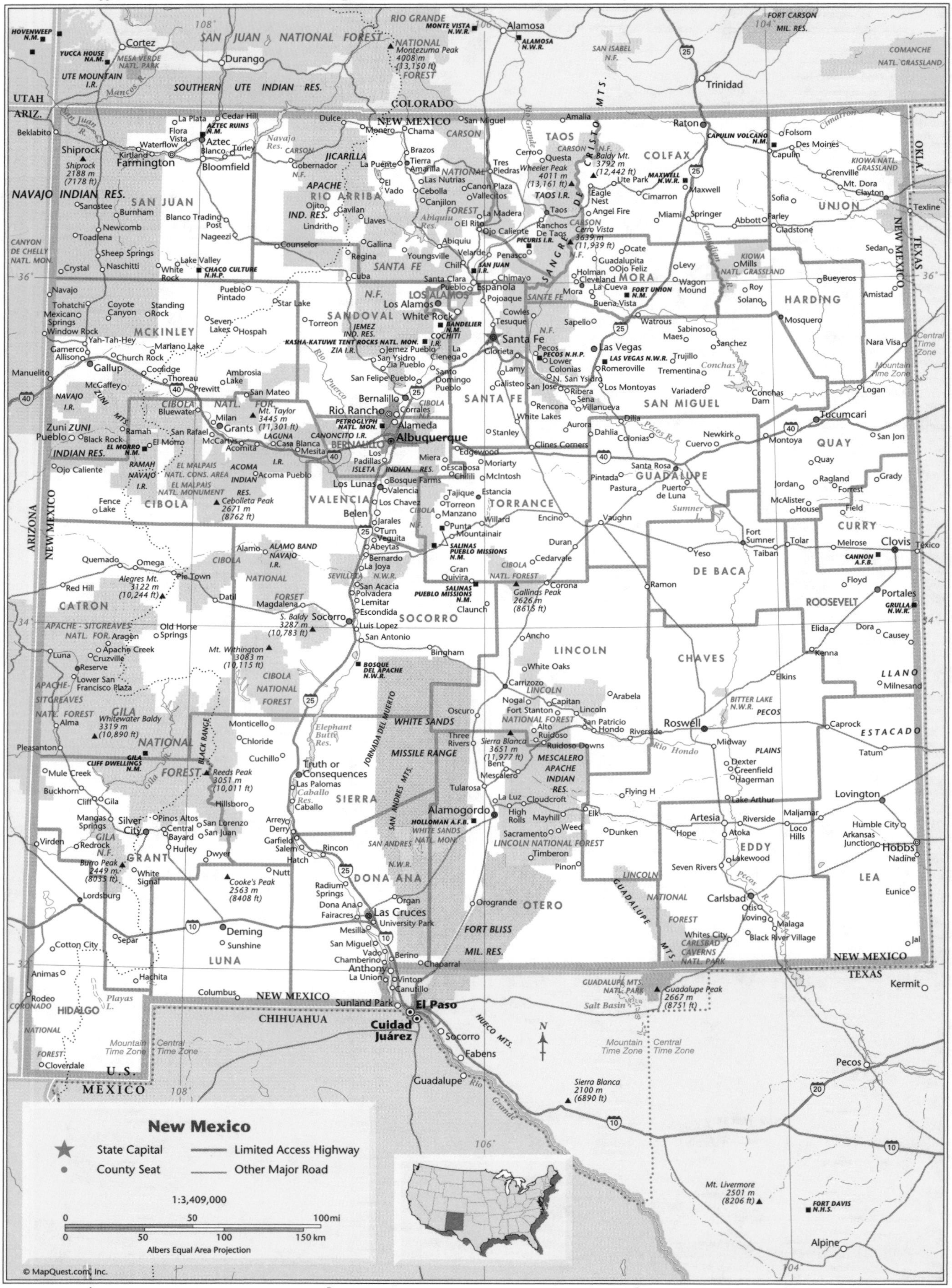

New Mexico

★ State Capital
• County Seat
— Limited Access Highway
— Other Major Road

1:3,409,000

0   50   100mi
0   50   100   150 km

Albers Equal Area Projection

© MapQuest.com Inc.

UTAH · ARIZ. · COLORADO · NEW MEXICO · TEXAS · OKLA. · U.S. MEXICO · CHIHUAHUA

Counties: SAN JUAN, RIO ARRIBA, TAOS, COLFAX, UNION, McKINLEY, SANDOVAL, LOS ALAMOS, SANTA FE, SAN MIGUEL, MORA, HARDING, QUAY, GUADALUPE, CIBOLA, BERNALILLO, VALENCIA, TORRANCE, DE BACA, CURRY, CATRON, SOCORRO, LINCOLN, ROOSEVELT, CHAVES, SIERRA, GRANT, LUNA, DONA ANA, OTERO, EDDY, LEA, HIDALGO

Major cities/towns: Shiprock, Farmington, Aztec, Bloomfield, Cortez, Durango, Gallup, Grants, Rio Rancho, Albuquerque, Bernalillo, Los Alamos, Santa Fe, Las Vegas, Taos, Raton, Tucumcari, Clovis, Portales, Socorro, Truth or Consequences, Silver City, Lordsburg, Deming, Las Cruces, Alamogordo, Roswell, Artesia, Carlsbad, Hobbs, Lovington, El Paso, Ciudad Juárez, Roswell

Peaks: Wheeler Peak 4011 m (13,161 ft), Baldy Mt. 3792 m (12,442 ft), Cerro Vista 3639 m (11,939 ft), Mt. Taylor 3445 m (11,301 ft), Truchas Peak, S. Baldy 3287 m (10,783 ft), Whitewater Baldy 3319 m (10,890 ft), Alegres Mt. 3122 m (10,244 ft), Mt. Withington 3083 m (10,115 ft), Reeds Peak 3051 m (10,011 ft), Cebolleta Peak 2671 m (8762 ft), Gallinas Peak 2626 m (8615 ft), Guadalupe Peak 2667 m (8751 ft), Cooke's Peak 2563 m (8408 ft), Burro Peak 2449 m (8033 ft), Sierra Blanca 3651 m (11,977 ft), Shiprock 2188 m (7178 ft)

Montezuma Peak 4008 m (13,150 ft), Sierra Blanca 2100 m (6890 ft), Mt. Livermore 2501 m (8206 ft)

National Forests/Parks: SAN JUAN NATIONAL FOREST, MESA VERDE NATL. PARK, CARSON NATIONAL FOREST, SANTA FE N.F., CIBOLA NATIONAL FOREST, GILA NATIONAL FOREST, LINCOLN NATIONAL FOREST, APACHE-SITGREAVES NATL. FOR., CORONADO NATIONAL FOREST, CHACO CULTURE N.H.P., BANDELIER N.M., WHITE SANDS NATL. MON., CARLSBAD CAVERNS NATL. PARK, PETROGLYPH NATL. MON., SALINAS PUEBLO MISSIONS N.M., AZTEC RUINS N.M., CAPULIN VOLCANO N.M., EL MORRO N.M., EL MALPAIS NATL. MONUMENT, BOSQUE DEL APACHE N.W.R., BITTER LAKE N.W.R., GUADALUPE MTS. NATL. PARK, FORT DAVIS N.H.S.

Indian Reservations: NAVAJO INDIAN RES., ZUNI INDIAN RES., JICARILLA APACHE IND. RES., MESCALERO APACHE INDIAN RES., UTE MOUNTAIN I.R., SOUTHERN UTE INDIAN RES., ACOMA INDIAN RES., LAGUNA, ISLETA INDIAN RES., SANTA CLARA, TAOS I.R., SAN JUAN

Military: FORT BLISS MIL. RES., WHITE SANDS MISSILE RANGE, HOLLOMAN A.F.B., CANNON A.F.B., KIRTLAND, FORT CARSON MIL. RES.

Central Time Zone / Mountain Time Zone

Capital: Albany
Area: 54,700 sq. mi.
141,100 sq. km.

Pop. (2000): 18,976,457
Largest City: New York
8,008,278

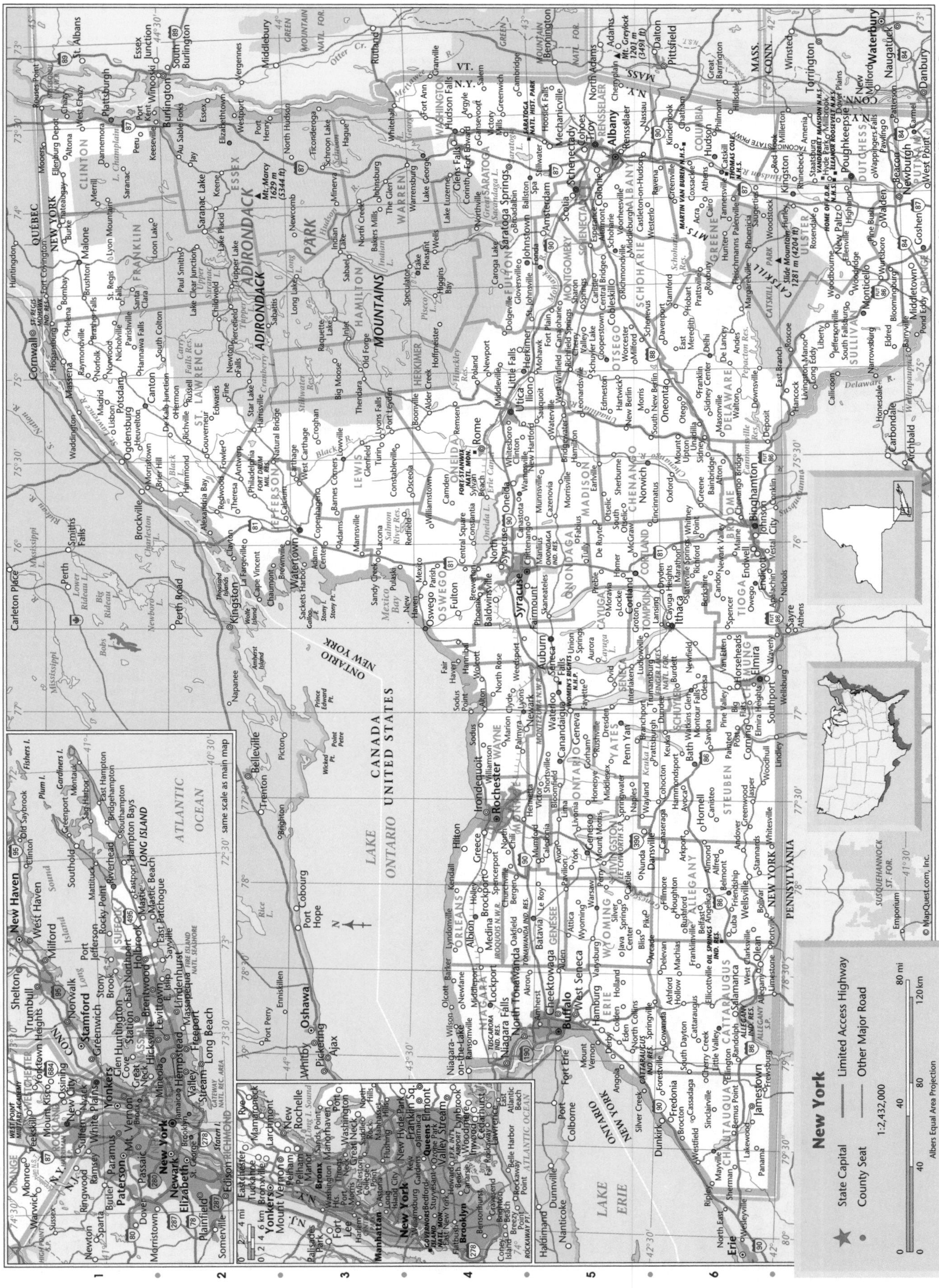
New York
State Capital
County Seat
Limited Access Highway
Other Major Road
1:2,432,000
Albers Equal Area Projection
same scale as main map
LAKE ONTARIO
LAKE ERIE
ATLANTIC OCEAN
ADIRONDACK MOUNTAINS
CANADA
UNITED STATES
PENNSYLVANIA
© MapQuest.com, Inc.

Capital: Raleigh
Area: 53,800 sq. mi.
139,400 sq. km.
Pop. (2000): 8,049,313
Largest City: Charlotte
540,828

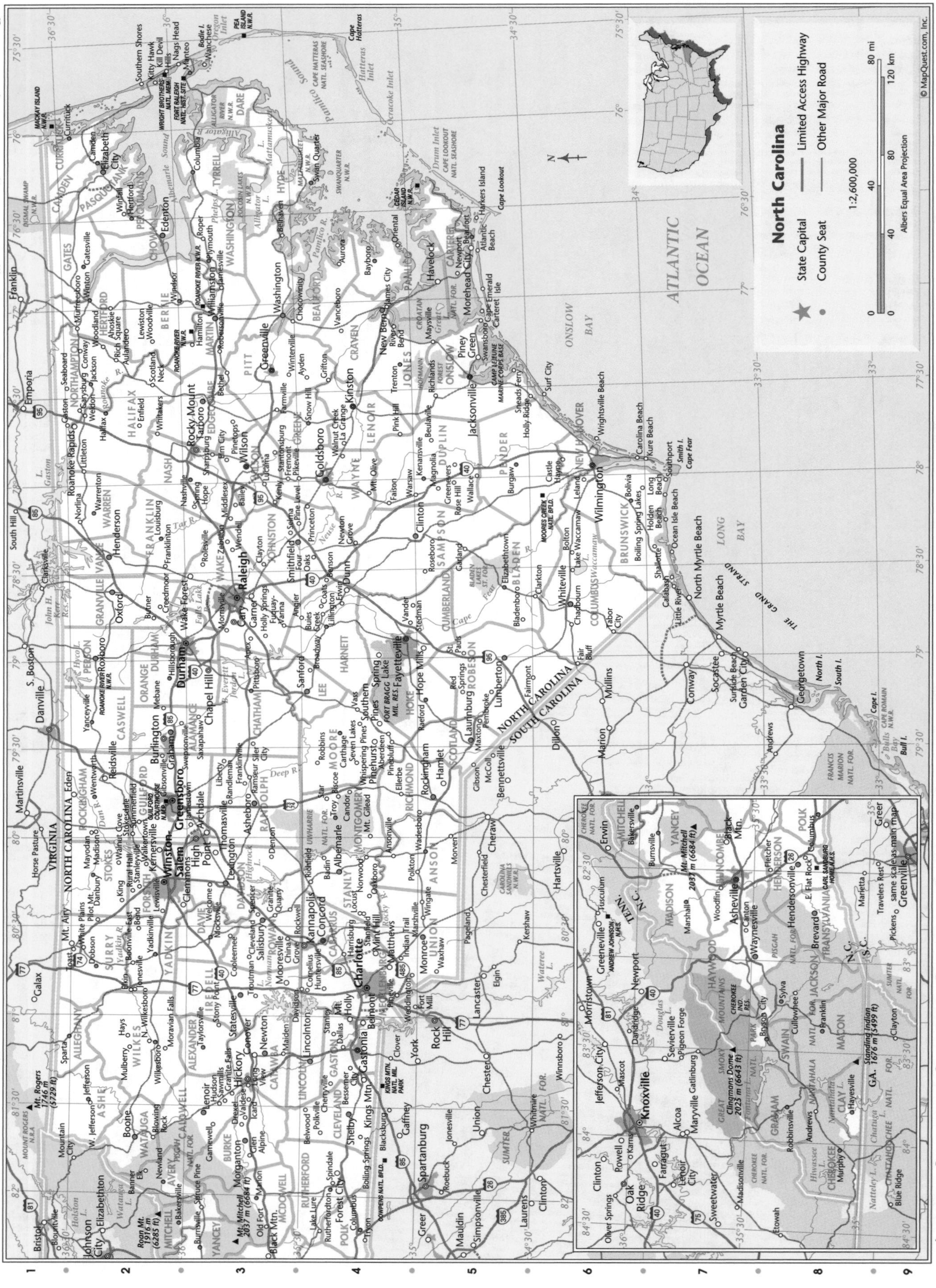

North Carolina

★ State Capital
• County Seat
— Limited Access Highway
— Other Major Road

1:2,600,000

Albers Equal Area Projection

ATLANTIC OCEAN

VIRGINIA

NORTH CAROLINA

SOUTH CAROLINA

TENN.

GA.

Raleigh

Charlotte

Greensboro

Winston-Salem

Durham

Fayetteville

Wilmington

Asheville

Knoxville

© MapQuest.com, Inc.

Capital: Bismarck
Area: 70,700 sq. mi.
       183,100 sq. km.
Pop. (2000): 642,200
Largest City: Fargo
                    90,599

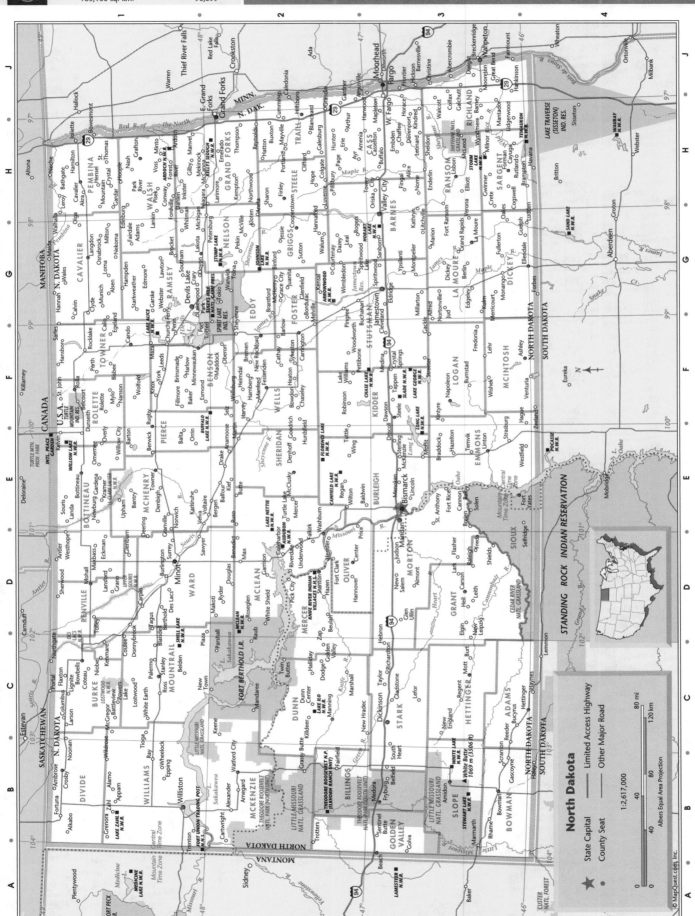

North Dakota

State Capital
County Seat

Limited Access Highway
Other Major Road

1:2,617,000

STANDING ROCK INDIAN RESERVATION

© MapQuest.com, Inc.

Capital: Columbus
Area: 44,800 sq. mi.
116,100 sq. km.
Pop. (2000): 11,353,140
Largest City: Columbus
711,470

Capital: Oklahoma City   Pop. (2000): 3,450,654
Area: 69,900 sq. mi.   Largest City: Oklahoma City
181,000 sq. km.   506,132

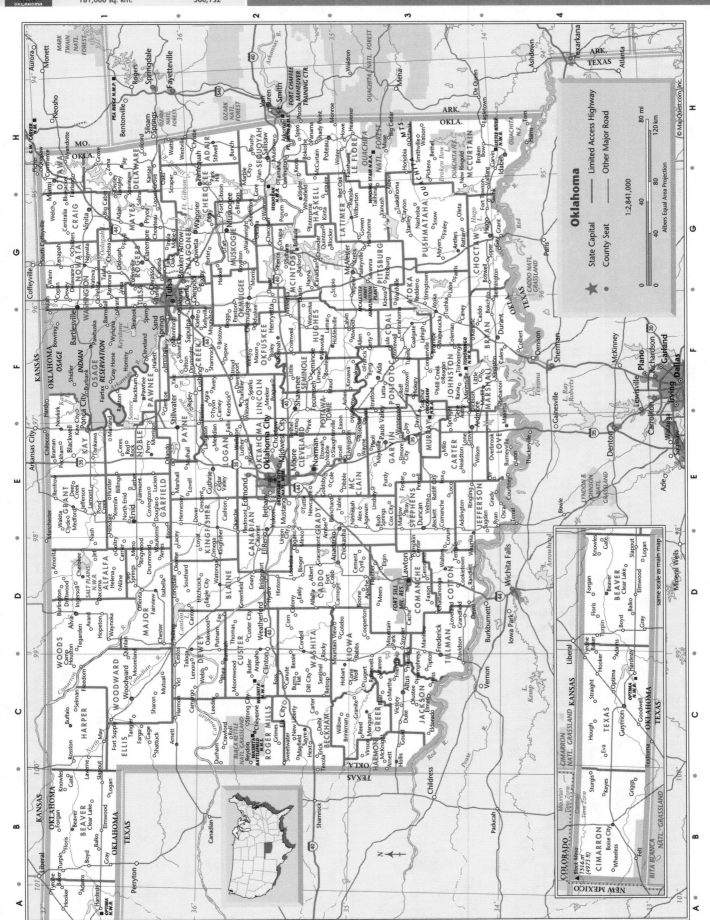

Capital: Salem	**Pop. (2000):** 3,421,399
Area: 98,400 sq. mi.	**Largest City:** Portland
254,800 sq. km.	529,121

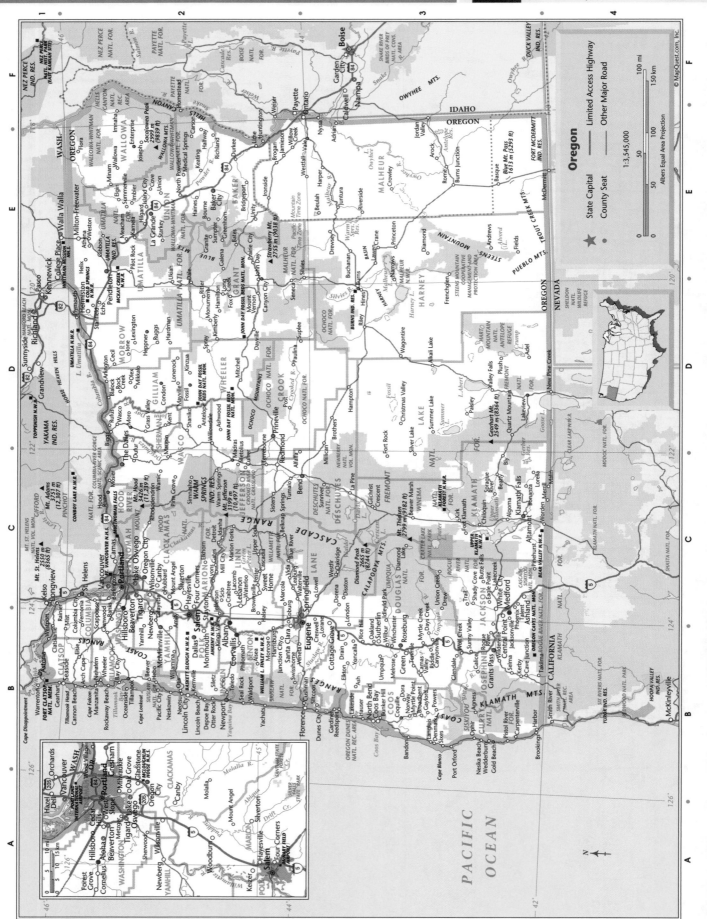

Oregon

1:3,545,000

State Capital ★
County Seat ●

Limited Access Highway
Other Major Road

Albers Equal Area Projection

© MapQuest.com, Inc.

PACIFIC OCEAN

Capital: Harrisburg **Pop. (2000):** 12,281,054
Area: 45,300 sq. mi. **Largest City:** Philadelphia
117,300 sq. km. 1,517,550

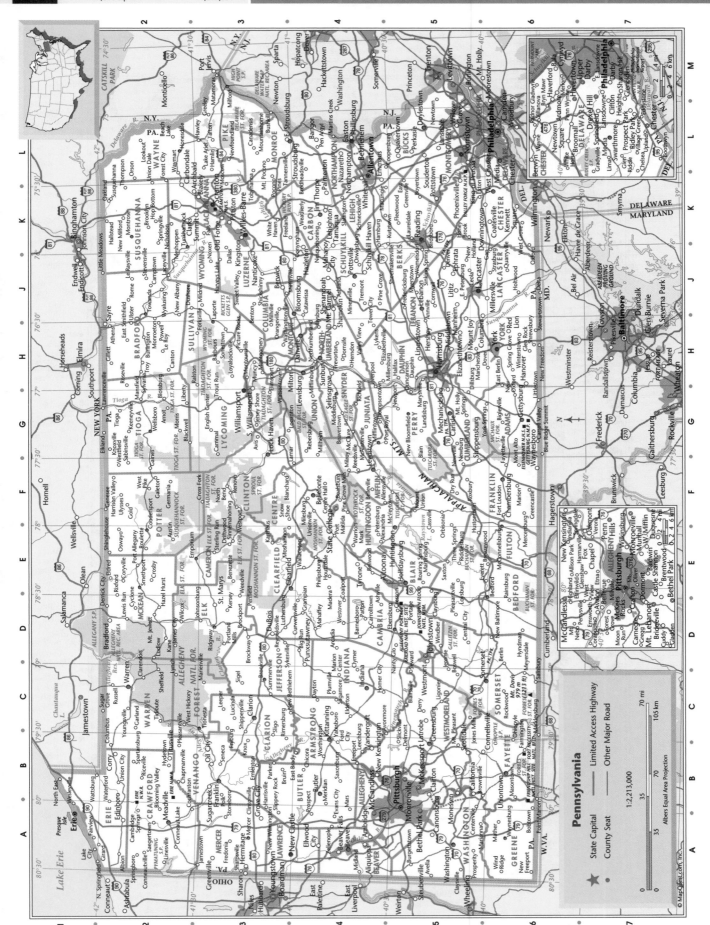

Pennsylvania

★ State Capital
• County Seat
— Limited Access Highway
— Other Major Road

1:2,213,000

Albers Equal Area Projection

© MapQuest.com, Inc.

Capital: Providence
Area: 1,500 sq. mi.
4,000 sq. km.
Pop. (2000): 1,048,319
Largest City: Providence
173,618

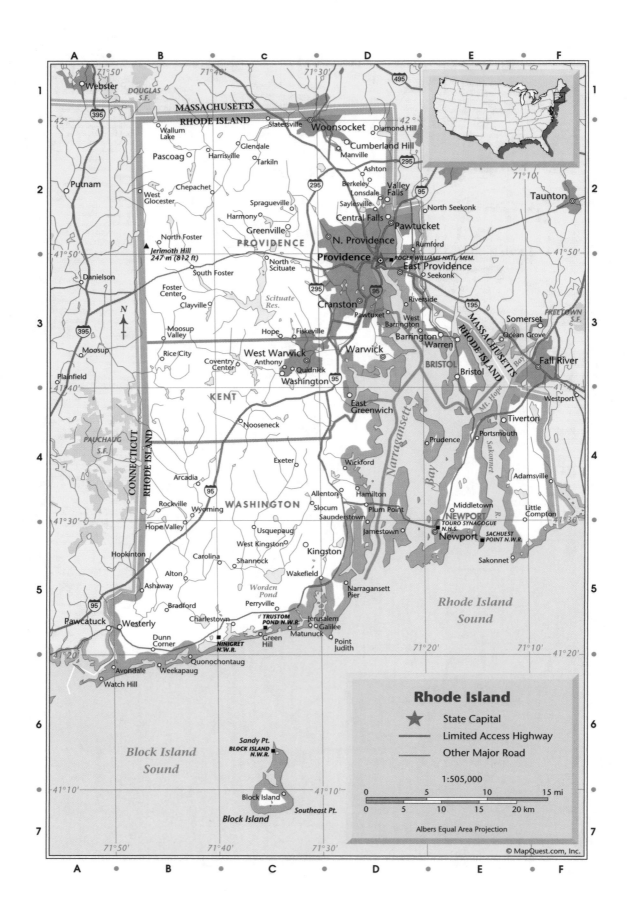

Rhode Island

★ State Capital

—— Limited Access Highway

—— Other Major Road

1:505,000

0   5   10   15 mi

0   5   10   15   20 km

Albers Equal Area Projection

© MapQuest.com, Inc.

Capital: Columbia
Area: 32,000 sq. mi.
82,900 sq. km.
Pop. (2000): 4,012,012
Largest City: Columbia
116,278

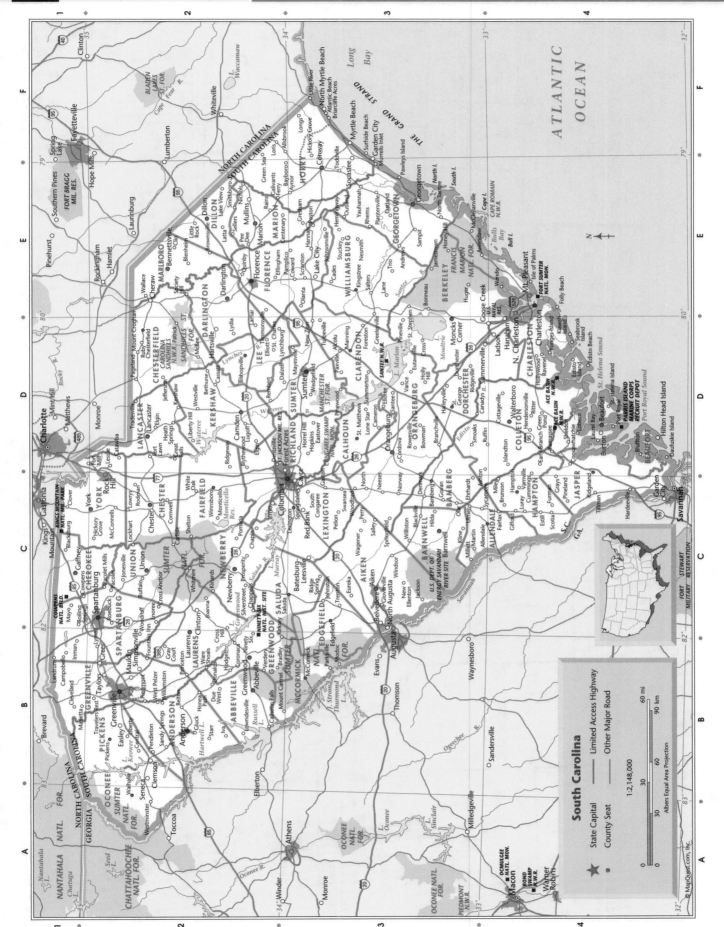

South Carolina

★ State Capital
• County Seat

— Limited Access Highway
— Other Major Road

1:2,148,000

Albers Equal Area Projection

© MapQuest.com, Inc.

Capital: Pierre
Area: 77,100 sq. mi.
199,700 sq. km.
Pop. (2000): 754,844
Largest City: Sioux Falls
123,975

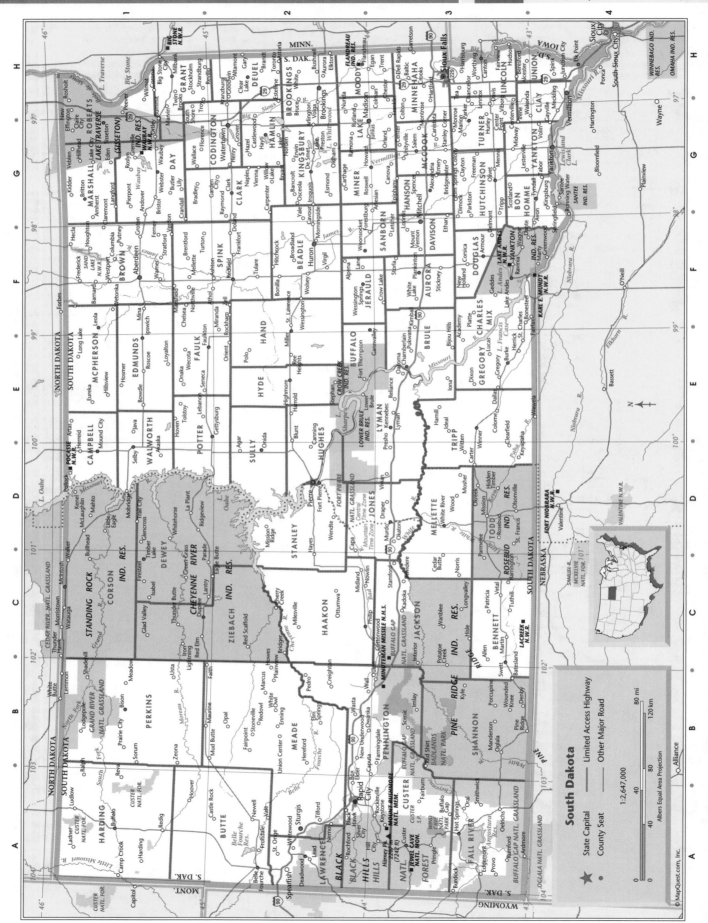

Capital: Nashville	Pop. (2000): 5,689,283
Area: 42,100 sq. mi.	Largest City: Memphis
109,200 sq. km.	650,100

TENNESSEE 169

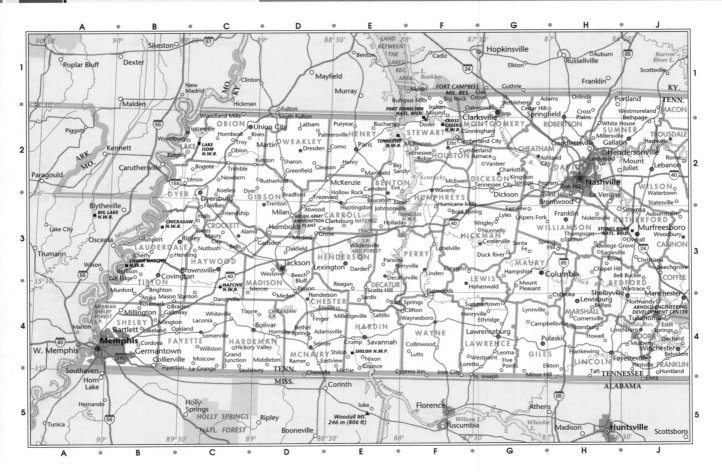

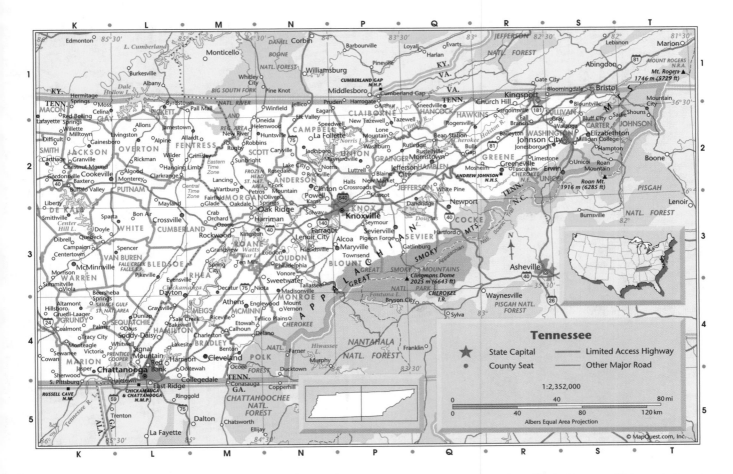

Tennessee

★ State Capital — Limited Access Highway
• County Seat — Other Major Road

1:2,352,000

0	40	80 mi
0	40	80	120 km

Albers Equal Area Projection

© MapQuest.com, Inc.

Capital: Austin
Area: 268,600 sq. mi.
695,700 sq. km.
Pop. (2000): 20,851,820
Largest City: Houston
1,953,631

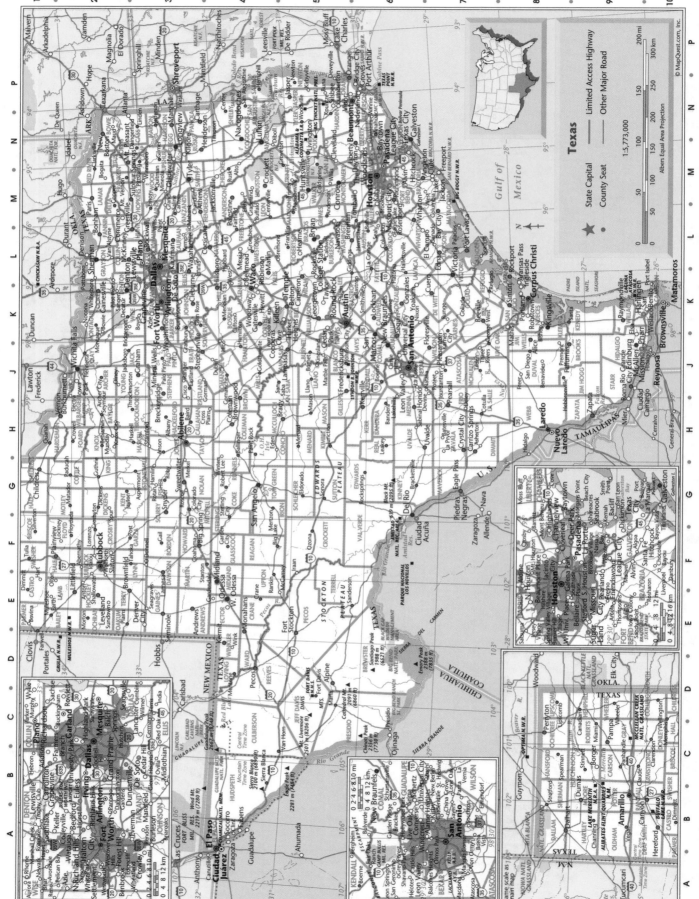

Texas
State Capital
County Seat
Limited Access Highway
Other Major Road
1:5,773,000
Albers Equal Area Projection

© MapQuest.com, Inc.

Capital: Salt Lake City
Area: 84,900 sq. mi.
219,900 sq. km.
Pop. (2000): 2,233,169
Largest City: Salt Lake City
181,743

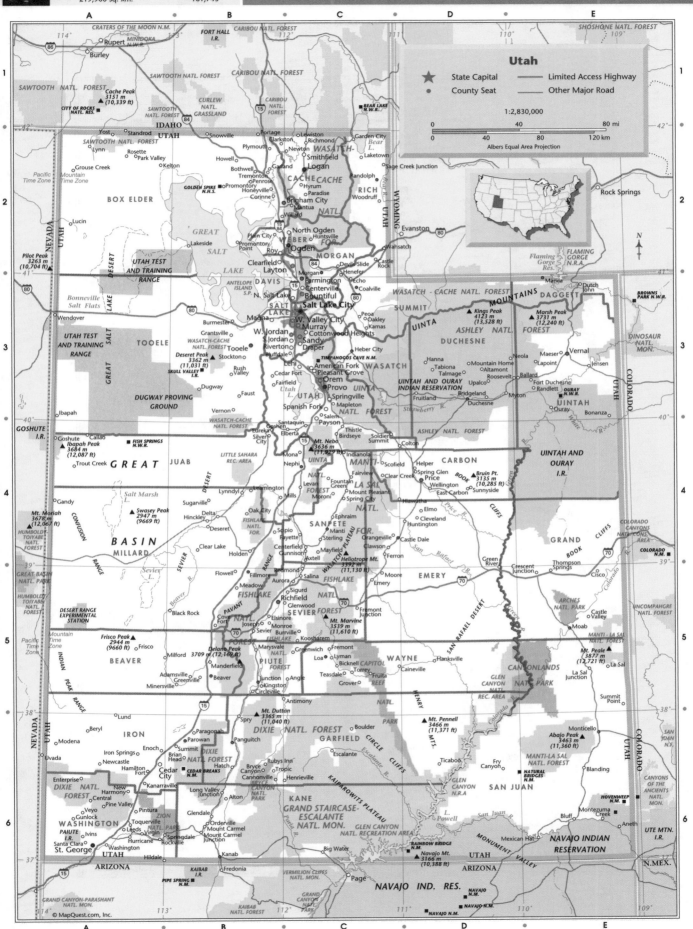

Utah

★ State Capital
● County Seat
── Limited Access Highway
── Other Major Road

1:2,830,000

0   40   80 mi
0   40   80   120 km

Albers Equal Area Projection

© MapQuest.com, Inc.

Capital:	Montpelier	Pop. (2000):	608,827
Area:	9,600 sq. mi.	Largest City:	Burlington
	24,900 sq. km.		38,889

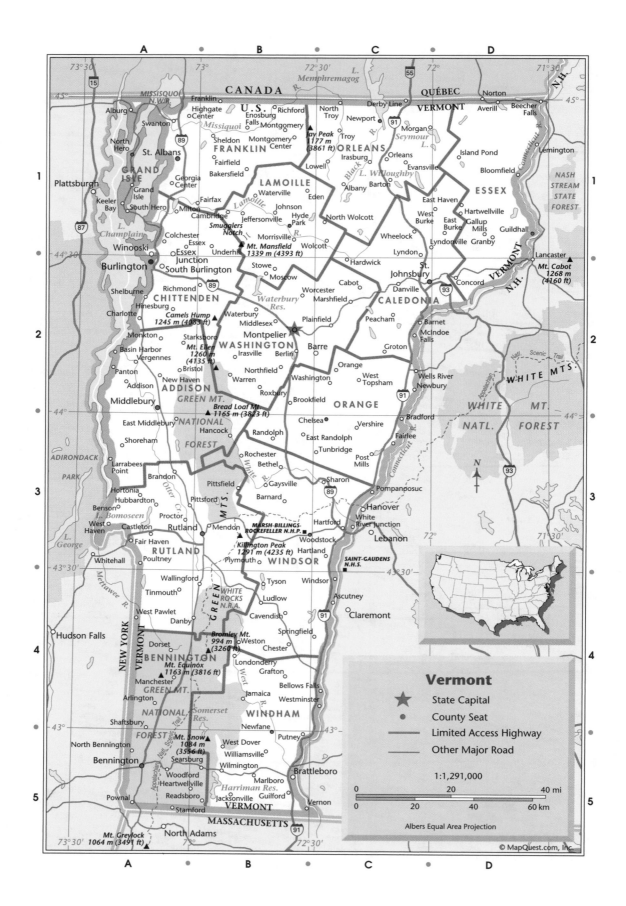

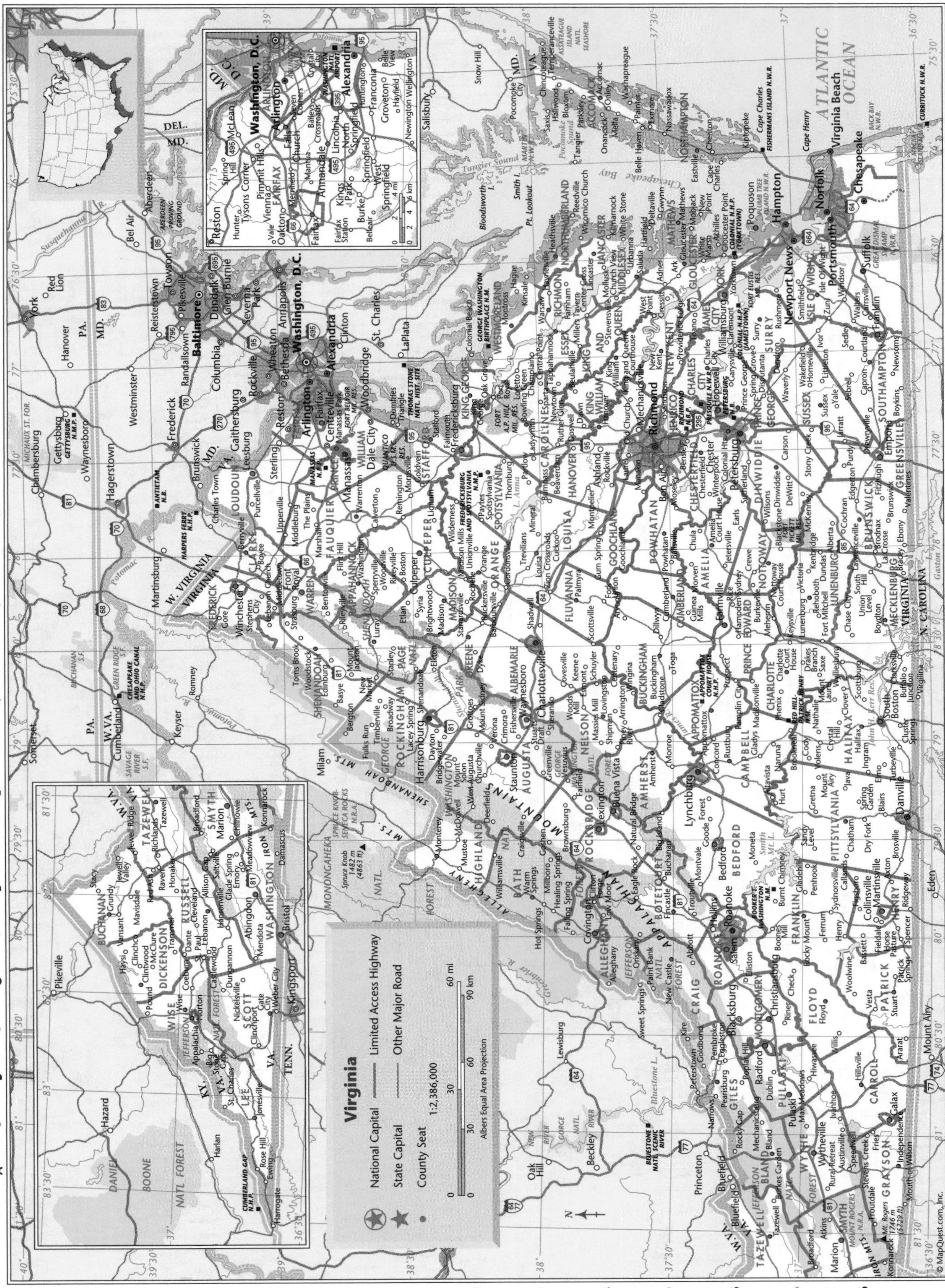

Capital: Richmond	Pop. (2000): 7,078,515
Area: 42,800 sq. mi.	Largest City: Virginia Beach
110,800 sq. km.	425,257

Virginia

Limited Access Highway
Other Major Road

National Capital ★
State Capital ☆
County Seat •

1:2,386,000

Albers Equal Area Projection

0 30 60 60 mi
0 30 60 90 km

© MapQuest.com, Inc.

Capital: Olympia
Area: 71,300 sq. mi.
184,700 sq. km.
Pop. (2000): 5,894,121
Largest City: Seattle
563,374

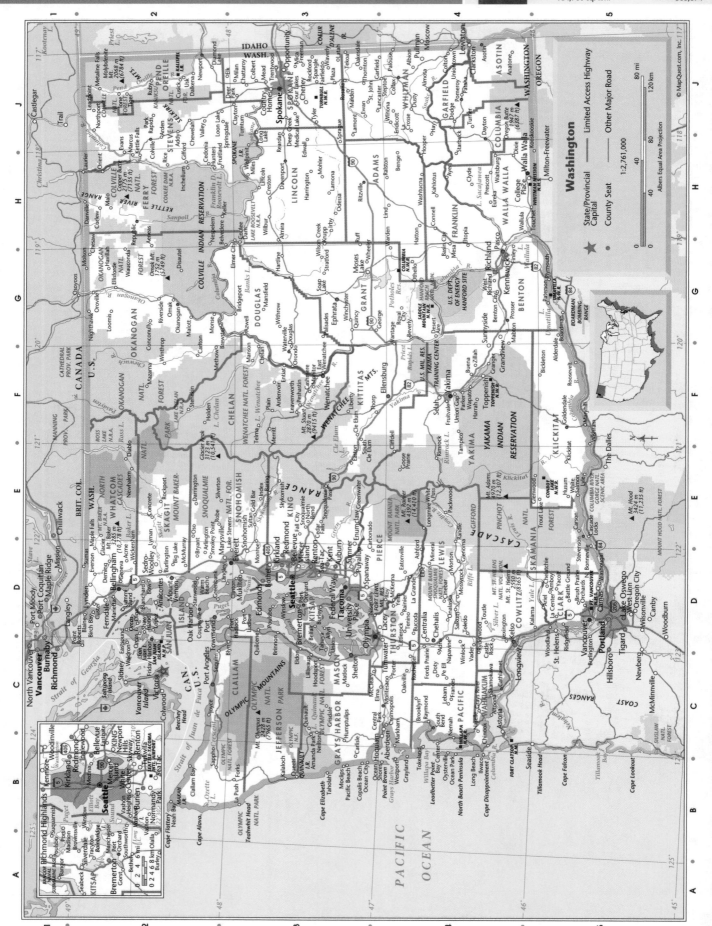

Washington

★ State/Provincial Capital
• County Seat
— Limited Access Highway
— Other Major Road

1:2,761,000

Albers Equal Area Projection

© MapQuest.com, Inc.

Capital: Charleston
Area: 24,200 sq. mi.
62,800 sq. km.
Pop. (2000): 1,808,344
Largest City: Charleston
53,421

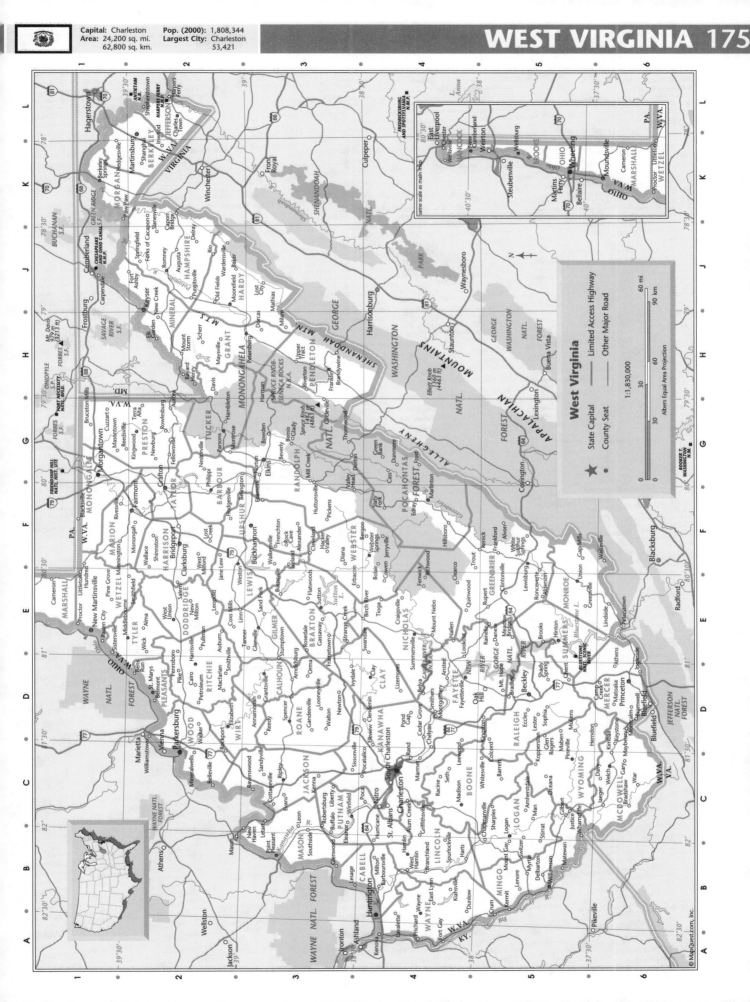

West Virginia

★ State Capital
● County Seat
— Limited Access Highway
— Other Major Road

1:1,830,000

Albers Equal Area Projection

© MapQuest.com, Inc.

WISCONSIN
1848

Capital: Madison
Area: 65,500 sq. mi.
169,600 sq. km.

Pop. (2000): 5,363,675
Largest City: Milwaukee
596,974

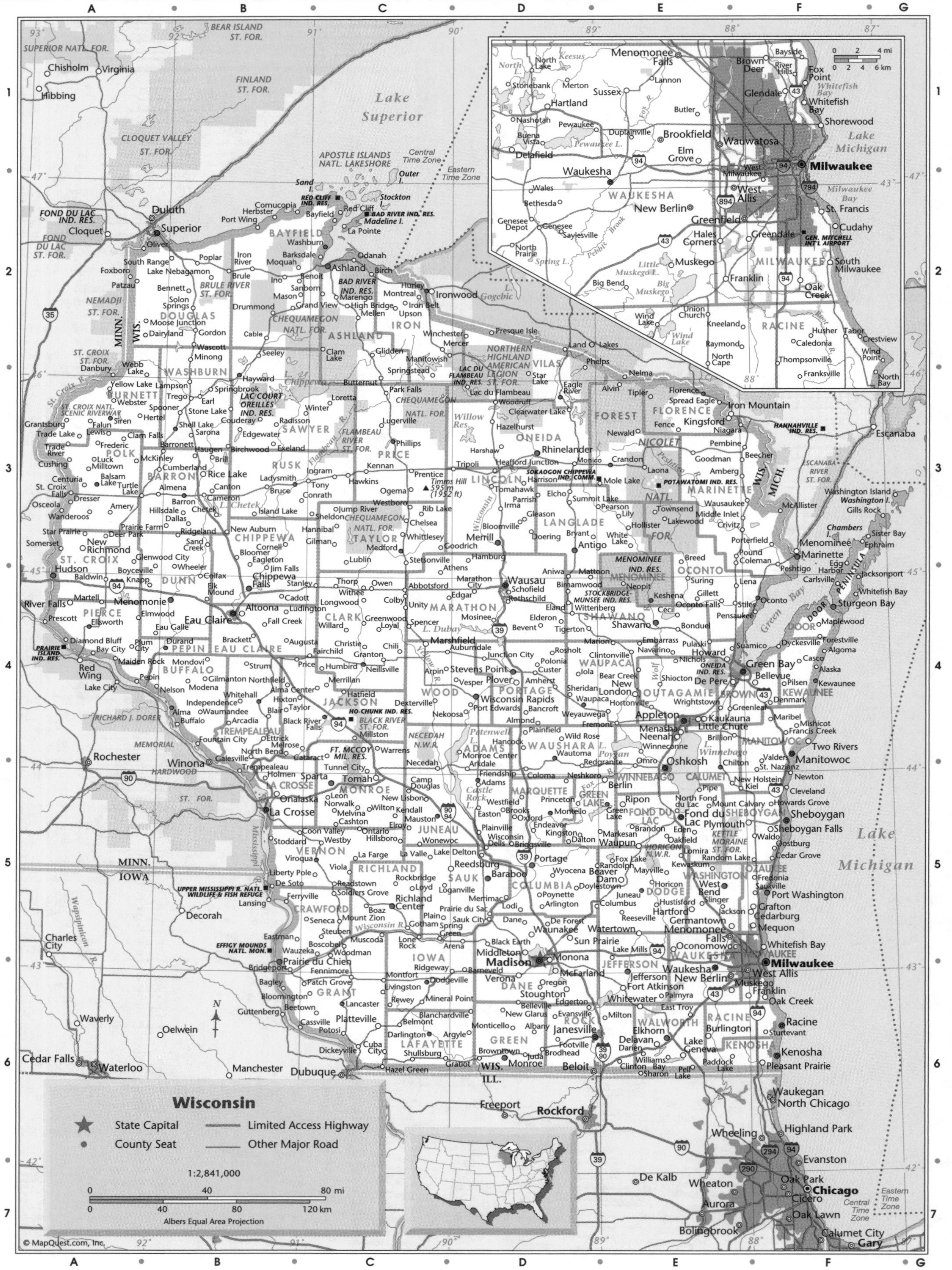

Wisconsin

★ State Capital
● County Seat
━━ Limited Access Highway
━━ Other Major Road

1:2,841,000

0   40   80 mi
0   40   80   120 km

Albers Equal Area Projection

© MapQuest.com, Inc.

Capital: Cheyenne
Area: 97,800 sq. mi.
253,300 sq. km.
Pop. (2000): 493,782
Largest City: Cheyenne
53,011

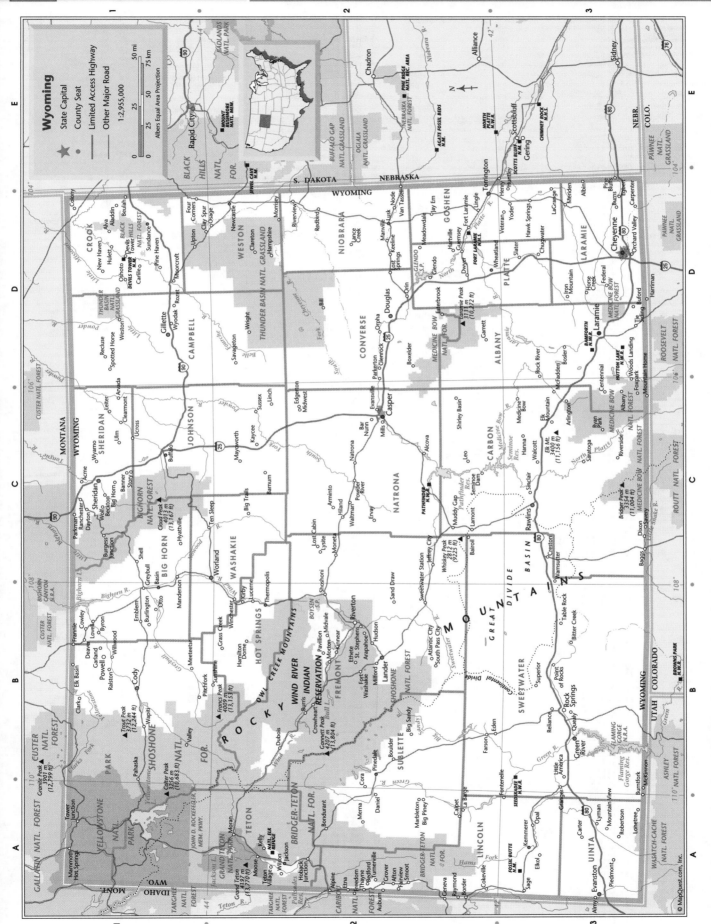

Wyoming
★ State Capital
• County Seat
— Limited Access Highway
— Other Major Road

1:2,955,000

© MapQuest.com, Inc.

178 ALABAMA–CALIFORNIA

Abbreviations
N.H.P. — National Historical Park
N.H.S. — National Historic Site
N.M. — National Monument
N.P. — National Park
N.R.A. — National Recreation Area

Alabama ....page 128

Cities and Towns (Key)
Abbeville D4
Adamsville C2
Alabaster C2
Albertville C1
Alexander City D3
Aliceville A2
Andalusia C4
Anniston D2
Arab C1
Ashford D4
Ashland D2
Ashville C2
Athens C1
Atmore B4
Attalla C1
Auburn D3
Bay Minette B5
Bayou La Batre A5
Bessemer C2
Birmingham C2
Blountsville C1
Boaz C1
Brent B3
Brewton B4
Bridgeport D1
Brundidge D4
Butler A3
Calera C2
Camden B4
Camp Hill D3
Carbon Hill B2
Carrollton A2
Center Point C2
Centre D1
Centreville B3
Chatom A4
Chelsea C2
Cherokee B1
Chickasaw A5
Childersburg C2
Citronelle A4
Clanton C3
Clayton D4
Clio D4
Collinsville D1
Columbiana C2
Cordova B2
Cottonwood D4
Creola A5
Crossville D1
Cullman C1
Dadeville D3
Daleville D4
Daphne B5
Decatur C1
Demopolis B3
Dora B2
Dothan D4
Double Springs B1
East Brewton B4
Elba C4
Enterprise D4
Eufaula D4
Eutaw B3
Evergreen C4
Fairfield C2
Fairhope B5
Falkville C1
Fayette B2
Flomaton B4
Florala C4
Florence B1
Foley B5
Fort Morgan A5
Fort Payne D1
Frisco City B4
Fultondale C2
Gadsden C1
Gardendale C2
Gasque B5
Geneva D4
Georgiana C4
Glencoe D2
Good Hope C1
Goodwater C2
Gordo B2
Grand Bay A5
Greensboro B3
Greenville C4
Grove Hill B4
Guin B2
Gulf Shores B5
Guntersville C1
Haleyville B1
Hamilton B1
Hanceville C1
Hartford D4
Hartselle C1
Hayneville C3
Hazel Green C1
Headland D4
Heflin D2
Helena C2
Henagar D1
Heron Bay A5
Hokes Bluff D2
Holt B2
Hoover C2
Hueytown B2
Huntsville C1
Irondale C2
Jackson B4
Jacksonville D2
Jasper B2
Jemison C3
Lafayette D3
Lanett D3
Leeds C2
Lincoln C2
Linden B3
Lineville D2
Livingston A3
Luverne C4
Madison C1
Marion B3
Meridianville C1
Midfield C2
Midland City D4
Millbrook C3
Mobile A5
Monroeville B4
Montevallo C2
Montgomery, *capital* C3
Moulton B1
Moundville B3
Muscle Shoals B1
New Hope C1
Newton D4
Northport B2
Oneonta C2
Opelika D3
Opp C4
Orange Beach B5
Oxford D2
Ozark D4
Parrish B2
Pelham C2
Pell City C2
Petersville B1
Phenix City D3
Phil Campbell B1
Piedmont D2
Pinson C2
Point Clear B5
Prattville C3
Priceville C1
Prichard A5
Ragland C2
Rainbow City C2
Rainsville D1
Reform A2
Roanoke D2
Robertsdale B5
Rockford C3
Russellville B1
Samson C4
Saraland A5
Sardis City C1
Satsuma A5
Scottsboro C1
Selma B3
Sheffield B1
Slocomb D4
Smiths D3
Southside C2
Spanish Fort B5
Springville C2
Stevenson D1
Sulligent A2
Sumiton B2
Sylacauga C2
Talladega C2
Tallassee D3
Taylor D4
Theodore A5
Thomasville B4
Thorsby C3
Tillmans Corner A5
Town Creek B1
Trinity B1
Troy D4
Trussville C2
Tuscaloosa B2
Tuscumbia B1
Tuskegee D3
Union Springs D3
Uniontown B3
Valley D3
Vernon A2
Vestavia Hills C2
Vincent C2
Warrior C2
Weaver D2
Wedowee D2
West Blocton B2
Wetumpka C3
Winfield B2
York A3

Other Features
Alabama, *river* B4
Appalachian, *mts.* D1
Bear Creek, *reservoir* B1
Black Warrior, *river* B3
Bon Secour, *bay* B5
Cahaba, *river* B3
Cheaha, *mt.* D2
Conecuh, *river* C4
Coosa, *river* D1
Dauphin, *island* A5
Guntersville, *lake* C1
Jordan, *lake* C3
Lewis Smith, *lake* B1
Logan Morgan, *lake* C2
Lookout, *mt.* D1
Martin, *lake* D3
Mitchell, *lake* C3
Mobile, *bay* A5
Neely Henry, *lake* C2
Pickwick, *lake* A1
R.L. Harris, *reservoir* D2
Russell Cave Natl. Monument D1
Tallapoosa, *river* D2
Tennessee, *river* A1
Tombigbee, *river* A4
Tuscaloosa, *lake* B2
Tuskegee Institute Natl. Hist. Site D3
Weiss, *lake* D1
Wheeler, *lake* B1
William "Bill" Dannelly, *reservoir* B3
Wilson, *lake* B1

Alaska ....page 129

Cities and Towns
Adak Inset
Anchorage F2
Barrow D1
Bethel C2
Big Delta F2
College F2
Cordova F2
Craig J3
Delta Jct. F2
Dillingham D3
Fairbanks F2
Haines H3
Homer E3
Juneau, *capital* J3
Kenai E2
Ketchikan J3
Kodiak E3
Kotzebue C1
McKinley Park F2
Metlakatla J3
Nikiski E2
Nome B2
North Pole F2
Palmer F2
Petersburg J3
Prudhoe Bay F1
Seward F2
Sitka H3
Skagway H3
Soldotna E2
Talkeetna E2
Tok G2
Unalaska B4
Valdez F2
Wasilla F2
Whittier F2
Wrangell J3

Other Features
Adak, *island* Inset
Admiralty Island Natl. Monument J3
Agattu, *island* Inset
Alaska, *gulf* F3
Alaska, *peninsula* C3
Alaska, *range* E2
Aleutian, *islands* A4, Inset
Alexander, *archipelago* H3
Amchitka, *island* Inset
Amlia, *island* Inset
Andreanof, *islands* Inset
Aniakchak N.M. and Preserve D3
Atka, *island* Inset
Attu, *island* Inset
Barrow, *point* D1
Beaufort, *sea* H1
Becharof, *lake* D3
Bering, *sea* B3
Bering, *strait* B2
Blackburn, *mt.* G2
Bristol, *bay* C3
Brooks, *range* D1
Cape Krusenstern N.M. C1
Chirikof, *island* D3
Chukchi, *sea* A1
Colville, *river* E1
Cook, *inlet* E3
Copper, *river* G2
Denali Natl. Park and Preserve E2
Fairweather, *mt.* H3
Gates of the Arctic N.P. and Preserve E1
Glacier Bay N.P. and Preserve H3
Iliamna, *lake* D3
Inside Passage, *waterway* J3
Kanaga, *island* Inset
Katmai Natl. Park and Preserve D3
Kenai, *peninsula* E2
Kenai Fjords Natl. Park F3
Kiska, *island* Inset
Klondike Gold Rush N.H.P H3
Kobuk, *river* D1
Kobuk Valley Natl. Park D1
Kodiak, *island* E3
Kotzebue, *sound* C1
Koyukuk, *river* D1
Kuskokwim, *bay* C3
Kuskokwim, *mts.* D2
Kuskokwim, *river* D2
Lake Clark Natl. Park and Preserve E2
Lisburne, *cape* B1
Lisburne, *peninsula* C1
Logan, *mt.* G2
Lynn, *canal* J3
McKinley, *mt.* E2
Malaspina, *glacier* G3
Michelson, *mt.* G1
Mohican, *cape* B2
Muir, *glacier* F2
Near, *islands* Inset
Noatak, *river* D1
Norton, *sound* C2
Nunivak, *island* B3
Porcupine, *river* G1
Pribilof, *islands* B3
Prince of Wales, *island* J3
Progromni, *volcano* C4
Rat, *islands* Inset
St. Elias, *mt.* G2
St. George, *island* B3
St. Lawrence, *island* A2
St. Matthew, *island* A2
St. Paul, *island* A3
Samalga, *pass* B4
Sanak, *island* C4
Seguam, *island* Inset
Semisopochnoi, *island* Inset
Seward, *peninsula* C1
Shishaldin, *volcano* C4
Shumagin, *islands* D4
Sitka N.H.P. H3
Stikine, *river* J3
Tanaga, *island* F3
Tanana, *river* E2
Tikchik, *lakes* D2
Trinity, *islands* E3
Umnak, *island* Inset
Unalaska, *island* B4
Unga, *island* C3
Unimak, *island* C4
Utukok, *river* C1
White Mts. Natl. Rec. Area F1
Wrangell, *mts.* G2
Wrangell-St. Elias N.P. and Preserve G2
Yukon, *river* D2
Yukon-Charley Rivers Natl. Preserve G2
Yunaska, *island* Inset

Arizona ....page 130

Cities and Towns
Ajo C5
Apache Junction D4
Avondale C4
Bagdad B3
Benson E6
Bisbee F6
Bitahochee E2
Buckeye C4
Bullhead City A2
Camp Verde D3
Carefree D4
Casa Grande D5
Catalina E5
Cave Creek D4
Chandler D4
Chinle F1
Chino Valley C3
Cibecue E3
Clarkdale C3
Claypool E4
Clifton F4
Colorado City C1
Coolidge D5
Cornville D3
Cow Springs E1
Crown King C3
Douglas F6
Dudleyville E5
Eagar F3
El Mirage C4
Eloy D5
Flagstaff D2
Florence D4
Fort Defiance F2
Fountain Hills D4
Ganado F2
Geronimo E4
Gila Bend C5
Gilbert D4
Globe E4
Goodyear C4
Grand Canyon C1
Greaterville E6
Green Valley E6
Guthrie F5
Happy Jack D3
Holbrook E3
Huachuca City E6
Kayenta E1
Kearny E4
Kingman A2
Kirkland Junction C3
Lake Havasu City A3
Lake Montezuma D3
Litchfield Park C4
Mammoth E5
Many Farms F1
Marana D5
Mesa D4
Miami E4
Nogales E6
Oracle E5
Oro Valley E5
Page D1
Paradise Valley D4
Parker A3
Payson D3
Peoria C4
Phoenix, *capital* C4
Pima F5
Pinetop-Lakeside F3
Prescott C3
Prescott Valley C3
Quartzsite A4
Queen Creek D4
Randolph D5
Sacaton D4
Safford F5
Sahuarita E6
St. David E6
St. Johns F3
San Carlos E4
Sanders F2
San Manuel E5
Scottsdale D4
Sedona D3
Sells D6
Show Low E3
Sierra Vista E6
Snowflake E3
Somerton A5
South Tucson E5
Springerville F3
Sun City C4
Sun Lakes D4
Superior D4
Surprise C4
Taylor E3
Tempe D4
Thatcher F5
Three Points D5
Tolleson C4
Tombstone E6
Tuba City D1
Tucson E5
Whiteriver F4
Wickenburg C4
Willcox F5
Williams C2
Window Rock F2
Winslow E2
Yuma A5

Other Features
Agua Fria, *river* C4
Alamo, *lake* B3
Apache, *lake* D4
Aztec Peak, *mt.* E4
Baldy, *mt.* F4
Bartlett, *reservoir* D4
Big Horn, *mts.* B4
Bill Williams, *river* A3
Black, *mesa* E1
Black, *river* E4
Canyon De Chelly N.M. F1
Casa Grande Ruins N.M. D5
Castle Dome, *mts.* A4
Castle Dome Peak, *mt.* A4
Chiricahua Natl. Monument F6
Colorado, *river* B2, D1
Coronado Natl. Mem. E6
Gila, *river* B5, D4, F4
Glen Canyon, *dam* D1
Glen Canyon Natl. Rec. Area D1
Grand, *canyon* C1
Grand Canyon Natl. Park B2, C1
Grand Canyon-Parashant N.M. B1
Harcuvar, *mts.* B4
Havasu, *lake* A3
Hide Creek, *mt.* C3
Hoover, *dam* A1
Hopi Indian Res. E2
Horseshoe, *reservoir* D4
Hualapai, *mt.* B2
Hubbell Trading Post N.H.S. F2
Humphreys Peak, *mt.* D2
Lake Mead Natl. Rec. Area B1
Little Colorado, *river* D2
Many Farms, *lake* F1
Maple Peak, *mt.* F4
Mazatzal Peak, *mt.* D3
Mohave, *lake* A2
Montezuma Castle N.M. D3
Monument, *valley* F1
Mormon, *lake* D3
Navajo Indian Res. E1, E2
Navajo Natl. Monument E1
Organ Pipe Cactus N.M. C5
Painted, *desert* D2
Parker, *dam* A3
Petrified Forest Natl. Park F3
Pipe Spring Natl. Monument C1
Pleasant, *lake* C4
Point Imperial, *mt.* D1
Powell, *lake* D1
Red, *lake* B2
Saguaro Natl. Monument E5
Salt, *river* E4
San Carlos, *lake* E4
San Pedro, *river* E5
Santa Cruz, *river* D5
Sonoran, *desert* B5
Sunset Crater Volcano N.M. D2
Theodore Roosevelt, *lake* D4
Tipton, *mt.* A2
Tonto Natl. Monument D4
Trumbull, *mt.* B1
Tumacacori Natl Hist. Park D6
Tuzigoot Natl. Monument C3
Ventana, *cave* C5
Verde, *river* D3
Virgin, *river* A1
Walnut Canyon Natl. Monument D2
White, *mts.* F4
White House, *ruin* F1
Wupatki Natl. Monument D2
Yuma, *desert* A5

Arkansas ....page 131

Cities and Towns
Alicia D2
Alma A2
Arkadelphia B3
Arkansas City D4
Ashdown A4
Ash Flat D1
Atkins C2
Augusta D2
Bald Knob D2
Barling A2
Batesville D2
Bay E2
Beebe D2
Bella Vista A1
Benton C3
Bentonville A1
Berryville B1
Blytheville F2
Bodcaw B4
Booneville B2
Brinkley D3
Bryant C3
Bull Shoals C1
Cabot D3
Camden C4
Caraway E2
Carlisle D3
Cave City D2
Charleston A2
Clarendon D3
Clarksville B2
Clinton C2
Conway C2
Corning E1
Crossett D4
Daisy B3
Damascus C2
Danville B2
Dardanelle B2
De Queen A3
Dermott D4
Des Arc D3
De Valls Bluff D3
De Witt D3
Dierks A3
Dumas D4
Earle E2
El Dorado C4
England D3
Eudora D4
Eureka Springs B1
Fairfield Bay C2
Fallsville B2
Farmington A1
Fayetteville A1
Fordyce C4
Foreman A4
Forrest City E2
Fort Smith A2
Fountain Hill D4
Gentry A1
Glenwood B3
Gosnell F2
Gould D4
Gravette A1
Greenbrier C2
Green Forest B1
Greenwood A2
Griffithville D2
Gurdon B4
Hamburg D4
Hampton C4
Harrisburg E2
Harrison B1
Haskell C3
Hatfield A3
Hazen D3
Heber Springs C2
Helena E3
Hope B4
Horseshoe Bend D1
Hot Springs National Park B3
Hot Springs Village B3
Hoxie E1
Hughes E3
Hunter D2
Huntsville B1
Jacksonville C3
Jasper B1
Jonesboro E2
Lake City E2
Lake Hamilton B3
Lake Village D4
Lepanto E2
Lewisville B4
Lincoln A2
Little Rock, *capital* C3
Lonoke D3
Luxora F2
McCrory D2
McGehee D4
McNeil B4
McRae D2
Magnolia B4
Malvern C3
Manila E2
Marianna E3
Marion E2
Marked Tree E2
Marshall C2
Marvell E3
Maumelle C3
Mayflower C3
Melbourne D1
Mena A3
Monticello D4
Morrilton C2
Mountain Home C1
Mountain View C2
Mount Ida B3
Mulberry A2
Murfreesboro B3
Nashville B4
Newport D2
North Crossett D4
North Little Rock C3
Oden B3
Osceola F2
Ozark B2
Paragould E1
Paris B2
Parkin E2
Pea Ridge A1
Pelsor B2
Perryville C2
Piggott E1
Pine Bluff D3
Pocahontas E1
Prescott B4
Rector E1
Rison C4
Rogers A1
Rose Bud C2
Russell D2
Russellville B2
St. Charles D3
St. Paul B2
Salem D1
Searcy D2
Sheridan C3
Sherwood C3
Siloam Springs A1
Smackover C4
Springdale A1
Springhill B4
Star City D4
Stuttgart D3
Texarkana A4
Tillar D4
Trumann E2
Tuckerman D2
Tupelo D2
Van Buren A2
Waldo B4
Waldron A3
Walnut Ridge E1
Warren C4
Washington B4
West Fork A2
West Helena E3
West Memphis E2
White Hall C3
Wynne E2
Yellville C1

Other Features
Arkansas, *river* D3
Arkansas Post Natl. Mem. D3
Beaver, *lake* B1
Black, *river* D2
Boston, *mts.* B2
Buffalo, *river* B1
Buffalo Natl. River C2
Bull Shoals, *lake* C1
Cache, *river* E2
Catherine, *lake* C3
Dardanelle, *reservoir* B2
DeGray, *lake* B3
Erling, *lake* B4
Fort Smith Natl. Hist Site A2
Greers Ferry, *lake* C2
Greeson, *lake* B3
Hamilton, *lake* B3
Hot Springs Natl. Park B3
Little Missouri, *river* B4
Little Rock Central H.S N.H.S. C3
Magazine, *mt.* B2
Maumelle, *lake* C3
Millwood, *lake* B4
Mississippi, *river* E3
Nimrod, *lake* B3
Norfork, *lake* C1
Ouachita, *lake* B3
Ouachita, *mts.* A3
Ouachita, *river* B3, C4
Ozark, *plateau* B1
Pea Ridge Natl. Mil. Park A1
Red, *river* B4
St. Francis, *river* E2
Saline, *river* C3
Table Rock, *lake* B1
White, *river* C2, D3

California ....page 132

Cities and Towns
Adelanto H8
Alameda K2
Alamo L2
Albany K1
Alhambra D10
Alpine J10
Altadena D10
Alturas E1
Anaheim E11, H9
Anderson C2
Antioch D4, L1
Apple Valley H8
Aptos D5
Arcadia D10
Arcata A2
Arnold E4
Arroyo Grande E7
Arvin G7
Ashland K2
Atascadero E7
Atherton K3
Atwater E5
Auberry F5
Auburn E4
Avalon G9
Avenal E6
Azusa E10
Bakersfield G7
Baldwin Park E10
Barstow H8
Bell D10
Bellflower D11
Belmont K3
Belvedere J1
Benicia K1
Berkeley C5, K2
Beverly Hills C10
Big Bear Lake J8
Bishop G5
Black Point J1
Blythe L9
Bonita C9
Boron H8

	Key
Borrego Springs	J9
Brawley	K10
Brea	E11
Bridgeport	F4
Brisbane	J2
Broadmoor	J2
Buellton	E8
Buena Park	E11
Burbank	C10
Burlingame	J3
Burney	D2
Buttonwillow	F7
Calabasas	B10
Calexico	K10
California City	H7
Calipatria	K9
Calistoga	C4
Cambria	D7
Campbell	L4
Canyon	K2
Carlsbad	H9
Carmel	D6
Carmel Valley	D6
Carpinteria	F8
Carson	D11
Castroville	D6
Cathedral City	J9
Cayucos	C7
Central Valley	C2
Ceres	E5
Chester	D2
Chico	D3
Chino	F10
Chowchilla	E5
Chula Vista	C9, H10
Claremont	F10
Clayton	L1
Clearlake	C4
Cloverdale	B4
Clovis	F6
Clyde	L1
Coachella	J9
Coalinga	E6
Cobb	C4
Colfax	E3
Colusa	D3
Compton	D11
Concord	L1
Corcoran	F6
Corning	C3
Corona	F11
Coronado	C8
Corte Madera	J1
Costa Mesa	E11
Cottonwood	C2
Covina	E10
Cowan Heights	E11
Crescent City	A1
Crestline	H8
Crockett	K1
Culver City	C10
Cupertino	L4
Cypress	D11
Daly City	J2
Danville	L2
Davis	D4
Delano	F6
Del Mar	H10
Desert Hot Springs	J9
Diablo	L2
Diamond Bar	E10
Dinuba	F6
Dos Palos	E5
Downey	D11
Downieville	E3
Dublin	L2
Dunsmuir	C1
Earlimart	F7
East Los Angeles	D10
Easton	F6
East Palo Alto	K3
El Cajon	C8, J10
El Centro	K10
El Cerrito	K1
El Granada	J3
Elk Grove	D4
El Monte	D10
El Segundo	C11
El Sobrante	K1
Emeryville	K2
Encinitas	H9
Escondido	H9
Eureka	A2
Exeter	F6
Fairfax	H1
Fairfield	D4
Fallbrook	H9
Ferndale	A2
Firebaugh	E6
Florence	D11
Florin	D4
Fort Bragg	B3
Fortuna	A2
Foster City	K3
Fountain Valley	E11
Frazier Park	G8
Fremont	D5, L3
Fresno	F6
Fullerton	E11
Galt	D4
Garden Grove	E11
Gilroy	D5
Glendale	D10, G8
Glendora	E10
Glenview	B10
Gonzales	D6
Grass Valley	D3
Greenacres	F7
Greenbrae	J1
Greenfield	D6
Greenville	E2
Gridley	D3
Groveland	E5
Guadalupe	E8
Half Moon Bay	J3
Hanford	F6
Hawthorne	C11
Hayfork	B2
Hayward	C5, L2
Healdsburg	C4
Hemet	J9
Hercules	K1
Hermosa Beach	C11
Hesperia	H8
Hidden Hills	B10
Hillsborough	J3
Hollister	D6
Holtville	K10
Huntington Beach	E11, C9
Huron	E6
Ignacio	J1
Imperial Beach	B9, H10

	Key
Independence	G6
Indio	J9
Inglewood	C11, C9
Ingot	C2
Inyokern	H7
Ione	K1
Irvine	E11, H9
Isla Vista	F8
Jackson	E4
Joshua Tree	J8
Julian	J9
Kelseyville	C4
Kensington	K1
Kentfield	J1
Kerman	E6
Kernville	G7
Kettleman City	F6
King City	D6
La Cañada-Flintridge	D10
La Crescenta	D10
Lafayette	K1
La Habra	E11
La Honda	K4
Lake Isabella	G7
Lakeport	C3
Lakeside	J10
Lakewood	D11
La Mesa	C8
La Mirada	D11
Lamont	G7
Lancaster	G8
La Puente	E10
Larkspur	J1
Laton	F6
Lawndale	C11
Lee Vining	F5
Lemon Grove	C8
Lemoore	F6
Lincoln	D4
Lindsay	F6
Littlerock	H8
Livermore	D5
Livingston	E5
Lockeford	D4
Lodi	D4
Loma Mar	K4
Lomita	C11
Lompoc	E8
Long Beach	D11, C9
Los Altos	K3
Los Altos Hills	K4
Los Angeles	D10, G8
Los Banos	E5
Los Molinos	C2
Los Osos	E7
Lynwood	D11
McCloud	C1
McFarland	F7
McKinleyville	A2
Madera	E6
Malibu	B10
Mammoth Lakes	G5
Manhattan Beach	C11
Manteca	D5
Marina	D6
Marina del Rey	C11
Marin City	J1
Marinwood	J1
Mariposa	F5
Markleeville	F4
Martinez	C4, K1
Marysville	D3
Maywood	D10
Mecca	J9
Mendota	E6
Menlo Park	K3
Merced	E5
Midway City	E11
Millbrae	J3
Mill Valley	J1
Milpitas	L3
Miranda	B2
Modesto	E5
Mojave	G7
Monrovia	E10
Montara	J3
Montclair	K1
Montebello	D10
Monte Nido	B10
Monterey	D6
Monterey Park	D10
Monte Sereno	L4
Moraga	K2
Moreno Valley	H9
Morgan Hill	D5
Morongo Valley	J8
Morro Bay	E7
Moss Beach	J3
Mountain View	K3
Mount Shasta	C1
Muir Beach	H1
Napa	C4
National City	C9
Needles	L8
Nevada City	D3
Newark	L3
Newberry Springs	J8
Newport Beach	H9
Nicasio	H1
Nice	C3
Nipomo	F7
Nipton	K7
Norco	F11
North Edwards	H7
North Fair Oaks	K3
Novato	H1
Oakdale	E5
Oakhurst	F5
Oakland	K2, C5
Oildale	F7
Ojai	F8
Olema	H1
Olivehurst	D3
Ontario	F10, H8
Orange	E11
Orinda	K1
Orland	C3
Oroville	D3
Otay	C9
Oxnard	F8
Pacheco	L1
Pacifica	J2
Palermo	D3
Palmdale	G8
Palm Desert	J9
Palm Springs	J9
Palo Alto	K3
Palos Verdes Estates	C11
Paradise	D3
Pasadena	D10, G8

	Key
Patterson	D5
Petaluma	C4
Pico Rivera	D10
Piedmont	K2
Pine Valley	J10
Pinole	K1
Pismo Beach	E7
Pittsburg	L1
Placentia	E11
Placerville	E4
Pleasant Hill	L1
Pleasanton	L2
Pomona	E10, H8
Port Costa	K1
Porterville	G6
Portola	E2
Poway	H10
Prunedale	D6
Quartz Hill	G8
Quincy	E3
Ramona	J9
Rancho Cucamonga	F10
Rancho Palos Verdes	C11
Rancho Rinconada	L4
Rancho Santa Margarita	F11
Red Bluff	C2
Redding	C2
Redlands	H8
Redondo Beach	C11
Redwood City	C5, K3
Reedley	F6
Richgrove	F7
Richmond	J1
Ridgecrest	H7
Rio Dell	A2
Riverside	H9
Rodeo	K1
Rolling Hills	C11
Rolling Hills Estates	C11
Rosamond	G8
Roseville	D4
Sacramento, capital	D4
Salinas	D6
San Andreas	E4
San Anselmo	H1
San Bernardino	H8
San Bruno	J2
San Carlos	K3
San Clemente	H9
San Diego	B8, H10
San Francisco	C5, J2
San Gabriel	D10
San Gregorio	J4
San Jose	D5, L4
San Juan Bautista	D6
San Juan Capistrano	H9
San Leandro	K2
San Lorenzo	K2
San Luis Obispo	E7
San Mateo	C5, K3
San Pablo	J1
San Quentin	J1
San Rafael	C5, J1
San Ramon	L2
Santa Ana	E11, H9
Santa Barbara	F8
Santa Clara	L4
Santa Clarita	G8
Santa Cruz	C6
Santa Maria	E8
Santa Monica	C10
Santa Paula	F8
Santa Rosa	C4
Santa Venetia	J1
Santa Ynez	E8
Santee	C8
Saratoga	L4
Sausalito	J2
Scotts Valley	C5
Seal Beach	D11
Sebastopol	C4
Selma	F6
Shafter	F7
Shingletown	D2
Shoshone	J7
Simi Valley	F8
Soledad	D6
Solvang	E8
Sonoma	C4
Sonora	E5
South Lake Tahoe	F4
South San Francisco	J2
Spring Valley	C8
Squaw Valley	F6
Stanford	K3
Stinson Beach	H1
Stockton	C5, L3
Sunnyvale	K3
Sunol	L3
Sunset Beach	D11
Susanville	E2
Taft	F7
Tamalpais Valley	J1
Tehachapi	G7
Temecula	H9
Templeton	E7
Terra Bella	F7
Thermalito	D3
Thousand Oaks	G8
Tiburon	J1
Tipton	F6
Topanga	B10
Torrance	C11, C9
Tracy	D5
Truckee	E3
Tulare	F6
Turlock	E5
Tustin	E11
Twain Harte	E4
Twentynine Palms	J8
Ukiah	B3
Union City	L3
Upland	F10
Vacaville	D4
Vallejo	C4, K1
Vandenberg Village	E8
Ventucopa	F8
Ventura	F8
Victorville	H8
Villa Park	E11
Vine Hill	K1
Visalia	F6
Vista	H9
Walnut	E10
Walnut Creek	L2
Wasco	F7
Watsonville	D6
Weaverville	C2
Weed	C1
West Covina	E10
West Hollywood	C10

	Key
Westminster	E11
Westmorland	K9
West Pittsburg	L1
Westwood	D3
Wheatland	D3
Whittier	D10
Willits	B3
Willow Creek	B2
Willows	C3
Windsor	C4
Wofford Heights	G7
Woodlake	F6
Woodland	D4
Woodside	K3
Wrightwood	H8
Yorba Linda	E11
Yosemite Village	F5
Yreka	C1
Yuba City	D3
Yucaipa	H8
Yucca Valley	J8
Zenia	B2

Other Features

	Key
Alameda, river	L3
Alcatraz, island	J2
Allison, mt.	D2
Almanor, lake	D2
Amargosa, range	J6
Amargosa, river	J7
Angel, island	J1
Balboa, park	B8
Berryessa, lake	C4
Boundary, peak	G5
Bullion, mts.	J8
Cascade, range	D1
Central, valley	C2
Chabot, lake	K2
Channel, islands	E9, F9
Channel Islands Natl. Park	E9, F9
Chatsworth, reservoir	B10
Chino, river	F10
Chocolate, mts.	K9
Clair Engle, lake	C1
Clear, lake	C3
Clear Lake, reservoir	D1
Coast, ranges	C2, D6
Colorado, desert	J9
Colorado, river	L9
Cucamonga, river	F11
Death, valley	H6
Death Valley Natl. Park	H6
Devils Postpile Natl. Monument	F5
Diablo, mt.	L2
Eagle, lake	E2
Eagle, peak	E1
Eel, river	B2
Estero, bay	E7
Eugene O'Neill Natl. Hist. Site	K2
Farallon, islands	B5
Farallones, gulf	H2
Giant Sequoia Natl. Mon.	F6, G6
Golden Gate Natl. Rec. Area	C5, J2
Goose, lake	E1
Grizzly, bay	L1
Half Moon, bay	J3
Honey, lake	E2
Humboldt, bay	A2
Imperial, valley	K9
Inyo, mts.	H6
Irvine, lake	F11
Joshua Tree Natl. Park	K8
Kern, river	G6
Kings, river	F6
Kings Canyon Natl. Park	G5
Klamath, mts.	B1
Klamath, river	B1
Lanfair, valley	K7
Lassen, peak	D2
Lassen Volcanic Natl. Park	D2
Lava Beds Natl. Monument	D1
McCoy, mts.	L9
Mad, river	B2
Manzanar Natl. Hist. Site	G6
Merced, river	F5
Middle Alkali, lake	E1
Mission, bay	B8
Mission Bay, park	B8
Mojave, desert	H7
Mojave, river	J8
Mono, lake	G4
Monterey, bay	D6
Morgan, mt.	G5
Morris, reservoir	E10
Muir Woods Natl. Monument	H1
Nacimiento, reservoir	D7
Napa, river	K1
Nicasio, reservoir	H1
Old Woman, mts.	K8
Oroville, reservoir	D3
Otay, river	C9
Panamint, range	H6
Panamint, valley	H6
Pescadero, river	J4
Pinnacles Natl. Monument	D6
Point Reyes Natl. Seashore	B4
Redwood Natl. Park	A1
Ritter, mt.	F5
Sacramento, river	C3
Salton, sea	K9
San Antonio, reservoir	J8
San Bernardino, mts.	J8
San Clemente, island	G10
San Diego, bay	B9
San Diego, river	B8
San Fernando, valley	B10
San Francisco, bay	J2
San Gabriel, mts.	G8
San Gabriel, reservoir	E10
San Joaquin, river	E5
San Luis Obispo, bay	E7
San Miguel, island	D8
San Nicolas, island	F9
San Pablo, bay	C4, K1
San Rafael, mts.	F8
Santa Ana, river	F11
Santa Barbara, channel	E8
Santa Barbara, island	F9
Santa Catalina, island	G9
Santa Cruz, island	F8
Santa Cruz, mts.	J3
Santa Lucia, range	D6
Santa Monica, bay	B11
Santa Monica, mts.	B10
Santa Monica Mts. N.R.A.	B10
Santa Rosa, island	E9
Santa Rosa and San Jacinto Mountains N.M.	J9
Santiago, river	F11
Sequoia Natl. Park	G6
Shasta, lake	C2
Shasta, mt.	C1

	Key
Sierra, peak	E11
Sierra Nevada, range	D3, G5
Siskiyou, mts.	B1
Smith River N.R.A.	B1
Tahoe, lake	E3
Tehachapi, mts.	G8
Telescope, peak	H6
Trinity, river	B2
Tule, river	F6
Turtle, mts.	L8
Upper, lake	E1
Upper San Leandro, reservoir	L2
Vizcaino, cape	B3
Whiskeytown-Shasta-Trinity N.R.A.	D1
White, mts.	G5
Whitney, mt.	G6
Wilson, mt.	D10
Yosemite Natl. Park	F5

Colorado ....page 133

Cities and Towns

	Key
Akron	G1
Alamosa	E4
Arvada	E2
Aspen	D2
Aurora	D2
Avon	D2
Bennett	F2
Berthoud	E1
Black Forest	F2
Boulder	E1
Breckenridge	D2
Brighton	F2
Broomfield	E2
Brush	G1
Buena Vista	D3
Burlington	H2
Canon City	E3
Carbondale	C2
Castle Rock	F2
Cedaredge	C3
Center	D4
Central City	E2
Cheyenne Wells	H3
Clifton	B2
Colorado Springs	F3
Conejos	D4
Cortez	B4
Craig	C1
Crawford	C3
Creede	D4
Cripple Creek	E3
Dacono	F1
Del Norte	D4
Delta	B3
Denver, capital	E2
Dinosaur	A1
Dove Creek	B4
Durango	C4
Eads	H3
Eagle	D2
Eaton	F1
Englewood	F2
Estes Park	E1
Evans	F1
Evergreen	E2
Fairplay	E2
Florence	E3
Fort Collins	E1
Fort Lupton	F1
Fort Morgan	G1
Fountain	F3
Frisco	D2
Fruita	B2
Fruitvale	B2
Georgetown	E2
Glenwood Springs	C2
Golden	E2
Grand Junction	B2
Greeley	F1
Gunnison	D3
Gypsum	D2
Haswell	G3
Hayden	C1
Holyoke	H1
Hot Sulphur Springs	D1
Hugo	G2
Idaho Springs	E2
Johnstown	F1
Julesburg	H1
Keota	F1
Kiowa	F2
Kit Carson	H3
Lafayette	E2
La Junta	G4
Lake City	C3
Lakewood	E2
Lamar	H3
Las Animas	G3
Leadville	D2
Limon	G2
Littleton	E2
Longmont	E1
Louisville	E2
Loveland	E1
Manitou Springs	F3
Meeker	C1
Milliken	F1
Monte Vista	D4
Montrose	C3
Niwot	E1
Northglenn	F2
Olathe	C3
Orchard City	B2
Orchard Mesa	B2
Ordway	G3
Ouray	C3
Pagosa Springs	C4
Palisade	B2
Palmer Lake	F2
Paonia	C3
Parker	F2
Platteville	F1
Pritchett	H4
Pueblo	F3
Pueblo West	F3
Rangely	B1
Rifle	C2
Rocky Ford	G3
Saguache	D3
Salida	E3
San Luis	E4
Security	F3
Silverthorne	D2
Silverton	C4
Snowmass Village	D2
Springfield	H4
Steamboat Springs	D1
Sterling	G1
Telluride	C4

	Key
Thornton	F2
Trinidad	F4
Vail	D2
Vilas	H4
Walden	D1
Walsenburg	F4
Wellington	E1
Westcliffe	E3
Westminster	E2
Wheat Ridge	E2
Wiley	H3
Windsor	F1
Woodland Park	E3
Wray	H1
Yuma	H1

Other Features

	Key
Animas, river	C4
Apishapa, river	F4
Arapahoe, peak	E1
Arapaho Natl. Rec. Area	E1
Arikaree, river	G2
Arkansas, river	F3
Bent's Old Fort Natl. Hist. Site	G3
Black Canyon of the Gunnison Natl. Park	C3
Blanca, peak	E4
Blue Mesa, reservoir	H2
Bonny, reservoir	C8
Canyons of the Ancients N.M.	B4
Castle, peak	D2
Colorado, plateau	A4
Colorado, river	C2
Colorado Natl. Monument	B2
Crestone, peak	E4
Cucharas, river	F4
Curecanti Natl. Rec. Area	C3
Dinosaur Natl. Monument	B1
Dolores, river	B3
Elbert, mt.	D2
Eolus, mt.	C4
Evans, mt.	E2
Florissant Fossil Beds N.M.	E3
Front, range	E1
Great Sand Dunes N.P.	E4
Green, river	B1
Gunnison, mt.	C3
Gunnison, river	B3
Hovenweep Natl. Monument	B4
John Martin, reservoir	G3
Laramie, mts.	E1
Laramie, river	E1
Little Snake, river	B1
Longs, peak	E1
Mancos, river	B4
Medicine Bow, mts.	D1
Mesa Verde Natl. Park	B4
Montezuma, peak	D4
North Fork Cimarron, river	H4
North Fork Smoky Hill, river	H2
North Platte, river	D1
Park, range	D1
Pikes, peak	E3
Purgatoire, river	G4
Rio Grande, river	E4
Roan, plateau	B2
Rocky, mts.	D1
Rocky Mt. Natl. Park	E1
Royal Gorge, canyon	E3
Sand Creek Massacre N.H.S.	H3
Sangre de Cristo, mts.	E3
San Juan, mts.	C4
San Luis, valley	E4
Sawatch, range	D3
South Fork Republican, river	G2
South Platte, river	E2, G1
Uncompahgre, peak	C3
U.S. Air Force Academy	F3
White, river	B1
Wilson, mt.	B4
Yampa, river	B1
Yucca House Natl. Monument	B4
Zirkel, mt.	D1

Connecticut ....page 134

Cities and Towns

	Key
Abington	G2
Andover	F3
Ansonia	C4
Attawaugan	H2
Avon	D2
Bakersville	C2
Ballouville	H2
Baltic	G3
Beacon Falls	C4
Berkshire	B4
Berlin	E3
Bethany	C4
Bethel	B4
Bethlehem	C3
Black Point	G4
Bloomfield	E2
Blue Hills	E2
Boardman Bridge	B3
Bolton	F2
Botsford	B4
Branford	D4
Bridgeport	C5
Bridgewater	B3
Bristol	D3
Broad Brook	F2
Brookfield	B4
Brookfield Center	B4
Brooklyn	H2
Burlington	D2
Burrville	C2
Cannondale	B5
Canterbury	H3
Canton	D2
Canton Center	D2
Centerbrook	F4
Central Village	H3
Chaplin	G2
Cheshire	D3
Chester	F4
Chesterfield	G4
Clarks Falls	H4
Clinton	E4
Colchester	F3
Colebrook	C2
Collinsville	D2
Columbia	F3
Cornwall	C2
Cornwall Bridge	B2
Coventry	F2
Cromwell	E3
Danbury	B4
Danielson	H2
Darien	B5
Dayville	H2

	Key
Deep River	F4
Derby	C4
Durham	E4
Eagleville	F2
East Brooklyn	H2
Eastford	H2
East Glastonbury	E3
East Granby	E2
East Haddam	F4
East Hampton	E3
East Hartford	E2
East Hartland	D2
East Haven	D4
East Killingly	H2
East Litchfield	C2
East Lyme	G4
Easton	B5
East Thompson	H1
East Village	F2
East Woodstock	H2
Ellington	E2
Enfield	E2
Essex	F4
Fairfield	B5
Falls Village	B2
Farmington	D3
Fitchman	G3
Flanders	B3
Franklin	G3
Gales Ferry	G4
Gaylordsville	B3
Georgetown	B5
Gilead	F3
Gilman	G3
Glasgo	H3
Glastonbury	E3
Goodrich Heights	E3
Goshen	C2
Granby	D2
Greenwich	A5
Grosvenor Dale	H2
Groton	G4
Groton Long Point	G4
Guilford	E4
Gurleyville	G2
Haddam	E4
Haddam Neck	E3
Hadlyme	F4
Hamburg	F4
Hamden	D4
Hampton	G2
Hanover	G3
Hartford, capital	E3
Harwinton	C3
Hawleyville	B4
Hazardville	E2
Hebron	F3
Higganum	E4
Hotchkissville	C3
Indian Neck	D5
Jewett City	H3
Kensington	D3
Killingworth	E4
Knollcrest	B4
Knollwood	B4
Lake Pocotopaug	E3
Lakeside	B3
Lakeside	C4
Laysville	F4
Lebanon	G3
Ledyard Center	G4
Liberty Hill	F3
Lime Rock	B2
Litchfield	C3
Lyons Plain	B5
Madison	E4
Manchester	E2
Mansfield Center	G3
Mansfield Four Corners	F2
Marble Dale	B3
Marion	D3
Meriden	D3
Merrow	F2
Middlebury	C3
Middlefield	E3
Middle Haddam	E3
Middletown	C5
Milford	C5
Mill Plain	A4
Milton	B2
Mohegan	G4
Monroe	C4
Montville	G4
Moosup	H3
Mystic	H4
Naugatuck	C4
New Britain	D3
New Canaan	B5
New Fairfield	B4
New Hartford	D2
New Haven	D4
Newington	E3
New London	G4
New Milford	B4
Newtown	B4
Niantic	G4
Noank	H4
Norfolk	C2
North Branford	D4
North Canton	D2
Northfield	C3
North Franklin	G3
North Grosvenor Dale	H2
North Guilford	E4
North Haven	D4
North Stonington	H4
Northville	B3
North Westchester	F3
North Windham	G3
Norwalk	B5
Norwich	G3
Oakdale	G4
Oakville	C3
Old Lyme	F4
Old Mystic	H4
Old Saybrook	F4
Oneco	H3
Orange	C4
Oxford	C4
Park Lane	B3
Pawcatuck	H4
Perkins Corner	F3
Phoenixville	G2
Plainfield	H3
Plainville	D3
Plantsville	D3
Pleasant Valley	D2
Pleasure Beach	G4
Plymouth	C3
Pomfret	H2
Poquetanuck	G4

	Key
Poquonock	E2
Poquonock Bridge	G4
Portland	E3
Preston City	H3
Prospect	D4
Putnam	H2
Quaddick	H2
Quaker Hill	G4
Redding	B4
Redding Ridge	B4
Ridgebury	A4
Ridgefield	B4
Riverton	C2
Robertsville	C2
Rockfall	E3
Rockville	F2
Rocky Hill	E3
Roxbury	B3
Sachem Head	E5
Salem	F4
Salisbury	B2
Scantic	E2
Scitico	E2
Scotland	G3
Seymour	C4
Sharon	B2
Shelton	C4
Sherman	B3
Short Beach	D5
Simsbury	D2
Somers	F2
Sound View	F4
Southbury	C4
South Canaan	B2
South Chaplin	G2
South Glastonbury	E3
Southington	D3
South Kent	B3
South Killingly	H2
South Willington	F2
South Windham	G3
South Windsor	E2
Stafford	F2
Stafford Springs	F2
Staffordville	F2
Stamford	A5
Sterling	H3
Stevenson	C4
Stony Creek	E4
Storrs	F2
Straitsville	C4
Stratford	C5
Suffield	E2
Taconic	B1
Talcottville	F2
Tariffville	D2
Terryville	C3
Thompson	H2
Thompsonville	E2
Tolland	F2
Torrington	C2
Trumbull	C5
Uncasville	G4
Union	G2
Unionville	D2
Vernon	F2
Versailles	F3
Voluntown	H3
Wallingford	D4
Warren	B3
Warrenville	G2
Washington	B3
Washington Depot	B3
Waterbury	C3
Waterford	G4
Watertown	C3
Weatogue	D2
Westbrook	F4
West Cornwall	B2
Westford	G2
West Granby	D2
West Hartford	E2
West Hartland	D1
West Haven	D4
West Mystic	H4
West Norfolk	C1
Weston	B5
Westport	B5
West Redding	B4
West Simsbury	D2
West Stafford	F2
West Suffield	E2
West Willington	F2
Wethersfield	E3
Whigville	D3
Willimantic	G3
Wilton	B5
Winchester Center	C2
Windham	G3
Windsor	E2
Windsor Locks	E2
Winsted	C2
Winthrop	F4
Wolcott	D3
Woodbridge	C4
Woodmont	D5
Woodstock	H2
Woodstock Valley	G2
Woodville	B3
Yalesville	D4

Other Features

	Key
Appalachian Natl. Scenic Trail	B2
Bantam, lake	C3
Barkhamsted, reservoir	D2
Candlewood, lake	B4
Connecticut, river	E4
Easton, reservoir	B4
Farmington, river	D3
Frissell, mt.	B1
Gaillard, lake	D4
Hammonasset, river	E4
Hop, river	F3
Housatonic, river	B4
Long Island, sound	D5
Mt. Hope, river	G2
Natchaug, river	G2
Naugatuck, river	C4
Nepaug, reservoir	D2
Norwalk, islands	B5
Norwalk, river	B5
Quinebaug, river	H3
Saugatuck, reservoir	B4
Shenipsit, lake	F2
Shetucket, river	G3
Thames, river	G4
Waramaug, lake	B3
Weir Farm Natl. Hist. Site	B5
Willimantic, river	F2
Yantic, river	G3

Delaware ....page 135

Cities and Towns

	Key
Adamsville	A3
Andrewville	A3
Argos Corner	A3
Blackbird	A2
Broadkill Beach	B3
Brookside	A1
Burrsville	A3
Camden	A2
Cannon	A3
Canterbury	A2
Capitol Park	A1
Clarksville	B3
Claymont	B1
Collins Park	A1
Delaware City	A1
Dover, capital	A2
Edgemoor	A1
Elsmere	A1
Fairfax	A1
Georgetown	A3
Glasgow	A1
Gumboro	B4
Harbeson	B3
Harrington	A3
Hartley	A2
Hazlettville	A3
Hickman	A3
Hockessin	A1
Indian Beach	B3
Jimtown	A3
Kirkwood	A1
Kitts Hummock	B2
Laurel	A4
Lewes	B3
Lincoln	B3
Little Heaven	B2
Llangollen Estates	A1
Lynch Heights	B3
McClellandville	A1
Marshallton	A1
Marydel	A2
Mastens Corner	A2
Middletown	A2
Midway	B3
Milford	B3
Millsboro	B3
Milton	B3
Nassau	B3
Newark	A1
New Castle	B1
Oak Orchard	B3
Owens	A3
Petersburg	A2
Pinetown	A3
Primehook Beach	B3
Reeves Crossing	A3
Rehoboth Beach	B3
Reliance	A3
Rosedale Beach	B3
Roxana	B3
Sandtown	A2
Seaford	A3
Selbyville	B4
Smyrna	B2
Stanton	A1
Swann Keys	B4
Talleyville	A1
Taylors Bridge	A2
Whitesville	B4
Williamsville	A3
Williamsville	B4
Wilmington	A1
Wilmington Manor	A1
Woodenhawk	A3
Woodland Beach	B2
Workmans Corners	B3

Other Features

	Key
Broadkill, river	B3
Chesapeake & Delaware, canal	A1
Delaware, bay	B2
Delaware, river	A1
Henlopen, cape	B3
Indian River, bay	B3
Mispillion, river	B3
Murderkill, river	A3
Nanticoke, river	A3
Rehoboth, bay	B3
Smyrna, river	A2

Florida ....page 136

Cities and Towns

	Key
Alachua	C2
Altamonte Springs	D3
Anna Maria	C4
Apalachicola	A2
Apollo Beach	C4
Apopka	D3
Arcadia	D4
Archer	C2
Astor	D2
Atlantic Beach	D1
Auburndale	D3
Aventura	B3
Avon Park	D4
Baldwin	D1
Bal Harbour	B3
Bartow	D4
Bay Harbor Islands	B3
Bayonet Point	C3
Bee Ridge	C4
Belle Glade	E5
Belleview	C2
Beverly Hills	C3
Big Pine Key	D7
Biscayne Park	A3
Blountstown	A1
Boca Raton	E5
Bonifay	C6
Bonita Springs	D5
Boynton Beach	E5
Bradenton	C4
Brandon	C4
Bristol	A1
Bronson	C2
Brooksville	C3
Buckhead Ridge	E4
Bunnell	D2
Bushnell	C3
Callaway	C6
Cape Canaveral	E3
Cape Coral	D5
Carol City	A3, E6
Chattahoochee	A1
Chiefland	C2
Chipley	C6
Clearwater	C4

	Key
Clermont	D3
Clewiston	E5
Cocoa	E3
Cocoa Beach	E3
Coconut Grove	A3
Cooper City	A3
Coral Gables	A3, E6
Coral Springs	E5
Crawfordville	A1
Crescent City	D2
Crestview	B6
Cross City	B2
Crystal River	C3
Dade City	C3
Dania	B2
Davie	A2, E5
Daytona Beach	D2
De Bary	D3
Deerfield Beach	E5
De Funiak Springs	B6
De Land	D2
Delray Beach	E5
Deltona	D3
Destin	B6
Dunedin	C3
Dunnellon	C2
East Naples	D5
Eastpoint	A2
Edgewater	E3
El Portal	A3
Elfers	C3
Englewood	D3
Eustis	D3
Fellsmere	E4
Fernandina Beach	D1
Flagler Beach	D2
Florida City	E6
Fort Lauderdale	B2, E5
Fort Meade	D4
Fort Myers	D5
Fort Myers Beach	D5
Fort Myers Villas	D5
Fort Pierce	E4
Fort Walton Beach	B6
Frostproof	D4
Gainesville	C2
Gifford	E4
Golden Gate	D5
Gonzalez	A6
Goulds	E6
Greenacres City	E5
Green Cove Springs	D2
Gretna	A1
Gulf Breeze	A6
Haines City	D3
Hallandale	B3, E6
Havana	A1
Hawthorne	D2
Hialeah	A3, E6
Hialeah Gardens	A3
High Springs	C2
Holiday	C3
Holly Hill	D2
Hollywood	A3, E5
Holmes Beach	C4
Homestead	E6
Homosassa Springs	C3
Hudson	C3
Immokalee	D5
Indian Harbour Beach	E3
Indian Rocks Beach	C4
Indiantown	E4
Inverness	C3
Jacksonville	D1
Jacksonville Beach	D1
Jasper	C1
Jensen Beach	E4
Jupiter	E5
Kendall	A4, E6
Key Biscayne	B4
Key Largo	E6
Keystone Heights	D2
Key West	D7
Kissimmee	D3
La Belle	D5
La Crosse	C2
Lady Lake	D3
Lake Buena Vista	D3
Lake Butler	C1
Lake City	C1
Lakeland	D3
Lake Mary	D3
Lake Panasoffkee	C3
Lake Wales	D4
Lake Worth	E5
Land O' Lakes	C3
Lantana	E5
Largo	C4
Lauderdale Lakes	A2
Lauderdale-by-the-Sea	B2
Lauderhill	A2
Lawtey	C1
Layton	E7
Leesburg	D3
Live Oak	C1
Longboat Key	C4
Lutz	C3
Lynn Haven	C6
Macclenny	C1
Madison	B1
Marathon	D7
Marco	D6
Margate	E5
Marianna	C6
Marineland	D2
Mayo	B1
Merritt Island	E3
Miami	A3, E6
Miami Beach	B3, E6
Miami Lakes	A3, A5
Miami Shores	A3, A5
Miami Springs	A3, A5
Middleburg	D1
Milton	A6
Mims	E3
Miramar	A3, E6
Monticello	B1
Moore Haven	D5
Mount Dora	D3
Naples	D5
Naples Manor	D5
Naples Park	D5
Naranja	E6
New Port Richey	C3
New Smyrna Beach	E2
Niceville	B6
Noma	B6
North Bay Village	A3
North Fort Myers	D5
North Miami	A3, E6
North Miami Beach	A3

	Key
North Naples	D5
North Port	C4
Oakland Park	B2, E5
Ocala	C2
Ocoee	D3
Okeechobee	E4
Oldsmar	C3
Olympia Hts.	A3
Opa-Locka	A3
Orange City	D3
Orange Park	D1
Orlando	D3
Ormond Beach	D2
Ormond-by-the-Sea	D2
Otter Creek	C2
Oviedo	D3
Pace	A6
Pahokee	E5
Palatka	D2
Palm Bay	E3
Palm Beach	E5
Palm Beach Gardens	E5
Palm Coast	D2
Palmetto	C4
Palm Harbor	C3
Panama City	C6
Pembroke Park	A3
Pembroke Pines	A3
Pennsuco	A3
Pensacola	A6
Perrine	E6
Perry	B1
Pierson	D2
Pine Castle	D3
Plantation	A2, E5
Plant City	C3
Polk City	D3
Pomona Park	D2
Port Charlotte	C5
Port Orange	E2
Port St. Joe	C7
Port St. Lucie	E4
Port Salerno	E4
Punta Gorda	C5
Quincy	A1
Raiford	C1
Ridge Manor	C3
Riverview	C4
Riviera Beach	E5
Rockledge	E3
Royal Palm Beach	E5
St. Augustine	D2
St. Augustine Shores	D2
St. Cloud	D3
St. Pete Beach	C4
St. Petersburg	C4
San Carlos Park	D5
Sanford	D3
Sanibel	C5
Sarasota	C4
Satellite Beach	E3
Sebastian	E4
Sebring	D4
Silver Springs	C2
Sneads	A1
South Miami	A3
South Venice	C4
Springfield	C6
Spring Hill	C3
Starke	C2
Stuart	E4
Sunrise	A2
Surfside	B3
Sweetwater	A3, E6
Tallahassee, capital	A1
Tamarac	A2, E5
Tampa	C4
Tarpon Springs	C3
Tavares	D3
Tavernier	E6
Temple Terrace	C3
Titusville	E3
Treasure Island	C4
Trenton	C2
Umatilla	D3
Venice	C4
Vero Beach	E4
Vilano Beach	D2
Virginia Gardens	A3
Warrington	A6
Wauchula	D4
Webster	C3
Weeki Wachee	C3
Welaka	D2
West Melbourne	E3
West Miami	A3
Weston	A2
West Palm Beach	E5
West Pensacola	A6
Westwood Lakes	A3
Wildwood	C3
Williston	C2
Wilton Manors	B2
Winter Garden	D3
Winter Haven	D3
Winter Park	D3
Woodville	A1
Yulee	D1
Zephyrhills	C3

Other Features

	Key
Amelia, island	D1
Apalachee, bay	A2
Apalachicola, bay	A2
Apalachicola, river	A1
Aucilla, river	B1
Big Cypress, swamp	D5
Biscayne, bay	B3, E6
Biscayne Natl. Park	E6
Boca Chica Key, island	D7
Caloosahatchee, river	D5
Canaveral, cape	E3
Canaveral Natl. Seashore	E3
Castillo de San Marcos N.M.	D2
Cedar Keys, islands	B2
Charlotte, harbor	C5
Chattahoochee, river	A1
Choctawhatchee, bay	B6
Crooked, island	C6
De Soto Natl. Memorial	C4
Deadman, bay	B2
Dog, island	A2
Dry Tortugas Natl. Park	C7
Elliott Key, island	E6
Escambia, river	A5
Everglades, swamp	A5, E6
Everglades Natl. Park	E6
Florida, bay	E6
Florida, straits	E7
Florida Keys, islands	D7
Fort Caroline Natl. Memorial	D1

	Key
Fort Matanzas Natl. Monument	D2
Gasparilla, island	C5
George, lake	D2
Gulf Islands Natl. Seashore	A6
Homosassa, bay	B6
Indian, river	D4
Iron, mt.	D4
Istokpoga, lake	D4
John F. Kennedy Space Center	E3
Key Biscayne, island	E6
Key Largo, island	E6
Kissimmee, lake	D4
Lochloosa, lake	D2
Marquesas Keys, islands	C7
Mexico, gulf	B5, B6
Ochlockonee, river	A1
Okeechobee, lake	D5
Okefenokee, swamp	C1
Peace, river	D4
Pensacola, bay	A6
Ponce de Leon, bay	D6
Romano, cape	D6
Sable, cape	D6
St. Andrews, bay	B6
St. George, island	A2
St. Johns, river	D2
St. Joseph, bay	C7
St. Marys, river	D1
St. Vincent, island	A2
San Blas, cape	C7
Sands Key, island	E6
Sanibel, island	C5
Santa Rosa, island	A6
Seminole, lake	A1
Sugarloaf Key, island	D7
Suwannee, river	C1, C2
Talquin, lake	A1
Tamiami, canal	A3
Tampa, bay	C4
Virginia Key, island	B3
Waccasassa, bay	C2
Withlacoochee, river	B1
Yellow, river	A6

Georgia ....page 137

Cities and Towns

	Key
Abbeville	E8
Adairsville	B3
Adel	E9
Alamo	F7
Albany	C8
Alma	G8
Alpharetta	C3
Americus	C7
Appling	G4
Arlington	B9
Ashburn	D8
Athens	E3
Atlanta, capital	C4, J3
Augusta	H5
Bainbridge	B10
Barnesville	C5
Baxley	G8
Belvedere	K3
Blackshear	G9
Blairsville	D2
Blakely	B9
Blue Ridge	C2
Boston	D10
Bremen	A4
Brookhaven	J2
Brunswick	H9
Buchanan	A4
Buena Vista	B7
Buford	C3
Butler	C6
Byron	D6
Cairo	C10
Calhoun	B2
Camilla	C9
Canton	C3
Carnesville	E3
Carrollton	A4
Cartersville	B3
Cedar Grove	J4
Cedartown	A3
Chamblee	J2
Chatsworth	B2
Clarkesville	E2
Clarkston	K2
Claxton	G7
Clayton	E2
Cleveland	D2
Cochran	E7
College Park	H3
Colquitt	B9
Columbus	B7
Commerce	E3
Conley	J4
Constitution	J4
Conyers	D4
Cordele	D8
Cornelia	E2
Covington	D4
Crawfordville	F4
Cumming	D3
Cusseta	B7
Cuthbert	B8
Dahlonega	D2
Dallas	B4
Dalton	B2
Danielsville	E3
Darien	H9
Dawson	C8
Dawsonville	D2
Decatur	K3
Donalsonville	B9
Doraville	K2
Douglas	F8
Douglasville	B4
Druid Hills	J3
Dublin	F6
Dunwoody	J2
Eastman	E7
East Point	C4, H3
Eatonton	E5
Elberton	F3
Ellaville	C7
Ellijay	C2
Evans	H2
Fair Oaks	H2
Fairview	K4
Fayetteville	C5
Fitzgerald	E8
Folkston	G10
Forest Park	J4
Forsyth	D5
Fort Gaines	A8
Fort Oglethorpe	A2
Fort Valley	D6

Key

Franklin ... A5
Gainesville ... D3
Garden City ... J7
Georgetown ... A8
Gibson ... F5
Gilmore ... H2
Glennville ... H8
Gordon ... E6
Gray ... D5
Greensboro ... E4
Greenville ... B5
Gresham Park ... J3
Griffin ... C5
Hahira ... E10
Hamilton ... B6
Hampton ... C5
Hapeville ... J3
Hartwell ... F3
Hawkinsville ... E7
Hazlehurst ... F8
Hephzibah ... G5
Hiawassee ... D2
Hinesville ... H8
Hogansville ... B5
Homer ... D3
Homerville ... F9
Irwinton ... E6
Jackson ... D5
Jasper ... C3
Jefferson ... E3
Jeffersonville ... E6
Jesup ... H8
Jonesboro ... C4
Kennesaw ... B3
Kingsland ... H10
Knoxville ... D6
La Fayette ... A2
La Grange ... A5
Lakeland ... E9
Lavonia ... E3
Lawrenceville ... D4
Leesburg ... C8
Lexington ... E4
Lincolnton ... G4
Locust Grove ... C5
Louisville ... G5
Ludowici ... H8
Lumber City ... F8
Lumpkin ... B7
Lyons ... G7
Mableton ... B4, G2
McDonough ... C5
McIntyre ... E6
Macon ... D6
McRae ... F7
Madison ... E4
Manchester ... B6
Marietta ... B4, H1
Marshallville ... D7
Metter ... G7
Milledgeville ... E5
Millen ... H6
Monroe ... D4
Monticello ... D5
Morgan ... B8
Moultrie ... D9
Mount Vernon ... F7
Mt. Bethel ... J1
Nashville ... E9
Newnan ... C9
Newton ... C9
Oakdale ... H2
Ocilla ... E8
Oglethorpe ... C7
Panthersville ... K3
Peachtree City ... B5
Pearson ... F9
Pembroke ... H7
Perry ... D7
Pooler ... J7
Powder Springs ... B4
Preston ... B7
Quitman ... E10
Red Oak ... H4
Reidsville ... G7
Richland ... B7
Richmond Hill ... J8
Rincon ... J7
Ringgold ... A2
Riverdale ... J4
Rochelle ... E8
Rockmart ... A3
Rome ... A3
Roswell ... C3
Royston ... E3
Sandersville ... F6
Sandy Springs ... J2
Savannah ... J7
Scottdale ... K3
Skyland ... J2
Smyrna ... H2
Snellville ... D4
Social Circle ... D4
Soperton ... F7
Sparta ... F5
Springfield ... H10
St. Marys ... H10
St. Simons Island ... J9
Statenville ... E10
Statesboro ... H7
Statham ... D4
Stone Mountain ... C4
Summerville ... A3
Swainsboro ... G6
Sylvania ... H6
Sylvester ... D8
Talbotton ... B6
Tennille ... F6
Thomaston ... C6
Thomasville ... D10
Thomson ... G5
Tifton ... E9
Toccoa ... E2
Toco Hills ... J2
Trenton ... A2
Trion ... A2
Tucker ... K2
Tybee Island ... K8
Unadilla ... D7
Union City ... B4, H4
Union Point ... E4
Valdosta ... E10
Vienna ... D7
Villa Rica ... B4
Wadley ... G6
Warner Robins ... D6
Warrenton ... F5
Washington ... F4
Watkinsville ... E4
Waycross ... G9
Waynesboro ... G5

Key

Westoak ... H1
Winder ... D4
Woodbine ... H10
Wrens ... G5
Wrightsville ... F6
Zebulon ... C5

Other Features

Alapaha, river ... E9
Allatoona, lake ... B3
Altamaha, river ... G8
Appalachian, mts. ... D2
Blackshear, lake ... D8
Blue, ridge ... C2
Brasstown Bald, mt. ... D2
Burton, lake ... D2
Carters, lake ... B2
Chattahoochee, river ... A5, A9, G3
Chattahoochee River N.R.A. ... J1
Chattooga, river ... E2
Chatuge, lake ... D1
Chickamauga and Chattanooga Natl. Military Park ... A2
Coosa, river ... D2
Cumberland, island ... J10
Cumberland Island Natl. Seashore ... J10
Ed Jenkins Natl. Rec. Area ... C2
Etowah, river ... B3
Flint, river ... C9
Fort Frederica Natl. Monument ... J9
Fort Pulaski Natl. Monument ... K7
Hartwell, lake ... F2
Jackson, lake ... D5
Jekyll, island ... J9
Jimmy Carter Natl. Hist. Site ... C7
J. Strom Thurmond, lake ... G4
Lookout Mt., ridge ... A2
Martin Luther King Jr. N.H.S. ... J3
Ocmulgee Natl. Monument ... D6
Ochlockonee, river ... C10
Ocmulge, river ... E7
Oconee, lake ... E5
Oconee, river ... F6
Ogeechee, river ... F5
Ohoopee, river ... G7
Okefenokee, swamp ... G10
Ossabaw, island ... J8
Russell, lake ... F3
St. Catherines, island ... J8
St. Marys, river ... H10
St. Simons, island ... J9
Sapelo, island ... J9
Savannah, river ... H5
Seminole, lake ... B10
Sidney Lanier, lake ... C3
Sinclair, lake ... E5
Stone Mt. State Park ... C4
Suwannee, river ... F10
Tallapoosa, river ... A4
Tybee, island ... K7
Walter F. George, reservoir ... A8
Wassaw, island ... J8
Weiss, lake ... A3
West Point, lake ... A6
Withlacoochee, river ... E10

Hawaii ... page 138

Cities and Towns

Ahuimanu ... J2
Aiea ... F1, J2
Captain Cook ... G6
Crestview ... E1, J2
Eleele ... C2
Ewa ... D2, J2
Ewa Beach ... E2, J3
Foster Village ... F1, J2
Halawa ... B3
Halawa Heights ... F1, J2
Haleiwa ... H1
Hana ... D4
Hanamaulu ... D1
Hanapepe ... C2
Hauula ... H1
Heeia ... G1, K2
Hilo ... E7, J5
Holualoa ... G5
Honalo ... G5
Honokaa ... H4
Honolulu, capital ... C5, F2, J2
Iroquois Point ... E2, J2
Kaanapali ... B3
Kahana ... B3, J1
Kahului ... C3, D6
Kailua ... C5, K2
Kailua-Kona ... D7, G5
Kalaheo ... C2
Kalaoa ... F5
Kalaupapa ... B3
Kaneohe ... C5, G1, K2
Kapaa ... A5, D1
Kaunakakai ... J5
Keaau ... J5
Kealakekua ... G5
Kealia ... D1, G6
Kekaha ... B2
Kihei ... C4, D6
Kilauea ... C1
Koloa ... C2
Kualapuu ... A3
Kula ... C5
Lahaina ... B3, D6
Laie ... C5, J1
Lanai City ... B3
Lawai ... C2
Lihue ... A5, D2
Maili ... H2
Makaha ... H2
Makakilo City ... H2
Makawao ... C3
Maunawili ... K2
Mililani Town ... J2
Mokuleia ... H1
Mountain View ... J5
Nanakuli ... B5, H2
Pacific Palisades ... E1, J2
Pahala ... H6
Papaikou ... J5
Pearl City ... C5, E1, J2
Pepeekeo ... J5
Pohakupu ... K2
Pukalani ... C3, D6
Pupukea ... J1
Volcano ... J6
Waialua ... B3, H1
Waianae ... B5, H2
Waihee ... C3
Waikiki ... G3
Waikoloa Village ... G4

Key

Wailua ... C3, D1
Wailuku ... C3, D6
Waimalu ... E1, J2
Waimanalo ... K2
Waimanalo Beach ... K2
Waimea ... C2, D6, H1
Waipahu ... E1, J2
Waipio ... H4
Waipio Acres ... J2
Whitmore Village ... J2

Other Features

Alenuihaha, channel ... D6
Alika Cone, mt. ... G6
Diamond Head, point ... G3
Ford, channel ... E1
Haleakala Natl. Park ... C4, D6
Hamakua, coast ... H4
Hawaii, island ... E6, G5
Hawaii Volcanoes Natl. Park ... E7, H6
Hilo, bay ... J5
Hualalai, mt. ... G5
Kaala, mt. ... G2
Kaena, point ... B5, H1
Kahoolawe, island ... B4, D6
Kahului, bay ... C3
Kaikipauula, mt. ... H4
Kailua, bay ... K2
Kaiwi, channel ... C5, K3
Ka Lae (South Cape), cape ... D7, G7
Kalalua, mt. ... J6
Kalaupapa, peninsula ... B3
Kalaupapa Natl. Hist. Park ... B3
Kaloko-Honokohau Natl. Hist. Park ... F5
Kamakou, mt. ... B3
Kau, desert ... H6
Kauai, channel ... B5, D2
Kauai, island ... A5, B1
Kaulakahi, channel ... A5, B1
Kawaikini, mt. ... C1
Kiholo, bay ... G4
Kilauea, crater ... J6
Kilohana, crater ... C2
Kinau, cape ... C4
Kipuka Puaulu, mt. ... H6
Kohala, coast ... F5
Kohala, mt. ... G4
Kohala, mts. ... G4
Kona, coast ... G6
Konahuanui, mt. ... G2, K2
Koolau Range, mts. ... F1, J1
Kulani, mt. ... H5
Lanai, island ... B3, C6
Lehua, island ... A1
Lua Makika, mt. ... B4
Maalaea, bay ... C4
Makalena, mts. ... H4
Makapuu, point ... C5, K2
Mamala, bay ... E2, J3
Maui, island ... C3, D6
Mauna Iki, mt. ... H6
Mauna Kea, mt. ... E6, H5
Mauna Loa, mt. ... D7, H6
Maunalua, bay ... K3
Mokolii, island ... J2
Mokuauia, island ... J1
Mokulua, island ... K2
Moku Manu, island ... K2
Molokai, island ... A3, C5
Molokini, island ... C4
Na Pali, coast ... B1
Niihau, island ... A2, A5
Oahu, island ... B5, D2, K1
Pearl, harbor ... E2
Punchbowl, crater ... G2
Pu'uhonua O Honaunau N.H.P. ... G6
Puu Kainapuaa, mt. ... J1
Puu Kaua, mt. ... H2
Puukohola Heiau Natl. Hist. Site ... G4
Puu Kukui, mt. ... B3
Puu Kulua, mt. ... H5
Puu Loa, mt. ... H5
Puu O Keokeo, mt. ... G6
Puu Ulaula, mt. ... C4
Sand, island ... F2
Sulphur Cone, mt. ... G6
U.S.S. Arizona Memorial ... E1
Upolu, point ... D6, G3
Waialeale, mt. ... A5, C1
Waianae Range, mts. ... H1
Wailuku, river ... H5
Waimea, canyon ... C2
West Maui, mts. ... B3

Idaho ... page 139

Cities and Towns

Aberdeen ... E7
American Falls ... E7
Ammon ... F6
Arco ... D6
Banks ... A5
Bellevue ... C6
Bennington ... F7
Blackfoot ... E6
Boise, capital ... A6
Bonners Ferry ... A1
Buhl ... C7
Burley ... D7
Caldwell ... A6
Cascade ... A5
Challis ... C5
Chubbuck ... E7
Coeur d'Alene ... A2
Council ... A5
Driggs ... F6
Dubois ... E5
Eagle ... A6
Emmett ... A6
Fairfield ... C6
Filer ... C7
Fish Haven ... F7
Fruitland ... A6
Fruitvale ... A5
Garden City ... A6
Garden Valley ... B5
Glenns Ferry ... B7
Gooding ... C7
Grangeville ... A4
Hailey ... C6
Hayden ... A2
Idaho City ... B6
Idaho Falls ... E6
Jerome ... C7
Kamiah ... A3
Kellogg ... A2
Ketchum ... C6
Kuna ... A6
Laclede ... A1
Lewiston ... A3

Key

McCall ... A5
Malad City ... E7
May ... D5
Middleton ... A6
Montpelier ... F7
Moscow ... A3
Mountain Home ... B6
Murphy ... A6
Nampa ... A6
New Plymouth ... A6
Nezperce ... A3
Orofino ... A3
Osburn ... A2
Paris ... F7
Parma ... A6
Patterson ... D5
Pauline ... E7
Payette ... A5
Pinehurst ... A2
Pocatello ... E7
Post Falls ... A2
Preston ... F7
Priest River ... A1
Rathdrum ... A2
Rexburg ... F6
Rigby ... F6
Rupert ... D7
St. Anthony ... F6
St. Maries ... A2
Salmon ... D4
Sandpoint ... A1
Shelley ... E6
Shoshone ... C7
Soda Springs ... F7
Sugar City ... F6
Sun Valley ... C6
Thatcher ... F7
Twin Falls ... C7
Wallace ... B2
Weiser ... A5
Wendell ... C7

Other Features

American Falls, reservoir ... E7
Bear, lake ... F7
Bear, river ... F7
Big Lost, river ... D6
Bitterroot, range ... B3, D4
Blackfoot, reservoir ... F7
Blackfoot, river ... F6
Bruneau, river ... B7
Cache, mt. ... D7
Caribou, range ... F6
Cascade, reservoir ... A5
Castle, mt. ... C5
Clearwater, mts. ... B3
Clearwater, river ... B3
Craters of the Moon N.M. ... D6
Dworshak, reservoir ... A3
Grays, lake ... F6
Hagerman Fossil Beds N.M. ... C7
Hells, canyon ... A4
Hells Canyon Natl. Recreation Area ... A4
Kootenai, river ... A1
Lemhi, river ... D5
Lochsa, river ... B3
Middle Fork Salmon, river ... C5
Minidoka Interment Natl. Mon. ... C7
Nez Perce N.H.P. ... A3, B3
North Fork Clearwater, river ... B3
Owyhee, mts. ... A6
Owyhee, river ... A6
Palisades, reservoir ... F6
Payette, lake ... A5
Payette, river ... A5
Pend Oreille, lake ... A1
Pend Oreille, river ... A1
Priest, lake ... A1
Ryan, mt. ... C6
St. Joe, river ... A2
Salmon, river ... B4
Salmon River, mts. ... C5
Sawtooth, range ... B5
Sawtooth Natl. Recreation Area ... C5
Scott, mt. ... E5
Snake, river ... A4
South Fork Selway, river ... B3
Teton, river ... F6
Weiser, river ... A5
Yellowstone Natl. Park ... F5

Illinois ... page 140

Cities and Towns

Abingdon ... C3
Addison ... B5
Albion ... E5
Alsip ... B6
Altamont ... E4
Alton ... C5
Amboy ... D2
Anna ... D6
Antioch ... A4, E1
Arcola ... E4
Arlington Heights ... A5
Arthur ... E4
Ashland ... C4
Athens ... D4
Atlanta ... D3
Atwood ... E4
Auburn ... D4
Aurora ... E2
Barrington ... A5
Bartlett ... A5
Bartonville ... D3
Batavia ... A5
Beach Park ... B4
Beardstown ... C3
Beecher ... F2
Belleville ... D5
Belvidere ... E1
Bement ... E4
Benld ... D4
Benton ... E6
Berwyn ... B6
Bethany ... E4
Bloomington ... D3
Blue Island ... B6
Bolingbrook ... A6, E2
Bourbonnais ... E2
Braidwood ... E2
Breese ... D5
Bridgeport ... F5
Brighton ... C4
Brookfield ... B6
Buffalo Grove ... B5
Bunker Hill ... D4
Burbank ... B6
Bushnell ... C3

Key

Byron ... D1
Cahokia ... C5
Cairo ... D7
Calumet City ... C6, F2
Cambridge ... C2
Canton ... C3
Capron ... E1
Carbondale ... D6
Carlinville ... D4
Carlyle ... D5
Carmi ... E5
Carol Stream ... A5
Carpentersville ... E1
Carrier Mills ... E6
Carrollton ... C4
Carterville ... D6
Carthage ... B3
Cary ... E1
Casey ... F4
Catlin ... F3
Centralia ... D5
Cerro Gordo ... E4
Champaign ... E3
Channahon ... E2
Charleston ... E4
Chatham ... D4
Chenoa ... E3
Chester ... D6
Chicago ... B5, F2
Chicago Heights ... B6
Chillicothe ... D3
Christopher ... D6
Cicero ... B6, F2
Clifton ... F3
Clinton ... E3
Coal City ... E2
Colchester ... C3
Collinsville ... D5
Columbia ... C5
Crest Hill ... A6
Crete ... F2
Crystal Lake ... E1
Cuba ... C3
Danville ... F3
Decatur ... D4
Deerfield ... B5
De Kalb ... E2
Delavan ... D3
De Soto ... D6
Des Plaines ... B5
Dixon ... D2
Dolton ... B6
Downers Grove ... B6
Du Quoin ... D5
Dwight ... E2
Earlville ... D2
East Dubuque ... C1
East Moline ... C2
East Peoria ... D3
East St. Louis ... C5
Edwardsville ... D5
Effingham ... E4
Elburn ... E2
Eldorado ... E6
Elgin ... E1
Elizabethtown ... E6
Elk Grove Village ... B5
Elmhurst ... B5
Elmwood ... D3
Elmwood Park ... B5
Erie ... C2
Eureka ... D3
Evanston ... B5, F1
Evergreen Park ... B6
Fairbury ... E3
Fairfield ... E5
Farmer City ... E3
Farmington ... D3
Fisher ... E3
Flora ... E5
Forrest ... E3
Forsyth ... D4
Fox Lake ... A4, E1
Fox Lake Hills ... A4
Fox River Grove ... A5
Frankfort ... B6, F2
Freeburg ... D5
Freeport ... D1
Fulton ... C2
Gages Lake ... B4
Galena ... C1
Galesburg ... C3
Galva ... C2
Geneseo ... C2
Geneva ... E2
Genoa ... E1
Georgetown ... F3
Gibson City ... E3
Gillespie ... D4
Gilman ... F3
Girard ... D4
Glen Ellyn ... A5
Glencoe ... B5
Glenwood ... B6
Godfrey ... C5
Golconda ... E6
Granite City ... C5
Granville ... D2
Grayslake ... A4
Grayville ... E5
Green Oaks ... B4
Greenup ... E4
Greenville ... D5
Gridley ... E3
Gurnee ... B4
Hainesville ... A4
Hamilton ... B3
Hampshire ... E1
Hanover Park ... A5
Hardin ... C4
Harrisburg ... E6
Harristown ... D4
Harvard ... E1
Harvey ... B6
Havana ... C3
Hennepin ... D2
Henry ... D2
Herrin ... D6
Herscher ... E2
Heyworth ... D3
Hickory Hills ... B6
Highland ... D5
Highland Park ... B5, F1
Highwood ... B5
Hillsboro ... D4
Hinckley ... E2
Hinsdale ... B6
Hoffman Estates ... A5
Homer ... F3
Homewood ... B6

Key

Hoopeston ... F3
Huntley ... E1
Island Lake ... A5
Jacksonville ... C4
Jerseyville ... C4
Johnston City ... E6
Joliet ... A6, E2
Jonesboro ... D6
Justice ... B6
Kankakee ... F2
Kaskaskia ... C6
Kewanee ... D2
Kincaid ... D4
Knoxville ... C3
Lacon ... D2
La Grange ... B6
La Harpe ... C3
Lake Bluff ... B5
Lake Forest ... B5
Lake Zurich ... A5
Lanark ... D1
La Salle ... D2
Lansing ... B6
Lawrenceville ... F5
Lemont ... B6
Lena ... D1
Le Roy ... E3
Lewistown ... C3
Lexington ... E3
Libertyville ... B5
Lilymoor ... A4
Lincoln ... D3
Lincolnwood ... B5
Lindenhurst ... A4
Lisle ... A6
Litchfield ... D4
Lockport ... A6
Lombard ... B6
Louisville ... E5
Loves Park ... D1
Lynwood ... C6
McHenry ... E1
Machesney Park ... D1
Mackinaw ... D3
McLeansboro ... E5
Macomb ... C3
Macon ... E4
Mahomet ... E3
Manhattan ... F2
Manito ... D3
Manteno ... E2
Marengo ... E1
Marion ... E6
Marissa ... D5
Marley ... B6
Maroa ... E3
Marseilles ... E2
Marshall ... F4
Mascoutah ... D5
Mason City ... D3
Matteson ... B6
Mattoon ... E4
Maywood ... B5
Melrose Park ... B5
Mendota ... D2
Metamora ... D3
Metropolis ... E6
Milan ... C2
Milford ... F3
Minonk ... D3
Minooka ... E2
Mokena ... B6
Moline ... C2
Momence ... F2
Monmouth ... C3
Monticello ... E3
Morris ... E2
Morrison ... D2
Morton ... D3
Morton Grove ... B5
Mound City ... D6
Mounds ... D6
Mount Carmel ... F5
Mount Carroll ... D1
Mount Morris ... D1
Mount Olive ... D4
Mount Prospect ... B5
Mount Pulaski ... D3
Mount Sterling ... C4
Mount Vernon ... E5
Mount Zion ... E4
Mowequa ... D4
Mundelein ... A5
Murphysboro ... D6
Naperville ... A6
Nashville ... D5
Neoga ... E4
New Athens ... D5
New Baden ... D5
New Lenox ... B6
Newton ... E5
Niles ... B5
Nokomis ... D4
Normal ... D3
Norridge ... B5
Northbrook ... B5
North Chicago ... B4, F1
Northfield ... B5
Oak Brook ... B6
Oak Forest ... B6
Oak Lawn ... B6, F2
Oak Park ... B5, F2
Oakwood ... F3
Oblong ... F4
O'Fallon ... D5
Oglesby ... D2
Okawville ... D5
Old Mill Creek ... B4
Olney ... E5
Onarga ... F3
Oquawka ... C3
Oregon ... D1
Orion ... C2
Orland Hills ... B6
Orland Park ... B6
Ottawa ... E2
Palatine ... A5
Palestine ... F4
Palos Heights ... B6
Palos Hills ... B6
Pana ... D4
Paris ... F4
Park City ... B4
Park Forest ... B6
Park Ridge ... B5
Pawnee ... D4
Paxton ... E3
Pecatonica ... D1
Pekin ... D3
Peoria ... D3
Peoria Heights ... D3
Peotone ... F2

	Key
Peru	D2
Petersburg	D4
Pinckneyville	D5
Pittsfield	C4
Plainfield	A6, E2
Plano	E2
Polo	D2
Pontiac	E3
Princeton	D3
Princeville	D3
Prophetstown	D2
Quincy	B4
Rantoul	E3
Red Bud	D5
Richton Park	B6
Riverdale	B6
Riverton	D4
Riverwoods	B5
Roanoke	D3
Robinson	F4
Rochelle	D2
Rochester	D4
Rock Falls	D2
Rock Island	C2
Rockford	D1
Rockton	D1
Rome	D3
Romeoville	A6
Roodhouse	C4
Roscoe	D1
Rosiclare	E6
Rossville	F3
Round Lake Beach	A4
Rushville	C3
Russell	B4
St. David	C3
St. Elmo	E4
St. Joseph	E3
St. Libory	D5
Salem	E5
Sandoval	D5
Sandwich	E2
Sauk Village	C6
Savanna	C1
Savoy	E3
Schaumburg	A5
Schiller Park	B5
Seneca	E2
Sesser	D5
Shawneetown	E6
Shelbyville	E4
Sheridan	E2
Sherman	D4
Shorewood	A6, E2
Skokie	B5
Somonauk	E2
South Beloit	D1
South Elgin	A5
South Holland	B6
South Jacksonville	C4
Sparta	D5
Spring Valley	D2
Springfield, capital	D4
Staunton	D4
Steeleville	D5
Sterling	D2
Stockland	F3
Stockton	C1
Streamwood	A5
Streator	E2
Sullivan	E4
Summit	B6
Sycamore	E2
Taylorville	D4
Teutopolis	E4
Tilton	F3
Tinley Park	B6, F2
Toledo	E4
Tolono	E4
Toluca	D3
Toulon	D2
Tower Lakes	A5
Tremont	D3
Trenton	D5
Tuscola	E4
Urbana	E3
Vandalia	D5
Vernon Hills	B5
Vienna	E6
Villa Grove	E4
Villa Park	B5
Virden	D4
Virginia	C4
Volo	A4
Wadsworth	B4
Walnut	D2
Wapella	E3
Warren	D1
Warrensburg	D4
Warrenville	A6
Warsaw	B3
Washington	D3
Waterloo	C5
Watseka	F3
Wauconda	A5
Waukegan	B4, F1
Waverly	D4
Westchester	B6
West Chicago	A5
West Frankfort	E6
Westville	F3
Wheaton	A6, E2
Wheeling	B5, F1
White Hall	C4
Wilmette	B5
Wilmington	B5
Winchester	C4
Winnebago	D1
Winnetka	B5
Winthrop Harbor	B4
Woodridge	A6
Wood River	C5
Woodstock	E1
Wyoming	D2
Yorkville	E2
Zeigler	D6
Zion	B4, F1

Other Features

	Key
Carlyle, lake	D5
Chautauqua, lake	C3
Chicago, river	B5
Clinton, lake	E3
Crab Orchard, lake	D6
Des Plaines, river	A6, B4
Du Page, river	A6
Fox, lake	A4
Fox, river	A4
Illinois, river	D3
Ind. Dunes Natl. Lakeshore	C6
Kankakee, river	E2
Kaskaskia, river	E4

	Key
Lincoln Home Natl. Hist. Site	D4
Marie, lake	A4
Michigan, lake	F1
O'Hare, airport	B5
Ohio, river	D6
Orland, lake	B6
Rend, lake	D5
Rock, river	D2
Sangamon, river	C3
Shelbyville, lake	E4
Spoon, river	C3
Wabash, river	E6

Indiana ....page 141

Cities and Towns

	Key
Albany	F4
Albion	F2
Alexandria	E4
Anderson	E4
Angola	G1
Arcadia	D4
Argos	D2
Atlanta	D4
Attica	B4
Auburn	F2
Aurora	G6
Austin	E7
Avila	F2
Bargersville	D5
Batesville	F5
Bedford	D7
Berne	G3
Bicknell	B7
Bloomfield	C6
Bloomington	C6
Bluffton	F3
Boonville	B8
Bourbon	D2
Brazil	B5
Bremen	D2
Brookston	C3
Brookville	F6
Brownsburg	D5
Brownstown	D7
Butler	G2
Cambridge City	F5
Cannelton	C9
Carmel	D5
Chandler	B8
Charlestown	E8
Chesterton	B1
Churubusco	F2
Cicero	D4
Clayton	C5
Clinton	B5
Cloverdale	C5
Columbia City	E2
Columbus	E6
Connersville	F5
Corydon	D8
Covington	B4
Crawfordsville	C4
Crothersville	E7
Crown Point	B2
Culver	D2
Dale	C8
Daleville	E4
Danville	C5
Darmstadt	A8
Decatur	G3
Delphi	C3
Demotte	B2
Dunlap	E1
East Chicago	B1
Eaton	F4
Edinburgh	E6
Elkhart	E1
Ellettsville	C6
Elwood	E4
English	D8
Evansville	A9
Fairmount	E4
Farmland	F4
Ferdinand	C8
Fishers	D5
Flora	C3
Fort Branch	A8
Fort Wayne	F2
Fowler	B3
Frankfort	C4
Franklin	D6
Fremont	G1
French Lick	C7
Galveston	D3
Garrett	F2
Gary	B1
Gas City	E4
Geneva	G3
Georgetown	E8
Goshen	E1
Greencastle	C5
Greenfield	E5
Greensburg	F6
Greentown	E4
Greenwood	D5
Hagerstown	F5
Hammond	A1
Hanover	F7
Hartford City	F4
Hebron	B2
Highland	B1
Hope	E6
Huntertown	F2
Huntingburg	C8
Huntington	F3
Indianapolis, capital	D5
Jasonville	B6
Jasper	C8
Jeffersonville	E8
Kendallville	F2
Kentland	B3
Kingsford Heights	C2
Knox	C2
Kokomo	D3
Kouts	B2
Lafayette	C4
Lagrange	F1
Lakeville	D1
La Porte	C1
Lawrence	D5
Lawrenceburg	G6
Lebanon	D4
Ligonier	E2
Liberty	G5
Lincoln City	B8
Linton	B6
Logansport	D3
Loogootee	C7
Lowell	B2
Madison	F7

	Key
Marion	E3
Martinsville	D6
Merrillville	B2
Michigan City	C1
Middlebury	E1
Milan	F6
Milford	E1
Mishawaka	D1
Mitchell	D7
Monon	C3
Monticello	C3
Montpelier	F3
Mooresville	D5
Mount Vernon	A9
Mulberry	C4
Muncie	F4
Nappanee	D2
Nashville	D6
New Albany	E8
Newburgh	B9
New Carlisle	C1
New Castle	F5
New Haven	F2
Newport	B5
New Whiteland	D5
Noblesville	D4
North Judson	C2
North Liberty	D1
North Manchester	E2
North Terre Haute	B5
North Vernon	E6
Notre Dame	D1
Oakland City	B8
Odon	C7
Orleans	D7
Osgood	F6
Ossian	F3
Otterbein	B3
Oxford	B3
Paoli	D7
Pendleton	E4
Peru	D3
Petersburg	B8
Plainfield	D5
Plymouth	D2
Portland	G4
Princeton	A8
Redkey	F4
Rensselaer	B3
Richmond	G5
Rising Sun	G7
Rochester	D2
Rockport	B9
Rockville	B5
Rushville	F5
Salem	D7
Schererville	B2
Scottsburg	E7
Sellersburg	E8
Seymour	E7
Shadeland	C4
Shelbyville	E5
Sheridan	D4
Shoals	C7
South Bend	D1
South Whitley	E2
Speedway	D5
Spencer	C6
Sullivan	B6
Syracuse	E2
Tell City	C9
Terre Haute	B6
Thorntown	C4
Tippecanoe	D2
Tipton	D4
Union City	G4
Upland	F4
Valparaiso	C2
Veedersburg	B4
Vernon	E6
Versailles	F6
Vevay	F7
Vincennes	A7
Wabash	E3
Wakarusa	E1
Walkerton	D2
Warsaw	E2
Washington	B7
Waterloo	F1
Westfield	D4
West Lafayette	C4
Westport	E6
Westville	C1
Williamsport	B4
Winamac	C2
Winchester	G4
Winona Lake	E2
Woodburn	G2
Worthington	C6
Yorktown	F4
Zionsville	D5

Other Features

	Key
Big Blue, river	E5
Brookville, lake	F5
Eel, river	F2
George Rogers Clark N.H.P.	A7
Indiana Dunes Natl. Lakeshore	B1
Kankakee, river	C2
Lemon, lake	D6
Lincoln Boyhood Natl. Memorial	C8
Maumee, river	G2
Michigan, lake	B1
Mississinewa, lake	E3
Monroe, lake	D6
Ohio, river	A9
Patoka, lake	B8
St. Joseph, river	G2
Salamoni, river	F3
Tippecanoe, river	C2
Wabash, river	A8
Wawasee, lake	E2
White, river	C6
Whitewater, river	F6

Iowa ....page 142

Cities and Towns

	Key
Ackley	H2
Adel	F4
Akron	A2
Albia	J5
Algona	F1
Allison	J2
Alta	D2
Altoona	H4
Ames	G3
Anamosa	M3
Ankeny	N3
Atlantic	D5

	Key
Audubon	E4
Avoca	D5
Batavia	K5
Bayard	E4
Bedford	E6
Belle Plaine	K4
Bellevue	P3
Belmond	G2
Bettendorf	P4
Bloomfield	K6
Boone	G3
Brighton	L5
Britt	G1
Brooklyn	K4
Burlington	M6
Camanche	P4
Carlisle	G5
Carroll	E3
Carter Lake	C5
Cascade	N3
Cedar Falls	K3
Cedar Rapids	L4
Center Point	L3
Centerville	J6
Chariton	H5
Charles City	J1
Cherokee	C2
Clarinda	D6
Clarion	G2
Clarksville	J2
Clear Lake	H1
Clinton	P4
Colfax	H4
Columbus Junction	M5
Coon Rapids	E4
Coralville	L4
Corning	E6
Corydon	H6
Council Bluffs	C5
Cresco	K1
Creston	F5
Dakota City	F2
Dallas Center	G4
Davenport	N4
Decorah	L1
Denison	D4
Denver	K2
Des Moines, captial	G4
De Witt	N4
Dubuque	N2
Dunlap	C4
Durant	N4
Dyersville	M3
Eagle Grove	G2
Eldora	H3
Eldridge	N4
Elgin	L2
Elkader	M2
Emmetsburg	E1
Epworth	N3
Estherville	E1
Evansdale	K3
Fairfield	L6
Farley	M3
Fayette	L2
Forest City	G1
Fort Dodge	F2
Fort Madison	M6
Garner	G1
Gilmore City	F2
Glenwood	C5
Greenfield	F5
Grimes	G4
Grinnell	J4
Grundy Center	J3
Guthrie Center	E4
Guttenberg	M2
Hampton	H2
Harlan	D4
Hartley	D1
Hawarden	B1
Hiawatha	L3
Holstein	C3
Hudson	K3
Hull	B1
Humboldt	F2
Huxley	G4
Ida Grove	D3
Independence	M3
Indianola	G5
Iowa City	L4
Iowa Falls	H2
Jefferson	F4
Jesup	K3
Johnston	G4
Kalona	L5
Keokuk	M7
Keosauqua	L6
Knoxville	H5
Lake City	E3
Lake Mills	G1
Lake View	D3
Lamoni	G6
La Porte City	K3
Laurens	E2
Le Claire	P4
Le Mars	B2
Lenox	E6
Leon	G6
Logan	C4
Lovilia	J5
Madrid	G3
Manchester	M3
Manly	H1
Manning	E4
Manson	E2
Mapleton	C3
Maquoketa	N3
Marengo	K4
Marion	L4
Marshalltown	J3
Mason City	H1
Mediapolis	M5
Melcher-Dallas	H5
Milford	D1
Missouri Valley	C4
Monroe	H4
Montezuma	J4
Monticello	M3
Mount Ayr	F6
Mount Pleasant	L6
Mount Vernon	M4
Moville	B3
Muscatine	M5
Nashua	J2
Nevada	H3
New Hampton	K1
New London	M6
Newton	H4
Nora Springs	J1
North Liberty	L4

	Key
Northwood	H1
Norwalk	G5
Oakland	D5
Oelwein	L2
Ogden	F3
Onawa	B3
Orange City	B1
Osage	J1
Osceola	G5
Oskaloosa	J5
Ottumwa	K5
Park View	N4
Parkersburg	J2
Pella	J5
Perry	F4
Pleasantville	H5
Pocahontas	E2
Polk City	G4
Postville	L1
Prairie City	H4
Primghar	D1
Red Oak	D5
Reinbeck	J3
Remsen	C2
Rock Rapids	B1
Rock Valley	B1
Rockwell City	E3
Sac City	D2
Sanborn	C1
Sergeant Bluff	B3
Sheldon	C1
Shell Rock	J2
Shenandoah	D6
Sibley	C1
Sidney	C6
Sigourney	K5
Sioux Center	B1
Sioux City	B2
Spencer	D1
Spirit Lake	D1
Storm Lake	D2
Story City	G3
Strawberry Point	L2
Stuart	F4
Sumner	K2
Tama	J4
Tipton	M4
Toledo	J4
Traer	K3
Urbandale	E4
Villisca	E6
Vinton	K3
Walcott	N4
Wapello	M5
Washington	L5
Waterloo	K3
Waukee	G4
Waukon	M1
Waverly	K2
Webster City	G2
West Branch	M4
West Burlington	M6
West Des Moines	G4
West Liberty	M4
West Union	L2
Williamsburg	K4
Wilton	M4
Windsor Heights	G4
Winterset	F5
Woodbine	C4

Other Features

	Key
Big Sioux, river	A1
Boone, river	G2
Cedar, river	K3
Chariton, river	H6
Clear, lake	H1
Coralville, lake	L4
Des Moines, river	F3
Effigy Mounds Natl. Monument	M1
Floyd, river	B2
Fox, river	K6
Herbert Hoover Natl. Hist. Site	M4
Iowa, river	K4
Little Sioux, river	D2
Maple, river	D2
Mississippi, river	M2
Missouri, river	C4
Rathbun, lake	J5
Red Rock, lake	J5
Saylorville, reservoir	G4
Skunk, river	L5
Spirit, lake	D1
Storm, lake	D2
Turkey, river	L2
Wapsipinicon, river	K2
West Nishnabota, river	K2

Kansas ....page 143

Cities and Towns

	Key
Abilene	E3
Adrian	G3
Alma	F3
Andover	D4
Anthony	D4
Arkansas City	D4
Arma	H4
Ashland	C4
Atchison	G2
Atwood	A2
Augusta	F4
Baldwin City	G3
Baxter Springs	H4
Belle Plaine	E4
Belleville	E2
Beloit	D2
Bonner Springs	H2
Buhler	E3
Burlington	G3
Butler	G3
Caldwell	E4
Caney	G4
Carbondale	G3
Chanute	G4
Chapman	E3
Cherryvale	G4
Chetopa	G4
Cimarron	B4
Clay Center	E3
Clearwater	E4
Clifton	E2
Coffeyville	G4
Colby	A2
Coldwater	C4
Columbus	H4
Concordia	E2
Conway Springs	E4
Coolidge	A3
Cottonwood Falls	F3

	Key
Council Grove	F3
Derby	E4
De Soto	H3
Dighton	B3
Dodge City	B4
Douglass	F4
El Dorado	F4
Elkhart	A4
Ellinwood	D3
Ellis	C3
Ellsworth	D3
Emporia	F3
Erie	G4
Eudora	H3
Eureka	F4
Florence	E3
Fort Scott	H4
Fredonia	G4
Frontenac	H4
Galena	H4
Garden City	B4
Gardner	H3
Garnett	G3
Girard	H4
Goddard	E4
Goodland	A2
Gove	B3
Great Bend	D3
Greensburg	C4
Halstead	E4
Harper	D4
Hays	C3
Haysville	E4
Herington	E3
Hesston	E3
Hiawatha	G2
Hill City	C2
Hillsboro	E3
Hoisington	D3
Holcomb	B4
Holton	G2
Horton	G2
Howard	F4
Hoxie	B2
Hugoton	A4
Humboldt	G4
Hutchinson	E3
Independence	G4
Iola	G4
Iuka	D4
Jetmore	C3
Johnson	A4
Junction City	F2
Kansas City	H2
Kansas City	H2
Kingman	D4
Kinsley	C3
La Crosse	A4
Lakin	A4
Lansing	H2
Larned	C3
Lawrence	G3
Leavenworth	H2
Leoti	A3
Liberal	B4
Lincoln	D2
Lindsborg	E3
Lorraine	D3
Louisburg	H3
Lyndon	G3
Lyons	D3
McPherson	E3
Maize	E4
Manhattan	F2
Mankato	D2
Marion	E3
Marysville	F2
Meade	B4
Medicine Lodge	D4
Minneapolis	E3
Mound City	H3
Moundridge	E3
Mulvane	E4
Neodesha	G4
Newton	E3
North Newton	E3
Norton	C2
Oakley	B2
Oberlin	B2
Ogden	F2
Olathe	H3
Osage City	G3
Osawatomie	H3
Osborne	D2
Oskaloosa	G2
Oswego	G4
Ottawa	G3
Overland Park	H3
Paola	H3
Park	B2
Park City	E4
Parsons	G4
Peabody	E3
Phillipsburg	C2
Pittsburg	H4
Plainville	C2
Pratt	D4
Rich Hill	G3
Rose Hill	E4
Rose Hill	E4
Russell	D3
Sabetha	G2
St. Francis	A2
St. John	D3
St. Marys	F2
Salina	E3
Scott City	B3
Sedan	G4
Sedgwick	E4
Seneca	F2
Sharon Springs	A3
Silver Lake	F2
Smith Center	D2
South Hutchinson	E3
Spring Hill	H3
Stafford	D3
Sterling	D3
Stockton	C2
Sublette	A4
Syracuse	A3
Tecumseh	G2
Tonganoxie	G2
Topeka, capital	F2
Towanda	F4
Tribune	A3
Troy	G2
Ulysses	A4
Valley Center	E4
Valley Falls	G2
Wakeeney	C3
Wamego	F2

	Key
Washington	E2
Waterville	F2
Wellington	E4
Wellsville	G3
Westmoreland	F2
Wichita	E4
Winfield	E4
Yates Center	G4

Other Features

	Key
Arkansas, river	A4, D3
Big Blue, river	F2
Cedar Bluff, reservoir	C3
Cheney, reservoir	E4
Chikaskia, river	D4
Cimarron, river	A4
Clinton, lake	G3
Fall, river	F4
Flint Hills	F4
Fort Larned Natl. Hist. Site	C3
Fort Scott Natl. Hist. Site	H4
Kanapolis, lake	E3
Kansas, river	F2
Kirwin, reservoir	C2
Little Blue, river	E1
Marion, lake	E3
Medicine Lodge, river	C4
Melvern, lake	G3
Milford, lake	F2
Missouri, river	G2
Neosho, river	G3
Nicodemus Natl. Hist. Site	C2
North Fork Solomon, river	B2
Republican, river	D1
Saline, river	C2
Smoky Hill, river	B3
Solomon, river	D2
South Fork Republican, river	A2
Sunflower, mt.	A2
Tuttle Creek, lake	F2
Verdigris, river	F3
Waconda, lake	D3
Wilson, lake	D3

Kentucky..................page 144

Cities and Towns

	Key
Aberdeen	F2
Albany	D4
Alexandria	E2
Allensville	B4
Ashland	G2
Auburn	C4
Augusta	E2
Barbourville	F4
Bardstown	D3
Bardwell	B2
Beattyville	F3
Beaver Dam	C3
Bedford	D2
Benton	C2
Berea	E3
Berry	E2
Booneville	F3
Bowling Green	C4
Brandenburg	C3
Brooks	D2
Brooksville	E2
Brownsville	C3
Burkesville	D4
Burlington	E1
Butler	E2
Cadiz	B4, C2
Calhoun	B3
Calvert City	C2
Campbellsville	D3
Campton	F3
Carlisle	E2
Carrollton	D2
Carrsville	C1
Catlettsburg	G2
Cave City	D3
Central City	B3
Clay City	F3
Clinton	B2
Columbia	D3
Concord	F2
Corbin	E4
Corinth	E2
Covington	E1
Crestwood	D2
Cumberland	G4
Cynthiana	E2
Danville	E3
Dawson Springs	B3, C1
Dixon	B3, C1
Dry Ridge	E2
Earlington	B3
Eddyville	A3, C2
Edmonton	D4
Ekron	C3
Elizabethtown	D3
Elkton	B4
Eminence	D2
Fairfield	D3
Falmouth	E2
Flatwoods	G2
Flemingsburg	F2
Florence	E2
Foster	E2
Frankfort, capital	E2
Franklin	C4
Frenchburg	F3
Fulton	B2
Georgetown	E2
Glasgow	D3
Gratz	E2
Grayson	G2
Greensburg	D3
Greenup	G2
Greenville	B3
Guthrie	B4
Hardinsburg	C3
Harlan	F4
Harrodsburg	E3
Hartford	C3
Hawesville	C3
Hazard	F3
Henderson	B3
Hickman	B2
Hindman	G3
Hiseville	D3
Hobson	D3
Hodgenville	D3
Hopkinsville	B4
Horse Cave	D3
Hyden	F3
Independence	E2
Inez	G3
Irvine	F3
Jackson	F3
Jamestown	D4
Jeffersontown	D2
Jeffersonville	F3
Jenkins	G3
Junction City	E3
La Fayette	B4, C2
La Grange	D2
Lancaster	E3
Lawrenceburg	E2
Leatherwood	F3
Lebanon	D3
Leitchfield	C3
Lewisport	C3
Lexington	E2
Liberty	E3
Livermore	B3
Livingston	E3
London	E3
Louisa	G2
Louisville	D2
McKee	F3
Mackville	D3
Madisonville	B3
Manchester	F3
Marion	A3, C1
Mayfield	B2
Maysville	F2
Middlesboro	F4
Middletown	D2
Monterey	E2
Monticello	E4
Morehead	F2
Morganfield	B3, C1
Morgantown	C3
Mt. Olivet	E2
Mt. Sterling	F2
Mt. Vernon	E3
Mt. Washington	D2
Muldraugh	D3
Munfordville	D3
Murray	B3
Nebo	B3
New Castle	D2
Nicholasville	E3
Oak Grove	B4
Okolona	D2
Olive Hill	F2
Owensboro	B3
Owenton	E2
Owingsville	F2
Paducah	C2
Paris	E2
Patesville	C3
Phelps	G3
Pikeville	G3
Pine Knot	E4
Pineville	F4
Pleasure Ridge Park	D2
Prestonsburg	G3
Princeton	B3, C2
Providence	B3, C1
Raceland	G2
Radcliff	D3
Richmond	E3
Rochester	C3
Russell Springs	D3
Russellville	C4
St. Matthews	D2
Salyersville	F3
Sandy Hook	F2
Scottsville	C4
Sebree	B3
Shelbyville	D2
Shepherdsville	D3
Slaughters	B3
Smithland	C1
Somerset	E3
South Shore	G2
Springfield	D3
Stanford	E3
Stanton	F3
Sturgis	A3, C1
Taylorsville	D2
Tompkinsville	D4
Valley Station	D2
Vanceburg	F2
Versailles	E2
Vicco	F3
Vine Grove	D3
Walton	E2
Warsaw	E2
West Liberty	F3
Wheelwright	G3
Whitesburg	G3
Whitley City	E4
Wickliffe	B2
Williamsburg	E4
Williamstown	E2
Wilmore	E3
Winchester	E3
Woodbury	C3
Zion	B3

Other Features

	Key
Barkley, lake	B4, C2
Barren, river	C3
Barren River, lake	C4
Big Sandy, river	G2
Big South Fork Natl. River and Rec. Area	E4
Buckhorn, lake	F3
Cave Run, lake	F2
Cumberland, lake	E4
Cumberland, river	E4
Cumberland Gap Natl. Hist. Park	F4
Dale Hollow, lake	D4
Fish Trap, lake	G3
Green, river	B3, D3
Green River, lake	D3
Kentucky, lake	C2
Kentucky, river	D2, E3
Licking, river	F2
Lincoln Birthplace Natl. Hist. Site	D3
Mammoth Cave Natl. Park	C3
Nolin River, lake	C3
Ohio, river	F2
Rough, river	C3
Rough River, lake	C3
Tennessee, river	C2
Tug Fork, river	G3

Louisiana ....page 145

Cities and Towns

	Key
Abbeville	E7
Abita Springs	J6
Alexandria	D4
Ama	Inset
Amelia	G7
Amite	J5
Arabi	Inset
Arcadia	D1
Arnaudville	F6
Avondale	Inset
Baker	G5
Baldwin	F7
Ball	E4
Basile	D6
Bastrop	F1
Baton Rouge, capital	G6
Bayou Cane	H7
Bayou Vista	G7
Belle Chasse	Inset
Bentley	E3
Bernice	D1
Bertrandville	Inset
Bogalusa	K5
Bossier City	B1
Boyce	D4
Braithwaite	Inset
Breaux Bridge	F6
Bridge City	Inset
Broussard	F6
Bunkie	E5
Buras	K8
Caernarvon	Inset
Cameron	C7
Carencro	E6
Carville	G6
Cecilia	F6
Chalmette	Inset, K7
Charenton	F7
Chauvin	H8
Church Point	E6
Clinton	G5
Colfax	D3
Columbia	E2
Cottonport	E5
Coushatta	C2
Covington	J6
Crowley	E6
Crown Point	Inset
Cullen	C1
Cut Off	J7
Dalcour	Inset
Delcambre	E7
Delhi	G2
Denham Springs	H5
De Quincy	C6
De Ridder	C5
Des Allemands	J7
Destrehan	Inset
Donaldsonville	H6
Edgard	H6
Elton	D6
English Turn	Inset
Erath	E7
Estelle	Inset
Eunice	E6
Farmerville	E1
Ferriday	F3
Franklin	F7
Franklinton	J5
Frenier	Inset
Galliano	J8
Garyville	H6
Glenmora	D5
Gonzales	H6
Grambling	D1
Grand Isle	K8
Gray	H7
Greensburg	H5
Greenwood	B2
Gretna	Inset, J7
Gueydan	E6
Hackberry	C6
Hahnville	Inset, J7
Hammond	J5
Harahan	Inset
Harrisonburg	E2
Harvey	Inset
Haughton	C1
Haynesville	C1
Henderson	F6
Homer	C1
Houma	H7
Independence	J5
Inniswold	G6
Iota	D6
Iowa	C6
Jackson	G5
Jeanerette	F7
Jean Lafitte	J7
Jefferson	Inset
Jena	E3
Jennings	D6
Jesuit Bend	Inset
Jonesboro	D2
Jonesville	F3
Kaplan	E6
Kenilworth	Inset
Kenner	Inset, J7
Kentwood	J5
Killona	Inset
Kinder	D6
Krotz Springs	F5
Labadieville	H7
Lacombe	K6
Lafayette	E6
Lafitte	J7
Lake Arthur	D6
Lake Charles	C6
Lake Providence	G1
Laplace	Inset, J6
Larose	J7
Lecompte	E4
Leesville	C4
Livingston	H5
Lockport	H7
Logansport	B3
Luling	Inset
Mamou	E5
Mandeville	J6
Mansfield	B3
Mansura	E4
Many	C3
Marion	E1
Marksville	E4
Marrero	Inset, J7
Melder	D4
Melville	F5
Meraux	Inset
Metairie	Inset, J7
Mimosa Park	Inset
Minden	C1
Monroe	E2
Montegut	H8
Montz	Inset
Morgan City	G7
Moss Bluff	C6
Napoleonville	G7
Natalbany	J5
Natchitoches	C3
Newellton	G2
New Iberia	F6
New Llano	C4
New Orleans	Inset, J7
New Roads	F5
New Sarpy	Inset
Norco	Inset
Oakdale	D5
Oak Grove	G1
Oakville	Inset
Oberlin	D5
Oil City	B1
Olla	E3
Opelousas	E5
Paincourtville	G6
Paradis	Inset
Patterson	G7
Plaquemine	G6
Point a la Hache	K7
Ponchatoula	J6
Port Allen	G5
Port Barre	F5
Port Sulphur	K8
Poydras	Inset
Raceland	H7
Rayne	E6
Rayville	F2
Reserve	H6
Richwood	E2
Ringgold	C2
River Ridge	Inset
Ruston	D1
St. Bernard	Inset
St. Francisville	G5
St. Joseph	G3
St. Martinville	F6
St. Rose	Inset
Scarsdale	Inset
Schriever	H7
Scott	E6
Shreveport	B2
Simmesport	F5
Slidell	K6
Springhill	C1
Stonewall	B2
Sulphur	C6
Sunset	E6
Swartz	F1
Taft	Inset
Tallulah	G2
Terrytown	Inset
Thibodaux	H7
Toca	Inset
Vidalia	G3
Ville Platte	E5
Vinton	B6
Violet	Inset, K7
Vivian	B1
Waggaman	Inset
Walker	H6
Washington	E5
Welsh	D6
West Monroe	E2
Westwego	Inset, J7
White Castle	G6
Winnfield	D3
Winnsboro	F2
Zachary	G5
Zwolle	B3

Other Features

	Key
Atchafalaya, bay	G8
Atchafalaya, river	F5
Barataria, bay	K8
Bistineau, lake	C2
Black, river	E4
Borgne, lake	Inset, K6
Breton, islands	L8
Caddo, lake	A1
Caillou, bay	G8
Calcasieu, lake	C7
Caney, lake	C2
Cane River Creole Natl. Hist. Park	D3
Catahoula, lake	E4
Chandeleur, islands	M7
Driskill, mt.	D2
Grand, lake	D7
Jean Lafitte N.H.P. and Preserve	J7
Little, river	D2
Marsh, island	F7
Mississippi, river	G3
Ouachita, river	E2
Pearl, river	K5
Pontchartrain, lake	Inset, J6
Red, river	C3
Sabine, lake	B7
Sabine, river	H8
Terrebonne, bay	J8
Timbalier, bay	J8
Toledo Bend, reservoir	B4
Vermilion, bay	F7
West Cote Blanche, bay	F7
White, lake	E7

Maine ....page 146

Cities and Towns

	Key
Alfred	B5
Amherst	D4
Athens	C4
Auburn	B4
Augusta, capital	C4
Bangor	D4
Bar Harbor	D4
Bass Harbor	D4
Bath	C4
Belfast	C4
Berwick	B5
Biddeford	B5
Boothbay Harbor	C4
Brewer	D4
Bridgton	B4
Brunswick	C4
Bucksport	D4
Calais	E3
Camden	C4
Cape Elizabeth	B5
Caribou	D2
Chisholm	B4
Clinton	C4
Conway	A4
Damariscotta	C4
Dexter	C4
Dixfield	B4
Dover-Foxcroft	C3
East Millinocket	D3
Eastport	F4
Ellsworth	D4
Fairfield	C4
Falmouth	B5, F3
Farmington	B4
Fort Fairfield	E2
Fort Kent	D1
Frankfort	D4
Franklin	B5
Freeport	B5
Frenchboro	D4
Frenchville	D1
Fryeburg	B4
Gardiner	C4
Greene	B4
Hallowell	C4
Hampden	D4
Houlton	E2
Howland	D3
Kennebunk	B5
Kittery	B5
Lewiston	B4
Lincoln	D3
Lisbon Falls	B4
Livermore Falls	B4
Machias	E4
Madawaska	D1
Madison	C4
Mars Hill	E2
Mechanic Falls	B4
Mexico	B4
Milbridge	E4
Milford	D4
Millinocket	D3
Milo	D3
Norridgewock	C4
North Amity	E3
North Berwick	B5
North Conway	A4
North East Carry	C3
North Windham	B5
Norway	B4
Oakland	C4
Old Orchard Beach	B5
Old Town	D4
Orono	D4
Oxford	B4
Patten	D3
Portland	B5
Presque Isle	D2
Richmond	C4
Rockland	C4
Rumford	B4
Saco	B5
Sanford	B5
Skowhegan	C4
South Paris	B4
South Portland	B5
Springvale	B5
Thomaston	C4
Van Buren	E1
Waldoboro	C4
Waterville	C4
Westbrook	B5
Westfield	E2
Wilsons Mills	A4
Wilton	B4
Winslow	C4
Winthrop	C4
Wiscasset	C4
Woodland	E3
Yarmouth	B5
York	B5

Other Features

	Key
Acadia Natl. Park	D4
Androscoggin, river	B4
Appalachian, mts.	A3
Aroostook, river	D2
au Haut, island	D4
Aziscohos, lake	A3
Baskahegan, lake	E3
Baxter State Park	D2
Big, lake	E3
Casco, bay	C4
Chamberlain, lake	C2
Chesuncook, lake	C2
Churchill, lake	C2
Cross, island	E4
Deer, island	D4
Elizabeth, cape	B4
Flagstaff, lake	B3
Grand, lake	E3
Grand Matagamon, lake	D2
Grand Seboeis, lake	D2
Great Wass, island	E4
Islesboro, island	D4
Katahdin, mt.	D3
Kennebec, river	C3
Long, island	C4
Maine, gulf	C4
Matinicus, island	C4
Mattawamkeag, river	D2
Millinocket, lake	D3
Monhegan, island	C4
Moosehead, lake	C3
Mooselookmeguntic, lake	B4
Mt. Desert, island	D4
Munsungan, lake	D2
Nicatous, lake	D3
Pemadumcook, lake	C3
Penobscot, bay	D4
Penobscot, river	D3
Piscataquis, river	C3
Richardson, lakes	B4
Saco, bay	B5
Saco, river	B5
Saddleback, mt.	B4
St. Croix, river	E3
St. John, river	D1
Sebago, lake	B5
Sebec, lake	C3
Seboeis, lake	D3
Seboomook, lake	C3
Snow, mt.	B3
Sugarloaf, mt.	B3
Swans, island	D4
Telos, lake	C2
Umbagog, lake	A4
Vinalhaven, island	D4
West Grand, lake	E3
West Quoddy Head, peninsula	F4
White Cap, mt.	C3

Maryland ....page 147

Cities and Towns

	Key
Aberdeen	K2
Accident	A6
Accokeek	F5
Adelphi	H3
Annapolis, capital	J4
Arden-on-the-Severn	H3
Arnold	J3
Aspen Hill	B3, F3
Avenue	G7
Baltimore	H2
Bel Air	J1
Beltsville	C3, G3
Berlin	P6
Berwyn Heights	C4
Bethesda	B4, F4
Bladensburg	C4
Boonsboro	D1
Bowie	G4
Bowleys Quarters	J2
Braddock Heights	D2
Brandywine	G5
Brentwood	C4
Brunswick	D2
Burtonsville	K6
Burtonsville	C3
Cabin John	B3
California	J6
Calverton	C3
Cambridge	K5
Cape St. Claire	J3
Camp Springs	C5
Carney	H2
Cascade	D1
Catonsville	H2
Centreville	K3
Chesapeake Beach	H5
Chesapeake Ranch Estates	J6
Chestertown	K3
Cheverly	C4
Chillum	C4, G4
Clinton	G4
Clover Hill	E2
Cloverly	C3
Cockeysville	H2
Colesville	C3
College Park	C4, G4
Columbia	G3
Contee	G3
Copenhaver	A3
Coral Hills	C5
Cresaptown	C6
Crisfield	L7
Crofton	H3
Crownsville	H3
Cumberland	D6
Damascus	F2
Deale	H4
Delmar	M6
Denton	L4
Derwood	A3
District Heights	D5
Dufief	A3
Dundalk	H2
Easton	K4
Edgemere	J3
Edgewood	J2
Eldersburg	G2
Elkridge	G3
Elkton	L1
Ellicott City	G3
Emmitsburg	E1
Essex	J2
Fair Hill	L1
Fallston	J1
Federalsburg	L5
Ferndale	H3
Forest Heights	B5, G4
Forestville	G4
Fountain Head	D1
Frederick	E2
Friendship	A6
Frostburg	C6
Fruitland	M6
Gaithersburg	F3
Garrison	G2
Germantown	E3
Glen	A3
Glenarden	D4
Glen Burnie	H3
Glen Echo Heights	B4
Glen Hills	A3
Glenmont	C3
Golden Beach	H6
Grantsville	B6
Grasonville	K4
Green Haven	H3
Greenbelt	D4, G3
Greensboro	L4
Hagerstown	D1
Halfway	C1
Hampstead	G1
Hampton	H2
Hancock	B1
Havre de Grace	K1
Herald Harbor	H3
High Ridge	C3
Hillandale	C3
Hillcrest Heights	C5
Hillsmere Shores	J4
Hughesville	G5
Hunting Hill	A3
Hurlock	L5
Hyattstown	F2
Hyattsville	C4, G4
Indian Head	F5
Jarrettsville	J1
Jessup	G3
Joppatowne	J2
Kemptown	F2
Kensington	B3, F3
Kentland	D4, G4
Kettering	D4
Keysers Ridge	B6
Kingstown	K3
Kingsville	J2
Knollwood	C3
Lake Shore	J3
Landover	C4, G4
Langley Park	C4
Lanham	D4
Lansdowne	H3
Largo	G4
Laurel	D3, G3
LaVale	C6
Lawsonia	L7
Layhill	B3
Leonardtown	H6
Lewisdale	C4
Lexington Park	J6
Linthicum	H3
Lochearn	H2
Londontown	H4
Lutherville	H2
Luxmanor	B3
Manchester	G1
Marlton	G4
Maydale	C3
Middle River	J2

	Key
Middletown	D2
Milford	G2
Montgomery Village	F3
Montpelier	D3
Mount Aetna	D1
Mountain Lake Park	A7
Mount Airy	F2
Mount Rainier	C4
Muirkirk	D3
New Carrollton	D4
Norbeck	B3
North Chevy Chase	B4
North East	L1
Oak Crest	D3
Oakland	A7
Oakland	G2
Oakview	C3
Ocean City	P6
Ocean Pines	P6
Odenton	H3
Olney	F3
Overlea	H2
Owings Mills	G2
Oxon Hill	C5
Palmer Park	D4
Parkville	H2
Parole	H4
Perry Hall	J2
Perryman	K2
Perryville	K1
Pikesville	H2
Pleasant Hills	J2
Pocomoke City	M7
Poolesville	E3
Potomac	A3, F3
Potomac Heights	F5
Preston	L5
Prince Frederick	H5
Princess Anne	M7
Randallstown	G2
Randolph Hills	B3
Redhouse	A7
Reisterstown	G2
Rising Sun	K1
Ritchie	D5
Riverdale	C4
Riviera Beach	H3
Rock Hall	K3
Rockville	A3, F3
Rosedale	H2
Rossmoor Leisure World	B3
Rossville	J2
St. Charles	G5
St. Michaels	K4
Salisbury	M6
Seabrook	D4
Seat Pleasant	D5
Severn	H3
Severna Park	H3
Shady Side	H4
Shawsville	H1
Silver Hill	C5
Silver Spring	B4, F4
Snow Hill	N7
South Gate	C3
Spencerville	C3
Stevensville	J4
Suitland	C5, G4
Sykesville	G2
Takoma Park	C4
Taneytown	F1
Temple Hills	C5, G4
Thurmont	E1
Timonium	H2
Towson	H2
Upper Marlboro	H4
Waldorf	G5
Walker Mill	D5
Walkersville	E2
Westernport	B7
Westminster	F1
West Ocean City	P6
Wheaton	B3, F3
White Marsh	J2
White Oak	C3, G3
White Plains	G5
Wildwood Hills	A3
Williamsport	C1
Woodlawn	G2
Woodyard	G4

Other Features

	Key
Allegheny Front, mt. ridge	C7
Antietam Natl. Battlefield	D2
Appalachian Natl. Scenic Trail	D2
Assateague Island Natl. Seashore	P7
Assawoman, bay	P6
Backbone, mt.	A7
Chesapeake, bay	J5
Chesapeake and Ohio Canal N.H.P.	A4, D2
Chester, river	K3
Chincoteague, bay	N7
Choptank, river	K5
Deep Creek, lake	A6
Liberty, reservoir	G2
North Branch Potomac, river	C7
Nanticoke, river	L6
Patapsco, river	H3
Patuxent, river	H4
Potomac, river	G6
Susquehanna, river	J1
Thomas Stone Natl. Hist. Site	F5
Wicomico, river	G6
Youghiogheny, river	A6

Massachusetts .... page 148

Cities and Towns

	Key
Abington	L4
Acton	A5, J3
Acushnet	L6
Adams	B2
Amesbury	L1
Amherst	D3
Andover	K2
Arlington	C6, K3
Ashby	G2
Ashfield	C2
Ashland	J3
Assinippi	F8
Assonet	K5
Athol	F2
Attleboro	J5
Auburn	G4
Avon	D8, K4
Ayer	H2
Baldwinville	F2
Barnstable	N6
Becket	B3
Bedford	B5, J3

	Key
Belchertown	E3
Bellingham	J4
Belmont	C6
Berkley	K5
Bernardston	D2
Beverly	F5, L2
Billerica	B5, J2
Blackstone	H4
Blandford	C4
Bliss Corner	L6
Bolton	H3
Bondsville	E3
Boston, capital	D6, K3
Boxford	K2
Braintree	E8, K4
Brewster	P5
Bridgewater	L5
Brimfield	F4
Brockton	F4
Brookfield	F4
Brookline	C7, K3
Burlington	C5, K2
Buzzards Bay	M5
Cambridge	D6, K3
Canton	C8, K4
Carlisle	B5
Cedarville	M5
Centerville	N6
Central Village	K6
Charlton	G4
Charlton City	G4
Chatham	Q6
Chelmsford	J2
Chelsea	D6
Cheshire	B2
Chester	C3
Chicopee	D4
Chilmark	M7
Clarksburg	B2
Clinton	H3
Cochituate	B7, J3
Cohasset	L4
Concord	B6, J3
Cotuit	N6
Dalton	B3
Danvers	E5, L2
Dartmouth	K6
Dedham	C7, K4
Dennis	P6
Douglas	H4
Dover	B8, J4
Dracut	J2
Duxbury	M4
East Brookfield	F4
East Dennis	P6
East Douglas	H4
East Falmouth	M6
East Freetown	L5
Eastham	Q5
Easthampton	D3
East Longmeadow	D4
East Orleans	Q5
East Pepperell	H2
East Wareham	M5
Edgartown	M7
Erving	E2
Essex	L2
Everett	D6
Fall River	K6
Falmouth	M6
Feeding Hills	D4
Fiskdale	F4
Fitchburg	G2
Florida	B2
Foxboro	J4
Framingham	A7, J3
Franklin	H4
Gardner	G2
Gay Head	L7
Georgetown	L2
Gloucester	M2
Granby	D3
Granville	C4
Great Barrington	A4
Greenfield	D2
Green Harbor	M4
Halifax	L5
Hamilton	L2
Hanover	L4
Hanson	L4
Haverhill	K1
Hingham	F8, L4
Holbrook	E8, K4
Holland	F4
Holliston	A8, J4
Holyoke	D4
Hopedale	H4
Hopkinton	H3
Hubbardston	G3
Hudson	H3
Hull	F7, L3
Huntington	C4
Hyannis	N6
Ipswich	L2
Kingston	M5
Lakeville	L5
Lawrence	K2
Lee	B3
Lenox	A3
Leominster	G2
Lexington	C6, K3
Lincoln	B6
Littleton	J2
Littleton Common	J2
Longmeadow	D4
Lowell	J2
Ludlow	E4
Lunenburg	H2
Lynn	E6, L3
Lynnfield	D5, K2
Madaket	P7
Malden	D6, K3
Manchester-by-the-Sea	L2
Mansfield	K4
Marblehead	F5, L3
Marion	L6
Marlborough	H3
Marshfield	M4
Marshfield Hills	M4
Mashpee	N6
Mattapoisett	L6
Maynard	H3
Medfield	B8, J4
Medford	D6, K3
Medway	A8
Melrose	D6, K3
Mendon	H4
Methuen	K2
Middleboro	L5
Milford	H4
Millis	B8
Milton	D7, K3

	Key
Monson	E4
Monterey	B4
Monument Beach	M6
Nahant	E6, L3
Nantucket	P7
Natick	B7, J3
Needham	C7, K3
New Ashford	B2
New Bedford	L6
New Boston	B4
Newburyport	L1
New Marlborough	B4
Newton	C7, K3
North Adams	B2
North Amherst	D3
Northampton	D3
North Andover	K2
North Attleboro	J5
Northborough	H3
Northbridge	H4
North Brookfield	F3
North Carver	L5
North Falmouth	M6
Northfield	E2
North Grafton	H4
North Pembroke	L4
North Plymouth	M5
North Reading	D5, K2
North Scituate	L4
North Sudbury	A7
North Tisbury	M7
Norton	K5
Norwell	L4
Norwood	C8, K4
Oakham	F3
Ocean Bluff	M4
Ocean Grove	K6
Orange	E2
Orleans	Q5
Osterville	N6
Otis	B4
Oxford	G4
Palmer	E4
Paxton	G3
Peabody	E5, L2
Pelham	E3
Pembroke	L4
Pepperell	H2
Petersham	F3
Phillipston	F2
Pinehurst	C5, K2
Pittsfield	B3
Plainfield	C3
Plainville	J4
Plymouth	M5
Pocasset	M6
Provincetown	P4
Quincy	E7, K3
Randolph	D8, K4
Raynham	K5
Raynham Center	K5
Reading	D5, K2
Rehoboth	K5
Revere	E6, K3
Rochester	L6
Rockland	E8, L4
Rockport	M2
Rutland	G3
Sagamore	M5
Salem	F5, L2
Salisbury	L1
Sandwich	N5
Saugus	E6, K3
Savoy	B2
Scituate	L4
Sharon	C8, K4
Sheffield	A4
Shelburne Falls	C2
Sherborn	B8
Shirley	H2
Shrewsbury	H3
Shutesbury	E3
Somerset	K5
Somerville	D6, K3
South Amherst	D3
Southbridge	F4
South Carver	M5
South Deerfield	D3
South Dennis	P6
South Duxbury	M4
South Lancaster	H3
South Sudbury	A7
South Wellfleet	P5
South Yarmouth	P6
Spencer	G4
Springfield	D4
Sterling	G3
Stoneham	D5
Stoughton	D8, K4
Sturbridge	F4
Sudbury	A6, J3
Sutton	G4
Swampscott	E6, L3
Taunton	K5
Teaticket	M6
Templeton	F2
Tewksbury	K2
Three Rivers	E4
Tolland	B4
Topsfield	L2
Truro	P5
Turners Falls	D2
Tyngsborough	J2
Upton	H4
Uxbridge	H4
Vineyard Haven	M7
Wakefield	D5, K2
Wales	F4
Walpole	C8, J4
Waltham	C6, B6
Ware	F3
Wareham	M5
Warren	F4
Warwick	E2
Washington	B3
Watertown	C6
Wauwinet	P7
Wayland	B7
Webster	G4
Wellesley	B7, J3
West Barnstable	N6
Westborough	H3
West Boylston	G3
West Brookfield	F4
West Concord	J3
West Cummington	C3
West Falmouth	M6
Westfield	D4
West Granville	C3
Westhampton	C3
West Medway	A8

	Key
Westminster	F2
Weston	B6, J3
Westport	K6
Westport Point	K6
West Springfield	D4
West Wareham	L5
Westwood	C8, K4
West Yarmouth	P6
Weymouth	E8, L4
Whately	D3
White Island Shores	M5
Whitinsville	H4
Whitman	L4
Wilbraham	E4
Williamstown	B2
Wilmington	C5, K2
Winchendon	F2
Winchester	C6
Windsor	B3
Winthrop	E6
Woburn	C5, K3
Worcester	G3
Worthington Center	C3
Wrentham	J4
Yarmouth Port	P6

Other Features

	Key
Adams Natl. Hist. Park	E8, L4
Ann, cape	M2
Berkshire, hills	B4
Boston, bay	E6
Boston, capital	D6
Boston Harbor Islands N.R.A.	E7
Boston Natl. Hist. Park	D6
Buzzards, bay	M6
Cape Cod, bay	N5
Cape Cod, canal	M5
Cape Cod Natl. Seashore	P5
Charles, river	B7
Chicopee, river	D4
Cobble Mt., reservoir	C4
Cod, cape	P4
Connecticut, river	D2
Deer, island	E7
Elizabeth, islands	L7
Frederick Law Olmsted N.H.S.	C7
Georges, island	E7
Greylock, mt.	B2
Hingham, bay	E7
Housatonic, river	A4
J.F.K. Birthplace Natl. Hist. Site	D7
Long, island	E7
Longfellow Natl. Hist. Site	D6
Lowell Natl. Hist. Park	J2
Maine, gulf	M1
Martha's Vineyard, island	M7
Massachusetts, bay	F6, M3
Merrimack, river	K1
Minute Man Natl. Hist. Park	B6, J3
Monomoy, island	P6
Muskeget, channel	N7
Nantucket, island	P7
New Bedford Whaling N.H.P.	L6
Neponset, river	C7
Otis, reservoir	B4
Peddocks, island	E7
Quabbin, reservoir	F3
Quincy, bay	E7
Salem Maritime N.H.S.	F5, L2
Saugus Iron Works N.H.S.	E6
Shawsheen, river	B6
Spectacle, island	E7
Swift, river	E4
Taconic, mts.	A2
Wachusett, reservoir	G3
Wachusett, river	G3
Walden, pond	B6

Michigan .... page 149

Cities and Towns

	Key
Adrian	E8
Albion	E7
Algonac	G7
Allegan	D7
Allendale	C7
Allen Park	A7
Alma	E6
Alpena	F4
Ann Arbor	F7
Atlanta	E5
Bad Axe	G6
Baldwin	D6
Battle Creek	D7
Bay City	F6
Belding	D6
Bellaire	D5
Belleville	F7
Benton Harbor	C7
Berkley	A6
Bessemer	C2
Beulah	C5
Beverly Hills	A6
Big Rapids	D6
Birmingham	A6
Blissfield	F8
Bloomfield Hills	A6
Boyne City	D4
Bridgeport	F6
Brighton	F7
Buchanan	C8
Burton	F6
Cadillac	D5
Carleton	F7
Caro	F6
Carrollton	F6
Cassopolis	C8
Cedar Springs	D6
Center Line	B6
Centreville	D8
Charlevoix	D4
Charlotte	E7
Cheboygan	E4
Chelsea	E7
Chesaning	E6
Chesterfield	C6
Christmas	C3
Clare	E6
Clawson	B6
Clio	F6
Coldwater	D8
Connorville	C2
Coopersville	C6
Crystal Falls	A3
Cutlerville	D7
Davison	F6
Dearborn	A7, F7
Dearborn Hts.	A7
Detroit	B7, F7
De Witt	E6
Dowagiac	C8

	Key
Dundee	F8
Durand	F7
Eagle River	A2
East Lansing	E7
Eastpointe	B6
East Tawas	F5
Eaton Rapids	E7
Ecorse	B7
Escanaba	B4
Essexville	F6
Farmington	A6
Farmington Hills	A6
Fenton	F7
Ferndale	B6
Ferrysburg	C6
Flat Rock	F7
Flint	F6
Flushing	F6
Fowlerville	F7
Frankenmuth	F6
Franklin	A6
Fraser	B6
Fremont	D6
Garden City	A7
Gaylord	E4
Gladstone	B4
Gladwin	E6
Grand Blanc	F7
Grand Haven	C6
Grand Ledge	E7
Grand Rapids	D6
Grayling	E5
Greenville	D6
Grosse Pointe	B7
Grosse Pointe Farms	B6
Grosse Pointe Park	B6
Grosse Pointe Shores	B6
Grosse Pointe Woods	B7
Hamtramck	B7
Hancock	A2
Harper Woods	B6
Harrison	E5
Harrisville	F5
Hart	C6
Hastings	D7
Hazel Park	B6
Highland Park	B7
Hillsdale	E8
Holland	C7
Holly	F7
Holt	E7
Houghton	A2
Houghton Lake	E5
Howell	F7
Hudson	E8
Hudsonville	D7
Huntington Woods	A6
Huron Heights	A6
Imlay City	F6
Inkster	A7
Ionia	D6
Iron Mountain	A4
Ironwood	C2
Ishpeming	B3
Ithaca	E6
Jackson	E7
Jenison	D7
Kalamazoo	D7
Kalkaska	D5
Keego Harbor	A6
Kentwood	D7
Kingsford	A4
Lake City	D5
Lake Orion	F7
Lambertville	F8
L'Anse	A3
Lansing, capital	E7
Lapeer	F6
Lincoln Park	A7
Livonia	A7, F7
Lowell	D7
Ludington	C6
Madison Hts.	B6
Manistee	C5
Manistique	C4
Marenisco	D2
Marine City	G7
Marquette	B3
Marshall	E7
Marysville	G7
Mason	E7
Melvindale	A7
Menominee	B4
Merriweather	D2
Michigan Center	E7
Midland	E6
Milan	F7
Milford	F7
Mio	E5
Monroe	F8
Mount Clemens	B6
Mount Morris	F6
Mount Pleasant	E6
Munising	C3
Muskegon	C6
Muskegon Hts.	C6
Negaunee	B3
New Baltimore	G7
Newberry	D3
Niles	C8
North Muskegon	C6
Norton Shores	C6
Norway	B4
Oak Park	A6
Okemos	E7
Ontonagon	D1
Orchard Lake	A6
Otsego	D7
Owosso	E6
Oxford	F7
Paw Paw	D7
Paw Paw Lake	C7
Petoskey	E4
Plainwell	D7
Pontiac	A6, F7
Portage	D7
Port Huron	G7
Portland	E6
Rapid River	C4
Reed City	D6
Richmond	G7
River Rouge	B7
Rochester	F7
Rochester Hills	A6
Rockford	D6
Rockwood	F7
Rogers City	F4
Romeo	F7
Romulus	A7
Roscommon	E5
Roseville	B6
Royal Oak	B6
Saginaw	F6

	Key
St. Clair	G7
St. Clair Shores	B6
St. Ignace	E4
St. Johns	E6
St. Joseph	C7
St. Louis	E6
Saline	F7
Sandusky	G6
Sault Ste. Marie	E3
Shields	F6
Silver City	D1
Skidway Lake	E5
Southfield	A6
Southgate	A7
South Haven	C7
South Lyon	F7
Sparta	C6
Spring Lake	C6
Standish	F6
Stanton	D6
Sterling Heights	F7
Sturgis	D8
Sylvan Lake	A6
Tawas City	F5
Taylor	A7, F7
Tecumseh	F8
Temperance	F8
Three Rivers	D7
Traverse City	D5
Troy	B6
Union Lake	A6
Utica	B6
Vassar	F6
Wakefield	C2
Waldenburg	B6
Walker	D7
Warren	B6, F7
Wayland	D7
Wayne	A7
West Acres	A6
West Branch	E5
Westland	A7
White Cloud	D6
Whitehall	C6
White Pine	D2
Whitmore Lake	F7
Williamston	E7
Wixom	F7
Wolf Lake	C6
Wyandotte	B7
Wyoming	D7
Ypsilanti	F7
Zeeland	C7

Other Features

	Key
Arvon, mt.	A3
Au Sable, river	E5
Beaver, island	D4
Big Bay De Noc, bay	C4
Big Sable, point	C5
Bois Blanc, island	E4
Cass, river	F6
Chambers, island	B4
Detroit, river	B7
Drummond, island	F4
Erie, lake	G8
Escanaba, river	B4
Glen, lake	D5
Gogebic, lake	D2
Government Peak, mt.	D1
Grand, island	C3
Grand Island Natl. Rec. Area	C3
Grand Traverse, bay	D4
Green, bay	B5
Hamlin, lake	C5
Hammond, bay	E4
Higgins, lake	E5
High, island	D4
Hog, island	D4
Houghton, lake	E5
Hubbard, lake	F5
Huron, lake	A3
Huron, lake	G5
Huron, lake	A3
Indian, lake	C3
Isle Royale, island	A1
Isle Royale Natl. Park	A2
Keweenaw, bay	A3
Keweenaw, peninsula	A2
Keweenaw, point	B2
Keweenaw Natl. Hist. Park	A2
Lookout, point	F5
Manistee, river	D5
Manitou, island	B2
Menominee, river	B4
Michigamme, reservoir	A3
Michigan, lake	C5
North Manitou, island	C4
Paint, river	A3
Pictured Rocks Natl. Lakeshore	C3
Porcupine, mts.	D2
Saginaw, bay	F6
St. Martin, island	C4
Sleeping Bear Dunes Natl. Lakeshore	C5
South Fox, island	D4
South Manitou, island	C4
Straits of Mackinac	E4
Sturgeon, bay	D4
Superior, lake	A2
Thunder, bay	F5
Whitefish, bay	E3
Wixom, lake	E6

Minnesota .... page 150

Cities and Towns

	Key
Ada	A3
Aitkin	D4
Albany	C5
Albert Lea	D7
Albertville	D5
Alexandria	B5
Annandale	C5
Anoka	D5
Appleton	A5
Arlington	C6
Aurora	E3
Austin	E7
Babbitt	F3
Bagley	B3
Barnesville	A4
Baudette	C2
Baxter	C4
Bayport	E6
Belle Plaine	D6
Bemidji	C3
Benson	B5
Big Lake	D5
Bird Island	C6

	Key
Blooming Prairie	D7
Bloomington	D6
Blue Earth	C7
Brainerd	C4
Breckenridge	A4
Brooklyn Center	E5
Buffalo	D5
Burnsville	D6
Caledonia	F7
Cambridge	D5
Canby	A6
Cannon Falls	E6
Carlton	E4
Center City	E5
Chanhassen	D6
Chaska	D6
Chatfield	E7
Chisholm	E3
Clara City	B6
Clarks Grove	D7
Clearwater	C5
Cloquet	E4
Cokato	C5
Cold Spring	C5
Columbia Hts.	F5
Coon Rapids	D5
Corcoran	D5
Crookston	A3
Crosby	D4
Dawson	A6
Detroit Lakes	B4
Dilworth	A4
Dodge Center	E6
Duluth	E4
Eagan	F6
Eagle Lake	D6
East Bethel	D5
East Grand Forks	A3
Edina	D6
Elbow Lake	B5
Elk River	D5
Ely	F3
Evansville	B4
Eveleth	E3
Eyota	E7
Fairmont	C7
Falcon Heights	F5
Faribault	D6
Farmington	D6
Fergus Falls	A4
Foley	D5
Forest Lake	E5
Fosston	B3
Fridley	E5
Gaylord	C6
Glencoe	C6
Glenwood	B5
Golden Valley	E5
Goodview	F6
Grand Forks	A3
Grand Marais	F5
Grand Portage	F4
Grand Rapids	D3
Granite Falls	B6
Hallock	A2
Hastings	E6
Hawley	A4
Hayfield	E7
Hermantown	E4
Hibbing	E3
Hokah	F7
Hopkins	E5
Hovland	F4
Howard Lake	C5
Hutchinson	C6
International Falls	D2
Ivanhoe	A6
Jackson	B7
Janesville	D6
Jordan	D6
Kasson	E6
Kenyon	E6
La Crescent	F7
Lake Crystal	C6
Lakefield	B7
Lakeville	D6
Le Center	D6
Le Sueur	D6
Lewiston	F7
Litchfield	C5
Little Canada	F5
Little Falls	C5
Long Prairie	C5
Lonsdale	D6
Lutsen	E5
Luverne	A7
McIntosh	B3
Madelia	C6
Madison	A5
Mahnomen	B3
Mankato	D6
Mantorville	E6
Maple Grove	D5
Maple Lake	C5
Mapleton	D7
Maplewood	F5
Marshall	B6
Melrose	C5
Mendota	F6
Milaca	D5
Minneapolis	D6
Minneota	B6
Montevideo	B6
Montgomery	D6
Monticello	D5
Moorhead	A4
Mora	D5
Morris	B5
Mound	D6
Mountain Iron	E3
Mountain Lake	C7
New Hope	E5
Newport	F6
New Prague	D6
New Ulm	C6
Nisswa	C4
North Branch	E5
Northfield	D6
North Mankato	C6
North Oaks	F5
Olivia	C6
Orono	D6
Oronoco	E6
Osakis	B5
Ortonville	A5
Owatonna	D6
Park Rapids	C4
Paynesville	C5
Pelican Rapids	A4
Perham	B4
Pigeon River	F4
Pine City	E5

	Key
Pine Island	E6
Pipestone	A7
Plainview	E6
Plymouth	D5
Preston	E7
Princeton	D5
Prinsburg	B6
Prior Lake	D6
Proctor	E4
Ramsey	D5
Red Lake Falls	A3
Red Wing	E6
Redwood Falls	B6
Renville	B6
Richfield	E6
Robbinsdale	E5
Rochester	E6
Roseau	B2
Rushford	F7
St. Anthony	F5
St. Charles	E7
St. Cloud	C5
St. Francis	D5
St. James	C7
St. Joseph	C5
St. Louis Park	E5
St. Michael	D5
St. Paul, *capital*	D6
St. Peter	D6
Sandstone	E4
Sartell	C5
Sauk Centre	C5
Sauk Rapids	C5
Shakopee	D6
Silver Bay	B7
Slayton	B7
Sleepy Eye	C6
South St. Paul	F6
Spring Valley	E7
Springfield	C6
Staples	C5
Stewartville	E7
Stillwater	E5
Thief River Falls	A2
Tracy	B6
Truman	C7
Two Harbors	F3
Tyler	A6
Virginia	E3
Wabasha	E6
Wadena	B4
Waite Park	C5
Walker	C3
Warren	A2
Warroad	B2
Waseca	D6
Waterville	D6
Wells	D7
Wheaton	A5
White Bear Lake	F5
Willmar	B5
Windom	B7
Winnebago	C7
Winona	F6
Winsted	C6
Winthrop	C6
Worthington	B7
Wyoming	E5
Young America	D6
Zimmerman	D5
Zumbrota	E6

Other Features

	Key
Big Fork, *river*	D2
Brule, *lake*	E4
Buffalo, *lake*	A4
Chippewa, *river*	B5
Clearwater, *river*	B3
Cloquet, *river*	F3
Des Moines, *river*	B6
Eagle, *mt.*	F4
Grand Portage Natl. Monument	F4
Gull, *lake*	C4
Lake of the Woods, *lake*	C1
Leech, *lake*	C3
Little Fork, *river*	D2
Lower Red, *lake*	B3
Lower Whitefish, *lake*	C4
Mall of America	F6
Mesabi, *range*	D3
Mille Lacs, *lake*	D4
Minnesota, *river*	B6
Mississippi, *river*	C3
Mud, *lake*	B2
Namakan, *lake*	E2
Pipestone Natl. Monument	A6
Pokegama, *lake*	D3
Rainy, *river*	C2
Red River of the North, *river*	A3
Root, *river*	E7
Rum, *river*	D5
St. Croix, *river*	E5
St. Louis, *river*	E3
Superior, *lake*	F3
Upper Red, *lake*	C2
Vermilion, *range*	F3
Voyageurs Natl. Park	E2
Winnibigoshish, *lake*	D3

Mississippi .... page 151

Cities and Towns

	Key
Aberdeen	D2
Ackerman	C2
Alligator	B1
Amory	D2
Ashland	C1
Baldwyn	D1
Bassfield	C4
Batesville	C1
Bay St. Louis	C5
Bay Springs	C4
Beauregard	B4
Belmont	D1
Belzoni	B2
Biloxi	D5
Blue Springs	D1
Booneville	D1
Brandon	C3
Braxton	C3
Brookhaven	B4
Bruce	C2
Calhoun City	C2
Canton	C3
Carrollton	C2
Carthage	C3
Centreville	A4
Charleston	C1
Clarksdale	B1
Cleveland	B2
Clinton	B3

	Key
Coahoma	B1
Coffeeville	C2
Coldwater	C1
Collins	C4
Collinsville	D3
Columbia	C4
Columbus	D2
Como	C1
Corinth	D1
Crystal Springs	B4
Decatur	C3
De Kalb	D3
Diamondhead	C5
D'Iberville	D5
Doddsville	B2
Drew	B2
Durant	C2
Eden	B3
Edwards	B3
Ellisville	C4
Eupora	C2
Falcon	B1
Falkner	D1
Fayette	A4
Flora	B3
Florence	C3
Forest	C3
Friars Point	B1
Fulton	D1
Gautier	D5
Glendora	B2
Gloster	A4
Golden	D1
Goodman	C3
Greenville	A2
Greenwood	B2
Grenada	C2
Gulfport	C5
Hattiesburg	C4
Hazlehurst	B4
Hernando	C1
Hollandale	B2
Holly Springs	C1
Horn Lake	B1
Houston	D2
Indianola	B2
Itta Bena	B2
Iuka	D1
Jackson, *capital*	B3
Jonestown	B1
Kiln	C5
Kosciusko	C2
Kossuth	D1
Laurel	C4
Leakesville	D4
Learned	B3
Leland	B2
Lena	C3
Lexington	B2
Liberty	B4
Long Beach	C5
Louisville	C2
Lucedale	D5
Lula	B1
Lumberton	C4
Lyman	C5
McComb	B4
McCool	C2
Macon	D2
Madison	B3
Magee	C3
Magnolia	B4
Mantee	C2
Marion	D3
Marks	B1
Mayersville	A3
Meadville	B4
Mendenhall	C4
Meridian	D3
Monticello	B4
Montrose	C3
Moorhead	B2
Morton	C3
Moss Point	D5
Mound Bayou	B1
Natchez	A4
Nettleton	D1
New Albany	D1
New Augusta	C4
Newton	C3
Ocean Springs	D5
Okolona	D1
Olive Branch	C1
Oxford	C1
Paden	D1
Pascagoula	D5
Pass Christian	C5
Paulding	C3
Pearl	B3
Pearlington	C5
Pelahatchie	C3
Petal	C4
Philadelphia	C3
Picayune	C5
Pickens	C3
Pittsboro	C2
Polkville	C3
Pontotoc	D1
Pope	C1
Poplarville	C5
Port Gibson	B4
Prentiss	C4
Purvis	C4
Quitman	D3
Raleigh	C3
Raymond	B3
Richland	B3
Ridgeland	B3
Ripley	D1
Rolling Fork	B3
Rosedale	A2
Ruleville	B2
Sallis	C2
Saltillo	D1
Sardis	C1
Satartia	B3
Seminary	C4
Senatobia	C1
Shannon	D1
Shaw	B2
Shelby	B2
Shubuta	D4
Silver Creek	B4
Slate Spring	C2
Southaven	B1
Starkville	D2
Summit	B4
Sumner	B2
Sylvarena	C3
Taylorsville	C4
Tchula	B2
Tillatoba	C2

	Key
Toccopola	C1
Tunica	B1
Tupelo	D1
Tutwiler	B1
Tylertown	B4
Union	C3
Vaiden	C2
Vancleave	D5
Verona	D1
Vicksburg	B3
Walthall	C2
Water Valley	C1
Waveland	C5
Waynesboro	D4
Wesson	B4
West	C2
West Point	D2
Wiggins	C3
Winona	C2
Woodland	C2
Woodville	A4
Yazoo City	B3

Other Features

	Key
Arkabutla, *lake*	B1
Big Black, *river*	B3
Big Springs, *lake*	D1
Big Sunflower, *river*	B2
Bogue Chitto, *river*	B4
Buttahatchee, *river*	D2
Cat, *island*	C5
Chickasawhay, *river*	D4
Coldwater, *river*	B1
Columbus, *lake*	D2
Enid, *lake*	C1
Grenada, *lake*	C2
Gulf Island Natl. Seashore	D5
Homochitto, *river*	A4
Horn, *island*	D5
Leaf, *river*	C4
Mississippi, *river*	B1
Mississippi, *sound*	D5
Natchez Natl. Hist. Park	A4
Noxubee, *river*	D2
Okatibbee, *lake*	D3
Pascagoula, *river*	D5
Pearl, *river*	C3
Petit Bois, *island*	D5
Pickwick, *lake*	D1
Pontotoc, *mt. ridge*	D1
Ross Barnett, *reservoir*	C3
Sardis, *lake*	C1
Ship, *island*	D5
Tallahatchie, *river*	B1
Tombigbee, *river*	D1
Tupelo Natl. Battlefield	D1
Vicksburg Natl. Mil. Park	B3
Woodall, *mt*	D1
Yazoo, *river*	B2

Missouri .... page 152

Cities and Towns

	Key
Adrian	B3
Affton	H3
Albany	B1
Alton	E5
Anderson	B5
Appleton City	B3
Ashland	D3
Atherton	J4
Aurora	C5
Ava	D5
Barnett	D3
Belton	B3
Benton	G4
Bernie	G5
Bethany	B1
Birmingham	J4
Bloomfield	G5
Blue Springs	J4
Bolivar	C4
Bonne Terre	F4
Boonville	D3
Bowling Green	E2
Branson	C5
Brentwood	H2
Bridgeton	H2
Brookfield	C2
Buckner	J4
Buffalo	C4
Butler	B3
Caboool	D4
California	D3
Calverton Park	H2
Camdenton	D4
Cameron	B2
Campbell	F5
Canton	E1
Cape Girardeau	G4
Carrollton	C2
Carthage	B4
Caruthersville	G5
Cassville	C5
Cedar Hill	F3
Centerville	F4
Centralia	D2
Chaffee	G4
Charleston	G5
Chesterfield	F3
Chillicothe	C2
Claycomo	J4
Clayton	F3, H2
Clinton	C3
Columbia	D3
Concord	H3
Concordia	C3
Crestwood	H3
Creve Coeur	H2
Cuba	E3
Dellwood	H2
Desloge	F4
De Soto	F3
Des Peres	H2
Dexter	G5
Dixon	D3
Doniphan	F5
East Prairie	G5
Edina	D1
Eldon	D3
El Dorado Springs	B4
Elsberry	F2
Eminence	E4
Eureka	F3
Excelsior Springs	B2, J3
Farley	H3
Farmington	F4
Fayette	D2
Fenton	G3
Ferguson	H2
Festus	F3

	Key
Florissant	H2
Forsyth	C5
Fredericktown	F4
Fulton	E3
Gainesville	D5
Galena	C5
Gallatin	C2
Gladstone	B2, J3
Glasgow	D2
Glasgow Village	H2
Glendale	H3
Grain Valley	J4
Granby	B5
Grandview	J4
Grant City	B1
Greenfield	C4
Greenville	F4
Hamilton	C2
Hannibal	E2
Harrisonville	B3
Hartville	D4
Hayti	G5
Hazelwood	H2
Hermann	E3
Hermitage	C4
Higginsville	C2
Hillsboro	F3
Holden	C3
Hollister	C5
Houston	E4
Huntsville	D2
Independence	B2, J4
Ironton	F4
Jackson	G4
Jefferson City, *capital*	D3
Jennings	H2
Joplin	B4
Kahoka	E1
Kansas City	B2, H4
Kennett	F5
Keytesville	D2
Kingston	B2
Kinloch	H2
Kirksville	D1
Kirkwood	H3
Knob Noster	C3
Ladue	H2
Lake Lotawana	J4
Lake St. Louis	F3
Lamar	B4
Lancaster	D1
La Plata	D1
Lathrop	B2
Lawson	B2
Lebanon	D4
Lee's Summit	B3, J4
Lemay	H3
Lexington	C2
Liberty	B2, J3
Licking	E4
Lilbourn	G5
Linn	D3
Linneus	C2
Louisiana	E2
Mackenzie	H3
Macon	D2
Malden	G5
Manchester	G3
Mansfield	D4
Maplewood	H2
Marble Hill	G4
Marceline	D2
Marionville	C5
Marshall	C2
Marshfield	D4
Maryland Heights	H2
Maryville	B1
Mattese	H3
Maysville	B2
Mehlville	H3
Memphis	E1
Mexico	E2
Milan	C1
Millard	D1
Moberly	D2
Monett	C5
Monroe City	E2
Montgomery City	E3
Monticello	E1
Mosby	J3
Mound City	A1
Mountain Grove	D4
Mountain View	E4
Mt. Vernon	C5
Murphy	G3
Neosho	B5
Nevada	B4
New Haven	E3
New London	E2
New Madrid	G5
Nixa	C4
North Kansas City	H4
Northwoods	H2
Oaks	J4
O'Fallon	F3
Olivette	H2
Oregon	A2
Osage Beach	D3
Osceola	C4
Overland	H2
Owensville	E3
Ozark	C4
Pacific	F3
Pagedale	H2
Palmyra	E2
Paris	D2
Park Hills	F4
Parkville	H4
Peculiar	B3
Peerless Park	G3
Perryville	G4
Pevely	F4
Piedmont	F4
Pierce City	C5
Pine Lawn	H2
Pineville	B5
Platte City	B2, H3
Plattsburg	B2
Pleasant Hill	B3
Poplar Bluff	F5
Portageville	G5
Potosi	F4
Princeton	C1
Randolph	J4
Raymore	B3
Raytown	J4
Republic	C4
Rich Hill	B3
Richland	D4
Richmond	C2
Richmond Heights	H2
Riverside	H4

	Key
Rock Hill	H2
Rock Port	A1
Rolla	E4
St. Ann	H2
St. Charles	F3, G2
St. Clair	F3
Ste. Genevieve	F4
St. James	E3
St. John	H2
St. Joseph	B2
St. Louis	F3, H2
St. Peters	F3
St. Robert	D4
Salem	E4
Salisbury	D2
Sappington	H3
Sarcoxie	B4
Savannah	B2
Scott City	G4
Sedalia	C3
Senath	F5
Seymour	D4
Shelbina	D2
Shelbyville	D2
Shirley	F4
Sikeston	G5
Slater	C2
Smithville	B2
Springfield	C4
Stanberry	B1
Steele	G5
Steelville	E4
Stockton	C4
Stoutsville	E2
Sugar Creek	J4
Sullivan	E3
Sweet Springs	C3
Tarkio	A1
Thayer	E5
Town and Country	G2
Trenton	C1
Troy	F3
Tuscumbia	D3
Union	F3
Unionville	C1
Unity Village	J4
University City	H2
Van Buren	F4
Vandalia	E2
Versailles	D3
Vienna	E3
Villa Ridge	F3
Waldron	H3
Warrensburg	C3
Warrenton	E3
Warsaw	C3
Washington	E3
Watson	A1
Waynesville	D4
Weatherby Lake	H3
Webb City	B4
Webster Groves	H3
Wellsville	E2
Wentzville	F3
West Plains	E5
Weston	B2
Willard	C4
Willow Springs	E4
Windsor	C3

Other Features

	Key
Bull Shoals, *lake*	D5
Eleven Point, *river*	E5
Fox, *river*	E1
G.W. Carver Natl. Monument	B5
Grand, *river*	B1
Harry S. Truman, *reservoir*	C3
Lake of the Ozarks, *lake*	D3
Mark Twain, *lake*	E2
Meramec, *river*	G4
Mississippi, *river*	G2
Missouri, *river*	C2
Osage, *river*	B4, D3
Ozark Natl. Scenic Riverways	E4
Platte, *river*	B2
St. Francis, *river*	F4
Stockton, *lake*	C4
Table Rock, *lake*	C5
Taum Sauk, *mt.*	F4
Thomas Hill, *reservoir*	D2
Weldon, *river*	C2

Montana .... page 153

Cities and Towns

	Key
Anaconda	D3
Baker	M3
Belgrade	E4
Big Timber	F4
Billings	H4
Boulder	D3
Bozeman	E4
Bridger	H4
Broadus	L4
Butte	D3
Chester	E1
Chinook	G1
Choteau	D2
Circle	L2
Columbus	G4
Conrad	E1
Crow Agency	J4
Cut Bank	D1
Deer Lodge	D3
Dell	D5
Dillon	D4
East Helena	E3
Ekalaka	M4
Evergreen	B1
Forsyth	K3
Fort Benton	F2
Gardiner	F4
Glasgow	K1
Glendive	M2
Great Falls	E2
Hamilton	B3
Hardin	J4
Harlowton	G3
Hathaway	K3
Havre	G1
Helena, *capital*	D3
Kalispell	B1
Lame Deer	K4
Laurel	H4
Lewistown	G2
Libby	A1
Lincoln	D3
Livingston	F4
Lolo Hot Springs	B3
Malta	J1
Miles City	L3

Montana

	Key
Missoula	C3
Orchard Homes	B3
Philipsburg	C3
Plentywood	M1
Polson	B2
Pony	E4
Red Lodge	G4
Ronan	B2
Roundup	H3
Rudyard	F1
St. Regis	A2
Scobey	L1
Shelby	E1
Sidney	M2
Somers	B1
Stanford	F2
Superior	B2
Terry	L3
Thompson Falls	A2
Townsend	E3
West Yellowstone	E5
Whitefish	B1
Wibaux	M3
Wolf Point	L1

Other Features

	Key
Bighorn, river	J4
Bighorn Canyon Natl. Rec. Area	H4
Bitterroot, river	B3
Bull, mts.	H3
Canyon Ferry, lake	E3
Clark Fork, river	D3
Cleveland, mt.	C1
Custer Battlefield Natl. Monument	J4
Elwell, lake	E1
Flathead, river	B2
Flathead, lake	B1
Fort Peck, lake	K2
Fresno, reservoir	F1
Glacier Natl. Park	C1
Granite Peak, mt.	D4
Granite Peak, mt.	G4
Grant-Kohrs Ranch N.H.S.	D3
Homer Youngs Peak, mt.	C4
Hungry Horse, reservoir	C1
Koocanusa, lake	A1
Kootenai, river	A1
Little Missouri, river	M5
Madison, river	E4
Marias, river	E1
Middle Fork, river	C1
Milk, river	D1
Missouri, river	G2
Musselshell, river	H3
Northwest Peak, mt.	A1
Pompeys Pillar Natl. Mon.	H3
Powder, river	L3
Rocky, mts.	C2
St. Mary, river	C1
St. Regis, river	B2
Scarface Peak, mt.	C2
South Fork, river	C2
Swan, river	C2
Teton, river	E2
Tongue, river	K4
Upper Missouri River Breaks N.M.	G2
Warren Peak, mt.	C4
Yellowstone, river	L3
Yellowstone Natl. Park	F5

Nebraska ....page 154

Cities and Towns

	Key
Ainsworth	E2
Albion	G3
Alliance	B2
Alma	E4
Ashland	H3
Atkinson	F2
Auburn	J4
Aurora	F4
Bartlett	F3
Bassett	E2
Beatrice	H4
Beaver City	E4
Bellevue	J3
Benkelman	C4
Blair	H3
Brewster	E3
Bridgeport	A3
Broken Bow	E3
Burwell	E3
Butte	F2
Center	G2
Central City	F3
Chadron	B2
Chapman	F3
Chappell	B3
Clay Center	F4
Columbus	G3
Cozad	E4
Crete	H4
Dakota City	H2
David City	G3
Elkhorn	H3
Elwood	E4
Exeter	G4
Fairbury	G4
Falls City	J4
Franklin	F4
Fremont	H3
Fullerton	G3
Geneva	G4
Gering	A3
Gibbon	F4
Gordon	B2
Gothenburg	D4
Grand Island	F4
Grant	C4
Greeley	F3
Gretna	H3
Guide Rock	F4
Harrisburg	A3
Harrison	A2
Hartington	G2
Hastings	F4
Hayes Center	C4
Hebron	G4
Holdrege	E4
Hyannis	C3
Imperial	C4
Kearney	F4
Kimball	A3
La Vista	H3
Leigh	G3
Lexington	E4
Lincoln, capital	H4
Loomis	E4
Loup City	F3
McCook	D4
Madison	G3
Milford	G4
Minden	F4
Mitchell	A3
Mullen	C2
Nebraska City	J4
Neligh	F2
Nelson	F4
Norfolk	G2
North Platte	D3
Oakland	H3
Ogallala	C3
O'Neill	F2
Ord	F3
Osceola	G3
Oshkosh	B3
Omaha	J3
Papillion	J3
Pawnee City	H4
Paxton	C3
Pender	H2
Pierce	G2
Plainview	G2
Plattsmouth	J3
Plymouth	H4
Ponca	H2
Prague	H3
Ravenna	F3
Red Cloud	F4
Rushville	B2
St. Paul	F3
Schuyler	G3
Scottsbluff	A3
Seward	G4
Sidney	B3
South Sioux City	H2
Springfield	H3
Springview	E2
Stanton	G3
Stapleton	D3
Stockville	D4
Superior	F4
Sutton	G4
Syracuse	H4
Taylor	E3
Tecumseh	H4
Thedford	D3
Trenton	C4
Tryon	D3
Valentine	D2
Valley	H3
Wahoo	H3
Waverly	H4
Wayne	G2
West Point	H3
Wilber	H4
Wisner	H3
Wymore	H4
York	G4

Other Features

	Key
Agate Fossil Beds N.M.	A2
Arikee, river	B5
Big Blue, river	G4
C.W. McConaughy, lake	C3
Calamus, reservoir	E3
Calamus, river	E2
Cedar, river	F3
Chimney Rock Natl. Hist. Site	A3
Elkhorn, river	E2, G3
Harlan Co., lake	E4
Homestead Natl. Monument	H4
Lewis and Clark, lake	G2
Little Blue, river	G4
Loup, river	F3
Middle Loup, river	D3
Missouri, river	J4
Niobrara, river	B2, E2
North Loup, river	C2, E3
North Platte, river	B3
Pine, mt. ridge	B2
Pine Ridge Natl. Rec. Area	A2
Platte, river	D4, G3
Republican, river	D4
Sand, hills	D3
Scotts Bluff Natl. Monument	A3
South Fork Republican, river	B5
South Loup, river	E3

Nevada ....page 155

Cities and Towns

	Key
Alamo	C3
Battle Mountain	B1
Beatty	B3
Boulder City	C4
Carlin	B1
Carson City, capital	A2
Elko	C1
Ely	C2
Eureka	C2
Fallon	A2
Fernley	A2
Gardnerville	A2
Goldfield	B3
Hawthorne	A2
Henderson	C3
Incline Village	A2
Las Vegas	C3
Laughlin	C4
Lovelock	A1
McGill	C2
Mesquite	C3
Minden	A2
North Fork	C1
North Las Vegas	C3
Pahrump	B3
Paradise	C3
Pioche	C3
Reno	A2
Silver Peak	B3
Sparks	A2
Spring Creek	C1
Spring Valley	C3
Sun Valley	A2
Tonopah	B2
Virginia City	A2
Wells	C1
West Wendover	C1
Winnemucca	B1
Yerington	A2
Zephyr Cove	A2

Other Features

	Key
Arc Dome, mt.	B2
Black Rock, desert	A1
Boundary Peak, mt.	A3
Colorado, river	C4
Desert, valley	A1
Egan, range	C2
Goshute, lake	C1
Grant, mts.	C2
Grant, mt.	A2
Great Basin	B2
Great Basin Natl. Park	C2
Hoover Dam	C3
Hot Creek, range	B2
Humboldt, river	B1
Independence, mts.	B1
Jefferson, mt.	B2
Lake Mead Natl. Rec. Area	C3
Marys, river	C1
Matterhorn, mt.	C1
Mead, lake	C3
Mohave, lake	C4
Monitor, range	B2
Moriah, mt.	C2
North Toiyabe Peak, mt.	B2
Owyhee, desert	B1
Owyhee, river	B1
Pilot Peak, mt.	C1
Pyramid, lake	A1
Quinn, river	B1
Ruby, mts.	C1
Ruby Dome, mt.	C1
Rye Patch, reservoir	A1
Schell Creek, range	C2
Shoshone, mts.	B2
Shoshone, range	B2
Smoky, valley	B2
Snake, range	C2
Summit, mt.	B2
Tahoe, lake	A2
Tobin, mt.	B1
Toiyabe, range	B2
Toquima, range	B2
Tuscarora, mts.	B1
Virgin, river	C3
Walker, lake	A2
Wheeler Peak, mt.	C2
White, river	C3

New Hampshire ....page 156

Cities and Towns

	Key
Albany	B3
Amherst	B4
Antrim	B3
Barnstead	B3
Bartlett	B2
Benton	B2
Berlin	B2
Blair	B3
Bradford	B3
Bretton Woods	B2
Bristol	B3
Candia	B3
Cascade	B2
Claremont	A3
Concord, capital	B3
Contoocook	B3
Conway	B2
Cornish City	A3
Dalton	B2
Deerfield	B3
Deering	B3
Derry	B4
Dixville Notch	B2
Dover	C3
Dunbarton Center	B3
Durham	C3
Easton	B2
Enfield	A3
Epping	B3
Exeter	C4
Farmington	B3
Franklin	B3
Gilmanton	B3
Glencliff	B3
Gorham	B2
Groveton	B2
Hampstead	B4
Hampton	C4
Hanover	A3
Haverhill	B2
Henniker	B3
Hillsboro	B3
Hinsdale	A4
Hollis	B4
Hooksett	B3
Hudson	B4
Jackson	B2
Jaffrey	A4
Jefferson	B2
Keene	A4
Laconia	B3
Lancaster	B2
Lebanon	A3
Littleton	B2
Loudon	B3
Lyman	B2
Manchester	B4
Meredith	B3
Merrimack	B4
Milan	B2
Milford	B4
Monroe	A2
Munsonville	A3
Nashua	B4
New Castle	C3
New London	B3
Newmarket	C3
Newport	A3
North Conway	B2
Northfield	B3
North Haverhill	A3
North Walpole	A3
North Woodstock	B2
Orford	A3
Ossipee	B3
Pelham	B4
Percy	B2
Peterborough	B4
Pinardville	B4
Pittsfield	B3
Plymouth	B3
Portsmouth	C3
Quaker City	A3
Randolph	B2
Raymond	B3
Rochester	B3
Rumney	B3
Rye	C4
Sandwich	B3
Sharon	B4
Shelburne	B2
Silver Lake	B3
Somersworth	C3
South Hooksett	B3
Stewartstown Hollow	B2
Strafford	B3
Stratford	B2
Suncook	B3
Sutton	B3
Tilton	B3
Warner	B3
Waterville Valley	B3
Westport	A4
West Rindge	A4
West Stewartstown	B2
Whittier	B3
Willey House	B2
Winchester	A4
Wolfeboro	B3
Woodsville	A2

Other Features

	Key
Appalachian Natl. Scenic Trail	A3
Blackwater, reservoir	B3
Blue, mt.	B2
Cabot, mt.	B2
Cardigan, mt.	B3
Connecticut, river	A3
First Connecticut, lake	B1
Franconia, notch	B2
Great, bay	C3
Indian, lake	B1
Kearsarge, mt.	B3
Merrimack, river	B4
Monadnock, mt.	B4
Newfound, lake	B3
Ossipee, lake	B3
Presidential, mt. range	B2
Saint-Gaudens Natl. Hist. Site	A3
Second Connecticut, lake	B1
Smarts, mt.	B3
Squam, lake	B3
Sunapee, lake	A3
Swift, river	B3
Umbagog, lake	B2
Washington, mt.	B2
White, mts.	B2
Winnipesaukee, lake	B3
Winnisquam, lake	B3

New Jersey ....page 157

Cities and Towns

	Key
Absecon	E5
Allendale	E1
Allentown	D3
Alloway	C4
Alpine	C1
Asbury Park	E3
Atlantic City	E5
Atlantic Highlands	E3
Atsion	D4
Avalon	D5
Barrington	B3
Basking Ridge	D2
Batsto	D4
Bay Point	C5
Bayonne	E2
Bayside	C5
Beachwood	E4
Beattyestown	D2
Beckett	C4
Belle Mead	D3
Belleville	B2
Bellmawr	B3, C4
Belmar	E3
Belvidere	C2
Bergenfield	C1
Berkeley Heights	E2
Berlin	D4
Bernardsville	D2
Blackwood	C4
Blairstown	D2
Bloomfield	B1
Bogota	B1
Boonton	E2
Bordentown	D3
Bound Brook	D2
Bradley Beach	E3
Brass Castle	C2
Brick	E3
Bridgeboro	C3
Bridgeton	C5
Brielle	E3
Brigantine	E5
Brookdale	B1
Browns Mills	D4
Budd Lake	D2
Buena	D4
Burlington	D3
Butler	E1
Caldwell	A1
Camden	B3, C4
Cape May	D6
Cape May Court House	D5
Carlstadt	B1
Carneys Point	C4
Carteret	E2
Carteret	E2
Cedar Grove	B1
Centerton	C4
Centerville	D2
Chatham	E2
Cherry Hill	B3, C4
Chesilhurst	D4
Chesterfield	D3
Cinnaminson	B3, D4
Clark	A2
Clayton	C4
Cliffside Park	C2
Clifton	B1
Clinton	D2
Closter	F2
Colesville	D1
Collings Lakes	D4
Collingswood	B3
Colonia	E2
Cranford	E2
Deerfield	C4
Delanco	D3
Denville	E2
Deptford	B4
Dover	D2
Dumont	C1
Dunellen	E2
East Brunswick	E3
East Orange	E2
East Rutherford	B1
Eatontown	E3
Edgewater	C1
Edison	E2
Egg Harbor City	D4
Elizabeth	E2
Elmer	C4
Elmwood Park	B1
Elwood	D4
Emerson	E2
Englewood	C1
Englewood Cliffs	C1
Englishtown	E3
Erma	D6
Estell Manor	D5
Evesboro	C3
Ewing	D3
Fair Lawn	B1, E2
Fairfield	C1
Fairton	C5
Fairview	B2
Fanwood	E2
Farmingdale	E3
Fellowship	C3
Fieldsboro	D3
Flemington	D3
Folsom	D4
Fords	D3
Forked River	E4
Fort Lee	C1
Franklin	D1
Franklinville	C4
Freehold	E3
Frenchtown	C3
Garfield	E2
Gilford Park	E4
Glassboro	C4
Glen Gardner	D2
Glen Ridge	B2
Glendora	B4
Gloucester City	B3, C4
Goshen	D5
Great Notch	B2
Green Bank	D4
Greenwich	C5
Guttenberg	F2
Hackensack	E2
Hackettstown	D2
Haddon Heights	B3
Haddonfield	C4
Hainesville	D1
Haledon	B1
Hamburg	D1
Hammonton	D4
Hampton	D2
Harrison	B2
Haworth	C1
Hawthorne	B1
Hedger House	D4
High Bridge	D2
Highland Lakes	E1
Highland Park	E3
Highlands	E3
Hightstown	D3
Hillsdale	E1
Hillside	B2
Hoboken	E2
Hopatcong	D2
Hopewell	D3
Howardsville	E4
Indian Mills	D4
Irvington	B2
Jamesburg	E3
Jersey City	E2
Keansburg	E3
Kearny	B2
Kendall Park	D3
Kenilworth	E2
Kinnelon	E2
Lakehurst	E3
Lakewood	E3
Lambertville	D3
Lavallette	E3
Lawnside	B3
Lawrenceville	D3
Leeds Point	E5
Leisure Village	E3
Leisuretowne	D4
Leonardo	E3
Lincroft	E3
Linden	E2
Lindenwold	B4, C4
Linwood	D5
Little Falls	B1
Livingston	E2
Lodi	B1
Long Branch	E3
Long Valley	D2
Lyndhurst	B2
Madison	E2
Mahwah	E1
Manahawkin	E4
Manalapan	E3
Manasquan	E3
Manumuskin	D5
Manville	D2
Maple Shade	B3, D4
Maplewood	E2
Marcella	E3
Margate City	E5
Marlboro	E3
Marlton	C3, D4
Matawan	E3
Mays Landing	D5
Maywood	B1
Medford Lakes	D4
Mendham	D2
Menlo Park	E2
Merchantville	B3
Metuchen	E2
Middlesex	E2
Middletown	E3
Midland Park	E1
Milford	C2
Millburn	E2
Millville	C5
Monmouth Beach	F3
Montclair	E2
Montvale	E1
Moorestown	C3, D4
Morris Plains	E1
Morristown	E2
Mountain Lakes	E2
Mount Holly	D4
Mount Laurel	D4
Mystic Islands	E4
National Park	B3
Neptune City	E3
Netcong	D2
Newark	E2
New Brunswick	E3
New Egypt	D3
Newfield	C4
New Gretna	E4
Newfoundland	E2
Newton	D1
Normandy Beach	E3
North Arlington	B2
North Bergen	B2
North Cape May	D6
Northfield	D5
North Wildwood	D5
Nutley	B2
Oakland	E1
Oaklyn	B3
Ocean City	D5
Oceanport	E3
Ogdensburg	D1
Olivet	C4
Oradell	B1
Orange	B2
Othello	C5
Oxford	D2
Palisades Park	B1
Palmyra	B3, C3
Paramus	B1, E1
Park Ridge	E1
Passaic	E2
Paterson	E1
Paulsboro	A4, C4
Pemberton	D4
Pennington	D3
Penns Grove	C4
Pennsauken	B3
Pennsville	B4
Perth Amboy	E2
Phillipsburg	C2
Piscataway	E2
Pine Hill	D4
Pitman	C4
Pittstown	D2
Plainfield	E2
Pleasant Plains	E3
Pleasantville	D5
Point Pleasant	E3
Pomona	D5
Port Monmouth	E3
Port Norris	C5
Princeton	D3
Princeton Junction	D3
Prospect Park	B1
Quinton	C4
Rahway	E2
Ramblewood	D4
Ramsey	E1
Raritan	D2
Red Bank	E3
Ridgefield	B1
Ridgefield Park	B1, E2
Ridgewood	E1
Ringoes	D3
Ringwood	E1
Rio Grande	D5
River Edge	B1
Riverside	C3, D3
Riverton	B3, C3
Robertsville	E3
Rochelle Park	B1
Rocktown	D3
Roselle	A2
Roselle Park	A2
Rumson	F3
Runnemede	B4, C4
Rutherford	B2
Salem	C4
Sayreville	E3
Seabrook	C4
Sea Girt	E3
Sea Isle City	D5
Seaside Heights	E4
Seaside Park	E4
Secaucus	E2
Ship Bottom	E4
Shrewsbury	E3
Silverton	E3
Smithville	E5
Somerdale	B4
Somers Point	D5
Somerset	D2
Somerville	D2
South Amboy	E3
South Orange	A2
South River	E3
Sparta	D1
Spotswood	E3
Spring Lake Heights	E3
Stanhope	D2
Stillwater	D1
Stockholm	D1
Stratford	B4, C4
Strathmere	D5
Summit	E2
Surf City	E4
Sussex	D1
Swedesboro	C4
Teaneck	B1
Tenafly	F2
Tinton Falls	E3
Toms River	E4
Totowa	B1
Trenton, capital	D3
Tuckahoe	D5
Tuckerton	E4
Turnersville	C4
Twin Rivers	E3
Union	E2
Union Beach	E3
Union City	E2
Upton	D4
Vauxhall	A2
Ventnor City	E5
Vernon	D1
Verona	A1
Villas	D5
Vineland	C5
Voorhees	C4
Waldwick	E1
Wanamassa	E3
Wanaque	E1
Waretown	E4
Warren Glen	C2
Warren Grove	E4
Washington	D2
Washington Crossing	D3
Watchung	E2
Wayne	A1, E2
Weehawken	B2
Welchville	C4
Wenonah	B3
Westfield	E2
West Milford	E1
Westmont	B3
West New York	B2
West Orange	B1
West Paterson	B1
Westville	B3
Wharton	D2
White Horse	D3
White House Station	D2
White Meadow Lake	D2

	Key
Whiting	E4
Wildwood	D6
Wildwood Crest	D6
Williamstown	D4
Willingboro	D3
Woodbine	D5
Woodbridge	E2
Woodbury	B4, C4
Woodlynne	B3
Wood Ridge	B1
Woodstown	C4
Woodstream	C3
Wrightstown	D3
Wyckoff	E1

Other Features

	Key
Cape May, point	D6
Cooper, river	B4
Delaware, bay	C5
Delaware, river	D3
Delaware Water Gap N.R.A.	D1
Edison Natl. Hist. Site	B2
Gateway Natl. Rec. Area	F3
Great, bay	E5
Hudson, river	E2
Morristown Nat. Hist. Park	D2
Pines, lake	B1
Raritan, bay	E3
Statue of Liberty N.M.	B2

New Mexico .... page 158

Cities and Towns

	Key
Acoma Pueblo	B2
Acomita	B2
Alameda	C3
Alamogordo	C3
Albuquerque	B2
Anthony	B4
Artesia	C3
Aztec	B1
Bayard	A3
Belen	B2
Bernalillo	B1
Bloomfield	B1
Bosque Farms	B2
Carlsbad	C3
Carrizozo	C3
Central	A3
Chaparral	B3
Chimayo	C1
Clayton	D1
Clovis	D2
Corrales	B2
Deming	B3
Dulce	B1
Elida	D3
Elk	C3
Elkins	C3
Española	B2
Estancia	B2
Eunice	D3
Fairacres	B3
Farmington	A1
Floyd	D2
Fort Sumner	C2
Gallup	A2
Grants	B2
Greenfield	C3
Hobbs	D3
Hurley	A3
Jal	D3
Jemez Pueblo	B2
Kirtland	A1
La Luz	C3
Las Cruces	B3
Las Vegas	C2
Lordsburg	A3
Los Alamos	B2
Los Chavez	B2
Los Lunas	B2
Los Padillas	D3
Lovington	C2
Lower Colonias	C2
Lower San Francisco Plaza	A3
Maxwell	C1
Mayhill	C3
Mesilla	B3
Milan	B2
Mora	C2
Moriarty	B2
Mosquero	D2
Navajo	A2
Polvadera	B2
Portales	D2
Questa	C1
Rancho De Taos	C1
Raton	C1
Reserve	A3
Rio Rancho	B2
Roswell	C3
Ruidoso	C3
Sabinoso	C2
San Felipe Pueblo	B2
San Miguel	B1
San Miguel	B3
Santa Fe, capital	C2
Santa Rosa	C2
Santo Domingo Pueblo	B2
Shiprock	A1
Silver City	A3
Socorro	B2
Springer	C1
Sunland Park	B4
Taos	C1
Tesuque	C2
Tierra Amarilla	B1
Truth or Consequences	B3
Tucumcari	D2
Tularosa	B3
University Park	B3
Ute Park	C1
Valencia	B2
Waterflow	A1
Zuni Pueblo	A2

Other Features

	Key
Abiquiu, reservoir	B1
Alegres, mt.	A2
Aztec Ruins Natl. Monument	B1
Baldy, mt.	C1
Bandelier Natl. Monument	B2
Black, mt. range	A3
Burro, mt.	A3
Caballo, res.	B3
Canadian, river	C1
Capulin Volcano N.M.	D1
Carlsbad Caverns Natl. Park	C3
Cebolleta, mt.	B2
Cerro Vista, mt.	C1
Chaco Culture Natl. Hist. Park	B1

	Key
Cimarron, river	D1
Conchas, lake	C2
Contintal Divide, mt. ridge	B2
Cooke's, mt.	B3
Elephant Butte, res.	B3
El Malpais Natl. Monument	A2
El Morro Natl. Monument	A2
Fort Union Natl. Monument	C2
Gallinas, mt.	C2
Gila, mt.	A3
Gila, river	A3
Gila Cliff Dwellings N.M.	A3
Guadalupe, mts.	C2
Jornada Del Muerto	B3
Kasha-Katuwe Tent Rocks N.M.	B2
Llano Estacado, plateau	D3
Navajo, reservoir	B1
Navajo Indian Res.	A1
Pecos, river	C2, C3
Pecos, plains	C3
Pecos N.H.P.	C2
Petroglyph Natl. Monument	B2
Playas, lake	A3
Reeds, mt.	B3
Rio Grande, river	C1
Rio Hondo, river	C3
Rio Puerco, river	B2
Salinas Pueblo Missions N.M.	B2
San Andres, mts.	B3
San Juan, river	A1
Sangre De Cristo, mts.	C1
Shiprock, mt.	A1
Sierra Blanca, mt.	C3
South Baldy, mt.	B3
Sumner, lake	C2
Taylor, mt.	B2
Wheeler, mt.	C1
White Sands Natl. Monument	B3
Whitewater Baldy, mt.	A3
Withington, mt.	B3
Zuni, mts.	A2

New York .... page 159

Cities and Towns

	Key
Adams	H3
Adams Center	H3
Akron	C4
Albany, capital	N5
Albion	D4
Alden	D5
Alfred	E6
Allegany	D6
Altamont	M5
Amsterdam	M5
Angola	B5
Arcade	D5
Astoria	A3
Athens	N6
Attica	D5
Auburn	G5
Avon	E5
Bainbridge	J6
Baldwinsville	H4
Ballston Spa	N4
Batavia	D4
Bath	F6
Beacon	N7
Bedford-Stuyvesant	A4
Belle Harbor	A4
Belmont	D6
Bensonhurst	A4
Big Flats	G6
Binghamton	J6
Bloomfield	F5
Bolivar	D6
Boonville	K4
Breezy Point	A4
Brentwood	C1
Brewerton	H4
Bridgehampton	E1
Brighton Beach	A4
Broadalbin	M4
Brockport	E4
Brocton	B6
Bronx	A3, B1
Bronxville	A2
Brooklyn	A4, B2
Buffalo	C5
Cairo	M6
Calcium	J2
Caledonia	E5
Cambridge	P4
Camden	J4
Canajoharie	L5
Canandaigua	F5
Canarsie	A4
Canastota	J4
Canisteo	E6
Canton	K1
Carmel	N7
Carthage	J3
Castleton-on-Hudson	N5
Catskill	N6
Cayuga Heights	H6
Cazenovia	J5
Cedarhurst	A4
Central Square	H4
Chatham	N6
Cheektowaga	C5
Chittenango	J4
Churchville	E4
Clayton	H2
Clinton	K4
Clyde	G4
Cobleskill	L5
Cohoes	N5
College Point	A3
Colonie	N4
Coney Island	A4
Cooperstown	L5
Corinth	N4
Corning	F6
Cortland	H5
Coxsackie	N6
Cuba	D6
Dannemora	N1
Dansville	E5
Delhi	L6
De Ruyter	J5
Deposit	K6
Dolgeville	L4
Dover Plains	N7
Dryden	H6
Dundee	G6
Dunkirk	B6
East Atlantic Beach	B4
Eastchester	A2
East Hampton	E1
East Islip	C2
East New York	A4
East Northport	C1

	Key
East Patchogue	D1
Eden	C5
Elizabethtown	N2
Ellenville	M7
Elmira	G6
Elmira Heights	G6
Elmont	B4
Endicott	H6
Endwell	H6
Fairmount	H4
Far Rockaway	B4
Fayette	G5
Fine	K2
Flatbush	A4
Flushing	A3
Fonda	M5
Fort Edward	N4
Fort Plain	L5
Franklin Sq.	B4
Franklinville	D6
Fredonia	B6
Freeport	C2
Frewsburg	B6
Friendship	D6
Fulton	H4
Geneseo	E5
Geneva	G5
Glen Cove	B1
Glens Falls	N4
Gloversville	M4
Goshen	M7
Gouverneur	K2
Gowanda	C6
Granville	P4
Gravesend	A4
Great Neck	B1
Greece	E4
Greene	J6
Greenport	E1
Greenwich	P4
Groton	H5
Hamburg	C5
Hamilton	J5
Hampton Bays	E1
Hancock	K7
Harlem	A3
Hempstead	B2
Herkimer	L4
Hicksville	C1
Highland	N7
Hilton	E4
Holbrook	C1
Holland	C5
Holley	D4
Homer	H5
Hoosick Falls	P5
Hornell	G6
Horseheads	G6
Houghton	D6
Howard Beach	A4
Hudson	N6
Hudson Falls	N4
Huntington Station	C1
Hurley	M7
Ilion	K4
Inwood	B4
Irondequoit	E4
Ithaca	H6
Jamaica	B2
Jamestown	B6
Johnson City	J6
Johnstown	M4
Keeseville	P1
Kew Gardens	A4
Kinderhook	N6
Kingston	N7
Lake George	N4
Lake Placid	M2
Lake Pleasant	M4
Lakewood	H5
Lansing	H5
Larchmont	B2
Lawrence	B4
Le Roy	D5
Levittown	C1
Liberty	L7
Lima	E5
Lindenhurst	C2
Little Falls	L4
Little Valley	C6
Livingston Manor	L7
Livonia	E5
Lockport	C4
Long Beach	B2
Long Eddy	K7
Long Island City	A3
Long Lake	M3
Loon Lake	M1
Lowville	K3
Lynbrook	B4
Lyons	G4
Malone	M1
Mamaroneck	B2
Manhasset Hills	B3
Manhattan	A3
Manlius	J4
Manorhaven	B3
Massapequa	C2
Massena	L1
Mastic	D1
Mastic Beach	D1
Mattituck	E1
Mayville	A6
Mechanicville	N5
Medina	D4
Mexico	H4
Middleburgh	M5
Middleport	D4
Middletown	M7
Millbrook	N7
Mineola	B1
Mohawk	K5
Monroe	A1
Montauk	F1
Monticello	L7
Montour Falls	G6
Moravia	H5
Mount Kisco	B1
Mount Morris	E5
Mount Vernon	B1, C5
Munnsville	J5
Nassau	N5
Newark	F4
Newburgh	M7
New City	B1
Newfane	C4
New Hartford	K4
New Hyde Park	B4
New Paltz	M7
New Rochelle	B2
New York	B2
Niagara Falls	B4

	Key
Norfolk	L1
North Collins	C5
North Hills	B3
North Syracuse	H4
North Tonawanda	C4
Norwich	J5
Norwood	L1
Nunda	E5
Nyack	B1
Oakfield	D4
Ogdensburg	K1
Olcott	C4
Olean	D6
Oneida	J4
Oneonta	K6
Ossining	N7
Oswego	H4
Owego	H6
Oxford	J6
Ozone Park	A4
Painted Post	F6
Pawling	N7
Peekskill	B1
Pelham	A3
Pelham Manor	A3
Penn Yan	F5
Peru	N1
Philadelphia	J2
Philmont	N6
Phoenix	H4
Pine Bush	M7
Plattsburgh	P1
Port Henry	P2
Port Jefferson	D1
Port Morris	A3
Port Washington	B3
Potsdam	L1
Poughkeepsie	N7
Pulaski	H3
Queens	B4
Randolph	C6
Ransomville	C4
Ravena	N6
Red Hook	N7
Rensselaer	N5
Rhinebeck	N7
Richfield Springs	L5
Riverhead	D1
Rochester	E4
Rockaway Point	A4
Rocky Point	D1
Rome	K4
Rosendale	M7
Rouses Point	P1
Rye	B2
Sackets Harbor	H3
Sag Harbor	E1
St. George	A2
St. Johnsville	L4
Salamanca	C6
Sands Point	B3
Saranac Lake	M2
Saratoga Springs	N6
Saugerties	N6
Sayville	C1
Schenectady	N5
Schoharie	M5
Scotia	N5
Seneca Falls	G5
Sherburne	K5
Shortsville	F5
Sidney	K6
Silver Creek	B5
Skaneateles	H5
Sodus	F4
Southampton	E1
South Fallsburg	L7
Southold	E1
Southport	G6
Spencerport	E4
Springville	C5
Stillwater	N5
Stony Brook	C1
Suffern	A1
Syracuse	H4
Throgs Neck	B2
Ticonderoga	P3
Troy	N5
Trumansburg	G6
Tupper Lake	M2
Unadilla	K6
Utica	K4
Valley Stream	B2
Victory Mills	N4
Voorheesville	N5
Walden	M7
Walton	K6
Wampsville	J4
Wappingers Falls	N7
Warrensburg	N4
Warsaw	D5
Warwick	A1
Waterloo	G5
Watertown	J3
Waterville	K5
Watkins Glen	G6
Waverly	G6
Wayland	E5
Weedsport	G4
Wellsville	E6
West Carthage	J3
Westfield	A6
West Point	N7
West Seneca	C4
Whitehall	P3
White Plains	B1
Whitesboro	K4
Whitestone	A3
Williamsburg	A4
Wilson	C4
Wolcott	G4
Woodmere	B4
Woodstock	M6
Yonkers	B1
Yorktown Heights	B1

Other Features

	Key
Adirondack, mts.	L2
Adirondack Park	M2
Appalachian Natl. Scenic Trail	A1
Black, lake	J2
Black, lake	J2
Cannonsville, reservoir	K6
Catskill, mts.	L7
Catskill Park	L6
Cayuga, lake	G5
Champlain, lake	P1
Chenango, river	J6
Cranberry, lake	L2
Delaware, river	K7

	Key
Eleanor Roosevelt N.H.S.	N7
Erie, canal	J4
Erie, lake	A5
Fire Island Natl. Seashore	D2
Fishers, island	E3
Fort Stanwix Natl. Monument	K4
Galloo, island	H3
Gardiners, island	F1
Gateway Natl. Rec. Area	B2
Genesee, river	D6
George, lake	N3
Governors Island Natl. Mon.	A4
Great Sacandaga, lake	M4
Hinckley, reservoir	K4
Home of F.D.R. Natl. Hist Site	N7
Hudson, river	M3
Indian, lake	M3
J.F.K. Int'l Airport	B4
Keuka, lake	F5
Long, island	E1
Long, lake	M3
Long Island, sound	C1
Marcy, mt.	M2
Martin Van Buren Natl. Hist. Site	N6
Mettawee, river	P3
Mohawk, river	L5
Oneida, lake	J4
Ontario, lake	E3
Pepacton, reservoir	L6
Piseco, lake	L4
St. Lawrence, river	K1
Salmon River, reservoir	J3
Saratoga, lake	N4
Saratoga Natl. Hist. Park	N4
Schoharie, reservoir	M6
Schroon, lake	N3
Slide, mt.	M7
Staten, island	A2
Stony, island	H3
Susquehanna, river	J6
Thomas Cole Natl. Hist. Site	N6
Thousand, islands	H2
Tupper, lake	M2
Unadilla, river	K5
Upper Saranac, lake	M2
Vanderbilt Mansion N.H.S.	N7
West Point Military Academy	A1
Women's Rights N.H.P.	G5

North Carolina .... page 160

Cities and Towns

	Key
Aberdeen	G4
Ahoskie	L2
Albemarle	C8
Andrews	C8
Angier	H3
Apex	H3
Archdale	F3
Asheboro	F3
Asheville	E7
Atlantic Beach	M5
Ayden	L4
Badin	A2
Bakersville	D4
Bayboro	M4
Beaufort	M5
Belhaven	M3
Belmont	C4
Benson	H4
Bessemer City	C4
Bethel	L3
Biscoe	F4
Black Mt.	A3
Bladenboro	B2
Blowing Rock	J6
Boiling Spring Lakes	B4
Boiling Springs	J6
Bolivia	J6
Boone	B2
Brevard	E8
Bryson City	C8
Buies Creek	H4
Burgaw	K5
Burlington	G2
Burnsville	H2
Butner	N2
Camden	N2
Canton	E7
Carolina Beach	K6
Carthage	G4
Cary	H3
Chadbourn	H6
Chapel Hill	G3
Charlotte	D4
Cherryville	C4
China Grove	D3
Clayton	J3
Clemmons	J5
Clinton	J5
Coats	H4
Columbia	N3
Columbus	A4
Concord	D4
Conover	C3
Cornelius	D4
Creedmoor	H2
Cullowhee	D8
Currituck	N2
Dallas	C4
Danbury	E2
Davidson	D3
Denton	E3
Dobson	D2
Drexel	B3
Dunn	H4
Durham	H2
E. Flat Rock	E8
Eden	F2
Edenton	M2
Elizabeth City	N2
Elizabethtown	H5
Elkin	D2
Elm City	K3
Emerald Isle	L5
Enfield	K2
Erwin	H4
Fairmont	G5
Farmville	K3
Fayetteville	H4
Fletcher	E8
Forest City	B4
Four Oaks	J4
Franklin	C8
Franklinton	J2
Fremont	K3
Fuquay-Varina	H3
Gamewell	B3
Garner	H3
Gastonia	C4
Gatesville	M2

	Key
Gibsonville	F2
Goldsboro	K4
Graham	G2
Granite Falls	C3
Granite Quarry	E3
Greensboro	F2
Greenville	L3
Grifton	L4
Halifax	K2
Hamlet	F5
Harkers Island	M5
Harrisburg	D4
Havelock	M5
Hayesville	C8
Hays	C2
Henderson	J2
Hendersonville	E8
Hertford	N2
Hickory	C3
High Point	E3
Hillsborough	G2
Hope Mills	H5
Hudson	C3
Huntersville	D4
Icard	C3
Indian Trail	D4
Jackson	L2
Jacksonville	L5
Jamestown	F3
Jefferson	C2
Jonesville	D2
Kannapolis	D4
Kenansville	K5
Kenly	J3
Kernersville	E2
Kill Devil Hills	P2
King	E2
Kings Mt.	C4
Kinston	K4
Kitty Hawk	P2
La Grange	K4
Laurinburg	G5
Leland	J6
Lenoir	B3
Lewisville	E2
Lexington	E3
Liberty	F3
Lillington	H4
Lincolnton	C4
Locust	E4
Long Beach	J7
Long View	C3
Louisburg	J2
Lumberton	H5
Madison	F2
Maiden	C3
Manteo	P3
Marion	A3
Marshall	E7
Marshville	E5
Matthews	D4
Maxton	G5
Mayodan	F2
Mebane	G2
Mint Hill	D4
Mocksville	D3
Monroe	D5
Mooresville	D3
Moravian Falls	C2
Morehead City	M5
Morganton	B3
Mt. Airy	D2
Mt. Gilead	F4
Mt. Holly	C4
Mt. Olive	J4
Mulberry	C2
Murfreesboro	L2
Murphy	B8
Nags Head	P3
Nashville	K3
New Bern	L4
Newland	B2
Newport	M5
Newton	C3
Norwood	E4
North Wilkesboro	C2
Oxford	H2
Pembroke	G5
Pinehurst	G4
Pinetops	K3
Pineville	D4
Piney Green	L5
Pittsboro	G3
Plymouth	M3
Polkville	B4
Raeford	G5
Raleigh, capital	H3
Randleman	F3
Red Springs	G5
Reidsville	F2
River Bend	L4
Roanoke Rapids	K2
Robbinsville	C8
Robersonville	L3
Rockingham	F5
Rockwell	E3
Rocky Mount	K3
Rolesville	J5
Rose Hill	J5
Roseboro	H5
Roxboro	H2
Rural Hall	E2
Rutherfordton	B4
Salisbury	D3
Sanford	G4
Sawmills	C3
Scotland Neck	L2
Selma	J3
Seven Lakes	F4
Sharpsburg	K3
Shelby	B4
Siler City	G3
Smithfield	J3
Sneads Ferry	L5
Snow Hill	K4
Southern Pines	G4
Southern Shores	P2
Southport	J7
Sparta	C1
Spencer	E3
Spindale	B4
Spring Lake	H4
Spruce Pine	A3
St. Pauls	H5
Stanley	C4
Stanleyville	E2
Statesville	D3
Stokesdale	F2
Stony Point	D3
Summerfield	F2
Swan Quarter	N4
Sylva	D8

Key

Tabor City H6
Tarboro K3
Taylorsville C3
Thomasville E3
Toast D2
Trenton L4
Troutman D3
Troy F4
Valdese B3
Wadesboro E5
Wake Forest H3
Wallace K5
Wanchese P3
Warrenton J2
Warsaw J5
Washington L3
Waxhaw D5
Waynesville D4
Weddington D4
Welcome E3
Weldon K2
Wendell J3
Wentworth F2
W. Jefferson C2
Whiteville H6
Wilkesboro C2
Williamston L3
Wilmington K6
Wilson K3
Windsor M2
Winfall N2
Wingate E5
Winston-Salem E2
Winterville L3
Winton M2
Woodfin E7
Wrightsville Beach K6
Yadkinville D2
Yanceyville G2
Zebulon J3

Other Features

Albemarle, sound N3
Alligator, lake N3
Alligator, river N3
B. Everett Jordan, lake G3
Bodie, island P3
Cape Fear, river H5
Cape Hatteras Natl. Seashore P4
Cape Lookout Natl. Seashore N5
Chatuga, lake C8
Clingmans Dome, mt. C7
Dan, river F2
Deep, river F3
Falls Lake, reservoir G3
Fear, cape K7
Fontana, lake C7
Fort Raleigh Natl. Hist. Site P3
Gaston, lake K1
Great, lake L5
Great Smoky Mts. Natl. Park C7
Hatteras, cape P4
Hatteras, inlet P4
Highrock, lake E3
Hiwassee, lake B8
Hyco, lake G2
John H. Kerr, reservoir H1
Lookout, cape M5
Mattamuskeat, lake M3
Mitchell, mt. A3
Nantahala, lake C8
Neuse, river J4
Norman, lake D3
Ocracoke, inlet N4
Oregon, inlet P3
Pamlico, river M4
Pamlico, sound P4
Phelps, lake N3
Roan, mt. A2
Roanoke, river K2
Rocky, river E4
Smith, island K7
Standing Indian, mt. C8
Tar, river J2
Waccamaw, lake J6
Wright Brothers Natl. Memorial ..P2
Yadkin, river D2

North Dakota ....page 161

Cities and Towns

Ashley F3
Beach A3
Belcourt F1
Beulah D2
Bismarck, capital E3
Bowman B3
Cando F1
Carrington F2
Casselton H3
Cavalier H1
Center D2
Cooperstown G2
Crosby B1
Devils Lake G1
Dickinson C3
Ellendale G3
Fargo J3
Fessenden F2
Finley H2
Forman H3
Fort Yates E3
Garrison D2
Grafton H1
Grand Forks H2
Harvey F2
Hazen D2
Hettinger C3
Hillsboro H2
Jamestown G3
Lakota G1
La Moure G3
Langdon G1
Larimore H2
Linton E3
Lisbon H3
McClusky E2
Mandan E3
Mayville H2
Mohall D1
Mott C3
Napoleon F3
New Rockford F2
New Town C1
Oakes G3
Park River H1
Rolla F1
Rugby F1
Stanley C1
Stanton D2
Steele F3

Key

Tioga C1
Towner E1
Valley City H3
Wahpeton J3
Washburn D2
Watford City B2
West Fargo J3
Williston B1

Other Features

Cannonball, river D3
Devils, lake G1
Fort Union Trading Post N.H.S. ..A1
Green, river B2
Heart, river D3
Intl. Peace Garden E1
James, river F2
Jamestown, reservoir G2
Knife, river D2
Knife River Indian Villages N.H.S. ..D2
Little Missouri, river B3
Long, lake E3
Maple, lake G3, H2
Missouri, river D2
Oahe, lake E3
Pembina, river G1
Sakakawea, lake C2
Sheyenne, river E2, G2, H3
Souris, river D1
Theodore Roosevelt N.P. B2, B3
White Butte, mt. B3
Wild Rice, river H3

Ohio ....page 162

Cities and Towns

Aberdeen C8
Ada C4
Akron G3
Alliance H4
Ansonia A5
Antrim A3
Antwerp A3
Arabia F8
Arcanum A6
Archbold B2
Arlington C4
Ashland F4
Ashtabula J2
Athens F7
Aurora H3
Avon Lake F2
Baltimore E6
Barberton G3
Barnesville H5
Batavia B7
Bay Village G9
Beachwood J9
Bedford J9
Bedford Heights J9
Bellaire J5
Bellefontaine C5
Bellevue E3
Bellville E4
Berea G9
Berlin Heights F3
Bethel B8
Beverly G6
Blanchester C7
Blissfield G5
Blue Ash C9
Bluffton C4
Boardman J3
Bowling Green C3
Bradford B5
Bremen F6
Brewster G4
Bridgetown B9
Broadview Heights H10
Brook Park G9
Brooklyn H9
Brookville B6
Brunswick G3
Bryan A3
Bucyrus E4
Burton H3
Cadiz J5
Caldwell G6
Cambridge G5
Camden A6
Canal Fulton G4
Canal Winchester E6
Canfield J3
Canton H4
Cardington E5
Carey D4
Carrollton H4
Cedarville C6
Celina A4
Centerburg E5
Chagrin Falls H3
Chardon H2
Chesterhill G6
Cheviot B9
Chillicothe E7
Cincinnati A7
Circleville E6
Cleveland G2
Cleveland Heights G2
Cleves A9
Clyde E3
Coldwater A5
Columbiana J4
Columbus, capital D6
Columbus Grove B4
Congress F4
Conneaut J2
Cortland J3
Coshocton G5
Covington B5
Crestline E4
Creston G4
Crooksville F6
Cuyahoga Falls H3
Dalton G4
Dayton B6
De Graff C5
Deer Park C9
Defiance B3
Delaware D5
Delhi Hills B9
Delphos B4
Delta C2
Deshler C3
Dover H4
Dresden F5
Dublin D5
Dunkinsville D8
E. Cleveland H8
East Liverpool J4
East Palestine J4

Key

Eaton A6
Edgerton A3
Elida B4
Elyria F3
Euclid G2
Fairborn C6
Fairfield A7
Fairport Harbor H2
Fairview Park G9
Findlay C3
Fitchville F3
Forest C4
Forest Park B8
Forestville B7
Fort Recovery A5
Fort Shawnee B4
Fostoria D3
Franklin B6
Fredericktown E5
Fremont D3
Fresno G5
Gahanna E5
Galion E4
Gallipolis F8
Gambier F5
Garfield Hts. H9
Geneva J2
Genoa D2
Georgetown C8
Germantown B6
Gibsonburg D3
Grafton F3
Granville E5
Green E5
Green Springs D3
Greenfield D7
Greenville A5
Greenwich E3
Grove City D6
Hamilton A7
Hannibal J6
Harrisburg D6
Harrison A9
Heath F5
Hebron F5
Hicksville A3
Hillsboro C7
Hiram H3
Holgate B3
Hubbard J3
Huron E3
Independence H9
Jackson E7
Jackson Center B5
Jefferson J2
Jeffersonville C6
Johnstown E5
Keene G5
Kent H3
Kenton C4
Kettering B6
Kimbolton G5
Kirtland H2
Lakewood G9
Lancaster E6
Lebanon B7
Leipsic C3
Lewisburg A6
Lexington E4
Lima B4
Lisbon J4
Lodi G3
Logan F6
London D6
Lorain F3
Loudonville F4
Louisville H4
Loveland B7
Lucasville E8
Lyndhurst J9
McArthur F7
McConnelsville G6
Macedonia J10
Macksburg H6
Madeira C9
Manchester C8
Mansfield E4
Maple Hts. J9
Marietta H7
Marion D4
Martins Ferry J4
Marysville D5
Mason B7
Massillon G4
Maumee C2
Mayfield Hts. J9
Mechanicsburg C5
Medina G3
Mentor H2
Miamitown B9
Middleburg Heights G9
Middlefield H3
Middletown B6
Milan E3
Milford B7
Millersburg G4
Minerva H4
Minster B5
Monfort Heights B9
Monroe B7
Montgomery C9
Montpelier A2
Mount Gilead E4
Mount Healthy B9
Mount Orab C7
Mount Sterling D6
Mount Vernon E5
Napoleon B3
Nelsonville F7
Newark F5
New Baltimore B9
New Boston E8
New Bremen B5
New Carlisle B6
Newcomerstown G5
New Concord G6
New Lebanon B6
New Lexington F6
New London F3
New Paris A6
New Philadelphia H4
New Richmond B8
Newtown C9
Niles J3
North Baltimore C3
North Canton H4
North College Hill B9
North Kingsville J2
North Olmsted G3
North Royalton H10
Northfield J9
Northridge C6

Key

Norwalk E3
Norwood C9
Oak Harbor D2
Oak Hill E8
Oberlin F3
Olmsted Falls G9
Oregon D2
Orrville G4
Orwell J2
Otsego B3
Ottawa B3
Painesville H2
Parma G3
Parma Heights H9
Pataskala E6
Paulding A3
Peebles D8
Pepper Pike J9
Perrysburg C2
Pickerington E6
Piketon E7
Pioneer A2
Piqua B5
Plain City D5
Plymouth E4
Pomeroy F7
Port Clinton D2
Portsmouth E8
Powhatan Point J6
Ravenna H3
Reading B7
Reynoldsburg E6
Richmond Heights J8
Richwood D5
Ripley C8
Rittman G3
Roseville F6
Russells Point C5
Sabina C7
Sagamore Hills J9
St. Bernard C9
St. Clairsville J5
St. Henry A5
St. Louisville F5
St. Marys B4
St. Paris C5
Salem J4
Salineville J4
Sandusky E3
Selma C6
Seven Hills H9
Shadyside J6
Shaker Hts. J9
Sharonville C9
Shelby E4
Shreve F4
Sidney B5
Silverton C9
Smithville G4
Solon J9
Somerset F6
South Charleston C6
South Euclid J8
South Point E9
Springdale C9
Springfield C6
Steubenville J5
Strasburg G4
Streetsboro H3
Strongsville H3
Stryker B3
Sugarcreek G5
Sunbury E5
Sylvania C2
The Village of Indian Hill C9
Tiffin D3
Tipp City B6
Toledo C2
Troy B5
Twinsburg J10
Uhrichsville H5
University Hts. J9
Upper Sandusky D4
Urbana C5
Utica F5
Van Wert A4
Vandalia B6
Venedocia B4
Vermilion F3
Versailles B5
Wapakoneta B4
Warren J3
Warrensville Heights J9
Warsaw G5
Washington Court House D6
Waterville C2
Wauseon B2
Waverly E7
Waynesville B6
Wellington F3
Wellston E7
Wellsville J4
West Alexandria A6
West Jefferson D6
West Lafayette G5
West Liberty C5
West Milton B6
West Salem F4
West Union C8
West Unity B2
Westerville E5
Westlake G9
Weston C3
Wheelersburg E8
Wickliffe J8
Wilkesville F7
Willard E3
Williamsburg B7
Williamsport D6
Williamsport E4
Wilmington C7
Woodsfield H6
Woodville D3
Wooster G4
Wyoming C9
Xenia C6
Yellow Springs C6
Youngstown J3

Other Features

Clendening, lake H5
Cuyahoga Valley N.P. G3, H9
Dayton Aviation N.H.P. B6
Erie, lake G1
First Ladies Natl. Hist. Site H4
Hocking, river F7
Hopewell Culture N.H.P. E7
James A. Garfield N.H.P. H2
Kelleys, island E2
Mohican, river F4
Muskingum, river G6
Ohio, river J6

Key

Salt Fork, lake H5
Sandusky, river D3
Scioto, river D4
Senecaville, lake H6
William H. Taft Natl. Hist. Site C9

Oklahoma ....page 163

Cities and Towns

Ada F3
Agawam E3
Altus C3
Alva D1
Anadarko D2
Antlers G3
Apache D3
Arapaho D2
Ardmore E3
Arkoma H2
Atoka F3
Barnsdall F1
Bartlesville F1
Beaver B1
Bethel Acres E2
Bixby G2
Blackwell E1
Blanchard E2
Boise City B4
Bristow F2
Broken Arrow G1
Broken Bow H3
Buffalo C1
Cache D3
Calera F4
Carnegie D2
Catoosa G1
Chandler F2
Checotah G2
Chelsea G1
Cherokee D1
Cheyenne C2
Chickasha E2
Choctaw E2
Chouteau G1
Claremore G1
Cleveland F1
Clinton D2
Coalgate F3
Collinsville G1
Comanche E3
Commerce H1
Cordell D2
Corum D3
Coweta G2
Cushing F2
Davis E3
Dewey G1
Drumright F2
Durant F4
Eagletown H3
Edmond E2
Elk City C2
Enid E1
Eufaula G2
Fairfax F1
Fairview D1
Farris G3
Fittstown F3
Floris B1
Forgan B1
Fort Gibson G1
Frederick D3
Geary D2
Glenpool G2
Granite C3
Grove H1
Guthrie E2
Guymon C4
Harmon C1
Hartshorne G3
Haskell G2
Headlton G3
Heavener H3
Hennessey E1
Henryetta F2
Hobart D2
Holdenville F2
Hollis C3
Hominy F1
Hooker A1
Hugo G3
Idabel H4
Inola G1
Jay H1
Jenks G1
Joy E3
Kingfisher E2
Konawa F3
Krebs G2
Laverne C1
Lawton D3
Lenora C1
Lindsay E3
Locust Grove G1
Lone Grove E3
Loveland D3
Lovell E2
McAlester G3
McCurtain H2
McKnight C3
Madill F3
Mangum C3
Mannford F1
Marietta E4
Marlow E3
Medford E1
Midwest City E2
Minco E2
Moore E2
Muskogee H2
Mustang E2
Newcastle E2
Newkirk E1
Norman E2
Nowata G1
Oakhurst F2
Okeene D1
Okemah F2
Oklahoma City, capital E2
Okmulgee G2
Owasso G1
Panama H2
Pawhuska F1
Pawnee F1
Perkins F2
Perry E1
Picher H1
Piedmont E2
Ponca City E1
Poteau H2
Prague F2

Key

Pryor Creek G1
Purcell E2
Roll C2
Sallisaw H2
Sand Springs F1
Sapulpa F1
Sayre C2
Seminole F2
Shattuck C1
Shawnee F2
Skiatook F1
Slaughterville E2
Snyder D3
Sparks F2
Spiro H2
Stanley G2
Stigler G2
Stillwater F2
Stilwell H2
Stratford F3
Stroud F2
Sulphur F3
Tahlequah H2
Talihina G3
Tecumseh F2
Tishomingo F3
Tonkawa E1
Tulsa G1
Turley G1
Tuttle E2
Vian H2
Vinita G1
Wagoner G2
Walters D3
Wanette E3
Warner G2
Warren C3
Watonga D2
Watova G1
Waukomis E1
Waurika D3
Weatherford D2
Westville H1
Wetumka F2
Wewoka F2
Wilburton G3
Wilson E3
Woodward C1
Wynnewood E3
Yale F1
Yukon E2

Other Features

Arkansas, river F1
Black Mesa, mt. B4
Broken Bow, lake H3
Canadian, river C2
Canton, lake D1
Chickasaw Natl. Rec. Area E3
Cimarron, river C1
Fort Gibson, lake G1
Hugo, lake G3
Illinois, river H2
Kaw, lake F1
Keystone, lake F1
North Canadian, river C1
Oklahoma City Natl. Memorial E2
Oologah, lake G1
Ouachita, mts. G3
Red, river F4
Sooner, lake F1
Texoma, lake F4
Washita Battlefield N.H.S. C2
Winding Stair Natl. Rec. Area H3

Oregon ....page 164

Cities and Towns

Albany B2
Aloha A2
Altamont C3
Ashland C3
Astoria B1
Baker City E2
Bandon B3
Beaverton A2, C2
Bend C2
Brookings B3
Brownsville B2
Burns D3
Canby A2, C2
Canyon City E2
Cedar Hills A2
Central Point C3
Clatskanie B1
Condon D2
Coos Bay B3
Coquille B3
Cornelius A2
Corvallis B2
Cottage Grove B3
Creswell B3
Crowley E3
Dallas B2
Eagle Point C3
Elgin E2
Enterprise E2
Eugene B2
Florence B3
Forest Grove A2
Fossil D2
Four Corners A2, C2
Glendale B3
Gold Beach B3
Grants Pass B3
Green B2
Gresham B2
Harbor B3
Harrisburg B2
Hayesville A2, C2
Heppner D2
Hermiston D2
Hillsboro A2, C2
Hines D3
Homestead F2
Hood River C2
Hubbard C2
Jacksonville C3
Jefferson B2
John Day E2
Junction City B2
Juntura E3
Keizer B2
Klamath Falls C3
Lafayette B2
La Grande E2
Lakecreek C3
Lake Oswego A2, C2
Lakeside B3
Lakeview D3
Lebanon B2

Key

Lexington D2
Lincoln Beach B2
Lincoln City B2
McMinnville C2
Madras C2
Meacham E2
Medford C3
Metzger A2
Mill City C2
Milton-Freewater E2
Milwaukie A2
Molalla A2
Monument D2
Moro D2
Mount Angel A2, C2
Mount Vernon D2
Myrtle Creek B3
Myrtle Point B3
Newberg A2, B2
Newport B2
North Bend B3
Nyssa E3
Oak Grove A2
Oakridge C3
Ontario F2
Oregon City A2, C2
Pendleton E2
Philomath B2
Phoenix C3
Pilot Rock E2
Portland A2, C2
Post D2
Prineville D2
Rainier C1
Redmond C2
Reedsport B3
Riley D3
Rogue River B3
Roseburg B3
Rufus D2
St. Helens C2
Stanfield D2
Salem, capital A2, B2
Santa Clara B2
Scappoose B2
Seaside B2
Seneca E2
Shady Cove C3
Sherwood A2
Silverton A2, C2
Springfield C2
Stayton C2
Sunriver C3
Sutherlin B3
Sweet Home C2
Talent C3
The Dalles D2
Tigard A2, C2
Tillamook B2
Toledo B2
Umpqua B3
Union E2
Vale E3
Veneta B2
Vernonia B2
Waldport B2
Warm Springs C2
Warrenton B1
Waterloo C2
West Slope A2
White City C3
Willamina B2
Wilsonville A2, C2
Woodburn A2
Wood Village B2

Other Features
Abert, lake D3
Blue, mts. E2
Calapooya, mts. C3
Cascade, range C3
Cascade-Siskiyou Natl. Mon. C3
Clackamas, river C2
Coast, mt. ranges B2
Columbia, river D2
Coos, bay B3
Crater, lake C3
Crater Lake Natl. Park C3
Crescent, lake C3
Crooked, river D2
Davis, lake C3
Deschutes, river C3
Diamond Peak, mt. C3
Gearhart Mtn., mt. D3
Green Peter, lake C2
Harney, basin D3
Harney, lake D3
Hells, canyon F2
Hells Canyon Natl. Rec. Area F2
Hood, mt. C2
Jefferson, mt. C2
John Day, river D2
John Day Fossil Beds N.M. D2
Klamath, mts. B3
Lookout, lake B2
McLoughlin house N.H.S. A2
Malheur, lake E3
Malheur, river E3
Molalla, river B2
Multnomah, waterfalls C2
Ochoco, river D2
Oregon Caves Natl. Monument B3
Oregon Dunes Natl. Rec. Area B3
Owyhee, lake E3
Owyhee, river E3
Powder, river E2
Pudding, river A2
Pueblo, mts. E3
Rogue, river B3
Sacajawea Peak, mt. E2
Silvies, river D3
Siuslaw, river B3
Snake, river F2
South Umpqua, river B3
Steens, mts. E3
Strawberry Mt., mt. E2
Summer, lake D3
Thielsen, mt. C3
Tillamook, bay B2
Trout Creek, mts. E3
Umatilla, lake D2
Upper Klamath, lake C3
Waldo, lake C3
Wallowa, lake E2
Willamette, river A2

Pennsylvania ....page 165
Cities and Towns
Albion A2
Aliquippa A4
Allensville F4
Allentown L4
Allison Park L6
Altoona E5
Ambridge A4
Amity H5
Annville K5
Archbald K2
Ardmore M6
Arnot G2
Ashland J4
Athens H2
Austin E2
Avalon D7
Avis G3
Bala Cynwyd M6
Baldwin E7
Bangor L4
Barnesboro D4
Beaver A4
Beaver Falls A4
Beavertown G4
Bedford E5
Bellefonte F4
Belleville F4
Bellevue D7
Bellwood E4
Berlin D6
Berwick J3
Berwyn L6
Bethel Park A5, D7
Bethlehem L4
Birdsboro K5
Blairsville C5
Blakely K3
Bloomsburg J4
Blossburg G2
Boalsburg F4
Boothwyn L7
Boswell C5
Boyertown K5
Bradford D2
Brentwood E7
Bridgeville D7
Brockport D3
Brockway D3
Brodheadsville L4
Brooklyn K2
Brookville C3
Broomall L6
Brownsville B5
Bryn Mawr L6
Burgettstown A5
Butler B4
California B5
Cambridge Springs A2
Canonsburg A5
Canton H2
Carbondale K2
Carlisle G5
Carnegie D7
Carroll Valley G6
Carrolltown D4
Castle Shannon E7
Catawissa J4
Chambersburg F6
Chelsea L7
Chester L6, L7
Clairton B5
Clarion C3
Clarks Summit K2
Claysburg E5
Clearfield E3
Clifton Heights L7
Clymer C4
Coatesville K6
Columbia H5
Connellsville B6
Conyngham L4
Coopersburg L5
Coraopolis D7
Cornwall J5
Corry B2
Coudersport E2
Crafton D7
Cresson D5
Crosby E2
Cuddy D7
Curwensville D4
Dallas K3
Danville H4
Darby M7
Delmont B5
Denver J5
Derry C5
Dillsburg G5
Dormont D7
Dover H5
Downingtown K5
Doylestown L5
Drexel Hill M7
DuBois D3
Duncannon G4
Duquesne E7
Dushore J2
Glenolden M7
Glen Riddle L7
Glen Rock H6
Gradyville L7
Greencastle F6
Greensburg B5
Greenville A3
Gregg D7
Grove City A3
Hallstead K2
Hamburg K4
Hanover H6
Harmarville E6
Harrisburg, capital H5
Harrisville A3
Harveys Lake J3
Haverford M6
Havertown M6
Hazel Hurst D2
Hazleton K4
Hermitage A3
Herndon H4
Hershey H5
Highland D6
Hollidaysburg E5
Homer City C4
Honesdale L2
Huntingdon E5
Hyndman D6
Indiana C4
Indianola E6
Jersey Shore G3
Jim Thorpe K4
Johnsonburg D3
Johnstown D5
Kane D2
Kennett Square K6
King of Prussia L5
Kingston K3
Kittanning B4
Kutztown K5
Lake City A1
Lancaster J5
Lansdale L5
Lansdowne M7
Laporte J3
Latrobe C5
Lebanon J5
Leechburg B4
Lehighton K4
Levittown M5
Lewisburg H4
Lewistown H4
Ligonier C5
Lima L7
Linglestown H5
Lititz J5
Littlestown G6
Lock Haven G3
Lykens H4
McCandless A4, D6
McConnellsburg E6
McKees Rocks D7
McKeesport B5
Macungie K4
Mahanoy City J4
Manchester H5
Manheim J5
Mansfield G2
Mars A4
Martinsburg E5
Marysville H5
Masontown B6
Matamoras M3
Meadville A3
Mechanicsburg H5
Media L6, L7
Mercer A3
Mercersburg F6
Meridian B4
Merion M6
Meyersdale C6
Middleburg G4
Middletown H5
Midland A4
Mifflinburg G4
Mifflintown G4
Mifflinville J3
Milford M3
Millersburg H4
Millersville J6
Millheim G4
Millvale E7
Milroy F4
Milton H3
Minersville J4
Monessen B5
Monroeville B5, F7
Mont Alto F6
Montgomery H3
Montoursville H3
Montrose K2
Moon Run D7
Moscow K3
Mt. Carmel J4
Mt. Holly Springs G5
Mount Joy H5
Mt. Lebanon D7
Mt. Nebo D6
Mt. Oliver E7
Mt. Pleasant B5
Mt. Pocono L3
Mount Union F5
Muncy H3
Munhall E7
Myerstown J5
Nanticoke J3
Nanty Glo D5
Nazareth L4
Nesquehoning K4
New Bloomfield G5
New Castle A4
New Freedom H6
New Holland J5
New Kensington B4, F6
New Oxford G6
Newport G5
Newtown M5
Newtown Square L6
Newville G5
New Wilmington A3
Norristown L5
North East B1
Northampton L4
North Springfield A1
Northumberland H4
Oakmont E7
Oil City B3
Old Forge K3
Orwigsburg J4
Oxford J6
Palmerton K4
Patton D4
Pen Argyl L4
Penn Hills F7
Penn Wynne M6
Perkasie L5
Philadelphia L6, M7
Philipsburg E4
Phoenixville K5
Picture Rocks H3
Pine Grove J4
Pittsburgh B5, E7
Pittston K3
Pleasantville B2
Pleasantville D5
Point Marion B6
Polk A3
Port Allegany E2
Port Matilda E4
Portage D5
Portland Mills D3
Pottstown K5
Pottsville J4
Powell H2
Prospect Park L7
Punxsutawney D4
Quakertown L5
Quarryville J6
Radnor L6
Rainsburg D6
Reading K5
Red Lion H6
Renovo F3
Reynoldsville D3
Ridgway D3
Ridley Park L7
Roaring Spring E5
St. Marys D3
Saxonburg B4
Sayre H2
Schnecksville K4
Schuylkill Haven J4
Scottdale B5
Scranton K3
Selinsgrove H4
Shamokin H4
Sharon A3
Sharon Hill M7
Sharpsville A3
Sheffield C2
Shenandoah J4
Shippensburg F5
Shoemakersville K5
Shrewsbury H6
Sinking Spring K5
Slatington K4
Slippery Rock A3
Smethport E2
Somerset C5
Souderton L5
South Williamsport G3
Spring Grove H6
Springdale F6
Springfield L7
State College F4
Stewartstown H6
Strasburg J6
Stroudsburg L4
Sugarcreek B3
Sunbury H4
Susquehanna K2
Swarthmore L7
Sykesville D3
Tamaqua K4
Tionesta B2
Titusville B2
Tobyhanna L3
Towanda J2
Tower City H4
Tremont J4
Trevorton H4
Troy H2
Tunkhannock K2
Tyrone E4
Union City B2
Uniontown B6
Upland L7
Valley View H4
Vandergrift B4
Verona E7
Village Green L7
Villanova L6
Warren C2
Washington A5
Waterford B2
Watsontown H3
Waymart L2
Wayne L6
Waynesboro F6
Waynesburg A6
Weatherly K4
Wellsboro G2
Wesleyville A1
West Chester K6
West Grove K6
West Mifflin E7
Westmont D5
West Pike F2
West View E7
Whitehall K4
White Horse L6
Wilcox D2
Wilkes-Barre K3
Wilkinsburg E7
Williamsport H3
Willow Grove L5
Windber D5
Womelsdorf J5
York H6
York Springs G5
Youngsville C2
Zelienople A4

Other Features
Allegheny, reservoir D2
Allegheny, river B3
Allegheny Natl. Rec. Area D2
Allegheny Portage Railroad N.H.S. D5
Appalachian, mts. F5
Clarion, river C3
Conemaugh, river C4
Davis, mt. C6
Delaware, river L2
Delaware Water Gap N.R.A. M3
Eisenhower Natl. Hist. Site G6
Erie, lake A1
Friendship Hill Natl. Hist. Site B6
Gettysburg Natl. Mil. Park G6
Johnstown Flood Natl. Memorial D5
Juniata, river F5
Lehigh, river K3
Ohio, river A1
Presque Isle, island A1
Raystown, lake E5
Schuylkill, river K5
Steamtown Natl. Hist. Site K3
Susquehanna, river J2
Tioga, river G2
Valley Forge Natl. Hist. Park L5

Rhode Island ....page 166
Cities and Towns
Adamsville F4
Allenton D4
Alton C3
Anthony B4
Arcadia B4
Ashaway B5
Ashton D2
Avondale A6
Barrington E3
Berkeley D2
Bradford B5
Bristol E3
Carolina C5
Central Falls D2
Charlestown C5
Chepachet B2
Clayville C3
Coventry Center C3
Cranston D3
Cumberland Hill D2
Diamond Hill D2
Dunn Corner B5
East Greenwich D4
East Providence D3
Exeter C4
Fiskeville C3
Foster Center B3
Galilee C5
Green Hill C5
Greenville C2
Hamilton D4
Harmony C2
Harrisville B2
Hope C3
Hope Valley B5
Hopkinton B5
Jamestown D4
Jerusalem C5
Kingston C5
Little Compton E4
Lonsdale D2
Matunuck C5
Middletown E4
Moosup Valley B3
Narragansett Pier D5
Newport E5
Nooseneck C4
North Foster B2
North Providence D2
North Scituate C2
Pascoag B2
Pawtucket D2
Pawtuxet D3
Perryville C5
Plum Point D4
Point Judith D5
Portsmouth E4
Providence, capital D3
Prudence E4
Quidnick C3
Quonochontaug B6
Rice City B3
Riverside D3
Rockville B4
Rumford D2
Sakonnet E5
Saunderstown D5
Saylesville D2
Shannock C5
Slatersville C1
Slocum C4
South Foster B3
Spragueville C2
Tarkiln C2
Tiverton E4
Usquepaug C5
Valley Falls D2
Wakefield C5
Wallum Lake B2
Warren E3
Warwick D3
Washington C3
Watch Hill A6
Weekapaug B6
West Barrington D3
Westerly B5
West Glocester B2
West Kingston C5
West Warwick C3
Woonsocket C1
Wyoming B4

Other Features
Block, island C7
Block Island, sound B6
Mt. Hope, bay E4
Narragansett, bay D4
Rhode Island, sound E5
Roger Williams Natl. Mem. D3
Sakonnet, river E4
Scituate, reservoir C3
Touro Synagogue N.H.S. E5

South Carolina ....page 167
Cities and Towns
Abbeville B2
Aiken C3
Allendale C3
Anderson B2
Andrews E3
Bamberg C3
Barnwell C3
Batesburg-Leesville C3
Beaufort D4
Belton B2
Belvedere C3
Bennettsville E2
Bishopville D2
Blacksburg C1
Blackville C3
Boiling Springs C2
Brownsville E2
Buffalo C1
Burton D4
Calhoun Falls B2
Camden D2
Cayce C3
Central B2
Charleston E4
Cheraw E2
Chester C2
Chesterfield D2
Clemson B2
Clinton C2
Clover C1
Columbia, capital C2
Conway E3
Cowpens C1
Darlington E2
Denmark C3
Dentsville D2
Dillon E2
Easley B2
Edgefield C3
Elgin C2
Enoree C2
Estill C4
Fairfax C4
Florence E2
Folly Beach E4
Forest Acres D2
Foreston D3
Fort Mill D1
Fountain Inn B2
Furman C4
Gaffney C1
Garden City F3
Georgetown E3
Gifford C4
Gloverville C3
Goose Creek D3
Great Falls D2
Greeleyville E3
Greenville B2
Greenwood B2
Greer B2
Hampton C4
Hanahan C4
Hardeeville C4
Harleyville D3
Hartsville D2
Hickory Grove C2
Hemingway F3
Hilda C3
Hilton Head Island D4
Holly Hill D3
Hollywood D4
Honea Path B2
Horrel Hill D2
Inman B1
Irmo C2
Isle of Palms E4
Jackson C3
Jefferson D2
Joanna C2
Johnsonville E3
Johnston C3
Kershaw D2
Kiawah Island D4
Kingstree E3
Kline C3
Ladson D4
Lake City E3
Lancaster D2
Landrum B1
Lane E3
Latta E2
Laurel Bay D4
Laurens B2
Lexington C3
Liberty B2
Little River F3
Little Rock E2
Loris F2
Lugoff D2
Lyman B2
Lynchburg D2
McBee D2
McClellanville E3
McCormick B3
Manning D3
Marion E2
Mauldin B2
Mayesville D3
Mayo C1
Moncks Corner D3
Mt. Pleasant E4
Mullins E2
Murrells Inlet F3
Myrtle Beach F3
Neeses C3
New Ellenton C3
Newberry C2
Nichols E2
Ninety Six B2
North Augusta B3
North Charleston E4
North Myrtle Beach F3
Norway C3
Olanta E3
Olar C3
Orangeburg D3
Pacolet C2
Pacolet Mills C2
Pageland D2
Pamplico E3
Patrick D2
Pelion C3
Pendleton B2
Pickens B2
Piedmont B2
Pinewood D3
Pomaria C2
Port Royal D4
Ravenel D4
Red Bank C3
Ridgeland C4
Ridgeville D3
Ridgeway D2
Rock Hill C2
Roebuck C2
Rowesville D3
Ruby D2
St. George D3
St. Matthews D3
St. Stephen E3
Salley C3
Salters E3
Saluda C3
Santee D3
Sellers E2
Seneca B2
Simpsonville B2
Society Hill E2
Socastee F3
South Congaree C3
Spartanburg C2
Springfield C3
Starr B2
Stuckey E3

Key

Summerville ... D3
Sumter ... D3
Surfside Beach ... F3
Swansea ... C3
Sycamore ... C3
Taylors ... B2
Timmonsville ... E2
Travelers Rest ... B2
Trenton ... C3
Turbeville ... D3
Union ... C2
Varnville ... C4
Wagener ... C3
Walhalla ... A2
Walterboro ... D4
Ware Shoals ... B2
Westminster ... A2
Whitmire ... C2
Williamston ... B2
Williston ... C3
Winnsboro ... C2
Woodruff ... B2
Yemassee ... D4
York ... C2

Other Features
Bull, *island* ... E4
Bulls, *bay* ... E4
Cape, *island* ... E3
Congaree Swamp N.M. ... D3
Cowpens Natl. Bfld. ... C1
Edisto, *river* ... D3
Fort Sumter Natl. Monument ... E4
Greenwood, *lake* ... C2
Hartwell, *lake* ... B2
J. Strom Thurmond, *lake* ... B3
Keowee, *lake* ... B2
Kings Mt. Natl. Mil. Park ... C1
Long, *bay* ... P3
Lynches, *river* ... D2
Marion, *lake* ... D3
Monticello, *reservoir* ... C2
Moultrie, *lake* ... D3
Murray, *lake* ... C2
Ninety Six Natl. Hist. Site ... B2
North, *island* ... E3
Port Royal, *sound* ... D4
Russell, *lake* ... B2
St. Helena, *sound* ... D4
Saluda, *river* ... C3
Santee, *river* ... E3
Savannah, *river* ... B3
South, *island* ... E3
The Grand Strand ... F3
Wateree, *lake* ... D2
Wateree, *river* ... D2

South Dakota ... page 168

Cities and Towns
Aberdeen ... F1
Alexandria ... G3
Armour ... F3
Belle Fourche ... A2
Beresford ... H3
Black Hawk ... A2
Box Elder ... A2
Britton ... G1
Brookings ... H2
Burke ... E3
Canton ... H3
Chamberlain ... E3
Cherry Creek ... C2
Clark ... G2
Clear Lake ... H2
Custer ... A3
Deadwood ... A2
Dell Rapids ... H3
De Smet ... G2
Dupree ... C1
Elk Point ... H4
Faulkton ... E1
Flandreau ... H2
Fort Pierre ... D2
Freeman ... G3
Gettysburg ... E1
Hartford ... H3
Highmore ... E2
Hot Springs ... A3
Howard ... G2
Huron ... F2
Ipswich ... E1
Kadoka ... C3
Lake Andes ... F3
Lead ... A2
Lemmon ... B1
Lennox ... G3
Leola ... F1
Madison ... G2
Martin ... C3
Milbank ... H1
Miller ... E2
Mitchell ... G3
Mobridge ... D1
Murdo ... D3
Onida ... D2
Parker ... G3
Parkston ... G3
Philip ... C2
Pierre, *capital* ... D2
Pine Ridge ... B3
Plankinton ... F3
Platte ... F3
Rapid City ... A2
Redfield ... F2
Rosebud ... D3
Salem ... G3
Selby ... D1
Sioux Falls ... H3
Sisseton ... G1
Spearfish ... A2
Sturgis ... A2
Timber Lake ... D1
Tyndall ... G4
Vermillion ... H4
Volga ... H2
Wagner ... F3
Watertown ... G2
Webster ... G1
Wessington Springs ... F2
White River ... D3
Winner ... E3
Woonsocket ... F2
Wounded Knee ... B3
Yankton ... G4

Other Features
Andes, *lake* ... F3
Angostura, *reservoir* ... A3
Bad, *river* ... C2
Badlands Natl. Park ... B3

Key

Belle Fourche, *reservoir* ... A2
Belle Fourche, *river* ... A2
Big Sioux, *river* ... G2
Big Stone, *lake* ... H1
Black, *hills* ... A2
Bois de Sioux, *river* ... H1
Cheyenne, *river* ... C2
Francis Case, *lake* ... F3
Grand, *river* ... C1
Harney Peak, *mt.* ... A3
James, *river* ... F1
Jewel Cave Natl. Monument ... A3
Keya Paha, *river* ... D3
Lewis and Clark, *lake* ... G4
Little Missouri, *river* ... A1
Little White, *river* ... D3
Minuteman Missile N.H.S. ... B3, C3
Missouri, *river* ... E3
Moreau, *river* ... B1
Mount Rushmore Natl. Memorial ... A3
North Fork Grand, *river* ... B1
Oahe, *lake* ... D2
Pine, *ridge* ... B3
Sharpe, *lake* ... E2
South Fork Grand, *river* ... A1
Traverse, *lake* ... H1
Vermillion, *river* ... G3
Waubay, *lake* ... G1
White, *river* ... D3
Whitewood, *river* ... G2
Wind Cave Natl. Park ... A3

Tennessee ... page 169

Cities and Towns
Adamsville ... E4
Alamo ... C3
Alcoa ... P3
Algood ... L2
Altamont ... K4
Arlington ... B4
Ashland City ... G2
Athens ... M4
Bartlett ... B4
Baxter ... K2
Bells ... C3
Benton ... M4
Bethel Springs ... D4
Bethpage ... J2
Blaine ... P2
Blountville ... S1
Bluff City ... S2
Bolivar ... D4
Brentwood ... H2
Bristol ... S1
Brownsville ... C3
Bruceton ... E2
Buffalo Valley ... K2
Byrdstown ... L1
Camden ... E2
Campaign ... K2
Carthage ... K2
Caryville ... N2
Celina ... K1
Centerville ... G3
Charlotte ... G2
Chattanooga ... L4
Church Hill ... R1
Clarksville ... G1
Cleveland ... M4
Clinton ... N2
Collegedale ... L4
Collierville ... B4
Columbia ... G3
Conasauga ... M4
Cookeville ... L2
Covington ... B3
Cowan ... J4
Crossville ... L3
Dandridge ... Q2
Dayton ... L3
Decatur ... M3
Decaturville ... E3
Decherd ... J4
Dickson ... G2
Dover ... F2
Dresden ... D2
Dunlap ... L4
Dyer ... C2
Dyersburg ... C2
East Ridge ... L4
Elizabethton ... S2
Englewood ... N4
Erin ... F2
Erwin ... S2
Estill Springs ... J4
Etowah ... M4
Fairfield Glade ... M2
Farragut ... N3
Fayetteville ... H4
Forest Hills ... H2
Frankewing ... H4
Franklin ... H3
Gainesboro ... K2
Gallatin ... J2
Gatlinburg ... P3
Germantown ... B4
Gleason ... D2
Goodlettsville ... H2
Granville ... K2
Graysville ... L4
Greeneville ... R2
Greenfield ... D2
Grimsley ... M2
Gruetli-Laager ... K4
Halls ... C3
Halls Crossroads ... P2
Hampshire ... G3
Harriman ... M3
Hartsville ... J2
Henderson ... D4
Hendersonville ... H2
Humboldt ... D3
Huntingdon ... E3
Huntsville ... N2
Jacksboro ... N2
Jackson ... D3
Jamestown ... M2
Jasper ... K4
Jefferson City ... Q2
Jellico ... N1
Johnson City ... S2
Jonesborough ... S2
Karns ... N3
Kenton ... C2
Kingsport ... R1
Kingston ... M3
Kingston Springs ... G2
Knoxville ... P3
Lafayette ... J1
La Follette ... N2

Key

Lake City ... N2
Lakewood ... H2
La Vergne ... H2
Lawrenceburg ... G4
Lebanon ... J2
Lenoir City ... N3
Lewisburg ... H4
Lexington ... E3
Linden ... F3
Livingston ... L2
Loretto ... G4
Loudon ... N3
Lynchburg ... J4
McEwen ... F2
McKenzie ... E2
McKinnon ... F2
McMinnville ... K3
Madisonville ... N3
Manchester ... J4
Martin ... D2
Maryville ... P3
Mascot ... P2
Maynardville ... P2
Medon ... D4
Memphis ... A4
Middleton ... D4
Milan ... D3
Millersville ... H2
Milligan College ... S2
Millington ... B4
Monterey ... L2
Morristown ... Q2
Mosheim ... R2
Mountain City ... T1
Mount Juliet ... H2
Mount Pleasant ... G3
Munford ... B4
Murfreesboro ... J3
Nashville, *capital* ... H2
Newbern ... C2
New Johnsonville ... F2
New Tazewell ... P2
Nolensville ... H3
Norris ... N2
Oak Hill ... H2
Oak Ridge ... N2
Oliver Springs ... N2
Oneida ... M2
Overall ... H2
Paris ... E2
Parsons ... E3
Pegram ... G2
Pigeon Forge ... P3
Pikeville ... L3
Portland ... H1
Powell ... N2
Pulaski ... G4
Reagan ... E3
Red Bank ... L4
Ridgely ... C2
Ripley ... B3
Rockwood ... M3
Rogersville ... R2
Rutherford ... C2
Rutledge ... Q2
Savannah ... E4
Selmer ... D4
Sevierville ... P3
Sewanee ... K4
Shelbyville ... J4
Signal Mountain ... L4
Smithville ... K3
Smyrna ... H3
Sneedville ... Q1
Soddy-Daisy ... L4
Somerville ... C4
South Fulton ... D2
South Pittsburg ... K4
Sparta ... L3
Spencer ... L3
Spring City ... M3
Spring Hill ... H3
Springfield ... H1
Stanton ... C4
Surgoinsville ... R2
Sweetwater ... N3
Taft ... H4
Tazewell ... P2
Tellico Plains ... N4
Tennessee Ridge ... F2
Tiptonville ... C2
Tracy City ... K4
Trenton ... D3
Trimble ... C2
Tullahoma ... J4
Tusculum ... R2
Union City ... C2
Wartburg ... M2
Waverly ... F2
Waynesboro ... F4
Westmoreland ... J1
White House ... H2
White Pine ... Q2
Whitwell ... K4
Winchester ... J4
Woodbury ... J4

Other Features
Andrew Johnson Natl. Hist. Site ... R2
Appalachian, *mts.* ... N4
Appalachian Natl. Scenic Trail ... Q3
Barkley, *lake* ... F1
Big South Fork Natl.
  River and Rec. Area ... M1
Center Hill, *lake* ... K3
Cherokee, *lake* ... Q2
Chickamauga & Chattanooga
  Natl. Mil. Park ... L5
Chickamauga, *lake* ... M3
Clinch, *river* ... Q2
Clingmans Dome, *mt.* ... Q3
Cumberland, *river* ... G2
Dale Hollow, *lake* ... L1
Douglas, *lake* ... Q2
Duck, *river* ... H3
Great Smoky, *mts.* ... Q3
Great Smoky Mts. Natl. Park ... Q3
Holston, *river* ... R2
Kentucky, *lake* ... F2
Mississippi, *river* ... B3
Norris, *lake* ... P2
Roan, *mt.* ... S2
Shiloh Natl. Mil. Park ... E4
Tennessee, *river* ... E5, K5
Watts Bar, *lake* ... M3
Woods, *reservoir* ... J4

Texas ... page 170

Cities and Towns
Abernathy ... F2

Key

Abilene ... H3
Addison ... C1
Alamo Heights ... B7
Albany ... H3
Algoa ... F9
Alice ... J8
Alpine ... D5
Alvin ... M6
Amarillo ... B9
Anahuac ... N6
Anderson ... M5
Andrews ... E3
Angleton ... M6
Anson ... H3
Anthony ... A3
Aransas Pass ... K8
Archer City ... J2
Arlington ... L3
Asherton ... H7
Aspermont ... G2
Atascosa ... A7
Athens ... M3
Atlanta ... N2
Austin, *capital* ... K5
Avondale ... A1
Azle ... K3
Baird ... H3
Balch Springs ... C2
Balcones Heights ... A7
Ballinger ... H4
Bandera ... H6
Barrett ... F8
Bastrop ... K5
Batesville ... H7
Bay City ... M7
Baytown ... N6
Beaumont ... N5
Beaumont Place ... F8
Beaver ... C8
Bedford ... B2
Beeville ... K7
Bellaire ... E8
Bellmead ... K4
Belton ... K4
Benavides ... J8
Benbrook ... A2
Benjamin ... H2
Bergheim ... A6
Big Lake ... F4
Big Spring ... F3
Bishop ... K8
Boerne ... A6
Bogata ... M2
Bonham ... L2
Borger ... C9
Bovina ... E1
Bowie ... K2
Bracken ... B6
Brackettville ... G6
Brady ... H4
Breckenridge ... J3
Brenham ... L5
Briar ... A1
Bridge City ... P5
Bridgeport ... K2
Brookshire ... M6
Brookside Village ... F9
Brownfield ... E2
Brownsville ... K10
Brownwood ... J4
Bryan ... L5
Buckingham ... C1
Buena Vista ... B7
Buffalo ... L4
Bulverde ... A6
Buna ... P5
Bunker Hill Village ... E8
Burkburnett ... J1
Burleson ... A3
Burleson ... K3
Burnet ... J5
Caldwell ... L5
Cameron ... L5
Canadian ... C10
Canton ... M3
Canutillo ... A4
Canyon ... B9
Carrizo Springs ... H7
Carrollton ... B1
Carthage ... N3
Castle Hills ... A6
Castle Hills ... J6
Cedar Hill ... B3
Cedar Park ... K5
Center ... N4
Centerville ... M3
Chandler ... M3
Channelview ... F8
Channing ... B9
Childress ... G1
Chocolate Bayou ... F10
Cisco ... J3
Clarendon ... C10
Clarksville ... M2
Claude ... C9
Cleburne ... K3
Cleveland ... M5
Clifton ... K4
Cloverleaf ... F8
Clute ... M6
Cockrell Hill ... B2
Coldspring ... M5
Coleman ... H4
College Station ... L5
Colleyville ... A2
Colorado City ... G3
Columbus ... L6
Comanche ... J4
Combine ... D2
Commerce ... L2
Conroe ... M5
Converse ... B6
Cooper ... M2
Copperas Cove ... J4
Corpus Christi ... K8
Corsicana ... L3
Cotulla ... H7
Crane ... E4
Crockett ... M4
Crosby ... F8
Crosbyton ... F2
Crowell ... H2
Crowley ... A3
Crystal City ... H7
Cuero ... K6
Daingerfield ... N2
Dalhart ... B8
Dallas ... L3
Dalworthington Gardens ... B2
Danbury ... F10

Key

Dayton ... N5
Decatur ... K2
Deer Park ... F8
Del Rio ... G6
Denison ... L2
Denton ... K2
Denver City ... E3
De Soto ... L3
Devine ... J6
Diboll ... N4
Dickens ... G2
Dickinson ... N6
Dilley ... H7
Dimmitt ... E1
Dublin ... J3
Dumas ... B9
Duncanville ... B2
Eagle Lake ... L6
Eagle Pass ... G7
Eastland ... J3
Eden ... H4
Edgecliff ... A3
Edinburg ... J9
Edna ... L7
El Campo ... L6
Eldorado ... G5
El Paso ... A4
Electra ... J1
Elgin ... K5
Elsa ... J9
Emory ... M3
Ennis ... L3
Euless ... B2
Everman ... A3
Fabens ... A4
Fair Oaks Ranch ... A6
Fairfield ... L4
Falfurrias ... J8
Farmers Branch ... B1
Farwell ... D1
Ferris ... C3
Flatonia ... K6
Floresville ... J6
Floydada ... F2
Forest Hill ... A3
Fort Davis ... D5
Fort Stockton ... E5
Fort Worth ... K3
Franklin ... L4
Fredericksburg ... J5
Freeport ... M7
Freer ... J8
Friendswood ... F9
Gail ... F3
Gainesville ... L2
Galena Park ... F8
Galveston ... N6
Ganado ... L7
Garden City ... F4
Garden Ridge ... B6
Gardendale ... B7
Garland ... C2
Gatesville ... K4
George West ... J7
Georgetown ... K5
Germann ... C5
Giddings ... L5
Gilmer ... N3
Gladewater ... N3
Glen Rose ... K3
Glenn Heights ... B3
Goldthwaite ... J4
Goliad ... K7
Gonzales ... K6
Graham ... J3
Granbury ... K3
Grand Prairie ... B2
Grand Saline ... M3
Grapeland ... M4
Grapevine ... B1
Grapevine ... K3
Greenville ... L2
Groesbeck ... L4
Groves ... P6
Groveton ... M4
Guthrie ... G2
Hallettsville ... L6
Haltom City ... A2
Hamilton ... J4
Hamlin ... G3
Harker Heights ... K4
Harlingen ... K9
Haskell ... H2
Hearne ... L5
Hebbronville ... J8
Helotes ... A6
Hemphill ... P4
Hempstead ... L5
Henderson ... M3
Henrietta ... J2
Hereford ... B10
Hewitt ... K4
Hico ... K4
Hidalgo ... J9
Highland Park ... C2
Highlands ... F8
Hillsboro ... K3
Hitchcock ... F9
Hitchcock ... M6
Hollywood Park ... A6
Hondo ... H6
Houston ... M6
Hubbard ... L4
Huntsville ... M5
Hurst ... A2
Hutchins ... C2
Idalou ... F2
India ... C3
Ingleside ... K8
Iowa Park ... J2
Irving ... B2
Jacinto City ... F8
Jacksboro ... J2
Jacksonville ... M4
Jasper ... P5
Jayton ... G2
Jefferson ... N3
Jersey Village ... E8
Johnson City ... J5
Jourdanton ... J7
Juliff ... E9
Junction ... H5

Key

Kingsland ... J5
Kingsville ... K8
Kirby ... B7
Kirbyville ... P5
Knox City ... H2
Kountze ... N5
La Grange ... L6
Lake Jackson ... M7
Lakehills ... H6
La Marque ... G9
Lamesa ... F3
Lampasas ... J4
Lancaster ... C3
La Porte ... F9
La Pryor ... H7
Laredo ... H8
League City ... N6
Leakey ... H6
Leon Springs ... A6
Leon Valley ... A7
Levelland ... E2
Lewisville ... L2
Liberty ... N5
Linden ... N3
Lipscomb ... D8
Littlefield ... E2
Live Oak ... B6
Livingston ... N5
Llano ... J5
Lockhart ... K5
Lockney ... F1
Longview ... N4
Lubbock ... F2
Lufkin ... N4
Luling ... K6
Lumberton ... N5
Mabank ... L3
McAllen ... J9
McCamey ... E4
Macdona ... A7
McKinney ... L2
Madisonville ... M5
Mangus Corner ... A7
Mansfield ... K3
Manvel ... F9
Marble Falls ... J5
Marfa ... C5
Marlin ... L4
Marshall ... N3
Mason ... H5
Matador ... G1
Mathis ... K8
Memphis ... C10
Menard ... H5
Mentone ... D4
Meridian ... K3
Merkel ... G4
Mertzon ... G4
Mesquite ... C2
Mesquite ... L3
Mexia ... L4
Miami ... C9
Midland ... E4
Midlothian ... B3
Mineola ... M3
Mineral Wells ... J3
Mission ... J9
Missouri City ... M6
Monahans ... E4
Mont Belvieu ... G8
Montague ... K2
Morgans Point ... G8
Morton ... E2
Moss Bluff ... F8
Mt. Houston ... F8
Mt. Pleasant ... N2
Mt. Vernon ... M2
Muleshoe ... D1
Munday ... H2
Murphy ... C1
Nacogdoches ... N4
Nassau Bay ... F9
Navasota ... L5
Nederland ... N6
New Berlin ... C7
New Boston ... N2
New Braunfels ... J6
Newton ... P5
Nixon ... K6
Nocona ... K2
North Houston ... E8
North Richland Hills ... A2
Odessa ... E4
Olmos Park ... A7
Olney ... J2
Olton ... E1
Orange ... P5
Ovilla ... B3
Ozona ... F5
Paducah ... G1
Paint Rock ... H4
Palacios ... L7
Palestine ... M4
Palo Pinto ... J3
Pampa ... C9
Panhandle ... C9
Pantego ... B2
Paris ... M2
Parita ... B7
Parker ... C1
Pasadena ... M6
Pearland ... F9
Pearsall ... H7
Pecos ... D4
Pelican Bay ... A1
Perryton ... C8
Pharr ... J9
Pilot Point ... L2
Pittsburg ... N2
Plains ... E2
Plainview ... F1
Plano ... L2
Pleasanton ... J7
Port Arthur ... P6
Port Bolivar ... G9
Port Isabel ... K9
Port Lavaca ... L7
Portland ... K8
Post ... F2
Poteet ... J6
Premont ... J8
Presidio ... C6
Quanah ... H1
Quitman ... M3
Ranger ... J3
Rankin ... F4
Raymondville ... K9
Red Oak ... C3
Refugio ... K7
Reno ... A1
Richardson ... C1
Richland Hills ... A2

	Key
Richmond	M6
Rio Grande City	J9
Roanoke	A1
Robert Lee	G4
Robinson	K4
Robstown	K8
Roby	G3
Rockdale	L5
Rockport	K7
Rocksprings	G5
Rockwall	L3
Roma	H9
Roscoe	G3
Rosenberg	M6
Rosharon	E9
Rotan	G3
Round Rock	K5
Rowlett	C2
Rusk	M4
Sabinal	H6
Sachse	C1
St. Hedwig	B7
San Angelo	G4
San Antonio	J6
San Augustine	N4
San Benito	K9
Sanderson	E5
San Diego	J8
Sandy Point	E9
Sanger	K2
San Geronimo	A6
San Leon	G9
San Marcos	K6
San Saba	J4
Sansom Park	A2
Sarita	K8
Satsuma	E8
Sayers	B7
Schertz	B6
Schumansville	C6
Seabrook	F9
Seadrift	L7
Seagoville	C2
Seagraves	E3
Sealy	L6
Seguin	K6
Selma	B6
Seminole	E3
Seymour	H2
Shallowater	E2
Shavano Park	A6
Sherman	L2
Shoreacres	G9
Sierra Blanca	B4
Silsbee	N5
Silverton	F1
Sinton	K7
Slaton	F2
Smith Point	G9
Smithville	K5
Snyder	G3
Socorro	A4
Sonora	G5
South Houston	F9
Southlake	A1
Southside Place	E8
Southton	B7
Spearman	C8
Spring Valley	E8
Spur	G2
Stafford	E9
Stamford	H3
Stanton	F3
Stephenville	J3
Sterling City	G4
Stratford	B8
Sugar Land	E9
Sulphur Springs	M2
Sundown	E2
Sunnyvale	C2
Sweetwater	G3
Tahoka	F2
Taylor	K5
Temple	K4
Texarkana	N2
Texas City	N6
The Woodlands	M5
Thompsons	E9
Three Rivers	J7
Throckmorton	H2
Tilden	J7
Tomball	M5
Trinity	M5
Trophy Club	A1
Tulia	F1
Tyler	M3
Universal City	J6
University Park	C2
Uvalde	H6
Van Alstyne	L2
Van Horn	B9
Vega	B9
Vernon	H1
Victoria	L7
Vidor	N5
Von Ormy	A7
Waco	K4
Waskom	N3
Watauga	A2
Waxahachie	L3
Weatherford	K3
Webster	F9
Wellington	D10
Weslaco	K9
West	K4
West Columbia	M6
West Odessa	A2
Westover Hills	A2
West University Place	E8
Westworth	A2
Wharton	L6
Wheatland	A3
Wheeler	D9
White Settlement	A2
Whitesboro	L2
Wichita Falls	J2
Willis	M5
Wills Point	L3
Wilmer	C3
Windcrest	B6
Winnie	N6
Winnsboro	M3
Winters	H4
Wolfforth	F2
Woodville	N5
Woodway	K4
Wylie	D1
Yoakum	K6
Zapata	H9
Zuehl	B7

	Key
Other Features	
Alibates Flint Quarries N.M.	B9
Amistad, reservoir	F6
Amistad Natl. Rec. Area	G6
Balcones, escarpment	J5
Big Bend Natl. Park	D6
Big Thicket Natl. Preserve	N5
Black, mt.	G6
Canadian, river	C9
Cathedral, mt.	D5
Chamizal Natl. Mem.	A4
Chinati Peak, mt.	C6
Dallas-Fort Worth Intl. Airport	B2
Davis, mts.	C5
Eagle Peak, mt.	B5
Edwards, plateau	H6
Emory Peak, mt.	D6
Falcon, reservoir	H9
Fort Davis Natl. Hist. Site	D5
Galveston, bay	G9
Galveston, island	N6
Guadalupe, mts.	C3
Guadalupe Mts. Natl. Park	C4
Guadalupe Peak, mt.	C4
Kemp, lake	H2
Lake Meredith Natl. Rec. Area	C9
Livermore, mt.	C5
Livingston, lake	M5
Lyndon B. Johnson N.H.P.	J5
Meredith, lake	C9
Nueces, river	J7
O.H. Ivie, lake	H4
Padre Island Natl. Seashore	K8
Pecos, river	E4
Pelican, island	G9
Red, river	H1
Red Bluff, lake	D4
Rio Grande, river	F6
Sabine, pass	P6
Sabine, river	P5
Sam Rayburn, reservoir	N4
Santiago Peak, mt.	D6
Sierra Del Carmen, mt.	D6
Stockton, plateau	E5
Toledo Bend, reservoir	P4

Utah ....page 171

Cities and Towns

	Key
American Fork	C3
Beaver	B5
Bicknell	C5
Blanding	E6
Bluffdale	C3
Bountiful	C3
Brigham City	C2
Castle Dale	C4
Cedar City	A6
Centerville	C3
Clearfield	B2
Coalville	C3
Cottonwood Heights	C3
Delta	B4
Draper	C3
Duchesne	D3
East Carbon	D4
Enoch	A6
Ephraim	C4
Farmington	C2
Ferron	C4
Fillmore	B5
Garland	B2
Grantsville	B3
Gunnison	C4
Heber City	D4
Helper	A6
Hildale	A6
Huntington	D4
Hurricane	A6
Hyrum	C2
Ivins	A6
Junction	B5
Kanab	B6
Lapoint	E3
Layton	C2
Lehi	C3
Lewiston	C2
Loa	C5
Logan	C2
Long Valley Junction	B6
Maeser	E3
Magna	B3
Manila	E3
Manti	C4
Mapleton	C3
Moab	E5
Monroe	B5
Monticello	E6
Morgan	C2
Mount Pleasant	C4
Murray	C3
Mytton	D3
N. Salt Lake	C3
Nephi	C4
North Ogden	C2
Ogden	C2
Orangeville	C4
Orem	C3
Panguitch	B6
Parowan	B6
Payson	C3
Plain City	B2
Pleasant Grove	C3
Price	D4
Provo	C3
Randolph	C2
Richfield	B5
Richmond	C2
Riverton	C3
Roosevelt	D3
Roy	B2
St. George	A6
Salem	C3
Salina	C5
Salt Lake City, capital	C3
Sandy	C3
Santa Clara	A6
Santaquin	C4
Smithfield	C2
South Jordan	C3
Spanish Fork	C3
Springville	C3
Sugarville	B4
Tooele	B3
Tremonton	B2
Vernal	E3
Washington	A6
Wellington	D4
West Jordan	C3
West Valley City	C3
Willard	B2

	Key
Other Features	
Abajo Peak, mt.	E6
Arches Natl. Park	E5
Bear, lake	C2
Bear, river	C2
Beaver, river	B5
Bonneville Salt Flats	A3
Bruin Point, mt.	D4
Bryce Canyon Natl. Park	B6
Canyonlands Natl. Park	E5
Capitol Reef Natl. Park	C5
Cedar Breaks Natl. Monument	B6
Colorado, river	E5
Delano Peak, mt.	B5
Deseret Peak, mt.	B3
Dinosaur Natl. Monument	E3
Dutton, mt.	B5
Escalante, river	C6
Flaming Gorge, reservoir	E2
Flaming Gorge Natl. Rec. Area	E2
Frisco Peak, mt.	A5
Glen Canyon Natl. Rec. Area	D6
Golden Spike Natl. Hist. Site	B2
Grand Staircase-Escalante N.M.	C6
Great, basin	A4
Great Salt, lake	B2
Great Salt Lake, desert	A3
Green, river	D4
Heliotrope, mt.	C5
Henry, mts.	D6
Ibapah Peak, mt.	A4
Kings Peak, mt.	D3
Marsh Peak, mt.	E3
Marvine, mt.	C5
Monument, valley	D6
Natural Bridges Natl. Monument	E6
Navajo, mt.	D6
Navajo Indian Res.	E6
Nebo, mt.	C4
Paria, river	C6
Pavant, range	B5
Peale, mt.	E5
Pennell, mt.	D6
Powell, lake	D6
Price, river	D4
Rainbow Bridge Natl. Monument	D6
Salt Marsh, lake	A4
San Juan, river	D6
San Rafael, river	D4
Sevier, desert	B4
Sevier, lake	A5
Strawberry, river	D3
Swasey Peak, mt.	A4
Timpanogos Cave N.M.	D3
Uinta, mts.	C3
Utah, lake	C3
Wasatch, plateau	C5
White, river	E3
Zion Natl. Park	A6

Vermont ....page 172

Cities and Towns

	Key
Addison	A2
Albany	C1
Ascutney	C4
Averill	D1
Bakersfield	B1
Barnard	B3
Barnet	C2
Barre	C2
Basin Harbor	A2
Beecher Falls	D1
Bellows Falls	B5
Bennington	A5
Benson	A3
Berlin	B2
Bethel	B3
Bloomfield	D1
Bradford	C3
Brandon	A3
Brattleboro	B5
Bristol	A2
Brookfield	B2
Burlington	A2
Cabot	C2
Cambridge	B1
Castleton	A3
Cavendish	B4
Charlotte	A2
Chelsea	C3
Colchester	A1
Concord	D2
Danby	B4
Danville	C2
Dorset	A4
East Burke	D1
East Haven	D1
East Middlebury	A3
East Randolph	B3
Eden	B1
Enosburg Falls	B1
Essex	A1
Essex Junction	A1
Evansville	C1
Fair Haven	A3
Fairfax	B1
Fairfield	B1
Fairlee	C3
Franklin	B1
Gallup Mills	D1
Gaysville	B3
Georgia Center	A1
Grafton	B4
Granby	D1
Grand Isle	A1
Groton	C2
Guildhall	D1
Guilford	B5
Hancock	B3
Hanover	C3
Hardwick	C2
Hartford	C3
Hartland	C3
Hartwellville	A5
Heartwellville	A5
Highgate Center	A1
Hinesburg	A2
Hortonia	A3
Hubbardton	A3
Hyde Park	B1
Irasburg	C1
Irasville	B2
Jacksonville	B5
Jamaica	B4
Jeffersonville	B1
Johnson	B1
Keeler Bay	A1
Larrabees Point	A3
Lemington	D1

	Key
Londonderry	B4
Lowell	C1
Lyndon	C1
Lyndonville	C1
McIndoe Falls	C2
Marlboro	B5
Mendon	B3
Middlebury	A2
Middlesex	B2
Milton	A1
Monkton	A2
Montgomery	B1
Montgomery Center	B1
Montpelier, capital	B2
Morgan	C1
Morrisville	B1
Moscow	B2
Newbury	C2
Newfane	B4
New Haven	A2
Newport	C1
North Bennington	A5
Northfield	B2
North Hero	A1
North Wolcott	C1
Norton	D1
Orange	C2
Panton	A2
Peacham	C2
Pittsfield	B3
Pittsford	A3
Plainfield	C2
Plymouth	B3
Pompanoosuc	C3
Post Mills	C3
Poultney	A3
Pownal	A5
Proctor	A3
Putney	B5
Randolph	B3
Readsboro	A5
Richford	B1
Richmond	A2
Rochester	B3
Roxbury	B2
Rutland	B3
St. Albans	A1
St. Johnsbury	C2
Searsburg	B5
Shaftsbury	A4
Sharon	C3
Shelburne	A2
Sheldon	B1
Shoreham	A2
South Burlington	A2
South Hero	A1
Springfield	C4
Stamford	A5
Starksboro	A2
Swanton	A1
Tinmouth	A4
Troy	C1
Tunbridge	C3
Tyson	B4
Underhill	B1
Vergennes	A2
Vernon	B5
Vershire	C3
Warren	B2
Washington	C2
Waterbury	B2
Waterville	B1
Wells River	C2
West Burke	D1
West Dover	B5
West Haven	A3
Westminster	C4
Weston	B4
West Pawlet	A4
West Topsham	C2
Wheelock	C1
White River Junction	C3
Williamsville	B5
Wilmington	B5
Windsor	C4
Winooski	A1
Wolcott	C1
Woodford	A5
Woodstock	B3
Worcester	B2

Other Features

	Key
Appalachian Natl. Scenic Trail	A5
Black, river	C1
Bomoseen, lake	A3
Bread Loaf, mt.	B2
Bromley, mt.	B4
Camels Hump, mt.	B2
Champlain, lake	A1
Connecticut, river	B2
Ellen, mt.	B2
Equinox, mt.	A4
Green, mts.	B4
Harriman, reservoir	B5
Jay Peak, mt.	B1
Killington Peak, mt.	B3
Lamoille, river	B1
Mansfield, mt.	B1
Marsh-Billings-Rockefeller N.H.P.	B3
Mettawee, river	A3
Missisquoi, river	B1
Seymour, lake	C1
Smugglers Notch, pass	B1
Somerset, reservoir	B4
Waterbury, reservoir	B2
West, river	B4
White, river	B3
White Rocks N.R.A.	B4
Willoughby, lake	C1

Virginia ....page 173

Cities and Towns

	Key
Abingdon	D1
Accomac	M4
Achilles	L5
Alberta	H6
Alexandria	J2
Allison Gap	D1
Altavista	E5
Amelia Court House	H5
Amherst	E4
Annandale	M2
Appalachia	B1
Appomattox	F5
Arlington	J2
Ashland	H4
Baileys Crossroads	M2
Bassett	C6
Basye	F2

	Key
Bedford	D5
Belleair	L2
Belle Haven	L4
Belle View	M2
Bensley	J5
Berryville	H1
Big Stone Gap	B1
Blacksburg	B5
Blackstone	H5
Bland	A5
Bloxom	M4
Bluefield	A5
Bon Air	H4
Bowling Green	J3
Boyce	G1
Boydton	G6
Boykins	J6
Bridgewater	F3
Bristol	D2
Brodnax	G6
Brookneal	F5
Brunswick	H6
Buckingham	F4
Buena Vista	E4
Burke	L2
Burkeville	G5
Callands	D6
Cape Charles	L5
Castlewood	C1
Centreville	J2
Charles City	J5
Charlotte Court House	F5
Charlottesville	F4
Chase City	G6
Chatham	E6
Cheriton	M5
Chesapeake	L6
Chester	H5
Chesterfield	H5
Chilhowie	E1
Chincoteague	M4
Christiansburg	C5
Chula	H5
Claremont	K5
Clifton Forge	D4
Clinchco	C1
Clintwood	C1
Coeburn	C1
Collinsville	D6
Colonial Beach	K3
Colonial Hts.	J5
Concord	E5
Courtland	J6
Covington	C4
Crewe	G5
Crimora	F3
Crystal City	M2
Crystal Hill	F6
Culpeper	G3
Cumberland	G4
Dale City	J2
Danville	E6
Dendron	K5
Dillwyn	G4
Dinwiddie	H5
Drakes Branch	F6
Dublin	B5
Dumfries	J2
Dungannon	C1
Eastville	M5
Elkton	F3
Emory	D1
Emporia	H6
Ewing	J2
Fairfax	J2
Fairfax Station	L2
Falls Church	M2
Falmouth	J3
Farmville	G5
Ferrum	D6
Figsboro	D6
Fincastle	D4
Fishersville	F3
Flint Hill	G2
Floyd	C6
Forest	E5
Fort Mitchell	G6
Franconia	M2
Franklin	K6
Fredericksburg	J3
Fries	B6
Front Royal	G2
Galax	B6
Gate City	C1
Glade Spring	D1
Gloucester	K5
Gloucester Point	L5
Goochland	H4
Gordonsville	G3
Goshen	E3
Gretna	E6
Grottoes	F3
Groveton	M2
Grundy	D1
Halifax	F6
Hampton	L5
Hanover	J4
Harrisonburg	F3
Harrogate	A1
Heathsville	L4
Hillsville	B6
Hollins	D5
Hopewell	J5
Horse Pasture	D6
Huntington	M2
Hurt	E5
Independence	A6
Isle of Wight	K6
Jetersville	G5
Jonesville	A1
Kenbridge	G6
King and Queen Courthouse	K4
King George	J3
Kings Park	L2
King William	J4
Lancaster	L4
Lawrenceville	H6
Lebanon	D1
Leesburg	H1
Lexington	E4
Lincolnia	M2
Louisa	G4
Lovingston	F4
Lunenburg	G6
Luray	G2
Lynchburg	E5
McLean	M1
Madison	G3
Manakin	H4
Manassas	J2
Manassas Park	J2
Mantua	L2
Marion	A6

	Key
Martinsville	D6
Mathews	L5
Mechanicsburg	A5
Mechanicsville	J4
Meherrin	G5
Millboro	D4
Monterey	D3
Montross	K3
Mount Jackson	F2
Narrows	B5
New Castle	C4
New Kent	K4
New Market	F2
Newport News	L6
Newsoms	J6
Norfolk	L6
North Springfield	M2
Norton	C1
Nottoway Court House	G5
Oakton	L2
Onancock	M4
Orange	G3
Palmyra	G4
Pearisburg	B5
Petersburg	J5
Peterstown	B5
Pimmit Hills	M1
Poquoson	L5
Portsmouth	L6
Powhatan	H4
Prince George	J5
Pulaski	B5
Purcellville	H1
Radford	B5
Raven	D1
Reston	J2
Richlands	D1
Richmond, capital	J4
Ridgeway	D6
Roanoke	D5
Rocky Mount	D6
Rustburg	E5
Ruther Glen	J4
Salem	C5
Saltville	D1
Saluda	K4
Shenandoah	F3
Smithfield	K6
South Boston	F6
South Hill	G6
Spotsylvania	H3
Springfield	M1
Spring Hill	M1
Stafford	J3
Stanardsville	G3
Staunton	E3
Sterling	J1
Stony Creek	J6
Strasburg	G2
Stuart	C6
Stuarts Draft	E3
Suffolk	K6
Surry	K5
Sussex	J6
Tappahannock	K4
Tazewell	A5
Timberville	F2
Triangle	J2
Tysons Corner	M1
Vale	L1
Verona	E3
Victoria	G6
Vienna	L1
Virginia Beach	M6
Warm Springs	D3
Warrenton	H2
Warsaw	K4
Washington	G2
Waverly	J5
Waynesboro	F3
Weber City	C1
Wellington	M3
West Point	K4
West Springfield	M2
Williamsburg	K5
Winchester	G1
Wise	C1
Woodbridge	J2
Woodstock	F2
Wytheville	A6
Yorktown	L5

Other Features

	Key
Allegheny, mts.	D3
Anna, lake	H3
Appalachian, mts.	D3
Appomattox Court House N.H.P.	F5
Arlington Natl. Cem.	M2
Assateague Island Natl. Seashore	M4
Booker T. Washington N.M.	D5
Charles, cape	M5
Chesapeake, bay	L5
Colonial Natl. Hist. Park	K5
Fredericksburg & Spotsylvania Natl. Mil. Park	H3
Gaston, lake	G6
George Washington Birthplace N.M.K	K3
Henry, cape	M6
Iron, mts.	A6
James, river	K5
John H. Kerr, reservoir	G6
Manassas Natl. Battlefield Park	H2
Mount Rogers Natl. Rec. Area	A6
Petersburg Natl. Battlefield	J5
Potomac, river	K3
Rappahannock, river	J3
Rogers, mt.	A6
Shenandoah, mts.	E3
Shenandoah, river	F3
Shenandoah Natl. Park	G2
Smith Mtn., lake	D5
York, river	K5

Washington ....page 174

Cities and Towns

	Key
Aberdeen	C4
Amboy	D5
Anacortes	D2
Arlington	D2
Asotin	J4
Auburn	D3
Bangor	A1
Battle Ground	D5
Bellingham	D1
Belvedere	H2
Benton City	G4
Bethel	A1
Birch Bay	D1
Blaine	D1
Boardman	G5

Washington (continued)

Name	Key
Bothel	D3
Bremerton	D3
Brewster	G2
Bridgeport	G2
Bucoda	D4
Burien	B2
Burlington	D2
Camas	D5
Cashmere	F3
Castle Rock	D4
Cathlamet	C4
Central Park	C3
Centralia	D4
Chelan	F3
Chehalis	D4
Cheney	J3
Chewelah	J2
Clarkston	J4
Cle Elum	F3
Clinton	D3
Colfax	J4
College Place	H4
Colville	J2
Connell	H4
Cosmopolis	C4
Country Homes	J3
Coupeville	D2
Davenport	H3
Dayton	J4
Deer Park	J3
Dusty	J4
Eastgate	B2
Easton	E3
Eastsound	D2
East Wenatchee	F3
Eatonville	D4
Edmonds	D3
Ellensburg	F3
Elma	D4
Elmer City	H3
Enumclaw	E3
Ephrata	G3
Everett	D2
Everson	D2
Fall City	E3
Federal Way	D3
Ferndale	D2
Fords Prairie	C4
Forks	B3
Four Lakes	J3
Friday Harbor	C2
Fruitvale	F4
Goldendale	F5
Gorst	A2
Grandview	G4
Granger	F4
Hoquiam	C3
Inglewood	C2
Kelso	D4
Kenmore	B1
Kennewick	G4
Kent	D3
Kettle Falls	H2
Kirkland	D3
Lacey	D3
La Grande	D4
Lake Stevens	D2
Leavenworth	F3
Lexington	D4
Longmire	E4
Longview	D4
Lynden	D2
Mabton	G4
McKenna	D4
McMurray	D2
Markham	C4
Marysville	D2
Medical Lake	J3
Medina	B2
Mercer Island	D3
Merritt	F3
Monroe	D3
Montesano	C3
Moses Lake	G3
Mount Vernon	D2
Mukilteo	D3
Newhalem	E2
Newport	J2
Newport Hills	B2
Normandy Park	B2
North Bend	E3
Oak Harbor	D2
Ocean Park	B4
Ocean Shores	B3
Okanogan	G2
Olalla	D3
Olympia, capital	D3
Omak	G2
Opportunity	J3
Orchards	D5
Oroville	G2
Othello	G4
Oysterville	B4
Pasco	G4
Plymouth	G5
Pomeroy	J4
Port Angeles	C2
Port Hadlock	D2
Port Ludlow	D3
Port Orchard	D3
Port Townsend	D2
Poulsbo	D3
Prosser	G4
Pullman	J4
Puyallup	D3
Quincy	G3
Raymond	C4
Redmond	D3
Renton	D3
Republic	H2
Richland	G4
Richmond Highlands	B1
Ridgefield	D5
Ritzville	H3
St. John	J3
Seabeck	D3
Sea-Tac	D3
Seattle	D3
Sedro-Woolley	D2
Selah	F4
Sequim	C2
Shelton	C3
Silverton	E2
Skyway	D2
Smokey Point	D2
Snohomish	D3
Snoqualmie	E3
South Bend	C4
Southworth	B2
Spanaway	D3
Spokane	J3
Stanwood	D2
Stevenson	E5
Sultan	E3
Sumas	D2
Sumner	D3
Sunnyside	F4
Suquamish	A1
Tacoma	D3
Tekoa	J3
Tenino	D4
Tiger	J2
Toppenish	F4
Tracyton	A2
Trentwood	J3
Tukwila	B2
Tumwater	D4
Union Gap	F4
University Place	D3
Vancouver	D5
Vashon	B2
Walla Walla	H4
Wapato	F4
Warden	G4
Washougal	D5
Waterville	F3
Westport	B4
West Richland	G4
White Center	B2
White Salmon	E5
Winslow	D3
Woodinville	B1
Woodland	D5
Yakima	F4
Yelm	D4
Zillah	F4

Other Features

Name	Key
Adams, mt.	E4
Bainbridge, island	B2
Baker, mt.	E2
Banks, lake	G3
Cascade, range	E4
Chelan, lake	F2
Chewuch, river	F2
Columbia, river	G2
Copper Butte, mt.	H2
Cowlitz, river	E4
Disappointment, cape	B4
Elliott, bay	B2
Flattery, cape	B2
Franklin D. Roosevelt, lake	H2
Glacier Peak, mt.	E2
Grays, harbor	B4
Green, river	E3
Hanford Reach Natl. Mon.	G4
Hood, canal	C3
Kettle River, range	H2
Klickitat, river	E4
Lake Chelan Natl. Rec. Area	F2
Lake Roosevelt Natl. Rec. Area	H2
Lewis, river	E4
Mt. Baker Natl. Rec. Area	E2
Mount Rainier Natl. Park	E4
Mt. St. Helens Natl. Vol. Mon.	D4
North Cascades Natl. Park	E2
Okanogan, river	G2
Olympic, mts.	C3
Olympic Natl. Park	C3
Olympus, mt.	C3
Omak, mt.	G2
Orcas, island	D2
Oregon Butte, mt.	J4
Ozette, lake	B2
Pasayten, river	F2
Pend Oreille, river	J2
Potholes, reservoir	G3
Priest Rapids, lake	G4
Puget, sound	B1, D2
Rainier, mt.	E4
Riffe, lake	D4
Rimrock, lake	E4
Ross, lake	F2
Ross Lake Natl. Rec. Area.	H2
Sacajawea, lake	H4
St. Helens, mt.	D4
San Juan, island	C2
Sanpoil, river	H2
Selkirk, mts.	J2
Skagit, river	E2
Skykomish, river	E3
Snake, river	J4
Spokane, river	H3
Strait of Juan de Fuca	B2
Stuart, mt.	F3
Umatilla, lake	G5
Vashon, island	B2
Wallula, lake	H4
Washington, lake	B1
Wenatchee, lake	F3
Wenatchee, mts.	F3
Wenatchee, river	F3
White, pass	E4
Whitman Mission Natl. Hist. Site	H4
Willapa, bay	B4
Yakima, river	F4
Yale, lake	D4

West Virginia ....page 175

Cities and Towns

Name	Key
Ansted	D4
Barboursville	B4
Beckley	D5
Belington	G2
Berkeley Springs	K1
Bluefield	D6
Bradley	D5
Bridgeport	F2
Buckhannon	F3
Charles Town	L2
Charleston, capital	C4
Chester	K4
Circleville	G3
Clarksburg	F2
Clay	D4
Clendenin	D4
Craigsville	E4
Davis	H2
East Liverpool	K4
Edray	E4
Eleanor	C3
Elizabeth	E2
Elkins	G3
Fairmont	F2
Fayetteville	D4
Fort Ashby	J2
Franklin	H3
Gary	C6
Glenville	E3
Grafton	F2
Grantsville	D3
Hamlin	B4
Harpers Ferry	L2
Harrisville	E2
Hinton	E5
Huntington	B4
Hurricane	B4
Inwood	K2
Kenova	A4
Keyser	J2
Kingwood	G2
Lewisburg	F5
Logan	C5
Madison	C4
Mannington	F1
Marlinton	F4
Marmet	C4
Martinsburg	L2
Matewan	B5
Middlebourne	E2
Milton	B4
Montgomery	D4
Moorefield	J2
Morgantown	G1
Moundsville	K6
Mt. Hope	D5
Mullens	D5
Newburg	G2
New Cumberland	K4
New Haven	C3
New Martinsville	E1
New Milton	E2
Nitro	C4
Oak Hill	D5
Oceana	C5
Orma	D3
Paden City	E1
Parkersburg	C2
Parsons	G2
Pennsboro	E2
Petersburg	H3
Peterstown	E6
Philippi	F2
Pineville	C5
Point Pleasant	B3
Princeton	D6
Rainelle	E5
Ravenswood	C3
Reedy	D3
Richwood	E4
Ripley	C3
Romney	J2
Ronceverte	F5
Rupert	E5
St. Albans	C4
St. Marys	D2
Salem	E2
Shady Spring	D5
Shepherdstown	L2
Shinnston	F2
Sistersville	E1
Slanesville	J2
South Charleston	C4
Spencer	D3
Summersville	E4
Sutton	E3
Terra Alta	G2
Union	E5
Vienna	C2
Wayne	B4
Webster Springs	F4
Weirton	K5
Welch	C6
Wellsburg	K5
Wellsville	K4
West Milford	F2
Weston	F2
West Union	E2
Wheeling	K5
White Sulphur Springs	F5
Whitesville	C5
Williamson	B5
Williamstown	D2
Winfield	C3

Other Features

Name	Key
Allegheny, mts.	G4
Big Sandy, river	B5
Bluestone, lake	E5
Bluestone Natl. Scenic River	E5
Gauley River Natl. Rec. Area	D4
Greenbrier, river	F4
Harpers Ferry Natl. Hist. Park	L2
Kanawha, river	B3
New River Gorge Natl. River	D5
Ohio, river	E1
Potomac, river	J2
Shenandoah, mts.	H3
Spruce Knob, mt.	G3
Spruce Knob-Seneca Rocks N.R.A.	H3
Sutton, lake	E3

Wisconsin ....page 176

Cities and Towns

Name	Key
Abbotsford	C4
Adams	D5
Algoma	F4
Alma	B4
Altoona	B4
Amery	A3
Antigo	D3
Appleton	E4
Arcadia	B4
Ashland	C2
Augusta	B4
Baldwin	A4
Balsam Lake	A3
Baraboo	D5
Barronett	A3
Bayside	F1
Beaver Dam	E5
Belleville	D6
Bellevue	E4
Beloit	D6
Bennett	B2
Berlin	E5
Bethesda	D2
Big Bend	F5
Black River Falls	C4
Bloomer	B3
Bloomville	D3
Boscobel	C5
Breed	E3
Brodhead	D6
Brookfield	E1
Brown Deer	F1
Bryant	D3
Buena Vista	E6
Burlington	E6
Butler	E1
Cadott	B4
Cameron	B3
Canton	B3
Carlsville	F4
Cedarburg	F5
Cedar Grove	F5
Chelsea	C3
Chetek	B3
Chili	C4
Chilton	E4
Chippewa Falls	B4
Cleveland	F5
Clinton	E6
Clintonville	E4
Colby	C4
Coloma	D5
Columbus	D5
Conrath	B3
Cornell	B3
Cornucopia	B1
Crandon	E3
Crestview	A3
Cuba City	C6
Cudahy	F2
Cumberland	A3
Darlington	C6
De Forest	D5
De Pere	E4
Delafield	D1
Delavan	E6
Denmark	F4
Dodgeville	C6
Duplainville	E1
Durand	B4
Eagle River	D3
Easton	D5
East Troy	E6
Eau Claire	B4
Edgar	C4
Edgerton	D6
Elkhorn	E6
Ellsworth	A4
Elm Grove	E1
Elroy	C5
Evansville	D6
Fennimore	C6
Florence	E3
Fond du Lac	E5
Forestville	F4
Fort Atkinson	E6
Fox Lake	E5
Fox Point	F1
Fredonia	F5
Friendship	D5
Galesville	B4
Genesee	D2
Genesee Depot	D2
Germantown	E5
Gillett	E4
Glendale	F1
Grafton	F5
Green Bay	F4
Greendale	F2
Greenfield	F2
Green Lake	E5
Greenleaf	E4
Hales Corners	E2
Hamburg	D3
Harrison	H3
Hartford	E5
Hartland	D1
Hayward	B2
Hillsboro	C5
Hollister	E3
Holmen	B5
Horicon	E5
Hortonville	E4
Howard	E4
Howards Grove	F5
Hudson	A4
Hurley	C2
Husher	F2
Jackson	E5
Janesville	D6
Jefferson	D6
Juda	D6
Jump River	C3
Juneau	E5
Kaukauna	E4
Kenosha	F6
Keshena	E4
Kewaskum	E5
Kewaunee	F4
Kiel	E5
Kneeland	F2
Lac du Flambeau	D3
La Crosse	B5
Ladysmith	B3
Lake Delton	D5
Lake Geneva	E6
Lake Mills	E6
Lampson	B3
Lancaster	C6
La Pointe	C2
Little Chute	E4
Lodi	D5
Lomira	E5
McFarland	D6
Madison, capital	D6
Maiden Rock	A4
Manitowish	C2
Manitowoc	F4
Marathon City	D4
Marinette	F3
Markesan	E5
Marshfield	C4
Mason	B2
Mattoon	D3
Mauston	C5
Mayville	E5
Medford	C3
Menasha	E4
Menomonee Falls	E5
Menomonie	B4
Mequon	F5
Merrill	D3
Middleton	D5
Milton	E6
Milwaukee	F5
Mineral Point	C6
Mishicot	F4
Modena	B4
Mole Lake	E3
Mondovi	B4
Monona	D5
Monroe	D6
Montello	D5
Montfort	C6
Mosinee	D4
Muscoda	C6
Muskego	E6
Neenah	E4
Neillsville	C4
Nekoosa	D4
New Berlin	E6
New Glarus	D6
New Holstein	E5
New Lisbon	C5
New London	E4
New Richmond	A3
Newton	F3
Niagara	F3
North Fond du Lac	E5
North Lake	D1
North Prairie	D2
Oak Creek	F6
Oconto	F4
Oconto Falls	E4
Odanah	C2
Omro	E4
Onalaska	B5
Oostburg	F5
Oregon	D6
Osceola	A3
Oshkosh	E4
Paddock Lake	E6
Palmyra	E6
Park Falls	C3
Pell Lake	E6
Peshtigo	F3
Pewaukee	E1
Phillips	C3
Platteville	C6
Pleasant Prairie	F6
Plover	D4
Plymouth	F5
Polonia	D4
Portage	D5
Port Edwards	D4
Porterfield	F3
Port Washington	F5
Port Wing	B1
Poynette	D5
Prairie du Chien	B6
Prairie du Sac	D5
Prescott	A4
Princeton	D5
Pulaski	E4
Racine	F6
Randolph	E5
Random Lake	F5
Raymond	E6
Reedsburg	C5
Rhinelander	D3
Rice Lake	B3
Richland Center	C5
Ridgeway	D5
Ripon	E5
River Falls	A4
River Hills	F1
Rothschild	D4
St. Croix Falls	A3
St. Francis	F2
Sauk City	D5
Saukville	F5
Saylesville	E1
Schofield	D4
Shawano	E4
Sheboygan	F5
Sheboygan Falls	F5
Shell Lake	B3
Shorewood	F1
Slinger	E5
South Milwaukee	F2
Sparta	C5
Spencer	C4
Spooner	B3
Spread Eagle	E3
Spring Green	C5
Stanley	C4
Stevens Point	D4
Stonebank	D1
Stoughton	D6
Sturgeon Bay	F4
Sturtevant	F6
Summit Lake	D3
Sun Prairie	D5
Superior	A2
Sussex	E1
Tabor	F2
Thompsonville	F2
Thorp	C4
Tomah	C5
Tomahawk	D3
Tony	C3
Two Rivers	F4
Verona	D6
Viola	C5
Viroqua	C5
Wales	D2
Wauneroos	A3
Washburn	C2
Watertown	E5
Waukesha	E6
Waunakee	D5
Waupaca	D4
Waupun	E5
Wausau	D4
Wautoma	D4
Wauwatosa	E1
Wauzeka	C5
West Allis	F6
West Bend	E5
Westby	C5
West Milwaukee	F1
Weyauwega	E4
Whitehall	B4
Whitewater	E6
Williams Bay	E6
Wind Lake	E2
Wind Point	G2
Winneconne	E4
Wisconsin Dells	D5
Wisconsin Rapids	D4
Wrightstown	E4

Other Features

Name	Key
Apostle Islands Natl. Lakeshore	C1
Big Muskego, lake	E2
Castle Rock, lake	D5
Chetek, lake	B3
Chippewa, lake	B3
Door, peninsula	F4
Dubay, lake	D4
Flambeau, river	C3
Green, bay	F4
Madeline, island	C2
Michigan, lake	G5
Mississippi, river	B5
Monona, lake	D5
Outer, island	C1
Peshtigo, river	E3
Petenwell, lake	D4
Pewaukee, lake	D1
Poygan, lake	E4
St. Croix Natl. Scenic Riverway	A3
Sand, island	C2
Spring, lake	D5
Stockton, island	C2
Superior, lake	C1
Timms Hill, mt.	C3
Winnebago, lake	E4
Wisconsin, river	D3
Wolf, river	E4
Yellow, river	C4

Wyoming ....page 177

Cities and Towns

Name	Key
Afton	A2
Basin	B1
Boxelder	D2
Buffalo	C1
Byron	B1
Casper	C2
Cheyenne, capital	D3
Cody	A1
Cokeville	A2
Deaver	B1
Douglas	D2
Evanston	A3
Evansville	C2
Gillette	D1
Glenrock	D2
Green River	B3
Greybull	B1
Jackson	A2
Kemmerer	A3
Lander	B2
Laramie	D3
Lovell	B1
Lusk	D2
Lyman	A3
Medicine Bow	C3
Mills	C2
Newcastle	D2
Pinedale	B2
Powell	B1
Rawlins	C3
Reliance	B3
Riverton	B2
Rock Springs	B3
Saratoga	C3
Sheridan	C1
Sundance	D1
Thermopolis	B2
Torrington	D2
Wamsutter	C3
Wheatland	D2
Worland	C1

Other Features

Name	Key
Absaroka, range	A1
Belle Fourche, river	D1
Big Sandy, river	B2
Bighorn, lake	B1
Bighorn, mts.	C1
Bighorn Canyon Natl. Rec. Area	B1
Bridger Peak, mt.	C3
Clarks Fork Yellowstone, river	B1
Cloud Peak, mt.	C1
Colter Peak, mt.	A1
Continental Divide, mt. ridge	B3
Devils Tower Natl. Monument	D1
Elk, mt.	C3
Flaming Gorge, reservoir	B3
Flaming Gorge Natl. Rec. Area	B3
Fort Laramie Natl. Hist. Site	D2
Fossil Butte Natl. Monument	A3
Francs Peak, mt.	B2
Gannett Peak, mt.	B2
Grand Teton, mt.	A2
Grand Teton Natl. Park	A2
Great Divide, basin	B3
Green, river	B3
Greybull, river	B1
Jackson, lake	A2
Laramie, mts.	C2
Laramie, river	D3
Laramie Peak, mt.	D2
Little Bighorn, river	C1
Little Missouri, river	D1
Little Powder, river	D1
Little Snake, river	C3
Medicine Bow, river	C2
North Platte, river	D2
Nowood, river	C1
Owl Creek, mts.	B2
Pathfinder, reservoir	C2
Powder, river	C1
Rocky, mts.	B2
Seminoe, reservoir	C3
South Fork Cheyenne, river	D2
South Fork Powder, river	C2
Sweetwater, river	B2
Teton, range	A2
Tongue, river	C1
Trout Peak, mt.	B1
Whiskey Peak, mt.	B2
Wind, river	B2
Wind River, range	B2
Yellowstone, lake	A1
Yellowstone Natl. Park	A1